Acting Out CULTURE

Readings for Critical Inquiry

Third Edition

James S. Miller
University of Wisconsin, Whitewater

Bedford/St. Martin's Boston ◆ New York

For Henry, Eliza, and Hope

For Bedford/St. Martin's

Vice President, Editorial, Macmillan Higher Education Humanities: Edwin Hill
Editorial Director for English and Music: Karen S. Henry
Publisher for Composition and Business and Technical Writing: Leasa Burton
Executive Editor for Readers: John Sullivan
Developmental Editor: Jill Gallagher
Assistant Production Editor: Lidia MacDonald-Carr
Senior Production Supervisor: Lisa McDowell
Marketing Manager: Jane Helms
Editorial Assistant: Kathleen Wisneski
Project Management: Katrina Ostler, Jouve North America
Senior Art Director: Anna Palchik
Cover Design: Billy Boardman
Composition: Jouve
Printing and Binding: RR Donnelley and Sons

Manufactured in the United States of America.

9 8 7 6
f e

For information, write: Bedford/St. Martin's, 75 Arlington Street, Boston, MA 02116 (617-399-4000)

ISBN 978-1-4576-4007-0 (Student Edition)

Acknowledgments

Acknowledgments and copyrights appear on the same page as the text and art selections they cover; these acknowledgments and copyrights constitute an extension of the copyright page. It is a violation of the law to reproduce these selections by any means whatsoever without the written permission of the copyright holder.

At the time of publication all Internet URLs published in this text were found to accurately link to their intended Web site. If you do find a broken link, please forward the information to Kathleen.Wisneski@macmillan.com so that it can be corrected for the next printing.

Preface for Instructors

A Critical Eye

James Dean's leather jacket in *Rebel Without a Cause* and Katniss Everdeen's mockingjay pin in *The Hunger Games* have become symbols of rebellion in American popular culture. But what does it really mean to rebel? True rebellion can begin with a question, with taking another look at the traditions and rituals that form the fabric of society and asking, "Why?"

Acting Out Culture encourages students to train a critical eye on American culture, instructing them how to challenge the norms and scripts society sets forth instead of simply accepting them at face value. It takes as a given that students have already internalized countless rules and are bombarded every day with media messages that dictate how they should think, feel, and behave. *Acting Out Culture* urges them to recognize these rules and prescriptions that they may adhere to unthinkingly, probe them, and imagine alternatives. Although scripts for their lives abound, the endings are not yet written. Working with the readings and assignments in *Acting Out Culture* gives students the opportunity to think critically about the norms and roles handed to or imposed on them and, as it were, devise their own scripts in response to what they discover. On the stage of a composition classroom where popular culture is the subject of inquiry, they have the chance to "act out" through writing that positions them as citizens making informed decisions about their world.

Why These Themes?

Because they start where students are and encourage them to exceed their own comfort zones of belief and action. The thematic organization of *Acting Out Culture* focuses students' attention not only on *what* our culture tells us but also on *how* it establishes those rules and disseminates those norms. The chapter themes explore questions of what and how we believe, watch, eat, work, learn, and connect — questions that get to the heart of who students are and how they behave. Do they count themselves among the "we"s? As students evaluate, negotiate, and resist the roles and stances reflected in the chapters, their critical responses begin to emerge.

Moreover, the specific topics and readings within the chapters use students' own knowledge of popular culture as a springboard to deeper analysis. For example, Chapter 2, "How We Watch," covers several types of seeing and makes connections between what it means to watch and be watched. Students are asked to draw on *what* they know about diverse topics such as reality TV, physical disabilities, and advertising as a first step in considering broader questions of *how* this knowledge might connect to the culture at large.

Students today are highly culturally attuned. They are surrounded by marketing and are adept at paying attention to huge streams of competing cultural data. In order to help them translate these native skills to the college classroom, the third edition of *Acting Out Culture* provides extensive support for doing critical analysis in academic work. The introduction, "How We Read and Write about Culture (and How We Ought To)," gives students a brief crash course in the vocabulary of cultural analysis with extended, real-life examples and an annotated professional essay that walks students step by step through performing cultural analysis. In addition, a complete student essay in MLA format in the introduction makes it easier for students to see how to integrate cultural analysis into academic writing.

Why These Readings?

Because they are exceptional models of writing and thinking by contemporary writers who have important things to say about issues students care about. Each chapter includes longer pieces that support sustained reading and model in-depth critical analysis, as well as more popular pieces that go beyond trend spotting to tackle the question "How does America tick?" — with often surprising conclusions. The writers include academics such as Michael Eric Dyson (writing on the perception of African American patriotism), journalists such as Barbara Ehrenreich (who exposes the ways in which the American poor are victimized), and activists such as Naomi Klein (who objects to sex being sold to women as a form of empowerment). Although the readings approach the book's main themes from different angles, the overall focus on making and breaking the sometimes unspoken rules that govern our everyday lives creates a dialogue that will challenge students' critical thinking skills.

Why These Features in Each Chapter?

Because they introduce a variety of approaches to thinking and writing about cultural norms and rules. To analyze culture, students need to notice what they often overlook or take for granted, so each chapter opens with a photograph that captures for analysis the rules that often fly beneath students' radar. Another recurring feature that makes the often-invisible visible is **"What is normal?"** which appears in the margins of the chapter introductions. These callouts list common rules that reflect conventional wisdom and invite students to move what's in the margins of their awareness to front and center, the better to unpack and examine the assumptions nested in the norms.

Students also need to see that cultural analysis moves beyond binary thinking — the impulse to frame issues in black-and-white terms. Therefore, each chapter includes a **Rule Maker/Rule Breaker** box, which presents opposing points of view on a cultural issue in the opponents' own words.

By looking into debates such as whether Whole Foods is truly good for the organic food movement or whether the purpose of education is to train thinkers or workers, students can discover that there are more than two sides to every issue, which prepares them for the multiple perspectives and complex dialogues in the ensuing chapter.

Because students increasingly receive their daily doses of popular culture via visual media, *Acting Out Culture* presents advertisements, movies, television, and news photos as objects of analysis. Throughout, the book provides opportunities for students to respond to images as conductors of cultural messages.

The images in **Then and Now** depict popular thinking from the past to the present. Students can compare and contrast the images, but they can also use the accompanying contextual information to think further about what *hasn't* changed over time. In the "How We Believe" chapter, for example, a news photo of a Cold War-era duck-and-cover air raid drill is paired with a recent news photo showing bottles of shampoo and mouthwash being confiscated at the airport. Students are asked to consider, then and now, "What's more important? To feel safe or to be safe?" Do the images suggest similarly futile responses to overwhelming perils? If not, why not? If so, what are some alternatives?

Scenes and Un-Scenes track cultural norms in visual media by juxtaposing images on a central topic. These topics range from patriotic symbols in political speeches to the importance of victory as an American ideal. Students are encouraged to see the images as texts, composed to persuade audiences to interpret the world in a certain way. Discussion and writing prompts then direct students to think about how visual media portray, navigate, and reframe social rules and norms. What's in the pictures, and what's been left out?

Why These Writing Assignments?

Because writing is the best way for students to harness their own thinking and take control of what the culture wants them to believe. Writing is one of the most powerful tools we have for participating as active members of society, and the assignments in *Acting Out Culture* help students get a grip on the issues and construct sturdy arguments for action and change. After reading each selection, students are asked to identify the norms the piece addresses, think critically about the issues at hand, and take a stand on these topics by analyzing a writer's argument, examining the point of view, or evaluating the effectiveness of the language.

In particular, the **Putting It into Practice** assignments that close each chapter put students in the driver's seat. Often rooted in field research, these assignments urge students to consider how the issues in a chapter play out in their communities and in their personal lives. For example, in the "How We Work" chapter, students are asked to research mean salaries for a range of jobs and write about why we value different types of work in different ways, using what they've discovered by reading the chapter selections to frame their own thoughts.

Tying It All Together, a set of questions and writing prompts that close each chapter, encourages students to think about the essays in relation to one another, independent of the chapter themes. These writing prompts challenge students to consider issues such as poverty, the relationship between education and work, and consumerism on a broader level, using multiple essays from the book.

What's New in the Third Edition?

*Because American culture evolves at such a rapid pace, there are **thirty-one new readings about current and relevant issues.*** More than half of the reading selections are new, featuring up-and-coming and established voices that think through and challenge established rules and norms, whether these are online, on television, at the dinner table, or at the cash register. The new readings feature the brightest writers, educators, journalists, and activists who challenge our thinking on the issues that matter in America today. From Catherine Rampell's intelligent defense of this generation's work ethic, to Amitava Kumar's exploration of faith-based justice, to Mac McClelland's journey into the dark world of warehouse fulfillment centers, each new reading addresses issues students encounter as they move through every role they play in life.

Whether through writing or social interaction, social norms evolve around us every day. **A new chapter, "How We Connect,"** explores how we interact with, respond to, and foster the notion of connection and community, reinforcing *Acting Out Culture*'s overall belief that writing and action give students the power to change their world. The chapter addresses the theme of connection on both societal and personal levels, covering topics as timely and engaging as communication in the age of Instagram, Peter Lovenheim's campaign to spend a night in each of his neighbor's homes, and the changing definition of friendship.

For the first time, the print book is complemented by **multimodal media content,** including videos, infographics, tutorials, quizzes, and online articles. The readings and videos are supported by critical thinking and writing questions. The Instructor's Manual featured in the Instructor's Edition contains suggestions on how to integrate these media resources into your course.

What Resources Are Available to Support Teaching and Learning?

INSTRUCTOR RESOURCES

Instructor's Edition for *Acting Out Culture*, Third Edition

ISBN 978-1-4576-8735-8

The instructor's edition features *Resources for Teaching Acting Out Culture,* a manual that offers helpful suggestions for integrating the selections into your writing course and includes discussion starters and tips for using the book's many special features to get your students thinking about the rules we live by. Also available in PDF that can be downloaded from the Bedford/St. Martin's online catalog, this manual supports every selection in the book and includes overviews, discussion starters, and ideas for clustering the readings into topical or thematic units. To download this manual, visit **macmillanhighered.com/actingout/catalog**.

TeachingCentral offers the entire list of Bedford/St. Martin's print and online professional resources in one place. You'll find landmark reference works, sourcebooks on pedagogical issues, award-winning collections, and practical advice for the classroom — all free for instructors. Visit **macmillanhighered.com/teachingcentral**.

Bits collects creative ideas for teaching a range of composition topics in an easily searchable blog. A community of teachers — leading scholars, authors, and editors — discuss revision, research, grammar and style, technology, peer review, and much more. Take, use, adapt, and pass the ideas around. Then come back to the site to comment or share your own suggestions. Visit **bedfordbits.com.**

STUDENT RESOURCES

LaunchPad Solo for *Acting Out Culture*, at **macmillanhighered.com/actingout**, provides students with integrated media including videos, multimodal readings, tutorials, and access to LearningCurve—innovative, adaptive online quizzes that let students learn at their own pace, with a game-like interface that keeps them at it.

Re:Writing 3 New open online resources with videos and interactive elements engage students in new ways of writing. You'll find tutorials about using common digital writing tools, an interactive peer review game, Extreme Paragraph Makeover, and more—all for free and for fun. Visit **macmillanhighered.com/rewriting**.

ACKNOWLEDGMENTS

As befits its focus on "acting," this book owes its existence to the contributions of a truly ensemble cast. First of all, I would like to thank Alanya Harter and Leasa Burton, whose early insights and guidance several years ago helped get this project off the ground. Thanks as well to Joan Feinberg, Denise Wydra, Karen Henry, Steve Scipione, Adam Whitehurst, and Jane Carter, whose combined wealth of experience and ideas added immeasurable depth and purpose to the book.

Once again, I'd like to extend my thanks to the countless students and instructors intrepid enough to have taken a chance on a new cultural studies reader. The anecdotes, reflections, and suggestions I have received over the last three years provided me with exactly the right foundation for thinking about what this book really needs to be. In particular, I would like to single out the contributions of my own students at University of Wisconsin-Whitewater, who never stinted in offering candid and constructive feedback about both what did and did not work. Thank you to the following instructors for their valuable input on the third edition:

Olga Abella, Eastern Illinois University
Christy Ball, San Diego City College
Joyce Biletz, Bucks County Community College
Jane Blankenship, Southern Union State Community College
Krista Callahan-Caudill, University of Kentucky
Susan Cooper, Roosevelt University
John Eliason, Gonzaga University
Gareth Euridge, Tallahassee Community College
Jason Fichtel, Joliet Junior College
Loretta Henry, Montgomery County Community College
Parmita Kapadia, Northern Kentucky University
Jennifer Kluck, South Dakota State University
Melissa Miller-Waters, Houston Community College-Northwest
Alberta Miranda, California State Polytechnic University of Pomona
Geneva Cobb Moore, University of Wisconsin-Whitewater
James Scannell, Middle Tennessee State University
Karen Stewart, Norwich University
Susan Strom, Rider University
Stephanie Tingley, Youngstown State University
Selena Zeledon, California State Polytechnic University of Pomona
Richard Zuras, University of Maine at Presque Isle

This book would never have made it past manuscript without the careful work of managing editor Elise Kaiser and production editors Lidia MacDonald-Carr and Katrina Ostler. And there'd be very little in it without Linda Winters and Margaret Gorenstein to hammer out the text permissions and without Martha Friedman and Jennifer Atkins applying their expert research skills to the visuals.

Of course *Acting Out Culture* would never have rounded the corner into a third edition were it not for the stalwart efforts of my new editor, Jill Gallagher. Jill brought a degree of insight and enthusiasm to this project that reinvigorated this book precisely when it was needed most. My heartfelt thanks. My continuing affection and gratitude, as well, go to the gang at EVP Coffee in Madison. When you're lucky enough to have discovered the perfect place for writing a book, why mess with a good thing? And finally, to Emily Hall, whose belief in and support for this project continues to make it all possible. My love and thanks.

Contents

5 How We Work:

What do our jobs say about us? 337

6 How We Connect:
What forces help — and hinder — our relationships with others? 439

Introduction: How We Read and Write about Culture (and How We Ought To)

These Are the Rules

Why do you act differently at a job interview than on a night out with friends? Why do we so rarely see people wearing their pajamas to church? What accounts for the fact that you're far more likely to be on a first-name basis with a classmate than with a professor? Why does your Thanksgiving dinner conversation with a grandparent sound so different from your e-mail exchanges with friends? Whether sitting in class or working an off-campus job, chatting with family on the phone or meeting a roommate for coffee, it's hardly a secret that different situations require different standards of behavior. And while this may seem like a fairly obvious observation, it is also an important one because it raises other questions whose answers aren't nearly as simple or straightforward. Namely, why do we accept *these* standards instead of others? Why do we regard only certain ways of acting, talking, and dressing as acceptable, appropriate, *normal*? Who, or what, teaches us to be normal?

This book invites you to look at and think more deeply about the countless rules that operate in our world: where they come from, how they shape our actions and attitudes, and whether ultimately they can be questioned, challenged, or even rewritten. From the shopping mall to the classroom, from the jobs we hold to the parties we attend, from family holidays to first dates, our world abounds with an almost endless array of instructions: different collections of "dos" and "don'ts" that, while generally unspoken, nonetheless influence how we act. This book asks you to consider writing about the world around you by asking yourself a series of questions:

- *What* is it that producers of popular culture want me to do?
- *How* do they use our common cultural beliefs, identities, or fears to persuade me to do it?
- How do I *really* want to do it, or do I want to do it at all?

Unlike other books that focus on popular culture, this book asks you to begin by examining the ordinary details of your daily life. Rather than exploring the texts and products of pop culture in isolation, you will be asked to uncover and make sense of

e macmillanhighered.com/actingout
LearningCurve > Commas
> Fragments
> Run-ons and comma splices
> Active and passive voice
> Appropriate language
> Subject-verb agreement
> Working with sources (MLA)
> Working with sources (APA)

the complex connections between this material and your personal actions. It is the goal of this book to direct your attention not just to what our popular culture *says* but to what it asks you to *do* (or *think* or *feel*) as well. You probably already know quite a bit about some of the ways that popular culture attempts to influence you. For example, you already have a working understanding of what mass media has as its primary goals: ads exist to sell you products, political commentary influences you to vote a certain way, and TV producers want you to watch their programs. But deciding for yourself which pitches to tune in and which to tune out means looking deeper, beyond *what's* being sold to you to *how* it's being sold. How do writers, advertisers, politicians, and activists use common cultural ideas about normality to influence the ways you believe and behave?

Norms, Scripts, Roles, Rules: Analyzing Popular Culture

Although you are surrounded by the messages of popular culture every day, the act of talking and writing about it can seem a little foreign. How do we talk about something we all experience but none of us experience the same way? Because this analysis of popular culture emphasizes how it influences us to "act," this book invites you to take up your investigation of culture by using a set of terms borrowed from the theatre as well as cultural studies. What happens, we ask, when we begin looking at our daily actions and choices as if they were highly choreographed *performances*? When we begin thinking about the rules that define the different settings in our world, not just as instructions per se, but as *scripts* to be followed? When we start redefining our own individual behavior as *roles* we have been assigned to play? What do we gain, in sum, by thinking about our world as a kind of *stage* on which we are encouraged to *act out* parts written for us in advance?

Rule:

A spoken or unspoken directive for how people should or should not act in a given situation.

To get a handle on what this work actually looks like, let's examine one of those everyday situations as a case study. Imagine for a moment you're sitting in a college composition classroom on the first day of the semester. If we wanted to attempt the kind of analysis of our lives as performances described above, we might begin by itemizing all of the different **rules** that, while often not spelled out explicitly, nonetheless govern within this particular environ-

Norm:

A widely held cultural belief about what is appropriate in a given situation.

macmillanhighered.com/actingout
LearningCurve > Topic sentences and supporting details > Topics and main ideas

ment: sit attentively, listen to the instructor, write down all the information we are told is especially important, agree to complete the readings, compose the essays, hand in other assignments by the due dates. Likewise, there are an equal number of rules that set the standard for how we may and may not talk: no interruptions or random interjections; respond on point when questioned by the instructor; speak in a measured tone of voice and make sure to use a formal, more academic vocabulary than you might elsewhere; restrict your conversation to topics and issues that fit the course themes.

Rather than conclude our investigation here, however, we would next delve more deeply into these rules in search of what ideas they invite us to accept as **norms,** or widely held cultural ideas about what is proper thinking or behavior in a given situation. For example, we might focus on the rules around student speech in order to figure out the more fundamental messages they simultaneously convey, such as "real" learning happens only when power is shared unequally within the classroom or "quality" education requires that instructors lead and students follow. In a similar vein, we could view the rule establishing formal standards for classroom discussion as an effort to impose a value system on different types of talk, one that defines so-called personal stories as being less legitimate than more abstract forms of argumentation. When figuring out what the norms are for a given situation, it is often helpful to think about what they *aren't*. In this case, you might ask yourself what you'd think about a classmate who constantly interrupted others or an instructor who told you you'd be graded solely on your penmanship.

Social script:

A set of behavioral instructions reinforced by norms and rules.

Conducting this kind of analysis sets us up nicely for the next step in a performative approach: one that involves defining these classroom rules as **social scripts,** the ways that following the rules and accepting the norms require us to behave. Building on the connection uncovered between rules and norms, following a social script in the classroom would be performing a task like reading the assigned selections in this book both because the rules require it and because the norms tell you that reading the assigned selections will help you in your quest for education. Doing this would then allow us to move to the final phase of this analysis: thinking of your actions and choices within the classroom as if you are performing a **role,** that is, "acting out" a social script for a given situation as part of your relationship to the larger culture. In this class, for example, your role as student means that you will most likely perform the social script of participating in class because the norms tell you that education is valuable and rules of the course require your participation. The relationship between these four

Role:

How people act in relation to their standing or environment.

terms can be applied to an analysis of any topic in this book, and the more you practice them in your writing, the more this analysis will become second nature.

EXERCISE:

Think of two or three roles you are often required to play in your life (e.g., student, sibling, friend, consumer) and write a paragraph for each in which you describe the scripts you follow as a part of performing these roles. What norms and rules do you think influence how effectively you play these roles?

How Culture Shapes Us: Rules of the Road

Lest you think the classroom is an isolated example, consider how many other settings in your life are defined and governed by a similar set of rules. Whether in the classroom or on the job, at our computers or riding on the bus, we constantly find ourselves in situations that call on us to navigate the boundary separating what is acceptable to do from what is not. We don't always think about our lives in these terms because, day to day, it's easier to take for granted the way the world works, the rules we are taught to follow, and the roles we are expected to play. But the truth is that these rules and roles are anything but timeless or universal. They are rather the product of extended, often contested, efforts to define what is normal. Norms, scripts, roles, and rules have been influenced and shaped over time, products of forces that we can learn to recognize.

Jeffrey Coolidge/Getty Images

To illustrate, let's choose an example from daily life to which we can all relate: seat belts. Have you ever known a time when you weren't aware that you are supposed to wear your seat belt every time you are inside a moving car? Don't most of us think of buckling up as a normal part of our driving? Wasn't it always this way? Among all the rules we (hopefully) follow when we drive — stop on red, go on green, obey the speed limit, use the turn signals — wearing a seat belt sits squarely among them as one of the most important. The 2012 U.S. average for seat belt use was 83 percent, according to the National Highway Traffic Safety Administration.

It might surprise you to learn that although seat belts were invented in the mid-1800s, they first appeared as standard equipment in the United States in 1958, in cars made by Swedish car manufacturer Saab. Only when a federal law was passed in 1968 did it become mandatory for car manufacturers to install seat belts in every car they sold.

At first, few people wore them. Seat belts were seen as uncomfortable and inconvenient. America's car culture has always used buzz words like *freedom* to describe the experience of driving, and what feels less like being free than being — literally — restrained in your seat? Seat belt laws have always been left to states, and throughout the 1960s and 1970s, attempts to pass mandatory seat belt laws repeatedly failed in many states. New York passed the first law requiring drivers to wear seat belts — after many defeated attempts — in 1984.

Steve Hathaway/Getty Images

But although seat belt use became the law of the land (currently New Hampshire, the "Live Free or Die" state, is the only one without any seat belt laws), penalizing drivers was not enough to make wearing seat belts seem like a normal thing to do. It would take the passage of time and a concerted public service campaign, including the popular 1980s campaign featuring Vince and Larry, two crash test dummies who walked away from accidents while a voiceover intoned, "You can learn a lot from a dummy. Buckle your safety belt."

In the time since seat belts first appeared in cars, many small changes to our car culture have made wearing them seem like a good thing to do. From the accident statistics cited in the evening news, to road signs telling us how many of our fellow drivers are similarly buckled in, to dashboard lights in our cars that blink and beep until we strap ourselves in, reminders to wear our seat belts shape our thinking and our actions every time we get into a car. Playing the role of good driver now makes wearing seat belts more than a rule we obey or a script we follow. It is a social norm.

Martin Hospach/Getty Images

This historical overview of public seat-belt habits highlights another important aspect of the relationship between rules and norms. It reminds us that the process by which a rule transforms itself into a norm is neither seamless nor quick. Rather, it happens gradually and is always the product of concerted, often contentious, effort. This is important to keep in mind because it reminds us that these norms are actually subject to greater change and influence by us than at first might seem to be the case. As you hear or read debates about issues such as taxes, same-sex marriage, or the budget deficit, think about what messages each side is sending out. The more you practice, the better you'll become at understanding how these messages seep in and interact with our larger culture, as well as with our individual lives.

The World in Words

While they may be produced and promoted by our larger pop culture, the rules and norms that surround us are far from set in stone. Indeed, one of the primary goals of this book is to underscore our own ability to engage, comment upon, and (potentially) change the messages we encounter. The ways we think about and respond to popular culture are constantly changing, and these changes are often brought about by one common act: questioning the norm through writing. To see examples of how writing helps us question and rewrite norms, you need look no further than the selections in this book. Only by reading and writing about the world we live in can we understand it and learn to navigate it on our own terms.

The selections in this book are designed to challenge the ways many of us think about a wide range of topics. What they're *not* designed to do is to inspire you to agree with everything their authors say. Each of the authors in this book is using writing as a way to explore, influence, or protest against different aspects of our larger culture. By responding to their ideas with your own writing, you are entering a larger dialogue in which you begin to defend and define your place as part of that culture.

As you read these selections, remember that your ultimate goal is to talk back to these writers, to analyze and respond to their key ideas and claims, and to synthesize ideas from sources with ideas of your own. To do this, you will have to think critically about the rules, norms, social scripts, and roles involved. You may also find it useful to analyze these selections in rhetorical terms. *Rhetoric,* in the most basic sense, refers to the strategies writers use to persuade an audience to accept their point of view. We can't effectively respond to the main point unless we fully grasp the persuasive strategies used to get this point across. One of the most effective ways to do this is to look at what is called the **rhetorical situation** — the context for a writer's argument that influences the form this argument ultimately takes. Here is a set of steps that will help you analyze the rhetorical situation:

- **Question the Author:** Who is this author? What is her level of expertise about this topic? What else has she written? Is she an academic, a journalist, an activist, a politician? How do those roles influence the way she communicates her opinions? What is the author's purpose? What prompted the author to write this piece? What is the author trying to say, and why is she trying to say it? What larger goal does she seem to have in mind? What is the author's attitude toward her topic or her readers, and what words or sentences convey this attitude?
- **Question the Audience (Including Yourself):** Toward whom is this piece directed? Which words or sentences help to create the overall tone or level of formality, and what do the tone and level tell me about the intended audience? What evidence or arguments were

chosen to appeal to this audience? How do I react to this piece? Does it support or go against my own experience and exposure to this topic?

- **Question the Context:** What is the setting within which this argument is made? The classroom? The workplace? An online community? Through what medium is the writing created? If, for example, the selection is delivered online, what visuals or links are included, and how do these features affect the overall message?
- **Question the Genre:** What form does this argument take? An academic essay? A memo? A blog post? What are the conventions particular to this genre, and how might genre expectations have affected the form or content of the selection?
- **Question the Rules, Norms, and Scripts:** What rules, norms, or scripts is this author writing about? Is the author writing in support of or in opposition to them?
- **Question the Argument:** What are the main points of this piece? How does the author support his point of view? Are his examples scientific, derived from interviews, or part of his own experience? What are the possible counterarguments? How does the author anticipate and refute them?

Guided Reading: Anne Trubek's "Stop Teaching Handwriting"

To figure out how to analyze this material most effectively, let's take a look at a sample essay. The classroom, as we have already seen, offers a perfect example of how forces beyond our immediate control can shape our actions and assumptions. In this setting, we are told to obey certain rules, asked to share certain norms, expected to follow certain scripts, and called on to play certain roles. Anne Trubek's "Stop Teaching Handwriting" challenges one of these norms and presents an impassioned plea for changing it. Seeking to question a long-standing classroom practice, Trubek asks: What are the goals this handwriting rule is designed to achieve? What broader assumptions about children and learning do these goals reflect? And are these assumptions valid? This essay is annotated with the sorts of questions you might ask while reading many of the essays in this book, questions about where an essay fits in relation to established norms and how it seeks to question them. As you review the annotations, think about how the questions and observations they raise help you put the essay in perspective. Once you've done this, take a look at the analysis of the rhetorical situation that follows the essay. How does this information help prepare you to analyze this essay more effectively? And how might you use it as a model for analyzing the rhetorical situation of other essays?

This title is very direct. How do I feel about this command?

The author is a parent whose son struggles with handwriting. What sort of qualities does the role of "parent" entail?

The state has rules and expectations that students should be able to write a certain way by third grade. Do I agree? Is this rule reasonable?

Other roles. How do these affect how I perceive Trubek as an author? Is she now more of an authority?

Trubek's thesis statement challenges the rule that teaching handwriting is important. She advocates changing it. What would she prefer?

Trubek makes a claim about what society considers normal. Do I agree that traditional handwriting rules inhibit or undermine self-expression? Why might we think this way?

The norms have changed over time. How did handwriting go from being considered "formulaic" to "self-expressive"?

A famous writer. Why does Trubek invoke his name?

ANNE TRUBEK

Stop Teaching Handwriting

MY SON, WHO IS IN THIRD GRADE, SPENDS MUCH OF HIS SCHOOL day struggling to learn how to form the letter "G." Sometimes he writes it backwards. Sometimes the tail on his lowercase "T" goes the wrong way. His teachers keep telling him he may fail the state assessment standards. We have had several "interventions." Simon now fears taking up a pencil. Repeatedly being told his handwriting is bad (a fine-motor-skill issue) has become, in his mind, proof that he is a bad writer (an expression issue). He now hates writing, period.

This is absurd: I am a college professor and a freelance writer, and the only time I pick up a pen is to sign a credit-card receipt. Let's stop brutalizing our kids with years of drills on the proper formation of a cursive capital "S"—handwriting is a historical blip in the long history of writing technologies, and it's time to consign to the trash heap this artificial way of making letters, along with clay tablets, smoke signals, and other arcane technologies.

Many will find this argument hard to swallow because we cling to handwriting out of a romantic sense that script expresses identity. But only since the invention of the printing press has handwriting been considered a mark of self-expression. Medieval monks first worried that the invention of printing would be the ruin of books, as presses were more idiosyncratic and prone to human error than manuscripts produced in scriptoriums. And the monks never conceived of handwriting as a sign of identity: For them, script was formulaic, not self-expressive. That concept did not appear until the early 18th century. Still later came the notion that personality and individuality could be deduced by analyzing handwriting. All the while, print became widely available, and handwriting lost its primacy as a vehicle of mass communication.

The typewriter took handwriting down another notch. Henry James took up the then-new writing machine in the 1880s, most likely because he, like my son, had poor handwriting. By the 1890s, James was dictating all his novels to a secretary. And as novelists and businesses were putting down their pens, others started to valorize handwriting as somehow more pure and more authentic, infusing script with nostalgic romanticism. The philosopher Martin Heidegger was particularly guilty of this, writing in 1940 of the losses wrought by typewriters: "In handwriting the relation of Being to man, namely the word, is inscribed in beings themselves. . . . When writing was withdrawn from the origin of its essence, i.e. from the hand, and was transferred to the machine, a transformation occurred in the relation of Being to man."

Why do people think that handwritten script is more personal than typewritten script? Trubek provides a quote that reinforces this point of view. Do I think that way? Why?

Meanwhile, back in school, teachers were trying to get student papers to look like typewritten documents: letter characters, the students were told, should look like fonts.

The pattern doesn't change: As writing technologies evolve, we romanticize the old and adapt to the new. This will happen with keyboards, too—some contemporary novelists have ceased using them already. Richard Powers uses voice-recognition software to compose everything, including his novels. "Except for brief moments of duress, I haven't touched a keyboard for years," he says. "No fingers were tortured in producing these words—or the last half a million words of my published fiction." Powers is wonderfully free of technological nostalgia: "Writing is the act of accepting the huge shortfall between the story in the mind and what hits the page. . . . For that, no interface will ever be clean or invisible enough for us to get the passage right," he says to his computer.

Why might a writer, and the mother of a struggling child, be in favor of these changing norms? What is the purpose of writing, according to Trubek or Powers?

That shortfall is exactly how my son describes his writing troubles: "I have it all in my memory bank and then I stop and my memory bank gets wiped out," he explains. Voice-recognition software—judging from the rapid-fire monologues he delivers at dinner about Pokémon and Yu-Gi-Oh!—would help.

Do I think of writing similarly?

Pokémon and Yu-Gi-Oh! are role-playing games that are very popular with children. What does this reference suggest about the audience Trubek is addressing?

No matter what we use to write, something will be lost between conception and execution. I have yet to be convinced that making a graphite stick go in certain directions enhances intellectual development. Let us teach our kids to use the best tools at our disposal: There are plenty of cool toys out there. Boys and girls, it is time to put down your pencils.

She concludes using a play on words involving classroom rules. Why?

Analyzing the Rhetorical Situation

- **Question the Author:** Anne Trubek is a professor of English and rhetoric at Oberlin College, where she teaches a range of courses on argumentation and persuasive writing. She is currently conducting research for her upcoming book, *The History and Uncertain Future of Handwriting*. She is also the mother of a child who struggles with penmanship.
- **Question the Audience (Including Yourself):** The intended audience here seems to be parents who have children currently learning these handwriting norms or those interested in educational reform. What are your own views about handwriting? Are these skills useful in your daily life? Did you struggle with handwriting as her son does? Did this struggle affect the way you think about writing?

- **Question the Context:** Trubek's essay first appeared in *Good*, a magazine published by a group that describes itself as "pragmatic idealists working toward individual and collective progress" on social, cultural, and political issues. What does this description suggest about the audience Trubek intends to reach? About how she views the issue of handwriting instruction?
- **Question the Genre:** This piece follows the format of an opinion piece that might be found on the editorial page of a newspaper or a selection in a mainstream magazine.
- **Question the Rules:** Trubek is directly challenging the rule that requires students to be taught proper handwriting. In this sense, she seems to be calling for a change in one of the key social scripts defining life in the elementary-school classroom.
- **Question the Argument:** Trubek's main argument revolves around whether or not traditional handwriting instruction fosters meaningful learning. Claiming that it doesn't, Trubek argues that we should "adapt to the new" and regard handwriting as an obsolete skill. Is she right? Is there really no value, in this day and age, to learning handwriting? Or is Trubek overlooking ways such instruction might still be useful?

A Student's Response to Trubek

After reading Trubek's essay and considering the questions posed about her argument, you probably have your own reaction to it. Thinking about her argument in terms of rules, roles, scripts, and norms, as well as the rhetorical situation, can help you analyze the selection and come up with something to say about it. In order to convey your assessment as clearly and cogently as possible, make sure that your own written response includes several key elements:

- **Thesis:** One main claim stated clearly and directly, usually in one (or sometimes two) sentences; your thesis should be the conclusion you want your reader to draw or the point of view you want your reader to share. The thesis usually occurs at the end of the introduction, but it may be held back until the conclusion, and in some cases may be implied rather than stated directly (although this strategy is less common in academic writing).
- **Introduction:** A compelling opening paragraph or section that announces your topic, engages your intended audience, and prepares readers for what follows. An effective introduction often ends with the thesis, and in a response essay, the introduction often includes a brief summary of the reading selection, including its main point and key supporting points.

e macmillanhighered.com/actingout
Tutorials > Working with Sources
> Do I need to cite that?
> How to cite a book in MLA style
> How to cite an article in MLA style
> How to cite a database in MLA style
> How to cite a Web site in MLA style
> How to cite a database in APA style
> How to cite a Web site in APA style

- **Supporting Paragraphs:** Paragraphs that provide the reasons and evidence needed to convince readers to accept the thesis. Supporting paragraphs usually include a topic sentence that states the main point of the paragraph (a point supporting the thesis) and also include reasons and evidence that support the topic sentence. They also usually include transitions, words or phrases (such as *however, therefore, for example, granted, at first, next, finally*) that show how previous or subsequent paragraphs or sentences connect with one another.
- **Concession and Rebuttal:** A concession acknowledges that opposing points of view may be valid, and a rebuttal shows how that position is flawed. Concessions often suggest to readers that the author is reasonable and has considered others' views, while rebuttals provide authors with an opportunity to respond.
- **Conclusion:** A final paragraph or section that reminds readers of your thesis and leaves them feeling that you have delivered what your thesis and introduction promised. An effective conclusion may summarize your argument (if it is lengthy or complex), may suggest why your position is important or relevant, or may encourage the audience to take action.

Let's look at a student response to Trubek's essay. Creating an effective response to an essay requires you to do a number of things: first, identify and summarize the basic argument the author is making; second, restate the author's main points one by one; and third, explain how and why you either agree or disagree with each of these points. As you read, pay special attention to the annotations included in the margins. How do these annotations help you identify the specific elements this writer uses to make his own argument?

DON'T ERASE HANDWRITING

Jordan Radziecki

In "Stop Teaching Handwriting," Anne Trubek argues that it's time to stop teaching handwriting and to throw this "historical blip in the long history of writing technologies" on the "trash heap" (p. 8). According to Trubek, new technologies make handwriting instruction unnecessary. She thinks schools still teach it because of a "nostalgic romanticism" (p. 8) and a mistaken belief that "script expresses identity" (p. 8). While she is correct that handwriting has become less important in recent years, Trubek is wrong in her overall argument. It is only when one examines her argument in light of her roles as a

Identifies the selection by author and title; presents a summary of Trubek's argument

Summarizes Trubek's main argument, using quotations from the text to illustrate

Author's thesis statement (two sentences)

Author's thesis statement (two sentences)

Concession

Rebuttal

First supporting reason

Supporting evidence

freelance writer and professor, and also as the mother of a child who struggles with his handwriting because of poor fine-motor skills, that one begins to see that the roles she plays in her life limit her willingness to see the usefulness of handwriting to others.

While it may be true that Trubek only picks up a pen to "sign a credit-card receipt" (p. 8), she cannot assume that this is true of everyone. The ability to write is fundamental to our society's understanding of what it means to be an educated person. Students must often take quizzes, tests, and exams, and they need to be able to write legibly and with minimal effort. Moreover, how much valuable teachers' time is wasted trying to decipher illegible handwriting? Many classes tend to focus on group work, papers, and projects. Trubek doesn't consider the reality that writing for students goes beyond work done outside of class.

Author restates one of Trubek's key claims

Author's second main point

Concession and rebuttal, with author's supporting reasons

As a mother, Trubek sees her son struggle with writing and decides based on his difficulties that teaching handwriting is "brutalizing our kids" (p. 8). She sees handwriting as a problem because it is not her son's strength in school. This doesn't automatically make handwriting useless. Of course, learning fundamental skills can be difficult, and no one thinks "drills" are fun. Yet education at the elementary school level is mostly about mastering the basics. After all, you are not learning history, economics, or high-level math at that age. The subject matter is often secondary. Instead, in the third grade you are learning the rules and scripts of the educational process: you are learning how to learn inside a classroom and outside it, too. You are learning how to perform your role as a student. In a sense, knowing how to write is not much different than knowing how to sit still at your desk or knowing how to raise your hand to answer a question rather than just shouting out a response.

Transition sentence

When we get out of school or look for work as students, we still must be able to write, even though it's likely that most of our writing will be done on computers, BlackBerry devices, or iPads. Trubek's argument that technology continually advances doesn't mean that we should willingly become dependent on it to do everything for us. For a long, long time, students have been required to learn the three Rs: "reading, writing, and 'rithmetic." Despite Trubek's belief that handwriting's time has passed, educated and capable people are still expected to be able to write legibly. As a professor, Trubek should understand that technology is still too expensive for many students to own. She might see a great advantage to using voice-recognition software, but students, especially in college, will always struggle to keep money in their pockets. Some of us cannot afford to have laptops with us every second, and we shouldn't be denied education because of costly technology.

Restatement of another of Trubek's main points (in a sentence responding to her claim)

Author uses his own experience as evidence

Like Trubek, I am among those lucky enough to be able to afford a laptop, and so do most of my writing on a computer, at least outside the classroom. Trubek argues that handwriting has long been viewed, incorrectly, as an expression of one's true self, but I was never taught that handwriting expresses my true identity, nor, as Trubek says, do I "romanticize the old" (p. 9). At the same time, I do like to send handwritten "Thank You" notes: nearly everyone agrees that they are more personal and show more thought. When I write a love note or Valentine to my girlfriend, I do it by hand. Who wants to receive a word-processed love letter? I appreciate the time and care put into such letters on special occasions. I like to know that her pen has pressed down and shaped each letter. But that doesn't mean that I am sentimental about handwriting in general or that I am romanticizing an old technology in a silly way. We all value handmade things, and I am sure that Trubek is no exception to that rule in some aspect of her life. In some respects, however, the argument she makes here leaves the impression that she doesn't value such traditional practices or values at all.

Concession

Rebuttal of Trubek's claim

Author's claim, rebutting Trubek; based on personal experiences

While I sympathize with Trubek's son's problems as a third grader and understand Trubek's own frustration as a

Author restates his thesis and highlights his key difference with Trubek parent, she takes her argument too far. The answer is for her young son to get the extra help he needs (don't many students struggle with some aspect of elementary school?) to learn a crucial and fundamental skill for school—and for life.

Work Cited

Trubek, Anne. "Stop Teaching Handwriting." *Acting Out Culture: Readings for Critical Inquiry.* 3rd ed. Ed. James S. Miller. Boston: Bedford/St. Martin's, 2015. Print.

Reading Multimodal Texts

More and more frequently, the messages we receive about popular culture come in forms that extend well beyond the written word. From news photos to cartoons, blogs to YouTube videos, advertisements to magazine covers, our world is increasingly filled with media that combine elements — textual, visual (still and video), graphic, audio — to convey a message. Because multimodal texts combine many elements, fully understanding them may require careful analysis. Consider, for example, the screenshot from Edudemic, a website dedicated to providing the latest in educational research, "not by offering access to huge volumes of information, but rather by pulling back the curtains on the learning process. Public and private, K–12 and higher ed, formal and informal, academic and authentic, our goal is to mainstream the learning process."

As you look over this website, think back to the outline of the rhetorical situation presented above. How do these categories provide you with a framework for beginning your own analysis? Then take a look at the annotations included with the screenshot. How do these annotations help you read this multimodal text more rhetorically and critically?

Most of the multimodal texts in this book can be read independently or as part of a series. Just like with texts, considering images together can show you a larger picture about how our culture depicts any action or belief as normal. Imagine if you were to look at this PSA, which details the dangers that bullying poses to school-age kids, side by side with a website promoting the Department of Education's "Race to the Top" initiative. Considering the images as a pair and thinking about the current state of public schools, how would looking at the second image influence how you read the first?

e macmillanhighered.com/actingout
LearningCurve > Critical reading
Tutorials > Critical Reading > Active reading strategies

What is Edudemic? Who are its organizers, what are its goals, who are its sponsors?

Think about how textual, visual, and video elements work together. How do they present a coherent message?

What do these headers suggest about the larger goals of Edudemic and the audience this website aims to address? Is there a connection between the issues raised here and the problem of school bullying?

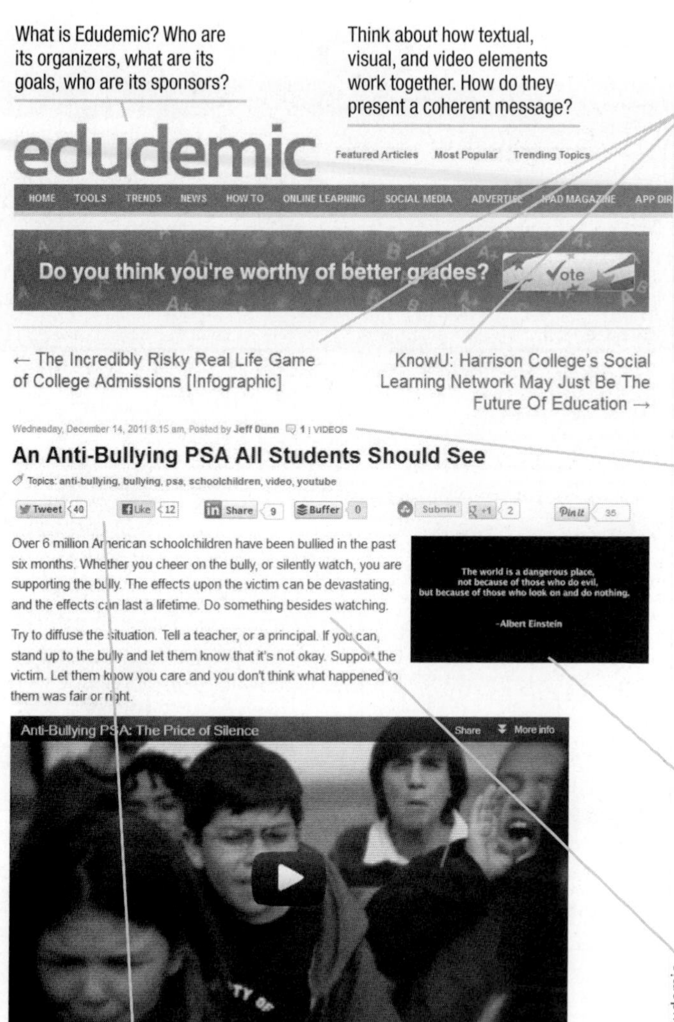

Edudemic

This story is framed to seem like a news report, but it also conveys an opinion and includes an embedded Public Service Announcement (PSA), a message disseminated by the media without charge to raise awareness of or change behavior regarding an important social issue. How do these three categories — news story, editorial, and PSA — help you make sense of the main message this website is presenting?

Einstein was celebrated not only for his revolutionary theories of mathematics and physics, but also as one of the great humanists of the twentieth century. Why include a quote from such a renowned figure? How does his statement relate to bullying?

Who is the audience for this argument? What role do the statistics play? How does this text relate to the Einstein quotation?

This website allows users to comment on and share the article or video. How does this medium foster this organization's goal(s)? What audience feedback is the statement "An anti-bullying PSA all students should see" designed to evoke?

How does this visual relate to the textual elements of this website? Does the scenario depicted here illustrate or reinforce the Einstein statement above? Who is the target audience for the embedded PSA? How does the image of the playground appeal to the intended audience?

Race to the Top

Race to the Top marks a historic moment in American education. This initiative offers bold incentives to states willing to spur systemic reform to improve teaching and learning in America's schools. Race to the Top has ushered in significant change in our education system, particularly in raising standards and aligning policies and structures to the goal of college and career readiness. Race to the Top has helped drive states nationwide to pursue higher standards, improve teacher effectiveness, use data effectively in the classroom, and adopt new strategies to help struggling schools.

To date, President Obama's Race to the Top initiative has dedicated over $4 billion to 19 states that have created robust plans that address the four key areas of K-12 education reform as described below. These states serve 22 million students and employ 1.5 million teachers in 42,000 schools, representing 45 percent of all K-12 students and 42 percent of all low-income students nationwide. The four key areas of reform include:

- Development of rigorous standards and better assessments
- Adoption of better data systems to provide schools, teachers, and parents with information about student progress
- Support for teachers and school leaders to become more effective
- Increased emphasis and resources for the rigorous interventions needed to turn around the lowest-performing schools

Forty-six states and the District of Columbia submitted comprehensive reform plans to compete in the Race to the Top competition. While 19 states have received funding so far, 34 states modified state education laws or policies to facilitate needed change, and 48 states worked together to create a voluntary set of rigorous college- and career-ready standards.

Race to the Top – District competition

In 2012, the Obama Administration launched a Race to the Top competition at the school district level. Known as Race to the Top – District, this program will invest nearly $400 million in 2012 in schools to create new models to personalize learning for students, so that they can engage their interests and take responsibility for their success.

Inspired by the education reform taking place in state K-12 systems nationwide, this next phase of RTT will build on the four core principles of reform at the classroom level, supplying teachers with the strategies and tools they need to help every student learn and succeed. The Race to the Top – District competition will encourage transformative change within schools, targeted toward leveraging, enhancing, and improving classroom practices and resources.

RELATED VIDEOS

APRIL 18, 2014 12:00 AM

West Wing Week: 4/18/14 or, "Pull Together, Fight Back, and Win"

APRIL 11, 2014 8:00 AM

West Wing Week 4/11/14 or, "Love Never Ends"

WHITEHOUSE.GOV IN YOUR INBOX

Sign up for education updates

Your Email Address

Making Yourself Heard

The bulk of this book consists of readings from a range of writers who've accepted the task of analyzing the rules we live by. You will be familiar with many of these topics, but some may be new to you. Whether you've had any exposure to these topics or not, each selection is part of a chapter that examines one of the roles we all play: believers, watchers, eaters, learners, workers, and communicators. The writing assignments in this book will ask you to consider what you know about these topics side by side with these authors so that you can ultimately decide for yourself how *you* want to play life's roles.

Why should we care about analyzing popular culture? Consider this: In the presidential campaign of 2012, the two candidates, Barack Obama and Mitt Romney, spent a combined total of $800 million on Internet advertising and outreach. Whereas sites like YouTube and Facebook were once designed for killing time, watching clips of strangers' home movies, or keeping in touch with friends, the power of popular culture has forced contenders for the biggest job in the United States to use the methods of dissemination perfected by popular culture to spread very serious promises about the future of America itself. By writing about popular culture, you become a part of the fabric of cultural conversation. This book will ask you to analyze and write about the world around you, but more importantly, it will ask you to analyze the world and to rewrite it on your own terms. You're not only about to read the writing of people who have used words as a way to navigate thousands of competing media messages. You're about to become one of them.

e macmillanhighered.com/actingout
e-Readings > Edudemic.com, *Anti-Bullying Public Service Announcement*

Alex Wong/Getty Images

1 How We BELIEVE

In what way does what we know shape our daily actions?

Introduction

Believing in "Belief"

Imagine yourself as the central actor in the following scenarios:

- First-time voter contemplating the choice between candidates in the presidential election
- Pacifist member of the National Guard summoned to active military duty overseas
- Graduating senior considering employment offers from both the Peace Corps and Goldman Sachs
- Student in a college physics class who has happened onto the answers to an upcoming midterm exam
- Shopper deciding whether to spend rent money on a new outfit
- Pedestrian on a city street approached by a homeless person asking for money
- Journalist ordered by a judge to divulge a confidential news source

Although these examples touch on different issues, they are alike in one crucial way: Each situation requires you to make a value judgment, to choose between what matters more and what matters less. In other words, each choice hinges on *what you believe*.

The concept of belief turns our attention to what lies *underneath* the choices we make: to the embedded, unspoken, and often subconscious assumptions that make these choices feel natural or normal. It's easy for most of us, given a set of circumstances, to say *what* we believe. But how often do any of us stop to think about *how* we came to hold the beliefs we take for granted? When we really stop to think about it, *how* do we make up our minds about what are the right and wrong things to do? Who or what teaches us to draw these kinds of distinctions? And how do these lessons come to feel so natural to us? Beliefs are not hypotheses. Grounded as they are in faith, in our intuitive or instinctive conviction that something is so, they require no recourse to empirical proof, factual data, or concrete evidence in order to stand in our minds as truth. Indeed, it might be said that belief encompasses all the things in our lives we're convinced are true simply because they *feel* right.

Of course, this is also what makes explaining or defending our beliefs such a tricky matter. If ultimately we can't prove the validity of our beliefs, then how can we ever hope to make others understand, accept, or share them? This dilemma — which in many ways seems hardwired into the very concept of belief — explains in part why our society is marked by so many disputes and controversies over what is and is not proper for us to believe.

If beliefs are not hypotheses that can be proved but rather convictions that are "right" because they feel so to their believers, how can different members of society ever establish common ground?

Although it is often assumed that belief applies only to questions of religion, it lies at the heart of some of our most urgent and intractable debates: from gay marriage to abortion to the war against terrorism. Belief also underlies countless decisions we confront every day in our personal lives: from how (or even whether) we vote to where we shop, from the work we perform to the money we earn, from the movies and television we watch or the books and magazines we read to the clothes we wear. Whatever the individual focus or context, belief always boils down to the same basic questions: What are the ideas and values we feel most committed to? Which ones end up just feeling right?

What is normal?

Sandra Dawes/The Image Works

What does this image ask us to believe? What are the ideas/values/ attitudes it asks us to accept as normal?

If we are not born already hardwired with ingrained assumptions about what is and is not right, then how did it happen that our beliefs feel like second nature to us now? By what process did we learn to regard only certain viewpoints and values as articles of faith?

Personal Beliefs, Cultural Norms, and Scripting Belief

To pose questions like these is to begin connecting belief to the broader question of social *norms*. Stated differently: It is to wonder about the ways our own assumptions about right and wrong intersect with — perhaps even derive from — the standards and instructions mapped by our larger culture. Indeed, such questions might even prompt us to rethink the idea of *personal* belief altogether. To be sure, we are far more used to thinking of our personal beliefs as things that belong exclusively to ourselves: those values, ethics, and priorities that, in the final analysis, remain beyond the influence of our larger culture. This definition is an attractive one because it not only reaffirms our faith in our individuality but also seems to confirm our irreducible *agency*: our ability to control and determine the choices we make. But this conceit misrepresents our fundamental relationship to the larger culture around us. Far from being tangential or irrelevant, our culture plays a central role in shaping what we come to believe, suggesting that the values we consider to be our own private domain do not belong to us alone.

What is normal?

"All in one rhythm."

The official slogan of the FIFA 2014 World Cup in soccer

TOSHIFUMI KITAMURA/AFP/Getty Images

Do you share this belief? Should we automatically accept it as normal?

We do, after all, live in a world that promotes very specific messages about what is right and what is wrong, a world in which countless instructions get issued telling us what we should and should not care about. From political campaigns to our Facebook news feed, from *Cosmopolitan* magazine to the *New York Times* business section, our cultural landscape is littered with sources that tell us, often in very authoritative tones, which things truly matter and which things do not. To compile even so cursory a list as this is to shift the terms of our conversation from individual or personal *choice* to cultural and social *power*; to confront the possibility that our own distinctions and value judgments are better understood as *scripts* we are encouraged to follow. In attempting to make sense of all this, our goal is less to "pick sides," to vote up or down on the validity of a given belief, than to better understand how beliefs take shape in the first place, how certain ideas come to acquire this special status as unexamined and cherished norms. Stated a bit more abstractly, our job is to assess the process of *legitimation*: the operations through which only select ideas and actions come to be promoted as the proper role models for the rest of us.

"Pledging Allegiance": Acting On and Acting Out Our Commitments

An example from everyday life will clarify the kind of work this involves, as well as the implications for us in undertaking it. Virtually all of us are familiar with reciting the Pledge of Allegiance. The Pledge offers an especially useful case study because it underscores how intimately connected belief is to issues of social scripts and role-playing. Whether it involves the reverential pose we are supposed to maintain toward the flag, the obligatory "hand-over-the-heart" gesture, or the language through which we express our "allegiance," the rules by which this ritual is defined couldn't be more detailed. One way to better apprehend the values underlying this performance is to ask what kind of objectives stand behind this kind of mandatory performance. Why have schoolchildren been required to recite the Pledge as a daily part of their scholastic lives? This line of inquiry leads us to wonder next about the particular assumptions this ritual reinforces — assumptions defining what our proper duties to the nation are supposed to be or the role that such patriotic expressions are supposed to play in our educational system. Building on this, we then consider the implications of endorsing these assumptions. We ponder, for instance, what it means for children to memorize and recite the loyalty oath at the center of the Pledge. What would be different if the words of the Pledge were different, if students were allowed to recite the oath silently or even to opt out from it altogether? Finally, we ask where else in our culture we are presented with opportunities to demonstrate our "allegiance" to the nation.

What is normal?

"I believe in . . . an America that lives by a Constitution that inspires freedom and democracy around the world. An America with a big, open, charitable heart that reaches out to people in need around the world. . . . An America that is still the beacon of light to the darkest corner of the world."

***Colin Powell, "The America I Believe In" from the National Public Radio series* This I Believe**

What kind of social script does this norm create? What would it feel like to act out this script in our personal lives?

It is precisely this kind of work that each of the selections included in this chapter invites us to conduct. Referencing a wide range of contemporary issues — from patriotism to consumerism, environmentalism to race — this collection shows how complex and overlapping the connection between personal beliefs and social scripts can be. Stephen Asma starts us off with an ironic and critical look at the ways our culture has turned eco-friendly behavior into a barometer of our moral character. Next, Ty Burr directs our attention to the culture of fame, asking why we invest so much time and energy tracking the lives of celebrities. Thinking about beliefs that underlie current economic orthodoxy, Michael Sandel tests the limits of our faith in markets by drawing a distinction between the kinds of things money can and cannot buy. Michael Eric Dyson, on the other hand, complicates our received ideas about patriotism, detailing how racial difference can shape the various ways "love-of-country" gets expressed. Switching from race to gender, Katie Roiphe offers a pointed defense of single motherhood, challenging what she views as our culture's all-too-easy assumptions about what does and does not get to count as a "real" family. David Brooks, meanwhile, enters into the debate over racial and gender difference

What is normal?

"I pledge allegiance to the Flag of the United States of America, and to the Republic for which it stands, one Nation under God, indivisible, with liberty and justice for all."

Can this social script be rewritten? Is there an alternative way to act upon or act out the norms promoted here?

from another angle, pushing back against what he claims is our unthinking embrace of "diversity" as a social ideal. Pursuing her own investigation of what it means to be nonwhite, Debra Dickerson digs into this debate even more deeply, offering a historically rooted challenge to our assumptions of what constitutes "race" altogether. And finally, Amitava Kumar rounds out our investigation by making a powerful case for forgiveness through the concept of "restorative justice."

e macmillanhighered.com/actingout
e-Readings > Duke University, Fuqua School of Business, *The Context of Our Character*

STEPHEN ASMA

Green Guilt

Can political convictions become so intense that they rise to the level of a religious belief? In our increasingly secular age, Stephen Asma argues, we seem to have increasingly turned our debates about social and political issues into theological disputes. Assessing the scope and intensity of current debates over "going green," Asma considers where the line between political conviction and personal belief should be drawn. Have modern politics, he asks, become our preferred vehicle for airing our moral differences? And if so, is this a good thing? Stephen Asma is a professor of philosophy at Columbia College Chicago. His books include *On Monsters: An Unnatural History of Our Worst Fears* (2009) and *Why I Am a Buddhist* (2010). This essay appeared in the *Chronicle of Higher Education* in 2010.

RECENTLY WHILE I WAS BRUSHING MY TEETH, MY 6-YEAR-OLD SON scolded me for running the water too long. He severely reprimanded me, and at the end of his censure asked me, with real outrage, "Don't you love the earth?" And lately he has taken up the energy cause, scampering virtuously around the house turning off lights, even while I'm using them. He seems as stressed and anxious about the sins of environmentalism as I was about masturbation in the days of my Roman Catholic childhood.

Not too long ago, at a party, a friend confessed in a group conversation that he didn't really recycle. It was as if his casual comment had sucked the air out of the room—I think the CD player even skipped. He suddenly became a pariah. A heretic had been detected among the orthodox flock. During the indignant tongue-lashing that followed, people's faces twisted with moral outrage.

Many people who feel passionate about saving the planet justify their intense feelings by pointing to the seriousness of the problem and the high stakes involved. No doubt they are right about the seriousness. There are indeed environmental challenges, and steps must be taken to ameliorate them. But there is another way to understand the unique passion surrounding our need to go green.

Not too long ago, at a party, a friend confessed . . . that he didn't really recycle. It was as if his casual comment had sucked the air out of the room.

Friedrich Nietzsche was the first to notice that religious emotions, like guilt and indignation, are still with us, even if we're not religious. He claimed that we were living in a post-Christian world—the church no longer dominates political and economic life—but we, as a culture, are still dominated by Judeo-Christian values. And those values are not obvious—they are not the Ten Commandments or any particular doctrine, but a general moral outlook.

You can see our veiled value system better if you contrast it with the one that preceded Christianity. For the pagans, honor and pride were valued, but for the Christians it is meekness and humility; for the pagans it was public shame, for Christians, private guilt; for pagans there was a celebration of hierarchy, with superior and inferior people, but for Christians there is egalitarianism; and for pagans there was more emphasis on justice, while for Christians there is emphasis on mercy (turning the other cheek). Underneath all these values, according to Nietzsche, is a kind of psychology—one dominated by resentment and guilt.

Every culture feels the call of conscience—the voice of internal self-criticism. But Western Christian culture, according to Nietzsche and then Freud, has conscience on steroids, so to speak. Our sense of guilt is comparatively extreme, and, with our culture of original sin and fallen status, we feel guilty about our very existence. In the belly of Western culture is the feeling that we're not worthy. Why is this feeling there?

All this internalized self-loathing is the cost we pay for being civilized. In a very well-organized society that protects the interests of many, we have to refrain daily from our natural instincts. We have to repress our own selfish, aggressive urges all the time, and we are so accustomed to it as adults that we don't always notice it. But if I was in the habit of acting on my impulses, I would regularly kill people in front of me at coffee shops who order elaborate whipped-cream mocha concoctions. In fact, I wouldn't bother to line up in a queue, but would just storm the counter (as I regularly witnessed people doing when I lived in China) and muscle people out of my way. But there is a small wrestling match that happens inside my psyche that keeps me from such natural aggression. And that's just morning coffee—think about how many times you'd like to strangle somebody on public transportation.

Instead of religious sins plaguing our conscience, we now have the transgressions of leaving the water running, leaving the lights on, failing to recycle, and using plastic grocery bags instead of paper.

When aggression can't go out, then it has to go inward. So we engage in a kind of self-denial, or self-cruelty. Ultimately this self-cruelty is necessary and good for society—I cannot unleash my murderous tendencies on the whipped-cream-mocha-half-decaf latte drinkers. But my aggression doesn't disappear, it just gets beat down by my own discipline. Subsequently, I feel bad about myself, and I'm supposed to. Magnify all those internal daily struggles by a hundred and you begin to see why Nietzsche thought we were always feeling a little guilty. But historically speaking we didn't really understand this complex psychology—it was, and still is, invisible to us. We just felt bad about ourselves, and slowly developed a theology that made sense out of it. God is perfect and pristine and pure, and we are sinful, unworthy maggots who defile the creation by our very presence. According to Nietzsche, we have historically needed an ideal God because we've needed to be cruel to ourselves, we've needed to feel guilty. And we've needed to feel guilty because we have instincts that cannot be discharged externally—we have to bottle them up.

Feeling unworthy is still a large part of Western religious culture, but many people, especially in multicultural urban centers, are less religious. There are still those who believe that God is watching them and judging them, so their feelings of guilt and moral indignation are couched in the traditional theological furniture. But increasing numbers, in the middle and upper classes, identify themselves as being secular or perhaps "spiritual" rather than religious.

Now the secular world still has to make sense out of its own invisible, psychological drama—in particular, its feelings of guilt and indignation. Environmentalism, as a substitute for religion, has come to the rescue. Nietzsche's argument about an ideal God and guilt can be replicated in a new form: We need a belief in a pristine environment because we need to be cruel to ourselves as inferior beings, and we need that because we have these aggressive instincts that cannot be let out.

Instead of religious sins plaguing our conscience, we now have the transgressions of leaving the water running, leaving the lights on, failing to recycle, and using plastic grocery bags instead of paper. In addition, the righteous pleasures of being more orthodox than your neighbor (in this case being more green) can still be had—the new heresies include failure to compost, or refusal to go organic. Vitriol that used to be reserved for Satan can now be discharged against evil corporate chief executives and drivers of gas-guzzling vehicles. Apocalyptic fear-mongering previously took the shape of repent or burn in hell, but now it is recycle or burn in the ozone hole. In fact, it is interesting the way environmentalism takes on the apocalyptic aspects of the traditional religious narrative. The idea that the end is nigh is quite central to traditional Christianity—it is a jolting wake-up call to get on the righteous path. And we find many environmentalists in a similarly earnest panic about climate change and global warming. There are also high priests of the new religion, with Al Gore ("the Goracle") playing an especially prophetic role.

We even find parallels in environmentalism of the most extreme, self-flagellating forms of religious guilt. Nietzsche claims that religion has fostered guilt to such neurotic levels that some people feel culpable and apologetic about their very existence. Compare this with extreme conservationists who want to sacrifice themselves for trees and whales. And teachers, like myself, will attest to significant numbers of their students who feel that their cats or whatever are equal to human beings. And not only are members of the next generation egalitarian about all life, but they often feel positively awful about the way that their species has corrupted and defiled the whole beautiful symphony of nature. The planet, they feel, would be better off without us. We are not worthy. In this extreme form, one does not seek to reduce one's carbon footprint so much as eliminate one's very being.

Pointing out these parallels is not meant to diminish the environmental cause. We should indeed do the things in our power, and within reason, to sustain the planet. But we have a tendency to become neurotic and overly anxious, especially when we are regularly told, via green marketing ploys, that each one of us is responsible for the survival of the planet. That's a heavy guilt trip.

The same demographic group for whom religion has little or no hold (namely white liberals) turns out to be the most virulent champion of all things green. Is it possible that these folks must vent their moral spleen on environmentalism because they don't have all the theological campaigns (e.g., opposing gay marriage, opposing abortion, etc.) on which social conservatives exercise *their* indignation?

If environmentalism is a substitute for religion—a way of validating certain emotions—then we might expect to find other secular surrogates for guilt and indignation. Our tendencies to sin, repent, and generally indulge in self-cruelty can be seen cropping up in our obsessions about health and fitness, for example. Struggling with our weight (diet and relapse) has risen above the other deadly sins to take a dominant position in our secular self-persecution. And our resentful aggression still manages to find some occasional pathways to the external world. We may not be able to punch the people we want to punch in real life, but we can turn some of our aggression outward at the reprobates of TV land. What a joyful hatred we all felt at the Octomom or Britney. It was a thoroughly cleansing bit of moral outrage. Or consider the inflamed moral drama for viewers of the *Jon & Kate Plus Eight* debacle. And more of this kind of indignation, previously reserved for religious condemnation, can be seen and heard everywhere on the screens and airwaves of the 24-hour "news" cycle. Large segments of the news seem calculated to facilitate the catharsis of our built-up resentment. Daytime talk shows and reality shows seem similarly designed to elicit our righteous anger. They form the other side of the religious coin—in addition to the self-cruelty of guilt, we can vent our aggression outwardly (like a crowd at a witch drowning) as long as it's justified by piety and the defense of virtue and orthodoxy.

Environmentalism is a much better hang-up than worrying about the spiritual pitfalls of too much masturbation. Even if it's neurotic, it's still doing some good. But environmentalism, like every other ism, has the potential for dogmatic zeal and obsession. Do we really need one more humorless religion? Let us save the planet, by all means. But let's also admit to ourselves that we have a natural propensity toward guilt and indignation, and let that fact temper our fervor to more reasonable levels.

DISCUSSION

1. Asma refers to contemporary politics as our "veiled value system" (p. 26). What do you think he means by this phrase? What vision of political life does this suggest? Does this vision accord with your own views?
2. In our day, writes Asma, environmentalism has come to serve as "a substitute for religion" (p. 27). How do you respond to this claim? In your view, is it valid to liken this kind of political stance to religious belief? And how does such a comparison change the way we typically think about environmentalism?
3. In Asma's reading of Western history, guilt has long served as the glue for keeping society intact. "All this internalized self-loathing," he writes, "is the cost we pay for being civilized" (p. 26). Do you agree? Is "guilt" or "self-loathing" necessary to maintaining social cohesion? Can you think of an example that confirms this hypothesis?

WRITING

4. For Asma, the intense debates around environmentalism are but one example of a much broader trend within our current pop culture: "Large segments of the news seem calculated to facilitate the catharsis of our built-up resentment. Daytime talk shows and reality shows seem similarly designed to elicit our righteous anger" (p. 28). Conduct your own pop culture analysis to assess the validity of Asma's claim. First, choose a cultural text (i.e., TV show, website, advertisement, etc.) that, in your view, seems designed to elicit audience anger. Then use this text as a case study for testing out Asma's hypothesis. Given the issues it raises, the tone it strikes, the audience it addresses, does this text seem "calculated to facilitate catharsis"? If so, what kind? And how do you evaluate the ultimate effect? Is it positive? Negative?
5. "Instead of religious sins plaguing our conscience," Asma declares, "we now have the transgressions of leaving the water running, leaving the lights on, failing to recycle, and using plastic grocery bags instead of paper" (p. 27). Write a longer essay (three to five pages) in which you identify and evaluate the comparison Asma is making here. According to Asma, what are the key differences between the "religious sins" of the past and the "transgressions" that characterize everyday life today? And what larger point is he trying to make here about the way our understanding of "sin" has changed? Then take a closer look at each of the "transgressions" he lists here. To what extent, in your view, is it valid to feel "guilty" about each? Is it helpful, necessary, and/or right for these oversights to "plague our conscience"? Why or why not?
6. "[L]ike every other ism," writes Asma, environmentalism "has the potential for dogmatic zeal and obsession" (p. 29). In light of his own examination of an "ism" — in this case, "patriotism" — do you think Michael Eric Dyson (p. 52) would agree? Given what he has to say about different forms patriotism can take in modern America, do you think Dyson would express sympathy or agreement with Asma's point regarding the "dogmatic" or "obsessive" nature of all "isms"? Why or why not? As you answer this question, look for passages from Dyson's essay that seem most pertinent, and spend some time explaining how they help support your own argument here.

TY BURR

The Faces in the Mirror

Celebrities have beguiled us since the days of the earliest silent movies. But why we have remained so fascinated for so long is far from a straightforward matter. Do we obsessively focus on celebrities because we love them or loathe them? Do we look upon their lives as an unattainable ideal or a cautionary tale? Taking up these kinds of questions, Ty Burr presents us with a brief history of celebrity and celebrity worship in modern America. When we look at celebrities, he asks, what exactly do we see? To what extent do we use celebrities as a kind of mirror, reflecting back what we wish (or fear) to see in ourselves? Ty Burr is film critic for the *Boston Globe*. He is the author of two books: *The Best Old Movies for Families: A Guide to Watching Together* (2007) and *Gods Like Us: On Movie Stardom and Modern Fame* (2012), from which the selection below is excerpted.

WHAT ARE THE STARS REALLY LIKE?

That question is not the subject of this book. The subject of this book is why we ask the question in the first place.

Still, people want to know. In my day job, I'm a professional film critic for a major metropolitan daily newspaper and throughout the 1990s I wrote reviews and articles for a national weekly entertainment magazine. Over the years, I've interviewed a number of actors and directors, ingénues and legends, and often the first question I'm asked by people is just that: What are they *really like?*

The answers always disappoint. Always. They range from "Pretty much what you see on the screen" to "Not all that interesting sometimes" to "Pleasantly professional" to an unspoken "Why do you care?" When pressed (and I'm usually pressed), I'll allow that Keira Knightley and I had a lovely chat once and Lauren Bacall was nastier than she needed to be to a young reporter just starting out. That Laura Linney seemed graciously guarded, Steve Carell centered and sincere, Kevin Spacey cagey and smart. I once took the young Elijah Wood to a Hollywood burger joint while interviewing him for the magazine. He was a kid who really liked that burger, no more and no less.

They are, in short, working actors, life-sized and fallible. There is no mystery here. But this is not what you want to hear, is it? If there's nothing genuinely special about movie stars, why do we give them our money? Why do we pay for cheaper and cheaper substitutes—reality stars, hotel heiresses, the Kardashians? Are we interested in the actual person behind the star façade, or just desperate to believe the magic has a basis in reality?

In truth, the relationship between persona and person can be problematic. Of all the celebrity encounters I've experienced, the one that sticks with me is the briefest, most random, possibly the saddest. Early one morning, many years ago, I came out of my apartment building on the Upper West Side of Manhattan and got ready to go for a run. As I breathed the spring air, the door to the adjoining building opened and another jogger emerged. We started stretching our hamstrings side by side, and I glanced over and acknowledged the other man with a friendly nod.

Three almost invisible things happened in rapid succession. First, he nodded back with a pleasant smile. Second, I realized that he was Robin Williams. Third, he realized that I realized he was Robin Williams, and his eyes went dead. Not just dead: empty. It was as if the storefront to his face had been shuttered, cutting off any possibility of interaction. There wasn't anything rude about this, and I respected his privacy, honoring the code observed by all New Yorkers who know they can potentially cross paths with an A-list name at any corner deli. Or was it his celebrity I was respecting? Whichever, a very small moment of human connection between two people had been squelched by the appearance of a third, not-quite-real person: the movie star. The second I recognized who the other jogger was, his persona got in the way. I couldn't not see him as "Robin Williams." And he knew it.

This happens dozens of times in any well-known person's day. It's why Williams's eyes shut down so completely; it's why I left him alone and went for my run. I felt bad for the man, even if I hadn't actually done anything. Because people do, in fact, do things. Think of all those fans who meet movie stars and insist on being photographed with them, the snapshot serving as both proof and relic. Think, too, of the man who shot and killed John Lennon but made sure to get his autograph first.

As the twenty-first century settles into its second decade, we are more than ever a culture that worships images and shrinks from realities.

Why a history of movie stardom? To celebrate, interrogate, and marvel over where we've been, and to weigh where we are now. As the twenty-first century settles into its second decade, we are more than ever a culture that worships images and shrinks from realities. Once those images were graven; now they are projected, broadcast, podcast, blogged, and streamed. There is not a public space that doesn't have a screen to distract us from our lives, nor is there a corner of our private existence that doesn't offer an interface, wireless or not, with the Omniverse, that roiling sea of infotainment we jack into from multiple access points a hundred times a day. The

Omniverse isn't real, but it's never turned off. You can't touch it, but you can't escape from it. And its most common unit of exchange, the thing that attracts so many people in the hopes of becoming it, is celebrity. Famous people. Stars.

Or what we've traditionally called stars, which traditionally arose from a place called the movies. As originally conceived during the heyday of the Hollywood studio system, movie stars were bigger and more beautiful than they are now, domestic gods who looked like us but with our imperfections removed (or, in some cases, gorgeously heightened). Our feelings about them were mixed. We wanted to be these people, and we were jealous of them too. We paid to see them in the stories the movie factories packaged for us, but we were just as *fascinated*—more fascinated, really—with the stories we believed happened offscreen, to the people the stars seemed to be.

Not many of us remember those days. Moreover, few are interested in connecting the dots between what we want from the movie stars now and what we wanted from them then—and the "then" before that, and the "then" before that, all the way back to the first flickering images in Thomas Edison's laboratory. The desires have changed, but so has the intensity. Mass media fame, a cultural concept that arose a century ago as a side effect of a new technology called moving pictures, now not only drives the popular culture of America (and, by extension, much of the world), but has become for many people a central goal and measure of self-worth.

When we were content to gaze up at movie stars on a screen that seemed bigger than life, the exchange was fairly simple. We paid money to watch our daily dilemmas acted out on a dreamlike stage, with ourselves recast as people who were prettier, smarter, tougher, or just not as scared. The stories illustrated the dangers of ambition, the ecstasies of falling in love, the sheer delight of song and dance. Because certain people embodied uniquely charismatic variations on how to react in certain situations—Bogart's street smarts, Kate Hepburn's gumption, Jimmy Stewart's bruised decency, Bette Davis's refusal ever to budge—we wanted to see them over and over again.

We want the stars, but we want what they have even more.

We wanted to *be* them. Why else would women have bought knock-offs of Joan Crawford's white organdy dress in 1932's *Letty Linton* (half a million sold through Macy's) or men have chosen to go without an undershirt like Clark Gable in 1934's *It Happened One Night*? On an even deeper level, we also burned with resentment at the stars' presumption to set themselves up as gods when our egos told us we were the ones deserving of attention. Behind every adoring fan letter is the urge to murder and replace. An image that reoccurs time and again in the pages that follow is that of a star out in public, surrounded by a mob that grabs and tears, ripping off buttons, chunks of clothing, as if to simultaneously absorb and obliterate the object of affection. There is love there and also a powerful, inarticulate rage. We want the stars, but we want what they have even more.

The strange part is that we got it . . . The history of modern stardom isn't just a roll call of icons but a narrative of how those icons affected the people and society that watched them, what psychic and cultural needs each star answered, and how that has changed over time. It's an ever-evolving story of industrial consolidation intertwined with technological advancement, each wondrous new machine bringing the dream tantalizingly closer to the control of the *dreamers*—to us.

The early cinema, for instance, allowed audiences to see actors close up, which rendered them both more specific and more archetypal than the players of the stage. The arrival of sound then let us hear the new stars' voices. Radio brought those voices into our homes; TV brought the rest of the performer, repackaged for fresh rules of engagement. Home video let us own the stars and watch them when we wanted; video cameras allowed us to play at being stars ourselves. The Internet has merely completed the process by providing an instant worldwide distribution and exhibition platform for our new star-selves, however many of them we want to manufacture.

In addition, an extremely profit-driven group of entertainment conglomerates now keeps the popular culture rapt in a feedback loop of movie stars, TV stars, pop stars, rap stars, tweener stars, reality stars, and Internet stars, all mutable, all modeling ways in which consumers can alter their own homemade identities for maximum appeal to friends and strangers. The revolution is complete. One hundred years ago, Charlie Chaplin, Mary Pickford, and a handful of others became the very first living human beings to be simultaneously recognizable to, in theory, everyone on earth. Today, a twelve-year-old child can achieve the same status with an afternoon, a digital camera, and a YouTube account. We have built the mirror we always dreamed about, and we cannot look away.

. . . The classic star system—as created by the Hollywood studios in the teens and twenties and sustained through the 1960s and, although much diminished, into the present day—was modern humanity's Rorschach test. We looked at those inkblots on the screen and saw what we needed: proof of discrete, individual, desirable human types. The system evolved, with stars falling away and new ones rising as necessary to the cultural demands of the time. Marlon Brando would have been unthinkable before World War II, and yet postwar Hollywood would be unthinkable without him. Each era has its own yearnings, pop star responses, and technological developments that change how the machine works, and each is a further step toward where we are now.

Where *are* we now? A way station, I believe, on the way to someplace very different, more truthful in some aspects, profoundly less so in others. A century of mass media and the concept of "stardom" have changed human society in ways we can barely encompass, but the one constant has been an urge toward personal fulfillment and freedom of identity that would have seemed perverse, if not sacrilegious, to our grandparents' grandparents.

Centuries ago, the common man's worth was marked primarily by *duty*—how hard he worked and how hard he prayed. The notion of "ego," of something unique within each individual person that needed to be expressed, was alien. What stars there were tended to be generals and kings, religious leaders and charlatans, and you didn't aspire to be like them. You simply followed where they led, or you kept your head down and worked the farm.

The movies helped change that. (All votes for movable type, the Enlightenment, the decline of the agrarian state, Sigmund Freud, and the rise of constitutional self-government will be counted.) The new medium tricked us, though, because it turned flesh-and-blood actors into dream-like phantoms writ large upon a wall. They didn't speak at first, either, so you could impose upon them any voice, any meaning, you wished. The stars thus became better versions of ourselves, idealized role models who literally acted out the things we wanted to do but didn't dare. If they died, as Cagney always seemed to, we still got safely up and went home.

Somewhere along the line, after many decades, we learned *not* to trust these role models anymore. Technology is inextricable in this, because each new medium effectively disproves the one preceding it. TV is somehow "better" than the movies, video and cable are "better" than network TV, the Internet is "better" than five hundred channels of Comcast. "Better" means less restricted in location and time, more portable, and more directly serving the immediate needs of you and me. We plug into star culture and its discontents on our cell phones now. The latest slice of the Lindsay Lohan/Mel Gibson/Charlie Sheen Meltdown Show is right there any time we want it.

When a specific medium is put out to pasture, so are its most representative figures, as the stars of the silent era would be the first to tell you. At the same time, that primal ache has never gone away. If anything, it has gotten stronger, because each wave of technology doesn't always make our lives better. Busier, yes, and faster. More than anything else, it just brings us closer to the mirror in which we reflect ourselves to the world. We still each in our own way ache to be somebody, to make our mark, to stand out from the crowd, *to be seen*. Otherwise, who are we? What's life for? Uniqueness of identity is the promise movie stars hold out to us; if they're able to separate themselves from the swarm of humanity, so might we.

I wonder what Marlene Dietrich would make of all this. *There* was a woman who knew from desire and who trusted a cameraman to keep her secret—that the magnificently shadowed creature of all those early '30s classics was an ordinary German girl with bedroom eyes. Or the other Hollywood gods—what would they think? Archie Leach and Ruby Stevens, Frances Gumm and Marion Morrison and Norma Jean Mortenson.

Who? Well, yes, you know them as Cary Grant and Barbara Stanwyck, Judy Garland and John Wayne and Marilyn Monroe. Those original names were left in the closet, along with Roy Scherer's—excuse me, Rock Hudson's—homosexuality. Entire pasts were abridged or erased because they didn't jibe with the luxuriant beauty onscreen, the gorgeous lie. The movie moguls kept the secrets, and the press played along because they understood that, really, we didn't want to know.

With some exceptions, though, the mystery that surrounded movie stars for the better part of a century is now highly suspect. Indeed, many pop consumers consider it their duty to pull down the idols and pass their dirty secrets around the Web. How can we trust Tom Cruise the movie star when we can Google the "real" one bouncing on Oprah's couch? We now have as much control over the idea of celebrity as the studio publicity departments once did, and is it any wonder that movie stars are ruthlessly mocked while our own sweet selves are headlining on YouTube?

Sometime in the past two decades, between video and pay cable and the rise of the World Wide Web, the walls were breached and the masses poured in.

Is this something like revenge? Or is it just the evolution of a species gradually conditioned to narcissism? For a century we accepted stardom as a blessing visited on those more gifted than we, a state of grace to which you and I in our drabness could not, and should not, aspire. We knew our place, and it was in the fifth row of the Bijou, worshiping as MGM chief Louis B. Mayer handed out the communion wafers. In 1919, when Chaplin and Pickford joined with Douglas Fairbanks and D.W. Griffith in creating United Artists, the first movie studio run by the talent, the other movie moguls complained "that the inmates had taken over the asylum." If only they knew. Sometime in the past two decades, between video and pay cable and the rise of the World Wide Web, the walls were breached and the masses poured in. The asylum is now ours.

You could see it coming a long way off, actually—since the late 1960s, with their anarchic overturning of the old ways. (Or maybe even further back, when Elvis arrived—an outsider who didn't need a new name.) The acknowledged motto of the new star order is Andy Warhol's much-abused announcement in the catalog of a 1968 Swedish art show that "in the future everyone will be world-famous for 15 minutes." A better, more concise variation came a year later, when Sly Stone recorded the number one pop hit "Everybody Is a Star."

The song's title was offered in a spirit of blissful hippie democracy, a counterculture version of the same promise that had lured tens of thousands of men and women to California and the entertainment industry over the decades. That promise said that you are the center of the universe, if only you can get the rest of the world to see it. Sly tweaked it enough to take the desperate edge off. Stay home, the song advises, and take heart. You are *already* your own star. Technology would eventually prove Stone correct. In effect, he predicted the Internet down to the size of a blogger's bedroom.

What happens to stardom, then, when we at last become stars ourselves? It mutates and spreads in a thousand directions. From our new perch we can now ridicule stars like Cruise, Gibson, Christian Bale, disseminating their audiovisual missteps to the world at large. We can lightly or wholly fictionalize our existence on Facebook or Second Life, developing plot threads, heroes, villains as we go: life not lived but shaped and produced. The new rules have also helped establish the half-lit world of reality TV, with its stars who are not stars because they are us (or less), as well as grotesque mash-ups of fame-mongering like *I Want a Famous Face!*, the 2004 MTV series that featured regular folks who volunteered to undergo surgery to look like their favorite celebrity. One wonders what these people felt when they came out of anesthesia and found they were still the same inside. . . .

. . . If there's a thematic through-line, it's in the ways the gods and goddesses of Hollywood were yanked off their thrones over the years as audiences increasingly demanded stars who looked and acted like them—i.e., people who seemed real rather than fake—and as the industry got better at the job of providing those stars. In 1949, Marlon Brando made every other Hollywood actor look like a fraud; twenty years later, Dustin Hoffman, Jack Nicholson, and Robert De Niro served as the new benchmarks in realism. Today it's the cast of *Jersey Shore* who are signifiers of actuality at its most extreme—a "realness" that makes us feel better about our own.

Yes the classic movie star lives on—has to live on, if only to give us something better to aspire to than Snookie and the Situation. We still have a varied buffet of star types before us, from the impenetrable Hollywood gloss of Jolie and Brad Pitt to the scruffy approachability of recent arrivals like Ellen Page and Joseph Gordon-Levitt. Younger audiences respond to those last two because they speak and act in ways that resonate with how people their age actually see themselves, as Hoffman did in the 1960s, as Mickey Rooney did in the 1930s. We want performers who reflect our reality—who seem to order that reality, comment on it, laugh at it, blow it up. The ones who do so with an appealing consistency of persona across a range of movies or other forms of media are those we call stars.

A distinction can and should be made between stars and actors. All stars are actors one way or another; not all actors are stars. Great actors—the true master craftsmen and women—transform themselves in role after role, and if the projects are successful and the actor is celebrated enough, that changeability becomes his or her persona, whether it's Lon Chaney in the silent era, Alec Guinness after World War II, Meryl Streep in the 1980s, or Cate Blanchett today.

Stars, by contrast, don't hide themselves. On the contrary, the great movie stars each construct an image that is bigger than their individual films even as it connects those films in a narrative of unfolding personality. This is important. . . . every successful star creates a persona and within that persona is an idea. The films are merely variations on the idea. The idea can be expressed as action or as attitude or simply as an unstated philosophy of how to live and behave in this world (or how not to live and how not to behave) that the player embodies in charismatic, two-dimensional human form. You could call it identity, too, but it's identity so contained, defined, and appealing that moviegoers grasp at it in an attempt to define their own senses of self. . . .

Some of the questions we need to ask ourselves are the same as they've been for decades. Why does a particular star speak to one era but not another? How much of any celebrity is his or her own invention and how much our projection? Other questions are vastly different from those of a century, half a century, even a decade ago. Why do we pay to see famous actors in a movie theater, then go home and make fun of them on the Web? Why do we still need Hollywood's manufactured identities when we can create them for ourselves? Am I my Facebook page, or the other way around? Why, oh Lord, do we Google ourselves? And how are we supposed to stop when it feels so good?

DISCUSSION

1. How are we taught to think about fame? To what extent is the prospect of "being famous" promoted in our popular culture as a social script? Can you think of any settings in contemporary life where we are especially encouraged to act out this script?
2. The book from which this selection is excerpted is titled *Gods Like Us* (2012). What do you make of this title? What larger point about our cultural obsession with celebrity is Burr making by choosing this title?
3. When it comes to celebrities, Burr declares, there is an important distinction to draw between *personality* and *persona*. How do you understand the difference between these two terms? And what larger point about fame and famous people is Burr trying to make by drawing this distinction?

WRITING

4. Among other things, Burr is interested in exploring the effect the rise of digital culture has had on the ways we think about fame. "There is not a public space that doesn't have a screen to distract us from our lives, nor is there a corner of our private existence that doesn't offer an interface, wireless or not, with the Omniverse, that roiling sea of infotainment we jack into from multiple access points a hundred times a day" (p. 32). In a short essay, analyze and evaluate the specific claim Burr is making here. What point is he trying to make about the new roles the Web has created for us and about the way these roles have changed how we think about celebrity? Do you agree? Why or why not?
5. "One hundred years ago, Charlie Chaplin, Mary Pickford, and a handful of others became the very first living human beings to be simultaneously recognizable to, in theory, everyone on earth. Today, a twelve-year-old child can achieve the same status with an afternoon, a digital camera, and a YouTube account. We have built the mirror we always dreamed about, and we cannot look away" (p.34). In a three- to five-page essay, describe, analyze, and evaluate the thesis Burr is advancing here. What larger point is Burr trying to make by comparing the Hollywood stars of old to a twelve-year-old with a YouTube account, the tools of digital culture to a mirror from which we "cannot look away"? How valid are his points?
6. Burr's essay describes the commodification of people: images that end up as brands and marketed like any other product. How do you think Michael Sandel (p. 40) would respond to this idea? Given the argument he makes about the "morality of markets," do you think he would assess our contemporary culture of celebrity in positive or negative terms? Why?

MICHAEL SANDEL

Markets and Morals

In a world marked by an ever-growing penchant for privatization, one in which services and opportunities formerly considered part of the public domain are increasingly auctioned for sale, it is now an open question whether there still exist things in our culture that cannot be bought and sold. Taking stock of this situation, noted philosopher Michael Sandel offers a few cautionary thoughts about embracing a belief in money as the sole arbiter of value. Michael Sandel is the Anne T. and Robert M. Bass Professor of Government at Harvard University. His books include *Liberalism and the Limits of Justice* (1982), *Democracy's Discontent* (1996), *Public Philosophy: Essays on Morality in Politics* (2005), and *The Case against Perfection: Ethics in the Age of Genetic Engineering* (2007). His most recent book is *What Money Can't Buy: The Moral Limits of Markets* (2012). The essay below is excerpted from the book's introduction.

THERE ARE SOME THINGS MONEY CAN'T BUY, BUT THESE DAYS, NOT many. Today, almost everything is up for sale. Here are a few examples:

- *A prison cell upgrade: $82 per night.* In Santa Ana, California, and some other cities, nonviolent offenders can pay for better accommodations—a clean, quiet jail cell, away from the cells for nonpaying prisoners.
- *Access to the car pool lane while driving solo: $8 during rush hour.* Minneapolis and other cities are trying to ease traffic congestion by letting solo drivers pay to drive in car pool lanes, at rates that vary according to traffic.
- *The services of an Indian surrogate mother to carry a pregnancy: $6,250.* Western couples seeking surrogates increasingly outsource the job to India, where the practice is legal and the price is less than one-third the going rate in the United States.
- *The right to immigrate to the United States: $500,000.* Foreigners who invest $500,000 and create at least ten jobs in an area of high unemployment are eligible for a green card that entitles them to permanent residency.
- *The right to shoot an endangered black rhino: $150,000.* South Africa has begun letting ranchers sell hunters the right to kill a limited number of rhinos, to give the ranchers an incentive to raise and protect the endangered species.

- *The cell phone number of your doctor: $1,500 and up per year.* A growing number of "concierge" doctors offer cell phone access and same-day appointments for patients willing to pay annual fees ranging from $1,500 to $25,000.
- *The right to emit a metric ton of carbon into the atmosphere: €13 (about $18).* The European Union runs a carbon emissions market that enables companies to buy and sell the right to pollute.
- *Admission of your child to a prestigious university:* Although the price is not posted, officials from some top universities told *The Wall Street Journal* that they accept some less than stellar students whose parents are wealthy and likely to make substantial financial contributions.

Not everyone can afford to buy these things. But today there are lots of new ways to make money. If you need to earn some extra cash, here are some novel possibilities:

- *Rent out space on your forehead (or elsewhere on your body) to display commercial advertising: $777.* Air New Zealand hired thirty people to shave their heads and wear temporary tattoos with the slogan "Need a change? Head down to New Zealand."
- *Serve as a human guinea pig in a drug safety trial for a pharmaceutical company: $7,500.* The pay can be higher or lower, depending on the invasiveness of the procedure used to test the drug's effect, and the discomfort involved.
- *Fight in Somalia or Afghanistan for a private military company: $250 per month to $1,000 per day.* The pay varies according to qualifications, experience, and nationality.
- *Stand in line overnight on Capitol Hill to hold a place for a lobbyist who wants to attend a congressional hearing: $15–$20 per hour.* The lobbyists pay line-standing companies, who hire homeless people and others to queue up.
- *If you are a second grader in an underachieving Dallas school, read a book: $2.* To encourage reading, the schools pay kids for each book they read.
- *If you are obese, lose fourteen pounds in four months: $378.* Companies and health insurers offer financial incentives for weight loss and other kinds of healthy behavior.
- *Buy the life insurance policy of an ailing or elderly person, pay the annual premiums while the person is alive, and then collect the death benefit when he or she dies: potentially, millions (depending on the policy).* This form of betting on the lives of strangers has become a $30 billion industry. The sooner the stranger dies, the more the investor makes.

We live at a time when almost everything can be bought and sold. Over the past three decades, markets—and market values—have come to govern our lives as never before. We did not arrive at this condition through any deliberate choice. It is almost as if it came upon us.

As the Cold War ended, markets and market thinking enjoyed unrivaled prestige, understandably so. No other mechanism for organizing the production and distribution of goods had proved as successful at generating affluence and prosperity. And yet, even as growing numbers of countries around the world embraced market mechanisms in the operation of their economies, something else was happening. Market values were coming to play a greater and greater role in social life. Economics was becoming an imperial domain. Today, the logic of buying and selling no longer applies to material goods alone but increasingly governs the whole of life. It is time to ask whether we want to live this way.

We live at a time when almost everything can be bought and sold.

THE ERA OF MARKET TRIUMPHALISM

The years leading up to the financial crisis of 2008 were a heady time of market faith and deregulation—an era of market triumphalism. The era began in the early 1980s, when Ronald Reagan and Margaret Thatcher proclaimed their conviction that markets, not government, held the key to prosperity and freedom. And it continued in the 1990s, with the market-friendly liberalism of Bill Clinton and Tony Blair, who moderated but consolidated the faith that markets are the primary means for achieving the public good.

Today, that faith is in doubt. The era of market triumphalism has come to an end. The financial crisis did more than cast doubt on the ability of markets to allocate risk efficiently. It also prompted a widespread sense that markets have become detached from morals and that we need somehow to reconnect them. But it's not obvious what this would mean, or how we should go about it.

Some say the moral failing at the heart of market triumphalism was greed, which led to irresponsible risk taking. The solution, according to this view, is to rein in greed, insist on greater integrity and responsibility among bankers and Wall Street executives, and enact sensible regulations to prevent a similar crisis from happening again.

This is, at best, a partial diagnosis. While it is certainly true that greed played a role in the financial crisis, something bigger is at stake. The most fateful change that unfolded during the past three decades was not an increase in greed. It was the expansion of markets, and of market values, into spheres of life where they don't belong.

To contend with this condition, we need to do more than inveigh against greed; we need to rethink the role that markets should play in our society. We need a public debate about what it means to keep markets in their place. To have this debate, we need to think through the moral limits of markets. We need to ask whether there are some things money should not buy.

The reach of markets, and market-oriented thinking, into aspects of life traditionally governed by nonmarket norms is one of the most significant developments of our time.

Consider the proliferation of for-profit schools, hospitals, and prisons, and the outsourcing of war to private military contractors. (In Iraq and Afghanistan, private contractors actually outnumbered U.S. military troops.)

Paying kids to read books might get them to read more, but also teach them to regard reading as a chore rather than a source of intrinsic satisfaction.

Consider the eclipse of public police forces by private security firms—especially in the United States and Britain, where the number of private guards is more than twice the number of public police officers.

Or consider the pharmaceutical companies' aggressive marketing of prescription drugs to consumers in rich countries. (If you've ever seen the television commercials on the evening news in the United States, you could be forgiven for thinking that the greatest health crisis in the world is not malaria or river blindness or sleeping sickness, but a rampant epidemic of erectile dysfunction.)

Consider too the reach of commercial advertising into public schools; the sale of "naming rights" to parks and civic spaces; the marketing of "designer" eggs and sperm for assisted reproduction; the outsourcing of pregnancy to surrogate mothers in the developing world; the buying and selling, by companies and countries, of the right to pollute; a system of campaign finance that comes close to permitting the buying and selling of elections.

These uses of markets to allocate health, education, public safety, national security, criminal justice, environmental protection, recreation, procreation, and other social goods were for the most part unheard of thirty years ago. Today, we take them largely for granted.

EVERYTHING FOR SALE

Why worry that we are moving toward a society in which everything is up for sale?

For two reasons: one is about inequality; the other is about corruption. Consider inequality. In a society where everything is for sale, life is harder for those of modest means. The more money can buy, the more affluence (or the lack of it) matters.

If the only advantage of affluence were the ability to buy yachts, sports cars, and fancy vacations, inequalities of income and wealth would not matter very much. But as money comes to buy more and more—political influence, good medical care, a home in a safe neighborhood rather than a crime-ridden one, access to elite schools rather than failing ones—the distribution of income and wealth looms larger and larger. Where all good things are bought and sold, having money makes all the difference in the world.

In a society where everything is for sale, life is harder for those of modest means.

This explains why the last few decades have been especially hard on poor and middle-class families. Not only has the gap between rich and poor widened, the commodification of everything has sharpened the sting of inequality by making money matter more.

The second reason we should hesitate to put everything up for sale is more difficult to describe. It is not about inequality and fairness but about the corrosive tendency of markets. Putting a price on the good things in life can corrupt them. That's because markets don't only allocate goods; they also express and promote certain attitudes toward the goods being exchanged. Paying kids to read books might get them to read more, but also teach them to regard reading as a chore rather than a source of intrinsic satisfaction. Auctioning seats in the freshman class to the highest bidders might raise revenue but also erode the integrity of the college and the value of its diploma. Hiring foreign mercenaries to fight our wars might spare the lives of our citizens but corrupt the meaning of citizenship.

Economists often assume that markets are inert, that they do not affect the goods they exchange. But this is untrue. Markets leave their mark. Sometimes, market values crowd out nonmarket values worth caring about.

Of course, people disagree about what values are worth caring about, and why. So to decide what money should—and should not—be able to buy, we have to decide what values should govern the various domains of social and civic life. . . .

. . . when we decide that certain goods may be bought and sold, we decide, at least implicitly, that it is appropriate to treat them as commodities, as instruments of profit and use. But not all goods are properly valued in this way. The most obvious example is human beings. Slavery was appalling because it treated human beings as commodities, to be bought and sold at auction. Such treatment fails to value human beings in the appropriate way—as persons worthy of dignity and respect, rather than as instruments of gain and objects of use.

Something similar can be said of other cherished goods and practices. We don't allow children to be bought and sold on the market. Even if buyers did not mistreat the children they purchased, a market in children would express and promote the wrong way of valuing them. Children are not properly regarded as consumer goods but as beings worthy of love and care. Or consider the rights and obligations of citizenship. If you are called to jury duty, you may not hire a substitute to take your place. Nor do we allow citizens to sell their votes, even though others might be eager to buy them. Why not? Because we believe that civic duties should not be regarded as private property but should be viewed instead as public responsibilities. To outsource them is to demean them, to value them in the wrong way.

These examples illustrate a broader point: some of the good things in life are corrupted or degraded if turned into commodities. So to decide where the market belongs, and where it should be kept at a distance, we have to decide how to value the goods in question—health, education, family life, nature, art, civic duties, and so on. These are moral and political questions, not merely economic ones. To resolve them, we have to debate, case by case, the moral meaning of these goods and the proper way of valuing them.

This is a debate we didn't have during the era of market triumphalism. As a result, without quite realizing it, without ever deciding to do so, we drifted from *having* a market economy to *being* a market society.

The difference is this: A market economy is a tool—a valuable and effective tool—for organizing productive activity. A market society is a way of life in which market values seep into every aspect of human endeavor. It's a place where social relations are made over in the image of the market.

The great missing debate in contemporary politics is about the role and reach of markets. Do we want a market economy, or a market society? What role should markets play in public life and personal relations? How can we decide which goods should be bought and sold, and which should be governed by nonmarket values? Where should money's writ not run? . . .

RETHINKING THE ROLE OF MARKETS

Even if you agree that we need to grapple with big questions about the morality of markets, you might doubt that our public discourse is up to the task. It's a legitimate worry. Any attempt to rethink the role and reach of markets should begin by acknowledging two daunting obstacles.

One is the persisting power and prestige of market thinking, even in the aftermath of the worst market failure in eighty years. The other is the rancor and emptiness of our public discourse. These two conditions are not entirely unrelated.

The first obstacle is puzzling. At the time, the financial crisis of 2008 was widely seen as a moral verdict on the uncritical embrace of markets that had prevailed, across the political spectrum, for three decades. The near collapse of once-mighty Wall Street financial firms, and the need for a massive bailout at taxpayers' expense, seemed sure to prompt a reconsideration of markets. Even Alan Greenspan, who as chairman of the U.S. Federal Reserve had served as high priest of the market triumphalist faith, admitted to "a state of shocked disbelief" that his confidence in the self-correcting power of free markets turned out to be mistaken. The cover of *The Economist*, the buoyantly pro-market British magazine, showed an economics textbook melting into a puddle, under the headline WHAT WENT WRONG WITH ECONOMICS.

The era of market triumphalism had come to a devastating end. Now, surely, would be a time of moral reckoning, a season of sober second thoughts about the market faith. But things haven't turned out that way.

The spectacular failure of financial markets did little to dampen the faith in markets generally. In fact, the financial crisis discredited government more than the banks. In 2011, surveys found that the American public blamed the federal government more than Wall Street financial institutions for the economic problems facing the country—by a margin of more than two to one.

The financial crisis had pitched the United States and much of the global economy into the worst economic downturn since the Great Depression and left millions of people out of work. Yet it did not prompt a fundamental rethinking of markets. Instead, its most notable political consequence in the United States was the rise of the Tea Party movement, whose hostility to government and embrace of free markets would have made Ronald Reagan blush. In the fall of 2011, the Occupy Wall Street movement brought protests to cities throughout the United States and around the world. These protests targeted big banks and corporate power, and the rising inequality of income and wealth. Despite their different ideological orientations, both the Tea Party and Occupy Wall Street activists gave voice to populist outrage against the bailout.

Notwithstanding these voices of protest, serious debate about the role and reach of markets remains largely absent from our political life. Democrats and Republicans argue, as they long have done, about taxes, spending, and budget deficits, only now with greater partisanship and little ability to inspire or persuade. Disillusion with politics has deepened as citizens grow frustrated with a political system unable to act for the public good, or to address the questions that matter most.

This parlous state of public discourse is the second obstacle to a debate about the moral limits of markets. At a time when political argument consists mainly of shouting matches on cable television, partisan vitriol on talk radio, and ideological food fights on the floor of Congress, it's hard to imagine a reasoned public debate about such controversial moral questions as the right way to value procreation, children, education, health, the environment, citizenship, and other goods. But I believe such a debate is possible, and that it would invigorate our public life.

Some see in our rancorous politics a surfeit of moral conviction: too many people believe too deeply, too stridently, in their own convictions and want to impose them on everyone else. I think this misreads our predicament. The problem with our politics is not too much moral argument but too little. Our politics is overheated because it is mostly vacant, empty of moral and spiritual content. It fails to engage with big questions that people care about.

The moral vacancy of contemporary politics has a number of sources. One is the attempt to banish notions of the good life from public discourse. In hopes of avoiding sectarian strife, we often insist that citizens leave their moral and spiritual convictions behind when they enter the public square. But despite its good intention, the reluctance to admit arguments about the good life into politics prepared the way for market triumphalism and for the continuing hold of market reasoning.

In its own way, market reasoning also empties public life of moral argument. Part of the appeal of markets is that they don't pass judgment on the preferences they satisfy. They don't ask whether some ways of valuing goods are higher, or worthier, than others. If someone is willing to pay for sex or a kidney, and a consenting adult is willing to sell, the only question the economist asks is, "How much?" Markets don't wag fingers. They don't discriminate between admirable preferences and base ones. Each party to a deal decides for himself or herself what value to place on the things being exchanged.

This nonjudgmental stance toward values lies at the heart of market reasoning and explains much of its appeal. But our reluctance to engage in moral and spiritual argument, together with our embrace of markets, has exacted a heavy price: it has drained public discourse of moral and civic energy, and contributed to the technocratic, managerial politics that afflicts many societies today.

A debate about the moral limits of markets would enable us to decide, as a society, where markets serve the public good and where they don't belong. It would also invigorate our politics, by welcoming competing notions of the good life into the public square. For how else could such arguments proceed? If you agree that buying and selling certain goods corrupts or degrades them, then you must believe that some ways of valuing these goods are more appropriate than others. It hardly makes sense to speak of corrupting an activity—parenthood, say, or citizenship—unless you think that some ways of being a parent, or a citizen, are better than others.

Moral judgments such as these lie behind the few limitations on markets we still observe. We don't allow parents to sell their children or citizens to sell their votes. And one of the reasons we don't is, frankly, judgmental: we believe that selling these things values them in the wrong way and cultivates bad attitudes.

Thinking through the moral limits of markets makes these questions unavoidable. It requires that we reason together, in public, about how to value the social goods we prize. It would be folly to expect that a morally more robust public discourse, even at its best, would lead to agreement on every contested question. But it would make for a healthier public life. And it would make us more aware of the price we pay for living in a society where everything is up for sale.

When we think of the morality of markets, we think first of Wall Street banks and their reckless misdeeds, of hedge funds and bailouts and regulatory reform. But the moral and political challenge we face today is more pervasive and more mundane—to rethink the role and reach of markets in our social practices, human relationships, and everyday lives.

DISCUSSION

1. The title of this essay ("Markets and Morals") raises questions about the role ethics should play in assessing and/or regulating the commercial marketplace. Do you think the marketplace is in need of greater moral oversight? If so, what kind?
2. According to Sandel, we live at a cultural moment where commercial values are increasingly coming to "crowd out nonmarket values" (p. 44). What are the "nonmarket values" Sandel seems to have in mind? How does his definition of this term compare to your own?
3. "Markets," Sandel tells us, "don't wag fingers. They don't discriminate between admirable preferences and base ones" (p. 47). Do you agree with this assessment? Do you think markets should "wag fingers"? If so, what kinds of actions or attitudes should be discouraged? Why?

WRITING

4. Sandel opens this essay by listing some of the services that are now for sale on the open market. Choose one. Then write a short essay in which you argue either for or against the merits of treating this service as a purchasable commodity. In your view, what is or is not valid about putting this service up for sale? What rules would you establish for how this transaction should unfold?
5. According to Sandel, there are two reasons why we should worry about the societal trend toward treating everything as if it were up for sale: "inequality" and "corruption." Choose an example of a good or service that is possible to buy or sell on the open market. In an essay, analyze the particular ways this product raises questions or risks having to do with "inequality" or "corruption." In order to conduct this analysis, you need to make sure you are clear about what each of these terms means, and how each applies to the example you choose.
6. How does Sandel's discussion here compare to the argument about "going green" advanced by Stephen Asma (p. 25)? Does Asma's portrait of environmental practices and politics fit Sandel's definition of "nonmarket values"? To what extent does Asma's portrait support or reinforce Sandel's thesis about "markets and morals"? To what extent does his portrait challenge, complicate, or undermine Sandel's thesis?

Rule Maker >>>>>>>>> Rule Breaker

- *68% of consumers plan to complete their holiday shopping in December.*
- *The most popular gift that people wish to receive this holiday season is gift cards.*
- *The shopping-center industry directly accounts for 9.2% of the employed workforce. That is approximately 12.3 million jobs.*
- *Men are more inclined to want electronic gadgets for their holiday gifts than women (46% to 31%).*

— INTERNATIONAL COUNCIL OF SHOPPING CENTERS (ICSC) 2012 HOLIDAY FUN FACTS

"Until we challenge the entrenched values of capitalism — that the economy must always keep growing, that consumer wants must always be satisfied, that immediate gratification is imperative — we're not going to be able to fix the gigantic psycho-financial-eco crisis of our times.

The journey toward a sane sustainable future begins with a single step. It could all start with a personal challenge, such as this: make a vow to yourself to participate in Buy Nothing Day this year. This November 29th, go cold turkey on consumption for 24 hours ... see what happens ... you just might have an unexpected, emancipatory epiphany!

— BUY NOTHING CHRISTMAS HOMEPAGE, ADBUSTERS.ORG, 2012

Holiday Shopping vs. Buy Nothing Christmas

It seems like every holiday season brings a fresh batch of criticism about pairing commercialism with seasonal or religious festivities. Television newscasts report on decreases in holiday sales and air stories on the amount of personal debt the holidays bring, and then they cut to commercial, offering the audience a fresh onslaught of ads urging them to finish their holiday shopping. The two quotations above underscore how conflicted our beliefs about consumerism can sometimes be. In the first, the International Council of Shopping Centers presents some of its "Fun Facts" about holiday shopping. What do these tell you about how closely our American "belief" in shopping is tied to our religious beliefs? And how are these messages challenged by the second quotation, excerpted from the Adbusters' "Buy Nothing Day" initiative?

FIND THE RULES: Make a list of the different attitudes about consumerism that each of these quotations expresses. Then write a paragraph examining how each "sells" its point of view. What does each quotation say, and how does each appeal to its intended audience?

ANALYZE THE RULES: Write a brief essay in which you assess the merits and shortcomings of the attitudes each group endeavors to sell to its audience. Which set of rules do you find more compelling? Which underlying viewpoint are you more inclined to accept as normal? Why?

MAKE YOUR OWN RULES: Write a three- to five-page essay in which you make the case for what our attitude toward holiday shopping ought to be. How would you characterize the "proper" attitude we should have toward holiday shopping? What makes your view of this issue compelling? What reasons, factors, or evidence can you cite as support? How do your views compare to those expressed in the two quotations? To what extent can the points raised in each be used to support the thesis you are advancing here?

Adam Gault/Getty Images

MICHAEL ERIC DYSON

Understanding Black Patriotism

What are the acceptable forms for expressing one's love of country? And do these boundaries establish different standards for the way people of different races are allowed to voice these views? Taking up this provocative question, noted public intellectual Michael Eric Dyson maps the contours of what he calls "black patriotism." Given the history that defines the African American experience, he argues, we shouldn't be surprised to discover that nationalistic feelings skew along racial lines. Nor, he adds, should we shrink from confronting what these differences tell us about what it means to accept conventional patriotic ideals as a universal norm. Dyson is the University Professor of Sociology at Georgetown University. He is the author of numerous books, among them: *I May Not Get There With You: The True Martin Luther King, Jr.* (2000), *Is Bill Cosby Right?* (2005), and *Holler If You Hear Me: Searching for Tupac Shakur* (2006). The essay below was published by *Time* in 2008.

MAINSTREAM AMERICA HAS SHOWN LITTLE UNDERSTANDING lately of the patriotism that a lot of black people practice. Black love of country is often far more robust and complicated than the lapel-pin nationalism some citizens swear by. Barack Obama hinted at this when he declared in Montana a few weeks ago, "I love this country not because it's perfect but because we've always been able to move it closer to perfection. Because through revolution and slavery . . . generations of Americans have shown their love of country by struggling and sacrificing and risking their lives to bring us that much closer to our founding promise."

Mainstream America has shown little understanding lately of the patriotism that a lot of black people practice.

That's a far cry from the "My country, right or wrong" credo, which confuses blind boosterism with a more authentic, if sometimes questioning, loyalty. At their best, black folk offer critical patriotism, an exacting devotion that carries on a lover's quarrel with America while they shed blood in its defense.

It is easy to see why the words of black critics and leaders, taken out of context, can be read as cynical renunciations of country. Abolitionist and runaway slave Frederick Douglass gave a famous oration on the meaning of Independence Day, asking "What, to the American slave, is your Fourth of July? I answer, a day that reveals to him, more than all other days in the year, the gross injustice and cruelty to which he is the constant victim." But instead of joining the chorus of black voices swelling with nostalgia to return to their African roots, Douglass stayed put. Poet Langston Hughes grieved in verse that "(America never was America to me) . . . (There's never been equality for me,/ Nor freedom in this 'homeland of the free')." But his lament is couched in a poem whose title, like its author, yearns for acceptance: Let America Be America Again.

Even Martin Luther King Jr. was branded a traitor to his country because he opposed the war in Vietnam. When King announced his opposition in 1967, journalist Kenneth Crawford attacked him for his "demagoguery," while black writer Carl Rowan bitterly concluded that King's speech had created "the impression that the Negro is disloyal." Black dissent over war has historically brought charges of disloyalty despite the eagerness among blacks to defend on foreign soil a democracy they couldn't enjoy back home. Since the time of slavery, blacks have actively defended the U.S. in every war it has waged, from the Civil War down to the war on terrorism, a loyalty to the Federal Government conceived by black leaders as a critical force in gaining freedom. W. E. B. Du Bois argued in World War I that blacks should "forget our special grievances and close our ranks . . . with our white fellow citizens." Some 380,000 soldiers answered the call even as they failed to reap the benefits of their sacrifice when they came home.

Even the angry comments of Jeremiah Wright have to be read as the bitter complaint of a spurned lover. Like millions of other blacks, Wright was willing to serve the country while suffering rejection. He surrendered his student deferment in 1961, voluntarily joined the Marines and, after a two-year stint, volunteered to become a Navy corpsman. He excelled and became valedictorian, later a cardiopulmonary technician, and eventually a member of the President's medical team. Wright cared for Lyndon B. Johnson after his 1966 surgery, earning three White House letters of commendation.

Since the time of slavery, blacks have actively defended the U.S. in every war it has waged, from the Civil War down to the war on terrorism.

Dick Cheney, born in the same year as Wright, received five deferments—four while an undergraduate or graduate student and one as a prospective father. Both Bill Clinton and George W. Bush used their student deferments to remain in college until 1968. Clinton did not serve, and Bush was on active duty in the National Guard for two years. If time in uniform is any measure, Wright, much more than Cheney, Clinton, or

Bush, embodies Obama's ideal of "Americans [who] have shown their love of country by struggling and sacrificing and risking their lives to bring us that much closer to our founding promise."

Wright's critics have confused nationalism with patriotism. Nationalism is the uncritical support of one's country regardless of its moral or political bearing. Patriotism is the affirmation of one's country in light of its best values, including the attempt to correct it when it's in error. Wright's words are the tough love of a war-tested patriot speaking his mind—one of the great virtues of our democracy. The most patriotic thing his nation can do now is extend to him the same right for which he was willing to die.

DISCUSSION

1. "At their best," writes Dyson, "black folk offer critical patriotism, an exacting devotion that carries on a lover's quarrel with America while they shed blood in its defense" (p. 52). How does Dyson's definition challenge or rewrite the social scripts through which love of country typically gets expressed? In your view, are these changes for the better? Why or why not?
2. Dyson describes conventional forms of patriotism as "lapel-pin nationalism." What does he mean by this phrase? What definition of patriotism does it suggest to you? Do you think it accurately captures the form patriotic feeling conventionally takes in our culture?
3. Throughout American history, Dyson reminds us, patriotism and dissent have often been viewed as mutually exclusive. Do you agree? Can you think of an example of dissent that served simultaneously as an expression of patriotism?

WRITING

4. Those who have criticized black patriots for voicing dissent, Dyson contends, "have confused nationalism with patriotism. Nationalism is the uncritical support of one's country regardless of its moral or political bearing. Patriotism is the affirmation of one's country in light of its best values, including the attempt to correct it when it's in error" (p. 54). First, describe in your own words the distinction Dyson is drawing here. What, according to Dyson, are the key differences between "nationalism" and "patriotism"? Then choose a recent debate that you think illustrates this distinction: Who is part of this debate? What issue or controversy does it concern? And which view do you find most compelling or persuasive?
5. Quoting a speech by then-presidential candidate Barack Obama, Dyson draws a distinction between stereotypical expressions of patriotism and those that, in his view, capture the kind of nationalism often expressed by African Americans: "'I love this country not because it's perfect but because we've always been able to move it closer to perfection. Because through revolution and slavery . . . generations of Americans have shown their love of country by struggling and sacrificing and risking their lives to bring us that much closer to our founding promise.' That's a far cry from the 'My country, right or wrong' credo, which confuses blind boosterism with a more authentic, if sometimes questioning, loyalty" (p. 55). In a three- to five-page essay, describe, analyze, and assess the distinction Dyson is drawing here. What are the basic differences — in attitude, assumption, and viewpoint — between these contrasting expressions of patriotism? What factors, in Dyson's estimation, account for these differences? Do you agree with Dyson's characterization of each? How or how not?
6. How does Dyson's explication of a racially specific patriotism compare with the argument about diversity presented by David Brooks (p. 62)? Do you think Brooks would regard Dyson's discussion here as proof that his own argument is correct? And what are your own views here? Does a defense of "black patriotism" amount to a celebration or a critique of "diversity"?

Then and Now: **Feeling (In)Secure**

To be sure, belief is partly about those things we've been taught to value and embrace, but it's also about those things we've been taught to fear. When it comes to the threats we are told are most dangerous, what exactly are we supposed to believe? How are we taught to define these threats? What instructions are we issued for how to deal with them? These days, no danger looms more ominously or ubiquitously in our lives than the threat of terrorism. From nightly news broadcasts to political speeches, color-coded government alerts to made-for-TV dramas, it is made clear to us in countless different ways that the world is full of shadowy enemies who despise "our way of life" and are therefore intent on doing us harm. So ingrained has this belief in the omnipresent terrorist threat become, in fact, that we have reorganized major swaths of our public behavior to accommodate it. There is no more vivid illustration of this fact than in the changes that have reshaped modern air travel. For the millions of Americans who travel by plane, things like long lines at security checkpoints, constantly changing restrictions on what may and may not be brought on board, random body searches, and full body image scanners have come to be regarded as established facts of life. Less clear, though, are the particular anxieties and fears that these new security rituals have simultaneously normalized. Indeed, it could be argued that all of these precautions and prohibitions have served to make air travel itself into a kind of extended tutorial in how and what we are supposed to fear. Every time we remove our shoes at the security check-in or dispose of our contraband toothpaste before getting on board, we are acting on (and thereby reinforcing) a particular definition of who and what our enemies are.

American Stock Archive/Getty Images

When framed as an example of cultural instruction, our modern-day preoccupation with terrorist threats starts to look less new than it first appears. The twentieth century in America was marked by a series of "scares" — from the Palmer Raids fears about alien immigrants in the 1920s to the anticommunist "Red Menace" hysteria of the 1950s — which taught Americans to define and fear the threats to the nation in very specific ways. During the Cold War, for instance, which most historians believe started soon after the end of World War II, these fears revolved largely around the twin specters of Soviet communism and nuclear weapons. Anticipating in many ways the media coverage we see today, television broadcasts and newspaper headlines of this era were replete with warnings about the "enemies" who might be lurking "in our midst"; politicians regularly enjoined audiences to remain vigilant against "sneak attacks," which, they cautioned, could happen at any time. As a result, countless Americans became convinced that their highest civic duty was to prepare against a Soviet missile attack, digging bomb shelters or stocking basements with canned goods. In contrast to the airport restrictions of today, the rituals through which people acted out these fears centered on the classroom. For elementary schoolchildren of the 1950s, air-raid alerts and "duck and cover" drills came to stand as the norm, the mid-century equivalent to the metal detectors and bomb-sniffing dogs of today.

Pool/Getty Images

When we place these two sets of security rituals side by side, what (if any) differences do we see? On the basis of the roles scripted for us in these respective eras, does it seem that we've learned to define and deal with the threats confronting us in new and different ways? Or does it seem instead that we've simply carried old attitudes and anxieties forward?

WRITING

1. Compare the ways that each image demonstrates the concept of safety. How are the rituals depicted in these photos designed to make us *feel* about our own safety?
2. While they may seem at first glance merely to be objective portraits, the images can also be read as depicting *public performances* in which people are shown acting out social scripts that have been written for them. It is from this perspective that such activities can start to seem like tutorials in security, scenarios designed to teach us what and how to fear. For each set of activities shown in the photographs, create instructions that lay out the steps for the safety rituals depicted and state why Americans should perform these steps.

KATIE ROIPHE

In Defense of Single Motherhood

How do we define the ideal family? And should we even try? In an era where families come in all shapes and sizes, it may be time, writes Katie Roiphe, to set aside our long-standing, and largely fruitless, search for the ideal. Katie Roiphe is a journalist and the author of several books, including *The Morning After: Sex, Fear, and Feminism* (1993) and *Last Night in Paradise: Sex and Morals at the Century's End* (1997). This essay appeared in the *New York Times* in 2012.

IN A SEASON OF ARDENT PARTISAN CLASHING, AMERICANS SEEM united in at least one shared idea: Single mothers are bad. A Pew Research Center poll on family structures reports that nearly 7 in 10 Americans think single mothers are a "bad thing for society."

Conservatives obsess over moral decline, and liberals worry extravagantly—and one could argue condescendingly—about children, but all exhibit a fundamental lack of imagination about what family can be—and perhaps more pressingly—what family is: we now live in a country in which 53 percent of the babies born to women under 30 are born to unmarried mothers.

I happen to have two children with two different fathers, neither of whom I live with, and both of whom we are close to. I am lucky enough to be living in financially stable, relatively privileged circumstances, and to have had the education that allows me to do so. I am not the "typical" single mother, but then there is no typical single mother any more than there is a typical mother. It is, in fact, our fantasies and crude stereotypes of this "typical single mother" that get in the way of a more rational, open-minded understanding of the variety and richness of different kinds of families.

The structure of my household is messy, bohemian, warm. If there is anything that currently oppresses the children, it is the idea of the way families are "supposed to be," an idea pushed—in picture books and classrooms and in adults' casual conversation—on American children at a very early age and with surprising aggressiveness.

In a season of ardent partisan clashing, Americans seem united in at least one shared idea: Single mothers are bad.

At 2, my son, Leo, started to call his sister's father, Harry, "my Harry." When he glimpsed Harry's chocolate-brown 1980s car coming down our block he would say,

"My Harry's car!" To me this unorthodox use of "my" gets at the spirit of what we're doing: inventing a family from scratch. There are no words for what Harry is to him, but he is definitely his Harry.

The other day Leo brushed his mop of blond hair in front of the mirror and announced, "Now I look like Harry." People are quick to tell me that this is not the real thing. But is it necessarily worse than "the real thing"? Is the physical presence of a man in the home truly as transfiguring, magical, and unadulteratedly essential as people seem to think? One could argue that a well-loved child is a well-loved child.

To support the basic notion that single mothers are irresponsible and dangerous to the general order of things, people often refer vaguely to "studies." I am not a huge believer in studies because they tend to collapse the complexities and nuance of actual lived experience and because people lie to themselves and others. (One of these studies, for instance, in order to measure emotional distress asks teenagers to record how many times in a week "you felt lonely." Is there a teenager on earth who is a reliable narrator of her inner life? Can anyone of any age quantify how many times in a week they have felt lonely?) But since these studies provide fodder for those who want to blast single mothers, it's worth addressing what they actually say.

Studies like those done by the Princeton sociologist Sara S. McLanahan, who is one of the foremost authorities on single motherhood and its impact on children, show that conditions like poverty and instability, which frequently accompany single-mother households, increase the chances that the children involved will experience alcoholism, mental illness, academic failure, and other troubles. But there is no conclusive evidence that, absent those conditions, the pure, pared-down state of single motherhood is itself dangerous to children.

Professor McLanahan's studies over the years, and many others like them, show that the primary risks associated with single motherhood arise from financial insecurity. They also offer evidence that, to a lesser extent, particular romantic patterns of the mother—namely introducing lots of boyfriends into children's lives—contribute to the risk. What the studies don't show is that longing for a married father at the breakfast table injures children.

And Professor McLanahan's findings suggest that a two-parent, financially stable home with stress and conflict would be more destructive to children than a one-parent, financially stable home without stress and conflict.

There is no doubt, however, that single motherhood can be more difficult than other kinds of motherhood. In France, the response to the added difficulty is to give single mothers preferential access to excellent day care. Here the response is moralism disguised as concern and, at other times, simply moralism.

The idea of "single mothers" may itself be the convenient fiction of a fundamentally conservative society. In fact women move in and out of singleness, married parents break apart, men and women live together without marrying, spouses or partners die, romantic attachments form and dissolve. Those who brandish research like Professor McLanahan's ongoing Fragile Families study and Paul R. Amato's 2005 paper on changing family structures to critique "single mothers" conveniently ignore the fact that such investigations rely on shifting, differing, and extremely complex definitions of the households involved.

If there is anything that currently oppresses the children, it is the idea of the way families are "supposed to be."

What gets lost in the moralizing conversation is that there is a huge, immeasurable variety in households, and there are great ones and terrible ones, arduous ones and inventive ones, drab ones and exuberant ones, among families of all structures and economic strata.

It's useful and humbling to remember that no family structure guarantees happiness or ensures misery: real life is wilier and more fraught with accident and luck than that. If you think that being married ensures a good life for your children you need only enter a bookstore and open any novel, or go to the theater and watch practically any play, or have dinner with nearly anyone you know. Suffering is everywhere, and married parents, even happily married parents, raise screwed-up or alcoholic or lost children, just as single parents raise strong, healthy ones. What matters most, it should go without saying, is the kind of parent you are, not whom you sleep with, and even that matters only up to a point.

With the steep rise of children born to unmarried parents, America's prevailing fantasies of family life no longer match the facts on the ground. But as the children born to unmarried women under 30 come of age in the majority, these faded archetypes will have to evolve. Our narrow, constricting, airless sense of the isolated nuclear family has not always, if we are honest, served us well, and it may now be replaced by something more vivid and dynamic, and closer to the way we are actually living.

All of the liberal concern about single motherhood might more usefully be channeled into protecting single mothers, rather than the elaborate clucking and exquisite condescension that get us nowhere. Attention should be paid to the serious underlying economic inequities, without the colorful surface distraction of concerned or judgmental prurience. Let's abandon the fundamentally frothy question of who is wearing a ring. Young men need jobs so they can pay child support and contribute more meaningfully to the households they are living in. The real menace to America's children is not single mothers, or unmarried or gay parents, but an economy that stokes an unconscionable divide between the rich and the not rich.

DISCUSSION

1. Take a moment to consider the phrase "single mother." What image does it evoke for you? What type of person, what set of social circumstances, what issues or problems do we typically associate with "single motherhood"? In your view, are the ways this term gets scripted accurate? Fair? Why or why not?
2. "The idea of 'single mothers,'" Roiphe posits, "may itself be the convenient fiction of a fundamentally conservative society" (p. 60). What do you make of this hypothesis? Is single motherhood a "convenient fiction"? Convenient for whom? Fictional how? Do you agree that our ideas about single motherhood reflect an underlying social conservatism? Why or why not?
3. For Roiphe, the most important questions raised by the phenomenon of single parenting are economic: "The real menace to America's children is not single mothers, or unmarried or gay parents, but an economy that stokes an unconscionable divide between the rich and the not rich" (p. 60). To what extent does the "divide between the rich and the not rich" affect the roles and relationships that define the family?

WRITING

4. As she acknowledges, Roiphe's conception of the ideal family is quite different from the standards scripted by the dominant culture. "The structure of my household," she declares, "is messy, bohemian, warm" (p. 58). Use Roiphe's characterization of her family as the starting point for creating your own definition of the ideal family. What does this family look like? What roles best define it? What social scripts does it reflect? What underlying norms does it represent? Then indicate the specific ways your model challenges or revises the roles, scripts, and norms that define the "typical" American family.
5. "It is, in fact," writes Roiphe, "our fantasies and crude stereotypes of this 'typical single mother' that get in the way of a more rational, open-minded understanding of the variety and richness of different kinds of families" (p. 58). In a longer essay of your own, address the claim Roiphe makes here. First, assess the way she characterizes the situation: Do you agree that our culture supplies us with "fantasies" and "crude stereotypes" about single mothers? How do such characterizations function as social scripts, teaching us to pass judgment on those in this category? Then respond to the central assertion Roiphe makes: Do you agree that cultural stereotypes "get in the way" of a more "open-minded understanding" of what family can be? How specifically? And what do you think should be done to remedy this situation?
6. From very different vantage points, Roiphe and Michael Eric Dyson (p. 52) each focus on the ways cultural stereotypes (whether about gender or race) shape broader public attitudes. Take a closer look at the argument each writer advances. What assumptions or ideas do they share? What are the key differences? On what specific points do their arguments about cultural stereotypes diverge?

DAVID BROOKS

People Like Us

In this essay, David Brooks takes up some of the key terms that currently anchor our public discussions of race, prompting us to think about the assumptions we bring to bear on this question. Do we, he asks, really care about diversity? And even more provocatively, should we? Brooks, a prominent voice for conservative politics, has been a columnist at the *New York Times* since 2003. He has also worked at the *Weekly Standard, Newsweek,* and the *Atlantic Monthly* and is a regular commentator on NPR's *All Things Considered* and PBS's *NewsHour.* He has published two books of commentary on American culture, *Bobos in Paradise: The New Upper Class and How They Got There* (2000) and *On Paradise Drive: How We Live Now (and Always Have) in the Future Tense* (2004). The following essay first appeared in the September 2003 issue of the *Atlantic Monthly.*

MAYBE IT'S TIME TO ADMIT THE OBVIOUS. WE DON'T REALLY CARE about diversity all that much in America, even though we talk about it a great deal. Maybe somewhere in this country there is a truly diverse neighborhood in which a black Pentecostal minister lives next to a white anti-globalization activist, who lives next to an Asian short-order cook, who lives next to a professional golfer, who lives next to a postmodern-literature professor and a cardiovascular surgeon. But I have never been to or heard of that neighborhood. Instead, what I have seen all around the country is people making strenuous efforts to group themselves with people who are basically like themselves.

Human beings are capable of drawing amazingly subtle social distinctions and then shaping their lives around them. In the Washington, D.C., area Democratic lawyers tend to live in suburban Maryland, and Republican lawyers tend to live in suburban Virginia. If you asked a Democratic lawyer to move from her $750,000 house in Bethesda, Maryland, to a $750,000 house in Great Falls, Virginia, she'd look at you as if you had just asked her to buy a pickup truck with a gun rack and to shove chewing tobacco in her kid's mouth. In Manhattan the owner of a $3 million SoHo loft would feel out of place moving into a $3 million Fifth Avenue apartment. A West Hollywood interior decorator would feel dislocated if you asked him to move to Orange County. In Georgia a barista from Athens would probably not fit in serving coffee in Americus.

It is a common complaint that every place is starting to look the same. But in the information age, the late writer James Chapin once told me, every place becomes more like itself. People are less often tied down to factories and mills, and they can search for places to live on the basis of cultural affinity. Once they find a town in which people share their values, they flock there, and reinforce whatever was distinctive about the town in the first place. Once Boulder, Colorado, became known as congenial to politically progressive mountain bikers, half the politically progressive mountain bikers in the country (it seems) moved there; they made the place so culturally pure that it has become practically a parody of itself.

But people love it. Make no mistake—we are increasing our happiness by segmenting off so rigorously. We are finding places where we are comfortable and where we feel we can flourish. But the choices we make toward that end lead to the very opposite of diversity. The United States might be a diverse nation when considered as a whole, but block by block and institution by institution it is a relatively homogeneous nation.

We are increasing our happiness by segmenting off so rigorously.

When we use the word "diversity" today we usually mean racial integration. But even here our good intentions seem to have run into the brick wall of human nature. Over the past generation reformers have tried heroically, and in many cases successfully, to end housing discrimination. But recent patterns aren't encouraging: according to an analysis of the 2000 census data, the 1990s saw only a slight increase in the racial integration of neighborhoods in the United States. The number of middle-class and upper-middle-class African-American families is rising, but for whatever reasons—racism, psychological comfort—these families tend to congregate in predominantly black neighborhoods.

In fact, evidence suggests that some neighborhoods become more segregated over time. New suburbs in Arizona and Nevada, for example, start out reasonably well integrated. These neighborhoods don't yet have reputations, so people choose their houses for other, mostly economic reasons. But as neighborhoods age, they develop personalities (that's where the Asians live, and that's where the Hispanics live), and segmentation occurs. It could be that in a few years the new suburbs in the Southwest will be nearly as segregated as the established ones in the Northeast and the Midwest.

Even though race and ethnicity run deep in American society, we should in theory be able to find areas that are at least culturally diverse. But here, too, people show few signs of being truly interested in building diverse communities. If you run a retail company and you're thinking of opening new stores, you can choose among dozens of consulting firms that are quite effective at locating your potential customers. They can do this because people with similar tastes and preferences tend to congregate by ZIP code.

The most famous of these precision marketing firms is Claritas, which breaks down the U.S population into sixty-two psycho-demographic clusters, based on such factors as how much money people make, what they like to read and watch, and what products they have bought in the past. For example, the "suburban sprawl" cluster is composed of young families making about $41,000 a year and living in fast-growing places such as Burnsville, Minnesota, and Bensalem, Pennsylvania. These people are almost twice as likely as other Americans to have three-way calling. They are two and a half times as likely to buy Light n' Lively Kid Yogurt. Members of the "towns & gowns" cluster are recent college graduates in places such as Berkeley, California, and Gainesville, Florida. They are big consumers of Dove Bars and *Saturday Night Live*. They tend to drive small foreign cars and to read *Rolling Stone* and *Scientific American*.

Looking through the market research, one can sometimes be amazed by how efficiently people cluster—and by how predictable we all are. If you wanted to sell imported wine, obviously you would have to find places where rich people live. But did you know that the sixteen counties with the greatest proportion of imported-wine drinkers are all in the same three metropolitan areas (New York, San Francisco, and Washington, D.C.)? If you tried to open a motor-home dealership in Montgomery County, Pennsylvania, you'd probably go broke, because people in this ring of the Philadelphia suburbs think RVs are kind of uncool. But if you traveled just a short way north, to Monroe County, Pennsylvania, you would find yourself in the fifth motor-home-friendliest county in America.

Geography is not the only way we find ourselves divided from people unlike us. Some of us watch Fox News, while others listen to NPR. Some like David Letterman, and others—typically in less urban neighborhoods—like Jay Leno. Some go to charismatic churches; some go to mainstream churches. Americans tend more and more often to marry people with education levels similar to their own, and to befriend people with backgrounds similar to their own.

My favorite illustration of this latter pattern comes from the first, noncontroversial chapter of *The Bell Curve*. Think of your twelve closest friends, Richard J. Herrnstein and Charles Murray write. If you had chosen them randomly from the American population, the odds that half of your twelve closest friends would be college graduates would be six in a thousand. The odds that half of the twelve would have advanced degrees would be less than one in a million. Have any of your twelve closest friends graduated from Harvard, Stanford, Yale, Princeton, Caltech, MIT, Duke, Dartmouth, Cornell, Columbia, Chicago, or Brown? If you chose your friends randomly from the American population, the odds against your having four or more friends from those schools would be more than a billion to one.

Many of us live in absurdly unlikely groupings, because we have organized our lives that way.

It's striking that the institutions that talk the most about diversity often practice it the least. For example, no group of people sings the diversity anthem more frequently and fervently than administrators at just such elite universities. But elite universities are amazingly undiverse in their values, politics, and mores. Professors in particular are drawn from a rather narrow segment of the population. If faculties reflected the general population, 32 percent of professors would be registered Democrats and 31 percent would be registered Republicans. Forty percent would be evangelical Christians. But a recent study of several universities by the conservative Center for the Study of Popular Culture and the American Enterprise Institute found that roughly 90 percent of those professors in the arts and sciences who had registered with a political party had registered Democratic. Fifty-seven professors at Brown were found on the voter-registration rolls. Of those, fifty-four were Democrats. Of the forty-two professors in the English, history, sociology, and political-science departments, all were Democrats. The results at Harvard, Penn State, Maryland, and the University of California at Santa Barbara were similar to the results at Brown.

What we are looking at here is human nature. People want to be around others who are roughly like themselves. That's called community. It probably would be psychologically difficult for most Brown professors to share an office with someone who was pro-life, a member of the National Rifle Association, or an evangelical Christian. It's likely that hiring committees would subtly—even unconsciously—screen out any such people they encountered. Republicans and evangelical Christians have sensed that they are not welcome at places like Brown, so they don't even consider working there. In fact, any registered Republican who contemplates a career in academia these days is both a hero and a fool. So, in a semi-self-selective pattern, brainy people with generally liberal social mores flow to academia, and brainy people with generally conservative mores flow elsewhere.

People want to be around others who are roughly like themselves. That's called community.

The dream of diversity is like the dream of equality. Both are based on ideals we celebrate even as we undermine them daily. (How many times have you seen someone renounce a high-paying job or pull his child from an elite college on the grounds that these things are bad for equality?) On the one hand, the situation is appalling. It is appalling that Americans know so little about one another. It is appalling that many of us are so narrow-minded that we can't tolerate a few people with ideas significantly different from our own. It's appalling that evangelical Christians are practically absent from entire professions, such as academia, the media, and filmmaking. It's appalling that people should be content to cut themselves off from everyone unlike themselves.

The segmentation of society means that often we don't even have arguments across the political divide. Within their little validating communities, liberals and conservatives circulate half-truths about the supposed awfulness of the other side. These distortions are believed because it feels good to believe them.

On the other hand, there are limits to how diverse any community can or should be. I've come to think that it is not useful to try to hammer diversity into every neighborhood and institution in the United States. Sure, Augusta National should probably admit women, and university sociology departments should probably hire a conservative or two. It would be nice if all neighborhoods had a good mixture of ethnicities. But human nature being what it is, most places and institutions are going to remain culturally homogeneous.

It's probably better to think about diverse lives, not diverse institutions. Human beings, if they are to live well, will have to move through a series of institutions and environments, which may be individually homogeneous but, taken together, will offer diverse experiences. It might also be a good idea to make national service a rite of passage for young people in this country: it would take them out of their narrow neighborhood segment and thrust them in with people unlike themselves. Finally, it's probably important for adults to get out of their own familiar circles. If you live in a coastal, socially liberal neighborhood, maybe you should take out a subscription to the *Door*, the evangelical humor magazine; or maybe you should visit Branson, Missouri. Maybe you should stop in at a megachurch. Sure, it would be superficial familiarity, but it beats the iron curtains that now separate the nation's various cultural zones.

Look around at your daily life. Are you really in touch with the broad diversity of American life? Do you care?

DISCUSSION

1. According to Brooks, our good intentions to create a more racially integrated society have failed because they "have run into the brick wall of human nature" (p. 63). Do you agree? Is segregation in America largely or exclusively a matter of human nature? And what kinds of solutions to this problem does such an understanding imply?
2. What do you make of the title of Brooks's essay? What, in his view, makes choosing "people like us" a preferable option to that of integration?
3. One of the main assumptions behind Brooks's argument is that issues like where we live and whom we associate with are fundamentally matters of personal choice. How accurately do you think his discussion treats the issue of choice? Do we all possess this kind of freedom to choose? And if not, what factors or circumstances undermine this possibility?

WRITING

4. Brooks ends his essay by challenging his readers: "Look around at your daily life. Are you really in touch with the broad diversity of American life? Do you care?" (p. 66) Write an essay in which you respond directly to Brooks's questions. How does the organization of your life (for example, by community, by living situation, by leisure activities) either support or refute Brooks's argument? In a hypothetical world that reflected an idealized portrait of diversity, what would need to change in the ways your life is structured to bring you in line with the ideal?
5. What kind of reader do you think would respond most favorably to Brooks's argument? In a three- to five-page essay present a detailed portrait of the type of reader you feel would make the ideal audience for this essay. What background, education, or political beliefs would this ideal reader have? What attitudes, values, or worldview? Make sure to explain, using quotes from Brooks's essay, why you define this reader in the ways you do. In what ways does defining this ideal reader strengthen or diminish Brooks's argument?
6. To what extent does Brooks's discussion of diversity intersect with Debra Dickerson's (p. 68) critique of what could be called "scientific racism," or the notion that race is permanently fixed in biology? Write an assessment of the differing ways these two authors seem to understand the issue of racial difference. What particular features of each author's argument account for the contrasting conclusions?

DEBRA J. DICKERSON

The Great White Way

In this book review, Debra Dickerson questions the status of "whiteness" as our culture's preeminent racial and social norm, the standard against which all other racial and ethnic identity is defined as "different." Challenging the hegemony this term has long exerted over American thought, she offers a succinct historical overview of the ways the boundaries dividing white from nonwhite have shifted in America. Dickerson's work has appeared in many publications, including the *New Republic, Slate,* and *Vibe*. Her memoir, *An American Story* (2001), describes her move from the rough St. Louis neighborhood where she grew up to her success as a Harvard Law School–trained, award-winning journalist. Her most recent book is *The End of Blackness: Returning the Souls of Black Folk to Their Rightful Owners* (2005). The following book review discusses *Working Toward Whiteness: How America's Immigrants Became White* (2005) by David R. Roediger and *When Affirmative Action Was White: An Untold History of Racial Inequality in Twentieth-Century America* (2005) by Ira Katznelson. It was originally published in the September/October 2005 issue of *Mother Jones.*

WHEN SPACE ALIENS ARRIVE TO COLONIZE US, RACE, ALONG WITH the Atkins diet and Paris Hilton, will be among the things they'll think we're kidding about. Oh, to be a fly on the wall when the president tries to explain to creatures with eight legs what blacks, whites, Asians, and Hispanics are. Race is America's central drama, but just try to define it in 25 words or less. Usually, race is skin color, but our visitors will likely want to know what a "black" person from Darfur and one from Detroit have in common beyond melanin. Sometimes race is language. Sometimes it's religion. Until recently, race was culture and law: Whites in the front, blacks in the back, Asians and Hispanics on the fringes. Race governed who could vote, who could murder or marry whom, what kind of work one could do and how much it could pay. The only thing we know for sure is that race is not biology: Decoding the human genome tells us there is more difference within races than between them.

Hopefully, with time, more Americans will come to accept that race is an arbitrary system for establishing hierarchy and privilege, good for little more than doling out the world's loot and deciding who gets to kick whose butt and then write epic verse about it. A belief in the immutable nature of race is the only way one can still believe that socioeconomic outcomes in America are either fair or entirely determined by individual effort. [David Roediger's *Working Toward Whiteness* and Ira Katznelson's *When Affirmative Action Was White*] should put to rest any such claims.

If race is real and not just a method for the haves to decide who will be have-nots, then all European immigrants, from Ireland to Greece, would have been "white" the moment they arrived here. Instead, as documented in David Roediger's excellent *Working Toward Whiteness,* they were long considered inferior, nearly subhuman, and certainly not white. Southern and eastern European immigrants' language, dress, poverty, and willingness to do "nigger" work excited not pity or curiosity but fear and xenophobia. Teddy Roosevelt popularized the term "race suicide" while calling for Americans to have more babies to offset the mongrel hordes. Scientists tried to prove that Slavs and "dagoes" were incapable of normal adult intelligence. Africans and Asians were clearly less than human, but Hungarians and Sicilians ranked not far above.

It gives one cultural vertigo to learn that, until the 1920s, Americans from northern Europe called themselves "white men" so as not to be confused with their fellow laborers from southern Europe. Or that 11 Italians were lynched in Louisiana in 1891, and Greeks were targeted by whites during a 1909 Omaha race riot. And curiously, the only black family on the Titanic was almost lost to history because "Italian" was used to label the ship's darker-skinned, nonwhite passengers.

Race is an arbitrary system for establishing hierarchy and privilege.

Yet it was this very bureaucratic impulse and political self-interest that eventually led America to "promote" southern and eastern Europeans to "whiteness." The discussion turned to how to fully assimilate these much-needed, newly white workers and how to get their votes. If you were neither black nor Asian nor Hispanic, eventually you could become white, invested with enforceable civil rights and the right to exploit—and hate—nonwhites. World War II finally made all European Americans white, as the "Americans All" banner was reduced to physiognomy alone: Patriotic Japanese Americans ended up in internment camps while fascist-leaning Italian Americans roamed free. While recent European immigrants had abstained from World War I-era race riots, racial violence in the 1940s was an equal-opportunity affair. One Italian American later recalled the time he and his friends "beat up some niggers" in Harlem as "wonderful. It was new. The Italo-American stopped being Italo and started becoming American."

While European immigrants got the racial stamp of approval, the federal government was engaged in a little-recognized piece of racial rigging that resulted in both FDR's New Deal and Truman's Fair Deal being set up largely for the benefit of whites. As Ira Katznelson explains in

When Affirmative Action Was White, these transformative public programs, from Social Security to the GI Bill, were deeply—and intentionally—discriminatory. Faced with a de facto veto by Southern Democrats, throughout the 1930s and 1940s Northern liberals acquiesced to calls for "states' rights" as they drafted the landmark laws that would create a new white middle class. As first-generation white immigrants cashed in on life-altering benefits, black families who had been here since Revolutionary times were left out in the cold.

Race is America's central drama.

Disbursement of federal Depression relief was left at the local level, so that Southern blacks were denied benefits and their labor kept at serf status. In parts of Georgia, no blacks received emergency relief; in Mississippi, less than 1 percent did. Agricultural and domestic workers were excluded from the new Social Security system, subjecting 60 percent of blacks (and 75 percent of Southern blacks) to what Katznelson calls "a form of policy apartheid" far from what FDR had envisioned. Until the 1950s, most blacks remained ineligible for Social Security. Even across the North, black veterans' mortgage, education, and housing benefits lagged behind whites'. Idealized as the capstone of progressive liberalism, such policies were as devastatingly racist as Jim Crow.

To remedy this unacknowledged injustice, Katznelson proposes that current discussions about affirmative action refer to events that took place seven, rather than four, decades ago, when it wasn't called affirmative action but business as usual. He's frustrated by the anemic arguments of his liberal allies, who rely on the most tenuous, least defensible of grounds—diversity—while their opponents invoke color blindness, merit, and the Constitution. In short, affirmative action can't be wrong now when it was right—and white—for so long.

Together, these two books indict the notion of race as, ultimately, a failure of the American imagination. We simply can't imagine a world in which skin color does not entitle us to think we know what people are capable of, what they deserve, or their character. We can't imagine what America might become if true affirmative action—not the kind aimed at the Huxtable kids[1] but at poverty and substandard education—was enacted at anywhere near the level once bestowed on those fortunate enough to be seen as white.

NOTE

[1]The Huxtables are the fictional family that appeared on the popular sitcom *The Cosby Show* in the 1980s and 1990s.

DISCUSSION

1. Dickerson opens her essay with a hypothetical scenario in which space aliens are faced with the task of understanding how Americans have perceived and sought to deal with race. Why do you think she chooses to begin her discussion on race by focusing on it from an "alien" perspective? What kind of commentary on race does this particular strategy imply?
2. Dickerson refers to race as the "central drama" of American history. Why do you think she uses the term *drama*? Does her discussion of racial politics and racialist violence invite us in any way to think about this history in terms of role-playing, performance, or social and cultural scripts? If so, how?
3. According to Dickerson, race is best understood as a question of power. "Hopefully, with time," she writes, "more Americans will come to accept that race is an arbitrary system for establishing hierarchy and privilege." (p. 68). What do you make of this claim? To what extent do you share Dickerson's conviction about the arbitrariness of racial categories and racial difference?

WRITING

4. The dominant ways of thinking about race in America, argues Dickerson, are more the product of social fantasy than a reflection of objective reality. In a brief essay, evaluate the validity of this thesis. To what extent is it valid to think of the racial scripts that get taught in our culture as fantastic or fictional? Does this possibility diminish or accentuate the power they can wield?
5. One of the goals of this essay is to denaturalize the racial differences we've been taught to accept. Write a three- to five-page essay in which you analyze and evaluate this goal. Choose an example from our popular culture (for example, a television show, an advertisement, or a news story) that, in your view, encourages us to accept a view about race and racial difference that you consider artificial. First identify, describe, and analyze the views this example invites its audience to share: What is the main point this text attempts to convey? How does it represent this false view as right or normal? What are the particular strategies it uses to persuade readers to accept this view? Then evaluate the consequences you believe follow from accepting the argument being advanced. In your view, what is problematic, counterproductive, or just plain wrong about taking at face value the view advanced here?
6. Debra Dickerson shares with Michael Eric Dyson (p. 52) a concern about public attitudes about race as well as the implications of accepting these attitudes uncritically. How do you think Dickerson would respond to the arguments about "black patriotism" or religion in African American life advanced by Dyson? In your view, would Dickerson find his arguments to be in line with her own conclusions about race, power, and hierarchy? How or how not?

AMITAVA KUMAR

The Restoration of Faith

In many ways, our contemporary legal system encourages us to define justice in terms of punishment. Advocates for stricter penalties and harsher sentences for criminals often speak of the "closure" such treatment brings to victims. But might this conventional wisdom have it wrong? Is it possible that resolution happens more through forgiveness and understanding than vengeance and punishment? This is the possibility Amitava Kumar contemplates here. Sketching a compelling portrait of "restorative justice," he raises important questions about the ways we have been taught to think about crime and punishment. Amitava Kumar is a writer and professor of English at Vassar College. His books include *Husband of a Fanatic* (2005) and *A Foreigner Carrying in the Crook of His Arm a Tiny Bomb* (2010). This essay was published in *Caravan* magazine in 2013.

ON A RECENT WEEKEND I PICKED UP THE *NEW YORK TIMES* THAT IS delivered in a blue polythene bag outside my door each morning, and read a story about a young man who had fatally shot his girlfriend during a fight. The young man's name was Conor McBride and the victim's name was Ann Margaret Grosmaire. Both were 19 when this happened, in March 2010, in Tallahassee, Florida.

The reporter, Paul Tullis, introduced an early note about what made the story unusual. Ann's father, Andy Grosmaire, standing next to his "intubated and unconscious" daughter in hospital, heard her say before her death, "Forgive him." Conor, when he was booked, was asked to provide the names of five people who could visit him in jail. He included the name of Ann's mother, Kate Grosmaire. Talking to the reporter who had written the story, Kate explained her desire to go and see Conor in prison, "Before this happened, I loved Conor. I knew that if I defined Conor by that one moment—as a murderer—I was defining my daughter as a murder victim. And I could not allow that to happen."

The significance of restorative justice [lies] in "community-based processes that hold people who harm directly accountable to the people that they've harmed."

The state attorney's office had charged Conor McBride with first-degree murder; this meant that he was likely to spend the rest of his life in prison. (As the case didn't have any aggravating circumstances, like prior convictions or the victim being a child, the prosecutors were probably not likely to seek the death penalty.) But Ann's parents told the assistant state attorney that they didn't want Conor to spend the rest of his life in prison. The concept that the Grosmaires had embraced, together with Conor's parents, Julie and Michael McBride, was that of "restorative justice," a not very widely known practice based on the idea of victim–offender dialogue.

Where the report took a turn for me is that the lawyer they hired to facilitate this process was a woman named Sujatha Baliga. The reporter had mentioned that Baliga was born in Shippensburg, Pennsylvania, the child of Indian immigrants. As I read her name and then a few more lines about her, I wanted to ask Baliga a question about India.

Baliga told me that the significance of restorative justice lay in "community-based processes that hold people who harm directly accountable to the people that they've harmed." There was great faith invested there in face-to-face dialogue and participatory decision-making. Paraphrasing Howard Zehr, a pioneer in the field of restorative justice, Baliga said that rather than asking the traditional justice system questions of "What law was broken? Who broke it? How should we punish them?" the approach she was advocating asked instead, "What harm has been done? What needs have arisen? Whose obligation is it to meet those needs?" Evidence of this shift was present in the actions of the Grosmaires and the McBrides. They had each sought to honor the memory of Ann Grosmaire.

Even approaching Baliga couldn't have been easy for the Grosmaires and the McBrides. Restorative justice cases have usually involved burglaries or property disputes—not violent crimes, and certainly not homicides. To add to this, Florida is considered a law-and-order state with a strong leaning toward punitive justice. But Baliga facilitated a meeting in June 2011 in the jail where Conor was incarcerated. At that conference, Ann's parents spoke first, talking of the young woman's childhood and her dreams. They told the young man who had killed their daughter about the pain he had caused. Then, Conor told them the story of how he and Ann had been fighting for 38 hours. Conor told the group, "What I did was inexcusable. There is no why, there are no excuses, there is no reason."

[T]he Grosmaires said that they didn't forgive Conor for his sake, but their own.

Earlier, while reading the report in the *New York Times* I had been struck by the fact that Conor had made such an honest and open admission at the meeting. But it wasn't until I had my exchanges with Baliga that I learned that Conor's statement had not—rather, *could* not—have been a spontaneous process. Baliga told me that helping Conor remember the details of the crime so that he would be prepared to answer the Grosmaires' questions had been "heartbreaking." The young man appeared to be experiencing what Baliga called "participatory traumatic stress" and he "couldn't remember many of the details of Ann's last moments." At the conference meeting, however, he came clean, telling Ann's parents the story of how he and Ann had been fighting for two days; in person, by text, and over the phone. Ann was on her knees, her hand raised to stop him, when he fired. It had been difficult, and understandably painful, for the dead woman's parents to hear this account. In fact, everyone involved in the process found it difficult, including the lawyers. Baliga said that it was "always challenging to get people in the traditional system to understand what we are doing—explaining it to jail staff, to the prosecutor, to the defense attorney."

When the meeting was over, Baliga asked the Grosmaires what they wanted. Ann's mother said that he should get a five to 15-year term, and her father said ten to 15 years. Conor's parents agreed. The assistant state attorney was asked to speak. He didn't suggest a punishment, pointing out that even a statement like that required consideration. Later, he wrote to the Grosmaires and said that he was going to offer Conor a choice: 20 years in prison plus ten years probation, or 25 years in prison. Conor has chosen the former.

In the *New York Times*, Tullis had written that the Grosmaires said that they didn't forgive Conor for his sake, but their own. Ann's mother told Tullis, "Forgiveness for me was self-preservation." For his part, Conor told Tullis, "With the Grosmaires' forgiveness, I could accept the responsibility and not be condemned." If he had simply been turned into an enemy, he could have escaped the human contract, but by accepting him, the Grosmaires had drawn him into the circle of obligation. He was going to have to do good enough for two.

In my discussion with Baliga, I came to the question I had been meaning to ask her the moment I finished reading the piece by Tullis. I asked Baliga about the recent gang rape of the young woman in a moving bus in Delhi. The entire society had been galvanized and was demanding justice. The victim's family has demanded that the perpetrators be hanged. In such circumstances, would Baliga still want to advocate restorative justice?

Baliga's answer was a forthright no. She explained that "restorative justice is a voluntary process, and is best when driven by the desires of the victims. The victims in this case have been clear—the woman from her deathbed, and her father now—that they want the death penalty. The family has said they don't want to see the young men who did this. So this is not an appropriate case for restorative justice."

Having said that, Baliga added that she was opposed to the death penalty. And that more information was needed about the men involved before a recommendation could be made about how long they ought to remain inside prison. She doubted that the penal system had the capacity to "rehabilitate this level of sexualized violence," in part because she believes that such behavior "comes from either some mental health issues or a history of unthinkable trauma that is being passed on to others." What was key now, far greater than simply wanting to hang the men now, was "to get to the roots of how these horrors happened."

Tullis's report in the *New York Times* had introduced Baliga by telling readers that she was a former public defender who was now the director of the restorative justice project at the National Council on Crime and Delinquency. Tullis had also written that "from as far back as Baliga can remember, she was sexually abused by her father." As a teen, she was dyeing her hair and cutting herself. Later, while studying at Harvard, she wanted to become a prosecutor and lock up child molesters. During a visit to India, she got a chance to meet the Dalai Lama, from whom she sought advice about how she could go on with her work on the behalf of the oppressed without having anger as her motivating force. The Dalai Lama advised Baliga to meditate and then asked her to align herself with the enemy. Baliga wasn't prepared to follow the second part of his advice, but after checking into a meditation course she found herself freed from rage and a desire for revenge.

DISCUSSION

1. What do you make of the term "restorative justice"? What specifically does this approach to crime "restore"? And what about this approach is supposed to be more "just"? Do you agree? Why or why not?
2. Kumar quotes the victim's mother as saying that "forgiveness for me was self-preservation" (p. 74). What do you think she means by this? Does it make sense to you that forgiving someone who has harmed you can actually "preserve" you?
3. This essay draws a firm distinction between a willingness to forgive and a desire for vengeance. In your view, should vengeance play any role in the criminal justice system? And if so, what role specifically?

WRITING

4. In interviewing one of the lawyers involved, Kumar highlights the key difference between traditional notions of justice and restorative justice: "[Rather] than asking the traditional justice system questions of 'What law was broken? Who broke it? How should we punish them?' the approach [the lawyer] was advocating asked instead, 'What harm has been done? What needs have arisen? Whose obligation is it to meet those needs?' " (p. 73). In an essay, discuss what you see as the key differences between these two types of questions. What attitude toward crime and criminals does each set of questions imply? How does each set of questions define the concept of justice differently? And which definition do you find more valid? Why?
5. Kumar describes restorative justice as a "practice based on the idea of victim–offender dialogue" (p. 73). Write an essay in which you lay out the rules by which you think a dialogue between a victim and an offender should unfold. What types of statement or questions should each party be allowed to make? What (if any) limits should be placed around what each party is allowed to say? And how would these rules help achieve a "just" outcome?
6. In many ways, justice would seem a perfect example of the kind of "nonmarket value" Michael Sandel discusses in his essay (p. 40). How do you think Sandel would respond to the moral argument behind "restorative justice" that Kumar outlines here? Given what Sandel has to say about the need to preserve and nurture such "nonmarket values," do you think he would find the emphasis within restorative justice upon dialogue and forgiveness to be compelling? Why or why not?

Tying It All Together

Like Ty Burr, Jessica Bennett ("The Flip Side of Internet Fame," p. 90) is interested in exploring the ways we are taught to think about and look at those people who find themselves in the public eye. How do these two discussions compare? Does Bennett draw the same conclusions about "Internet fame" that Burr does regarding the culture of celebrity? Which argument do you find most compelling? Why?

A number of other chapters in the book contain selections that examine what Stephen Asma would describe as an *ism*: a system of beliefs or values that have gained wide currency within mainstream culture. Among the systems explored are vegetarianism (Schwennesen, "The Ethics of Eating Meat," p. 178), communitarianism (Kotkin, "There's No Place Like Home," p. 453), and academic plagiarism (Toor, "Unconscious Plagiarism," p. 296). In a two- to three-page essay, consider how one of these essays examines its particular "ism." What belief or value system does this essay explore? What conclusions about it does this essay encourage readers to draw? And how does this discussion compare with what Asma has to say in his piece about environmentalism?

Scenes and Un-Scenes: Political Protest

There is a long and storied tradition in America of social or political protest. From the Boston Tea Party to the women's suffrage movement, antisegregation campaigns to abortion rights rallies, civil rights demonstrations to Occupy Wall Street, our national history is replete with efforts to challenge the practices and beliefs that, at one time or another, have stood as unexamined norms. But how do these public demonstrations actually succeed — if indeed they do — in rewriting beliefs that, for any given era, have become so embedded, entrenched, assumed? The short answer, of course, is that these beliefs were never quite as universal as they may have appeared. Bringing together people who felt marginalized or oppressed by a given societal norm, these demonstrations were designed to challenge the beliefs on which such norms rested, to offer up for scrutiny the embedded practices and unspoken assumptions that justified the status quo. For each of the following examples, how fully would you say this objective is achieved? What particular beliefs does each put on display? What social scripts does each attempt to rewrite?

Hulton Archive/Getty Images

Even today, the civil rights movement led by Martin Luther King Jr. in the 1960s still stands as a model for how Americans think about social or political protest. The tradition of public, nonviolent protest that King pioneered persists within the public imagination as the blueprint for how "the people" can affect not only tangible changes in public policy but also meaningful shifts in social attitude. The famous 1963 March on Washington, for example, marks a watershed both for efforts to create new civil rights legislation and for the struggle to challenge and undo long-standing public attitudes about race.

Steve Heiber/AP Photo

The Million Man March sought to carry forward King's standard of public, nonviolent protest into the present day. At the same time, though, such spectacles make evident how much has changed over the last forty plus years. In updating King's messages for our contemporary "wired" age, for example, it reminds us how different the tactics of public protest have become. Availing itself of the same tools we might find at a sporting event or rock concert, this image shows how deeply shaped by our media culture political protest is these days.

Justin Sullivan/Getty Images

<< Over the years, in fact, King's legacy has moved well beyond the realm of racial politics, coming to underlie and inform all manner of different causes. His tradition of public, nonviolent protest as well as his rhetoric of civil and social rights have long been adopted by a va ety of other constituencies and used to advance a host of other interests. Not surprisingly, this has led to the marriage of these tactics to a number of seemingl unlikely causes. We might well wonder, for example, what parti ular "right" a celebrity-studded, Scientology-sponsored demonstration against the use of antidepressants is meant to advance. When you compare this spectacle to the March on Washington, how much commonality do you discern?

Alex Wong/Getty Images

Stan Honda/Getty Images

The legacy of the civil rights movement extends even to the financial realm, informing recent efforts to challenge and critique the role the financial industry played in causing the global recession. This image captures a moment from the Occupy Wall Street protests. To what extent does the Occupy movement reflect the core values of King's legacy?

Another arena in which King's tradition of public demonstration and civil rights protest has been taken up in recent years is gay rights — in particular, the much-publicized and highly contentious issue of gay marriage. In ways large and small, proponents of this movement have sought to model their efforts along the lines of the African American struggle for justice and equality before the law. Deploying some of the same rhetoric, many have framed the demand for legalized marriage as a natural extension of King's work. Do you agree with this analogy?

DISCUSSION

1. Which of these protests raises an issue that most resonates with your personal experience? Which one touches on an issue or conflict that you feel a personal stake in? To what extent does its embedded or unspoken critique reflect your own views?
2. Choose one of the previous examples. What relationship between public spectacle and societal belief does it showcase? That is, in what ways does this protest seem designed to affect or alter a more fundamental and underlying social norm?
3. What political or social controversy does this collection leave out? What protest would you add to this list, and what in your view would make it worthy of inclusion?

WRITING

4. Choose something from our popular culture (e.g., a television show, a commercial, a movie, or the like) that shows an example of a political or social protest challenging a particular societal rule. Describe how this protest gets depicted. How are the protesters presented? What specific issues or ideas are offered up for critique? How do the symbols match or differ from the images you've viewed in this feature? How compelling or convincing do you find this depiction? Why?
5. Choose one of the images above that offers a blueprint for social protest that you yourself would not follow. Identify and evaluate the particular aspects of this protest that you find problematic, inadequate, or otherwise ineffective. Then use this critique to create a model of the kind of protest you would endorse. What different sorts of tactics would your model utilize? What different objectives would it attempt to achieve? And finally, what, in your estimation, makes this alternative more preferable?
6. The role of social protest in our culture has gone a long way toward normalizing certain issues. In what ways can Katie Roiphe's discussion of single motherhood (p. 58) or Michael Sandel's reflections on the marketplace (p. 40) be read as their own forms of social protest? To what extent do their arguments challenge prevailing social scripts or underlying cultural norms?

Putting It into Practice: **Scripting Belief**

Now that you've read the chapter selections, try applying your conclusions to your own life by completing the following exercises.

SURVEYING OURSELVES How do you think "normal" Americans think? Visit the Gallup Poll website (www.galluppoll.com) and look at the home page. Choose two or three topics from the toolbar labeled "Hot Topics" and decide how you would answer the survey questions posed. Write an essay in which you compare your beliefs to those of the American majority. Are you "normal" or are you "different"? How do you respond to being categorized in either of those groups?

MARKETING BELIEF Choose some venue or organization that you think actively works to promote or market a set of beliefs to the general public (e.g., a church, a military recruitment center, a campus activist group, or a similar group). Research the ways that this group advertises itself to the larger community. Write an essay in which you explore what tactics the group uses to court new members. What symbols does it use in its advertising? What language do these ads include that is designed to inspire new believers?

SELL IT Try combining the two activities above. Choose one of the survey topics you wrote about in the first assignment and design an ad you think would be effective in appealing to nonbelievers. This ad could be anything from a speech to a commercial or billboard. What images or language do you believe is most important in convincing others to follow the particular belief you've chosen?

Brand New Images/Getty Images

2 How We WATCH

Does what we see depend on how we're looking?

Introduction

Seeing Is Believing?

Do the names Carrie Underwood and Adam Lambert mean anything to you? Do you let your incoming calls go straight to voicemail during *Project Runway*? Do you find yourself regularly debating who should have been voted off the show in the latest episode of *Big Brother*? If so, you are not alone. Reality TV draws millions of viewers like you who enjoy watching everyday people live out certain "realities" in front of the camera. And these viewers, also like you, accurately sense that few other television genres work as hard as reality TV to teach us how to play the *role* of viewer.

As anyone who has seen even an episode or two can attest, very clear but unspoken rules dictate the ways we are and are not supposed to watch reality television. Cardinal among these rules is the presumption that what we see on these shows truly is a snapshot of reality, a window through which we get to glimpse the personal, private details of real people in real situations feeling real emotions. At the same time, however, we are also aware that within the boundaries established by these shows not everything counts equally as reality. If we want to properly perform our role as viewer, we know that we need to keep our attention focused on very specific aspects of what is on display. We must view *selectively.* These shows work only if we suspend disbelief and buy into the idea that what we're seeing is more or less real.

This unspoken message doesn't pertain only to reality television. Indeed, few things are more widely available to us than the opportunity to play the role of watcher. Whether it is the candid photos that pop up on our cell phones, the billboards we drive past on the interstate, the clothing catalogs that litter our mailboxes, or the stories broadcast on the nightly news, we are called constantly to view things. So natural has the experience of watching become, however, that we sometimes miss the larger implication: at the same time we are being taught how to *watch,* we are also being taught how to *think* — about ourselves and the wider world around us.

Take, for example, the typical ad for a luxury car. Because we have grown so accustomed to seeing this sort of image in television commercials or online ads, we don't need any explicit instructions telling us how we are supposed to look at it. Through repeated exposure to examples just like it, we have internalized the form of watching we are expected to conduct. And because we have learned this role of watcher so well, we have also come to understand the particular ways we are supposed to think about this image: the associations we are supposed to make, the conclusions we are supposed to draw. We know, for example, that when we come across one of these glossy portraits, there is a very specific type of person we are allowed to imagine sitting behind the wheel — a person with a certain kind of look (young, fit, fashionable); a certain kind of lifestyle (yuppie professional but also rugged and outdoorsy); a particular circle of friends (similarly young, fit, and fashionable); and a certain level of income (comfortably upper middle class). And we further know that our job as viewers is not only to accurately define this hypothetical driver, but also to admire him, to see him as a stand-in for ourselves. Once we have taken this step, we are well on our way to accepting and adopting the other messages an image like this conveys (about, for instance, the desirability of wealth, the importance of status, or the proper definition of success).

To a very real degree, this same formula underlies our visual encounters with virtually everything in our popular culture: rules of spectatorship that turn the ever-expanding universe of images, signs, and messages surrounding us into a kind of classroom where we are taught the difference between what matters and what doesn't. And when this sort of thing happens in places other than our entertainment industry, the stakes involved can be even higher — as, for example, in our news industry. Whether it is a presidential press conference or footage of a natural disaster, a Sunday talk show roundtable on immigration reform or cable news coverage of an anti–Wall Street demonstration, every depiction or discussion of current events is underwritten by the same basic requirement: to accept the assumptions and norms being presented as our own. When we catch the tail end of a Fox News commentator attacking Gulf oil spill protesters or a mock news story on *The Daily Show* spoofing the role of Super PACs in presidential campaigns, we are no less intimately caught up in navigating our culture's ideals and expectations than when we catch a glimpse of A-list celebrities strolling down the red carpet.

To return one final time to the example of reality television, think for a moment about what these shows teach us about,

What is normal?

Jeff Mitchell/Getty Images

What does this logo ask you to believe? What are the ideas/values/ attitudes it asks you to accept as normal?

What is normal?

Tabloids like *US Weekly* tell us, "Stars are just like us!"

Alo Ceballos/Film Magic/Getty Images

Do you share this belief? Should we automatically accept it as normal?

What is normal?

"It is astonishing that gay and lesbian Americans are still treated as second-class citizens. I am confident that, very soon, the laws of this nation will reflect the basic truth that gay and lesbian people — like all human beings — are born equal in dignity and rights."

— George Clooney

AFP/Stringer/Getty Images

What kind of social script does this quotation advocate? What would it feel like to act out this script in our personal lives?

say, the importance of not only *watching* but also of being *watched*: about the pleasures and payoffs that supposedly result from turning ourselves into an entertainment spectacle. Since we rarely see a cast member on one of these shows expressing annoyance or dismay over having their lives filmed twenty-four hours a day, is it really all that strange to consider that we might begin to feel the same way — that we might start regarding the prospect of being scrutinized by others as ordinary, unremarkable, just "the way things are"?

To expand our inquiry, we might note how often this expectation gets reinforced elsewhere in popular culture. We need only take stock of the popularity of online sites like Facebook and Twitter, for example, to get a sense of how widespread this norm has become. Is the emergence of popular Internet sites like YouTube linked to a need to watch ourselves the way we have grown so accustomed to watching others? We certainly don't lack for images that encourage us to think about the private lives of other people as material fit for public consumption. As we've already seen, when we accept this premise — when we look at the websites, television shows, and magazines in the ways prescribed for us — we find ourselves confronting additional expectations as well: from the clothing brands we should wear to the body images we should cultivate to the reasonableness of being watched ourselves.

To sketch out this process does not by itself answer or resolve the thorny questions this introduction poses: Is seeing believing? In a world defined by Instagram and Photoshop, Pixar-animated movies and network television "docudramas," how do we know the difference between what is real and what is scripted? How does taking on the role of watcher affect our assumptions about the world around us? And does this role eventually blur the boundaries between watching and being watched? Given the volume and variety of what we are shown day to day, it should not surprise us that answering these questions gets pretty complicated pretty quickly.

Nonetheless, this task is taken up by each of the following selection's authors. The authors in this chapter fall into two basic categories: those exploring some aspect of how we are taught to look and those addressing some dimension of how we are looked at. Within the first are Virginia Heffernan, Naomi Klein, Heather Havrilesky, and John Paul Titlow. Pushing back against growing conviction that Americans have lost the capacity to concentrate, Heffernan points out that distraction has long been a feature of public life and argues for a more common-sense approach to what she calls the "attention-span myth." In her exploration of corporate branding, Naomi Klein shifts the focus from attention spans to consumer culture — pondering how campus activism these days has been co-opted and largely driven by the logic of commercial advertising. Exploring the world of pop culture from a different angle, Heather Havrilesky looks at the increasing use of the term *girl* to describe female characters on television. In what ways, she asks, does this term frame and/or limit our understanding of female experience and female power? Rounding out this group, John Paul Titlow shares some thoughts about the growing popularity of so-called "selfie" portraits online, wondering whether the rise of this trend marks the emergence of a new type of digitally driven narcissism. Within the second category are Harriet McBryde Johnson, Jessica Bennett, Don Tapscott, and Charles Duhigg. In recounting her debate with famed medical ethicist Peter Singer, Johnson, an American with disabilities, offers a startlingly blunt and thought-provoking meditation on what it means to be viewed — and stereotyped — as the "token cripple." Assessing the ways the Web has refashioned daily life, Tapscott makes the argument for a new visual norm, one that prizes the payoffs of disclosure and transparency over the benefits of keeping things private. Presenting her own take on the relentless visibility afforded by the Internet, Bennett portrays the ways that fast fame via viral videos can have a lasting impact on the lives of the reluctantly famous. And finally, Charles Duhigg culminates our examination of digital culture by tracking the growing efforts of online retailers to monitor and record every move their customers make.

What is normal?

AFP/Getty Images

Can social scripts be rewritten? What alternative norms does this image promote?

While they range widely across the landscape of our modern popular culture, these selections do remain linked in one fundamental way: By questioning some of the key visual roles that get scripted in our world, each in its own way inclines us to wonder whether what we *see* is truly what we *get*.

e macmillanhighered.com/actingout
Tutorials > Critical Reading > Reading visuals: Purpose
> Reading visuals: Audience
e-Readings > Linda Stone, *On Continuous Partial Attention*

JESSICA BENNETT

The Flip Side of Internet Fame

From YouTube to Facebook to Twitter, we have grown accustomed to the experience of being watched and followed online. Many of us simply take it as a given that our day-to-day activities will be captured and put on display for one audience or another. But is this situation really normal? What are the consequences of living in a world where what we do and what we say automatically become public? Taking up precisely these questions, Jessica Bennett looks more closely at our modern visual culture, examining the effects that such perpetual audienceship has on the ways we think and feel. Bennett was formerly an editor and senior writer for *Newsweek* and an executive editor of Tumblr. Her reporting about the rise in gay activism after the passage of Proposition 8, which overturned legalized gay marriage in California, earned her a 2009 award from the Gay and Lesbian Alliance Against Defamation (GLAAD). The following selection originally appeared in the February 21, 2008, edition of *Newsweek*.

IN 2002, GHYSLAIN RAZA, A CHUBBY CANADIAN TEEN, FILMED HIMself acting out a fight scene from *Star Wars* using a makeshift light saber. His awkward performance was funny, in part because it wasn't meant to be. And it certainly was never meant to be public: for nearly a year the video remained on a shelf in Raza's school's TV studio, where he'd filmed it. Sometime in 2003, though, another student discovered the video, digitized it, and posted it online—and Raza's nightmare began. Within days, "Star Wars Kid" had become a viral frenzy. It was posted on hundreds of blogs, enhanced by music and special effects, and watched by millions. Entire Web sites were dedicated to the subject; one, jedimaster.net, was even named one of *Time*'s 50 best sites of 2003. Had that teenager wanted to be famous, he couldn't have asked for anything better. But in Raza's case it became a source of public humiliation, precisely what every kid fears the most.

Razas of the world take note: among the generation that's been reared online, stories like this are becoming more and more common. They serve as important reminders of a dark side of instant Internet fame: humiliation. Already dozens of Web sites exist solely to help those who would shame others. There are sites for posting hateful rants about ex-lovers (DontDateHimGirl.com) and bad tippers (the S----ty Tipper Database), and for posting cell-phone images of public bad behavior (hollabackNYC.com) and lousy drivers. As a new book makes clear in powerful terms, such sites can make or break a person, in a matter of seconds.

"Anybody can become a celebrity or a worldwide villain in an instant," says Daniel Solove, a law professor at George Washington University and author of *The Future of Reputation: Gossip, Rumor, and Privacy on the Internet* (Yale). "Some people may revel in that. But others might say that's not the role they wanted to play in life."

"Dog poop girl" wasn't the public role a South Korean student had in mind when, in 2005, she refused to clean up after her dog in the subway in Seoul. A minor infraction, perhaps, but another passenger captured the act on a cellphone camera, posted it online, and created a viral frenzy. The woman was harassed into dropping out of college. More recently a student at Lewis & Clark University in Portland, Ore., was publicly accused—on Facebook, the social-networking site—of sexually assaulting another student. Normally, such allegations on campus are kept confidential. But in this case a Facebook group revealed his name, with the word "rapist" for the world to see, before the incident was ever even reported to the authorities. The accused teen was never arrested or charged, but he might as well have been: bloggers picked up the story, and a local alt-weekly put it on its cover, revealing graphic details of the encounter as described by the alleged victim, without including the supposed perpetrator's version of events.

Anybody can become a celebrity or a worldwide villain in an instant.

Public shaming, of course, is nothing new. Ancient Romans punished wrongdoers by branding them on the forehead—slaves caught stealing got *fur* (Latin for thief) and runaways got *fug* (fugitive). In Colonial America heretics were clamped into stocks in the public square, thieves had their hands or fingers cut off, and adulterers were forced to wear a scarlet A. More recently a U.S. judge forced a mail thief to wear a sign announcing his crime outside a San Francisco post office; in other places sex offenders have to post warning signs on their front lawns.

Although social stigma can be a useful deterrent, "the Internet is a loose cannon," says ethicist Jim Cohen of Fordham University School of Law in New York. Online there are few checks and balances and no due process—and validating the credibility of a claim is difficult, to say the least. Moreover, studies show that the anonymity of the Net encourages people to say things they normally wouldn't. JuicyCampus, a gossip Web site for U.S. college students, has made headlines by tapping into this urge. The site solicits juicy rumors under the protection of anonymity for sources. But what may have begun as fun and games has turned into a venue for bigoted rants and stories about drug use and sex that identify students by name. "Anyone with a grudge can maliciously and sometimes libelously attack defenseless students," Daniel Belzer, a Duke senior, told *Newsweek* in December.

Regulators find sites like JuicyCampus hard to control. Laws on free speech and defamation vary widely between countries. In the United States, proving libel requires the victim to show that his or her persecutor intended malice, while the British system puts the burden on the defense to show that a statement is not libelous (making it much easier to prosecute). A 1996 U.S. law—Section 230 of the Communications Decency Act—specifically protects the operators of Web sites from liability for the speech of their users. As long as the host of a site doesn't post or edit content, it has no liability. (If AOL, say, were held responsible for every poster, it would quickly go out of business.)

So, then, what's to stop a person from posting whatever he wants about you, if he can do so anonymously and suffer no repercussions? For people who use blogs and social-networking sites like diaries, putting their personal information out there for the world to see, this presents a serious risk. "I think young people are seduced by the citizen-media notion of the Internet: that everyone can have their minutes of fame," says Barry Schuler, the former CEO of AOL who is now the coproducer of a new movie, *Look*, about public video surveillance. "But they're also putting themselves out there—forever."

Public shaming, of course, is nothing new.

Shaming victims, meanwhile, have little legal recourse. Identifying posters often means having to subpoena an anonymous IP address. But that could lead nowhere. Many people share IP addresses on college networks or Wi-Fi hotspots, and many Web sites hide individual addresses. Even if a victim identifies the defamer, bloggers aren't usually rich enough to pay big damage awards. Legal action may only increase publicity—the last thing a shaming victim wants. "The law can only do so much," warns Solove.

Once unsavory information is posted, it's almost impossible to retrieve. The family of the "Star Wars Kid," who spent time in therapy as a result of his ordeal, filed suit against the students who uploaded his video, and settled out of court. But dozens of versions of his video are still widely available, all over the Net. One of the bad boyfriends featured on Don'tDateHimGirl.com also sued, but his case was dismissed due to lack of jurisdiction. The accused rapist at Lewis & Clark has also hired lawyers. But Google his name today, and the first entry has the word "rapist" in its title. If the "Star Wars Kid" has anything to teach us, it's that shame, like the force, will always be with you.

DISCUSSION

1. Bennett's essay poses fundamental questions about what it means in our culture to watch and be watched. What is the connection between how we view ourselves and how others view us? How does the Internet alter this dynamic? Can you think of a moment in your life when you had to confront a discrepancy between your self-image and the image others held of you? In the face of this discrepancy, what did you do?
2. Take a moment to focus on the title of this essay. To what extent does Bennett's portrait of online shaming challenge prevailing norms regarding fame? What, in your view, are the more typical ways we are taught in our culture to regard the prospect of being famous? What, according to the dominant scripts, is fame supposed to do to and for us? And how does Bennett's discussion uncover the "flip side" of such norms?
3. How do you understand the concept of public shaming? In your view, is this a defensible, even reasonable, practice? Or do its dangers outweigh its benefits?

WRITING

4. Part of the problem posed by online shaming has to do with the ways this behavior bumps up against our belief in free expression. How do we balance a belief in the freedom of speech against our concern for safeguarding people's reputations? In a brief essay, identify what limits, if any, you would place on the free exchange of ideas so fundamental to the Internet. If you were given the power to legislate these limits, where would you draw the line? What restrictions or guidelines would you mandate for how a viewer or reader could respond to or use somebody else's personal information? Quote some of Bennett's examples to support your argument.
5. Taken together, the examples Bennett cites amount to a case study in the dangers of our cultural obsession with fame. Write an essay in which you discuss your thoughts on fame and notoriety. How do you understand our society's celebration of being famous? Is this, in your view, a worthwhile ideal to pursue? Does our culture create scripts for how and why to become famous that are worth following? How or how not?
6. How do you think Don Tapscott (p. 117) would respond to Bennett's portrait of online shaming? In a one-page essay, identify and analyze what you see as the parallels between these two essays. Given what Tapscott has to say about self-disclosure online, do you think he would challenge the risks of "Internet fame" that Bennett profiles? Why or why not?

Rule *Maker* >>>>>>>>> Rule *Breaker*

“Certainly, reality TV is a very manipulated format where the basis of it is that real people are put into unreal situations to create a story. . . . What makes it so compelling is that you never know what a real person's reaction to an unreal situation will be. That's why you get such great stuff on reality TV.*

— J. RUPERT THOMPSON, DIRECTOR AND PRODUCER OF REALITY SHOWS *BIG BROTHER* AND *FEAR FACTOR*

QUOTED IN CNBC ARTICLE, APRIL 14, 2009.

“*It's an edited-for-television show. Each and every one of us works really, really hard to entertain you. For people to take it seriously, that really disturbs me.*

— KELLY BENSIMON, *REAL HOUSEWIVES OF NEW YORK CITY*

J. Rupert Thompson vs. Kelly Bensimon

Is what we are shown on reality television, in fact, *real*? It depends on whom you ask. For those who create and produce these shows, the answer could quite easily be “yes.” They might acknowledge that aspiring participants are put through a rigorous screening process or that specific story lines are tailored and polished in the editing room, but such producers would likely still maintain that these shows nonetheless bring viewers into contact with real people simply being *themselves.* Those on the other side of the camera, however, might easily argue that reality TV is less an opportunity to showcase the “real you” than a job: one that requires you to conform to a role you had no direct hand in creating. Every reality show has its villain, its crybaby, its average Joe, and those who aspire to be on these shows work hard to conform themselves to these pre-made categories.

FIND THE RULES: Choose a reality television show and write a profile of it. More specifically, summarize the goals of the show, analyze its participants, and evaluate the story lines it creates for them.

ANALYZE THE RULES: Write a brief essay in which you assess the merits and shortcomings of the rules that the reality-show producer and the reality-show actors attempt to promote. Which set of rules do you find more compelling? Which set are you more inclined to accept as normal? And why?

MAKE YOUR OWN RULES: Imagine that you are creating a reality television show that must be 100 percent real. In a brief essay, describe what this show would look like. What would be the show's format? Its setting and characters? Explain how this "100 percent real" show would rewrite the rules and norms by which reality television shows are conventionally created.

Taylor Hill/Getty Images

Kelly Bensimon

HARRIET McBRYDE JOHNSON

Unspeakable Conversations

What does it mean to be tokenized, to have the stereotypes based on how we look become the scripts by which others think about and define us? In recounting her two-day experience playing the role of what she calls the "token cripple" on a Princeton University visit, Harriet McBryde Johnson raises a series of provocative questions about the ways in which our physical appearance comes to stand as definitive proof of who and what we are. Johnson practiced law in Charleston, South Carolina. She earned a BS in history from Charleston Southern University (1978), a master's in public administration from the College of Charleston (1981), and a JD from the University of South Carolina (1985). She wrote about political and disability issues for a number of publications, such as *South Carolina Lawyer* and *Review of Public Personnel Administration.* She also wrote a novel titled *Accidents of Nature* (2006). Johnson died on June 4, 2008. This piece was first published in the *New York Times* in 2003.

HE INSISTS HE DOESN'T WANT TO KILL ME. HE SIMPLY THINKS IT would have been better, all things considered, to have given my parents the option of killing the baby I once was, and to let other parents kill similar babies as they come along and thereby avoid the suffering that comes with lives like mine and satisfy the reasonable preferences of parents for a different kind of child. It has nothing to do with me. I should not feel threatened.

Whenever I try to wrap my head around his tight string of syllogisms, my brain gets so fried it's . . . almost fun. Mercy! It's like *Alice in Wonderland.*

It is a chilly Monday in late March, just less than a year ago. I am at Princeton University.

My host is Prof. Peter Singer, often called—and not just by his book publicist—the most influential philosopher of our time. He is the man who wants me dead. No, that's not at all fair. He wants to legalize the killing of certain babies who might come to be like me if allowed to live. He also says he believes that it should be lawful under some circumstances to kill, at any age, individuals with cognitive impairments so severe that he doesn't consider them "persons." What does it take to be a person? Awareness of your own existence in time. The capacity to harbor preferences as to the future, including the preference for continuing to live.

At this stage of my life, he says, I am a person. However, as an infant, I wasn't. I, like all humans, was born without self-awareness. And eventually, assuming my brain finally gets so fried that I fall into that wonderland where self and other and present and past and future blur into one boundless, formless all or nothing, then I'll lose my personhood and therefore my right to life. Then, he says, my family and doctors might put me out of my misery, or out of my bliss or oblivion, and no one count it murder.

My host is Prof. Peter Singer. . . . He is the man who wants me dead.

I have agreed to two speaking engagements. In the morning, I talk to 150 undergraduates on selective infanticide. In the evening, it is a convivial discussion, over dinner, of assisted suicide. I am the token cripple with an opposing view.

I had several reasons for accepting Singer's invitation, some grounded in my involvement in the disability rights movement, others entirely personal. For the movement it seemed an unusual opportunity to experiment with modes of discourse that might work with very tough audiences and bridge the divide between our perceptions and theirs. I didn't expect to straighten out Singer's head. But maybe I could reach a student or two. Among the personal reasons: I was sure it would make a great story, first for telling and then for writing down.

By now I've told it to family and friends and colleagues, over lunches and dinners, on long car trips, in scads of e-mail messages and a couple of formal speeches. But it seems to be a story that just won't settle down. After all these tellings, it still lacks a coherent structure; I'm miles away from a rational argument. I keep getting interrupted by questions like these:

Q: Was he totally grossed out by your physical appearance?

A: He gave no sign of it. None whatsoever.

Q: How did he handle having to interact with someone like you?

A: He behaved in every way appropriately and treated me as a respected professional acquaintance and was a gracious and accommodating host.

Q: Was it emotionally difficult for you to take part in a public discussion of whether your life should have happened?

A: It was very difficult. And horribly easy.

Q: Did he get that job at Princeton because they like his ideas on killing disabled babies?

A: It apparently didn't hurt. But he's most famous for animal rights. He's the author of *Animal Liberation*.

Q: How can he put so much value on animal life and so little value on human life?

That last question is the only one I avoid. I used to say I don't know; it doesn't make sense. But now I've read some of Singer's writing, and I admit it does make sense—within the conceptual world of Peter Singer. But I don't want to go there. Or at least not for long.

So I will start from those other questions and see where the story goes this time.

That first question, about my physical appearance, needs some explaining.

It's not that I'm ugly. It's more that most people don't know how to look at me. The sight of me is routinely discombobulating. The power wheelchair is enough to inspire gawking, but that's the least of it. Much more impressive is the impact on my body of more than four decades of a muscle-wasting disease. At this stage of my life, I'm Karen Carpenter thin, flesh mostly vanished, a jumble of bones in a floppy bag of skin. When, in childhood, my muscles got too weak to hold up my spine, I tried a brace for a while, but fortunately a skittish anesthesiologist said no to fusion, plates, and pins—all the apparatus that might have kept me straight. At 15, I threw away the back brace and let my spine reshape itself into a deep twisty S-curve. Now my right side is two deep canyons. To keep myself upright, I lean forward, rest my rib cage on my lap, plant my elbows beside my knees. Since my backbone found its own natural shape, I've been entirely comfortable in my skin.

I am in the first generation to survive to such decrepitude. Because antibiotics were available, we didn't die from the childhood pneumonias that often come with weakened respiratory systems. I guess it is natural enough that most people don't know what to make of us.

Two or three times in my life—I recall particularly one largely crip, largely lesbian cookout halfway across the continent—I have been looked at as a rare kind of beauty. There is also the bizarre fact that where I live, Charleston, S.C., some people call me Good Luck Lady: they consider it propitious to cross my path when a hurricane is coming and to kiss my head just before voting day. But most often, the reactions are decidedly negative. Strangers on the street are moved to comment:

It's not that I'm ugly. It's more that most people don't know how to look at me.

> I admire you for being out; most people would give up.
> God bless you! I'll pray for you.
> You don't let the pain hold you back, do you?
> If I had to live like you, I think I'd kill myself.

I used to try to explain that in fact I enjoy my life, that it's a great sensual pleasure to zoom by power chair on these delicious muggy streets, that I have no more reason to kill myself than most people. But it gets tedious. God didn't put me on this street to provide disability awareness training to the likes of them. In fact, no god put anyone anywhere for any reason, if you want to know.

But they don't want to know. They think they know everything there is to know, just by looking at me. That's how stereotypes work. They don't know that they're confused. That they're really expressing the discombobulation that comes in my wake.

So. What stands out when I recall first meeting Peter Singer in the spring of 2001 is his apparent immunity to my looks. His apparent lack of discombobulation, his immediate ability to deal with me as a person with a particular point of view.

Then, 2001. Singer has been invited to the College of Charleston, not two blocks from my house. He is to lecture on "Rethinking Life and Death." I have been dispatched by Not Dead Yet, the national organization leading the disability-rights opposition to legalized assisted suicide and disability-based killing. I am to put out a leaflet and do something during the Q and A.

On arriving almost an hour early to reconnoiter, I find the scene almost entirely peaceful; even the boisterous display of South Carolina spring is muted by gray wisps of Spanish moss and mottled oak bark.

I roll around the corner of the building and am confronted with the unnerving sight of two people I know sitting on a park bench eating veggie pitas with Singer. Sharon is a veteran activist for human rights. Herb is South Carolina's most famous atheist. Good people, I've always thought—now sharing veggie pitas and conversation with a proponent of genocide. I try to beat a retreat, but Herb and Sharon have seen me. Sharon tosses her trash and comes over. After we exchange the usual courtesies she asks, "Would you like to meet Professor Singer?"

She doesn't have a clue. She probably likes his book on animal rights. "I'll just talk to him in the Q and A."

But Herb, with Singer at his side, is fast approaching. They are looking at me, and Herb is talking, no doubt saying nice things about me. He'll be saying that I'm a disability rights lawyer and that I gave a talk against assisted suicide at his secular humanist group a while back. He didn't agree with everything I said, he'll say, but I was brilliant. Singer appears interested, engaged. I sit where I'm parked. Herb makes an introduction. Singer extends his hand.

I hesitate. I shouldn't shake hands with the Evil One. But he is Herb's guest, and I simply can't snub Herb's guest at the college where Herb teaches. Hereabouts, the rule is that if you're not prepared to shoot on sight, you have to be prepared to shake hands. I give Singer the three fingers on my right hand that still work. "Good afternoon, Mr. Singer. I'm here for Not Dead Yet." I want to think he flinches just a little. Not Dead Yet did everything possible to disrupt his first week at Princeton. I sent a check to the fund for the 14 arrestees, who included comrades in power chairs. But if Singer flinches, he instantly recovers. He answers my questions about the lecture format. When he says he looks forward to an interesting exchange, he seems entirely sincere.

It is an interesting exchange. In the lecture hall that afternoon, Singer lays it all out. The "illogic" of allowing abortion but not infanticide, of allowing withdrawal of life support but not active killing. Applying the basic assumptions of preference utilitarianism, he spins out his bone-chilling argument for letting parents kill disabled babies and replace them with nondisabled babies who have a greater chance at happiness. It is all about allowing as many individuals as possible to fulfill as many of their preferences as possible.

As soon as he's done, I get the microphone and say I'd like to discuss selective infanticide. As a lawyer, I disagree with his jurisprudential assumptions. Logical inconsistency is not a sufficient reason to change the law. As an atheist, I object to his using religious terms ("the doctrine of the sanctity of human life") to characterize his critics. Singer takes a note pad out of his pocket and jots down my points, apparently eager to take them on, and I proceed to the heart of my argument: that the presence or absence of a disability doesn't predict quality of life. I question his replacement-baby theory, with its assumption of "other things equal," arguing that people are not fungible. I draw out a comparison of myself and my nondisabled brother Mac (the next-born after me), each of us with a combination of gifts and flaws so peculiar that we can't be measured on the same scale.

He responds to each point with clear and lucid counterarguments. He proceeds with the assumption that I am one of the people who might rightly have been killed at birth. He sticks to his guns, conceding just enough to show himself open-minded and flexible. We go back and forth for 10 long minutes. Even as I am horrified by what he says, and by the fact that I have been sucked into a civil discussion of whether I ought to exist, I can't help being dazzled by his verbal facility. He is so respectful, so free of condescension, so focused on the argument, that by the time the show is over, I'm not exactly angry with him. Yes, I am shaking, furious, enraged—but it's for the big room, 200 of my fellow Charlestonians who have listened with polite interest, when in decency they should have run him out of town on a rail.

My encounter with Peter Singer merits a mention in my annual canned letter that December. I decide to send Singer a copy. In response, he sends me the nicest possible e-mail message. Dear Harriet (if he may) . . . Just back from Australia, where he's from. Agrees with my comments on the world situation. Supports my work against institutionalization. And then some pointed questions to clarify my views on selective infanticide.

I reply. Fine, call me Harriet, and I'll reciprocate in the interest of equality, though I'm accustomed to more formality. Skipping agreeable preambles, I answer his questions on disability-based infanticide and pose some of my own. Answers and more questions come back. Back and forth over several weeks it proceeds, an engaging discussion of baby killing, disability prejudice, and related points of law and philosophy. Dear Harriet. Dear Peter.

Imagine a disabled child on the beach, watching the other children play.

Singer seems curious to learn how someone who is as good an atheist as he is could disagree with his entirely reasonable views. At the same time, I am trying to plumb his theories. What has him so convinced it would be best to allow parents to kill babies with severe disabilities, and not other kinds of babies if no infant is a "person" with a right to life? I learn it is partly that both biological and adoptive parents prefer healthy babies. But I have trouble with basing life-and-death decisions on market considerations when the market is structured by prejudice. I offer a hypothetical comparison: "What about mixed-race babies, especially when the combination is entirely nonwhite, who I believe are just about as unadoptable as babies with disabilities?" Wouldn't a law allowing the killing of these undervalued babies validate race prejudice? Singer agrees there is a problem. "It would be horrible," he says, "to see mixed-race babies being killed because they can't be adopted, whereas white ones could be." What's the difference? Preferences based on race are unreasonable. Preferences based on ability are not. Why? To Singer, it's pretty simple: disability makes a person "worse off."

Are we "worse off"? I don't think so. Not in any meaningful sense. There are too many variables. For those of us with congenital conditions, disability shapes all we are. Those disabled later in life adapt. We take constraints that no one would choose and build rich and satisfying lives within them. We enjoy pleasures other people enjoy, and pleasures peculiarly our own. We have something the world needs.

Pressing me to admit a negative correlation between disability and happiness, Singer presents a situation: imagine a disabled child on the beach, watching the other children play.

It's right out of the telethon. I expected something more sophisticated from a professional thinker. I respond: "As a little girl playing on the beach, I was already aware that some people felt sorry for me, that I wasn't frolicking with the same level of frenzy as other children. This annoyed me, and still does." I take the time to write a detailed description of how I, in fact, had fun playing on the beach, without the need of standing, walking, or running. But, really, I've had enough. I suggest to Singer that we have exhausted our topic, and I'll be back in touch when I get around to writing about him.

He responds by inviting me to Princeton. I fire off an immediate maybe.

Of course I'm flattered. Mama will be impressed.

But there are things to consider. Not Dead Yet says—and I completely agree—that we should not legitimate Singer's views by giving them a forum. We should not make disabled lives subject to debate. Moreover, any spokesman chosen by the opposition is by definition a token. But even if I'm a token, I won't have to act like one. Anyway, I'm kind of stuck. If I decline, Singer can make some hay: "I offered them a platform, but they refuse rational discussion." It's an old trick, and I've laid myself wide open.

My invitation is to have an exchange of views with Singer during his undergraduate course. He also proposes a second "exchange," open to the whole university, later in the day. This sounds a lot like debating my life—and on my opponent's turf, with my opponent moderating, to boot. I offer a counterproposal, to which Singer proves amenable. I will open the class with some comments on infanticide and related issues and then let Singer grill me as hard as he likes before we open it up for the students. Later in the day, I might take part in a discussion of some other disability issue in a neutral forum. Singer suggests a faculty-student discussion group sponsored by his department but with cross-departmental membership. The topic I select is "Assisted Suicide, Disability Discrimination, and the Illusion of Choice: A Disability Rights Perspective." I inform a few movement colleagues of this turn of events, and advice starts rolling in. I decide to go with the advisers who counsel me to do the gig, lie low, and get out of Dodge.

I ask Singer to refer me to the person who arranges travel at Princeton. I imagine some capable and unflappable woman like my sister, Beth, whose varied job description at a North Carolina university includes handling visiting artists. Singer refers me to his own assistant, who certainly seems capable and unflappable enough. However, almost immediately Singer jumps back in via e-mail. It seems the nearest hotel has only one wheelchair-accessible suite, available with two rooms for $600 per night. What to do? I know I shouldn't be so accommodating, but I say I can make do with an inaccessible room if it has certain features. Other logistical issues come up. We go back and forth. Questions and answers. Do I really need a lift-equipped vehicle at the airport? Can't my assistant assist me into a conventional car? How wide is my wheelchair?

By the time we're done, Singer knows that I am 28 inches wide. I have trouble controlling my wheelchair if my hand gets cold. I am accustomed to driving on rough, irregular surfaces, but I get nervous turning on steep slopes. Even one step is too many. I can swallow purées, soft bread, and grapes. I use a bedpan, not a toilet. None of this is a secret; none of it cause for angst. But I do wonder whether Singer is jotting down my specs in his little note pad as evidence of how "bad off" people like me really are.

I realize I must put one more issue on the table: etiquette. I was criticized within the movement when I confessed to shaking Singer's hand in Charleston, and some are appalled that I have agreed to break bread with him in Princeton. I think they have a very good point, but, again, I'm stuck. I'm engaged for a day of discussion, not a picket line. It is not in my power to marginalize Singer at Princeton; nothing would be accomplished by displays of personal disrespect. However, chumminess is clearly inappropriate. I tell Singer that in the lecture hall it can't be Harriet and Peter; it must be Ms. Johnson and Mr. Singer.

He seems genuinely nettled. Shouldn't it be Ms. Johnson and Professor Singer, if I want to be formal? To counter, I invoke the ceremonial low-country usage, Attorney Johnson and Professor Singer, but point out that Mr./Ms. is the custom in American political debates and might seem more normal in New Jersey. All right, he says. Ms./Mr. it will be.

I describe this awkward social situation to the lawyer in my office who has served as my default lunch partner for the past 14 years. He gives forth a full-body shudder.

"That poor, sorry son of a bitch! He has no idea what he's in for."

Being a disability rights lawyer lecturing at Princeton does confer some cachet at the Newark airport. I need all the cachet I can get. Delta Airlines has torn up my power chair. It is a fairly frequent occurrence for any air traveler on wheels.

When they inform me of the damage in Atlanta, I throw a monumental fit and tell them to have a repair person meet me in Newark with new batteries to replace the ones inexplicably destroyed. Then I am told no new batteries can be had until the morning. It's Sunday night. On arrival in Newark, I'm told of a plan to put me up there for the night and get me repaired and driven to Princeton by 10 A.M.

"That won't work. I'm lecturing at 10. I need to get there tonight, go to sleep, and be in my right mind tomorrow."

"What? You're lecturing? They told us it was a conference. We need to get you fixed tonight!"

Carla, the gate agent, relieves me of the need to throw any further fits by undertaking on my behalf the fit of all fits.

Carmen, the personal assistant with whom I'm traveling, pushes me in my disabled chair around the airport in search of a place to use the bedpan. However, instead of diaper-changing tables, which are functional though far from private, we find a flip-down plastic shelf that doesn't look like it would hold my 70 pounds of body weight. It's no big deal; I've restricted my fluids. But Carmen is a little freaked. It is her first adventure in power-chair air travel. I thought I prepared her for the trip, but I guess I neglected to warn her about the probability of wheelchair destruction. I keep forgetting that even people who know me well don't know much about my world.

We reach the hotel at 10:15 P.M., four hours late.

I wake up tired. I slept better than I would have slept in Newark with an unrepaired chair, but any hotel bed is a near guarantee of morning crankiness. I tell Carmen to leave the TV off. I don't want to hear the temperature.

I keep forgetting that even people who know me well don't know much about my world.

I do the morning stretch. Medical people call it passive movement, but it's not really passive. Carmen's hands move my limbs, following my precise instructions, her strength giving effect to my will. Carmen knows the routine, so it is in near silence that we begin easing slowly into the day. I let myself be propped up to eat oatmeal and drink tea. Then there's the bedpan and then bathing and dressing, still in bed. As the caffeine kicks in, silence gives way to conversation about practical things. Carmen lifts me into my chair and straps a rolled towel under my ribs for comfort and stability. She tugs at my clothes to remove wrinkles that could cause pressure sores. She switches on my motors and gives me the means of moving without anyone's help. They don't call it a power chair for nothing.

I drive to the mirror. I do my hair in one long braid. Even this primal hairdo requires, at this stage of my life, joint effort. I undo yesterday's braid. Fix the part and comb the hair in front. Carmen combs where I can't reach. I divide the mass into three long hanks and start the braid just behind my left ear. Section by section, I hand it over to her, and her unimpaired young fingers pull tight, crisscross, until the braid is fully formed.

A big polyester scarf completes my costume. Carmen lays it over my back. I tie it the way I want it, but Carmen starts fussing with it, trying to tuck it down in the back. I tell her that it's fine, and she stops.

On top of the scarf, she wraps the two big shawls that I hope will substitute for an overcoat. I don't own any real winter clothes. I just stay out of the cold, such cold as we get in Charleston.

We review her instructions for the day. Keep me in view and earshot. Be instantly available but not intrusive. Be polite, but don't answer any questions about me. I am glad that she has agreed to come. She's strong, smart, adaptable, and very loyal. But now she is digging under the shawls, fussing with that scarf again.

"Carmen. What are you doing?"

"I thought I could hide this furry thing you sit on."

"Leave it. Singer knows lots of people eat meat. Now he'll know some crips sit on sheepskin."

The walk in is cold but mercifully short. The hotel is just across the street from Princeton's wrought-iron gate and a few short blocks from the building where Singer's assistant shows us to the elevator. The elevator doubles as the janitor's closet—the cart with the big trash can and all the accouterments is rolled aside so I can get in. Evidently, there aren't a lot of wheelchair people using this building.

We ride the broom closet down to the basement and are led down a long passageway to a big lecture hall. As the students drift in, I engage in light badinage with the sound technician. He is squeamish about touching me, but I insist that the cordless lavaliere is my mike of choice. I invite him to clip it to the big polyester scarf.

The students enter from the rear door, way up at ground level and walk down stairs to their seats. I feel like an animal in the zoo. I hadn't reckoned on the architecture, those tiers of steps that separate me from a human wall of apparent physical and mental perfection, that keep me confined down here in my pit.

It is 5 before 10. Singer is loping down the stairs. I feel like signaling to Carmen to open the door, summon the broom closet, and get me out of here. But Singer greets me pleasantly and hands me Princeton's check for $500, the fee he offered with apologies for its inadequacy.

So. On with the show.

My talk to the students is pretty Southern. I've decided to pound them with heart, hammer them with narrative, and say "y'all" and "folks." I play with the emotional tone, giving them little peaks and valleys, modulating three times in one 45-second patch. I talk about justice. Even beauty and love. I figure they haven't been getting much of that from Singer.

Of course, I give them some argument too. I mean to honor my contractual obligations. I lead with the hypothetical about mixed-race, nonwhite babies and build the ending around the question of who should have the burden of proof as to the quality of disabled lives. And woven through the talk is the presentation of myself as a representative of a minority group that has been rendered invisible by prejudice and oppression, a participant in a discussion that would not occur in a just world.

I let it go a little longer than I should. Their faces show they're going where I'm leading, and I don't look forward to letting them go. But the clock on the wall reminds me of promises I mean to keep, and I stop talking and submit myself to examination and inquiry.

Singer's response is surprisingly soft. Maybe after hearing that this discussion is insulting and painful to me, he doesn't want to exacerbate my discomfort. His reframing of the issues is almost pro forma, abstract, entirely impersonal. Likewise, the students' inquiries are abstract and fairly predictable: anencephaly, permanent unconsciousness, eugenic abortion. I respond to some of them with stories, but mostly I give answers I could have e-mailed in.

I call on a young man near the top of the room.

"Do you eat meat?"

"Yes, I do."

"Then how do you justify —"

"I haven't made any study of animal rights, so anything I could say on the subject wouldn't be worth everyone's time."

The next student wants to work the comparison of disability and race, and Singer joins the discussion until he elicits a comment from me that he can characterize as racist. He scores a point, but that's all right. I've never claimed to be free of prejudice, just struggling with it.

Singer proposes taking me on a walk around campus, unless I think it would be too cold. What the hell? "It's probably warmed up some. Let's go out and see how I do."

He doesn't know how to get out of the building without using the stairs, so this time it is my assistant leading the way. Carmen has learned of another elevator, which arrives empty. When we get out of the building, she falls behind a couple of paces, like a respectful chaperone.

In the classroom, there was a question about keeping alive the unconscious. In response, I told a story about a family I knew as a child, which took loving care of a nonresponsive teenage girl, acting out their unconditional commitment to each other, making all the other children, and me as their visitor, feel safe. This doesn't satisfy Singer. "Let's assume we can prove, absolutely, that the individual is totally unconscious and that we can know, absolutely, that the individual will never regain consciousness."

I see no need to state an objection with no stenographer present to record it; I'll play the game and let him continue.

"Assuming all that," he says, "don't you think continuing to take care of that individual would be a bit—weird?"

"No. Done right, it could be profoundly beautiful."

"But what about the caregiver, a woman typically, who is forced to provide all this service to a family member, unable to work, unable to have a life of her own?"

"That's not the way it should be. Not the way it has to be. As a society, we should pay workers to provide that care, in the home. In some places, it's been done that way for years. That woman shouldn't be forced to do it, any more than my family should be forced to do my care."

Singer takes me around the architectural smorgasbord that is Princeton University by a route that includes not one step, unramped curb, or turn on a slope. Within the strange limits of this strange assignment, it seems Singer is doing all he can to make me comfortable.

He asks what I thought of the students' questions.

"They were fine, about what I expected. I was a little surprised by the question about meat eating."

"I apologize for that. That was out of left field. But—I think what he wanted to know is how you can have such high respect for human life and so little respect for animal life."

"People have lately been asking me the converse, how you can have so much respect for animal life and so little respect for human life."

"And what do you answer?"

"I say I don't know. It doesn't make a lot of sense to me."

"Well, in my view—"

"Look, I have lived in blissful ignorance all these years, and I'm not prepared to give that up today."

"Fair enough," he says and proceeds to recount bits of Princeton history. He stops. "This will be of particular interest to you, I think. This is where your colleagues with Not Dead Yet set up their blockade." I'm grateful for the reminder. My brothers and sisters were here before me and behaved far more appropriately than I am doing.

A van delivers Carmen and me early for the evening forum. Singer says he hopes I had a pleasant afternoon.

Yes, indeed. I report a pleasant lunch and a very pleasant nap, and I tell him about the Christopher Reeve Suite in the hotel, which has been remodeled to accommodate Reeve, who has family in the area.

"Do you suppose that's the $600 accessible suite they told me about?"

"Without doubt. And if I'd known it was the Christopher Reeve Suite, I would have held out for it."

"Of course you would have!" Singer laughs. "And we'd have had no choice, would we?"

We talk about the disability rights critique of Reeve and various other topics. Singer is easy to talk to, good company. Too bad he sees lives like mine as avoidable mistakes.

I'm looking forward to the soft vegetarian meal that has been arranged; I'm hungry. Assisted suicide, as difficult as it is, doesn't cause the kind of agony I felt discussing disability-based infanticide. In this one, I understand, and to some degree can sympathize with, the opposing point of view—misguided though it is.

My opening sticks to the five-minute time limit. I introduce the issue as framed by academic articles Not Dead Yet recommended for my use. Andrew Batavia argues for assisted suicide based on autonomy, a principle generally held high in the disability rights movement. In general, he says, the movement fights for our right to control our own lives; when we need assistance to effect our choices, assistance should be available to us as a matter of right. If the choice is to end our lives, he says, we should have assistance then as well. But Carol Gill says that it is differential treatment—disability discrimination—to try to prevent most suicides while facilitating the suicides of ill and disabled people. The social-science literature suggests that the public in general, and physicians in particular,

The case for assisted suicide rests on stereotypes.

tend to underestimate the quality of life of disabled people, compared with our own assessments of our lives. The case for assisted suicide rests on stereotypes that our lives are inherently so bad that it is entirely rational if we want to die.

I side with Gill. What worries me most about the proposals for legalized assisted suicide is their veneer of beneficence—the medical determination that, for a given individual, suicide is reasonable or right. It is not about autonomy but about nondisabled people telling us what's good for us.

In the discussion that follows, I argue that choice is illusory in a context of pervasive inequality. Choices are structured by oppression. We shouldn't offer assistance with suicide until we all have the assistance we need to get out of bed in the morning and live a good life. Common causes of suicidality—dependence, institutional confinement, being a burden—are entirely curable. Singer, seated on my right, participates in the discussion but doesn't dominate it. During the meal, I occasionally ask him to put things within my reach and he competently complies.

I feel as if I'm getting to a few of them, when a student asks me a question. The words are all familiar, but they're strung together in a way so meaningless that I can't even retain them—it's like a long sentence in Tagalog. I can only admit my limitations. "That question's too abstract for me to deal with. Can you rephrase it?"

He indicates that it is as clear as he can make it, so I move on.

A little while later my right elbow slips out from under me. This is awkward. Normally I get whoever is on my right to do this sort of thing. Why not now? I gesture to Singer. He leans over, and I whisper, "Grasp this wrist and pull forward one inch, without lifting." He follows my instructions to the letter. He sees that now I can again reach my food with my fork. And he may now understand what I was saying a minute ago, that most of the assistance disabled people need does not demand medical training.

A philosophy professor says, "It appears that your objections to assisted suicide are essentially tactical."

"Excuse me?"

"By that I mean they are grounded in current conditions of political, social, and economic inequality. What if we assume that such conditions do not exist?"

"Why would we want to do that?"

"I want to get to the real basis for the position you take."

I feel as if I'm losing caste. It is suddenly very clear that I'm not a philosopher. I'm like one of those old practitioners who used to visit my law school, full of bluster about life in the real world. Such a bore! A once-sharp mind gone muddy! And I'm only 44—not all that old.

The forum is ended, and I've been able to eat very little of my puréed food. I ask Carmen to find the caterer and get me a container. Singer jumps up to take care of it. He returns with a box and obligingly packs my food to go.

When I get home, people are clamoring for the story. The lawyers want the blow-by-blow of my forensic triumph over the formidable foe; when I tell them it wasn't like that, they insist that it was. Within the disability rights community, there is less confidence. It is generally assumed that I handled the substantive discussion well, but people worry that my civility may have given Singer a new kind of legitimacy. I hear from Laura, a beloved movement sister. She is appalled that I let Singer provide even minor physical assistance at the dinner. "Where was your assistant?" she wants to know. How could I put myself in a relationship with Singer that made him appear so human, even kind?

I struggle to explain. I didn't feel disempowered; quite the contrary, it seemed a good thing to make him do some useful work. And then, the hard part: I've come to believe that Singer actually is human, even kind in his way. There ensues a discussion of good and evil and personal assistance and power and philosophy and tactics for which I'm profoundly grateful.

I e-mail Laura again. This time I inform her that I've changed my will. She will inherit a book that Singer gave me, a collection of his writings with a weirdly appropriate inscription: "To Harriet Johnson, So that you will have a better answer to questions about animals. And thanks for coming to Princeton. Peter Singer. March 25, 2002." She responds that she is changing her will, too. I'll get the autographed photo of Jerry Lewis she received as an M.D.A. poster child. We joke that each of us has given the other a "reason to live."

I have had a nice e-mail message from Singer, hoping Carmen and I and the chair got home without injury, relaying positive feedback from my audiences—and taking me to task for a statement that isn't supported by a relevant legal authority, which he looked up. I report that we got home exhausted but unharmed and concede that he has caught me in a generalization that should have been qualified. It's clear that the conversation will continue.

I am soon sucked into the daily demands of law practice, family, community, and politics. In the closing days of the state legislative session, I help get a bill passed that I hope will move us one small step toward a world in which killing won't be such an appealing solution to the "problem" of disability. It is good to focus on this kind of work. But the conversations with and about Singer continue. Unable to muster the appropriate moral judgments, I ask myself a tough question: am I in fact a silly little lady whose head is easily turned by a man who gives her a kind of attention she enjoys? I hope not, but I confess that I've never been able to sustain righteous anger for more than about 30 minutes at a time. My view of life tends more toward tragedy.

The tragic view comes closest to describing how I now look at Peter Singer. He is a man of unusual gifts, reaching for the heights. He writes that he is trying to create a system of ethics derived from fact and reason, that largely throws off the perspectives of religion, place, family, tribe, community, and maybe even species—to "take the point of view of the universe." His is a grand, heroic undertaking.

But like the protagonist in a classical drama, Singer has his flaw. It is his unexamined assumption that disabled people are inherently "worse off," that we "suffer," that we have lesser "prospects of a happy life." Because of this all-too-common prejudice, and his rare courage in taking it to its logical conclusion, catastrophe looms. Here in the midpoint of the play, I can't look at him without fellow-feeling.

I am regularly confronted by people who tell me that Singer doesn't deserve my human sympathy. I should make him an object of implacable wrath, to be cut off, silenced, destroyed absolutely. And I find myself lacking an argument to the contrary.

I am talking to my sister Beth on the phone. "You kind of like the monster, don't you?" she says.

I find myself unable to evade, certainly unwilling to lie. "Yeah, in a way. And he's not exactly a monster."

"You know, Harriet, there were some very pleasant Nazis. They say the SS guards went home and played on the floor with their children every night."

She can tell that I'm chastened; she changes the topic, lets me off the hook. Her harshness has come as a surprise. She isn't inclined to moralizing; in our family, I'm the one who sets people straight.

When I put the phone down, my argumentative nature feels frustrated. In my mind, I replay the conversation but this time defend my position.

"He's not exactly a monster. He just has some strange ways of looking at things."

"He's advocating genocide."

"That's the thing. In his mind, he isn't. He's only giving parents a choice. He thinks the humans he is talking about aren't people, aren't 'persons.'"

"But that's the way it always works, isn't it? They're always animals or vermin or chattel goods. Objects, not persons. He's repacking some old ideas. Making them acceptable."

"I think his ideas are new, in a way. It's not old-fashioned hate. It's a twisted, misinformed, warped kind of beneficence. His motive is to do good."

"What do you care about motives?" she asks. "Doesn't this beneficent killing make disabled brothers and sisters just as dead?"

"But he isn't killing anyone. It's just talk."

"Just talk? It's talk with an agenda, talk aimed at forming policy. Talk that's getting a receptive audience. You of all people know the power of that kind of talk."

"Well, sure, but—"

"If talk didn't matter, would you make it your life's work?"

"But," I say, "his talk won't matter in the end. He won't succeed in reinventing morality. He stirs the pot, brings things out into the open. But ultimately, we'll make a world that's fit to live in, a society that has room for all its flawed creatures. History will remember Singer as a curious example of the bizarre things that can happen when paradigms collide."

"What if you're wrong? What if he convinces people that there's no morally significant difference between a fetus and a newborn, and just as disabled fetuses are routinely aborted now, so disabled babies are routinely killed? Might some future generation take it further than Singer wants to go? Might some say there's no morally significant line between a newborn and a 3-year-old?"

"Sure. Singer concedes that a bright line cannot be drawn. But he doesn't propose killing anyone who prefers to live."

"That overarching respect for the individual's preference for life—might some say it's a fiction, a fetish, a quasi-religious belief?"

"Yes," I say. "That's pretty close to what I think. As an atheist, I think all preferences are moot once you kill someone. The injury is entirely to the surviving community."

"So what if that view wins out, but you can't break disability prejudice? What if you wind up in a world where the disabled person's 'irrational' preference to live must yield to society's 'rational' interest in reducing the incidence of disability? Doesn't horror kick in somewhere? Maybe as you watch the door close behind whoever has wheeled you into the gas chamber?"

"That's not going to happen."

"Do you have empirical evidence?" she asks. "A logical argument?"

"Of course not. And I know it's happened before, in what was considered the most progressive medical community in the world. But it won't happen. I have to believe that."

Belief. Is that what it comes down to? Am I a person of faith after all? Or am I clinging to foolish hope that the tragic protagonist, this one time, will shift course before it's too late?

DISCUSSION

1. Johnson devotes a good deal of time acquainting her readers with the facts about her disability, itemizing the various things that, as a result of her physical condition, she can and cannot do. Why do you think she does this? How does this tactic help her advance her argument about the ways disabled people are seen in our culture?
2. Based on McBryde Johnson's descriptions of her physical appearance, what do you think she looked like? How do you think she was perceived by the general public? In what ways does our popular culture encourage us both to see and *not* see people with disabilities? That is to say, how do the images of and stories about disability we typically see teach us to judge people with disabilities in particular ways?
3. To what extent is it valid to think of Johnson's account here as expanding or enlarging the scope of the ways disabled people are conventionally seen? What quotes can you find from her essay to support your opinion?

WRITING

4. Spend some time reflecting on the specific language Johnson uses to describe her physical condition. What specific cultural norms do you think this description is intended to challenge? How does Johnson's language differ from the kind typically used to describe one's physical appearance? What larger point about the way we are taught to "see" disabled people do you think this description is designed to convey? Make sure to include quotations from Johnson's essay to support your analysis.
5. Have you ever felt "tokenized" because of your physical or external appearance? When people first meet you, what assumptions do you think they make about you based on your appearance? Write a personal essay in which you recount what the experience of being seen in this particular way was like. What perceptions of you did people have? What conclusions did they draw? And in what ways were they inaccurate, unfair, or otherwise limiting? Use quotes from Johnson's essay to pinpoint both the parallels and the key differences between your own experience and what Johnson recounts in her essay.
6. Johnson and Heather Havrilesky (p. 126) share an interest in cultural stereotyping. Each of their essays acknowledges the ways people can be mislabeled or misread by the public at large, and how this experience can lead to disenfranchisement or marginalization. Write an essay in which you compare and contrast the ways these two writers explore this question. Despite their shared concern over stereotyping, where do their discussions diverge?

VIRGINIA HEFFERNAN

The Attention-Span Myth

Has the emergence of our fast-paced, always-on, 24/7 media culture affected, even eroded, our powers of concentration? Taking a closer look at the culture of distraction to which the Web has given rise, Virginia Heffernan offers readers a more complex and nuanced view of what she calls "attention-span theory." Heffernan is a national correspondent for *Yahoo News*. A former editor at *Harper's* magazine and columnist for the *New York Times*, Heffernan has written extensively about digital and popular culture. Her most recent book is *Magic and Loss: The Pleasures of the Internet*. This essay appeared in the *New York Times* in 2010.

WE SEEM TO KNOW A GREAT DEAL ABOUT ATTENTION SPANS, those constituents of character that have become the digital-age equivalent of souls.

Everyone has an attention span. It can be short or long. Long is good. Good scholars, good citizens, and good children have long attention spans. Attention spans used to be robust; now they are stunted. Technology—MTV, the Internet, the iPhone—shriveled them. Nicholas Carr, who argued in *The Shallows* that Web use practically causes brain damage, told PBS that technology is "pushing even more distractions and interruptions on us" and thus will never "return to us our attention span."

At the same time, there is a pro-technology view of attention spans—rarer, but no less confident. Science writers like Jonah Lehrer have pointed to studies that seem to demonstrate perfectly respectable attention spans in gamers and Web users.

And so polemicists of various stripes continue to calibrate the effect of technology on attention spans. But I'm surprised that anyone ventures so far into this thicket of sophistry. I get stuck much earlier in the equation. Everyone has an attention span: really? And really again: an attention span is a freestanding entity like a boxer's reach, existing independently of any newspaper or chess game that might engage or repel it, and which might be measured by the psychologist's equivalent of a tailor's tape?

Maybe my own brain is faltering in a Web wasteland, but I don't get it. Whether the Web is making us smarter or dumber, isn't there something just unconvincing about the idea that an occult "span" in the brain makes certain cultural objects more compelling than others? So a kid loves the drums but can hardly get through a chapter of *The Sun Also*

Rises; and another aces algebra tests but can't even understand how Call of Duty is played. The actions of these children may dismay or please adults, but anyone who has ever been bored by one practice and absorbed by another can explain the kids' choices more persuasively than does the dominant model, which ignores the content of activities in favor of a wonky span thought vaguely to be in the brain.

So how did we find ourselves with this unhappy attention-span conceit, and with the companion idea that a big attention span is humankind's best moral and aesthetic asset?

So how did we find ourselves with this unhappy attention-span conceit, and with the companion idea that a big attention span is humankind's best moral and aesthetic asset? In other eras, distractibility wasn't considered shameful. It was regularly praised, in fact—as autonomy, exuberance, and versatility. To be brooding, morbid, obsessive, or easily mesmerized was thought much worse than being distractible. In *Moby-Dick*, Starbuck tries to distract Ahab from his monomania with evocations of family life in Nantucket. Under the spell of "a cruel, remorseless emperor"—his own single-mindedness—Ahab stays his fatal course. Ahab's doom comes from his undistractibility.

In 19th-century American literature, the resting state from which characters seek distraction is sorrow or fury. No wonder distraction seems kind. In *The Adventures of Tom Sawyer*, Tom, the prototypical hyperactive rascal who plays with a beetle rather than sit still in church, resists sadness "not because his troubles were one whit less heavy and bitter to him than a man's are to a man, but because a new and powerful interest bore them down and drove them out of his mind for the time—just as men's misfortunes are forgotten in the excitement of new enterprises."

In the 1920s, a decade before T. S. Eliot recognized being "distracted from distraction by distraction" as part of the modernist plight, Bertolt Brecht made the case for a "smokers' theater," which encouraged the audience to light up cigars during plays. Condemning his fellow Germans for being "uncommonly good at putting up with boredom," he hoped that by smoking during a play—or pacing, talking, walking out—they could also cultivate individuality and ideally an immunity to tyranny. A healthy fidgetiness would keep them from sitting silently, sheepish and spellbound.

And speaking of sitting silently without fidgeting: that's essentially what we want of children with bum attention spans, isn't it? The first sign that a distractible child is doing "better"—with age or Adderall, say—is that he sits still. This is why the A.D.H.D. diagnosis, which popularized the idea of an "attention span" that can be pathologically short, grew out of the old "hyperactive" diagnosis. The hyperactive child squirmed at church and at the dinner table, embarrassing his mother.

At some point, we stopped calling Tom Sawyer–style distractibility either animal spirits or a discipline problem. We started to call it sick, even after an early twin study showed that a relatively short attention span is virtually synonymous with standard-issue irritability and distemper. But the fact that the attention-span theory makes news of what was once considered ordinary or artistic behavior is not what's wrong with it. These cultural transitions—disruptive as they are—happen all the time as society's demands on individuals change.

We seem to know a great deal about attention spans, those constituents of character that have become the digital-age equivalent of souls.

Instead, the problem with the attention-span discourse is that it's founded on the phantom idea of an attention span. A healthy "attention span" becomes just another ineffable quality to remember having, to believe you've lost, to worry about your kids lacking, to blame the culture for destroying. Who needs it?

DISCUSSION

1. “The problem with the attention-span discourse,” Heffernan declares, “is that it's founded on the phantom idea of an attention span” (p. 115). How do you respond to this claim? In your view, is attention span really just a “phantom idea”? What does this term mean to you?
2. Heffernan refers to current debates over attention span as venturing into a “thicket of sophistry” (p. 113). Why do you think Heffernan draws this particular analogy? What larger point about this debate does she seem to be making here? Do you agree with this point?
3. “In other eras,” Heffernan writes, “distractibility wasn't considered shameful. It was regularly praised, in fact — as autonomy, exuberance, and versatility. To be brooding, morbid, obsessive, or easily mesmerized was thought much worse than being distractible” (p. 114). Why do you think Heffernan provides her readers with this quick historical overview? To what extent does it relate to or reinforce the larger argument she is making in this essay?

WRITING

4. As Heffernan notes, one of the most commonplace responses to changes in attention span is to diagnose it as a medical condition. Write a short essay in which you assess the validity of this strategy. In your view, is it reasonable or accurate to use medical terminology to describe this phenomenon? To what extent does such language create a social script for how those with different attention spans should be viewed?
5. Heffernan briefly outlines the pro- and anti-technology sides of the attention-span debate. Anti-technologists, she observes, view the rise of digital culture as a dire threat to our attention, while pro-technologists treat this development as an opportunity to create new forms of attention. In a three- to five-page essay identify, analyze, and evaluate the merits of each position. In what ways is each perspective on digital culture valid? Which perspective do you feel greater sympathy for, and why?
6. Like Heffernan, Don Tapscott (p. 117) argues for the need to rethink an established, even cherished, cultural norm. How does Heffernan's call to rethink the attention-span debate compare with Tapscott's injunction to “ditch privacy”? How do these two arguments compare? What are the key similarities and differences?

DON TAPSCOTT

Should We Ditch the Idea of Privacy?

Among pundits, observers, and critics of all stripes, it has become an article of faith that the rise of the Internet has led to a dramatic loss in personal privacy. But is it equally self-evident that we should regard this change as a problem? Posing precisely this question, Don Tapscott wonders whether we've reached a point in our social and technological evolution where we've simply outgrown the idea of privacy. Tapscott is a writer and business consultant who has written extensively about the Web and digital culture. He is the author of numerous books, including *Wikinomics: How Mass Collaboration Changes Everything* (2006) and *Grown Up Digital: How the Net Generation is Changing Your World* (2008). The following essay was published by Reuters in 2012.

SINCE I CO-AUTHORED A BOOK ON PRIVACY AND THE INTERNET 15 years ago I've been writing about how to manage the various threats to the security and control of our personal information. But today I find myself in a completely unexpected discussion. A growing number of people argue that the notion of having a private life in which we carefully restrict what information we share with others may not be a good idea. Instead, sharing our intimate, personal information with others would benefit us individually and as a society.

This is not a fringe movement. The proponents of this view are some of the smartest and most influential thinkers and practitioners of the digital revolution.

Jeff Jarvis, in his thoughtful book *Public Parts*, makes the case for sharing, and he practices what he preaches. We learn about everything from details of his personal income to his prostate surgery and malfunctioning penis. He argues that because privacy has its advocates, so should "publicness." "I'm a public man," says Jarvis. "My life is an open book." And he provides elaborate evidence on why this has benefited him, and says that if everyone followed his lead, the world would be a better place. He concludes that while releasing information should be a personal choice, privacy regulation should be avoided.

Facebook is the leading social-media site that promotes information sharing, and part of the company's mission is to "make the world more open." In his book *The Facebook Effect*, David Kirkpatrick explains that Facebook founders believe that "more visibility makes us better people. Some claim, for example, that because of Facebook, young people today have a harder time cheating on their boyfriends or girlfriends. They also say that more transparency should make for a more tolerant society in which people eventually accept that everybody sometimes does bad or embarrassing things." Some at Facebook refer to this as "radical transparency"—a term initially used to talk about institutions that is now being adapted to individuals. In other words, everyone should have just one identity, whether at their workplace or in their personal life.

In the course of a day, we generate the same amount of data as had been captured since the beginning of history up to the year 2003.

Stanford University professor Andreas Weigend, former chief scientist at Amazon.com, says that "the notion of privacy began with the creation of cities, and it's pretty much ended with Facebook." He says "our social norms are changing."

Other thought leaders like Tim O'Reilly (he coined the term "Web 2.0") or Stewart Brand (author of the *Whole Earth Catalog*) defend an individual's right to privacy. But they argue that the benefits of sharing personal information are becoming so beneficial to each of us and so widespread that we need to shift the discussion from *what* to share, to *how* to ensure the information we share is used appropriately. Says Brand: "I'd be totally happy if my personal DNA mapping was published."

It may well be that our fundamental ideas about identity and privacy, the strategies that we have collectively pursued and the technologies that we have adopted must change and adapt in a rapidly evolving world of connectivity, networking, participation, sharing, and collaboration. But this will take a long time, and in the meantime there are many challenges and even dangers.

To be sure, the digital technologies in general and social media in particular are providing new benefits to sharing personal information, and not just from getting more birthday wishes. There is a real upside to participating in communities, seeing photos, hearing stories, or knowing the location of friends and family. Sharing also helps companies deliver personalized products and services. It can improve advertising, as we are targeted for products and services that correspond to our interests.

When we reveal personal information we can help society too. Every time a gay person comes out or someone with depression opens up about his condition, it helps break down stigma and prejudice. Fully 20 percent of all patients with the fatal disease ALS share intimate information about their treatment and condition on the network PatientsLikeMe.com. And tens of thousands of others with rare diseases who use that website report that sharing has helped them better manage their illness.

It is important to understand the extraordinary volumes of data being generated and how this will increase exponentially in the near future. In the course of a day, we generate the same amount of data as had been captured since the beginning of history up to the year 2003. Much of this is information attached to individuals. Our digital footprints and shadows are being gathered together, bit by bit, megabyte by megabyte, terabyte by terabyte, into personas and profiles and avatars—virtual representations of us, in thousands of locations.

Every time a gay person comes out or someone with depression opens up about his condition, it helps break down stigma and prejudice.

In testimony before a congressional committee, Justin Brookman from the Center for Democracy & Technology, outlined the dilemma that citizens face when they want to participate fully in society yet not live under constant surveillance. "There is an incredible amount that we as a society have to gain from innovative new technologies, but there is also an incredible amount that we have to lose. Without a framework in place to assure everyday consumers of the ability to limit the collection and retention of the minutiae of their lives by unknown third parties, any sense of a realm of personal privacy may completely evaporate."

Brookman cites many examples, such as the record kept of stories read on a newspaper's website, compared with the anonymity of buying and reading a paper from a newsstand. Or going out for a drive, talking to friends, writing letters, watching TV—"all of these rights are eroding as these activities move into the networked world and surveillance technologies become more sophisticated." Brookman likens the decision to opt out of being party to the data collection as analogous to opting out of electricity 30 years ago: "To disconnect from the services that collect such personal, sensitive data would be to disconnect from society."

Before Facebook arrived, few would have predicted that hundreds of millions of people would voluntarily log on to the Internet and record detailed, almost minute-by-minute data about themselves, their activities, their likes and dislikes, and so on.

Soon smartphones (or other personal appliances like sunglasses with an internal screen) will have a persistent connection to the Internet and record nonstop video and audio of everything going on around us. This might strike some people as bizarre. They wonder: "What could I do throughout the day that's so important that I would want to record it?" This is like asking two decades ago: "What's so important that I would need to carry a phone everywhere so people could reach me?" Today most people view their cell phones as essential survival gear.

Soon a manager could ask her smartphone to retrieve the last five minutes of yesterday's meeting with a colleague when they agreed on action items. She'll transmit the video clip to her subordinates so they'll know what to do. Businesspeople will archive meetings with associates or suppliers, so that if a dispute arises, they can go back and prove they're right. Of course, since everybody knows everybody has a recording of the conversation, the dispute is less likely to arise.

Add to this the emerging "augmented reality" tools that can give you real-time information about the world around you when, say, you point your mobile device at the street. For augmented reality to work, the device must know precisely where you are and have a detailed understanding of what interests you. If you can annotate the physical world, a plethora of new capabilities open up. For example, when walking down the street and looking through the screen inside your sunglasses, perhaps you'll be able to see the names and profiles of people you're passing.

Lest you think managing all this data would be a nightmare, companies are already working to help ease the burden. Microsoft has a research program in progress called MyLifeBits. The program digitizes, catalogs, and retrieves every conceivable scrap of information about your own life that you could want, such as photos, rock-concert tickets, and wedding invitations. It acts as a surrogate memory. Google has a similar idea. The company sees the management and retrieval of the massive amounts of data each person will soon generate as an enormous business opportunity.

The tensions between information freedom and personal control are exploding today, and not simply because of the benefits of sharing information using new media.

The tensions between information freedom and personal control are exploding today, and not simply because of the benefits of sharing information using new media. Rather there are massive commercial and government interests, as well as malevolent individuals, that have a lot to gain from each of us revealing highly granular personal information, much of it in the public domain by default and in real time as we travel through life.

But given that there are few social and legal controls over what happens to our personal information, a life plan of "being open" is probably a big mistake. Personal information, be it biographical, biological, genealogical, historical, transactional, locational, relational, computational, vocational, or reputational, is the stuff that makes up our modern identity and is the foundation of our personal security. It must be managed responsibly—not just by others, but by each of us. The clear and present danger is the irreversible erosion of that most enabling of liberties: anonymity.

Yes, we need a broad discussion and new norms and even laws regarding what is done with this cornucopia of information. But each of us also needs a personal privacy strategy governing what information we release and to whom.

DISCUSSION

1. At the heart of current debates over Internet privacy, Tapscott argues, is a tension between "information freedom and personal control" (p. 120). How do you understand the difference between these two concepts? Do you agree with Tapscott that the rise of the Web has created a tension between them? And if so, how important an issue does this represent?
2. Tapscott lists a number of the benefits that follow from our ability to share personal information online. Can you think of any risks this ability poses? And do any of these risks outweigh benefits Tapscott outlines? How or how not?
3. Tapscott acknowledges that there are currently "few social and legal controls over what happens to our personal information" (p. 120) once it is posted online. Should there be? And if so, what do you think such controls should look like?

WRITING

4. In the course of making his argument about privacy, Tapscott notes how profoundly the Web has altered our social and communication norms. "Before Facebook arrived," he notes, "few would have predicted that hundreds of millions of people would voluntarily log on to the Internet and record detailed, almost minute-by-minute data about themselves, their activities, their likes and dislikes, and so on" (p. 119). Write a short essay in which you present your own views on the cultural shift Tapscott identifies here. How do you respond to people's increasing willingness to record and exhibit virtually every detail of their lives? In your view, is this a change in our social norms we should welcome? Why or why not?
5. "It may well be," writes Tapscott, "that our fundamental ideas about identity and privacy, the strategies that we have collectively pursued and the technologies that we have adopted must change and adapt in a rapidly evolving world of connectivity, networking, participation, sharing, and collaboration." In a three- to five-page essay, summarize and analyze the evolution Tapscott is describing here. What vision of the world is evoked by such terms as "connectivity," "participation," and "collaboration"? What kinds of rules and scripts is Tapscott suggesting will govern this world? And, in your view, does this evolution represent an improvement or not? Why?
6. In its own way, Harriet McBryde Johnson's essay (p. 96) can be read as a similar call to rethink our established ideas about privacy. Like Tapscott, Johnson sees a great deal of value in learning to look at what our larger culture has traditionally decreed should be off limits. Compare the arguments about privacy in each of these essays. What are the key similarities and differences?

JOHN PAUL TITLOW

#Me:

Instagram Narcissism and the Scourge of the Selfie

While many observers laud social media for its capacity to transcend boundaries and create new connections, an equal number worry about the opposite impact: the tendency of such tools to encourage a greater and greater concern for one's self. John Paul Titlow counts himself among those in this second camp. Taking aim at the growing popularity of the "selfie," he offers some reflections about the new, and increasingly self-centered, visual norms to which our media landscape is giving rise. Titlow is a technology journalist based in Philadelphia. He primarily writes about digital music, the future of TV, and new media trends. He also teaches journalism at Temple University. This essay was first posted on the website ReadWrite in January 2013.

THOSE OF US WHO USE INSTAGRAM EVERY DAY LIKE TO THINK OF IT in glowing terms. Not only is it a rapidly growing social media success story, but it's a place where we can go to see gorgeous, often creatively composed imagery. Our friends are there, documenting their world for us and reliably tapping the Like button every time we share our own photos. It's awesome.

That is, until you take a step back and look around.

As it turns out, Instagram is a breeding ground for many people's most narcissistic tendencies. It's a reality that comes into sharp focus as soon as you step outside of your circle of friends and look at what everybody else is posting. Turns out that as a group, Instagrammers are a pretty self-absorbed bunch.

Sure, you might say, we knew this. Mirror-shot, pouty-faced self-portraits of teenagers find their way to the "Popular" (now called "Explore") tab as often as sunsets, celebs, and food pics. But Instagram narcissism is more than a stereotype. There's actually data to back it up.

90 MILLION SELFIES...AND COUNTING

Consider this: The third most frequently used hashtag on Instagram is #me. Under it, you'll find more than 90 million self-portraits taken primarily by younger users, very few of them with any irony, or even much creativity.

Of course, there's nothing inherently wrong with publishing self-portraits. After all, your appearance is a very significant part of the life you're documenting using social services like Instagram. Taken tastefully and periodically, the "selfie" can add personality and context to your never-ending streams of lattes, power lines, cats, and skylines. And sure, just like in the real world, our brains love the ego boost we get from the compliments.

Turns out that as a group, Instagrammers are a pretty self-absorbed bunch.

Scrolling through the #me photos, you see images of varying quality, all displaying faces of different people. In a way, it's kind of fascinating to peruse. Here are all these people, broadcasting their own faces to the world. In one photo, you'll see an American kid with his collar popped and earbuds in, probably shirking some school-related responsibility. In the next, there's a Saudi Arabian man dressed in a traditional gutra headdress, snapping a self-portrait in the mirror. Some people have new haircuts. Some have new babies. One guy has several large nuggets of marijuana.

Some of these images feel a little too intimate. As you scroll through, you start to get the feeling that you're peeking through a window of a world you're not quite supposed to have access to. But mobile and social technology have given us millions of little windows into the worlds of others, so we keep scrolling.

The stream exposes nothing explicit, but it's peppered with what feels like far too many young, teenage girls lying in bed. Or 15-year-old boys standing shirtless in front of a mirror. Some of these kids are showing skin. Just about all of them—male and female alike—are seeking some kind of approval from their peers and the larger community, which thanks to the Internet, is now effectively infinite.

THE RISE OF THE NARCISSISTIC SOCIAL MEDIA STAR

Some are getting the approval they're seeking in a big way. Michael Saba is a 15-year-old from Boca Raton, Florida, whose Instagram photos often find their way to the app's Explore tab among teen pop stars, professional athletes, and professional photographers. But despite his 45,000 followers and hordes of teenage fans, Saba is not a celebrity. He is, as his Instagram profile says, "just a kid who takes pictures."

Saba's photo stream is comprised entirely of self-portraits, each one garnering between three and five thousand likes and hundreds of comments, mostly from adoring teenage girls who fawn over Saba with almost Bieber-esque intensity—and shower him in heart-shaped Emojis. The pictures are not particularly interesting or varied. It's just him, in similar-looking outfits, day after day. Sometimes in the mirror, sometimes making well-rehearsed "cute" faces directly into his phone's camera. Quite often, Saba poses with two other friends, also heartthrobs. Every photo is a massive hit. Meanwhile, he follows only one other user.

In our weird new world, it's not uncommon for young people to achieve this new type of pseudo-fame, fueled solely by social media. And we're not just talking the type of notoriety you can get from a viral YouTube video, which tends to require at least a sliver of talent, humor, or skill. Instead, these kids are amassing huge followings just for being attractive. It's like a high school popularity contest on digital steroids, but this homeroom has more than 45,000 kids in it.

INSTAGRAM AND SELF-IMAGE: IS THE IMPACT GOOD OR BAD?

Is this necessarily a bad thing? One has to wonder what this kind of existence must do to the ego of a 15-year-old kid. Or the weird new social dynamics it could produce at school. But some psychologists think that the self-image boosts offered by social networks like Instagram could be a good thing.

It used to be that most of the photographs of other people we encountered were carefully crafted images of the flawless-looking individuals portrayed in popular media and advertising. Psychologists have long had concerns about the distorted effect that's had on normal-looking people's self-images. Instagram and mobile photography more generally may be changing that.

As you scroll through, you start to get the feeling that you're peeking through a window of a world you're not quite supposed to have access to.

"I like to think that Instagram offers a quiet resistance to the barrage of perfect images that we face each day," writes Sarah J. Gervais in *Psychology Today*. "Rather than being bombarded with those creations... we can look through our Instagram feed and see images of real people—with beautiful diversity."

Of course, as Gervais acknowledges, there hasn't yet been much research into what sort of impact Instagram in particular is having on self-image or anything else. Indeed, when I reached out to Microsoft's Danah Boyd and several other academics who study social media and its effect on society, I wasn't able to turn up much.

The psychological impact of technology more generally *has* been a popular topic for a few years now. Narcissistic personality disorder has been on the rise for 20 years, according to a paper coauthored by Dr. Larry Rosen, who also wrote a book called *iDisorder: Understanding Our Obsession with Technology and Overcoming Its Hold on Us*.

Some research suggests a correlation between social media and narcissism, but the condition's increase long predates the rise of smartphones, says Jean Twenge, a researcher at San Diego State University who studies issues related to social media.

"It's probably both that higher narcissism causes people to use social media in narcissistic ways, and that some social media causes higher narcissism," says Twenge. "But it's definitely a two-way street."

DISCUSSION

1. In the subtitle to this piece, Titlow characterizes the popularity of the "selfie" portrait as a "scourge." What point is he trying to make by using this term? Do you think Titlow's word choice here is accurate? Appropriate? Why or why not?
2. According to data Titlow cites, the "third most frequently used hashtag on Instagram is #me" (p. 122). What do you think this statistic tells us about the social norms this particular tool is helping to create? How does your view compare with Titlow's?
3. Titlow refers to the recognition Instagram users achieve through self-portraiture as "pseudo-fame" (p. 124). What do you think he means? And what larger point is he trying to make by using this term?

WRITING

4. "As you scroll through [Instagram]," Titlow writes, "you start to get the feeling that you're peeking through a window of a world you're not quite supposed to have access to. But mobile and social technology have given us millions of little windows into the worlds of others, so we keep scrolling" (p. 123). In a short essay, identify and evaluate the argument Titlow seems to be making here. What point is he trying to make about the visual scripts Instagram promotes by describing this technology as "peeking through a window"? And what attitude toward "mobile and social technology" more generally is he encouraging his readers to adopt? Do you share this attitude? Why or why not?
5. Titlow also cites research that speculates about the potential benefits sites like Instagram may offer users: "It used to be that most of the photographs of other people we encountered were carefully crafted images of the flawless-looking individuals portrayed in popular media and advertising. Psychologists have long had concerns about the distorted effect that's had on normal-looking people's self-images. Instagram and mobile photography more generally may be changing that" (p. 124). In a three- to five-page essay, present your own response to this hypothesis. Do you agree that "mobile photography" tools have the potential to counter the "distorted" self-image standards often purveyed and promoted by our larger popular culture? How or how not? And can you offer some concrete examples or evidence to support your view?
6. Like John Paul Titlow, Jessica Bennett (p. 90) retains a healthy skepticism toward the supposed benefits of online self-display. What concerns about this practice do these two writers share? What risks or dangers do they believe these acts of disclosure pose? Can you make a counterargument that identifies and defends the advantages of this practice?

HEATHER HAVRILESKY

Some "Girls" Are Better Than Others

Our world abounds with examples of culturally loaded language: words or phrases that carry powerful but unspoken connotations, positive or negative. How do we respond to such language? To what extent do unspoken connotations shape our own assumptions, values, and views? Using these questions as her frame, Heather Havrilesky tries to make sense of the growing ubiquity of the term *girl* in popular culture. What particular assumptions, she asks, stand behind this term? And what portrait of contemporary female life do these assumptions create? Havrilesky, a former TV critic for Salon.com, is the author of *Disaster Preparedness: A Memoir* (2010). This essay appeared in the *New York Times* in April 2012.

AH, TO BE A GIRL AGAIN! NOT A CHILD, OF COURSE, BUT AN INHABItant of that rarefied, pH-balanced zone of romance and optimism where you might flirt and flounce and be easily bruised by a pea. Girls can put on a dress and twirl in a circle and others will clap and say, "How pretty!" Girls never question whether the attention they get is well-meaning. They skip through the forest with a basket full of treats for Grandma, happily telling every Big Bad Wolf they encounter exactly where they're headed.

Sooner or later, of course, some of us wise up. A combination of skepticism and feminist indignation sets in, and it becomes harder to wink coyly at strangers or to marvel innocently at Grandma's sharp and pointy teeth.

But for those of us who retain some sense memory of twirling and hearing someone coo, spotting the word *girl* in every other title these days (*2 Broke Girls*, *New Girl*, *The Girl with the Dragon Tattoo*, and, of course, *Girls*) or just hearing it in a line of dialogue (think *Sex and the City*, conspiratorial clinking of cosmopolitans, etc.) can bring on a faintly nostalgic twinge. Or is it a shudder? We recall that privileged but exasperating era when we were transfixing and special but also a little doomed. As a girl, you are a delicate glass vase, waiting to be broken. You are a sweet-smelling flower, waiting for life's hobnailed boots to trample you. That built-in suspense is part of your appeal.

"How will you make it on your own?" the theme song for *The Mary Tyler Moore Show* asks, hinting that the slightest pothole in the road might ruin everything for our hopeful heroine, peering worriedly from behind her steering wheel. When modern TV shows use the word *girl* in their titles, it's this state of uncertainty they're hoping to conjure. Forget that Mary Richards herself was done with twirling, if not hat tossing, well before she stepped into Mr. Grant's newsroom. Ever since she (and *That Girl* Marlo Thomas before her) turned the world on with her smile, we've been offered coquettish creatures who mimic her second-guessing and nervous tics but curiously lack her complexity and gravitas.

Witnessing the female characters on TV comedies today, I find it hard not to marvel at the effortful overcompensation at play here, as adult women are transformed into something lighter, perkier, less frightening.

With their forced laughs and their preening and those heavy bangs resting straight on their eyeballs, our current batch of TV ingénues seems designed to conjure the childlike poutiness of America's onetime sweetheart Ally McBeal. You can afford to be a little sassy and street smart when you have big doll eyes and the frame of a preteen.

Aside from a few exceptions—Tina Fey's Liz Lemon on *30 Rock*, Amy Poehler's Leslie Knope on *Parks and Recreation*, both farcical enough to have more in common with *S.N.L.* personas than actual characters—we've largely been spared confident, complicated, single comedic heroines for a few decades now. Each week on *2 Broke Girls*, the spunky leads flee confrontation, seek solace in each other's "You go, girl!" clichés, and then stride out from their hidey hole to shake a finger in someone's face (only to be rewarded with more humiliation). For all of the single-girl bluster of *Whitney*, our heroine seems to have few interests outside of her live-in boyfriend, whether turning him on, manipulating him, or distracting him from ogling another girl's assets. Even Jess (Zooey Deschanel) of *New Girl*, the least insipid of the lot, tends to go all bashful and pigeon-toed a few times per episode, forsaking weightier goals in favor of trotting out her oddball charms for the adoration of her male roommates.

After prolonged exposure to these smoldering doll-babies, it's hard not to long for some of the stubbornness of Lucy Ricardo (Lucille Ball), the insatiability and bad temper of Samantha Jones (Kim Cattrall), or the nerve and self-possession of Mary Richards. When Mary and Rhoda go to a party amid young hippies and Mary notices that they are the only ones wearing eyeliner, we understand Mary and Rhoda as real human beings, complex entities capable of layered reactions to their surroundings. If this were *2 Broke Girls*, Mary and Rhoda would dash off to the bathroom to giggle behind their hands, then wipe off their makeup and re-emerge, anxious to blend in with the crowd. Or Rhoda, after resolving to tell those nutty hippie kids a thing or two, would end up being humiliated by them in the process.

This discord between how vehemently we're told to believe in ourselves as young girls and how dismissively we're treated as young women...is part of what fuels the shudder brought on by that word, "girl."

Witnessing the female characters on TV comedies today, I find it hard not to marvel at the effortful overcompensation at play here, as adult women are transformed into something lighter, perkier, less frightening. Each character is outfitted with charming tics ("What an adorable sneeze!") and inoffensive mediocrities ("She's so clumsy!") and toothless yuppie righteousness ("You tell that snippy barista the customer is always right!") Our culture chooses the naïve audacity of girlhood over more robust concepts of femininity—even Madonna has taken to waving sparkly pompoms. If watching shows like *2 Broke Girls* and *Whitney* and *New Girl* brings on a certain nausea and dizziness, it's most likely a result of seeing the same grown women twirl and twirl and twirl endlessly for an imagined audience each week. Even Carrie Bradshaw, in all of her attention-seeking wishy-washiness, at least had the courage of conviction to dress like an extra in the Ziegfeld Follies.

It's against this backdrop that we encounter Lena Dunham's new HBO comedy, *Girls*, in which Dunham tosses the basket of cupcakes aside and rolls out the Big Bad Wolf instead. It's no mistake that we meet our lead, Hannah (played by Dunham), while she's slurping up pasta on her parents' dime. Just a few scenes later, she's having awkward sex on the couch with a guy who rarely returns her texts. The deliberately jarring juxtaposition of these images, one of an overgrown infant, the other of a sexually submissive woman, is at once horrifying and hilariously caustic.

Caught in that bewildering nowhereland between childhood and adulthood, Hannah demonstrates how easy it is to experience a loss of directional cues, if not a total shutdown of onboard instrument panels. The show's use of that ubiquitous term *girl* is less about offering up another candidate for America's sweetheart than it is about charting that unnerving intersection of giggly specialness and self-consciousness, coyness and skepticism, flirtation and feminist indignation. Hannah herself appears to have marched straight from a Take Back the Night rally to a booty call with a guy who wants her to pretend she's a lost girl on the street with a Cabbage Patch Kids lunchbox. She plays along, limply—"Yeah, I was really scared." But a few minutes later, when the guy calls her friend's abortion a "heavy situation," she asserts that it's less a tragic affair than a pragmatic concern. "What was she gonna do, like, have a baby and then take it to her baby-sitting job? It's not realistic."

If *Girls* has been heralded as game-changing television, there's a reason for that: the stuttered confessions, half-smiles, hissed warnings, and quiet shared confidences between Hannah and her friends make the empty sassing and high-fiving of existing girlie comedies look like the spasms of a bygone era. But what's most riveting about Hannah and her friends is not their wisdom, their righteousness, or their backbone—as we might imagine would be the antidote to the frothy pap of other girlie comedies—but their confusion, their vulnerability, and their ambivalence. Instead of clamoring for attention like Whitney or Jess, Hannah's roommate, Marnie (Allison Williams), who is beautiful and has a devoted boyfriend, is bored by his sensitivity, bored by his affection (she complains that "his touch now feels like a weird uncle putting his hand on my knee at Thanksgiving") but can't muster the resolve to dump him. This is not how the candy-coated ingénue of American imagining, poised on the doorstep of womanhood, is supposed to react to male attention.

Hannah, meanwhile, almost never takes a stand. She asks her boss at her publishing internship to give her a paid job, and he politely bids her farewell in that passive-aggressive professional way that's difficult to counter. After trading quips with a potential employer at an interview, she says something off-color and is summarily dismissed for her insensitivity. (She's baffled but doesn't protest.) Worst of all, she lets her sort-of-not-really-boyfriend call her a dirty little whore and smash her face into the mattress. Afterward, he asks her if she wants a Gatorade. "What flavor?" she asks. "Orange," he answers. "Um, no thanks, I'm good," she replies, politely.

Hannah, like so many women walking the line between the coddling of girlhood and the realities of adulthood, doesn't hoot or cackle or tell it like it is. Most young women, even if they're assertive and determined, still find themselves, in those forlorn in-between years, apologizing for themselves, blurting some muddled, half-finished thought, and, finally, resolving to take up less space.

This discord between how vehemently we're told to believe in ourselves as young girls and how dismissively we're treated as young women—captured so heartbreakingly in *Girls*—is part of what fuels the shudder brought on by that word, "girl." As vivid as our culture's fantasy of this magical juncture between childhood and adulthood might be, it's hardly a carefree time occupied by effusive pixies, let alone a period to which most of us would happily return. Because one day, we wake up ready—not to wag our fingers in someone's face (which is just another way of twirling when you get right down to it) but to present our true selves without apology. This is the trajectory that Lena Dunham and her collaborators have set out to portray, with humor and subtlety and realism. You can turn the world on with your smile for only so long before it gets a little dull. Or as Hannah tells her parents, trying to remain calm despite the fact that her extended childhood is suddenly in peril: "I have work, and then I have a dinner thing, and then I am busy, trying to become who I am."

Eventually, we learn to explain, calmly, who we are and what we will and won't accept. That's how you make it on your own, as Mary Richards often demonstrated, though her voice sometimes trembled and her hands sometimes shook. That's the reason that scene of Mary throwing her hat in the air still feels exhilarating, 42 years later. No, that girl didn't break. But she was never all that fragile to begin with.

DISCUSSION

1. What is your personal response to the term *girl*? What specific assumptions or stereotypes does it evoke? Do you think they are fair or accurate? Why or why not?
2. Havrilesky writes about the "discord between how vehemently we're told to believe in ourselves as young girls and how dismissively we're treated as young women" (p. 129). What does she mean by this? What specific gap between personal self-regard and public treatment is Havrilesky calling out? And do you agree it exists?
3. "Most young women," Havrilesky declares, "even if they're assertive and determined, still find themselves, in those forlorn in-between years, apologizing for themselves, blurting some muddled, half-finished thought, and, finally, resolving to take up less space" (p. 129). What kind of social script for "young women" does this passage describe? Is it one you have either encountered or experienced yourself?

WRITING

4. "As a girl," Havrilesky writes, "you are a delicate glass vase, waiting to be broken. You are a sweet-smelling flower, waiting for life's hobnailed boots to trample you. That built-in suspense is part of your appeal" (p. 126). Write a short essay in which you describe and analyze the description Havrilesky offers here. What portrait of "girlhood" does this passage create? What images or associations does her specific language evoke? In your view, does it create a social script worth following? How or how not?
5. Havrilesky cites numerous examples of pop culture shows (both past and present) that put the title girl front and center. Choose a pop culture example of your own (an ad, TV show, website, etc.) that does this same thing. Then write a three- to five-page essay in which you summarize, analyze, and evaluate the ways this text utilizes the term *girl*. What portrait of "girlhood" does this text present? What specific language and/or images does it use to create this portrait? In your view, is this a valid or appropriate portrait for our times? How or how not?
6. Havrilesky shares with Naomi Klein (p. 150) a common concern over the ways our entertainment media can shape public attitudes regarding social issues. What aspects of Havrilesky's essay do you think Klein would most likely endorse? Where might the two writers part ways? Offer a response to Havrilesky's argument that, in your view, Klein herself would write, using quotes from both writers to support your argument.

Then and Now: **Wearing Your Identity on Your Sleeve**

Merchandisers have long sought to sell their goods by appealing to our sense of personal style: by flattering our desire to make an impression or cultivate an image that reflects our unique individuality. For years, this goal revolved around a strategy known as niche marketing, a tactic designed to associate a given product with the interests, hobbies, or "look" of a particular group. To wear a specific brand of clothing, drive a certain model of car, drink a particular variety of soda was (according to this formulation) to demonstrate your membership within a cohort of people who wear, drive, and drink the same thing — in effect, to make a statement about the *type* of person you truly are. Niche marketing, in other words, has long encouraged us to treat commercial marketing as a viable blueprint for *self*-marketing. When you think of 1950s fashion, one word that might first come to mind is *conformity*, and indeed the picture at the left shows a group of teenage girls wearing more or less the teenage girl uniform of the 1950s.

Donald Uhrbrock/Getty Images

Fashions are often designed to appeal to members of a certain group, even as we talk about fashion as a way to express individual identity. These days, however, niche marketing is giving way to a new sales strategy, one that seems at first glance to resolve this contradiction. No longer content with associating their goods with a consumer type, many merchandisers nowadays promote products that they claim are tailored to nonconformist consumers. A website like Threadless.com, for example, allows artists to create designs that are then voted on by Threadless members, with the most popular designs being printed and sold by the company. For many, this change not only heralds the demise of niche marketing but also signals a movement beyond the outmoded ideas of self-marketing and image creation. With the advent of customized marketing, we are told, it is now possible for shopping to serve as a truly legitimate means of self-expression, a vehicle for defining and displaying our true individuality.

But how much has *really* changed? Just because merchandisers now market customized products doesn't necessarily mean they've gotten out of the business of creating and marketing different images. No matter how personalized the messages on these design-your-own T-shirts, they are still logos. Indeed we could well ask whether all of this so-called customized design is simply a different, admittedly more sophisticated, form of branding. At the end of the day, after all, customers who wear these products are still engaging in the same operation that customers always have, one in which they use brand images and logos to make statements about the types of people they are. Do we find ourselves drawn to these kinds of products because they really do help us showcase our genuine selves? Or do we respond to this come-on for the same old reasons — because these products promise to supply us with a genuine self that is made for us?

Threadless.com

WRITING

1. In a brief essay, compare the different directions each image lays out for how and why we should shop. What role for the average consumer does each example seem to create? What parallels or similarities do you note? What differences? Which is a more effective way to market clothing? Why?
2. Naomi Klein (p. 150) takes up the issue of consumerism, exploring the ways that commercial culture influences some of our personal attitudes and beliefs. Put yourself in the position of Klein for a moment and write a description of the ways you think she would evaluate or respond to the notion of "personalized marketing." On which aspects of this promotional campaign do you think Klein would focus most attention? How would she evaluate the messages about shopping and identity these products encourage us to accept?

CHARLES DUHIGG

How Companies Learn Your Secrets

We hear a lot these days about the dangers posed by government surveillance. Just as extensive, and perhaps even more troubling, however, is the phenomenon of corporate surveillance: the efforts of countless retail companies to monitor, and ultimately manipulate, our personal shopping behavior. What are the implications, Charles Duhigg asks, of living in a world where the stores we patronize may know more about us than we know about ourselves? Charles Duhigg is a staff writer for the *New York Times* and author of *The Power of Habit: Why We Do What We Do in Life and Business* (2012). The essay below appeared in the *New York Times Magazine* in 2012.

ANDREW POLE HAD JUST STARTED WORKING AS A STATISTICIAN for Target in 2002, when two colleagues from the marketing department stopped by his desk to ask an odd question: "If we wanted to figure out if a customer is pregnant, even if she didn't want us to know, can you do that?"

Pole has a master's degree in statistics and another in economics, and has been obsessed with the intersection of data and human behavior most of his life. His parents were teachers in North Dakota, and while other kids were going to 4-H, Pole was doing algebra and writing computer programs. "The stereotype of a math nerd is true," he told me when I spoke with him last year. "I kind of like going out and evangelizing analytics."

As the marketers explained to Pole—and as Pole later explained to me, back when we were still speaking and before Target told him to stop—new parents are a retailer's holy grail. Most shoppers don't buy everything they need at one store. Instead, they buy groceries at the grocery store and toys at the toy store, and they visit Target only when they need certain items they associate with Target—cleaning supplies, say, or new socks or a six-month supply of toilet paper. But Target sells everything from milk to stuffed animals to lawn furniture to electronics, so one of the company's primary goals is convincing customers that the only store they need is Target. But it's a tough message to get across, even with the most ingenious ad campaigns, because once consumers' shopping habits are ingrained, it's incredibly difficult to change them.

There are, however, some brief periods in a person's life when old routines fall apart and buying habits are suddenly in flux. One of those moments—*the* moment, really—is right around the birth of a child, when parents are exhausted and overwhelmed and their shopping patterns and brand loyalties are up for grabs. But as Target's marketers explained to Pole, timing is everything. Because birth records are usually public, the moment a couple have a new baby, they are almost instantaneously barraged with offers and incentives and advertisements from all sorts of companies. Which means that the key is to reach them earlier, before any other retailers know a baby is on the way. Specifically, the marketers said they wanted to send specially designed ads to women in their second trimester, which is when most expectant mothers begin buying all sorts of new things, like prenatal vitamins and maternity clothing. "Can you give us a list?" the marketers asked.

"We knew that if we could identify them in their second trimester, there's a good chance we could capture them for years," Pole told me. "As soon as we get them buying diapers from us, they're going to start buying everything else too. If you're rushing through the store, looking for bottles, and you pass orange juice, you'll grab a carton. Oh, and there's that new DVD I want. Soon, you'll be buying cereal and paper towels from us, and keep coming back."

Target can buy data about your ethnicity, job history, the magazines you read, if you've ever declared bankruptcy or got divorced, the year you bought (or lost) your house, where you went to college, what kinds of topics you talk about online, whether you prefer certain brands of coffee, paper towels, cereal, or applesauce, your political leanings, reading habits, charitable giving, and the number of cars you own.

The desire to collect information on customers is not new for Target or any other large retailer, of course. For decades, Target has collected vast amounts of data on every person who regularly walks into one of its stores. Whenever possible, Target assigns each shopper a unique code—known internally as the Guest ID number—that keeps tabs on everything they buy. "If you use a credit card or a coupon, or fill out a survey, or mail in a refund, or call the customer help line, or open an e-mail we've sent you or visit our Web site, we'll record it and link it to your Guest ID," Pole said. "We want to know everything we can."

Also linked to your Guest ID is demographic information like your age, whether you are married and have kids, which part of town you live in, how long it takes you to drive to the store, your estimated salary, whether you've moved recently, what credit cards you carry in your wallet and what Web sites you visit. Target can buy data about your ethnicity, job history, the magazines you read, if you've ever declared bankruptcy or got divorced, the year you bought (or lost) your house, where you went to college, what kinds of topics you talk about online, whether you prefer certain brands of coffee, paper towels, cereal, or applesauce, your political leanings, reading habits, charitable giving, and the number of cars you own. (In a statement, Target declined to identify what demographic information it collects or purchases.) All that information is meaningless, however, without someone to analyze and make sense of it. That's where Andrew Pole and the dozens of other members of Target's Guest Marketing Analytics department come in.

Almost every major retailer, from grocery chains to investment banks to the U.S. Postal Service, has a "predictive analytics" department devoted to understanding not just consumers' shopping habits but also their personal habits, so as to more efficiently market to them. "But Target has always been one of the smartest at this," says Eric Siegel, a consultant and the chairman of a conference called Predictive Analytics World. "We're living through a golden age of behavioral research. It's amazing how much we can figure out about how people think now."

The reason Target can snoop on our shopping habits is that, over the past two decades, the science of habit formation has become a major field of research in neurology and psychology departments at hundreds of major medical centers and universities, as well as inside extremely well financed corporate labs. "It's like an arms race to hire statisticians nowadays," said Andreas Weigend, the former chief scientist at Amazon.com. "Mathematicians are suddenly sexy." As the ability to analyze data has grown more and more fine-grained, the push to understand how daily habits influence our decisions has become one of the most exciting topics in clinical research, even though most of us are hardly aware those patterns exist. One study from Duke University estimated that habits, rather than conscious decision-making, shape 45 percent of the choices we make every day, and recent discoveries have begun to change everything from the way we think about dieting to how doctors conceive treatments for anxiety, depression, and addictions.

Researchers have figured out how to stop people from habitually overeating and biting their nails. They can explain why some of us automatically go for a jog every morning and are more productive at work, while others oversleep and procrastinate.

This research is also transforming our understanding of how habits function across organizations and societies. A football coach named Tony Dungy propelled one of the worst teams in the

N.F.L. to the Super Bowl by focusing on how his players habitually reacted to on-field cues. Before he became Treasury secretary, Paul O'Neill overhauled a stumbling conglomerate, Alcoa, and turned it into a top performer in the Dow Jones by relentlessly attacking one habit—a specific approach to worker safety—which in turn caused a companywide transformation. The Obama campaign has hired a habit specialist as its "chief scientist" to figure out how to trigger new voting patterns among different constituencies.

Researchers have figured out how to stop people from habitually overeating and biting their nails. They can explain why some of us automatically go for a jog every morning and are more productive at work, while others oversleep and procrastinate. There is a calculus, it turns out, for mastering our subconscious urges. For companies like Target, the exhaustive rendering of our conscious and unconscious patterns into data sets and algorithms has revolutionized what they know about us and, therefore, how precisely they can sell.

Inside the brain-and-cognitive-sciences department of the Massachusetts Institute of Technology are what, to the casual observer, look like dollhouse versions of surgical theaters. There are rooms with tiny scalpels, small drills, and miniature saws. Even the operating tables are petite, as if prepared for 7-year-old surgeons. Inside those shrunken O.R.'s, neurologists cut into the skulls of anesthetized rats, implanting tiny sensors that record the smallest changes in the activity of their brains.

An M.I.T. neuroscientist named Ann Graybiel told me that she and her colleagues began exploring habits more than a decade ago by putting their wired rats into a T-shaped maze with chocolate at one end. The maze was structured so that each animal was positioned behind a barrier that opened after a loud click. The first time a rat was placed in the maze, it would usually wander slowly up and down the center aisle after the barrier slid away, sniffing in corners and scratching at walls. It appeared to smell the chocolate but couldn't figure out how to find it. There was no discernible pattern in the rat's meanderings and no indication it was working hard to find the treat.

The probes in the rats' heads, however, told a different story. While each animal wandered through the maze, its brain was working furiously. Every time a rat sniffed the air or scratched a wall, the neurosensors inside the animal's head exploded with activity. As the scientists repeated the experiment, again and again, the rats eventually stopped sniffing corners and making wrong turns and began to zip through the maze with more and more speed. And within their brains, something unexpected occurred: as each rat learned how to complete the maze more quickly, its mental activity *decreased*. As the path became more and more automatic—as it became a habit—the rats started thinking less and less.

This process, in which the brain converts a sequence of actions into an automatic routine, is called "chunking." There are dozens, if not hundreds, of behavioral chunks we rely on every day. Some are simple: you automatically put toothpaste on your toothbrush before sticking it in your mouth. Some, like making the kids' lunch, are a little more complex. Still others are so complicated that it's remarkable to realize that a habit could have emerged at all.

Take backing your car out of the driveway. When you first learned to drive, that act required a major dose of concentration, and for good reason: it involves peering into the rearview and side mirrors and checking for obstacles, putting your foot on the brake, moving the gearshift into reverse, removing your foot from the brake, estimating the distance between the garage and the street while keeping the wheels aligned, calculating how images in the mirrors translate into actual distances, all while applying differing amounts of pressure to the gas pedal and brake.

Now, you perform that series of actions every time you pull into the street without thinking very much. Your brain has chunked large parts of it. Left to its own devices, the brain will try to make almost any repeated behavior into a habit, because habits allow our minds to conserve effort. But conserving mental energy is tricky, because if our brains power down at the wrong moment, we might fail to notice something important, like a child riding her bike down the sidewalk or a speeding car coming down the street. So we've devised a clever system to determine when to let a habit take over. It's something that happens whenever a chunk of behavior starts or ends—and it helps to explain why habits are so difficult to change once they're formed, despite our best intentions.

To understand this a little more clearly, consider again the chocolate-seeking rats. What Graybiel and her colleagues found was that, as the ability to navigate the maze became habitual, there were two spikes in the rats' brain activity—once at the beginning of the maze, when the rat heard the click right before the barrier slid away, and once at the end, when the rat found the chocolate. Those spikes show when the rats' brains were fully engaged, and the dip in neural activity between the spikes showed when the habit took over. From behind the partition, the rat wasn't sure what waited on the other side, until it heard the click, which it had come to associate with the maze. Once it heard that sound, it knew to use the "maze habit," and its brain activity decreased. Then at the end of the routine, when the reward appeared, the brain shook itself awake again and the chocolate signaled to the rat that this particular habit was worth remembering, and the neurological pathway was carved that much deeper.

The process within our brains that creates habits is a three-step loop. First, there is a cue, a trigger that tells your brain to go into automatic mode and which habit to use. Then there is the routine, which can be physical or mental or emotional. Finally, there is a reward, which helps your brain figure out if this particular loop is worth remembering for the future. Over time, this loop—cue, routine, reward; cue, routine, reward—becomes more and more automatic. The cue and reward become neurologically intertwined until a sense of craving emerges. What's unique about cues and rewards, however, is how subtle they can be. Neurological studies like the ones in Graybiel's lab have revealed that some cues span just milliseconds. And rewards can range from the obvious (like the sugar rush that a morning doughnut habit provides) to the infinitesimal (like the barely noticeable—but measurable—sense of relief the brain experiences after successfully navigating the driveway). Most cues and rewards, in fact, happen so quickly and are so slight that we are hardly aware of them at all. But our neural systems notice and use them to build automatic behaviors.

Habits aren't destiny—they can be ignored, changed, or replaced. But it's also true that once the loop is established and a habit emerges, your brain stops fully participating in decision-making. So unless you deliberately fight a habit—unless you find new cues and rewards—the old pattern will unfold automatically.

"We've done experiments where we trained rats to run down a maze until it was a habit, and then we extinguished the habit by changing the placement of the reward," Graybiel told me. "Then one day, we'll put the reward in the old place and put in the rat and, by golly, the old habit will re-emerge right away. Habits never really disappear."

Luckily, simply understanding how habits work makes them easier to control. Take, for instance, a series of studies conducted a few years ago at Columbia University and the University of Alberta. Researchers wanted to understand how exercise habits emerge. In one project, 256 members of a health-insurance plan were invited to classes stressing the importance of exercise. Half the participants received an extra lesson on the theories of habit formation (the structure of the habit loop) and were asked to identify cues and rewards that might help them develop exercise routines.

The results were dramatic. Over the next four months, those participants who deliberately identified cues and rewards spent twice as much time exercising as their peers. Other studies have yielded similar results. According to another recent paper, if you want to start running in the morning, it's essential that you choose a simple cue (like always putting on your sneakers before breakfast or leaving your running clothes next to your bed) and a clear reward (like a midday treat or even the sense of accomplishment that comes from ritually recording your miles in a log book). After a while, your brain will start anticipating that reward—craving the treat or the feeling of accomplishment—and there will be a measurable neurological impulse to lace up your jogging shoes each morning.

Our relationship to e-mail operates on the same principle. When a computer chimes or a smartphone vibrates with a new message, the brain starts anticipating the neurological "pleasure" (even if we don't recognize it as such) that clicking on the e-mail and reading it provides. That expectation, if unsatisfied, can build until you find yourself moved to distraction by the thought of an e-mail sitting there unread—even if you know, rationally, it's most likely not important. On the other hand, once you remove the cue by disabling the buzzing of your phone or the chiming of your computer, the craving is never triggered, and you'll find, over time, that you're able to work productively for long stretches without checking your in-box.

Habits aren't destiny—they can be ignored, changed, or replaced.

Some of the most ambitious habit experiments have been conducted by corporate America. To understand why executives are so entranced by this science, consider how one of the world's largest companies, Procter & Gamble, used habit insights to turn a failing product into one of its biggest sellers. P.&G. is the corporate behemoth behind a whole range of products, from Downy fabric softener to Bounty paper towels to Duracell batteries and dozens of other household brands. In the mid-1990s, P.&G.'s executives began a secret project to create a new product that could eradicate bad smells. P.&G. spent millions developing a colorless, cheap-to-manufacture liquid that could be sprayed on a smoky blouse, stinky couch, old jacket, or stained car interior and make it odorless. In order to market the product—Febreze—the company formed a team that included a former Wall Street mathematician named Drake Stimson and habit specialists, whose job was to make sure the television commercials, which they tested in Phoenix, Salt Lake City, and Boise, Idaho, accentuated the product's cues and rewards just right.

The first ad showed a woman complaining about the smoking section of a restaurant. Whenever she eats there, she says, her jacket smells like smoke. A friend tells her that if she uses Febreze, it will eliminate the odor. The cue in the ad is clear: the harsh smell of cigarette smoke. The reward: odor eliminated from clothes. The second ad featured a woman worrying about her dog, Sophie, who always sits on the couch. "Sophie will always smell like Sophie," she says, but with Febreze, "now my furniture doesn't have to." The ads were put in heavy rotation. Then the marketers sat back, anticipating how they would spend their bonuses. A week passed. Then two. A month. Two months. Sales started small and got smaller. Febreze was a dud.

The panicked marketing team canvassed consumers and conducted in-depth interviews to figure out what was going wrong, Stimson recalled. Their first inkling came when they visited a woman's home outside Phoenix. The house was clean and organized. She was something of a neat freak, the woman explained. But when P.&G.'s scientists walked into her living room, where her nine cats spent most of their time, the scent was so overpowering that one of them gagged.

According to Stimson, who led the Febreze team, a researcher asked the woman, "What do you do about the cat smell?"

"It's usually not a problem," she said.

"Do you smell it now?"

"No," she said. "Isn't it wonderful? They hardly smell at all!"

A similar scene played out in dozens of other smelly homes. The reason Febreze wasn't selling, the marketers realized, was that people couldn't detect most of the bad smells in their lives. If you live with nine cats, you become desensitized to their scents. If you smoke cigarettes, eventually you don't smell smoke anymore. Even the strongest odors fade with constant exposure. That's why Febreze was a failure. The product's cue—the bad smells that were supposed to trigger daily use—was hidden from the people who needed it the most. And Febreze's reward (an odorless home) was meaningless to someone who couldn't smell offensive scents in the first place.

P.&G. employed a Harvard Business School professor to analyze Febreze's ad campaigns. They collected hours of footage of people cleaning their homes and watched tape after tape, looking for clues that might help them connect Febreze to people's daily habits. When that didn't reveal anything, they went into the field and conducted more interviews. A breakthrough came when they visited a woman in a suburb near Scottsdale, Ariz., who was in her 40s with four children. Her house was clean, though not compulsively tidy, and didn't appear to have any odor problems; there were no pets or smokers. To the surprise of everyone, she loved Febreze.

"I use it every day," she said.

"What smells are you trying to get rid of?" a researcher asked.

"I don't really use it for specific smells," the woman said. "I use it for normal cleaning—a couple of sprays when I'm done in a room."

The researchers followed her around as she tidied the house. In the bedroom, she made her bed, tightened the sheet's corners, then sprayed the comforter with Febreze. In the living room, she vacuumed, picked up the children's shoes, straightened the coffee table, then sprayed Febreze on the freshly cleaned carpet.

"It's nice, you know?" she said. "Spraying feels like a little minicelebration when I'm done with a room." At the rate she was going, the team estimated, she would empty a bottle of Febreze every two weeks.

When they got back to P.&G.'s headquarters, the researchers watched their videotapes again. Now they knew what to look for and saw their mistake in scene after scene. Cleaning has its own habit loops that already exist. In one video, when a woman walked into a dirty room (cue), she started sweeping and picking up toys (routine), then she examined the room and smiled when she was done (reward). In another, a woman scowled at her unmade bed (cue), proceeded to straighten the blankets and comforter (routine), and then sighed as she ran her hands over the freshly plumped pillows (reward). P.&G. had been trying to create a whole new habit with Febreze, but what they really needed to do was piggyback on habit loops that were already in place. The marketers needed to position Febreze as something that came at the end of the cleaning ritual, the reward, rather than as a whole new cleaning routine.

The company printed new ads showing open windows and gusts of fresh air. More perfume was added to the Febreze formula, so that instead of merely neutralizing odors, the spray had its own distinct scent. Television commercials were filmed of women, having finished their cleaning routine, using Febreze to spritz freshly made beds and just-laundered clothing. Each ad was designed to appeal to the habit loop: when you see a freshly cleaned room (cue), pull out Febreze (routine), and enjoy a smell that says you've done a great job (reward). When you finish making a bed (cue), spritz Febreze (routine), and breathe a sweet, contented sigh (reward). Febreze, the ads implied, was a pleasant treat, not a reminder that your home stinks.

And so Febreze, a product originally conceived as a revolutionary way to destroy odors, became an air freshener used once things are already clean. The Febreze revamp occurred in the summer of 1998. Within two months, sales doubled. A year later, the product brought in $230 million. Since then Febreze has spawned dozens of spinoffs—air fresheners, candles, and laundry detergents—that now account for sales of more than $1 billion a year. Eventually, P.&G. began mentioning to customers that, in addition to smelling sweet, Febreze can actually kill bad odors. Today it's one of the top-selling products in the world.

Andrew Pole was hired by Target to use the same kinds of insights into consumers' habits to expand Target's sales. His assignment was to analyze all the cue-routine-reward loops among shoppers and help the company figure out how to exploit them. Much of his department's work was straightforward: find the customers who have children and send them catalogs that feature toys before Christmas. Look for shoppers who habitually purchase swimsuits in April and send them coupons for sunscreen in July and diet books in December. But Pole's most important assignment was to identify those unique moments in consumers' lives when their shopping habits become particularly flexible and the right advertisement or coupon would cause them to begin spending in new ways.

In the 1980s, a team of researchers led by a U.C.L.A. professor named Alan Andreasen undertook a study of people's most mundane purchases, like soap, toothpaste, trash bags, and toilet paper. They learned that most shoppers paid almost no attention to how they bought these products, that the purchases occurred habitually, without any complex decision-making. Which meant it was hard for marketers, despite their displays and coupons and product promotions, to persuade shoppers to change.

But when some customers were going through a major life event, like graduating from college or getting a new job or moving to a new town, their shopping habits became flexible in ways that were both predictable and potential gold mines for retailers. The study found that when someone marries, he or she is more likely to start buying a new type of coffee. When a couple move into a new house, they're more apt to purchase a different kind of cereal. When they divorce, there's an increased chance they'll start buying different brands of beer.

Consumers going through major life events often don't notice, or care, that their shopping habits have shifted, but retailers notice, and they care quite a bit. At those unique moments, Andreasen wrote, customers are "vulnerable to intervention by marketers." In other words, a precisely timed advertisement, sent to a recent divorcee or new homebuyer, can change someone's shopping patterns for years.

And among life events, none are more important than the arrival of a baby. At that moment, new parents' habits are more flexible than at almost any other time in their adult lives. If companies can identify pregnant shoppers, they can earn millions.

But Pole's most important assignment was to identify those unique moments in consumers' lives when their shopping habits become particularly flexible and the right advertisement or coupon would cause them to begin spending in new ways.

The only problem is that identifying pregnant customers is harder than it sounds. Target has a baby-shower registry, and Pole started there, observing how shopping habits changed as a woman approached her due date, which women on the registry had willingly disclosed. He ran test after test, analyzing the data, and before long some useful patterns emerged. Lotions, for example. Lots of people buy lotion, but one of Pole's colleagues noticed that women on the baby registry were buying larger quantities of unscented lotion around the beginning of their second trimester. Another analyst noted that sometime in the first 20 weeks, pregnant women loaded up on supplements like calcium, magnesium, and zinc. Many shoppers purchase soap and cotton balls, but when someone suddenly starts buying lots of scent-free soap and extra-big bags of cotton balls, in addition to hand sanitizers and washcloths, it signals they could be getting close to their delivery date.

As Pole's computers crawled through the data, he was able to identify about 25 products that, when analyzed together, allowed him to assign each shopper a "pregnancy prediction" score. More important, he could also estimate her due date to within a small window, so Target could send coupons timed to very specific stages of her pregnancy.

One Target employee I spoke to provided a hypothetical example. Take a fictional Target shopper named Jenny Ward, who is 23, lives in Atlanta and in March bought cocoa-butter lotion, a purse large enough to double as a diaper bag, zinc and magnesium supplements, and a bright blue rug. There's, say, an 87 percent chance that she's pregnant and that her delivery date is sometime in late August. What's more, because of the data attached to her Guest ID number, Target knows how to trigger Jenny's habits. They know that if she receives a coupon via e-mail, it will most likely cue her to buy online. They know that if she receives an ad in the mail on Friday, she frequently uses it on a weekend trip to the store. And they know that if they reward her with a printed receipt that entitles her to a free cup of Starbucks coffee, she'll use it when she comes back again.

In the past, that knowledge had limited value. After all, Jenny purchased only cleaning supplies at Target, and there were only so many psychological buttons the company could push. But now that she is pregnant, everything is up for grabs. In addition to triggering Jenny's habits to buy more cleaning products, they can also start including offers for an array of products, some more obvious than others, that a woman at her stage of pregnancy might need.

Pole applied his program to every regular female shopper in Target's national database and soon had a list of tens of thousands of women who were most likely pregnant. If they could entice those women or their husbands to visit Target and buy baby-related products, the company's cue-routine-reward calculators could kick in and start pushing them to buy groceries, bathing suits, toys and clothing, as well. When Pole shared his list with the marketers, he said, they were ecstatic. Soon, Pole was getting invited to meetings above his paygrade. Eventually his paygrade went up.

At which point someone asked an important question: How are women going to react when they figure out how much Target knows?

"If we send someone a catalog and say, 'Congratulations on your first child!' and they've never told us they're pregnant, that's going to make some people uncomfortable," Pole told me. "We are very conservative about compliance with all privacy laws. But even if you're following the law, you can do things where people get queasy."

About a year after Pole created his pregnancy-prediction model, a man walked into a Target outside Minneapolis and demanded to see the manager. He was clutching coupons that had been sent to his daughter, and he was angry, according to an employee who participated in the conversation.

"My daughter got this in the mail!" he said. "She's still in high school, and you're sending her coupons for baby clothes and cribs? Are you trying to encourage her to get pregnant?"

The manager didn't have any idea what the man was talking about. He looked at the mailer. Sure enough, it was addressed to the man's daughter and contained advertisements for maternity clothing, nursery furniture, and pictures of smiling infants. The manager apologized and then called a few days later to apologize again.

On the phone, though, the father was somewhat abashed. "I had a talk with my daughter," he said. "It turns out there's been some activities in my house I haven't been completely aware of. She's due in August. I owe you an apology."

When I approached Target to discuss Pole's work, its representatives declined to speak with me. "Our mission is to make Target the preferred shopping destination for our guests by delivering outstanding value, continuous innovation, and exceptional guest experience," the company wrote in a statement. "We've developed a number of research tools that allow us to gain insights into trends and preferences within different demographic segments of our guest population." When I sent Target a complete summary of my reporting, the reply was more terse: "Almost all of your statements contain inaccurate information and publishing them would be misleading to the public. We do not intend to address each statement point by point." The company declined to identify what was inaccurate. They did add, however, that Target "is in compliance with all federal and state laws, including those related to protected health information."

When I offered to fly to Target's headquarters to discuss its concerns, a spokeswoman e-mailed that no one would meet me. When I flew out anyway, I was told I was on a list of prohibited visitors. "I've been instructed not to give you access and to ask you to leave," said a very nice security guard named Alex.

Using data to predict a woman's pregnancy, Target realized soon after Pole perfected his model, could be a public-relations disaster. So the question became: how could they get their advertisements into expectant mothers' hands without making it appear they were spying on them? How do you take advantage of someone's habits without letting them know you're studying their lives?

Before I met Andrew Pole, before I even decided to write a book about the science of habit formation, I had another goal: I wanted to lose weight.

I had got into a bad habit of going to the cafeteria every afternoon and eating a chocolate-chip cookie, which contributed to my gaining a few pounds. Eight, to be precise. I put a Post-it note on my computer reading "NO MORE COOKIES." But every afternoon, I managed to ignore that note, wander to the cafeteria, buy a cookie, and eat it while chatting with colleagues. Tomorrow, I always promised myself, I'll muster the willpower to resist.

Tomorrow, I ate another cookie.

When I started interviewing experts in habit formation, I concluded each interview by asking what I should do. The first step, they said, was to figure out my habit loop. The routine was simple: every afternoon, I walked to the cafeteria, bought a cookie, and ate it while chatting with friends.

Next came some less obvious questions: What was the cue? Hunger? Boredom? Low blood sugar? And what was the reward? The taste of the cookie itself? The temporary distraction from my work? The chance to socialize with colleagues?

Rewards are powerful because they satisfy cravings, but we're often not conscious of the urges driving our habits in the first place. So one day, when I felt a cookie impulse, I went outside and took a walk instead. The next day, I went to the cafeteria and bought a coffee. The next, I bought an apple and ate it while chatting with friends. You get the idea. I wanted to test different theories regarding what reward I was really craving. Was it hunger? (In which case the apple should have worked.) Was it the desire for a quick burst of energy? (If so, the coffee should suffice.) Or, as turned out to be the answer, was it that after several hours spent focused on work, I wanted to socialize, to make sure I was up to speed on office gossip, and the cookie was just a convenient excuse? When I walked to a colleague's desk and chatted for a few minutes, it turned out, my cookie urge was gone.

All that was left was identifying the cue.

Deciphering cues is hard, however. Our lives often contain too much information to figure out what is triggering a particular behavior. Do you eat breakfast at a certain time because you're hungry? Or because the morning news is on? Or because your kids have started eating? Experiments have shown that most cues fit into one of five categories: location, time, emotional state, other people, or the immediately preceding action. So to figure out the cue for my cookie habit, I wrote down five things the moment the urge hit:

Where are you? (Sitting at my desk.)

What time is it? (3:36 P.M.)

What's your emotional state? (Bored.)

Who else is around? (No one.)

What action preceded the urge? (Answered an e-mail.)

The next day I did the same thing. And the next. Pretty soon, the cue was clear: I always felt an urge to snack around 3:30.

Once I figured out all the parts of the loop, it seemed fairly easy to change my habit. But the psychologists and neuroscientists warned me that, for my new behavior to stick, I needed to abide by the same principle that guided Procter & Gamble in selling Febreze: To shift the routine—to socialize, rather than eat a cookie—I needed to piggyback on an existing habit. So now, every day around 3:30, I stand up, look around the newsroom for someone to talk to, spend 10 minutes gossiping, then go back to my desk. The cue and reward have stayed the same. Only the routine has shifted. It doesn't feel like a decision, any more than the M.I.T. rats made a decision to run through the maze. It's now a habit. I've lost 21 pounds since then (12 of them from changing my cookie ritual).

After Andrew Pole built his pregnancy-prediction model, after he identified thousands of female shoppers who were most likely pregnant, after someone pointed out that some of those women might be a little upset if they received an advertisement making it obvious Target was studying their reproductive status, everyone decided to slow things down.

The marketing department conducted a few tests by choosing a small, random sample of women from Pole's list and mailing them combinations of advertisements to see how they reacted.

"We have the capacity to send every customer an ad booklet, specifically designed for them, that says, 'Here's everything you bought last week and a coupon for it,'" one Target executive told me. "We do that for grocery products all the time." But for pregnant women, Target's goal was selling them baby items they didn't even know they needed yet.

"With the pregnancy products, though, we learned that some women react badly," the executive said. "Then we started mixing in all these ads for things we knew pregnant women would never buy, so the baby ads looked random. We'd put an ad for a lawn mower next to diapers. We'd put a coupon for wineglasses next to infant clothes. That way, it looked like all the products were chosen by chance.

"And we found out that as long as a pregnant woman thinks she hasn't been spied on, she'll use the coupons. She just assumes that everyone else on her block got the same mailer for diapers and cribs. As long as we don't spook her, it works."

In other words, if Target piggybacked on existing habits—the same cues and rewards they already knew got customers to buy cleaning supplies or socks—then they could insert a new routine: buying baby products, as well. There's a cue ("Oh, a coupon for something I need!"), a routine ("Buy! Buy! Buy!"), and a reward ("I can take that off my list"). And once the shopper is inside the store, Target will hit her with cues and rewards to entice her to purchase everything she normally buys somewhere else. As long as Target camouflaged how much it knew, as long as the habit felt familiar, the new behavior took hold.

Soon after the new ad campaign began, Target's Mom and Baby sales exploded. The company doesn't break out figures for specific divisions, but between 2002—when Pole was hired—and 2010, Target's revenues grew from $44 billion to $67 billion. In 2005, the company's president, Gregg Steinhafel, boasted to a room of investors about the company's "heightened focus on items and categories that appeal to specific guest segments such as mom and baby."

Pole was promoted. He has been invited to speak at conferences. "I never expected this would become such a big deal," he told me the last time we spoke.

A few weeks before this article went to press, I flew to Minneapolis to try and speak to Andrew Pole one last time. I hadn't talked to him in more than a year. Back when we were still friendly, I mentioned that my wife was seven months pregnant. We shop at Target, I told him, and had given the company our address so we could start receiving coupons in the mail. As my wife's pregnancy progressed, I noticed a subtle upswing in the number of advertisements for diapers and baby clothes arriving at our house.

Pole didn't answer my e-mails or phone calls when I visited Minneapolis. I drove to his large home in a nice suburb, but no one answered the door. On my way back to the hotel, I stopped at a Target to pick up some deodorant, then also bought some T-shirts and a fancy hair gel. On a whim, I threw in some pacifiers, to see how the computers would react. Besides, our baby is now 9 months old. You can't have too many pacifiers.

When I paid, I didn't receive any sudden deals on diapers or formula, to my slight disappointment. It made sense, though: I was shopping in a city I never previously visited, at 9:45 P.M. on a weeknight, buying a random assortment of items. I was using a corporate credit card, and besides the pacifiers, hadn't purchased any of the things that a parent needs. It was clear to Target's computers that I was on a business trip. Pole's prediction calculator took one look at me, ran the numbers, and decided to bide its time. Back home, the offers would eventually come. As Pole told me the last time we spoke: "Just wait. We'll be sending you coupons for things you want before you even know you want them."

DISCUSSION

1. Take a moment to evaluate the title of this essay. How do you react to the prospect of retailers trying to "learn your secrets"? Do you find this possibility surprising? Troubling? Unremarkable? Why?
2. "Habits," writes Duhigg, "aren't destiny — they can be ignored, changed, or replaced. But it's also true that once the loop is established and a habit emerges, your brain stops fully participating in decision-making" (p. 139). How do you respond to this claim? Does your own personal experience reinforce or challenge this belief in the power of habit?
3. Underneath Duhigg's examination of corporate "snooping" is a deeper concern over what might be called corporate manipulation: the effort by retailers to use the personal data they collect to influence the ways we think, feel, and act. In your view, is this a valid concern to have? Should we be worried that our choices and actions are being scripted in this way? Why or why not?

WRITING

4. Duhigg connects the issue of corporate surveillance (i.e., how companies gather data about our shopping choices and behaviors) to the broader question of habituation (i.e., the degree to which these choices and behaviors are governed by deeply ingrained habit). Write an essay in which you use your own personal experience to test the validity of this connection. Do you feel that your personal shopping behavior is dictated largely by habit? Can you think of an example of your own that either confirms or refutes this hypothesis? And based on your own shopping behavior, do you think you would make a particularly valuable target for retailers intent on gathering information about their customers? How or how not?
5. Duhigg cites a number of experiments that seem to confirm the role that habituation plays in scripting our daily actions and choices. Create an experiment of your own that, in your view, could be used to measure the power of habit in everyday life. To get yourself started, think about the specific parameters you want to establish. What aspect of everyday life do you want to focus on? What particular behavior do you want to measure? Next speculate about the findings or results you think your experiment would produce.
6. In your view, how would Charles Duhigg respond to Virginia Heffernan's examination of the "attention-span myth" (p. 113)? Do you think he would find in Heffernan's argument a confirmation of or a challenge to his own thesis about the power of habit? And what specific aspects of Heffernan's discussion make you say so?

NAOMI KLEIN

Patriarchy Gets Funky:

The Triumph of Identity Marketing

To what extent do we turn to the world of commercial advertising for guidance about how to think through social and political questions? Tracking the growing phenomenon of identity marketing, Naomi Klein tells the story of how such companies as Benetton and MTV have learned to use mass-produced and mass-marketed models of racial and ethnic diversity as brand names for the products they sell. Wondering about and worrying over the growing indistinguishability between our political and commercial lives, Klein shows how intimately corporate iconography has insinuated itself into the ways we view not just the issue of social activism but the idea of social justice as well. Klein, a writer and activist, was born into a political family in Montreal, Quebec, and currently lives in Toronto. She has worked as the editor of *THIS Magazine* and as a weekly columnist for the *Toronto Star,* and she is currently a columnist for the *Nation* and the *Guardian.* Her books *No Logo* (2000), from which this selection is taken, and *Fences and Windows* (2002) discuss globalization and its countermovement. Her latest book is *The Shock Doctrine: The Rise of Disaster Capitalism* (2007).

AS AN UNDERGRADUATE IN THE LATE EIGHTIES AND EARLY NINEties, I was one of those students who took a while to wake up to the slow branding of university life. And I can say from personal experience that it's not that we didn't notice the growing corporate presence on campus—we even complained about it sometimes. It's just that we couldn't get particularly worked up about it. We knew the fast-food chains were setting up their stalls in the library and that profs in the applied sciences were getting awfully cozy with pharmaceutical companies, but finding out exactly what was going on in the boardrooms and labs would have required a lot of legwork, and, frankly, we were busy. We were fighting about whether Jews would be allowed in the racial equality caucus at the campus women's center, and why the meeting to discuss it was scheduled at the same time as the lesbian and gay caucus—were the organizers implying that there were no Jewish lesbians? No black bisexuals?

In the outside world, the politics of race, gender, and sexuality remained tied to more concrete, pressing issues, like pay equity, same-sex spousal rights, and police violence, and these serious movements were—and continue to be—a genuine threat to the economic and social order. But somehow, they didn't seem terribly glamorous to students on many university campuses, for whom identity politics had evolved by the late eighties into something quite different. Many of the battles we fought were over issues of "representation"—a loosely defined set of grievances mostly lodged against the media, the curriculum, and the English language. From campus feminists arguing over "representation" of women on the reading lists to gays wanting better "representation" on television, to rap stars bragging about "representing" the ghettos, to the question that ends in a riot in Spike Lee's 1989 film *Do the Right Thing*—"Why are there no brothers on the wall?"—ours was a politics of mirrors and metaphors.

These issues have always been on the political agendas of both the civil-rights and the women's movements, and later, of the fight against AIDS. It was accepted from the start that part of what held back women and ethnic minorities was the absence of visible role models occupying powerful social positions, and that media-perpetuated stereotypes—embedded in the very fabric of the language—served to not so subtly reinforce the supremacy of white men. For real progress to take place, imaginations on both sides had to be decolonized.

But by the time my generation inherited these ideas, often two or three times removed, representation was no longer one tool among many, it was the key. In the absence of a clear legal or political strategy, we traced back almost all of society's problems to the media and the curriculum, either through their perpetuation of negative stereotypes or simply by omission. Asians and lesbians were made to feel "invisible," gays were stereotyped as deviants, blacks as criminals, and women as weak and inferior: a self-fulfilling prophecy responsible for almost all real-world inequalities. And so our battlefields were sitcoms with gay neighbors who never got laid, newspapers filled with pictures of old white men, magazines that advanced . . . "the beauty myth," reading lists that we expected to look like Benetton ads, Benetton ads that trivialized our reading-list demands. So outraged were we media children by the narrow and oppressive portrayals in magazines, in books, and on television that we convinced ourselves that if the typecast images and loaded language changed, so too would the reality. We thought we would find salvation in the reformation of MTV, CNN, and Calvin Klein. And why not? Since media seemed to be the source of so many of our problems, surely if we could only "subvert" them to better represent us, they could save us instead. With better collective mirrors, self-esteem would rise and prejudices would magically fall away, as society became suddenly inspired to live up to the beautiful and worthy reflection we had retouched in its image.

For a generation that grew up mediated, transforming the world through pop culture was second nature. The problem was that these fixations began to transform us in the process. Over time, campus identity politics became so consumed by personal politics that they all but eclipsed the rest of the world. The slogan "the personal is political" came to replace the economic as political and, in the end, the Political as political as well. The more importance we placed on representation issues, the more central a role they seemed to elbow for themselves in our lives—perhaps because, in the absence of more tangible political goals, any movement that is about fighting for better social mirrors is going to eventually fall victim to its own narcissism.

Transforming the world through pop culture was second nature.

Soon "outing" wasn't about AIDS, but became a blanket demand for gay and lesbian "visibility"—all gays should be out, not just right-wing politicians but celebrities as well. By 1991, the radical group Queer Nation had broadened its media critique: it didn't just object to portrayals of homicidal madmen with AIDS, but any nonstraight killer at all. The group's San Francisco and L.A. chapters held protests against *The Silence of the Lambs,* objecting to its transvestite serial-killer villain, and they disrupted filming on *Basic Instinct* because it featured ice-pick-wielding killer lesbians. GLAAD (Gay and Lesbian Alliance Against Defamation) had moved from lobbying the news media about its use of terms like "gay plague" to describe AIDS, and had begun actively pushing the networks for more gay and lesbian characters in TV shows. In 1993, Torie Osborn, a prominent U.S. lesbian rights activist, said that the single biggest political issue facing her constituency was not same-sex spousal benefits, the right to join the military, or even the right of two women to marry and adopt children. It was, she told a reporter, "Invisibility. Period. End of sentence."[1]

Much like a previous generation of anti-porn feminists who held their rallies outside peep shows, many of the political demonstrations of the early nineties had shifted from the steps of government buildings and courthouses to the steps of museums with African art exhibits that were deemed to celebrate the colonial mindset. They massed at the theater entrances showing megamusicals like *Showboat* and *Miss Saigon,* and they even crept right up to the edge of the red carpet at the 1992 Academy Awards.

These struggles may seem slight in retrospect, but you can hardly blame us media narcissists for believing that we were engaged in a crucial battle on behalf of oppressed people everywhere: every step we took sparked a new wave of apocalyptic panic from our conservative foes. If we were not revolutionaries, why, then, were our opponents saying that a revolution was under way, that we were in the midst of a "culture war"? "The transformation of American campuses is so sweeping that it is no exaggeration to call it a revolution," Dinesh D'Souza, author of *Illiberal Education*, informed his readers. "Its distinctive insignia can be witnessed on any major campus in America today, and in all aspects of university life."[2]

Despite their claims of living under Stalinist regimes where dissent was not tolerated, our professors and administrators put up an impressively vociferous counteroffensive: they fought tooth and nail for the right to offend us thin-skinned radicals; they lay down on the tracks in front of every new harassment policy, and generally acted as if they were fighting for the very future of Western civilization. An avalanche of look-alike magazine features bolstered the claim that ID politics constituted an international emergency: "Illiberal Education" (*Atlantic Monthly*), "Visigoths in Tweed" (*Fortune*), "The Silences" (*Maclean's*), "The Academy's New Ayatollahs" (*Outlook*), "Taking Offense" (*Newsweek*). In *New York* magazine, writer John Taylor compared my generation of campus activists with cult members, Hitler Youth, and Christian fundamentalists.[3] So great was the threat we allegedly posed that George Bush even took time out to warn the world that political correctness "replaces old prejudices with new ones."

THE MARKETING OF ID

The backlash that identity politics inspired did a pretty good job of masking for us the fact that many of our demands for better representation were quickly accommodated by marketers, media makers, and pop-culture producers alike—though perhaps not for the reasons we had hoped. If I had to name a precise moment for this shift in attitude, I would say August of 1992: the thick of the "brand crisis" that peaked with Marlboro Friday. That's when we found out that our sworn enemies in the "mainstream"—to us a giant monolithic blob outside of our known university-affiliated enclaves—didn't fear and loathe us but actually thought we were sort of interesting. Once we'd embarked on a search for new wells of cutting-edge imagery, our insistence on extreme sexual and racial identities made for great brand-content and niche-marketing strategies. If diversity is what we wanted, the brands seemed to be saying, then diversity was exactly what we would get. And with that, the marketers and media makers swooped down, airbrushes in hand, to touch up the colors and images in our culture.

If diversity is what we wanted, the brands seemed to be saying, then diversity was exactly what we would get.

The five years that followed were an orgy of red ribbons, Malcolm X baseball hats, and Silence = Death T-shirts. By 1993, the stories of academic Armageddon were replaced with new ones about the sexy wave of "Do-Me Feminism" in *Esquire* and "Lesbian Chic" in *New York* and

Newsweek. The shift in attitude was not the result of a mass political conversion but of some hard economic calculations. According to *Rocking the Ages*, a book produced in 1997 by leading U.S. consumer researchers Yankelovich Partners, "Diversity" was the "defining idea" for Gen-Xers, as opposed to "Individuality" for boomers and "Duty" for their parents.

> Xers are starting out today with pluralistic attitudes that are the strongest we have ever measured. As we look towards the next twenty-five years, it is clear that acceptance of alternative lifestyles will become even stronger and more widespread as Xers grow up and take over the reins of power, and become the dominant buying group in the consumer marketplace. . . . *Diversity is the key fact of life for Xers, the core of the perspective they bring to the marketplace.* Diversity in all of its forms—cultural, political, sexual, racial, social—is a hallmark of this generation [italics theirs]. . . [4]

The Sputnik cool-hunting agency, meanwhile, explained that "youth today are one big sample of diversity" and encouraged its clients to dive into the psychedelic "United Streets of Diversity" and not be afraid to taste the local fare. Dee Dee Gordon, author of *The L. Report*, urged her clients to get into Girl Power with a vengeance: "Teenage girls want to see someone who kicks butt back";[5] and, sounding suspiciously like me and my university friends, brand man Tom Peters took to berating his corporate audiences for being "OWMs—Old White Males."

As we have seen, this information was coming hot on the heels of two other related revelations. The first was that consumer companies would only survive if they built corporate empires around "brand identities." The second was that the ballooning youth demographic held the key to market success. So, of course, if the market researchers and cool hunters all reported that diversity was the key character trait of this lucrative demographic, there was only one thing to be done: every forward-thinking corporation would have to adopt variations on the theme of diversity as their brand identities.

Which is exactly what most brand-driven corporations have attempted to do. In an effort to understand how Starbucks became an overnight household name in 1996 without a single national ad campaign, *Advertising Age* speculated that it had something to do with its tie-dyed, Third World aura. "For devotees, Starbucks' 'experience' is about more than a daily espresso infusion; it is about immersion in a politically correct, cultured refuge. . . ."[6] Starbucks, however, was only a minor player in the P.C. marketing craze. Abercrombie & Fitch ads featured guys in their underwear making goo-goo eyes at each other; Diesel went further, showing two sailors kissing; and a U.S. television spot for Virgin Cola depicted "the first-ever gay wedding featured in a commercial," as the press release proudly announced. There were also gay-targeted brands like Pride Beer and Wave Water, whose slogan is "We label bottles not people," and the gay community got its very own cool hunters—market researchers who scoured gay bars with hidden cameras.[7]

The Gap, meanwhile, filled its ads with racially mixed rainbows of skinny, childlike models. Diesel harnessed frustration at that unattainable beauty ideal with ironic ads that showed women being served up for dinner to a table of pigs. The Body Shop harnessed the backlash against both of them by refusing to advertise and instead filled its windows with red ribbons and posters condemning violence against women. The rush to diversity fitted in neatly with the embrace of African-American style and heroes that companies like Nike and Tommy Hilfiger had already pinpointed as a powerful marketing source. But Nike also realized that people who saw themselves as belonging to oppressed groups were ready-made market niches: throw a few liberal platitudes their way and, presto, you're not just a product but an ally in the struggle. So the walls of Nike Town were adorned with quotes from Tiger Woods declaring that "there are still courses in the U.S. where I am not allowed to play, because of the color of my skin." Women in Nike ads told us that "I believe 'babe' is a four-letter word" and "I believe high heels are a conspiracy against women."

And everyone, it seemed, was toying with the fluidity of gender, from the old-hat story of MAC makeup using drag queen RuPaul as its spokesmodel to tequila ads that inform viewers that the she in the bikini is really a he; from Calvin Klein's colognes that tell us that gender itself is a construct to Sure Ultra Dry deodorant that in turn urges all the gender benders to chill out: "Man? Woman? Does it matter?"

OPPRESSION NOSTALGIA

Fierce debates still rage about these campaigns. Are they entirely cynical or do they indicate that advertisers want to evolve and play more positive social roles? Benetton's mid-nineties ads careened wildly between witty and beautiful challenges to racial stereotypes on the one hand, and grotesque commercial exploitation of human suffering on the other. They were, however, indisputably part of a genuine attempt to use the company's vast cultural real estate to send a message that went beyond "Buy more sweaters"; and they played a central role in the fashion world's embrace of the struggle against AIDS. Similarly, there is no denying that the Body Shop broke ground by proving to the corporate sector that a multinational chain can be an outspoken and controversial political player, even while making millions on bubble bath and body lotion. The complicated motivations and stark inconsistencies inside many of these "ethical" businesses [are] explored [elsewhere]. But for many of the activists who had, at one point not so long ago, believed that better media representation would make for a more just world, one thing had become abundantly clear: identity politics weren't fighting the system, or even subverting it. When it came to the vast new industry of corporate branding, they were feeding it.

The crowning of sexual and racial diversity as the new superstars of advertising and pop culture has understandably created a sort of Identity Identity Crisis. Some ex-ID warriors are even getting nostalgic about the good old days, when they were oppressed, yes, but the symbols of their radicalism weren't for sale at Wal-Mart. As music writer Ann Powers observed of the much-vaunted ascendancy of Girl Power, "at this intersection between the conventional feminine and the evolving Girl, what's springing up is not a revolution but a mall . . . Thus, a genuine movement devolves into a giant shopping spree, where girls are encouraged to purchase whatever identity fits them best off the rack."[8] Similarly, Daniel Mendelsohn has written that gay identity has dwindled into "basically, a set of product choices . . . At least culturally speaking, oppression may have been the best thing that could have happened to gay culture. Without it, we're nothing."

The nostalgia, of course, is absurd. Even the most cynical ID warrior will admit, when pressed, that having Ellen Degeneres and other gay characters out on TV has some concrete advantages. Probably it is good for the kids, particularly those who live outside of larger urban settings—in rural or small-town environments, where being gay is more likely to confine them to a life of self-loathing. (The attempted suicide rate in 1998 among gay and bisexual male teens in America was 28.1 percent, compared with 4.2 percent among straight males of the same age group.)[9] Similarly, most feminists would concede that although the Spice Girls' crooning, "If you wanna be my lover, you have to get with my friends" isn't likely to shatter the beauty myth, it's still a step up from Snoop Dogg's 1993 ode to gang rape, "It ain't no fun if my homies can't have none."

And yet, while raising teenagers' self-esteem and making sure they have positive role models is valuable, it's a fairly narrow achievement, and from an activist perspective, one can't help asking: Is this it? Did all our protests and supposedly subversive theory only serve to provide great content for the culture industries, fresh new lifestyle imagery for Levi's new "What's True" ad campaign, and girl-power-charged record sales for the music business? Why, in other words, were our ideas about political rebellion so deeply non-threatening to the smooth flow of business as usual?

The question, of course, is not Why, but Why on earth not? Just as they had embraced the "brands, not products" equation, the smart businesses quickly realized that short-term discomfort—whether it came from a requirement to hire more women or to more carefully vet the language in an ad campaign—was a small price to pay for the tremendous market share that diversity promised. So while it may be true that real gains have emerged from this process, it is also true that Dennis Rodman wears dresses and Disney World celebrates Gay Day less because of political progress than financial expediency. The market has seized upon multiculturalism and gender-bending in the same ways that it has seized upon youth culture in general—not just as a market niche but as a source of new carnivalesque imagery. As Robert Goldman and Stephen Papson note, "White-bread culture will simply no longer do."[10] The $200 billion culture industry—now America's biggest export—needs an ever-changing, uninterrupted supply of street styles, edgy music videos, and rainbows of colors. And the radical critics of the media clamoring to be "represented" in the early nineties virtually handed over their colorful identities to the brandmasters to be shrink-wrapped.

The need for greater diversity—the rallying cry of my university years—is now not only accepted by the culture industries, it is the mantra of global capital. And identity politics, as they were practiced in the nineties, weren't a threat, they were a gold mine. "This revolution," writes cultural critic Richard Goldstein in *The Village Voice*, "turned out to be the savior of late capitalism."[11] And just in time, too.

NOTES

[1]Jeanie Russell Kasindorf, "Lesbian Chic," *New York*, 10 May 1993, 35.

[2]Dinesh D'Souza, "Illiberal Education," *Atlantic Monthly*, March 1991, 51.

[3]John Taylor, "Are You Politically Correct?" *New York*, 21 January 1991.

[4]J. Walker Smith and Ann Clurman, *Rocking the Ages* (New York: HarperCollins, 1997), 88.

[5] *Vogue*, November 1997.

[6]"Starbucks Is Ground Zero in Today's Coffee Culture," *Advertising Age*, 9 December 1996.

[7]Jared Mitchell, "Out and About," *Report on Business Magazine*, December 1996, 90.

[8]Ann Powers, "Everything and the Girl," *Spin*, November 1994, 74.

[9]Gary Remafedi, Simone French, Mary Story, Michael D. Resnick, and Robert Blum, "The Relationship between Suicide Risk and Sexual Orientation: Results of a Population-Based Study," *American Journal of Public Health*, January 1998, 88, no. 1, 57–60.

[10]Robert Goldman and Stephen Papson, *Sign Wars*, (New York: Guilford Press, 1996), v.

[11]Richard Goldstein, "The Culture War Is Over! We Won! (For Now)," *Village Voice*, 19 November 1996.

DISCUSSION

1. How do you respond to the term *identity marketing* as Klein defines it? Is identity something you naturally think of as marketable? How or how not?
2. Among the many problems with commercial marketing, Klein argues, is its tendency to define ethnic and racial difference in very limited ways. Choose one of the ad campaigns Klein references in her essay. In what particular ways might you alter the portrait of diversity so that it offers a more accurate or realistic depiction? In your view, would doing so enhance or inhibit the marketability of the product being sold?
3. In our culture, is there any social or political issue that could never be marketed? What would this issue be? And what aspect of it would make it impervious to commercial or corporate uses?

WRITING

4. Choose a commercial image you've come across recently that you think attempts to sell a particular definition of diversity. First, describe what definition or model this image endeavors to convey. Next, analyze the ways this definition seems connected to the particular product this commercial is also trying to sell. How (if at all) does this image of diversity shape viewer attitudes toward the product itself?
5. Klein asks whether identity marketing campaigns are "entirely cynical or do they indicate that advertisers want to evolve and play more positive social roles?" (p. 155). Write an essay in which you take a position on this question, using examples from ad campaigns you remember or those Klein discusses in her writing. Make sure that you consider both sides of the question in your argument.
6. Klein and Harriet McBryde Johnson (p. 96) are concerned with the ways our contemporary media teaches us both to see and not to see various types of difference. Write an essay in which you analyze how each writer discusses the idea of diversity and how it is portrayed in popular culture. What aspects of diversity are of particular concern to Klein? How do you think Johnson would respond to Klein's argument that diversity sells?

Tying It All Together

Implicit in Heather Havrilesky's effort to chronicle the complex history of the term *girl* is a recognition that social scripts and cultural norms have particular histories and that they evolve over time. Within very different contexts, this same recognition underlies a number of other essays in this book, among them: Francine Prose ("The Wages of Sin," p. 181), Alfie Kohn ("From Degrading to De-Grading," p. 238), and Matthew Crawford ("The Case for Working With Your Hands," p. 368). Choose one of these selections, and then write a short essay in which you identify and assess the ways this writer's discussion of social scripts and cultural norms compares to Havrilesky's. To what extent do both writers uncover the history behind a given social script or cultural norm? And in what ways does each use this history to make a larger argument about such scripts and/or norms?

Like Virginia Heffernan, Evgeny Morozov ("Open and Closed," p. 449) is interested in the ways modern technology influences what we do and do not see. In a three- to five-page essay, describe and evaluate how the arguments each writer makes compare. To what extent does Heffernan's examination of the "attention-span myth" echo — or challenge — Morozov's critique of Internet "openness"? What are the key assumptions or ideas these essays have in common? And which do you find more convincing? Why?

Scenes and Un-Scenes: **Picturing Disaster**

Whether it is a television commercial or a news broadcast, a web image or a blockbuster movie, virtually everything we see has been selectively shaped for our inspection. While it may purport to show us "the way things are," the truth is that every image bears traces of some slant or bias, intentional or not. And yet while it may be inevitable, this doesn't mean it is automatically excusable — that such bias doesn't warrant our attention, doesn't deserve to be challenged, critiqued, or changed. Certainly when it comes to something as politically important and personally catastrophic as Superstorm Sandy, the hurricane that devastated the New York/New Jersey area in the fall of 2012, it is no small matter to know whether the images we are shown tell the whole story.

AP Photo/NOAA

In the hours before it made landfall, media coverage tended to treat Superstorm Sandy as an entirely natural phenomenon. Tracking its movements from the supposedly objective vantage of outer space, for example, satellite photos like the one above reinforced an initial perception among many in the general public that no one was really to blame for this disaster.

AP Photo/Mike Groll

Mark Wilson/Getty Images

In the days immediately following Sandy's landfall, news organizations ran countless images documenting local residents' struggles to survive. In the weeks and months that followed, however, not all of the news coverage maintained this sympathetic focus. Take, for example, the two pictures featured above and on the following page. The first photo was published in the initial days following the storm. Capturing local residents' pleas for assistance, it focuses audience attention on the overwhelming plight and immediate needs of those devastated by Sandy's effects. The second, taken months later, records a moment in the contentious Congressional debate over how much federal assistance should have been devoted to Sandy relief. Many conservative congresspeople, angered at the prospect of such a large government expenditure, united in opposition to the relief bill. Presented above the caption, "Sandy Relief passes House despite conservative opposition," this image invites viewers to adopt a very different perspective, one that defines Sandy less as a natural disaster than a partisan political contest.

Another hallmark of the Sandy coverage involved what we might call the "sympathetic celebrity" story, in which a famous person toured the aftermath of the flooding in New Jersey to showcase her or his "personal" anguish or outrage at what was transpiring. What is the effect of casting Sandy as this type of human-interest story? What kind of reaction does it seem designed to elicit from viewers?

AP Photo /Julio Cortez

In contrast to much of the media coverage nationally, headlines such as these presented a view of the disaster informed by a far more immediate sense of suffering and emergency. Does this local perspective seem different from that modeled in other examples? More valuable?

RICHARD B. LEVINE/Newscom

Saul Loeb/Getty Images

One last frame within which the media depicted Superstorm Sandy was the 2012 presidential election campaign between Barack Obama and Mitt Romney. In the days following the storm, many conservative commentators expressed dismay over the words of praise and support for President Obama's assistance in providing aid offered by Republican New Jersey Governor, Chris Christie. Accusing Christie of undermining Republican candidate Romney's electoral chances in the waning days of the campaign, this backlash supplied Americans with yet another lens for viewing this disaster: namely, as a political controversy.

DISCUSSION

1. Are we always fully aware of the ways an image's bias shapes the conclusions we draw? Does it really matter? Would anything change if we were? How or how not?
2. In your view, does the regional identity of the viewer make any difference in what these images show or say? How might a local resident draw different conclusions than a member of the general public? Why?
3. Is the Sandy coverage an isolated or idiosyncratic example of media bias, or do you think it reflects a more wide-ranging pattern? Can you think of another news event or controversy that ended up being defined by such contrasting sorts of images?

WRITING

4. This portfolio makes clear that bias is a question not only of (mis)representation but also of omission. That is, it shows how bias reveals itself not simply in terms of what an image shows, but also by virtue of what it leaves out. Choose one of the images showcased in the preceding pages and write a one-page assessment of the things it does not show. What key aspects of its portrait are left out? How do these omissions influence the conclusions viewers are encouraged to draw?
5. As discussed throughout this chapter, our culture's visual rules teach us not only how to watch but also how to think. Choose one of the images from the preceding pages and write a one-page script for how the image is supposed to make us think about the politically loaded issue of federal disaster relief. What sorts of ideas concerning the responsibility of the government to aid those in need does it encourage viewers to adopt?
6. As her essay suggests, Harriet McBryde Johnson was someone interested in the ways that people's personal experiences and struggles can be misunderstood by the public at large. Choose three of the images previously listed and in two or three sentences write the kind of caption you think Johnson would create for each. What aspect of each image would she focus on? What specific sort of bias or slant would she identify? Then, write a second set of captions you think accurately describes what is happening in the photos you've chosen. How does your perspective compare to Johnson's?

Putting It into Practice: **Keeping an Eye Out**

Now that you've read the chapter selections, try applying your conclusions to your own life by completing the following exercises.

WINDOW SHOPPING Pay a visit to the retail website of your choice. Based on the marketing images it includes, what sort of customer do you think it is trying to attract? How do the site's layout, links, and icons stereotype this customer? Imagine that you are creating a website of your own, designed to attract a certain type of person, whether it is the soccer mom, macho guy, or hipster. Describe what your customer looks like, and then decide what sorts of elements and images you would use to draw the customer to your site.

RATING THE HEADLINES In television news, stories are typically covered in the order that news producers deem most important to least important. Watch a broadcast of the national evening news and keep a running record of the order in which the stories of the day are covered. What characterizing images stand out in your mind for each story? Write a brief essay in which you discuss why you think certain stories are given more weight or are broadcast earlier than others, and be sure to include examples from the broadcast you've just watched. If you were a news producer, in what order would you broadcast the same stories? Why?

THE REAL YOU Make a photo collage of images you think express facets of your identity, whether they are personal photos, advertisements for products you like, or pieces of art you find important. In class, swap collages with a peer and write a brief characterization of him or her based on the collage you've been given. Based on your collage, what do your classmates have to say about you? How closely does their description of you match your personality or identity? How might you have portrayed yourself differently to get them to describe you more accurately?

HUNGRY

3 How We EAT

Which rules dictate the foods we put in our bodies?

Introduction

Scripting the Perfect Meal

Few activities seem as straightforward as eating. We do it so regularly and for such apparently obvious reasons, it's hard at first to believe there's all that much to it. We're hungry, we eat. What's so complicated about that? Because we tend to treat eating as such a given, such an essential and unexamined part of our lives, it's easy to assume that the choices we make about it are entirely individual. Some people like Chicken McNuggets while others prefer sushi; some of us are die-hard vegetarians while others fall into the meat-and-potatoes camp. Whichever way we slice it, however, the underlying assumption is the same: How and what we eat are, in every sense of the phrase, matters of personal taste.

We might want to pause, however, before too quickly accepting this premise. We do, after all, live in a world that presents us with an almost endless array of food-related choices. For starters, there's the question of *what* to eat. Meat or tofu? Homemade or takeout? Organic or processed? High carb, low carb, or no carb? Following this, there is the question of *how* to eat. Alone or with friends? Driving in our cars or sitting in front of the TV? Fresh from a wok or out of a microwave? And then, there are those questions concerning the economics of eating: Do we shop at 7-11 or Whole Foods? Do we need to buy what's on sale, or can we splurge instead? When we really stop to think about it, how *do* we make up our minds?

In answering these questions, we would do well to start by acknowledging a basic (if often overlooked) fact about our modern food culture: No matter how instinctive our individual eating choices feel to us, they aren't, in the strictest sense, personal at all. We don't make our decisions about food all by ourselves; we get a lot of help. From diet books to FDA guidelines, fast-food commercials to gourmet magazines, we are surrounded by images and instructions, messages and advice — all of which aim to fix our "proper" relationship to food. Our culture has rules for what types of food we are supposed to eat, when we are supposed to eat them, and in what amounts. We have rules for how different meals should be prepared and others for how they should be hosted. And rules dictate how much all of these different things cost.

What is normal?

"Atkins Diet: The Rules of Induction

Rule 4. Eat nothing that isn't on the Acceptable Foods list. And that means absolutely nothing. Your 'just this one taste won't hurt' rationalization is the kiss of failure during this phase of Atkins."

Atkins Nutritional Approach

What does this diet advice ask you to believe? What are the ideas, values, or attitudes it asks you to accept as normal?

Whether these rules take the form of government-issued regulations about growth hormones, diet fads proscribing our daily allowance of carbohydrates, fast-food commercials instructing us to supersize our selections, or Web sites extolling the benefits of going vegan, every one of these rules reminds us of the same inescapable truth: Our food choices are framed long before we ever set foot in the kitchen, the grocery store, or the restaurant.

What is normal?

U.S. Department of Agriculture

Do you share the attitude toward eating presented here? Should we automatically accept it as normal?

Food for Thought

Nor are these rules concerned solely with how we *act*. They play just as important a role in shaping how we *think* as well. Whether this means following the 15 percent tipping rule or memorizing Dr. Phil's ten steps to a slimmer waistline, every time we live up to one of our culture's food-related instructions we simultaneously endorse the value or ideas that underlie it. To illustrate, let's compare two representative, if distinct, eating experiences: a Thanksgiving dinner and a McDonald's meal. In each case, there are well-established and universally recognized rules for how these two meals are supposed to unfold. We know, for example, to expect only a few select items on the menu for each. We are far more likely to come across turkey and cranberry sauce at the Thanksgiving table than veggie kabobs or tuna salad, and burgers and fries at the fast-food counter rather than tofu stir-fry. We also know that, in each case, very different dress codes apply. Cut-off jeans are far more appropriate when we are sitting in a plastic booth at McDonald's than when we are sitting at a holiday dinner table. And we know, finally, that there exist very different social rituals as well. Napkins go on laps and pleases and thank-yous accompany requests for food at a Thanksgiving gathering, while at McDonald's it is OK to eat with your hands and to throw away plates, containers, and napkins once the meal is finished.

These sorts of differences aren't terribly difficult to list. A bit trickier to discern, however, are the ways these instructions simultaneously function as social scripts. When we live up to the more formal expectations of a traditional Thanksgiving dinner, we are doing more than playing the role of a particular kind of diner. In donning this costume and adhering to this script, we are just as firmly giving our assent to a number of related notions: about the importance of tradition, about the special role that home and family should play in commemorating national holidays, even about which version of American history to accept as right. Similarly, when we assume the role of the typical fast-food consumer, our performance registers our tacit acceptance of a number of unspoken priorities: processed over "whole" foods, speed and efficiency over patience, convenience over nutrition.

This particular relationship — between the eating roles we take on and the eating rules we follow on the one hand and the social norms that underlie them on the other — links all of the readings in this chapter. Because our eating habits offer such a sensitive barometer of our current ideals and anxieties, each of the following selections uses its portrait of eating as a jumping-off point for investigating a larger issue or controversy to which food is connected. In several cases, writers focus their attention on the ways our contemporary food system is overseen and regulated. Pursuing this line of inquiry, Nicholas Kristof poses hard questions about our current food-stamp policy, calling legislative leaders to task for what he considers to be the government's callous "cruelty" toward poor Americans. Paul Schwennesen, on the other hand, offers a surprising defense of carnivorism, arguing for a radical revaluing of meat eating as an "ethical" act. Offering a unique twist on the locavore movement, Brendan Buhler makes the provocative case for roadkill as "the most ethical meat." Other selections focus on some of the different cultural attitudes embedded within our current eating practices. In what ways and for what reasons, these writers ponder, have we learned to differentiate ideal from taboo forms of eating? And what are the consequences of trying to live up to these distinctions? Surveying the cultural history of "gluttony," Francine Prose indicts our contemporary society for its long-standing demonization of overeating, a tradition that has led many of us to stigmatize our overweight population as victims of food, social misfits, or pariahs. Addressing what we might consider the flip side of this issue, Caroline Knapp chronicles her own decade-long struggle with anorexia, a struggle that revolved around an effort to make sense of our culture's treacherous and contradictory injunctions to be "slim" and "beautiful." In her journalistic account of eating in the inner city, Erika Nicole Kendall works to debunk a different kind of stereotype: those "food myths" that inaccurately and unjustly define the residents of these areas as

What is normal?

"How do I prepare my TOMBSTONE FOR ONE Pizza? Toaster Oven/ Conventional Oven Cooking Directions: Preheat the oven to 400 degrees Fahrenheit. Remove pizza from box and overwrap. Discard silver cooking circle. Place pizza directly on oven rack in Center Position (8 to 10 inches from bottom of oven). Bake according to the table below, or until the cheese is melted and edges are golden brown. Oven temperatures vary, so adjust baking time and oven temperature as necessary. Supreme: 12 to 16 minutes. Extra Cheese: 9 to 12 minutes. Pepperoni: 9 to 12 minutes. CAUTION: Do not use silver circle in toaster oven or conventional oven."

Frequently Asked Questions, www.kraftfoods.com

What kind of social script do these instructions write? What would it feel like to act out this script in our own lives? And can this kind of social script be rewritten?

helpless, benighted victims. Taking a look at the ways that eating intersects with social class, Tracie McMillan reflects on the ways food can serve as an instrument for distancing and dividing us. And finally, Sam Dolnick challenges some of the core assumptions about overeating and weight in an article that tries to make sense of what he terms the "obesity-hunger paradox."

e macmillanhighered.com/actingout
e-Readings > Casey Neistat, *Calorie Detective*

NICHOLAS KRISTOF

Prudence or Cruelty?

While it can often feel like an entirely personal activity, the truth is that eating is connected to some of the most pressing political, economic, and ethical questions of our day. It shapes not only how we approach health and nutrition but also how we think about such overtly political issues as poverty, social class, and social justice. It is this insight that underlies Nicholas Kristof's unsparing assessment of our federal food-stamp policy. Calling out congressional leaders for their callous indifference to the plight of hungry children, Kristof's essay highlights the social, economic, and moral issues our debates over food often involve. Kristof is a two-time Pulitzer Prize-winning columnist for the *New York Times*. He is also the coauthor of two books: *China Wakes: The Struggle for the Soul of a Rising Power* (1995) and *Thunder from the East: Portrait of a Rising Asia* (2000). This essay appeared in the *New York Times* in 2013.

WHEN MEMBERS OF CONGRESS DEBATE WHETHER TO SLASH THE food stamp program, they should ask if they really want more small children arriving at school having skipped breakfast.

As it is, in the last few days of the month before food stamps are distributed, some children often eat less and have trouble focusing, says Kisha Hill, a teacher in a high-poverty prekindergarten school in North Tulsa, Okla.

"Kids can't focus on studying when their stomachs are grumbling," Hill told me.

Some 47 million Americans receive food stamps, including some who would otherwise go hungry—or hungrier. A recent government study found that about 5 percent of American households have "very low food security," which means that food can run out before the end of the month. In almost a third of those households, an adult reported not eating for an entire day because there wasn't money for food.

In almost a third of those households, an adult reported not eating for an entire day because there wasn't money for food.

Meanwhile, 14 percent of American toddlers suffer iron deficiency. Malnutrition isn't the only cause, but it's an important one—and these children may suffer impaired brain development as a result. This kind of malnutrition in America is tough to measure, because some children are simultaneously malnourished and overweight, but experts agree it's a problem. We expect to find malnourished or anemic children in Africa and Asia, but it's dispiriting to see this in a country as wealthy as our own.

Let me take that back. It's not just dispiriting. It's also infuriating.

"The cutback in food stamps represents a clear threat to the nutritional status and health of America's children," says Dr. Irwin Redlener, the president of the Children's Health Fund and a professor of pediatrics at Columbia University. Dr. Redlener said that one result of cutbacks will be more kids with anemia and educational difficulties.

Food stamp recipients already took a cut in benefits this month, and they may face more. The Senate Democratic version of the farm bill would cut food stamps by $4 billion over 10 years, while the House Republican version would slash them by $40 billion.

We expect to find malnourished or anemic children in Africa and Asia, but it's dispiriting to see this in a country as wealthy as our own.

More than 90 percent of benefits go to families living below the poverty line, according to federal government data, and nearly two-thirds of the recipients are children, elderly, or disabled.

Let's remember that the government already subsidizes lots of food. When wealthy executives dine at fancy French restaurants, part of the bill is likely to be deducted from taxes, which amounts to a subsidy from taxpayers. How is it that food subsidies to anemic children are more controversial than food subsidies to executives enjoying coq au vin?

Meanwhile, the same farm bill that is hotly debated because of food stamps includes agricultural subsidies that don't go just to struggling farmers but also, in recent years, to 50 billionaires or companies they are involved in, according to the Environmental Working Group, a Washington research group.

Among the undeserving people receiving farm subsidies has been a *New York Times* columnist. Yes, I have been paid $588 a year not to grow crops on wooded land I own in Oregon (I then forward the money to a maternity hospital in Somaliland). When our country pays a New York journalist not to grow crops in an Oregon forest, there's a problem with the farm bill—but it's not food stamps.

Granted, safety-net spending is more about treating symptoms of poverty than causes, and we may get more bang for the buck when we chip away at long-term poverty through early education, home visitation for infants, job training, and helping teenagers avoid unwanted pregnancies.

That said, food stamps do work in important ways. For starters, they effectively reduce the number of children living in extreme poverty by half, according to the Center on Budget and Policy Priorities in Washington.

By improving nutrition of young children, food stamps also improve long-term outcomes. In recent years, mounting scholarship has found that malnutrition in utero or in small children has lasting consequences. One reason seems to be that when a fetus or small child is undernourished, it is programmed to anticipate food shortages for the remainder of its life. If food later becomes plentiful, the metabolic mismatch can lead to diabetes, obesity, and heart disease.

An excellent study last year from the National Bureau of Economic Research followed up on the rollout of food stamps, county by county, between 1961 and 1975. It found that those who began receiving food stamps by the age of 5 had better health as adults. Women who as small children had benefited from food stamps were more likely to go farther in school, earn more money, and stay off welfare.

So slashing food stamp benefits—overwhelmingly for children, the disabled, and the elderly—wouldn't be a sign of prudent fiscal management by Congress. It would be a mark of shortsighted cruelty.

DISCUSSION

1. How do you understand the juxtaposition within the title between the terms "prudence" and "cruelty"? Why do you think Kristof uses these two terms to frame his discussion of food stamps?
2. How do you think a member of Congress would respond to Kristof's essay? Do you think s/he would be persuaded by the argument Kristof makes? Why or why not?
3. Kristof repeatedly uses the word "slash" to describe the proposed cuts to food-stamp benefits Congress is currently considering. Why do you think he uses this particular term? How does it differ from a word like "reduce" or "cut"?

WRITING

4. Much of Kristof's critique here revolves around the statistics about childhood malnutrition he presents. Write an essay in which you analyze and evaluate the role this type of data plays in advancing Kristof's larger argument. What sort of connection between malnutrition and food-stamp policy is Kristof asserting here? Is it a connection that makes his call for changes to food-stamp legislation more credible or persuasive? How or how not?
5. Create a proposal that outlines what you believe should be the proper government policy concerning food stamps. How much support for this program should the government provide? What particular needs should it address? What limits should it establish? Then write a quick assessment of the ways your proposal compares to Kristof's. What are the key similarities and differences?
6. Erika Nicole Kendall's essay (p. 210) also links the discussion of food policy to the issue of poverty. In a brief essay, reflect on the key differences in the ways these two authors talk about food and poverty. To what extent does Kendall's account of "food deserts" (p. 210) provide further support for Kristof's call for greater governmental support for food stamps?

Rule **Maker** >>>>>>>>> *Rule* **Breaker**

"I am not sure if merely because of our size and success Whole Foods Market deserves the pejorative label 'Big Organic' or 'Industrial Organic,' or even to be linked to those categories. I would argue instead that organic agriculture owes much of its growth and success over the past 20 years to Whole Foods Market's successful growth and commitment to organic. As an organization we continually challenge ourselves to be responsible and ethical tenants of the planet. Through our stores, large and small organic farmers, both local and international, can offer their products to an increasingly educated population that is more interested in organics every day. . . . Whole Foods Market is one of the 'good guys' in this story about the 'industrialization of agriculture.' "

— JOHN MACKEY,
WHOLE FOODS CEO, 2006

"[T]he trickiest contradiction Whole Foods attempts to reconcile is the one between the industrialization of organic food and the pastoral ideals on which that industry has been built. The organic movement, as it was once called, has come a remarkably long way in the last thirty years, to the point where it now looks considerably less like a movement than a big business. . . . So is an industrial organic food chain finally a contradiction in terms? It's hard to escape the conclusion that it is. . . . As in so many other realms, nature's logic has proven no match for the logic of capitalism."

— MICHAEL POLLAN,
AUTHOR OF THE OMNIVORE'S DILEMMA, 2006

WHOLE FOODS VS. MICHAEL POLLAN

Since the 1960s and 1970s, the organic food industry has played a major role in reshaping how millions of Americans think about, shop for, and (of course) eat their food. Pioneered by a small cadre of local farmers, grocery co-op proprietors, and eco-conscious consumers, the organic movement cast itself in its early years as a revolutionary alternative to what was often termed the "corporate" or "industrial" food economy, a system typified by the giant, chain grocery store, with its row after row of frozen TV dinners, pesticide-coated oranges, canned vegetables, and potato chips. And yet, as such popular and profitable stores like Whole Foods and Trader Joe's have become national chains, many have begun to wonder whether any meaningful differences still exist between industrial and organic food. In a world where even Wal-Mart has begun marketing organic selections to its shoppers, does it still make sense to talk about this movement as a kind of anticorporate revolution? For observers like noted food author Michael Pollan, the answer is "not really." For people like Whole Foods CEO John Mackey, on the other hand, such doubts are shortsighted and unfair, overlooking the ways that the organic industry has succeeded in rewriting the rules by which countless Americans eat.

FIND THE RULES: Next time you're at the grocery store (whether it is an organic chain like Whole Foods or another corporate chain with an organic section), take notes on the way the store presents itself to you. In what ways is the décor designed to appeal to an organic foods shopper? How do the product labels and nutritional information for organic and nonorganic items compare? The price? After you have collected your observations, write a one-page summary describing your trip.

ANALYZE THE RULES: In a one-page essay, identify and evaluate the scripts and roles these rules create for the typical food consumer. What attitudes toward or feelings about organic food do these rules encourage shoppers to adopt? In your view, are they accurate or valid? Why?

MAKE YOUR OWN RULES: Proponents of organic farming and markets list many reasons for favoring these methods, including better nutrition, more responsible use of land, and reduced pollution from trucks that bring conventional products a long way to market. According to Michael Pollan, however, large organic grocery chains sometimes, to continue operating, resort to practices that are against their founding ideals. Write a one-page essay in which you propose a happy medium — that is, the type of shopping scenario that would preserve the organic ideals while allowing consumers to buy everything they needed. What complications might arise from the scenario you've proposed?

Erik Freeland/Corbis

PAUL SCHWENNESEN

The Ethics of Eating Meat

Is our willingness to consume animals for food evidence of our moral shortcomings as a society? Or is meat eating, rather, simply an expression of our essential natures? Schwennesen, a ranch owner with extensive experience raising and slaughtering animals for sale, argues emphatically for the latter view, offering readers a spirited defense of the morality of eating meat. Schwennesen appears frequently on FOX Business News and is a regular contributor to the Property and Environment Research Center. His writing has appeared in the *Freeman, American Spectator,* and the *Tucson Citizen*. This article appeared in the *Huffington Post* in 2012.

I KILL ANIMALS FOR A LIVING.

I do it so others, as well as myself, can eat them. This accident of circumstance probably disqualifies me from any serious ethical discussion of meat eating. After all, I can hardly claim objectivity. Then again, who can? I live very close to the forces of nature that give (and take) life and therefore have an informed, if undoubtedly nearsighted, sense of what it is I do.

But is it ethical?

Asking whether eating meat is "ethical" is like asking whether having sex is ethical. Biological imperatives do not pander to such arbitrary distinctions.

My meat-eating is ethical, in the sense that it is not gratuitous; I understand intimately the implications and contradictions of my consumption. I know how it is that my beeves are born, the grasses they like and the ones they don't. I've saved the lives of calves and butchered their mothers in the same afternoon. I thank each for the age-old sacrifice of prey to predator and I swear they understand. I neither rejoice in the blood nor shy from it. This is life. This is ethics.

Asking whether eating meat is "ethical" is like asking whether having sex is ethical.

For me, my proximate, deliberate understanding of what I do defines ethical behavior as a whole: the social moderation of otherwise unrestrained individual yearnings. In my mind, eating #906 (a red mottle-face cow with upturned horns currently braising in the slow cooker) is an ethically different activity than eating a Big Mac on the run.

The fact that I feel comfortable making such a distinction indicates something fundamental about ethics: they evolve. Our current handwringing over what we eat is clearly a privilege born of abundance. Room for such ruminations are only created after the belly hasn't room for anything else. We agonize over meat consumption because we can afford to. Lucky us.

"Ethics" exist as social shorthand; a distilled collective conscience that varies with the social reality it reflects. Ethics do not stand like clean-cut traffic cops in the path of natural urges; they are more like cautionary rumble-strips as we careen down lives strewn with choices. Ethical consumption of meat, therefore, is based upon timing, circumstance, and conscientious understanding of what society deems appropriate. In modern Western culture at least, you are "unethical" if you cannot moderate a biological sexual urge. It is likewise "unethical" to fulfill biological carnivorous urges upon, say, kittens.

We have evolved from a society in which nearly everyone knew the intimate realities and consequences of eating meat to one in which nearly no one does. We have commercially outsourced the twinge of guilt, the pang of discomfort, the heart-race of witnessing a death to just a handful among us. Is there an ethical distinction between the deaths caused by a yeoman farmer who grimly butchers a hog in the fall and a minimum-wage factory worker who mechanically butchers six thousand in a morning? Many of us now see an ethical nuance. Our physical capacities to produce and consume have altered dramatically in the last sixty years; our ethical capacity to accept these realities are altering as well.

Ethics do not stand like clean-cut traffic cops in the path of natural urges; they are more like cautionary rumble-strips as we careen down lives strewn with choices.

My occupation, as a result, caters to omnivores and more than a few "recovering vegetarians" who prefer (apparently) the conscientious killing I practice. I therefore raise my cattle with sentiment but cannot stray into the realm of sentimentality. I recognize that life rests upon the consumption of the unwilling. I obey this ecological truth while simultaneously working within the artificial, changeable lines society delineates. This too, is natural.

Eating meat, particularly #906, is ethical because most people think it is. That is, perhaps, about all one can say.

DISCUSSION

1. Schwennesen refers to the practice of eating meat as a "biological imperative" (p. 178). Do you agree? What attitude toward meat eating does this phrase suggest?
2. In recounting his experiences as a rancher, Schwennesen offers what he views as a crucial distinction: I "raise my cattle with sentiment but cannot stray into the realm of sentimentality" (p. 179). How do you understand the difference between "sentiment" and "sentimentality"? Do you see the same kind of ethical distinction Schwennesen perceives?
3. For Schwennesen, ethics are best understood as evolving and changeable social scripts: "'Ethics' exist as social shorthand; a distilled collective conscience that varies with the social reality it reflects" (p. 179). How do you respond to this assertion? Do you share the view that our ethical principles or moral stances depend upon the "social reality" they reflect? What are the strengths and weaknesses of this view?

WRITING

4. Here is how Schwennesen resolves the moral questions posed by raising and slaughtering animals for a living: "I've saved the lives of calves and butchered their mothers in the same afternoon. I thank each for the age-old sacrifice of prey to predator and I swear they understand. I neither rejoice in the blood nor shy from it. This is life. This is ethics" (p. 178). Write a short essay in which you describe and evaluate the model of "ethics" Schwennesen presents here. Does the relationship he sketches between humans and animals ("predator and prey") seem like a moral one? In your view, is he able to reconcile the contradiction between "saving" animals on the one hand and "butchering" them on the other? If not, what are the flaws or gaps in his argument?
5. "We have evolved," Schwennesen writes, "from a society in which nearly everyone knew the intimate realities and consequences of eating meat to one in which nearly no one does. We have commercially outsourced the twinge of guilt, the pang of discomfort, the heart-race of witnessing a death to just a handful among us" (p. 179). In a three- to five-page essay, offer an extended response to and evaluation of the claim Schwennesen makes here. As you do, pay particular attention to the language he uses to convey his point. How does such language help him make his larger argument about our growing disconnection from the "realities and consequences of eating meat"? And do you find this argument persuasive or not? Why?
6. From a very different perspective, Erika Nicole Kendall is also interested in debunking some of our culture's most entrenched assumptions about food. Write an essay in which you analyze the ways their respective commentaries compare. What are the similarities and differences between the stereotypes or "myths" each addresses? Which critique do you find more persuasive? Why?

FRANCINE PROSE

The Wages of Sin

When it comes to eating, how much is too much? And where do we learn to draw this line? Taking aim at our current fixation on food, dieting, and body image, Francine Prose contemplates whether ours has become a culture in which overeating now stands as the preeminent sign of our moral and physical failure. Prose graduated from Radcliffe College in 1968 and currently lives and writes in New York City. She is the author of nine novels, including *The Blue Angel* (2001), a finalist for the National Book Award, and *A Changed Man* (2005), which won the Dayton Literary Peace Prize. She has also published several nonfiction books, including *Gluttony* (2003), from which the following is excerpted, and *Reading Like a Writer* (2006). Her most recent works are the novel *Goldengrove* (2008), the nonfiction book *Anne Frank: The Book, the Life, the After Life* (2009), and the memoir *My New American Life* (2012).

MORE AND MORE OFTEN, WE READ ARTICLES AND HEAR TV commentators advocating government intervention to protect us from the greed of a corporate culture that profits from our unhealthy attraction to sugary and fatty foods. Legal experts discuss the feasibility of mounting class action suits—on the model of the recent and ongoing litigation against so-called big tobacco companies—against fast-food restaurants, junk-food manufacturers, and advertisers who target children with ads for salty fried snacks and brightly colored candy masquerading as breakfast cereal.

What's slightly more disturbing is the notion that not only do fat people need to be monitored, controlled, and saved from their gluttonous impulses, but that we need to be saved from them—that certain forms of social control might be required to help the overweight resist temptation. Writing in the *San Francisco Chronicle*, essayist Ruth Rosen has suggested that such actions might be motivated by compassion for such innocent victims as the parents of a child whose overweight helped lead to diabetes, or the child of a parent who died from weight-related causes. Of course the bottom line is concern for our pocketbooks, for the cost—shared by the wider population—of treating those who suffer from obesity-related ailments. As a partial remedy, Rosen proposes that schools and employers might forbid the sale of junk food on campus and in offices. Finally, she suggests that, in a more glorious future, the host who serves his guests greasy potato chips and doughnuts will incur the same horrified disapproval as the smoker who lights up—and blows smoke in our faces.

Rosen is not alone in her belief that legislation may be required to regulate the social costs of overeating. A recent item on CBS worriedly considered the alarming growth in the number of overweight and obese young people—a group that now comprises 14 percent of American children. According to the news clip, overweight was soon expected to surpass cigarette smoking as the major preventable cause of death: each year, 350,000 people die of obesity-related causes. Thirteen billion dollars is spent annually on food ads directed at children, and four out of five ads are for some excessively sugary or fatty product. The problem is undeniable, but once more the projected solution gives one pause; several interviewees raised the possibility of suing the purveyors of potato chips and candy bars. How far we have come from Saint Augustine and John Cassian and Chrysostom, taking it for granted that the struggle against temptation would be waged in the glutton's heart and mind—and not, presumably, in the law courts.

> You're so fat when they pierced your ears, they had to use a harpoon.
> You're so fat you've got to put on lipstick with a paint roller.

In studies that have examined the causes and motives behind the stigmatization of the overweight, such prejudice has been found to derive from the widely accepted notion that fat people are at fault, responsible for their weight and appearance, that they are self-indulgent, sloppy, lazy, morally lax, lacking in the qualities of self-denial and impulse control that our society (still so heavily influenced by the legacy of Puritanism) values and rewards. In a 1978 book, *The Seven Deadly Sins: Society and Evil,* sociologist Stanford M. Lyman takes a sociocultural approach to the reasons why we are so harsh in our condemnation of the so-called glutton.

> The apparently voluntary character of food gluttony serves to point up why it is more likely to seem "criminal" than sick, an act of moral defalcation rather than medical pathology. Although gluttony is not proscribed by the criminal law, it partakes of some of the social sanctions and moral understandings that govern orientations toward those who commit crimes. . . . Gluttony is an excessive *self*-indulgence. Even in its disrespect for the body it overvalues the ego that it slavishly satisfies.[1]

Most of us would no doubt claim that we are too sensible, compassionate, and enlightened to feel prejudice against the obese. We would never tell the sorts of cruel jokes scattered throughout this chapter. But let's consider how we feel when we've taken our already cramped seat in coach class on the airplane and suddenly our seatmate appears—a man or woman whose excessive weight promises to make our journey even more uncomfortable than we'd anticipated. Perhaps, contemplating a trip of this sort, we might find ourselves inclined to support Southwest Airline's discriminatory two-seats-per-large-passenger rule. Meanwhile, as we try not to stare at our sizable traveling companion, we might as well be the medieval monks glaring at the friar who's helped himself to an extra portion. For what's involved in both cases is our notion of one's proper share, of surfeit and shortage—not enough food in one case, not enough space in the other.

"The glutton is also noticeable as a defiler of his own body space. His appetite threatens to engulf the spaces of others as he spreads out to take more than one person's ordinary allotment of territory. If he grows too large, he may no longer fit into ordinary chairs . . . and require special arrangements in advance of his coming.[2] The glutton's "crime" is crossing boundaries that we jealously guard and that are defined by our most primitive instincts: hunger, territoriality—that is to say, survival.

So we come full circle back to the language of crime and innocence, sin and penance, guilt and punishment—a view of overweight frequently adopted and internalized by the obese themselves. "Many groups of dieters whom I studied," writes Natalie Allon, "believed that fatness was the outcome of immoral self-indulgence. Group dieters used much religious language in considering themselves bad or good dieters—words such as sinner, saint, devil, angel, guilt, transgression, confession, absolution, diet Bible—as they partook of the rituals of group dieting."[3] Nor does the association between gluttony and the language of religion exist solely in the minds of dieters, the obese, and the food-obsessed. In fact it's extremely common to speak of having overeaten as having "been bad"; rich, fattening foods are advertised as being "sinfully delicious"; and probably most of us have thought or confessed the fact that we've felt "guilty" for having eaten more than we should have.

The glutton's "crime" is crossing boundaries that we jealously guard and that are defined by our most primitive instincts: hunger, territoriality—that is to say, survival.

Like the members of other Twelve-Step programs, and not unlike the medieval gluttons who must have felt inspired to repent and pray for divine assistance in resisting temptation, the members of Overeaters Anonymous employ the terminology of religion. *Lifeline,* the magazine of Overeaters Anonymous, is filled with stories of healing and recovery, first-person accounts in which God was asked to intercede, to provide a spiritual awakening, and to remove the dangerous and destructive flaws from the recovering overeater's character.

Routinely, the capacity to achieve sobriety and abstinence—which for OA members means the ability to restrict one's self to three healthy and sensible meals a day—is credited to divine mercy and love, and to the good effects of an intimate and sustaining relationship with God. In one testimonial, a woman reports that coming to her first meeting and identifying herself as a recovering compulsive eater was more difficult for her than to say that she was a shoplifter, a serial killer, or a prostitute. Only after admitting that she was powerless over food and asking for the help of a higher power was she at last able to end her unhappy career as a "grazer and a binger."

For perhaps obvious reasons, the term "gluttony" is now rarely used as a synonym for compulsive eating. Yet Stanford Lyman conflates the two to make the point that our culture's attitude toward the obese is not unlike an older society's view of the gluttonous sinner:

> Societal opposition to gluttony manifests itself in a variety of social control devices and institutional arrangements. Although rarely organized as a group, very fat individuals at times seem to form a much beset minority, objects of calculating discrimination and bitter prejudice. Stigmatized because their addiction to food is so visible in its consequences, the obese find themselves ridiculed, rejected, and repulsed by many of those who do not overindulge. Children revile them on the streets, persons of average size refuse to date, dance, or dine with them, and many businesses, government, and professional associations refuse to employ them. So great is the pressure to conform to the dictates of the slimness culture in America that occasionally an overweight person speaks out, pointing to the similarities of his condition to that of racial and national minorities.[4]

Indeed, the overweight have found a forum in which to speak out, at the meetings, conventions, and in the bimonthly newsletter sponsored by NAAFA—the National Association to Advance Fat Acceptance. A recent issue of the newsletter, available on the internet, calls for readers to write to the government to protest the National Institutes of Health's ongoing studies of normal-sized children to find out if obesity might have a metabolic basis. There are directions for giving money and establishing a living trust to benefit NAAFA, reviews of relevant new books, a report on the Trunk Sale at a NAAFA gathering in San Francisco, an update on the struggle to force auto manufacturers to provide seat belts that can save the lives of passengers who weigh over 215 pounds, and an article on the problems—the fear of appearing in public in a bathing suit, the narrow ladders that often provide the only access to swimming pools—that make it more difficult for the overweight to get the exercise that they need. There is a brief discussion of how obesity should be defined, and another about the effectiveness of behavioral psychotherapy in helping patients lose weight. Finally, there are grateful letters from readers whose lives have been improved by the support and sustenance they gain from belonging to NAAFA.

Equally fervent—if somewhat less affirmative and forgiving—are the gospel tracts, also available on-line. One of the most heartfelt and persuasive is the work of a preacher identified only as George Clark:

> After conducting healing campaigns and mailing out thousands of anointed handkerchiefs—since 1930—I have learned that the greatest physical cause of sickness among the people of God is coming from this lust for overindulgence in eating. . . . Tens of thousands of truly converted people are sick and are suffering with heart trouble coming from high blood pressure and other ailments which result from overeating. . . . Did you ever wonder why artists have never depicted any of Jesus' disciples as being overweight or of the fleshy type? No one could have followed Jesus very long and remained overweight. . . . If eating too much has brought on high blood pressure, heart trouble, or many of the other diseases which come from being overweight, then God requires a reduction in your eating.

Given our perhaps misguided sense of living in a secular society, it's startling to find that our relationship with food is still so commonly translated directly into the language of God and the devil, of sin and repentance. But why should we be surprised, when we are constantly being reminded that our feelings about our diet and our body can be irrational, passionate, and closer to the province of faith and superstition than that of reason and science?

NOTES

[1]Stanford M. Lyman, *The Seven Deadly Sins: Society and Evil* (New York: St. Martin's Press, 1978), 220.

[2]Ibid., 223.

[3]Benjamin Wolman, ed., *Psychological Aspects of Obesity: A Handbook* (New York: Van Nostrand Reinhold, 1982), 148.

[4]Lyman, *Seven Deadly Sins,* 218.

BIBLIOGRAPHY

Albala, Ken. *Eating Right in the Renaissance.* Berkeley: University of California Press, 2002.

Augustine, Saint. *The Confessions of Saint Augustine,* trans. Edward B. Pusey, D. D. New York: The Modern Library, 1949.

Bell, Rudoph M. *Holy Anorexia.* Chicago: University of Chicago Press, 1985.

Chaucer, Geoffrey. *The Works of Geoffrey Chaucer,* ed. F. N. Robinson. Boston: Houghton Mifflin, 1957.

Chernin, Kim. *The Obsession*. New York: Harper Perennial, 1981.

Chesterton, G. K. *Saint Thomas Aquinas*. New York: Image Books, Doubleday, 2001.

Fielding, Henry. *Tom Jones*. New York: The Modern Library, 1994.

Fisher, M. F. K. *The Art of Eating*. New York: Vintage, 1976.

Lyman, Stanford M. *The Seven Deadly Sins: Society and Evil*. New York: St. Martin's Press, 1978.

Petronius. *The Satyricon*, trans. William Arrowsmith. New York: Meridian, 1994.

Pleij, Herman. *Dreaming of Cockaigne*, trans. Diane Webb. New York: Columbia University Press, 2001.

Rabelais, François. *Gargantua and Pantagruel*, trans. Burton Raffel. New York: W. W. Norton, 1991.

Roth, Geneen. *When Food Is Love*. New York: Plume, 1991.

Schwartz, Hillel. *Never Satisfied: A Cultural History of Fantasies and Fat*. New York: The Free Press, 1986.

Shaw, Teresa M. *The Burden of the Flesh: Fasting and Sexuality in Early Christianity*. Minneapolis: Fortress Press, 1996.

Spenser, Edmund. *The Faerie Queene*. New York: E. P. Dutton & Company, 1964.

Wolman, Benjamin, ed., with Stephen DeBerry, editorial associate. *Psychological Aspects of Obesity: A Handbook*. New York: Van Nostrand Reinhold, 1982.

DISCUSSION

1. Elsewhere in this essay Prose writes, "The so-called glutton is a walking rebuke to our self-control, our self-denial, and to our shaky faith that if we watch ourselves, then surely death cannot touch us." What exactly does she mean by this? Do you think she is right? In what ways do we use the images and examples of those body types that are regarded in our culture as deficient or abnormal as role models for what *not* to be ourselves?
2. From diet books to exercise videos, there is no shortage of material that scripts the ways we are and are not supposed to eat. Choose one such example from our current culture and describe the specific steps it itemizes. What does this list imply is the right attitude we should have toward food? How does it endeavor to get readers to adopt this view? What incentives does it offer? What punishments does it threaten?
3. There is, according to Prose, a close and complex connection between gluttony and guilt. Whether in the form of FDA warnings or ad copy for "sinfully delicious desserts," overeating is regularly associated in our culture with some kind of misbehavior or even moral failing. What do you make of this connection? Choose an example from our pop culture that you think is designed to teach this kind of guilt.

WRITING

4. Choose some venue (for example, a fast-food restaurant, health club, doctor's office, or similar place) that in your view endeavors to teach us specific attitudes about overeating. Spend a couple of hours there. First, write out as comprehensive a description of this place as you can. What kind of people do you observe? What sorts of equipment or décor are present? Next, write a short essay in which you speculate about the rules for eating that this venue attempts to instill. What relationship to food are people here encouraged to form? How does this relationship get presented or packaged as the norm?
5. One of the hallmarks of our contemporary culture, according to Prose, is that overeating is no longer viewed as a vice or sin but as an illness. Do you agree? What are some of the ways this change in thinking is communicated in popular culture or in the media? Write an essay in which you argue for or against gluttony as a moral issue.
6. Prose and Sam Dolnick (p. 219) address the issue of gluttony in very different ways. Write an essay in which you compare the ways each explores the issue of overeating. How does each of these writers define and understand this phenomenon? How does each writer use the issue of overeating as a lens for commenting upon other social rules? Do you think this strategy is effective? Why or why not?

CAROLINE KNAPP

Add Cake, Subtract Self-Esteem

When are our appetites about more than just food? Detailing her own struggle with anorexia, Caroline Knapp offers some pointed observations about the ways our contemporary culture fosters "disorders of appetite" in women, creating an environment in which it has become normal to define questions of female self-worth and female power in relation to what one does (or does not) eat. Knapp was a columnist for the *Boston Phoenix.* Some of the pieces she wrote as the anonymous "Alice K." are collected in *Alice K.'s Guide to Life* (1994). Her other books include *Drinking: A Love Story* (1996) and *Pack of Two: The Intricate Bond between People and Dogs* (1998). She died in 2002 from complications of lung cancer, just after completing her last book, *Appetites: Why Women Want* (2003), the book in which the following essay appears.

THE LURE OF STARVING—THE BAFFLING, SEDUCTIVE HOOK—WAS that it soothed, a balm of safety and containment that seemed to remove me from the ordinary, fraught world of human hunger and place me high above it, in a private kingdom of calm.

This didn't happen immediately, this sense of transcendent solace, and there certainly wasn't anything blissful or even long-lived about the state; starving is a painful, relentless experience, and also a throbbingly dull one, an entire life boiled down to a singular sensation (physical hunger) and a singular obsession (food). But when I think back on those years, which lasted through my mid-twenties, and when I try to get underneath the myriad meanings and purposes of such a bizarre fixation, that's what I remember most pointedly—the calm, the relief from an anxiety that felt both oceanic and nameless. For years, I ate the same foods every day, in exactly the same manner, at exactly the same times. I devoted a monumental amount of energy to this endeavor—thinking about food, resisting food, observing other people's relationships with food, anticipating my own paltry indulgences in food—and this narrowed, specific, driven rigidity made me feel supremely safe: one concern, one feeling, everything else just background noise.

Disorders of appetite—food addictions, compulsive shopping, promiscuous sex—have a kind of semiotic brilliance, expressing in symbol and metaphor what women themselves may not be able to express in words, and I can deconstruct anorexia with the best of them. Anorexia is a response to cultural images of the female body—waiflike, angular—that both capitulates to the ideal and also mocks it, strips away all the ancillary signs of sexuality, strips away breasts and hips and butt and leaves in their place a garish caricature, a cruel cartoon of flesh and bone. It is a form of silent protest, a hunger strike that expresses some deep discomfort with the experience of inhabiting an adult female body. It is a way of co-opting the traditional female preoccupation with food and weight by turning the obsession upside down, directing the energy not toward the preparation and provision and ingestion of food but toward the shunning of it, and all that it represents: abundance, plenitude, caretaking. Anorexia is this, anorexia is that. Volumes have been written about such symbolic expressions, and there's truth to all of them, and they are oddly comforting truths: They help to decipher this puzzle; they help to explain why eating disorders are the third most common chronic illness among females in the United States, and why fifteen percent of young women have substantially disordered attitudes and behaviors toward food and eating, and why the incidence of eating disorders has increased by thirty-six percent every five years since the 1950s. They offer some hope—if we can understand this particularly devastating form of self-inflicted cruelty, maybe we can find a way to stop it.

I, too, am tempted to comfort and explain, to look back with the cool detachment of twenty years and offer a crisp critique: a little cultural commentary here, a little metaphorical analysis there. But what recedes into the background amid such explanations—and what's harder to talk about because it's intangible and stubborn and vast—is the core, the underlying drive, the sensation that not only made anorexia feel so seductively viable for me some two decades ago but that also informs the central experience of appetite for so many women, the first feeling we bring to the table of hunger: anxiety, a sense of being overwhelmed.

There is a particular whir of agitation about female hunger, a low-level thrumming of shoulds and shouldn'ts and can'ts and wants that can be so chronic and familiar it becomes a kind of feminine Muzak, easy to dismiss, or to tune out altogether, even if you're actively participating in it. Last spring, a group of women gathered in my living room to talk about appetite, all of them teachers and administrators at a local school and all of them adamant that this whole business—weight, food, managing hunger—troubles them not at all. "Weight," said one, "is not really an issue for me." "No," said another, "not for me, either." And a third: "I don't really think about what I'm going to eat from day to day. Basically, I just eat what I want."

This was a cheerful and attractive group, ages twenty-two to forty-one, and they were all so insistent about their normalcy around food that, were it not for the subtle strain of caveat that ran beneath their descriptions, I might have believed them.

The caveats had to do with rules, with attitudes as ingrained as reflexes, and with a particularly female sense of justified reward: They are at the center of this whir, an anxious jingle of mandate and restraint. The woman who insisted that weight is "not really an issue," for instance, also noted that she only allows herself to eat dessert, or second helpings at dinner, if she's gone to the gym that day. No workout, no dessert. The woman who agreed with her (no, not an issue for her, either) echoed that sentiment. "Yeah," she nodded, "if I don't work out, I start to feel really gross about food and I'll try to cut back." A third said she eats "normally" but noted that she always makes a point of leaving at least one bite of food on her plate, every meal, no exceptions. And the woman who said she "basically just eats what she wants" added, "I mean, if someone brings a cake into the office, I'll have a tiny slice, and I might not eat the frosting, but it's not like a big deal or anything. I just scrape the frosting off."

Tiny slices, no frosting, forty-five minutes on the StairMaster: These are the conditions, variations on a theme of vigilance and self-restraint that I've watched women dance to all my life, that I've danced to myself instinctively and still have to work to resist. I walk into a health club locker room and feel an immediate impulse toward scrutiny, the kneejerk measuring of self against other: *That one has great thighs, this one's gained weight, who's thin, who's fat, how do I compare?* I overhear snippets of conversation, constraints unwittingly articulated and upheld in a dollop of lavish praise here *(You look fabulous, have you lost weight?)*, a whisper of recriminating judgment there *(She looks awful, has she gained weight?)*, and I automatically turn to look: Who looks fabulous, who looks awful? I go to a restaurant with a group of women and pray that we can order lunch without falling into the semi-covert business of collective monitoring, in which levels of intake and restraint are aired, compared, noticed: *What are you getting? Is that all you're having? A salad? Oh, please.* There's a persistent awareness of self in relation to other behind this kind of behavior, and also a tacit nod to the idea that there are codes to adhere to, and self-effacing apologies to be made if those codes are broken. *I'm such a hog*, says the woman who breaks rank, ordering a cheeseburger when everyone else has salad.

That one has great thighs, this one's gained weight, who's thin, who's fat, how do I compare?

Can't, shouldn't, I'm a moose. So much of this is waved away as female vanity—this tedious nattering about calories and fat, this whining, shallow preoccupation with surfaces—but I find it poignant, and painful in a low-level but chronic way, and also quite revealing. One of the lingering cultural myths about gender is that women are bad at math—they lack confidence for it, they have poor visual-spatial skills, they simply don't excel at numbers the way boys do. This theory has been widely challenged over the years, and there's scant evidence to suggest that girls are in any way neurologically ill-equipped to deal with algebra or calculus. But I'd challenge the myth on different grounds: Women are actually superb at math; they just happen to engage in their own variety of it, an intricate personal math in which desires are split off from one another, weighed, balanced, traded, assessed. These are the mathematics of desire, a system of self-limitation and monitoring based on the fundamental premise that appetites are at best risky, at worst impermissible, that indulgence must be bought and paid for. Hence the rules and caveats: Before you open the lunch menu or order that cheeseburger or consider eating the cake with the frosting intact, haul out the psychic calculator and start tinkering with the budget.

Why shouldn't you? I asked a woman that question not long ago while she was demurring about whether to order dessert at a restaurant.

Immediate answer: "Because I'll feel gross."

Why gross?

"Because I'll feel fat."

And what would happen if you felt fat?

"I hate myself when I feel fat. I feel ugly and out of control. I feel really un-sexy. I feel unlovable."

And if you deny yourself the dessert?

"I may feel a little deprived, but I'll also feel pious," she said.

So it's worth the cost?

"Yes."

These are big trade-offs for a simple piece of cake—add five hundred calories, subtract well-being, allure, and self-esteem—and the feelings behind them are anything but vain or shallow. Hidden within that thirty-second exchange is an entire set of mathematical principles, equations that can dictate a woman's most fundamental approach to hunger. Mastery over the body—its impulses, its needs, its size—is paramount; to lose control is to risk beauty, and to risk beauty is to risk desirability, and to risk desirability is to risk entitlement to sexuality and love and self-esteem. Desires collide, the wish to eat bumping up against the wish to be thin, the desire to indulge conflicting with the injunction to restrain. Small wonder food makes a woman nervous. The experience of appetite in this equation is an experience of anxiety, a burden and a risk; yielding to hunger may be permissible under certain conditions, but mostly it's something to be Earned or Monitored and Controlled. $E = mc^2$.

During the acute phases of my starving years, I took a perverse kind of pleasure in these exhibitions of personal calculus, the anxious little jigs that women would do around food. Every day at lunchtime, I'd stand in line at a café in downtown Providence clutching my 200-calorie yogurt, and while I waited, I'd watch the other women deliberate. I'd see a woman mince edgily around the glass case that held muffins and cookies, and I'd recognize the look in her eye, the longing for something sweet or gooey, the sudden flicker of *No*. I'd overhear fragments of conversation: debates between women (*I can't eat that, I'll feel huge*), and cajolings (*Oh, c'mon, have the fries*), and collaborations in surrender (*I will if you will*). I listened for these, I paid attention, and I always felt a little stab of superiority when someone yielded (*Okay, fuck it, fries, onion rings, PIE*). I would not yield—to do so, I understood, would imply lack of restraint, an unseemly, indulgent female greed—and in my stern resistance I got to feel coolly superior while they felt, or so it seemed to me, anxious.

But I knew that anxiety. I know it still, and I know how stubbornly pressing it can feel, the niggling worry about food and calories and size and heft cutting to the quick somehow, as though to fully surrender to hunger might lead to mayhem, the appetite proven unstoppable. If you plotted my food intake on a graph from that initial cottage cheese purchase onward, you wouldn't see anything very dramatic at first: a slight decline in consumption over my junior and senior years, and an increasing though not yet excessive pattern of rigidity, that edgy whir about food and weight at only the edges of consciousness at first. I lived off campus my senior year with a boyfriend, studied enormously hard, ate normal dinners at home with him, but permitted myself only a single plain donut in the morning, coffee all day, not a calorie more. The concept of "permission" was new to me—it heralded the introduction of rules and by-laws, a nascent internal tyrant issuing commands—but I didn't question it. I just ate the donut, drank the coffee, obeyed the rules, aware on some level that the rigidity and restraint served a purpose, reinforced those first heady feelings of will and determination, a proud sensation that I was somehow beyond ordinary need. I wrote a prize-winning honors thesis on two hundred calories a day.

The following year, my first out of college, the line on the graph would begin to waver, slowly at first, then peaking and dipping more erratically: five pounds up, five pounds down, six hundred calories here, six thousand there, the dieting female's private NASDAQ, a personal index of self-torture.

This was not a happy time. I'd taken a job in a university news bureau, an ostensible entree into writing and a fairly hefty disappointment (I was an editorial assistant in title, a glorified secretary in fact, bored nearly senseless from day one). The boyfriend had left for graduate school in California, and I was living alone for the first time, missing him with the particularly consuming brand of desperation afforded by long-distance love. I was restless and lonely and full of self-doubt, and the low-level tampering I'd been doing with my appetite began to intensify, my relationship with food thrown increasingly out of whack. This is familiar territory to anyone with a long history of dieting: a fundamental severing between need and want begins to take place, eating gradually loses its basic associations with nourishment and physical satisfaction and veers onto a more complex emotional plane in which the whole notion of hunger grows loaded and confusing. Sometimes I was very rigid with my diet during this period, resolving to consume nothing but coffee all day, only cheese and crackers at night. Other times I ate for comfort, or because I was bored, or because I felt empty, all reasons that frightened and confused me. I'd make huge salads at night, filled with nuts and cubes of cheese and slathered in creamy dressings; I'd eat big bowls of salty soups, enormous tuna melts, hideously sweet oversized chocolate chip cookies, purchased in little frenzies of preservation (should I? shouldn't I?) from a local bakery. I started drinking heavily during this period, too, which weakened my restraint; I'd wake up feeling bloated and hungover and I'd try to compensate by eating nothing, or next to nothing, during the day.

For a year, I gained weight, lost weight, gained the weight back, and I found this deeply unnerving, as though some critical sense of bodily integrity were at risk, my sense of limits and proportion eroding. I'd feel my belly protrude against the waistband of my skirt, or one thigh chafing against another, and I'd be aware of a potent stab of alarm: *Shit,* the vigilance has been insufficiently upheld, the body is growing soft and doughy, something central and dark about me—a lazy, gluttonous, insatiable second self—is poised to emerge. Women often brought pastries into the office where I worked. Sometimes I'd steadfastly avoid them, resolve not even to look; other times I'd eye the pastry box warily from across the room, get up periodically and circle the table, conscious of a new sensation of self-mistrust, questions beginning to flitter and nag. *Could I eat one pastry, or would one lead to three, or four, or six? Was I actually hungry for a Danish or a croissant, or was I trying to satisfy some other appetite? How hungry—how rapacious, greedy, selfish, needy—was I?* The dance of the hungry woman—two steps toward the refrigerator, one step back, that endless loop of hunger and indulgence and guilt—had ceased to be a game; some key middle ground between gluttony and restraint, a place that used to be easily accessible to me, had grown elusive and I didn't know how to get back there.

This, of course, is one of appetite's insidious golden rules: The more you meddle with a hunger, the more taboo and confusing it will become. Feed the body too little and then too much, feed it erratically, launch that maddening cycle of deprivation and overcompensation, and the sensation of physical hunger itself becomes divorced from the body, food loaded with alternative meanings: symbol of longing, symbol of constraint, form of torture, form of reward, source of anxiety, source of succor, measure of self-worth. And thus the simple experience of hunger—of wanting something to eat—becomes frightening and fraught. What does it mean this time? Where will it lead? Will you eat *everything* if you let yourself go? Will you prove unstoppable, a famished dog at a garbage bin? Young and unsure of myself and groping for direction, I was scared of many things that year—leaving the structure of college was scary, entering the work world was scary, living on my own was scary, the future loomed like a monumental question mark—but I suspect I was scared above all of hunger itself, which felt increasingly boundless and insatiable, its limits and possible ravages unknown.

I suspect, too, that this feeling went well beyond the specific issue of food, that anxiety about caloric intake and body size were merely threads in a much larger tapestry of feeling that had to do with female self-worth and power and identity—for me and for legions of other women. This time period—late 1970s, early 1980s—coincided with the early stages of the well-documented shift in the culture's collective definition of beauty, its sudden and dramatically unambiguous pairing with slenderness. There is nothing new about this today; the pressure (internal and external) to be thin is so familiar and so widespread by now that most of us take it for granted, breathe it in like air, can't remember a time when we weren't aware of it, can't remember how different the average model or actress or beauty pageant contestant looked before her weight began to plummet (in the last twenty-five years, it's dropped to twenty-five percent below that of the average woman), can't remember a world in which grocery store shelves didn't brim with low-cal and "lite" products, in which mannequins wore size eight clothes instead of size two, in which images of beauty were less wildly out of reach.

But it's worth recalling that all of this—the ratcheted-up emphasis on thinness, the aesthetic shift from Marilyn Monroe to Kate Moss, the concomitant rise in eating disorders—is relatively recent, that the emphasis on diminishing one's size, on miniaturizing the very self, didn't really heat up until women began making gains in other areas of their lives. By the time I started to flirt with anorexia, in the late 1970s, women had gained access to education, birth control, and abortion, as well as widespread protection from discrimination in most areas of their lives. At the same time, doctors were handing out some ten billion appetite-suppressing amphetamines per year, Weight Watchers had spread to forty-nine states, its membership three million strong, and the diet-food business was about to eclipse all other categories as the fastest-growing segment of the food industry.

The more you meddle with a hunger, the more taboo and confusing it will become.

This parallel has been widely, and sensibly, described as the aesthetic expression of the backlash against feminist strength that Susan Faludi would document in 1992. At a time when increasing numbers of women were demanding the right to take up more space in the world, it is no surprise that they'd be hit with the opposite message from a culture that was (and still is) both male-dominated and deeply committed to its traditional power structures. Women get psychically larger, and they're told to grow physically smaller. Women begin to play active roles in realms once dominated by men (schools, universities, athletic fields, the workplace, the bedroom), and they're countered with images of femininity that infantilize them, render them passive and frail and non-threatening. "The female body is the place where this society writes its messages," writes Rosalind Coward in *Female-Desires*, and its response to feminism was etched with increasing clarity on the whittled-down silhouette of the average American model: Don't get too hungry, don't overstep your bounds.

The whispers of this mandate, audible in the 1970s and 1980s, have grown far louder today; they are roars, howls, screams. The average American, bombarded with advertisements on a daily basis, will spend approximately three years of his or her lifetime watching television commercials, and you don't have to look too closely to see what that deluge of imagery has to say about the female body and its hungers. A controlled appetite, prerequisite for slenderness, connotes beauty, desirability, worthiness. An uncontrolled appetite—a fat woman—connotes the opposite; she is ugly, repulsive, and so fundamentally unworthy that, according to a *New York Times* report on cultural attitudes toward fat, sixteen percent of adults would choose to abort a child if they knew he or she would be untreatably obese.

Hatred of fat, inextricably linked to fear of fat, is so deeply embedded in the collective consciousness it can arouse a surprising depth of discomfort and mean-spiritedness, even among people who consider themselves to be otherwise tolerant and sensitive to women. Gail Dines, director of women's studies and professor of sociology at Wheelock College in Boston and one of the nation's foremost advocates of media literacy, travels around the country giving a slide show/lecture called "Sexy or Sexist: Images of Women in the Media." The first half of the presentation consists of images, one after the other, of svelte perfection: a sultry Brooke Shields clad in a blue bikini on a *Cosmo* cover, an achingly slender leg in an ad for Givenchy pantyhose, a whisper-thin Kate Moss. Then, about halfway into the presentation, a slide of a postcard flashes onto the screen, a picture of a woman on a beach in Hawaii. The woman is clad in a bright blue two-piece bathing suit, and she is very fat; she's shown from the rear, her buttocks enormous, her thighs pocked with fleshy folds, and the words on the postcard read: HAVING A WHALE OF A TIME IN HAWAII. The first time I saw this, I felt a jolt of something critical and mean—part pity, part judgment, an impulse to recoil—and I felt immediately embarrassed by this, which is precisely the sensation Dines intends to flush out. At another showing before a crowd at Northeastern University, the image appears on the screen and several people begin to guffaw, nervous titters echo across the room. Dines stops and turns to the audience. "Now why is this considered funny?" she demands. "Explain that to me. Does she not have the right to the dignity that you and I have a right to? Does having extra pounds on your body deny you that right?" The crowd falls silent, and Dines sighs. There it is: This obese woman, this object of hoots and jeers, is a tangible focus of female anxiety, a 350-pound picture of the shame and humiliation that will be visited upon a woman if her hunger is allowed to go unchecked.

Dines, among many others, might identify culture as the primary protagonist in this narrative, a sneering villain cleverly disguised as Beauty who skulks around injecting women with an irrational but morbid fear of fat. There is certainly some truth to that—a woman who isn't affected to some degree by the images and injunctions of fat-and-thin is about as rare as a black orchid. But I also think the intensity of the struggle around appetite that began to plague me twenty years ago, that continues to plague so many women today, speaks not just to cultural anxiety about female hunger, profound though it may be, but also to deep reservoirs of personal anxiety. Fear of fat merely exists on the rippled surface of that reservoir; mass-market images are mere reflections upon it. Underneath, the real story—each woman in her own sea of experience—is more individual and private; it's about what happens when hunger is not quite paired with power, when the license to hunger is new and unfamiliar, when a woman is teased with freedom—to define herself as she sees fit, to attend to her own needs and wishes, to fully explore her own desires—but may not quite feel that freedom in her bones or believe that it will last.

Fear of fat merely exists on the rippled surface of that reservoir; mass-market images are mere reflections upon it.

Once, several months into that first year of weight gain and weight loss, I met some friends for Sunday brunch, an all-you-can-eat buffet at a local hotel restaurant. All-you-can-eat buffets terrify me to this day—I find them sadistic and grotesque in a particularly American way, the emphasis on quantity and excess reflecting something insatiably greedy and short-sighted about the culture's ethos—and I date the onset of my terror to that very morning. Such horrifying abundance! Such potential for unleashed gluttony! The buffet table seemed to stretch out for a mile: at one station, made-to-order omelets and bacon and sausage; at another, waffles and pancakes and crêpes; at another, bagels and muffins and croissants and pastries; at yet another, an entire array of desserts, cakes and pies and individual soufflés. If you're confused about hunger, if the internal mechanisms that signal physical satiety have gone haywire, if food has become symbolically loaded, or a stand-in for other longings, this kind of array can topple you. I couldn't choose. More to the point, I couldn't trust myself to choose moderately or responsibly, or to stop when I was full, or even to know what I wanted to begin with, what would satisfy and how much. And so I ate everything. The suppressed appetite always rages just beneath the surface of will, and as often happened during that period, it simmered, then bubbled up, then boiled over. I ate. I ate eggs and bacon and waffles and slabs of cake. I ate knowing full well that I'd feel bloated and flooded with disgust later on and that I'd have to make restitution—I'd starve the next day, or go for a six-mile run, or both. I ate without pleasure. I ate until I hurt.

Years later, I'd see that brunch in metaphorical terms, a high-calorie, high-carbohydrate testament to the ambiguous blessings of abundance, its promise and its agonizing terror. As a rule, women of my generation were brought up without knowing a great deal about how to understand hunger, with very little discussion about how to assess and respond adequately to our own appetites, and with precious few examples of how to negotiate a buffet of possibility, much less embrace one. Eating too much—then as now—was a standard taboo, a mother's concern with her own body and weight handed down to her daughter in a mantle of admonishments: *Always take the smallest portion; always eat a meal before you go on a date lest you eat too much in front of him; don't eat that, it'll go straight to your hips.* Sexual hunger was at best undiscussed, at worst presented as a bubbling cauldron of danger and sin, potentially ruinous; the memory banks of women my age are riddled with images of scowling mothers, echoes of recriminating hisses (*Take that off, you look like a slut!*), fragments of threat-laden lectures about the predatory hunger of boys. And the world of ambition was in many ways uncharted territory, one that required qualities and skills—ego strength, competitiveness, intellectual confidence—that were sometimes actively discouraged in girls (*Don't brag, don't get a swelled head, don't be so smart*), rarely modeled.

This is a complicated legacy to bring to a world of blasted-open options, each *yes* in potential collision with an old *no*, and it makes for a great deal of confusion. The underlying questions of appetite, after all, are formidable—What *would* satisfy? How much *do* you need, and of what? What *are* the true passions, the real hungers behind the ostensible goals of beauty or slenderness?—and until relatively recently, a lot of women haven't been encouraged to explore them, at least not in a deep, concerted, uniform, socially supported way. We have what might be called post-feminist appetites, whetted and encouraged by a generation of opened doors and collapsed social structures, but not always granted unequivocal support or license, not always stripped of their traditional alarm bells and warnings, and not yet bolstered by a deeper sense of entitlement.

Freedom, it is important to note, is not the same as power; the ability to make choices can feel unsettling and impermanent and thin if it's not girded somehow with the heft of real economic and political strength. Women certainly have more of that heft than they did a generation ago; we are far less formally constrained, far more autonomous, and far more politically powerful, at least potentially so. Forty-three million women—forty percent of all adult women—live independently today, without traditional supports. Women make the vast majority of consumer purchases in this country—eighty-three percent—and buy one fifth of all homes. We have an unprecedented amount of legal protection, with equality on the basis of sex required by law in virtually every area of American life. We are better educated than the women of any preceding generation, with women representing more than half of full-time college enrollments. By all accounts, we ought to feel powerful, competent, and strong—and many women no doubt do, at least in some areas and at some times.

But it's also true that an overwhelming majority of women—estimates range from eighty to eighty-nine percent—wake up every morning aware of an anxious stirring of self-disgust, fixated on the feel of our thighs as we pull on our stockings, the feel of our bellies and hips as we zip up our pants and skirts. Women are three times as likely as men to feel negatively about their bodies. Eighty percent of women have been on a diet, half are actively dieting at any given time, and half report feeling dissatisfied with their bodies all the time. There is no doubt that this negativity is a culturally mediated phenomenon, that culture gives the female preoccupation with appearance (which in itself is nothing new) its particular cast, its particularly relentless focus on slenderness. But the sheer numbers, which indicate an unprecedented depth and breadth of anxiety about appearance in general and weight in particular, suggest that something more complex than imagery is at work, that our collective sense of power and competence and strength hasn't quite made it to a visceral level.

To be felt at that level, as visceral and permanent and real, entitlement must exist beyond the self; it must be known and acknowledged on a wider plane. And this is where women still get the short end of the stick; for all the gains of the last forty years, we are hardly ruling the world out there. Congress is still ninety percent male, as are ninety-eight percent of America's top corporate officers. Ninety-five percent of all venture capital today flows into men's bank accounts. The two hundred highest-paid CEOs in America are all men. Only three women head Fortune 500 companies, a number that hasn't budged in twenty years. We also have less visibility than men; women—our lives, issues, concerns—are still featured in only fifteen percent of page-one stories, and when we do make front-page news, it is usually only as victims or perpetrators of crime. And we still have less earning power: Women continue to make eighty-four cents for every dollar a man makes; women who take time off from work to have children make seventeen percent less than those who don't even six years after they return; men with children earn the most money while women with children earn the least.

This gap, I think—this persistent imbalance between personal freedom on the one hand and political power on the other—amps up the anxiety factor behind desire; it can leave a woman with a sense that something does not quite compute; it can give choices a partial, qualified feel. A woman, today, can be a neurosurgeon, or an astrophysicist; she can marry or not marry, leave her spouse, pack up, and move across the country at will. But can she take such choices a step further, or two or ten? Can a woman be not just an astrophysicist, but a big, powerful, lusty astrophysicist who feels unequivocally entitled to food and sex and pleasure and acclaim? Can she move across the country and also leave behind all her deeply ingrained feelings about what women are really supposed to look and act and be like? External freedoms may still bump up against a lot of ancient and durable internal taboos; they may still collide with the awareness, however vague, that women still represent the least empowered portion of the population, and these collisions help explain why appetites are so particularly problematic today; they exist in a very murky context, and an inherently unstable one, consistently pulled between the opposing poles of possibility and constraint, power and powerlessness.

The world mobilizes in the service of male appetite; it did during my upbringing and it does still. Whether or not this represents the actual experience of contemporary boys and men, our cultural stereotypes of male desire (and stereotypes exist precisely because they contain grains of truth) are all about facilitation and support: Mothers feed (Eat! Eat!), fathers model assertion and unabashed competitiveness, teachers encourage outspoken bravado. At home and at work, men have helpers, usually female, who clean and cook and shop and type and file and assist. And at every turn—on billboards, magazine covers, in ads—men are surrounded by images of offering, of breasts and parted lips and the sultry gazes of constant availability: Take me, you are entitled, I exist to please you. For all the expansion of opportunity in women's lives, there is no such effort on behalf of female appetite, there are no comparable images of service and availability, there is no baseline expectation that a legion of others will rush forward to meet our needs or satisfy our hungers. The striving, self-oriented man is adapted to, cut slack, his transgressions and inadequacies explained and forgiven. *Oh, well, you wouldn't expect him to cook or take care of his kids, who cares if he's put on a few pounds, so what if he's controlling or narcissistic, he's busy, he gets things done, he's running the show, he's running the company, he's running the* COUNTRY. That litany of understanding does not apply to women; it sounds discordant and artificial if you switch the genders, and if you need a single example of the double standard at work here, think about Bill and Hillary Clinton. Bill's pudginess and fondness for McDonald's was seen as endearing; his sexual appetite criticized but ultimately forgiven by most Americans, or at least considered irrelevant to his abilities on the job; Hillary got no such latitude, the focus on her appearance (hairstyle, wardrobe, legs) was relentless, the hostility released toward her ambition venomous.

The one exception to this rule, the one area where a legion of others might, in fact, rush forward in service to a woman's needs, is shopping, particularly high-end retail shopping, but in itself, that merely underscores how lacking the phenomenon is in other areas, and how constricted the realm of appetite is for women in general: We can want, and even expect, the world to mobilize on our behalf when we're equipped with an American Express gold card and an appetite for Armani. But beyond the world of appearances and consumer goods, expressions of physical hunger and selfish strivings rarely meet with such consistent support. Instead, the possibility of risk can hang in the air like a mildly poisonous mist; for every appetite, there may be a possible backlash, or a slap or a reprimand or a door that opens but has caveats stamped all over the welcome mat. A novelist tells me in a whisper about a glowing review she's received; she can barely get the words out, so strong are the chastising echoes of her family: *Now, don't you let it go to your head*, her mother used to say, and it took her decades to realize how truly defeating that phrase was. ("Where's it supposed to go," she asks today, "someone else's head?") A scientist, brilliant and respected, secures a major grant for a project she's dreamed of taking on for years and later describes what an emotional hurdle it was to fully take pride in the accomplishment, to really revel in it: "I couldn't say it aloud, I just couldn't get the words out," she says. "I don't think a man would *get* that." An educator, who's taught high school for thirteen years and is now pursuing a PhD in education, tells me, "For years, I've carried around the feeling that if I really allow myself to follow my passions, something bad will happen." She can't follow that line of thought to any logical conclusion; rather, it expresses an amalgam of worries, some specific (she's apprehensive about being consumed by work, and about making sacrifices in her personal life), but more of them generic, as though the admission of hunger and ambition is in itself a dangerous thing, quite likely a punishable offense.

This quiet, dogged anxiety, this internalized mosquito whine of caveat, may explain why the memory of that hotel brunch would stick with me for so long; the experience seemed to capture something about the times, about the onset of a complicated set of conflicts between an expansive array of options on the one hand and a sense of deep uncertainty on the other, a feeling that this freedom was both incomplete and highly qualified, full of risks. Certainly that's how I felt in those early unformed twentysomething years, as though I were standing before an enormous table of possibilities with no utensils, no serving spoons, no real sense that I was truly entitled to sample the goods, to experiment or indulge or design my own menu.

DISCUSSION

1. Knapp begins her personal account of anorexia by referring to the "lure of starving" (p. 188). How do you react to this provocative phrase? In your view, is it possible for something as harrowing and harmful as self-starvation to feel so compelling or desirable? If so, how?
2. For Knapp, anorexia is both a personal and a societal disease, starkly registering the ways women can be taught to internalize and act on destructive gender stereotypes. How valid does this hypothesis seem to you? Does it make sense to think about this illness as a blueprint for the scripts that get written out and imposed on women?
3. As Knapp relates, denying herself food felt for so long like the right thing to do in part because it gave her an enhanced sense of control. Choose one of the diets Knapp describes having followed during her anorexic years and evaluate it as a recipe for achieving a particular form of control. In your view, does the diet achieve this objective?

WRITING

4. Much of Knapp's writing of her own hunger centers around imaginary conversations or internal dialogue that expresses common embedded attitudes about eating and appetite. Write an essay in which you analyze how effective this approach to writing about appetite is. Who is Knapp talking to in these conversations, and how does she use this dialogue to highlight her own attitudes toward eating?
5. Here is a partial list of the words Knapp tells us she learned to associate with her own hunger: *rapacious*, *greedy*, *selfish*, *needy*, *unsexy*, *bad*. Write an essay in which you propose what scripts about food and eating have given rise to these kinds of associations. What scripts in food advertising, nutritional guidelines, or the popular media do you think reinforce this type of thinking? In your opinion, are these scripts intentional? How might you approach communicating messages about health or beauty without triggering the negative associations that Knapp discusses?
6. For Knapp, cultural attitudes about food formed "a low-level thrumming of shoulds and shouldn'ts and can'ts and wants," or what the author calls a kind of "feminine Muzak" (p. 189). In your view, does this analogy do a good or bad job of capturing the ways we learn to absorb or internalize cultural norms around eating? Write an essay in which you compare these messages and this process of internalization to what Francine Prose (p. 181) has to say in her piece on gluttony. Does Prose seem to share Knapp's view of where our norms vis-à-vis food typically come from and the ways they come to feel so normal? How or how not?

BRENDAN BUHLER

On Eating Roadkill

For most of us, our connection to the food we eat extends no further than the container in which it is packaged or the label with which it is affixed. For those in what has come to be known as the locavore movement, however, the connection goes all the way back to our food's former existence as a living thing. Offering an unexpected twist on this idea, Brendan Buhler makes a provocative case for roadkill as the ultimate locavore fare. And in doing so, he invites readers to think more deeply and more critically about where exactly our food comes from. Buhler is a freelance writer and former reporter for the *Las Vegas Sun*. This article appeared in *Modern Farmer* in 2013.

ETHICALLY SPEAKING, WE SHOULD ALL BE EATING ROADKILL.

Not just us carnivores, either. It is the perfect meat for vegetarians and vegans, too, provided their objections to meat are its murder or its environmental implications and not because it's icky-gross. The animal was not raised for meat, it was not killed for meat; it is just simply and accidentally meat—manna from minivans.

Practical, culinary, and even legal considerations make it hard for many to imagine cooking our vehicular accidents, but that needn't be the case. If the roadkill is fresh, perhaps hit on a cold day and ideally a large animal, it is as safe as any game. Plus, not eating roadkill is intensely wasteful: last year, State Farm Mutual Automobile Insurance Company estimated that some 1,232,000 deer were hit by cars in the United States. Now imagine that only a third of that meat could be salvaged. That'd be about 20 million pounds of free-range venison, perhaps not much compared to the 23 billion pounds of beef produced in the U.S. in 2011 but significant.

The animal was not raised for meat, it was not killed for meat; it is just simply and accidentally meat—manna from minivans.

(*Nota bene*: Deer are the important edible roadkill category for two reasons: money and physics. Insurance companies keep statistics on roadkill deer because hitting a deer messes up a car in a way a jackrabbit can't—State Farm estimates the average cost of collision with a deer is just over $3,300. The reporting of all other roadkill is sporadic and anecdotal. But what you really care about is that deer are large animals and more likely to remain edible. Their height means they're unlikely to be mashed under a car but thrown over or around it. Their mass means their guts are less likely to rupture and contaminate the surrounding meat. That's not to say there's never an edible Thumper or Flower lying by the roadside, but the star attraction remains Bambi.)

Roadkill arrived with the age of the automobile. The first study of roadkill was probably published by New England naturalist James Raymond Simmons, author of 1938's *Feathers and Fur on the Turnpike*—a rare book, for knowledge of which we are grateful to Roger Knutson's more recent work, *Flattened Fauna*. While little hard data exists in the critically understudied field of eating roadkill, it's probably safe to say people have been eating it as long as it's been around. Wisconsin, for instance, started issuing roadkill salvage tags for deer in the 1950s, and there was already a demand. Culturally, roadkill foraging is largely a rural practice, because that's where you find farmers and hunters accustomed to butchering animals, and that's where you find more animals—animals that haven't been hit multiple times and animals that aren't either pets or sewer-dwelling vermin.

While little hard data exists in the critically understudied field of eating roadkill, it's probably safe to say people have been eating it as long as it's been around.

For those new to eating roadkill, the best advice (other than trusting your eyes and nose) can be found in wild game cookbooks. Avoid roadkill-specific cookbooks, which tend to be jokey, like, you might be a redneck if you own this book.

The legal ramifications of eating roadkill are a bit dicey, though. In West Virginia, the roadkill must simply be reported to the state within 12 hours of its collection. Tennessee considered a similar law, but withdrew it under ridicule. In Massachusetts, you must obtain a permit after the fact and submit your roadkill to inspection by the state. In Illinois, the chain of title is somewhat complicated, and no one delinquent in child support may claim a dead deer. Alaska practices roadside socialism: all roadkill belongs to the state, which then feeds it to human families in need.

On the other hand, Texas, California, and Washington may not agree on much, but they are three of the very few states that agree that possession of roadkill is illegal. Apparently, they worry it will lead to poaching.

Carrie Wilson, a marine biologist with California's Department of Fish and Wildlife who writes a question and answer column for the state agency, said she's had to address the topic of roadkill a couple of times. She tells readers that even if they have a hunting license, smacking a deer with a Volvo does not constitute a legal method of taking game.

Now, I've been a passenger in a car that hit a deer. The deer bounded off in who knows what condition and the car limped home with shaken passengers and several hundred dollars worth of damage. It is not an experience I would repeat on purpose. I asked Wilson if she thought there was anyone out there who would try to run a deer down for meat.

"There are people who will do it, unfortunately," she said.

Facts don't really back up that fear, though. In Wisconsin, a state that has issued salvage tags since the '50s, officials say poaching is not an issue. Scott Roepke, an assistant big game ecologist with the state's Department of Natural Resources, notes the state issued 4,400 roadkill deer salvage tags in 2011—up about 1,000 from the previous three years' totals, but nowhere near the almost 14,000 deer salvaged in 1998.

"We have prosecuted a few people at least who do try and run down deer with their cars. There is a sizable fine associated with it," Roepke said. "We definitely wouldn't want to encourage people to try and run down a deer with their trucks and take it home for meat."

It's worth noting here that in the woodsy states of the Northeast, the states with the most deer and the most deer dead alongside the road—Pennsylvania, Michigan, New York, Ohio, and Wisconsin—it's legal to collect and eat roadkill deer.

The most recent state to legalize roadkill collection is Montana, with a bill introduced by Republican Representative Steve Lavin, a highway patrol sergeant in northwest Montana, near Glacier National Park. At first, Lavin says he laughed off the suggestion of one of his troopers that the meat be legalized, but the more he thought about it, the more it made sense. There is a lot of roadkill in the area; some of it's getting eaten, even taken to food banks. "What's happening is people are taking them already—essentially what this will do is legalize the process," he says.

Lavin's law will allow any peace officer to issue a permit for the salvage of roadkill antelope, deer, elk, or moose. (Bears, bighorn sheep, and other animals with valuable body parts are intentionally excluded from the statute, Lavin said.)

There are times, of course, when roadkill is not collected for human culinary purposes. In Wisconsin, and other states worried about the spread of a deer pathogen known as Chronic Wasting Disease, the deer are collected by contractors and hauled to nearby landfills. It's a patchwork system in California, Carrie Wilson said. If the state roads agency finds the animals, they tend to drag the carcasses off into the bushes for non-human scavengers. Some cities either have their own animal control agencies or hire animal shelters to collect carcasses. The carcasses are then either fed to rescued carnivores or taken to a rendering plant, from which they eventually exit as ingredients for pet food, glue, soap, pharmaceuticals, and gelatin.

So for those on the fence (or outright repelled) by the concept, consider this: because gelatin ends up in everything from marshmallows to gummy bears to ice cream, there's a good chance that you've already consumed, legally, some accidental meat.

DISCUSSION

1. What are some of the associations you bring to the term *roadkill*? And are any of these associations compatible with the idea of eating roadkill? Why or why not?
2. Take a moment to consider the claim implied by the essay's title. Do you agree that roadkill could very well constitute one of our most ethical eating choices? How or how not?
3. What would happen if eating roadkill were to become a more widely accepted social norm? What rules would you suggest for how this practice should be carried out? What guidelines? What limitations? And why?

WRITING

4. Buhler spends a good deal of time reviewing the different state laws that regulate and restrict treatment of roadkill. Write an assessment of this decision. Why do you think Buhler chooses to include this information? What is his larger goal in doing so? Did reading these descriptions affect your views about eating roadkill in any way?
5. Buhler concludes his essay with these thoughts: "[F]or those on the fence (or outright repelled) by the concept, consider this: because gelatin ends up in everything from marshmallows to gummy bears to ice cream, there's a good chance that you've already consumed, legally, some accidental meat" (p. 206). Write an essay in which you analyze the rhetorical strategy at work here. Why does Buhler conclude by pointing out the likelihood that we all have already consumed "accidental meat"? How does this statement relate to the larger argument he is trying to make?
6. Buhler's essay, like Paul Schwennesen's (p. 178), makes an argument that challenges some of our most deeply embedded food norms. In a two-page essay, discuss the ways each of these essays can be read as an attempt to rewrite conventional or mainstream eating scripts. What food-specific attitudes or behaviors do these two writers seem most directly to be questioning?

Then and Now: **How to Make Meatloaf**

Far more than a list of ingredients and steps, each of these recipes offers a quick snapshot of the sorts of attitudes toward eating that, at two different moments in our food culture's recent history, passed for the norm. Meatloaf is a classic American dish that first became popular on family dinner tables during the Great Depression. It's a dish families could make on a budget because the recipe relied on cheaper cuts of meat and included bread or cracker crumbs as a way to create more servings. The first recipe is a classic meatloaf recipe from the Heinz ketchup company. Looking at it, we may learn more about what the prevailing food attitudes were by focusing on what the recipe does *not* say — that is, on the things it simply takes for granted. The instructions are much less explicit than what we're used to today: no temperature setting for the oven, no specifications for the size of baking dish, and no order for the ingredients added. The recipe also omits nutritional information — no discussion of calories or cholesterol here or references to recommended daily allowances of fiber or calcium. These omissions stem in part from ingrained assumptions about eating that people of this era simply regarded as *common sense.* To put it mildly, any dish whose list of ingredients goes no further than pepper, ground beef, and bologna didn't achieve popularity at a historical moment that placed a terribly high premium on physical health. The point of eating, this recipe all but says out loud, is not to make us live longer; it is to put things into our bodies that conform to a particular standard of good taste or smart spending — a standard that in this case appears to have revolved primarily around adding flavor using the least expensive ingredients possible.

Circa 1956

HEINZ KETCHUP MEATLOAF RECIPE

2 lbs. ground beef
½ lb. bologna
1 tablespoon grated onion
1 cup moist cracker crumbs
1 egg
1 teaspoon salt
½ cup Heinz Tomato Ketchup
Pepper

Chop bologna finely and add to the meat. Add other ingredients, adding Tomato Ketchup last, and bake in a moderate oven, basting frequently.

Contrast the second recipe, which transforms the all-American dish. The tofu meatloaf recipe carefully acquaints its readers with the particular facts about the ingredients it assembles, a tactic exemplified in its references to "light miso," "tahini," and "dried dill." This difference underscores how much more diversified our culture's prevailing definitions of American cuisine have grown since the Depression era. But perhaps even more important, it suggests how much more worried we are about what we put into our bodies.

This recipe is meat free and includes all-natural ingredients and exotic flavors. Indeed, if this Moosewood Restaurant recipe is a reliable guide, we could well argue that ours has become a food culture in which concerns over physical health (as well as its corollary, physical appearance) and ideology now supplant expense as the primary standard by which we judge the quality of our food.

These recipes may represent night and day in terms of what goes in them, but both represent a certain anxiety over eating. The first recipe includes just a few inexpensive ingredients (and relies on ketchup to provide the zing), while the second includes numerous fresh and healthy ingredients that are tough to find in some areas and cost considerably more than a bottle of ketchup. While the first recipe's author is conscious of the cook's pocketbook, the second is conscious of his or her health and lifestyle. Each recipe provides a revealing glimpse into how meatloaf can reflect our cultural concerns.

2001

TOFU MEATLOAF

Serves 8
Prep time: 30 minutes
Baking time: 25–30 minutes
2 cakes firm tofu (16 ounces each)
2 tablespoons vegetable oil
2 cups diced onions
1 cup peeled and grated carrots
1 cup diced bell peppers
1 teaspoon dried oregano
1 teaspoon dried basil
1 teaspoon dried dill
⅔ cup chopped walnuts
1 cup bread crumbs
2 tablespoons tahini
2 tablespoons light miso
2 tablespoons soy sauce
1–2 tablespoons Dijon mustard

Press the tofu between two plates and rest a heavy weight on the top plate. Press for 15 minutes, then drain the liquid.

Meanwhile, heat the oil in a frying pan and sauté the onions, carrots, peppers, oregano, basil, and dill for about 7 minutes, until the vegetables are just tender. Crumble the pressed tofu into a large bowl, or grind it through a food processor. Stir in the walnuts, bread crumbs, tahini, miso, soy sauce, and mustard. Add the sautéed vegetables and mix well.

Preheat the oven to 350 or 375 degrees. Press the mix into an oiled casserole dish, and bake for about 30 minutes, until lightly browned.

— Reprinted from* Moosewood Restaurant New Classics*, Copyright © 2001 by the Moosewood Collective, Clarkson N. Potter, New York, publishers.

WRITING

1. How does each recipe seem to define "good" eating? What does each recipe seem to define its standards of good eating against? Why? Write a one-page essay in which you analyze and evaluate the key differences between these two scripts. In what ways have the norms around eating changed since the first recipe was popular?

2. Both Erika Nicole Kendall (p. 210) and Tracie McMillan (p. 215) write about food and economics. What do you think each author would have to say about these meatloaf recipes? Do they seem to confirm the kinds of connections between food and social class that these two authors identify? How or how not?

ERIKA NICOLE KENDALL

No Myths Here: Food Stamps, Food Deserts, and Food Scarcity

The last decade has witnessed a growing concern over what have come to be known as "food deserts": urban neighborhoods that lack any access to healthy, fresh food. But while much energy is expended on bemoaning this situation, comparatively little effort is devoted to figuring out the root causes behind it. Taking a hard look at food and the inner city, Erika Nicole Kendall argues that our attempt to deal with "food deserts" is hobbled by our refusal to confront the realities of the economic system that has created them. Kendall, a health and wellness expert, nutritionist, and blogger, has written for the *New York Times*, the *Huffington Post*, and *Black Enterprise*. She is the author of the award-winning blog A Black Girl's Guide to Weight Loss, where this piece first appeared in 2012.

WHEN I WAS ABOUT 5 OR SO, I USED TO GO TO MY GRANDMOTHER'S house during the day while my Mother went to work. I remember catching the bus and sleeping across my Mom's lap until we got there, and then her hugging me and heading off to do whatever it was she did all day. (I was five. Clearly, I had no idea.)

Grandma was cool, but there was always a bajillion people at her house. She lived in the projects, and spent a big portion of her day being "Mama" to *everyone* even though she was well into her 50s.

I remember, as a kid, how the big thing was for us to run across the street to the convenience store and get a Big Red pop and a bag of chips. All for $0.50. I mean, it was how we spent every afternoon. Because Grandma's house was full of people, it was never hard for me to get a hold of two quarters—ahhh, two shiny, glorious quarters—so that I could be like the rest of the kids and sit in the middle of the grass and eat my Funyuns or my Munchos and my Big Red pop. (I'm from the Midwest. We say pop, thank you very much.)

It wasn't that I was Grandma's favorite, but . . . well, I was Grandma's favorite. She invested a lot of time and effort into me. She taught me to read—she'd hand me the newspaper and make me read every page out loud—and she taught me how to be a little lady. She taught me how to love, as a young girl, because outside of that typical adoration that a young girl has for her mother, you learn that *thing* that binds you to Grandma emotionally and you understand it even more so once she's gone. That made her valuable.

However, I must admit. If there's one thing I don't remember, it's going to a grocery store with Grandma. We just . . . we never went together. At least, we didn't go to a grocery store as I know a grocery store to be today. The only store I ever saw her go to was the convenient store across the street.

And now that I think about it, there's a lot of things I don't remember about that time with Grandma.

I don't remember a lot of cooking going on. I don't even know that I remember any fresh vegetables there. I mean, I remember my Great Grandma—my Grandma's mother—having that gorgeous garden in her fenced-off backyard, but Grandma didn't have that kind of backyard. The soil didn't even have grass on it. It was just hard dirt. I know. I fell on it and scraped myself up a few times.

I guess that's to be expected. It's not like it was quality, "prime" real estate or anything. It's not even like anyone cares to maintain the area, I guess.

I remember running to one particular house in the building in the back of the projects where the free lunch was given out. Bologna, milk, cheese, bread, and little mustard packets to dress the makeshift sandwiches. All the kids used to make a mad dash back there because they were always limited in how much they had and how many kids would be able to sit in there, and if you were last, you went hungry.

As a different woman today, I can acknowledge that that housing project community was a food desert. That even though Grandma was doing all she could to make sure I never went hungry, there was rarely a vegetable on the plate. Even though she meant very well and did the best that she could, I know I picked up a lot of bad habits from that time in my life.

Are the ramifications of growing up in a food desert ever discussed? . . . Or are they never mentioned because it's assumed they don't matter?

In fact, it sounds a lot like this paragraph from the NYTimes blog:

> Poor urban neighborhoods in America are often food deserts—places where it is difficult to find fresh food. There are few grocery stores; people may do all their shopping at bodegas, where the only available produce and meat are canned peaches and Spam. If they want fruits and vegetables and chicken and fish, they have to take a bus to a grocery store. The lack of fresh food creates a vicious cycle; children grow up never seeing it or acquiring a taste for it. It is one reason that the poor are likelier to be obese than the rich.[1]

When I hear people complain about the *cost* of fresh food and use this as an excuse to not eat it, it makes me think about those projects where so many people who were, actually, given money *by* the government to eat couldn't even *access* the healthy food. My Grandma, while she might've been able to catch a bus to hit the grocery store, might've had difficulty doing this since she was the family babysitter. Her, four kids (one of them facing a mental disability), and countless bags with enough food to feed the numerous people that'd be in and out of her house to eat? On the bus? You're joking, right?

Back to the point. All that food stamp money in the projects, and no fresh food in the area to spend it on.

Whenever we talk about problems with our food system, we often talk about access . . . and yeah, we might toss around the phrase "food desert," but is that ever quantified? Are the ramifications of growing up in a food desert ever discussed? Do places like the Morris Brown projects ever come up for discussion? Or are they never mentioned because it's assumed they don't matter?

A while back, I wrote the following:

> I can specifically remember a time when I lived in a food desert, and the only food store nearby was a gas station. My daughter was on formula at the time, and I used to purchase that in bulk and have that shipped. For myself, though, it was whatever I could get at the store. A bag of chips for breakfast, a bag of chips for lunch, a bowl of ice cream for dinner. If I wanted to go to the grocery, I had to either beg one of my girls to take me or call a taxi. I eventually called the taxi and cut back on groceries so that I could afford the ride, but . . . it was a lonnng time before I came to that realization.
>
> It made perfect sense, though, that the grocery stores would be on the other side of town from me. The area where I lived was wholly college students living on that good ol' beer and pizza diet . . . as evidenced by the abundance of pizza joints, sub shops, and drive-thru liquor stores. The stores that a young Mom like me needed . . . were at least two miles away. With no car, that was quite the struggle.
>
> But if you think about it, isn't that how Capitalism works? When there is a demand, the promise of profit guarantees that there will always be someone willing and able to jump in and fulfill that need, right? In my neighborhood, there was a high demand for pizza joints and liquor stores. That's what the college kids wanted. I was the random weird outlier with an infant in a college apartment complex.

The reason that food deserts exist is because it is assumed that the people in those geographic locations cannot afford the products that a fresh food-selling store would provide. This is also an automatic assumption of the projects, because the implication is "if these people had any money, they wouldn't be living in the projects after all."

That's just how Capitalism works. Big C. Supply goes where the demand is located. If there's no money, then clearly there's no demand off which the investor can profit.

My question, really, is what do we gain from denying the realities of food deserts? How do we benefit from silencing the voices of the un-privileged? If we can identify that fresh food is expensive, why wouldn't we want to hear from the people most affected by that? If we deny the fact that food deserts exist, you silence the input of those of us who have been affected by this problem the most. Those of us who have been on government assistance and live in still-impoverished areas offer up the critique of the system that says that the government is giving away money to be spent on the very things making us ill and preventing us from healing ourselves.

My question, really, is what do we gain from denying the realities of food deserts? How do we benefit from silencing the voices of the un-privileged?

We also shoot ourselves in our collective feet when we decide to downplay food deserts because it prevents us from ever finding a solution to the problem. What about offering incentives to investors—franchise, corporate, and otherwise—who build in food deserts? Why can't we do that? Why not offer incentives up the chain—tax incentives for security measures (since a lot of these places fear theft and property damage), incentives for the space of the store dedicated solely to fresh produce? We can't do that because we're too busy debating their existence. Y'all know I have a problem with that.

So, it saddens me to know that the big politicians that I vote for to get the big checks are not offering up the answers that we need to solve this problem in particular, especially since they're never walking through (or helicoptering through, even) the projects (or a trailer park, or a low-income community in general) to see what struggles people like this face. Realistically speaking, they're facing the same struggles that "middle-class" Americans are facing. Middle-class America, for the most part, just knows how to hide it better. If anything would've taught us that, it would be the up-spring of foreclosure signs in our very nice, quaint neighborhoods.

NOTES

[1]Rosenberg, Tina. "In 'Food Deserts,' Oases of Nutrition." The New York Times, May 23, 2011.

DISCUSSION

1. How do you respond to Kendall's use of the term "myth" here? What does this term mean to you? Can you think of a specific myth that fits your definition?
2. Growing up, Kendall came to realize that the issue of one's access to food is no less important than its affordability: "All that food stamp money in the projects, and no fresh food in the area to spend it on" (p. 212). Do you share Kendall's view? Is access just as important as affordability? How do you understand the relationship between the two?
3. For Kendall, the problem of food scarcity persists in part because of the public's refusal to look squarely at the true causes behind it. What do you think accounts for the reluctance to look clearly at (and talk clearly about) this issue? What assumptions, what cultural norms, prevent us from doing so?

WRITING

4. Attempting to make sense of the root causes behind food deserts, Kendall offers the following hypothesis: "That's just how Capitalism works. Big C. Supply goes where the demand is located. If there's no money, then clearly there's no demand off which the investor can profit" (p. 212). Write an essay in which you analyze and evaluate the thesis Kendall advances here. What is Kendall identifying as the root cause behind food deserts? How does this view challenge the stereotypes or "myths" often invoked to explain this phenomenon? And how persuasive do you find her argument? Why?
5. Near the end of her essay, Kendall presents readers with a series of suggestions designed to move the public discussion of food scarcity forward: "What about offering incentives to investors — franchise, corporate, and otherwise — who build in food deserts? Why can't we do that? Why not offer incentives up the chain — tax incentives for security measures (since a lot of these places fear theft and property damage), incentives for the space of the store dedicated solely to fresh produce?" (p. 213). In a three- to five-page essay, analyze and evaluate the proposals Kendall offers here. How effective would they be in confronting and ameliorating the problem of food scarcity? What problems or shortcomings do you see? And what suggestions of your own would you add to this list?
6. Kendall and Tracie McMillan (p. 215) share an interest in challenging prevailing assumptions about "food deserts." How do their respective accounts compare? In your view, does McMillan's investigation into food and "class warfare" reinforce or extend Kendall's argument about food scarcity? How specifically?

TRACIE MCMILLAN

Food's Class Warfare

Whether it's advice about dieting or debates about nutrition, discussions about food frequently spill over into other, often more contentious, topics. Tracie McMillan's essay offers a case in point. What, she asks, are the unexamined assumptions about social class that underlie the current debate over Americans' eating habits? And to what extent does this debate become a forum for airing (and reinforcing) unhelpful class-based stereotypes? McMillan, a freelance journalist whose work centers on food and class, is a Senior Fellow at the Schuster Institute for Investigative Journalism at Brandeis University. Her first book *The American Way of Eating: Undercover at Walmart, Applebee's, Farm Fields and the Dinner Table* was published in 2012. This piece appeared in *Slate* in 2012.

A FEW YEARS AGO, THE CHEF AND ORGANIC PIONEER ALICE WATERS did a spin on *60 Minutes* that managed to showcase exactly why foodies get branded as elitist. "Some people want to buy Nikes, two pairs," she said in a casual moment at a farmers' market. "And some people want to eat Bronx grapes and nourish themselves."

This was vintage foodie-ism, a smug and irritating noblesse oblige transposed onto a discussion of our meals. That didn't change the fact that much of everything else Waters said was right: The way we eat is making us sick; it's a good idea for kids to learn to cook; even, in a more formal moment, "good food should be a right and not a privilege." But her aside about sneakers made it unlikely that anyone not yet onboard with Waters would listen to her in the first place.

I bring this up because roughly half of the conversation about how to secure the future of America's food supply has been driven by the same just-buy-better-stuff logic Waters embraces, despite its disturbing similarity to Marie Antoinette's "Let them eat cake." The other half of the discussion focuses on the structural challenges of eating well, sort of a caricature of liberal analysis. It's strikingly rare for those two halves to cleave together in public discourse—and that is a serious problem for anyone sincere about changing food and eating in America.

Foodie analysis like Waters' suggests that individual preferences, which are seen solely as a product of a person and her culture, are the key to fixing the American way of eating. This gives foodies some strange bedfellows, ranging from Sarah Palin brandishing cookies at a school fundraiser as a way of championing individual choice (much to the chagrin of fellow conservatives), to journalists parroting Waters, to the USDA's long-standing, often futile efforts to offer dietary guidance. Indeed, individual preference has arguably been our primary strategy in attempts to change both American diets and American agriculture for decades. (The obesity epidemic might be one reason to think this approach has largely failed.)

Foodie analysis like Waters' suggests that individual preferences, which are seen solely as a product of a person and her culture, are the key to fixing the American way of eating.

Then, a second, and no more perfect, strategy for changing America's food and diet emerged: treating it as a structural problem. In the last decade, concern over food deserts—neighborhoods with insufficient grocery stores, and thus insufficient supplies of healthy food—has boomed. The food desert analysis holds that access to a supermarket is a key part of making sure Americans eat healthier meals. It's an approach that is arguably more sympathetic to the poor, but can also imply that people are solely products of systems, rather than agents of free will.

The term "food desert" itself is relatively new. It wasn't even in circulation a decade ago, but last year the USDA began measuring the presence of food deserts nationwide. Last July, First Lady Michelle Obama put their eradication on her to-do list, announcing a series of partnerships with national grocers. "We can give people all of the information and advice in the world about healthy eating and exercise," she said. "But if parents can't buy the food they need to prepare those meals . . . then all that is just talk."

Food deserts are—and have always been—a flawed conceit. As a measure of access to healthy food, supermarkets are crude. Some are flush with high-quality produce, but others have little concern for quality control. And while all supermarkets sell produce, they are also rife with processed junk (even Whole Foods).

What's more, the method by which supermarkets are identified leaves out important nuances. Typically, a local list of food stores is screened for those that exceed a certain size. Modest green grocers, farmers' markets, or street vendors won't show up in the measure of "food access." Indeed, one of the more obscure debates in policy circles is whether "food swamps" or "food grasslands" might be more apt descriptors. And while early studies found links between food access and either lower obesity rates or better diets, more recent ones question whether access plays a role in the obesity epidemic at all.

Despite the divided national debate about food choice vs. food access, the two camps are not diametrically opposed. I've been covering food and class for nearly a decade, and I've yet to meet someone doing supermarket development work who doesn't think food education is important too. The efforts of Brahm Ahmadi, who's trying to open People's Community Market—a community grocery store in West Oakland, a textbook example of a food desert—is a case in point. And for all of Waters' foibles, most chefs I've met grasp the economic difficulty faced by working-class Americans (not to mention the problem of time). Check out Tamar Adler's *An Everlasting Meal* for an example of someone using the language of high culture to promote very proletarian ideals.

So here's one solution: Make class consciousness a central—but thoughtful—part of the discussion over our meals.

I can't quite pinpoint why journalists play up this divide. Surely some of it has to do with the way each approach, in caricature, lines up neatly with right wing (individualistic) and left wing (social) ideology. The clean lines of an absolute make for crisper copy—and sexier headlines—than nuance. And they are typically drawn, somewhat laboriously, around the elephant in the room: economic class.

So here's one solution: Make class consciousness a central—but thoughtful—part of the discussion over our meals. Right now, the affluent spend more at restaurants each year than the poor spend on all their food. The poor, interestingly, tend to make use of coupons at farmers' markets, suggesting that they are less in need of lectures than higher incomes.

Here's another, and one that many communities—and even the first lady—already make use of: Go at this from all sides. Supermarkets are important. So are cooking classes. So is agriculture. So are farmers' markets and work-life balance. We didn't end up with an obesity problem because of a single fatal flaw, and we're not going to solve it with a magic bullet.

At the end of the day, it's the overlap between the two sides that matters the most. How do we fix the American food system? The answer is going to include both individual changes and structural ones. The sooner we stop squabbling over which one is most important, the better.

DISCUSSION

1. McMillan takes aim at elitism she sees at the heart of our contemporary foodie culture, "a smug and irritating noblesse oblige transposed onto a discussion of our meals" (p. 215). Do you share this view? In your estimation, is our culture marked by a "smug" and "irritating" condescension toward those whose tastes are not gourmet?
2. We make a mistake, McMillan argues, when we assume that Americans' eating habits are solely the result of individual choice. Do you agree? Is there another explanation for these trends that makes more sense to you?
3. Chief among the recommendations McMillan offers here is this: "Make class consciousness a central — but thoughtful — part of the discussion over our meals" (p. 217). What do you think she means? What would introducing "class consciousness" into our discussions about food look like? And what kind of difference would it make?

WRITING

4. McMillan mentions the specific terms we use to discuss the problem of food access, saying that some debate the use of "food swamps" or "food grasslands." Write a short essay in which you analyze and assess these terms. How do they differ from the more conventional "food desert"? How do they change the ways we think about and engage the problem of food scarcity? And in your view, are these changes for the better? Why or why not?
5. In searching for a way to alter or rewrite the social scripts around eating, McMillan argues for an approach that reconciles two views that traditionally have been regarded as mutually exclusive: the view that poor eating habits are caused by structural factors like economics and the view that poor eating habits are the result of ill-advised individual choice. In a three- to five-page essay, write a detailed description of what you think this new approach might look like. What revised explanation for Americans' eating habits would it offer? What changes in public attitudes and public policy would it bring?
6. Both McMillan and Kristof (p. 172) use their examinations of public attitudes toward food as a platform to argue for specific changes in our official food policy. How do their recommendations compare? Can you imagine Kristof citing the points McMillan raises here as evidence or support for the argument he makes about food stamps? If so, how specifically?

SAM DOLNICK

The Obesity-Hunger Paradox

Accepted wisdom would have us believe that obesity is little more than the result of overeating. According to Sam Dolnick, however, this view radically misperceives the true causes behind one of America's most persistent and pernicious health problems. Dolnick is a reporter for the *New York Times,* where this article was published in 2010.

WHEN MOST PEOPLE THINK OF HUNGER IN AMERICA, THE IMAGES that leap to mind are of ragged toddlers in Appalachia or rail-thin children in dingy apartments reaching for empty bottles of milk.

Once, maybe.

But a recent survey found that the most severe hunger-related problems in the nation are in the South Bronx, long one of the country's capitals of obesity. Experts say these are not parallel problems persisting in side-by-side neighborhoods, but plagues often seen in the same households, even the same person: the hungriest people in America today, statistically speaking, may well be not sickly skinny, but excessively fat.

Call it the Bronx Paradox.

"Hunger and obesity are often flip sides to the same malnutrition coin," said Joel Berg, executive director of the New York City Coalition Against Hunger. "Hunger is certainly almost an exclusive symptom of poverty. And extra obesity is one of the symptoms of poverty."

The Bronx has the city's highest rate of obesity, with residents facing an estimated 85 percent higher risk of being obese than people in Manhattan, according to Andrew G. Rundle, an epidemiologist at the Mailman School of Public Health at Columbia University.

But the Bronx also faces stubborn hunger problems. According to a survey released in January by the Food Research and Action Center, an antihunger group, nearly 37 percent of residents in the 16th Congressional District, which encompasses the South Bronx, said they lacked money to buy food at some point in the past 12 months. That is more than any other Congressional district in the country and twice the national average, 18.5 percent, in the fourth quarter of 2009.

When most people think of hunger in America, the images that leap to mind are of ragged toddlers in Appalachia or rail-thin children in dingy apartments reaching for empty bottles of milk.

Such studies present a different way to look at hunger: not starving, but "food insecure," as the researchers call it (the Department of Agriculture in 2006 stopped using the word "hunger" in its reports). This might mean simply being unable to afford the basics, unable to get to the grocery, or unable to find fresh produce among the pizza shops, doughnut stores, and fried-everything restaurants of East Fordham Road.

Precious, the character at the center of the Academy Award-winning movie by the same name, would probably count as food insecure even though she is severely obese (her home, Harlem, ranks 49th on the survey's list, with 24.1 percent of residents saying they lacked money for food in the previous year). There she is stealing a family-size bucket of fried chicken from a fast-food restaurant. For breakfast.

That it is greasy chicken, and that she vomits it up in a subsequent scene, points to the problem that experts call a key bridge between hunger and obesity: the scarcity of healthful options in low-income neighborhoods and the unlikelihood that poor, food-insecure people like Precious would choose them.

A 2008 study by the city government showed that 9 of the Bronx's 12 community districts had too few supermarkets, forcing huge swaths of the borough to rely largely on unhealthful, but cheap, food.

Full-service, reasonably priced supermarkets are rare in impoverished neighborhoods, and the ones that are there tend to carry more processed foods than seasonal fruits and vegetables. A 2008 study by the city government showed that 9 of the Bronx's 12 community districts had too few supermarkets, forcing huge swaths of the borough to rely largely on unhealthful, but cheap, food.

"When you're just trying to get your calorie intake, you're going to get what fills your belly," said Mr. Berg, the author of *All You Can Eat: How Hungry Is America?* "And that may make you heavier even as you're really struggling to secure enough food."

For the center's survey, Gallup asked more than 530,000 people across the nation a single question: "Have there been times in the past 12 months when you did not have enough money to buy food that you or your family needed?"

The unusually large sample size allowed researchers to zero in on trouble spots like the South Bronx.

New York's 10th Congressional District, which zigzags across Brooklyn and includes neighborhoods like East New York and Bedford-Stuyvesant, ranked sixth in the survey, and Newark ranked ninth, both with about 31 percent of residents showing food hardship. (At the state level, the South is the hungriest: Mississippi tops the list at 26 percent, followed by

Arkansas, Alabama, Tennessee, Kentucky, Louisiana, the Carolinas, and Oklahoma. New York ranks 27th, with 17.4 percent; New Jersey is 41st, with 15.5 percent; and Connecticut is 47th, with 14.6 percent.)

The survey, conducted over the past two years, showed that food hardship peaked at 19.5 percent nationwide in the fourth quarter of 2008, as the economic crisis gripped the nation. It dropped to 17.9 percent by the summer of 2009, then rose to 18.5 percent.

Though this was the first year that the center did such a survey, it used a question similar to one the Department of Agriculture has been asking for years. The most recent survey by the agency, from 2008, found that 14.6 percent of Americans had low to very low food security.

Bloomberg administration officials see hunger and obesity as linked problems that can be addressed in part by making healthful food more affordable.

"It's a subtle, complicated link, but they're very much linked, so the strategic response needs to be linked in various ways," said Linda I. Gibbs, the deputy mayor for health and human services. "We tackle the challenge on three fronts—providing income supports, increasing healthy options, and encouraging nutritious behavior."

To that end, the city offers a Health Bucks program that encourages people to spend their food stamps at farmers' markets by giving them an extra $2 coupon for every $5 spent there.

The city has also created initiatives to send carts selling fresh fruits and vegetables to poor neighborhoods, and to draw grocery stores carrying fresh fruit and produce to low-income areas by offering them tax credits and other incentives. The city last month announced the first recipients of those incentives: a Foodtown store that burned down last year will be rebuilt and expanded in the Norwood section of the Bronx, and a Western Beef store near the Tremont subway station will be expanded.

But the Bronx's hunger and obesity problems are not simply related to the lack of fresh food. Experts point to a swirling combination of factors that are tied to, and exacerbated by, poverty.

Poor people "often work longer hours and work multiple jobs, so they tend to eat on the run," said Dr. Rundle of Columbia. "They have less time to work out or exercise, so the deck is really stacked against them."

Indeed, the food insecurity study is hardly the first statistical measure in which the Bronx lands on the top—or, in reality, the bottom. The borough's 14.1 percent unemployment rate is the highest in the state. It is one of the poorest counties in the nation. And it was recently ranked the unhealthiest of New York's 62 counties.

"If you look at rates of obesity, diabetes, poor access to grocery stores, poverty rates, unemployment, and hunger measures, the Bronx lights up on all of those," said Triada Stampas of the Food Bank for New York City. "They're all very much interconnected."

DISCUSSION

1. "When most people think of hunger in America," writes Dolnick, "the images that leap to mind are of ragged toddlers in Appalachia or rail-thin children in dingy apartments reaching for empty bottles of milk" (p. 219). Do you agree? What impression of or attitude toward hunger do images like these provide us? Can you think of other images we are taught to associate with hunger?
2. While we tend to think of obesity as evidence of excess or overindulgence, notes Dolnick, the truth is that obesity is much more often caused by poverty. How does this fact change your assumptions about eating, weight, and health?
3. In attempting to capture the paradox of hunger and obesity, Dolnick cites the government term "food insecurity." What does this term mean to you? What portrait of eating does it suggest? And do you think it is a useful term for helping to explain the hunger-obesity paradox itself?

WRITING

4. What are the particular assumptions and stereotypes our culture teaches us to associate with obesity? What sorts of judgments about obese people are we encouraged to pass? Once you've answered these questions, focus on the particular ways Dolnick's essay seeks to challenge or rewrite these proscriptions. To what extent does his discussion of the "obesity-hunger paradox" create an alternative script for viewing and thinking about the topic of obesity? In your view, is this a change for the better? Why or why not?
5. Dolnick lists a number of the initiatives New York City has considered in its effort to stem the rise of obesity. Among them: sending carts selling fresh fruit and vegetables to poor neighborhoods; using tax incentives to draw grocery stores to low-income areas; encouraging people to spend their food-assistance support on healthy food choices. Write an essay in which you evaluate the effectiveness of these strategies. In your view, are these strategies adequate responses to the problem of obesity? On what basis do you draw this conclusion? And how do your views on this topic compare to the view espoused by Dolnick?
6. Like Dolnick, Francine Prose (p. 181) is also interested in exploring cultural attitudes around eating and obesity. How does her examination of "gluttony" compare to Dolnick's discussion of the "obesity-hunger paradox"? Do you think Prose would find the data cited by Dolnick useful in her effort to challenge the cultural stigma around overeating?

Tying It All Together

One of the themes tying several of the chapter's readings together is poverty. Sam Dolnick (p. 219) and Erika Nicole Kendall (p. 210) in particular use their investigations into food-related topics as a way of opening up broader discussion about what it means to be poor in America. These writers are not alone. In the chapter "How We Work," for example, both Barbara Ehrenreich (p. 380) and Mac McClelland (p. 394) pose very similar questions. In an essay, compare one of the two essays from this chapter with one of these two essays from "How We Work." How do their respective commentaries about poverty relate? What are the key similarities and differences? Which do you find more persuasive? Why?

Caroline Knapp (p. 188) and Francine Prose (p. 181) both explore the ways one's body can be turned into an object of public scrutiny. In this sense, their essays cover the same ground as writers such as Jessica Bennett (p. 90) and Harriet McBryde Johnson (p. 96), both of whom write essays examining what it means to have one's physical self put on broader, public display. Compare the various and contrasting ways each of these essays goes about commenting upon this process. What perspective on or attitude about public display and public scrutiny does each writer offer? What are the key differences?

Scenes and Un-Scenes: **Giving Thanks**

Thanksgiving stands out as one of our few genuinely American holidays. Its rituals are rooted in American myth, one that is separate from religious doctrine. Regardless of who we are, where we come from, or what we do, virtually all Americans celebrate this holiday in one way or another. Of course, this doesn't mean we all share the same view of how this meal should go or what it means. We may all be familiar with the classic Thanksgiving stereotype (the harmonious and homogeneous nuclear family gathered around the well-stocked dinner table), but this doesn't mean our own holiday experiences conform to this template. It is precisely this question of difference, in fact, that the portraits assembled here highlight. Representing Thanksgiving dinner from a range of vantage points, the following images underscore various ways Americans observe and think about this national holiday. In each case, we can pose two related sets of questions. First, what vision of the typical holiday meal does it present? What typical ways of eating? What typical American family? What typical American values? And second, how does this depiction serve either to challenge or reinforce those traditional ideals this meal is supposed to symbolize?

>> ***Painted at the height of World War II, Norman Rockwell's*** **Freedom from Want** ***remains arguably the most well-known and influential depiction of Thanksgiving dinner ever created. For decades, its old-fashioned, homespun portrait has succeeded in setting the boundaries around how we are supposed to think about this particular holiday. Connecting this meal to one of the nation's core freedoms, it has encouraged countless Americans over the years to regard Thanksgiving as a celebration of the values (such as comfort, security, and abundance) universally available to all Americans. Given how this picture defines the typical American family and the typical American meal, however, do these values seem as universal as they are intended?***

N. Rockwell/Corbis

Created over a half century later, John Currin's **Thanksgiving** ***rewrites Rockwell's portrait in dramatic ways. Replacing*** **Freedom's** ***vision of comfort and plenitude with a darker and more anxiety-ridden image of thwarted desire and unfulfilled appetite, Currin makes this holiday meal into an occasion for critiquing our long-standing emphasis on excessive consumption. As one reviewer puts it, "We've come a long way from Norman Rockwell."***

John Holyfield

For artists of color, the effort to revise the Rockwell Thanksgiving vision has frequently revolved around challenging its assumptions about who gets to count as a typical American — a definition that treats being white as an unexamined given. Seeking to enlarge the boundaries of this definition, John Holyfield's Blessing II *does more than merely recapitulate the basic terms of the Thanksgiving myth; it also subtly alters them. What sorts of messages (about comfort and security, about family and tradition) would you say this image conveys? And to what extent do they either resemble or rework the messages discernible in the Rockwell portrait?*

The stereotypical Thanksgiving scene is so familiar to most Americans that it has become shorthand for visual artists seeking to comment on current events. This cartoon by Pat Oliphant adopts the traditional Thanksgiving scene in order to make a satirical point about paranoia surrounding recent news reports about possible bird flu outbreaks in the United States.

Warner Bros./Photofest

Not every modern portrayal of Thanksgiving, of course, adopts such an ironic, skeptical, or dismissive perspective. It could be argued, for example, that this image, from the 1990s sitcom **Friends** ***presents us with simply an updated version of the same ideals promoted in the iconic Rockwell image shown earlier. What do you think of this proposition? Does this portrait define the typical American family in the same ways? The typical American meal?***

Pool/Getty

Many of these old-fashioned Thanksgiving ideals have proved so enduring, in fact, that they have become woven into the fabric of our political life as well. No politician these days passes up an opportunity to be pictured celebrating this holiday meal with one or another group of "regular" Americans — a ritual designed to promote the same vision of America that we see in Norman Rockwell's painting. How well would you say this photo-op does this? Does it offer a similarly convincing portrait of community?

DISCUSSION

1. Which of these portraits most closely resembles your typical Thanksgiving experience? Which least resembles your experience? Why?
2. What does each of these images define its portrait of Thanksgiving against? In your view, which of these visions (ideal or anti-ideal) strikes you as more legitimate? How so?
3. As these pictures make clear, our eating attitudes and habits can serve as a revealing metaphor for the other kinds of things we think and care about. Based on the preceding portfolio, which cultural issues and debates would you say eating gets connected to most often in our culture?

WRITING

4. First, focus on how eating is being represented in one of the images you've just reviewed. What stands out? What seems most important or noteworthy? And what, by contrast, seems noticeably absent? Then, analyze the ways you think this image uses its dining portrait to define the typical or ideal American family. What behaviors and attitudes does it seem to present as normal? And what values, beliefs, or ideas does this portrait seem to endorse as right?
5. Taken together, the images assembled here make clear what boundaries exist around how we are and are not allowed to think about eating. On the basis of what this portfolio includes, where do these boundaries seem to get drawn? Write an essay in which you speculate about the kinds of activities, attitudes, assumptions, and values that this collection of images implies lie outside the norm. Make sure you argue either in favor of or against drawing the boundary in these particular ways, using details from these images and your own experience to reinforce your point of view.
6. Choose one of the preceding examples. How does its depiction of the typical meal compare to the eating practices described by Brendan Buhler (p. 203) or Caroline Knapp (p. 188)? In a page, evaluate how the norms promoted by this image compare to those profiled in one of these two essays. What are the similarities? The differences? To what extent do you think either Buhler or Knapp would subscribe to or choose to emulate them? Why do you think this?

Putting It into Practice: **Consumer Profiling**

Now that you've read the chapter selections, try applying your conclusions to your own life by completing the following exercises.

FOOD JOURNAL For one week, keep a written account of all your meals, including what you eat, what time you eat, where you eat, how healthy you believe your meal is, and how much it costs. At the end of the week, write a brief essay in which you reflect on the reasons or motives behind *why* you made these particular choices. Identify and evaluate the different scripts, rules, and norms you think may have played a part in your eating habits. How many of your choices were simply prompted by cravings and how many by nutritional concerns? How much did your physical appearance influence your choices? How much was determined by non-food-related factors (such as your time constraints or budget)? Do any of your decisions line up with the topics discussed by the authors in this chapter? How?

LOCAL CONTEXTS, LOCAL TASTES What and how we eat are greatly influenced by context. The cultural traditions in which we are raised, the neighborhood in which we live, and the social class to which we belong play significant roles in determining the particular eating practices we follow. Choose one of these factors (i.e., culture, geography, class) and research the ways it shapes the eating customs of a particular group. Within this group, what foods are most popular? How are they eaten? In what settings do meals take place? Then write a brief essay in which you discuss how the particular factor you chose influences these outcomes. Be sure to cite your research in your discussion.

WHOLESALE MESSAGES For this exercise, find some examples of the ways that food and eating are advertised: how restaurants, food brands, or diet gurus try to sell you on their products and on the idea that consuming them will be a positive experience. What elements of these products seem to have the most weight in terms of marketing? Taste? Fitness? Fun? Family? Write an essay in which you discuss which key elements seem to occur most often. Why do you think that is? Do you feel like food and eating are sold as part of a larger package? That is, when you are being sold the idea of eating, what other norms are you also buying, according to these advertisers?

Alex Wong/Getty

4 How We LEARN

What are our perceptions of knowledge and the ways we should acquire that knowledge?

Introduction

School Rules

If you were to create your own school, what would it look like? What kinds of courses would get taught? What kind of work would get assigned, and how would it be evaluated? What sorts of activities and routines would organize daily classroom life? What roles would you script for teachers and students? As you consider all this, think too about what such a school would *not* look like: what sorts of lessons would never get taught, what rules would never get written, what kinds of teachers and students you would never see. After you've considered these questions, ask yourself a final one: How much of your experience at school has ever measured up to this ideal?

It is difficult to think of an environment in contemporary life more rule bound than school. If you doubt this claim, take a moment to compile a mental list of all regulations by which a typical school day is organized. We all know firsthand that once we walk into the classroom, precious few activities are really up for debate. In ways that are perhaps a bit more explicit than elsewhere, school is a world defined by very firm boundaries and governed by very clear requirements. Rules tell us what kinds of homework we have to complete and what kinds of tests we have to take, decree which courses are mandatory and which ones are optional, mandate the number of hours per week and the number of weeks per semester we need to spend at school. In some cases, in fact, rules even set standards for what we can wear or how we can talk. Underlying and justifying these many regulations is one final expectation: that we look on the rigid organization of school life as something both indispensable and nonnegotiable, an essential component of a quality education. Without things like homework and pop quizzes, standardized testing and attendance policies, graduation requirements and semester schedules, P.E. and recess, we are supposed to believe, real learning simply wouldn't happen.

What is normal?

Jim West/Alamy

Detroit, Michigan, rules posted on a classroom door at Guyton Elementary School, part of the Detroit public school system

What do these rules ask you to believe? What actions and attitudes do they ask you to accept as normal?

But what exactly is *real* learning? And who should be given the authority to decide this? Do all the expectations and instructions we are called on to follow at school really turn us into better-educated people? While school is one of the few genuine touchstones in our lives — one of only a handful of institutions with which we all have had some degree of personal experience — it remains one of the most problematic as well. Because so many of the day-to-day decisions are taken out of our hands, it doesn't always feel as if the education we spend so many years pursuing actually belongs to us. We may wonder whether there is a logical connection between the tests we take and the grades we receive or between our personal opinions about a poem or short story and the views espoused by a professor in lecture, but given the way school is typically set up, there isn't a whole lot we can do about it. No matter what ideas we have about what rules should and should not govern our school experiences, we also know that subordinating these decisions to somebody else is part of our jobs.

For a particularly vivid illustration, take the example of grading. Grades are absolutely essential, so goes the conventional thinking, because they alone offer educators a reliable and verifiable way of assessing students' work. Without grades, how would we ever know if students were measuring up? But notice the unspoken assumptions that lie beneath this anxious query, most prominently among them the conviction that grades are accurate barometers of student ability and achievement. To believe in the validity and necessity of grading, we also have to believe that the standards on which they rest — the standards that differentiate, say, A-grade work from C-grade work — are grounded in a fair and universally applicable understanding of what good work involves. Nor do the assumptions stop here. We could easily probe the implications of this grading norm even further, posing questions about the ultimate wisdom of any system that so conspicuously emphasizes competition and rank. Does an arrangement that compels students to focus so much attention on the external markers of achievement really offer the best way to encourage meaningful learning? This question might well lead us to rethink the kinds of authority that typically get vested in teachers: the authority not only to grade student work, but also to evaluate, assess, and judge more generally. Posing these kinds of questions not only challenges some of the rules by which school

What is normal?

a. The Honor Code is an undertaking of the students, individually and collectively:

   1. that they will not give or receive aid in examinations; that they will not give or receive unpermitted aid in class work, in the preparation of reports, or in any other work that is to be used by the instructor as the basis of grading;
   2. that they will do their share and take an active part in seeing to it that others as well as themselves uphold the spirit and letter of the Honor Code.

From the Stanford University Honor Code

Do you share the attitudes and values scripted here? Should we automatically accept them as normal?

conventionally operates, but, even more fundamentally, also starts the process of unlearning the core lessons that have taught us what a worthwhile education is.

In many ways, this unlearning process is already taking place. Education is one of the most contentiously debated issues of our time. We argue over the merits of public versus private schooling, over the limits of free speech on campus, over the place of religious belief in the classroom, over how to best utilize the educational resources of the Internet. Educational issues anchor our debates about multiculturalism, about economic and social class, about free speech. Whether it involves a court case adjudicating the merits of teaching intelligent design or a state initiative to require school uniforms, a dispute over online university accreditation or protests regarding a college's financial ties to companies that exploit their workers, school-related issues and controversies remain at the very center of our national life. So engrossing and encompassing a topic has education become that we could easily extend the scope of this investigation well beyond the walls of the classroom. The other chapters in this book help illustrate the argument that our larger culture itself is a classroom in which we are all pupils.

Taken together, the readings assembled in this chapter provide some sense of how richly diverse and broadly encompassing the issue of education is. Mike Rose argues passionately about the assumptions we make about a link between education and intellect. Dan Hurley, meanwhile, chronicles recent efforts to use digital tools — in particular video gaming — as a vehicle for honing creative and critical thinking. Several writers examine some discrete aspect of our contemporary schooling practices. Alfie Kohn, for example, calls into question the conventional wisdom regarding grades and grading. Whereas Kohn criticizes specific aspects of formal schooling, former teacher John Taylor Gatto argues that we ought to dismantle the entire system. In a personal comment on the educational system, bell hooks recounts her experiences navigating the educational and social boundaries she encountered as

What is normal?

"The truth is — too many teachers are unprepared when they enter the classroom and the system fails to identify and reward good teachers, support those with potential or — when necessary — counsel out of the field those teachers who are just not suited for this challenging profession.

"The truth is — too many schools — including many charter schools — are simply not providing students with an education that prepares them for college and careers — and they need to change the way they do business — or go out of business.

"The truth is — there are indefensible inequities in our school system — in terms of funding, teacher quality, access to rigorous curriculum, and student outcomes. Half a century after *Brown versus Board of Education*, this is an epic injustice for our society."

Secretary of Education Arne Duncan in a speech to the National Press Club, July 27, 2010

What kind of script do these remarks write? What would it look like to act upon these scripts in your own life?

a working-class student of color. Taking a fresh look at public handwringing over academic plagiarism, Rachel Toor offers a more nuanced assessment of what it means — and what it doesn't mean — to "cheat." Jonathan Kozol's essay catalogs the insidious ways that business language and business logic have come to underlie much of what happens in our elementary classrooms. And finally, adding her voice to the call for education reform, Kristina Rizga talks back to the myths and stereotypes that teach us to fundamentally misunderstand why schools "fail."

What is normal?

"I support intelligent design. What I support is putting all science on the table and then letting students decide. I don't think it's a good idea for government to come down on one side of scientific issue or another, when there is reasonable doubt on both sides."

Speech by Representative Michele Bachmann to the Republican Leadership Council, July 2011.

Can social scripts be rewritten?

e macmillanhighered.com/actingout
Tutorials > Digital Writing > Online Research Tools
e-Readings > The American Academy of Arts & Sciences, *The Heart of the Matter*

ALFIE KOHN

From Degrading to De-grading

Are grades really necessary? Do they truly offer us an accurate, meaningful measure of student ability or achievement? Couldn't we have a quality education without them? Answering this final question with an emphatic "yes," Alfie Kohn makes the case that grades are not only irrelevant but actually antithetical to learning. Kohn has published eleven books on education and parenting, including *No Contest: The Case against Competition* (1986), *Unconditional Parenting: Moving from Rewards and Punishments to Love and Reason* (2005), *The Homework Myth: Why Our Kids Get Too Much of a Bad Thing* (2006), and most recently, *Feel-Bad Education* (2011). His articles have appeared in *Phi Delta Kappan*, the *Journal of Education*, the *Nation*, and the *Harvard Business Review.* As a public speaker, he has lectured school groups and corporations against competition in education. He has also appeared on the *Today* show and *The Oprah Winfrey Show*. The essay that follows was originally published in *High School Magazine* in 1999.

YOU CAN TELL A LOT ABOUT A TEACHER'S VALUES AND PERSONALITY just by asking how he or she feels about giving grades. Some defend the practice, claiming that grades are necessary to "motivate" students. Many of these teachers actually seem to enjoy keeping intricate records of students' marks. Such teachers periodically warn students that they're "going to have to know this for the test" as a way of compelling them to pay attention or do the assigned readings—and they may even use surprise quizzes for that purpose, keeping their grade books at the ready.

Frankly, we ought to be worried for these teachers' students. In my experience, the most impressive teachers are those who despise the whole process of giving grades. Their aversion, as it turns out, is supported by solid evidence that raises questions about the very idea of traditional grading.

THREE MAIN EFFECTS OF GRADING

Researchers have found three consistent effects of using—and especially, emphasizing the importance of—letter or number grades:

1. **Grades tend to reduce students' interest in the learning itself.** One of the best-researched findings in the field of motivational psychology is that the more people are rewarded for doing something, the more they tend to lose interest in whatever they had to do to get the reward (Kohn 1993). Thus, it shouldn't be surprising that when

students are told they'll need to know something for a test—or, more generally, that something they're about to do will count for a grade—they are likely to come to view that task (or book or idea) as a chore.

While it's not impossible for a student to be concerned about getting high marks and also to like what he or she is doing, the practical reality is that these two ways of thinking generally pull in opposite directions. Some research has explicitly demonstrated that a "grade orientation" and a "learning orientation" are inversely related (Beck, Rorrer-Woody, and Pierce 1991; Milton, Pollio, and Eison 1986). More strikingly, study after study has found that students—from elementary school to graduate school, and across cultures—demonstrate less interest in learning as a result of being graded (Benware and Deci 1984; Butler 1987; Butler and Nisan 1986; Grolnick and Ryan 1987; Harter and Guzman 1986; Hughes, Sullivan, and Mosley 1985; Kage 1991; Salili et al. 1976). Thus, anyone who wants to see students get hooked on words and numbers and ideas already has reason to look for other ways of assessing and describing their achievement.

2. **Grades tend to reduce students' preference for challenging tasks.** Students of all ages who have been led to concentrate on getting a good grade are likely to pick the easiest possible assignment if given a choice (Harter 1978; Harter and Guzman 1986; Kage 1991; Milton, Pollio, and Eison 1986). The more pressure to get an A, the less inclination to truly challenge oneself. Thus, students who cut corners may not be lazy so much as rational; they are adapting to an environment where good grades, not intellectual exploration, are what count. They might well say to us, "Hey, you told me the point here is to bring up my GPA, to get on the honor roll. Well, I'm not stupid: The easier the assignment, the more likely that I can give you what you want. So don't blame me when I try to find the easiest thing to do and end up not learning anything."

3. **Grades tend to reduce the quality of students' thinking.** Given that students may lose interest in what they're learning as a result of grades, it makes sense that they're also apt to think less deeply. One series of studies, for example, found that students given numerical grades were significantly less creative than those who received qualitative feedback but no grades. The more the task required creative thinking, in fact, the worse the performance of students who knew they were going to be graded. Providing students with comments in addition to a grade didn't help: The highest achievement occurred only when comments were given *instead* of numerical scores (Butler 1987; Butler 1988; Butler and Nisan 1986).

In another experiment, students told they would be graded on how well they learned a social studies lesson had more trouble understanding the main point of the text than did students who were told that no grades would be involved. Even on a measure of rote recall, the graded group remembered fewer facts a week later (Grolnick and Ryan 1987). And students who tended to think about current events in terms of what they'd need to know for a grade were less knowledgeable than their peers, even after taking other variables into account (Anderman and Johnston 1998).

MORE REASONS TO JUST SAY NO TO GRADES

The preceding three results should be enough to cause any conscientious educator to rethink the practice of giving students grades. But there's more.

Grades aren't valid, reliable, or objective. A B in English says nothing about what a student can do, what she understands, where she needs help.

Moreover, the basis for that grade is as subjective as the result is uninformative. A teacher can meticulously record scores for one test or assignment after another, eventually calculating averages down to a hundredth of a percentage point, but that doesn't change the arbitrariness of each of these individual marks. Even the score on a math test is largely a reflection of how the test was written: what skills the teacher decided to assess, what kinds of questions happened to be left out, and how many points each section was "worth."

A B in English says nothing about what a student can do, what she understands, where she needs help.

Moreover, research has long been available to confirm what all of us know: Any given assignment may well be given two different grades by two equally qualified teachers. It may even be given two different grades by a single teacher who reads it at two different times (for example, see some of the early research reviewed in Kirschenbaum, Simon, and Napier 1971). In short, what grades offer is spurious precision—a subjective rating masquerading as an objective evaluation.

Grades distort the curriculum. A school's use of letter or number grades may encourage a fact- and skill-based approach to instruction because that sort of learning is easier to score. The tail of assessment thus comes to wag the educational dog.

Grades waste a lot of time that could be spent on learning. Add up all the hours that teachers spend fussing with their grade books. Then factor in the (mostly unpleasant) conversations they have with students and their parents about grades. It's tempting to just roll our eyes when confronted with whining or wheedling, but the real problem rests with the practice of grading itself.

Grades encourage cheating. Again, we can either continue to blame and punish all the students who cheat—or we can look for the structural reasons this keeps happening. Researchers have found that the more students are led to focus on getting good grades, the more likely they are to cheat, even if they themselves regard cheating as wrong (Anderman, Griesinger, and Westerfield 1998; Milton, Pollio, and Eison 1986).

Grades spoil teachers' relationships with students. Consider this lament, which could have been offered by a teacher in your district:

> I'm getting tired of running a classroom in which everything we do revolves around grades. I'm tired of being suspicious when students give me compliments, wondering whether or not they are just trying to raise their grade. I'm tired of spending so much time and energy grading your papers, when there are probably a dozen more productive and enjoyable ways for all of us to handle the evaluation of papers. I'm tired of hearing you ask me, 'Does this count?' And, heaven knows, I'm certainly tired of all those little arguments and disagreements we get into concerning marks which take so much fun out of the teaching and the learning . . . (Kirschenbaum, Simon, and Napier 1971, p. 115).

Grades spoil students' relationships with one another. The quality of students' thinking has been shown to depend partly on the extent to which they are permitted to learn cooperatively (Johnson and Johnson 1989; Kohn 1992). Thus, the ill feelings, suspicion, and resentment generated by grades aren't just disagreeable in their own right; they interfere with learning.

The most destructive form of grading by far is that which is done "on a curve," such that the number of top grades is artificially limited: No matter how well all the students do, not all of them can get an A. Apart from the intrinsic unfairness of this arrangement, its practical effect is to teach students that others are potential obstacles to their own success. The kind of collaboration that can help all students to learn more effectively doesn't stand a chance in such an environment. Sadly, even teachers who don't explicitly grade on a curve may assume, perhaps unconsciously, that the final grades "ought to" come out looking more or less this way: a few very good grades, a few very bad grades, and the majority somewhere in the middle.

The competition that turns schooling into a quest for triumph and ruptures relationships among students doesn't only happen within classrooms, of course. The same effect is witnessed schoolwide when kids are not just rated but ranked, sending the message that the point isn't to learn, or even to perform well, but to defeat others. Some students might be motivated to improve their class rank, but that is completely different from being motivated to understand ideas. (Wise educators realize that it doesn't matter how motivated students are; what matters is *how* students are motivated. It is the type of motivation that counts, not the amount.)

EXCUSES AND DISTRACTIONS

Most of us are directly acquainted with at least some of these disturbing consequences of grades, yet we continue to reduce students to letters or numbers on a regular basis. Perhaps we've become inured to these effects and take them for granted. This is the way it's always been, we assume, and the way it has to be. It's rather like people who have spent all their lives in a terribly polluted city and have come to assume that this is just the way air looks—and that it's natural to be coughing all the time.

Oddly, when educators are shown that it doesn't have to be this way, some react with suspicion instead of relief. They want to know why you're making trouble, or they assert that you're exaggerating the negative effects of grades (it's really not so bad—cough, cough), or they dismiss proven alternatives to grading on the grounds that our school could never do what other schools have done.

It's rather like people who have spent all their lives in a terribly polluted city and have come to assume that this is just the way air looks.

The practical difficulties of abolishing letter grades are real. But the key question is whether those difficulties are seen as problems to be solved or as excuses for perpetuating the status quo. The logical response to the arguments and data summarized here is to say: "Good heavens! If even half of this is true, then it's imperative we do whatever we can, as soon as we can, to phase out traditional grading." Yet, many people begin and end with the problems of implementation, responding to all this evidence by saying, in effect, "Yeah, yeah, yeah, but we'll never get rid of grades because . . ."

It is also striking how many educators never get beyond relatively insignificant questions, such as how many tests to give, or how often to send home grade reports, or what number corresponds to what letter. Some even reserve their outrage for the possibility that too many students are ending up with good grades, a reaction that suggests stinginess with A's is being confused with intellectual rigor.

COMMON OBJECTIONS

Let's consider the most frequently heard responses to the above arguments—which is to say, the most common objections to getting rid of grades.

First, it is said that students expect to receive grades and even seem addicted to them. This is often true; I've taught high school students who reacted to the absence of grades with what I can only describe as existential vertigo. (*Who am I if not a B+?*) But as more elementary and even some middle schools move to replace grades with more informative (and less destructive) systems of assessment, the damage doesn't begin until students get to high school. Moreover, elementary and middle schools that *haven't* changed their practices often cite the local high school as the reason they must get students used to getting grades regardless of their damaging effects—just as high schools point the finger at colleges.

Even when students arrive in high school already accustomed to grades, already primed to ask teachers, "Do we have to know this?" or "What do I have to do to get an A?," this is a sign that something is very wrong. It's more an indictment of what has happened to them in the past than an argument to keep doing it in the future.

Perhaps because of this training, grades can succeed in getting students to show up on time, hand in their work, and otherwise do what they're told. Many teachers are loath to give up what is essentially an instrument of control. But even to the extent this instrument works (which is not always), we are obliged to reflect on whether mindless compliance is really our goal. The teacher who exclaims, "These kids would blow off my course in a minute if they weren't getting a grade for it!" may be issuing a powerful indictment of his or her course. Who would be more reluctant to give up grades than a teacher who spends the period slapping transparencies on the overhead projector and lecturing endlessly at students about Romantic poets or genetic codes? Without bribes (A's) and threats (F's), students would have no reason to do such assignments. To maintain that this proves something is wrong with the kids—or that grades are simply "necessary"—suggests a willful refusal to examine one's classroom practices and assumptions about teaching and learning.

"If I can't give a child a better reason for studying than a grade on a report card, I ought to lock my desk and go home and stay there." So wrote Dorothy De Zouche, a Missouri teacher, in an article published in February . . . of 1945. But teachers who *can* give a child a better reason for studying don't need grades. Research substantiates this: When the curriculum is engaging—for example, when it involves hands-on, interactive learning activities—students who aren't graded at all perform just as well as those who are graded (Moeller and Reschke 1993).

Another objection: It is sometimes argued that students must be given grades because colleges demand them. One might reply that "high schools have no responsibility to serve colleges by performing the sorting function for them"—particularly if that process undermines learning (Krumboltz and Yeh 1996, p. 325). But in any case the premise of this argument is erroneous: Traditional grades are not mandatory for admission to colleges and universities.

MAKING CHANGE

A friend of mine likes to say that people don't resist change—they resist being changed. Even terrific ideas (like moving a school from a grade orientation to a learning orientation) are guaranteed to self-destruct if they are simply forced down people's throats. The first step for an administrator, therefore, is to open up a conversation—to spend perhaps a full year just encouraging people to think and talk about the effects of (and alternatives to) traditional grades. This can happen in individual classes, as teachers facilitate discussions about how students regard grades, as well as in evening meetings with parents, or on a website—all with the help of relevant books, articles, speakers, videos, and visits to neighboring schools that are further along in this journey.

The actual process of "de-grading" can be done in stages. For example, a high school might start by freeing ninth-grade classes from grades before doing the same for upperclassmen. (Even a school that never gets beyond the first stage will have done a considerable service, giving students one full year when they can think about what they're learning instead of their GPAs.)

Another route to gradual change is to begin by eliminating only the most pernicious practices, such as grading on a curve or ranking students. Although grades, per se, may continue for a while, at least the message will be sent from the beginning that all students can do well, and that the point is to succeed rather than to beat others.

Anyone who has heard the term *authentic assessment* knows that abolishing grades doesn't mean eliminating the process of gathering information about student performance—and communicating that information to students and parents. Rather, abolishing grades opens up possibilities that are far more meaningful and constructive. These include narratives (written comments), portfolios (carefully chosen collections of students' writings and projects that demonstrate their interests, achievements, and improvement over time), student-led parent-teacher conferences, exhibitions, and other opportunities for students to show what they can do.

Of course, it's harder for a teacher to do these kinds of assessments if he or she has 150 or more students and sees each of them for forty-five to fifty-five minutes a day. But that's not an argument for continuing to use traditional grades; it's an argument for challenging these archaic remnants of a factory-oriented approach to instruction, structural aspects of high schools that are bad news for reasons that go well beyond the issue of assessment. It's an argument for looking into block scheduling, team teaching, interdisciplinary courses—and learning more about schools that have arranged things so each teacher can spend more time with fewer students (e.g., Meier 1995).

Administrators should be prepared to respond to parental concerns, some of them completely reasonable, about the prospect of edging away from grades. "Don't you value excellence?" You bet—and here's the evidence that traditional grading *undermines* excellence. "Are you just trying to spare the self-esteem of students who do poorly?" We are concerned that grades may be making things worse for such students, yes, but the problem isn't just that some kids won't get A's and will have their feelings hurt. The real problem is that almost all kids (including yours) will come to focus on grades and, as a result, their learning will be hurt.

If parents worry that grades are the only window they have into the school, we need to assure them that alternative assessments provide a far better view. But if parents don't seem to care about getting the most useful information or helping their children become more excited learners—if they demand grades for the purpose of documenting how much better their kids are than everyone else's—then we need to engage them in a discussion about whether this is a legitimate goal, and whether schools exist for the purpose of competitive credentialing or for the purpose of helping everyone to learn (Kohn 1998; Labaree 1997). Above all, we need to make sure that objections and concerns about the details don't obscure the main message, which is the demonstrated harm of traditional grading on the quality of students' learning and their interest in exploring ideas.

The real problem is that almost all kids . . . will come to focus on grades and, as a result, their learning will be hurt.

High school administrators can do a world of good in their districts by actively supporting efforts to eliminate conventional grading in elementary and middle schools. Working with their colleagues in these schools can help pave the way for making such changes at the secondary school level.

IN THE MEANTIME

Finally, there is the question of what classroom teachers can do while grades continue to be required. The short answer is that they should do everything within their power to make grades as invisible as possible for as long as possible. Helping students forget about grades is the single best piece of advice for those who want to create a learning-oriented classroom.

When I was teaching high school, I did a lot of things I now regret. But one policy that still seems sensible to me was saying to students on the first day of class that, while I was compelled to give them a grade at the end of the term, I could not in good conscience ever put a letter or number on anything they did during the term—and I would not do so. I would, however, write a comment—or, better, sit down and talk with them—as often as possible to give them feedback.

At this particular school I frequently faced students who had been prepared for admission to Harvard since their early childhood—a process I have come to call "Preparation H." I knew that my refusal to rate their learning might cause some students to worry about their marks all the more, or to create suspense about what would appear on their final grade reports, which of course would defeat the whole purpose. So I said that anyone who absolutely had to know what grade a given paper would get could come see me and we would figure it out together. An amazing thing happened: As the days went by, fewer and fewer students felt the need to ask me about grades. They began to be more involved with what we were learning, because I had taken responsibility as a teacher to stop pushing grades into their faces, so to speak, whenever they completed an assignment.

What I didn't do very well, however, was to get students involved in devising the criteria for excellence (what makes a math solution elegant, an experiment well designed, an essay persuasive, a story compelling) or in deciding how well their projects met those criteria. I'm afraid I unilaterally set the criteria and evaluated the students' efforts. But I have seen teachers who were more willing to give up control, more committed to helping students participate in assessment and turn that into part of the learning. Teachers who work with their students to design powerful alternatives to letter grades have a replacement ready to go when the school finally abandons traditional grading—and are able to minimize the harm of such grading in the meantime.

ADDENDUM: MUST CONCERNS ABOUT COLLEGE DERAIL HIGH SCHOOL LEARNING?

Here is the good news: College admissions practices are not as rigid and reactionary as many people think. Here is the better news: Even when that process doesn't seem to have its priorities straight, high schools don't have to be dragged down to that level.

Sometimes it is assumed that admissions officers at the best universities are eighty-year-old fuddy-duddies peering over their spectacles and muttering about "highly irregular" applications. In truth, the people charged with making these decisions are often just a few years out of college themselves, and after making their way through a pile of interchangeable applications from 3.8-GPA, student-council-vice-president, musically accomplished hopefuls from high-powered traditional suburban high schools, they are desperate for something unconventional. Given that the most selective colleges have been known to accept homeschooled children who have never set foot in a classroom, secondary schools have more latitude than they sometimes assume. It is not widely known, for example, that hundreds of colleges and universities don't require applicants to take either the SAT or the ACT.

Admittedly, large state universities are more resistant to unconventional applications than are small private colleges simply because of economics: It takes more time, and therefore more money, for admissions officers to read meaningful application materials than it does for them to glance at a GPA or an SAT score and plug it into a formula. But I have heard of high schools approaching the admissions directors of nearby universities and saying, in effect, "We'd like to improve our school by getting rid of grades. Here's why. Will you work with us to make sure our seniors aren't penalized?" This strategy may well be successful for the simple reason that not many high schools are requesting this at present and the added inconvenience for admissions offices is likely to be negligible. Of course, if more and more high schools abandon traditional grades, then the universities will have no choice but to adapt. This is a change that high schools will have to initiate rather than waiting for colleges to signal their readiness.

It takes more time . . . for admissions officers to read meaningful application materials than it does for them to glance at a GPA or an SAT score.

At the moment, plenty of admissions officers enjoy the convenience of class ranking, apparently because they have confused being better than one's peers with being good at something; they're looking for winners rather than learners. But relatively few colleges actually insist on this practice. When a 1993 survey by the National Association of Secondary School Principals asked eleven hundred admissions officers what would happen if a high school stopped computing class rank, only 0.5 percent said the school's applicants would not be considered for admission, 4.5 percent said it would be a "great handicap," and 14.4 percent said it would be a "handicap" (Levy and Riordan 1994). In other words, it appears that the absence of class ranks would not interfere at all with students' prospects for admission to four out of five colleges.

Even more impressive, some high schools not only refuse to rank their students but refuse to give any sort of letter or number grades. Courses are all taken pass/fail, sometimes with narrative assessments of the students' performance that become part of a college application. I have spoken to representatives and all assure me that, year after year, their graduates are accepted into large state universities and small, highly selective colleges. *Even the complete absence of high school grades is not a barrier to college admission*, so we don't have that excuse for continuing to subject students to the harm done by traditional grading.

REFERENCES

Anderman, E. M., T. Griesinger, and G. Westerfield. 1998. "Motivation and Cheating During Early Adolescence." *Journal of Educational Psychology* 90: 84–93.

Anderman, E. M., and J. Johnston. 1998. "Television News in the Classroom: What Are Adolescents Learning?" *Journal of Adolescent Research* 13: 73–100.

Beck, H. P., S. Rorrer-Woody, and L. G. Pierce. 1991. "The Relations of Learning and Grade Orientations to Academic Performance." *Teaching of Psychology* 18: 35–37.

Benware, C. A., and E. L. Deci. 1984. "Quality of Learning with an Active Versus Passive Motivational Set." *American Educational Research Journal* 21: 755–65.

Butler, R. 1987. "Task-Involving and Ego-Involving Properties of Evaluation: Effects of Different Feedback Conditions on Motivational Perceptions, Interest, and Performance." *Journal of Educational Psychology* 79: 474–82.

Butler, R. 1988. "Enhancing and Undermining Intrinsic Motivation: The Effects of Task-Involving and Ego-Involving Evaluation on Interest and Performance." *British Journal of Educational Psychology* 58: 1–14.

Butler, R., and M. Nisan. 1986. "Effects of No Feedback, Task-Related Comments, and Grades on Intrinsic Motivation and Performance." *Journal of Educational Psychology* 78: 210–16.

De Zouche, D. 1945. " 'The Wound Is Mortal': Marks, Honors, Unsound Activities." *The Clearing House* 19: 339–44.

Grolnick, W. S., and R. M. Ryan. 1987. "Autonomy in Children's Learning: An Experimental and Individual Difference Investigation." *Journal of Personality and Social Psychology* 52: 890–98.

Harter, S. 1978. "Pleasure Derived from Challenge and the Effects of Receiving Grades on Children's Difficulty Level Choices." *Child Development* 49: 788–99.

Harter, S., and M. E. Guzman. 1986. "The Effect of Perceived Cognitive Competence and Anxiety on Children's Problem-Solving Performance, Difficulty Level Choices, and Preference for Challenge." Unpublished manuscript, University of Denver.

Hughes, B., H. J. Sullivan, and M. L. Mosley. 1985. "External Evaluation, Task Difficulty, and Continuing Motivation." *Journal of Educational Research* 78: 210–15.

Johnson, D. W., and R. T. Johnson. 1989. *Cooperation and Competition: Theory and Research.* Edina, Minn.: Interaction Book Co.

Kage, M. 1991. "The Effects of Evaluation on Intrinsic Motivation." Paper presented at the meeting of the Japan Association of Educational Psychology, Joetsu, Japan.

Kirschenbaum, H., S. B. Simon, and R. W. Napier. 1971. *Wad-Ja-Get?: The Grading Game in American Education.* New York: Hart.

Kohn, A. 1992. *No Contest: The Case Against Competition.* Rev. ed. Boston: Houghton Mifflin.

Kohn, A. 1993. *Punished by Rewards: The Trouble with Gold Stars, Incentive Plans, A's, Praise, and Other Bribes.* Boston: Houghton Mifflin.

Kohn, A. 1998. "Only for My Kid: How Privileged Parents Undermine School Reform." *Phi Delta Kappan,* April: 569–77.

Krumboltz, J. D., and C. J. Yeh. 1996. "Competitive Grading Sabotages Good Teaching." *Phi Delta Kappan,* December: 324–26.

Labaree, D. F. 1997. *How to Succeed in School Without Really Learning: The Credentials Race in American Education.* New Haven, Conn.: Yale University Press.

Levy, J., and P. Riordan. 1994. *Rank-in-Class, Grade Point Average, and College Admission.* Reston, Va.: NASSP. (Available as ERIC Document 370988.)

Meier, D. 1995. *The Power of Their Ideas: Lessons for America from a Small School in Harlem.* Boston: Beacon.

Milton, O., H. R. Pollio, and J. A. Eison. 1986. *Making Sense of College Grades.* San Francisco: Jossey-Bass.

Moeller, A. J., and C. Reschke. 1993. "A Second Look at Grading and Classroom Performance: Report of a Research Study." *Modern Language Journal* 77: 163–69.

Salili, F., M. L. Maehr, R. L. Sorensen, and L. J. Fyans Jr. 1976. "A Further Consideration of the Effects of Evaluation on Motivation." *American Educational Research Journal* 13: 85–102.

DISCUSSION

1. Kohn has some pointed things to say about the connection often presumed to exist between traditional grading and student motivation. More specifically, he questions the long-standing educational norm that says students who do not receive grades have no incentive to work. What do you think of this claim? Is it valid? How does your own view compare to Kohn's?
2. Kohn's critique of conventional grading practices rests in part on his assertion that, no matter how minutely calculated, every letter or number grade is a subjective and arbitrary assessment. Do you agree? Can you think of an example from your own school experiences that either confirms or confounds this argument?
3. "Perhaps," Kohn speculates, "we've become inured to [the] effects [of grades] and take them for granted. This is the way it's always been, we assume, and the way it has to be. It's rather like people who have spent all their lives in a terribly polluted city and have come to assume that this is just the way air looks — and that it's natural to be coughing all the time" (p. 242). What do you make of this analogy? To what extent does it seem valid to think of our contemporary approach to grading as a kind of pollution? Does this analogy capture any aspect of your own educational experiences?

WRITING

4. Write a personal essay in which you either support or refute Kohn's argument about grading, using anecdotes from your experience as a student. Do you view grading in a negative or positive light? Why or why not? Make sure to structure your argument by addressing Kohn's multiple points directly.
5. Kohn writes about the need to move a school "from a grade orientation to a learning orientation" (pp. 239, 243). What do you think he means? How, according to Kohn, does grading make it harder to focus on learning? Write an essay in which you discuss the characteristics of these two orientations. Do you think it's possible to have an educational system that emphasizes both?
6. Write an essay in which you discuss how Kohn might use Rachel Toor's observations about plagiarism (p. 296) to support his argument against grading. Do you think Kohn would find Toor's approach to plagiarism compatible with his own vision of a grade-free classroom?

Then and Now: Encyclopedic Knowledge

For generations, the classic multivolume encyclopedia has epitomized what it means to be an educated person. Studded with dense descriptions and overviews of countless subjects — from astronomy to anatomy, geography to world history — these leather-bound tomes have long stood as tangible symbols of what we consider legitimate knowledge. Supporting these compendia of information were a number of unspoken assumptions: not only about the things we were expected to know, but also about the proper way we were expected to go about acquiring this knowledge. Widely respected as the arbiter of learning, the encyclopedia drew boundaries around what is and is not a worthwhile subject of study; and even more fundamentally, it conveyed a clear message about who was in charge of setting these boundaries. Legitimate knowledge, these monumental volumes implied, was not something we were allowed to define on our own; this task, rather, remained the purview of those with greater expertise and authority — namely, the experts and editors deemed educated enough to write the encyclopedia.

Neale Cousland/Shutterstock

With the explosion of digital technologies, however, many of these cherished norms have been turned on their head. Case in point: Wikipedia. As the latter half of the name implies, this site is designed to function as a comprehensive collection of entries on subjects of importance. On closer inspection, however, it becomes clear that the wiki does a good deal more than simply transpose old practices and old assumptions into a new century. Unlike the traditional encyclopedia, Wikipedia sets very different parameters around what constitutes legitimate knowledge. Rather than a collection of facts culled by a cadre of faceless experts, wikis offer themselves as clearinghouses for information to which virtually anyone — regardless of training, background, or expertise — can contribute. The prerogative to weigh in on a given subject — to present information — is not confined to so-called experts; it is an invitation, rather, for collaborative writing about subjects important to culture, revisable almost in real time. The result is not just a more democratic definition of knowledge, but also one that is far more fluid and dynamic — one that is constantly undergoing change as more and more contributors add to the body of information.

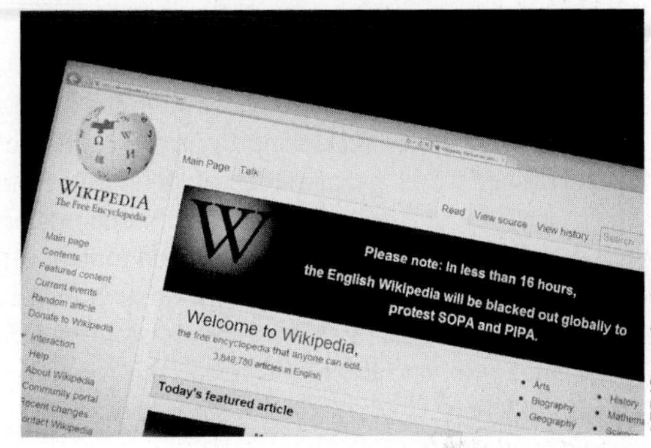

AFP/Getty Images

But are these changes for the better? To be sure, Wikipedia goes a long way toward broadening the range of information and perspectives that are allowed to be included: It makes great strides in reconfiguring research and knowledge sharing as collaborative undertakings, and it's interactive in ways that traditional encyclopedias aren't. But these changes give rise to important questions having to do with credibility and reliability of the information this new technology makes available. Are there adequate standards in place for determining what gets defined as legitimate knowledge? Have we lost a belief in the value of experts and expertise that perhaps we shouldn't have? What are the new norms, the new definitions, of education these sorts of changes have ushered in? Does this exciting new technology actually improve the ways we learn?

WRITING

1. How does technology such as Wikipedia redefine what it means to conduct research? Does knowing that the information contributed in a Wikipedia article comes from many anonymous sources change the way you evaluate its contents? Write a brief evaluation of the pros and cons of using Wikipedia versus a more traditional research source.
2. Pull up a Wikipedia article for a subject of your choosing that also has an entry in a traditional encyclopedia. Write a comparison of how each source treats the subject. Which is more useful to you, and why? What are the shortcomings of each source? In the end, does either source provide adequate information for research? Why or why not?

KRISTINA RIZGA

Everything You've Heard about Failing Schools is Wrong

We hear a lot these days about the crisis in public education. But how many discussions of this crisis are grounded in firsthand knowledge of what actually goes on in school? Seeking to provide just such a perspective, journalist Kristina Rizga takes a closer look at life in one school officially deemed to be "failing." What results is a surprising, enlightening, and complex portrait — one that challenges our received ideas about what is and isn't working in contemporary education. Kristina Rizga covers education for *Mother Jones* magazine. Her writing has appeared in the *Nation*, *Global Post*, Grist.com, and the *Bay Citizen*. This piece was published by *Mother Jones* in 2012.

"SPEEK EENGLISH, TACO," THE GIRL WITH THE GIANT BACKPACK yelled when Maria asked where to find a bathroom. The backpack giggled as it bounced down the hall. It had been hours since Maria began looking for a bathroom. Anger boiled inside her, but she didn't know any English words to yell back. That was the hardest part. Back in El Salvador she'd always had something to say.

The bell rang. A flood of shoulders and sneakers swirled around Maria, and she couldn't see much until the sea of strangers streamed back into classrooms. Then she stood alone in the hallway.

It was Maria's first day at school, her first week in the United States. Her middle school in San Francisco was the biggest building she'd ever seen. It was bigger than the entire Best Buy store she'd walked through in awe on her first day in the city.

Eventually, Maria found her way to class, a special setting for Spanish-speaking newcomers. There she would practice English words for colors and numbers, learn how to introduce herself and how to say thank you. By eighth grade she was moved into mainstream classes, where she struggled. It didn't help that her math teacher started each class by saying, "Okay, my little dummies." He spoke really fast. Maria never raised her hand in his class.

One day Maria stopped by the administrative office, looking for someone to help her with multiplication. She took her spot in line behind a middle-aged woman who chatted with her in Spanish as they waited.

Maria said school was really hard for her. The woman told her not to worry. "Latinas usually don't finish high school," she said. "They go to work or raise kids."

The woman was right, statistically speaking, and Maria's middle-school experience all but ensured she'd join the 52 percent[1] of foreign-born Latinos who drop out of high school. She graduated from eighth grade without learning to speak English. She had a hard time writing in Spanish and didn't know how to multiply.

And then everything changed. At Mission High, the struggling school she'd chosen against the advice of her friends and relatives, Maria earned high grades in math and some days caught herself speaking English even with her Spanish-speaking teachers. By 11th grade, she wrote long papers on complex topics like desegregation and the war in Iraq. She became addicted to winning debates in class, despite her shyness and heavy accent. In her junior year, she became the go-to translator and advocate for her mother, her aunts, and for other Latino kids at school. In March, Maria and her teachers were celebrating acceptance letters to five colleges and two prestigious scholarships, including one from Dave Eggers' writing center, 826 Valencia[2].

But on the big state tests—the days-long multiple-choice exams that students in California take once a year—Maria scored poorly. And these standardized tests, she understood, were how her school was graded. According to the scores, Mission High is among the lowest-performing 5 percent[3] of schools in the country, and it has consistently failed to meet the ever-rising benchmarks set by the federal No Child Left Behind Act[4]. The law mandates universal "proficiency" in math and reading by 2014—a deadline that weighs heavily on educators around the nation, since schools that don't meet it face stiff penalties.

It was with these penalties on his mind that Mission High principal Eric Guthertz got ready for work one morning in 2010. It was his wife's birthday, and also the day California was supposed to release its list of "persistently low-performing" schools—schools that the state deemed as urgently in need of improvement. As he put on his tie, he recalls, "I told my wife, 'I hope we dodged that bullet!' But I was kidding, because I was convinced we wouldn't be on that list. And on my ride to school, I was feeling bad for the principals" who would.

It wasn't long after he got to the office that the phone rang. It was the district. Mission was on the list.

Guthertz was in shock. His teachers had been working so hard, he thought. What would they say? How about the parents, the students? Where would he get extra resources to bring up the numbers? Mission's test scores and college acceptance rates had been going up. But for purposes of the list, that didn't matter.

A few months later, Guthertz got another call from the district. This one was of the good news/bad news variety: As a low-performing school, Mission qualified for additional funding—but only if it agreed to undergo a major restructuring[5]. Options included replacing the principal and either revamping the curriculum or replacing half the staff; closing the school; or turning it into a charter. Guthertz had been promoted to his job less than two years earlier, and the district was allowed to report this change to the federal government as a replacement of the principal—a loophole that bought Mission some time. But San Francisco's oldest comprehensive public high school[6], founded in 1890, would still have to show dramatic growth in scores by 2014 or face more interventions, including possible closure.

Judging from what I'd read about "troubled" schools, I'd expected noisy classrooms, hallway fights, and disgruntled staff. Instead I found a welcoming place that many students and staff called "family."

Around the same time that Guthertz was digesting this news, I was calling education officials in search of a school that would let me spend time inside its classrooms. I was looking for a grassroots view of America's latest run at school reform: How do we know when schools are failing, and why is it so hard to turn them around? Is the close to $4.4 billion spent on testing since 2002—with scores now used for everything from deciding teacher pay to allocating education budgets—getting results? Is all that data helping us figure out what really works, or seducing us into focusing only on what the tests can measure?

If you wonder why you haven't read many accounts of how these questions are playing out in real life, there's a reason: It's easier for a journalist to embed with the Army or the Marines than to go behind the scenes at a public school. It took months to find one that would let me play fly on the wall. Once Guthertz opened the door at Mission, it took months more for some teachers, wary of distortion and stereotyping, to warm to me. In the end, I'd spend more than 18 months in Mission's classrooms, cafeterias, and administrative offices, finally watching the Class of 2012—including a beaming Maria—show off their diplomas.

The surprises began almost right away. Judging from what I'd read about "troubled" schools, I'd expected noisy classrooms, hallway fights, and disgruntled staff. Instead I found a welcoming place that many students and staff called "family." After a few weeks of talking to students, I failed to find a single one who didn't like the school, and most of the parents I met were happy too. Mission's student and parent satisfaction surveys rank among the highest in San Francisco.

One of the most diverse high schools in the country, Mission has 925 students holding 47 different passports. The majority are Latino, African American, and Asian American, and 72 percent are poor. Yet even as the school was being placed on the list of lowest-performing schools, 84 percent of the graduating class went on to college, higher than the district average; this year, 88 percent were accepted. (Nationally, 32 percent of Latino and 38 percent of African American students[7] go to college.) That same year, Mission improved Latinos' test scores more than any other school in the district. And while suspensions are skyrocketing across the nation, they had gone down by 42 percent at Mission. Guthertz had seen dropout rates fall from 32 percent to 8 percent. Was this what a failing school looked like?

When Maria turned three, she stopped hearing the voice of her mother in the mornings. No one explained where she'd gone, but when Maria was seven, her grandmother explained that her mom had crossed three borders to find work in California. Maria and her older brother were raised by her grandparents in the village of San Juan Las Minas in El Salvador. Their aunt Angelica came to visit when she could.

Maria doesn't remember much from those days except for her auntie's soft, soothing voice. Angelica had two children of her own, but she didn't mind when Maria started calling her "mom." When Angelica left, Maria kept to herself. Her grandparents were busy growing vegetables, raising cows and chickens, and looking after Maria, her brother, and four cousins.

Angelica ran a corner liquor store in San Salvador, two hours away. To stay in business, she had to pay off the MS-13 gang each month. They left her alone most of the time, except the day they shot one of her customers in the store. Maria was there. A piece of the man's head dropped on her foot.

Angelica loved escaping the city for Las Minas. "I'm like you, Maria. Like a little girl," she used to say when they played soccer together or climbed the mango trees.

Maria remembers everything about the day of her auntie's funeral. Angelica's tall body in a light wooden coffin beside the kitchen table, surrounded by candles. The scent of wax giving way to the smell of beer and sticky sweat as the day wore on. The 20 strangers in the house, their shiny, shirtless bodies covered in tattoos of letters, numbers, and devil's horns: symbols for MS-13. As the house got hotter, the men's voices grew louder. They started playing poker, roaring at their own jokes.

Maria, now 12, was praying near the coffin. She could see her auntie's dark hair through the white lace covering her face. It had been a week since she'd last heard from her. "Don't worry," Angelica had said. "I'll take care of everything. I'll pay off MS-13."

But she couldn't. She didn't have enough money. Three days after that call, she was found at the entrance of a San Salvador hospital, naked and barely alive. The doctors said she'd been raped and tortured for days. There was nothing they could do to save her.

Maria tried to focus on praying, but the men who'd invaded her grandparents' house got louder, throwing cards across the table and spitting on the floors. Maria gathered her courage and walked toward them. "Be respectful or get out of my house!" she shouted. The men's heads turned. For a few moments, the house was quiet. Then the men started laughing.

They left only after Angelica was buried, and they'd taken all of Maria's grandparents' money.

"Why don't you come to America?" Maria's mother asked her on the phone a week after the funeral. She had been talking to her about coming to the States since she was seven. "I'd always say no," Maria recalls. "I loved my auntie more than anything. I didn't want to be in any other country but mine. But when my auntie died, I had no one close left."

Maria was the youngest passenger on the bus crossing El Salvador, Guatemala, and Mexico toward California. Her mom had paid the coyote $3,000, and Maria's ride was easy. No wandering through the desert. The coyote bought them chicken for dinner every night. At home, her grandparents cooked chicken only when relatives came over on Sunday.

The first time Maria set foot in Mission High, she thought it looked like a church. The facade and doorway were decorated with intricate Spanish Baroque moldings. Heavy iron chandeliers adorned the ornate ceiling above the entrance hall. The light glittered on spotless yellow linoleum. As Maria and her middle-school classmates toured the library, courtyards, and cafeteria, she noticed that people seemed friendly. Even the security guards were cracking jokes. Principal Guthertz regaled students with the school's history and famous alumni: Carlos Santana, Maya Angelou. There were after-school programs—the Latino student club, soccer, creative writing. Maria asked a few students if they liked Mission. To her surprise, all of them did.

Everyone Maria knew outside of Mission told her not to go there. Her mother's friends said she should pick a better school. Maria's friends said Mission had gangs.

Guthertz introduced Maria to Amadis Velez, who spoke to her in Spanish. He told her that he'd be her English teacher. On the wall, Maria noticed Velez's diploma from the University of California-Berkeley, surrounded by photos of Frida Kahlo, César Chávez, and Salvador Dalí. "He was so welcoming," Maria remembers. "He kept making jokes about our English, making us laugh. After I met Mr. Velez, I knew I'll be going to Mission."

"She didn't speak a lick of English when she started in my ninth-grade English class," Velez recalls. "That year, there were only two students whose English was worse than Maria's." Velez also noticed that Maria's Spanish grammar was about two years behind her Latino classmates'. Maria was 5 feet tall and weighed about 80 pounds. "She was tiny," Velez remembers, "but very spunky, and her leadership and popularity among students stood out to me right away."

Maria loved that she had a class with Velez every day. He taught her English and geography in the 9th grade, and history in the 10th. He often checked in with her in the afternoon. All kinds of worries kept pouring out in their conversations. Could Velez explain the word *tariffs*? What's this thing, *analysis*? Who could teach Maria how to multiply?

"I thought of myself as a really bad student back then," she recalls. "I didn't believe in myself. But Mr. Velez always told me not to give up, to keep going, keep pushing."

Overall, the last 10 years have revealed that while Big Data can make our questions more sophisticated, it doesn't necessarily lead to Big Answers.

One day, Velez sat her down, took out a piece of paper, and started charting her path to college. He said that she needed to transfer into regular English classes as soon as possible to prepare for college. He also explained that California was one of 12 states[8] that allow undocumented students like her to pay resident tuition rather than out-of-state rates, which can be twice as much. Velez said that Maria was not eligible for any government grants or student loans, but there were private scholarships, and he'd help her get them. All of this was possible, he said, if Maria kept her grades up, did all of her homework, and worked twice as hard as her classmates who already knew English. He said he'd be there for her no matter what. He told her to have fun and to laugh a lot.

Most days Maria did well and felt good about her progress. She met with Velez after class to review her grammar and plan for college. He urged her to write more complex sentences. By the end of 10th grade, she was writing essays that didn't fit on one page. She earned an A in Mr. Velez's modern world history class.

Then one morning, over breakfast, she found an envelope on her mother's kitchen table. Inside were the results of the standardized tests she'd taken a few months before. Her stomach tilted. She'd done much worse than she'd anticipated. In history her score was "far below basic," the lowest ranking.

What Maria didn't know was that only 19 percent[9] of Mission High's Latino students scored "proficient or above" in history. The vast majority of Latinos, at Mission High and statewide[10], scored similar to Maria.

She knew that Velez thought she was smart. But this was the first grade she'd gotten from people outside of Mission, and it made her wonder. Was Mr. Velez wrong?

Every spring across the nation, students in 3rd to 11th grade sit down to take standardized tests required by the federal No Child Left Behind Act (NCLB). Each state comes up with its own tests, based on its own list of curriculum standards students have to master in each grade. In most states, standardized tests consist primarily[11] of multiple-choice questions.

People who fought for these tests wanted to raise expectations for all students. They knew that for decades students of color, the learning disabled, and poor students weren't challenged, often stuck in segregated and underfunded schools and shuffled into vocational training. Education historian Larry Cuban pins the beginning of the move toward high-stakes testing to the passage of the Elementary and Secondary Education Act of 1965[12], which sent significant extra funding to low-income schools neglected by local school boards.

Closures or mass firings at low-performing schools, bonuses for high-scoring teachers, and an expansion of charter schools were supposed to disrupt a system that, in the reformers' view, had failed students and the companies for which they would one day work.

The policies were also designed to find out which reforms were improving achievement. "Class size reduction, whole language instruction, everything under the sun has been tried in our schools," Arun Ramanathan, the executive director of the Oakland think tank Education Trust-West[13], told me. "But how could we assess if there are any returns without reliable data? How could we know what we can scale up?"

As more states started using standardized testing, urban education reformers in the '70s and '80s were able to flag the outliers[14]: schools that were reducing the achievement gap between white, middle-class students and students of color and the poor. Cuban believes that this data helped to dismantle the idea that poor, minority, immigrant, or disabled students couldn't learn.

By 2001, when the Bush administration was pushing No Child Left Behind through Congress, testing had undergone a political transformation: Now it was at the core of a business-inspired approach championed by a loose coalition of corporate leaders like Bill Gates[15], idealists like Wendy Kopp[16] of Teach for America, and maverick education officials like Washington, DC, schools chief Michelle Rhee[17], the heroine of the documentary *Waiting for "Superman."* Standardized tests, many of these reformers believed, could bring hard-and-fast metrics—and hardcore sanctions—to a complacent world of bureaucrats and teachers' unions. Closures or mass firings at low-performing schools, bonuses for high-scoring teachers, and an expansion of charter schools were supposed to disrupt a system that, in the reformers' view, had failed students and the companies for which they would one day work.

No Child Left Behind was animated by this faith in metrics. It mandated that states use test scores to determine whether schools were succeeding or failing, with the latter required to improve or accept punitive measures. NCLB passed with bipartisan support, and many civil rights groups were behind it.

Ten years later, a growing number[18] of education advocates say they didn't anticipate how high-stakes testing would change instruction for the worse. Among the converts is education historian Diane Ravitch, who served as assistant secretary of education in George H. W. Bush's administration and was an ardent champion of NCLB. "Accountability turned into a nightmare for American schools," she wrote in a 2010 *Wall Street Journal* op-ed[19], "producing graduates who were drilled regularly on the basic skills but were often ignorant about almost everything else . . . This was not my vision of good education." In his studies, Cuban has also found that an increasing proportion of lesson time is spent preparing students for tests, and the curriculum is being narrowed to what is on those tests—even though many researchers agree that cramming for multiple-choice, a.k.a. "bubble," tests contributes very little[20] to actual learning.

The overwhelming emphasis on testing has led some schools and districts to cheat. An investigation[21] by the state of Georgia last year found widespread test-tampering in Atlanta, and the *Atlanta Journal-Constitution*[22] has identified similar patterns in hundreds of districts nationwide. Some schools have also cranked up discipline and school-based arrests, leading struggling students to drop out[23] — and thus improving scores.

Overall, the last 10 years have revealed that while Big Data can make our questions more sophisticated, it doesn't necessarily lead to Big Answers. The push to improve scores has left behind traditional assessments that, research indicates, work better to gauge performance: classroom work and homework[24], teachers' grades and quizzes, the opinions of students and parents about a school. In his recent book *The Social Animal*, conservative columnist and veteran education commentator David Brooks identifies this bias[25] — to emphasize and reward what we can measure, and ignore the rest—as a key reason why technocratic promises in social policy have largely failed to materialize. Research,

Brooks notes, shows that the key to success is more often found in realms that resist quantification—relationships, emotions, and social norms.

Even the godfather of standardized testing, the cognitive psychologist Robert Glaser[26], warned in 1987 about the dangers of placing too much emphasis on test scores. He called them "fallible and partial indicators of academic achievement" and warned that standardized tests would find it "extremely difficult to assess" the key skills people should gain from a good education: "resilience and courage in the face of stress, a sense of craft in our work, a commitment to justice and caring in our social relationships, a dedication to advancing the public good."

It was eight in the morning, and the lights were off in Mr. Roth's history class as winter rain tapped on the windowsills and warm moisture filled the room. In the flickering light of a television screen, Maria could see her friend Brianna breaking small pieces from a muffin and dropping them into her mouth. Maria lowered her chin into her hands. Her right leg, sheathed in dark blue jeans, bounced on the linoleum floor.

On the TV, Paula Crisostomo was waving a protest sign in the face of a police officer and arguing with her father, a Filipino immigrant wearing a blue work shirt. "I told you to stay away from these agitators!" he yelled at Paula. Based on a true story, *Walkout* captures the 1968 school protests[27] in East Los Angeles. About 22,000 Latino students participated, inspired by a teacher named Sal Castro. (One of them—Antonio Villaraigosa, né Antonio Villar—is now mayor of LA.) Back then, most Latinos were forbidden from speaking Spanish in class. Curricula largely ignored Mexican American history, and Latinos were steered toward menial labor.

In the film, students could be seen shaking the metal gate of their school, locked shut by officials to prevent them from walking out. The students rattled the bars chanting "*Viva la Raza!*" while police stood on the other side. The gate broke. Maria's entire class erupted in applause as the teens flooded into the street.

After the film ended, Robert Roth switched on the lights and turned to a class sitting in motionless silence. "Any thoughts, anyone?"

"It's incredible to see how courageous Paula was," said a student from Nicaragua named Catharine. "She lost confidence so many times, but whenever she lost it, her friends were there to support her."

"In middle school I was told to speak only English at home," Maria said next. "I think that's wrong. I already do at school. They shouldn't tell me how to live my life."

"I can relate to Paula, how people don't believe Latinos are smart enough for college," Yessenia added. "These stereotypes make me want to prove them wrong."

"Speaking of stereotypes," Brianna said, "I was in the bathroom with five other black girls, and we were fixing our hair. Two Asian American girls come in and they run out right away, thinking that we are going to bully them. I want to fix that. I'm a nice person!"

Roth jumped in, "Rebecca, you were talking to me about this kind of stereotype the other day. Do you mind sharing what you said?"

"When we moved to St. Louis from China," Rebecca said, "we went to an all African American school. My parents were telling me to stay away from black students. They said don't trust them, run away. But they were all really nice to us. A lot of times it's coming from parents, but they just don't know."

At the end of class, Brianna and her friend Destiny came up to Maria. "What's 'Viva la Raza'?"

"It kind of means being proud to be Latino," Maria explained.

"How do you say it?" Brianna asked, and Maria told them. "Viva la Raza! Viva la Raza! Viva la Raza!" the three chanted out loud, fists in the air, laughing.

As students shuffled out, Roth reminded them, "A short reflection on this film is due next time. And please! Don't summarize, analyze. Why is this important? How does it connect to other things we learned?"

The following Monday, Roth passed back his students' homework essays. On Maria's he'd written, "It's a B this time! See me about this, OK?"

Maria showed up at his office the next day. "Some of the stuff you've been writing is so powerful. You are really getting there, Maria," Roth said, lowering his reading glasses and putting down a folder.

"Why isn't it an A then?" Maria half-smiled, and pulled out her homework. "Is it because of bad grammar?" She pointed at Roth's corrections on her paper.

"Look, writing is primarily about ideas," Roth told her. "Language, grammar, and style are important tools to express those ideas. But don't start by focusing on a few grammar mistakes, or you'll get stuck and ignore the bigger issues." He explained why he made certain corrections, but he spent most of the time talking to Maria about the elements he deems essential "to getting your thoughts out": thesis, evidence, analysis, and conclusion. "Did you organize your thoughts in a way that made sense?" he asked her. "Did you back up your opinions with evidence? Did you go deep enough?"

Roth explained to Maria that she'd summarized and discussed *Walkout* really well, but when it came to analysis and conclusion, her writing seemed rushed. "What are the connections between these protests and the African American struggle for civil rights?" Maria gave a few examples. Roth suggested that she think more about why these efforts were successful. "How did these walkouts change things? Why are we studying this?"

A few weeks later, Maria presented a research paper on equal access to education. While rewriting her essay about *Walkout*, she'd discovered that some Latino parents were organizing school boycotts even before the onset of the civil rights movement. "Did you know that *Mendez v.* [28] *Westminster*[28] happened eight years before *Brown v. Board?*" Maria announced to her class. In the 1946 case, Latino parents won the first-ever anti-segregation lawsuit in federal courts. "It helped the *Brown v. Board* attorneys to win their arguments before the Supreme Court," she explained. "The *Mendez* case was the beginning of the end for *Plessy v. Ferguson*, which said that 'separate but equal' is fine."

"Listen! One more day before the big bad test," Roth announced one spring day as he passed out a test that included some practice questions from the California STAR test—the final exam in US history as far as the state was concerned.

Maria and her classmates had been working with their teachers for a month to prepare for the state exams. Principal Guthertz, who has been known to eat live worms in front of students as a reward for higher test scores, promised to get a famous chef to cook a free meal for the entire school if scores went up again, as they had in the past three years.

"All I'm asking you to do is to take it seriously. Do it for the school," Roth said as he passed out the test. "Let's do a quick review together."

"Who was the first Catholic president? Give me three things about the New Deal!" Dozens of students shouted out answers. "You are going to *nail* this test!"

As Roth retreated to his desk, Maria stared at the rows of empty bubbles. A sharp, pounding pain filled her head. She picked up a pencil and read the first question:

> *During the late 19th and 20th centuries, urban immigrants generally supported local political machines that:*
> *(a) discouraged the new immigrants from participating in civic affairs.*
> *(b) were usually supported by urban reformers.*
> *(c) provided essential services to the immigrants.*
> *(d) reminded immigrants of political practices in their homelands.*

As always, Maria started translating the words into Spanish. Then she got to *discouraged*. She'd seen the word many times before, but it was usually in a context where she could guess the meaning of the passage without knowing every term. In this short sentence, though, there were no hints.

She tried to remember the word's meaning for a few minutes. Nothing.

Affairs was another word she'd heard before but couldn't remember. She translated the rest of the sentence—*new immigrants from participating*—but that didn't help. She took a deep breath and translated the rest of the answers. B was a possibility, she thought, but something felt off. C seemed right. But what about A? What if that was really the answer? There was no way of knowing. She filled in C for now.

"Five more minutes, everyone!" Roth interrupted. An ambulance siren wailed outside. Maria had spent too much time on the first five questions, and now she had to rush. She translated another page and randomly bubbled in the rest.

When she switched to the written section of the test, her leg stopped bouncing. When the bell rang, Maria kept writing, and didn't stop until Roth collected the pages from her.

Roth waited until the last student had left the room, and we looked over Maria's test together. She got almost all the answers wrong on the practice multiple-choice section, the only one that would have counted for the state. On Roth's essay question, she got an A+.

In 2010, Latinos made up the majority[29] of California's public school students for the first time. At Mission High, more than half the students are immigrants, and Guthertz says 20 percent have been in the United States for less than two years.

At Mission High, many teachers told me that there was simply no way to cover all of the standards while also maintaining a rich curriculum and actual research projects.

After just one year in the country, Maria had to take the same test as native speakers, even though studies show[30] that immigrant teens take at least four years to become proficient in English—and that's with constant focus. Maria scored "proficient" in history for the first time in the 11th grade.

A look at Maria's schoolwork, on the other hand, is a glimpse at a learner's progress. In the quizzes and tests designed by her teachers, in her research papers, essays, art projects, class discussions, and presentations, what you see is an intellect battling to find its voice: developing research and analytical skills, the ambition and empathy to immerse herself in worlds beyond her own, and the tenacity and confidence to tackle challenging problems and keep rewriting her papers even as she wrestled with the basics of her new language.

Roth has been teaching in inner-city schools for 24 years. He has been able to find ways to cover most of the core standards for the high-stakes testing without neglecting courage, craft, intellectual curiosity, and justice. But he struggles to keep the balance, and study after study shows that's true for many teachers. At Mission High, many teachers told me that there is simply no way to cover all of the standards while also maintaining a rich curriculum and actual research projects.

Yet despite a mountain of evidence that standardized tests reveal a very narrow slice[31] of information, in most states they still determine a school's fate. In some, such as New York[32], students' scores on the standardized tests also play a major role in grade promotion and high school placement. And in several states[33], up to 50 percent of the evaluations that determine teachers' job security and sometimes pay are based on a week's worth of tests rather than a year's worth of learning.

In the broader context of education reform, standardized testing data has been seen as absolute proof of specific policies' effectiveness. Pick up almost any news story on education—whether it is about charter schools, teacher bonuses, class sizes, or teacher unions—and the go-to evidence is gains or losses on the tests without regard for other measures, even easily available quantitative data such as dropout rates, student attendance, teacher attrition, or college enrollment rates.

It's not that reporters are blind to the other factors. Just like overworked school administrators, they simply use the data everyone talks about. And while the perspective of actual teachers and students might provide more nuance, there are few opportunities for exploring them. *Washington Post* reporter Paul Farhi noted in an essay for the *American Journalism Review*[34] that access to schools has been greatly constrained as administrators, fearful of sanctions, increasingly seek to control the message. It doesn't help that most of today's newsrooms simply can't afford to let a reporter spend time in a school for a month, let alone a year, as I did for *Mother Jones*. It's more efficient to look up scores online and make a few phone calls.

Given all that, it's no surprise that much of the debate is reduced to stereotypes. *Waiting for "Superman"* is a perfect distillation of education clichés, pitting charter schools run by enthusiastic reformers against sclerotic unions and incompetent administrators.

"I have seen about 20 rounds of classroom reform in my teaching career," Roth told me recently. "You know what I haven't seen? Serious dialogue with teachers, students, and parents. They can identify successful teaching, but they are rarely a part of the discussion."

Seeking alternatives to high-stakes testing doesn't mean giving ineffective teachers a pass, Roth added. "With all of that testing money floating around, I hope education reformers can spend some of it on finding a more holistic instrument"—one that would include a wide range of hard data as well as a deep look at student work.

One day as we sat on a curb near her mother's apartment, Maria told me she'd learned more in her years at Mission than ever before. "I'm shy," she said. "I don't speak that much in other classes, but Mr. Roth teaches me how to do it. He taught me that it's okay to argue even when I still have a lot of questions. As long as I give examples, support my point, and stay with it. Before, I would give up easily and not defend my point of view." Beaming, she added, "Now I argue, and I love winning."

But while debating was one of Maria's favorite things about school, she spent most of her time in Roth's class researching and writing papers. "That's how I prepare for the debates and learn how to express myself clearly."

"Mr. Roth tells me that I will get an A, if I am dedicated to working on my weaknesses," she told me. "What I really like is that he shows me exactly how I improve each time. In the past two years, I've seen Mr. Roth probably a thousand times to discuss each written assignment."

Maria told me that she used the textbooks to make an outline of important dates, names, and events, and to look up definitions of new words like "laissez-faire." She used the outlines to write papers. But Maria didn't remember many of these facts from year to year. What she did recall were her research papers, presentations, and art posters.

She plugged a small memory card into my laptop to show me what she'd learned.

"Oh, I really liked this one," she exclaimed, opening a paper titled "Latinos in the 1920s." As her class focused on the Roaring '20s, Maria found that Latino dances like the bolero, rumba, and tango were entering mainstream American culture. This led her to research Hollywood, where she made her favorite discovery. "Dolores del Río was the first Mexican movie star to gain interest to white audiences," she wrote in her paper. "Dolores showed the world that height does not matter at all if you want to be an actor, because she was very famous and beautiful even though she was very short like me!"

"Last year, I became really interested in African American history and their struggles," she explained, clicking through presentation files on Ida B. Wells, Frederick Douglass, Ella Baker, and W. E. B. Du Bois. "Learning about this motivates me not to give up." She opened a "Reconstruction Defeated" paper from the previous year. "I wanted to find out how did government justify treating African Americans unfairly with Jim Crow even though the Constitution said that all men and women were equal," she told me. "Through this paper, I became really interested in the 14th and 15th Amendment."

As I handed the memory card back to her, Maria said that as a sophomore she'd been determined to go back to her middle school to find the woman who'd told her that she'd never go to college. With her senior year under way, there was simply no time for that. She'd soon be filling out college applications and had recently been elected Latino student club president. She helped new immigrants at school. She also volunteered at a senior housing project through the Latino club, helping older neighbors. "And in my free time, I babysit my little cousins," she told me. "From now on, I only have time to talk with you over lunch at school."

One day this past spring as I lingered in Roth's room after class, a young teacher rushed in. "Robert, I've been teaching for years, but I'm really struggling this semester." Her students' grades were not showing any progress, she said, and they seemed to be losing interest. As the two looked over her grading book together, they realized she was attaching most of the grade to homework assignments and wasn't giving significant points on the work students did in her class. Those assignments showed that they were learning, but since her struggling students only saw the Fs on their homework, their engagement was dropping.

Roth's colleague, Pirette McKamey, has been teaching English and history for 24 years and is now the instructional reform facilitator at Mission High. She calls this kind of one-on-one mentoring "mucking in the dirt." "Every day, there are hundreds of small intellectual conversations all over the school about student work," explains McKamey. Along with Roth, she also co-leads a committee focused on improving achievement for kids of color, in which faculty review student work and grading policies and read the latest research. "What did the kid write? What did the kid produce?" McKamey says. "That's all that should matter."

An ample body of research shows that this kind of mentoring and peer review helps teachers figure out ways for struggling students to improve. But it doesn't show up in standardized tests—and for many, it's pushed aside by the constant battle to ratchet up scores.

Before NCLB there was a movement[36] in many states, including California, to come up with reliable, unified rubrics for using classroom work to measure achievement—to move toward a mix of standardized tests and teacher assessments, something shared by most of the world's top-performing school systems, from Finland to Hong Kong. But that effort got largely steamrolled by NCLB's focus on high-stakes testing.

"I'm a history teacher," Roth says. "I believe in systemic change and macro-level conversations. But when it comes to schools, what most people don't realize is that it's about work at the micro level. The biggest reform at schools lives at the micro level, and it has to do with improving the craft of teaching."

There are some signs of a shift at the macro level. In 2009, President Obama asked[37] states to "develop standards and assessments that don't simply measure whether students can fill in a bubble on a test, but whether they possess 21st-century skills like problem-solving and critical thinking and entrepreneurship and creativity." The federal government has allocated $330 million for developing tests for a new set of standards, known as Common Core[38], that will hit classrooms in 2015. Supporters say that while the new tests will still include multiple-choice questions, they will also offer some opportunities for writing, and the lists of standards will be shorter, leaving teachers more freedom.

But many education experts are skeptical. A recent Brookings Institution study[39] finds no correlation at all between the testing standards and student achievement. Even Common Core advocates such as Ramanathan concede that there's a disconnect. "California has long been considered to have some of the best standards in the nation," he says, "but we also have some of the worst student outcomes."

Roth, who has been coaching fellow teachers for two decades, told me that standards can act as a "political security blanket" and a general guideline, but they can't help teachers with the more important tasks: figuring out how to apply the material in the classroom and gathering evidence to measure real understanding. Roth's filing cabinets are filled with different lesson plans. But every year, he creates another folder for each class, and approximately 50 percent of the material is new. He then adjusts everything throughout the year based on what works with his students.

I observed the same in other successful classrooms at Mission. "I adjust my lessons and tests every day," says a popular young math teacher named Taica Hsu. "The student body changes every semester, and what worked last year most likely won't work next year."

The Obama administration has softened some of NCLB's impact, granting waivers[40] to more than half of the states from the law's most punitive section, which calls for all students to score "proficient" in math and English by 2014. But even in the waiver states, standardized tests[41] remain the dominant measure for schools.

Midway through Maria's senior year in 2012, she was watching *Waiting for "Superman"* in Mr. Velez's college expository writing class. They were learning about achievement gaps, test scores, teacher unions, charter schools, and different solutions offered to "fix" schools like Mission. In one scene, DC's Michelle Rhee was shown firing the principal of a low-scoring school, and then the film cut to scenes of teachers and parents protesting school closures.

"Which facts in the movie shocked you?" Velez probed as the movie ended.

"What we spend on prison inmates," one student called out.

"Why is it so hard to fire a bad teacher?" said another, visibly upset.

"I was shocked how low test scores[42] are in California and DC," added a student with big headphones around his neck.

"California test scores are low, but the movie didn't mention we have the most immigrants here," countered a classmate. "Our English scores are bad, but that doesn't mean our school is bad."

"What would you do to fix schools?" Velez asked. Students took turns calling out responses as Velez wrote down their suggestions on a white-board: Make the tests more meaningful . . . Allow our teachers to write these tests . . . Don't test immigrant students in the first two years . . . Give more money to public schools in California . . . Make it easier to fire bad teachers . . . Ask students which schools are good and bad . . .

"Will they close Mission like those schools in DC?" Maria asked.

The shouting stopped.

"We won't let them," another kid responded, and the class burst out laughing. Velez kept writing.

NOTES

[1]http://blog.chron.com/immigration/2010/05/52-percent-of-adult-latino-immigrants-are-drop-outs/

[2]http://826valencia.org/

[3]http://www.cde.ca.gov/ta/ac/pl/tier2.asp

[4]http://thomas.loc.gov/cgi-bin/bdquery/z?d107:HR00001:@@@D&summ1&

[5]http://data.ed.gov/grants/school-improvement-grants

[6]http://mhs-sfusd-ca.schoolloop.com/aboutmhs

[7]http://www.pewhispanic.org/2011/08/25/hispanic-college-enrollment-spikes-narrowing-gaps-with-other-groups/

[8]http://www.ncsl.org/issues-research/immig/in-state-tuition-and-unauthorized-immigrants.aspx

[9]http://star.cde.ca.gov/star2010/ViewReport.asp?ps=true&lstTestYear=2010&lstTestType=C&lstCounty=38&lstDistrict=68478-000&lstSchool=3834082&lstGroup=5&lstSubGroup=78

[10]http://star.cde.ca.gov/star2010/ViewReport.asp?ps=true&lstTestYear=2010&lstTestType=C&lstCounty=&lstDistrict=&lstSchool=&lstGroup=5&lstSubGroup=78

[11]http://www.motherjones.com/documents/406650-gao-nclb-report

[12]http://www.motherjones.com/documents/406651-esea-of-1965

[13]http://www.edtrust.org/west

[14]http://www.motherjones.com/documents/406652-history-of-testing

[15]http://online.wsj.com/article/SB10001424052970204485304576641123767006518.html

[16]http://www.theatlantic.com/national/archive/2012/04/how-micromanaging-educators-stifles-reform/255543/#

[17]http://www.huffingtonpost.com/michelle-rhee/why-im-proud-of-student-a_b_848560.html

[18]http://www.reuters.com/article/2012/06/12/us-usa-education-testing-idUSBRE85B0EO20120612

[19]http://online.wsj.com/article/SB10001424052748704869304575109443305343962.html

[20]http://edpolicy.stanford.edu/sites/default/files/publications/beyond-basic-skills-role-performance-assessment-achieving-21st-century-standards-learning_4.pdf

[21]http://gov.georgia.gov/00/press/detail/0,2668,165937316_172445682_173112104,00.html

[22]http://www.ajc.com/news/cheating-our-children-suspicious-1397022.html

[23]http://advancementproject.org/sites/default/files/Federal%20Policy%20ESEA%20Reauthorization%20and%20the%20School-to-Prison%20Pipeline%20-%2003%2009%2011.pdf

[24]http://educationnext.org/portfolio-assessment/

[25]http://www.npr.org/2011/03/07/134329412/david-brooks-defines-the-new-social-animal

[26]http://www.nytimes.com/2012/02/16/us/robert-glaser-cognitive-psychologist-and-expert-on-student-testing-dies-at-91.html

[27]http://www.pomona.edu/magazine/PCMSP08/FSmaninthemiddle.shtml

[28]http://library.fullcoll.edu/friends/pdfs/Aguirre-MendezvWestminster.pdf

[29]http://www.sfgate.com/education/article/Latino-kids-now-majority-in-state-s-public-schools-3166843.php

[30]http://steinhardt.nyu.edu/scmsAdmin/uploads/004/297/AERJ%202008.pdf

[31]http://dissentmagazine.org/online.php?id=156

[32]http://www.nytimes.com/schoolbook/2012/05/23/more-parents-are-saying-no-to-pearsons-field-tests/

[33]http://www.nctq.org/p/publications/docs/nctq_stateOfTheStates.pdf

[34]http://www.ajr.org/Article.asp?id=5280

[35]http://www.motherjones.com/authors/erika-eichelberger

[36]http://edpolicy.stanford.edu/sites/default/files/publications/beyond-basic-skills-role-performance-assessment-achieving-21st-century-standards-learning_3.pdf

[37]http://www.whitehouse.gov/the-press-office/fact-sheet-race-top

[38]http://www.corestandards.org/about-the-standards

[39]http://www.brookings.edu/~/media/newsletters/0216_brown_education_loveless.pdf

[40]http://www.ed.gov/news/press-releases/26-more-states-and-dc-seek-flexibility-nclb-drive-education-reforms-second-round

[41]http://www.educationnews.org/education-policy-and-politics/nclb-waivers-could-signal-attempts-by-obama-to-undermine-law/

[42]http://nces.ed.gov/nationsreportcard/pdf/main2011/2012457.pdf

DISCUSSION

1. As Rizga notes, there exist very entrenched assumptions about what a “failing school” looks like. What images come to mind when you hear this phrase? What portrait of classroom life? What profile of students and teachers?
2. Rizga devotes a lot of attention in this essay to the experiences of students outside the classroom: their personal histories, family lives, economic circumstances. Why do you think Rizga chooses to include this information? In your view, is this helpful? How or how not?
3. “It is no surprise,” writes Rizga, “that much of the debate [about schools] is reduced to stereotypes” (p. 264). Do you agree? What are the particular stereotypes we are taught to use in such debates? What kind of attitude toward public education do such stereotypes script?

WRITING

4. According to Rizga, the primary factor responsible for designating a school as “failing” is our current reliance upon standardized tests. Write an essay in which you evaluate the validity or usefulness of using standardized tests to rank the performance of schools. Do such tests offer a fair, accurate, or helpful measure of a school’s performance or not? How? If you were charged with revamping the system for evaluating school performance, what kind of standardized test (if any) would you utilize? Why?
5. Here is how Rizga characterizes the work of one student at Mission High School: “In the quizzes and tests designed by her teachers, in her research papers, essays, art projects, class discussions, and presentations, what you see is an intellect battling to find its voice: developing research and analytical skills, the ambition and empathy to immerse herself in worlds beyond her own, and the tenacity and confidence to tackle challenging problems” (p. 263). Write an essay in which you describe and analyze the model of learning this passage outlines. What are the key abilities and skills Rizga highlights? What makes these abilities and skills so valuable? In your experience, is this learning model representative of the typical classroom experience? How or how not?
6. For John Taylor Gatto (p. 271) the reasons contemporary schools are failing can be summed up in a single word: “boredom.” How do you think Kristina Rizga would respond to this charge? Do you think her portrait of life at Mission High School is proof that Gatto is right? Or does it offer evidence that Gatto’s critique is off base? What specifically about Rizga’s essay makes you say so?

JOHN TAYLOR GATTO

Against School

Does boredom define the modern experience of being a student? And if so, who or what is to blame for this? Posing the provocative question "Do we really need school?" long-time educator and educational critic John Taylor Gatto offers a stinging rebuke to the practices and assumptions that underlie what passes for modern education. Gatto was born in Monongahela, Pennsylvania, and before becoming a schoolteacher and educational critic he held a number of jobs, including scriptwriter, taxi driver, and hot dog vendor. In 1991, he was named New York State Teacher of the Year. His books include *Dumbing Us Down: The Hidden Curriculum of Compulsory Schooling* (1992), *A Different Kind of Teacher: Solving the Crisis of American Schooling* (2000), *The Underground History of American Education* (2001), and, most recently, *Weapons of Mass Instruction: A Schoolteacher's Journey through the Dark World of Compulsory Schooling* (2009). He is now retired from teaching and is working on a documentary about compulsory education called *The Fourth Purpose.* The following piece originally appeared in the September 2003 issue of *Harper's Magazine.*

I TAUGHT FOR THIRTY YEARS IN SOME OF THE WORST SCHOOLS IN Manhattan, and in some of the best, and during that time I became an expert in boredom. Boredom was everywhere in my world, and if you asked the kids, as I often did, why they felt so bored, they always gave the same answers: They said the work was stupid, that it made no sense, that they already knew it. They said they wanted to be doing something real, not just sitting around. They said teachers didn't seem to know much about their subjects and clearly weren't interested in learning more. And the kids were right: their teachers were every bit as bored as they were.

Boredom is the common condition of schoolteachers, and anyone who has spent time in a teachers' lounge can vouch for the low energy, the whining, the dispirited attitudes, to be found there. When asked why they feel bored, the teachers tend to blame the kids, as you might expect. Who wouldn't get bored teaching students who are rude and interested only in grades? If even that. Of course, teachers are themselves products of the same twelve-year compulsory school programs that so thoroughly bore their students, and as school personnel they are trapped inside structures even more rigid than those imposed upon the children. Who, then, is to blame?

We all are. My grandfather taught me that. One afternoon when I was seven I complained to him of boredom, and he batted me hard on the head. He told me that I was never to use that term in his presence again, that if I was bored it was my fault and no one else's. The obligation to amuse and instruct myself was entirely my own, and people who didn't know that were childish people, to be avoided if possible. Certainly not to be trusted. That episode cured me of boredom forever, and here and there over the years I was able to pass on the lesson to some remarkable students. For the most part, however, I found it futile to challenge the official notion that boredom and childishness were the natural state of affairs in the classroom. Often I had to defy custom, and even bend the law, to help kids break out of this trap.

The empire struck back, of course; childish adults regularly conflate opposition with disloyalty. I once returned from a medical leave to discover that all evidence of my having been granted the leave had been purposely destroyed, that my job had been terminated, and that I no longer possessed even a teaching license. After nine months of tormented effort I was able to retrieve the license when a school secretary testified to witnessing the plot unfold. In the meantime my family suffered more than I care to remember. By the time I finally retired in 1991, I had more than enough reason to think of our schools — with their long-term, cell-block-style, forced confinement of both students and teachers — as virtual factories of childishness. Yet I honestly could not see why they had to be that way. My own experience had revealed to me what many other teachers must learn along the way, too, yet keep to themselves for fear of reprisal: if we wanted to we could easily and inexpensively jettison the old, stupid structures and help kids take an education rather than merely receive a schooling. We could encourage the best qualities of youthfulness — curiosity, adventure, resilience, the capacity for surprising insight — simply by being more flexible about time, texts, and tests, by introducing kids to truly competent adults, and by giving each student what autonomy he or she needs in order to take a risk every now and then.

But we don't do that. And the more I asked why not, and persisted in thinking about the "problem" of schooling as an engineer might, the more I missed the point: What if there is no "problem" with our schools? What if they are the way they are, so expensively flying in the face of common sense and long experience in how children learn things, not because they are doing something wrong but because they are doing something right? Is it possible that George W. Bush accidentally spoke the truth when he said we would "leave no child behind"? Could it be that our schools are designed to make sure not one of them ever really grows up?

Do we really need school?

Do we really need school? I don't mean education, just forced schooling: six classes a day, five days a week, nine months a year, for twelve years. Is this deadly routine really necessary? And if so, for what? Don't hide behind reading, writing, and arithmetic as a rationale, because 2 million happy homeschoolers have surely put that banal justification to rest. Even if they hadn't, a considerable number of well-known Americans never went through the twelve-year wringer our kids currently go through, and they turned out all right. George Washington, Benjamin Franklin, Thomas Jefferson, Abraham Lincoln? Someone taught them, to be sure, but they were not products of a school system, and not one of them was ever "graduated" from a secondary school. Throughout most of American history, kids generally didn't go to high school, yet the unschooled rose to be admirals, like Farragut; inventors, like Edison; captains of industry, like Carnegie and Rockefeller; writers, like Melville and Twain and Conrad; and even scholars, like Margaret Mead. In fact, until pretty recently people who reached the age of thirteen weren't looked upon as children at all. Ariel Durant, who co-wrote an enormous, and very good, multivolume history of the world with her husband, Will, was happily married at fifteen, and who could reasonably claim that Ariel Durant was an uneducated person? Unschooled, perhaps, but not uneducated.

We have been taught (that is, schooled) in this country to think of "success" as synonymous with, or at least dependent upon, "schooling," but historically that isn't true in either an intellectual or a financial sense. And plenty of people throughout the world today find a way to educate themselves without resorting to a system of compulsory secondary schools that all too often resemble prisons. Why, then, do Americans confuse education with just such a system? What exactly is the purpose of our public schools?

Mass schooling of a compulsory nature really got its teeth into the United States between 1905 and 1915, though it was conceived of much earlier and pushed for throughout most of the nineteenth century. The reason given for this enormous upheaval of family life and cultural traditions was, roughly speaking, threefold:

1. To make good people.

2. To make good citizens.

3. To make each person his or her personal best.

These goals are still trotted out today on a regular basis, and most of us accept them in one form or another as a decent definition of public education's mission, however short schools actually fall in achieving them. But we are dead wrong. Compounding our error is the fact that the national literature holds numerous and surprisingly consistent statements of compulsory schooling's true purpose. We have, for example, the great H. L. Mencken, who wrote in the *American Mercury* for April 1924 that

> the aim of public education is not to fill the young of the species with knowledge and awaken their intelligence. . . . Nothing could be further from the truth. The aim . . . is simply to reduce as many individuals as possible to the same safe level, to breed and train a standardized citizenry, to put down dissent and originality. That is its aim in the United States . . . and that is its aim everywhere else.

Because of Mencken's reputation as a satirist, we might be tempted to dismiss this passage as a bit of hyperbolic sarcasm. His article, however, goes on to trace the template for our own educational system back to the now vanished, though never to be forgotten, military state of Prussia. And although he was certainly aware of the irony that we had recently been at war with Germany, the heir to Prussian thought and culture, Mencken was being perfectly serious here. Our educational system really is Prussian in origin, and that really is cause for concern.

The odd fact of a Prussian provenance for our schools pops up again and again once you know to look for it. William James alluded to it many times at the turn of the century. Orestes Brownson, the hero of Christopher Lasch's 1991 book, *The True and Only Heaven*, was publicly denouncing the Prussianization of American schools back in the 1840s. Horace Mann's "Seventh Annual Report" to the Massachusetts State Board of Education in 1843 is essentially a paean to the land of Frederick the Great and a call for its schooling to be brought here. That Prussian culture loomed large in America is hardly surprising, given our early association with that utopian state. A Prussian served as Washington's aide during the Revolutionary War, and so many German-speaking people had settled here by 1795 that Congress considered publishing a German-language edition of the federal laws. But what shocks is that we should so eagerly have adopted one of the very worst aspects of Prussian culture: an educational system deliberately designed to produce mediocre intellects, to hamstring the inner life, to deny students appreciable leadership skills, and to ensure docile and incomplete citizens in order to render the populace "manageable."

It was from James Bryant Conant—president of Harvard for twenty years, WWI poison-gas specialist, WWII executive on the atomic-bomb project, high commissioner of the American zone in Germany after WWII, and truly one of the most influential figures of the twentieth century—that I first got wind of the real purposes of American schooling. Without Conant, we would probably not have the same style and degree of standardized testing that we enjoy today, nor would we be blessed with gargantuan high schools that warehouse 2,000 to 4,000 students at a time, like the famous Columbine High in Littleton, Colorado. Shortly after I retired from teaching I picked up Conant's 1959 book-length essay, "The Child, the Parent, and the State," and was more than a little intrigued to see him mention in passing that the modern schools we attend were the result of a "revolution" engineered between 1905 and 1930. A revolution? He declines to elaborate, but he does direct the curious and the uninformed to Alexander Inglis's 1918 book, *Principles of Secondary Education*, in which "one saw this revolution through the eyes of a revolutionary."

Inglis, for whom a lecture in education at Harvard is named, makes it perfectly clear that compulsory schooling on this continent was intended to be just what it had been for Prussia in the 1820s: a fifth column into the burgeoning democratic movement that threatened to give the peasants and the proletarians a voice at the bargaining table. Modern, industrialized, compulsory schooling was to make a sort of surgical incision into the prospective unity of these underclasses. Divide children by subject, by age-grading, by constant rankings on tests, and by many other more subtle means, and it was unlikely that the ignorant mass of mankind, separated in childhood, would ever re-integrate into a dangerous whole.

Inglis breaks down the purpose—the actual purpose—of modern schooling into six basic functions, any one of which is enough to curl the hair of those innocent enough to believe the three traditional goals listed earlier:

1. The adjustive or adaptive function. Schools are to establish fixed habits of reaction to authority. This, of course, precludes critical judgment completely. It also pretty much destroys the idea that useful or interesting material should be taught, because you can't test for reflexive obedience until you know whether you can make kids learn, and do, foolish and boring things.

2. The integrating function. This might well be called "the conformity function," because its intention is to make children as alike as possible. People who conform are predictable, and this is of great use to those who wish to harness and manipulate a large labor force.

3. The diagnostic and directive function. School is meant to determine each student's proper social role. This is done by logging evidence mathematically and anecdotally on cumulative records. As in "your permanent record." Yes, you do have one.

4. The differentiating function. Once their social role has been "diagnosed," children are to be sorted by role and trained only so far as their destination in the social machine merits—and not one step further. So much for making kids their personal best.

5. The selective function. This refers not to human choice at all but to Darwin's theory of natural selection as applied to what he called "the favored races." In short, the idea is to help things along by consciously attempting to improve the breeding stock. Schools are meant to tag the unfit—with poor grades, remedial placement, and other punishments—clearly enough that their peers will accept them as inferior and effectively bar them from the reproductive sweepstakes. That's what all those little humiliations from first grade onward were intended to do: wash the dirt down the drain.

6. The propaedeutic function. The societal system implied by these rules will require an elite group of caretakers. To that end, a small fraction of the kids will quietly be taught how to manage this continuing project, how to watch over and control a population deliberately dumbed down and declawed in order that government might proceed unchallenged and corporations might never want for obedient labor.

That, unfortunately, is the purpose of mandatory public education in this country. And lest you take Inglis for an isolated crank with a rather too cynical take on the educational enterprise, you should know that he was hardly alone in championing these ideas. Conant himself, building on the ideas of Horace Mann and others, campaigned tirelessly for an American school system designed along the same lines. Men like George Peabody, who funded the cause of mandatory schooling throughout the South, surely understood that the Prussian system was useful in creating not only a harmless electorate and a servile labor force but also a virtual herd of mindless consumers. In time a great number of industrial titans came to recognize the enormous profits to be had by cultivating and tending just such a herd via public education, among them Andrew Carnegie and John D. Rockefeller.

There you have it. Now you know. We don't need Karl Marx's conception of a grand warfare between the classes to see that it is in the interest of complex management, economic or political, to dumb people down, to demoralize them, to divide them from one another, and to discard them if they don't conform. Class may frame the proposition, as when Woodrow Wilson, then president of Princeton University, said the following to the New York City School Teachers Association in 1909: "We want one class of persons to have a liberal education, and we want another class of persons, a very much larger class, of necessity, in every society, to forgo the privileges of a liberal education and fit themselves to perform specific difficult manual tasks." But the motives behind the disgusting decisions that bring about these ends need not be class-based at all. They can stem purely from fear, or from the by now familiar belief that "efficiency" is the paramount virtue, rather than love, liberty, laughter, or hope. Above all, they can stem from simple greed.

There were vast fortunes to be made, after all, in an economy based on mass production and organized to favor the large corporation rather than the small business or the family farm. But mass production required mass consumption, and at the turn of the twentieth century most Americans considered it both unnatural and unwise to buy things they didn't actually need. Mandatory schooling was a godsend on that count. School didn't have to train kids in any direct sense to think they should consume nonstop, because it did something even better: it encouraged them not to think at all. And that left them sitting ducks for another great invention of the modem era—marketing.

School didn't have to train kids in any direct sense to think they should consume nonstop, because it did something even better: it encouraged them not to think at all.

Now, you needn't have studied marketing to know that there are two groups of people who can always be convinced to consume more than they need to: addicts and children. School has done a pretty good job of turning our children into addicts, but it has done a spectacular job of turning our children into children. Again, this is no accident. Theorists from Plato to Rousseau to our own Dr. Inglis knew that if children could be cloistered with other children, stripped of responsibility and independence, encouraged to develop only the trivializing emotions of greed, envy, jealousy, and fear, they would grow older but never truly grow up. In the 1934 edition of his once well-known book *Public Education in the United States*, Ellwood P. Cubberley detailed and praised the way the strategy of successive school enlargements had extended childhood by two to six years, and forced schooling was at that point still quite new. This same Cubberley—who was dean of Stanford's School of Education, a textbook editor at Houghton Mifflin, and Conant's friend and correspondent at Harvard—had written the following in the 1922 edition of his book *Public School Administration*: "Our schools are . . . factories in which the raw products (children) are to be shaped and fashioned. . . . And it is the business of the school to build its pupils according to the specifications laid down."

It's perfectly obvious from our society today what those specifications were. Maturity has by now been banished from nearly every aspect of our lives. Easy divorce laws have removed the need to work at relationships; easy credit has removed the need for fiscal self-control; easy entertainment has removed the need to learn to entertain oneself; easy answers have removed the need to ask questions. We have become a nation of children, happy to surrender our judgments and our wills to political exhortations and commercial blandishments that would insult actual adults. We buy televisions, and then we buy the things we see on the television. We buy computers, and then we buy the things we see on the computer. We buy $150 sneakers whether we need them or not, and when they fall apart too soon we buy another pair. We drive SUVs and believe the lie that they constitute a kind of life insurance, even when we're upside-down in them. And, worst of all, we don't bat an eye when Ari Fleischer tells us to "be careful what you say," even if we remember having been told somewhere back in school that America is the land of the free. We simply buy that one too. Our schooling, as intended, has seen to it.

Now for the good news. Once you understand the logic behind modern schooling, its tricks and traps are fairly easy to avoid. School trains children to be employees and consumers; teach your own to be leaders and adventurers. School trains children to obey reflexively; teach your own to think critically and independently. Well-schooled kids have a low threshold for boredom; help your own to develop an inner life so that they'll never be bored. Urge them to take on the serious material, the grown-up material, in history, literature, philosophy, music, art, economics, theology—all the stuff schoolteachers know well enough to avoid. Challenge your kids with plenty of solitude so that they can learn to enjoy their own company, to conduct inner dialogues. Well-schooled people are conditioned to dread being alone, and they seek constant companionship through the TV, the computer, the cell phone, and through shallow friendships quickly acquired and quickly abandoned. Your children should have a more meaningful life, and they can.

First, though, we must wake up to what our schools really are: laboratories of experimentation on young minds, drill centers for the habits and attitudes that corporate society demands. Mandatory education serves children only incidentally; its real purpose is to turn them into servants. Don't let your own have their childhoods extended, not even for a day. If David Farragut could take command of a captured British warship as a preteen, if Thomas Edison could publish a broadsheet at the age of twelve, if Ben Franklin could apprentice himself to a printer at the same age (then put himself through a course of study that would choke a Yale senior today), there's no telling what your own kids could do. After a long life, and thirty years in the public school trenches, I've concluded that genius is as common as dirt. We suppress our genius only because we haven't yet figured out how to manage a population of educated men and women. The solution, I think, is simple and glorious. Let them manage themselves.

DISCUSSION

1. Gatto repeatedly associates conventional compulsory schooling with entrapment. To what extent does this reflect your feelings and experiences? Has school ever made you feel trapped?
2. Gatto draws a distinction between helping children "take an education" and "receive a schooling" (p. 272). How do you understand the difference between the two? In your view, which of these phrases defines the superior model of education? Why?
3. "Boredom and childishness," writes Gatto, are too often "the natural state of affairs in the classroom" (p. 272). To what extent do you think this is true? And what factors account for why these things have come to stand as our current educational norms? What, in your view, would it take to denaturalize them – to get teachers and students to regard them as something other than "just the way school is"?

WRITING

4. At the heart of the problems around contemporary schooling, argues Gatto, is its compulsory nature. Think back on your experiences in school. How much of what typically defined your role was compulsory? What are some of the scripts (for how to act, talk, even think) that were required? Write an essay that argues in favor of or against the validity of implementing these particular requirements. What educational goals did they seem designed to accomplish, and were they worth it?
5. Gatto lists the three objectives that, he contends, we typically assume underlie contemporary education: "to make good people," "to make good citizens," "to make each person his or her personal best" (p. 273). Create a lesson plan that, in your view, would actually help fulfill these goals. What activities or assignments would it include? What would be the roles for teachers and students? Then, in an additional paragraph, sketch out an analysis or assessment of the ways this lesson plan would rewrite the script that you think more typically characterizes the modern classroom.
6. Much of Gatto's critique revolves around the charge of standardization. Modern American schools, he says, have become "factories" bent on mass-producing unimaginative, conformist, mediocre students. How do you think Alfie Kohn (p. 238) would respond to such a statement? Write an essay in which you compare each author's opinion on the state of education. What are the key problems each sees? Do you ultimately agree with their assessments of the education system? Why or why not?

MIKE ROSE

Blue-Collar Brilliance

Among the many stereotypes that shape cultural attitudes toward manual or blue-collar work is the assumption that such work is not intellectually challenging. Working with your head and working with your hands, the social script would have us believe, are fundamentally different, even incompatible, endeavors. Challenging this thinking, noted educator Mike Rose presents us with a portrait of blue-collar work that flouts this narrow view. Rose has spent his career studying literacy and the relationship of working-class Americans to the educational system. His books include *Possible Lives: The Promise of Public Education in America (1995)*, *The Mind at Work: Valuing the Intelligence of the American Worker* (2004), *An Open Language: Selected Writing on Literacy, Learning, and Opportunity* (2006), *Why School?: Reclaiming Education For All of Us (2009)*, and *Back to School: Why Everyone Deserves a Second Chance at Education (2012).* He is currently professor of social research methodology at the UCLA Graduate School of Education and Information Studies. This essay originally appeared in the Summer 2009 edition of the *American Scholar.*

MY MOTHER, ROSE MERAGLIO ROSE (ROSIE), SHAPED HER ADULT identity as a waitress in coffee shops and family restaurants. When I was growing up in Los Angeles during the 1950s, my father and I would occasionally hang out at the restaurant until her shift ended, and then we'd ride the bus home with her. Sometimes she worked the register and the counter, and we sat there; when she waited booths and tables, we found a booth in the back where the waitresses took their breaks.

There wasn't much for a child to do at the restaurants, and so as the hours stretched out, I watched the cooks and waitresses and listened to what they said. At mealtimes, the pace of the kitchen staff and the din from customers picked up. Weaving in and out around the room, waitresses warned *behind you* in impassive but urgent voices. Standing at the service window facing the kitchen, they called out abbreviated orders. *Fry four on two*, my mother would say as she clipped a check onto the metal wheel. Her tables were *deuces*, *four-tops*, or *six-tops* according to their size; seating areas also were nicknamed. The *racetrack*, for instance, was the fast-turnover front section. Lingo conferred authority and signaled know-how.

Rosie took customers' orders, pencil poised over pad, while fielding questions about the food. She walked full tilt through the room with plates stretching up her left arm and two cups of coffee somehow cradled in her right hand. She stood at a table or booth and removed a plate for this person, another for that person, then another, remembering who had the hamburger, who had the fried shrimp, almost always getting it right. She would haggle with the cook about a returned order and rush by us, saying, *He gave me lip, but I got him.* A minute to flop down in the booth next to my father. *I'm all in,* she'd say, and whisper something about a customer. Gripping the outer edge of the table with one hand, she'd watch the room and note, in the flow of our conversation, who needed a refill, whose order was taking longer to prepare than it should, who was finishing up.

I couldn't have put it in words when I was growing up, but what I observed in my mother's restaurant defined the world of adults, a place where competence was synonymous with physical work. I've since studied the working habits of blue-collar workers and have come to understand how much my mother's kind of work demands of both body and brain. A waitress acquires knowledge and intuition about the ways and the rhythms of the restaurant business. Waiting on seven to nine tables, each with two to six customers, Rosie devised memory strategies so that she could remember who ordered what. And because she knew the average time it took to prepare different dishes, she could monitor an order that was taking too long at the service station.

Like anyone who is effective at physical work, my mother learned to work smart, as she put it, *to make every move count.* She'd sequence and group tasks: What could she do first, then second, then third as she circled through her station? What tasks could be clustered? She did everything on the fly, and when problems arose—technical or human—she solved them within the flow of work, while taking into account the emotional state of her coworkers. Was the manager in a good mood? Did the cook wake up on the wrong side of the bed? If so, how could she make an extra request or effectively return an order?

And then, of course, there were the customers who entered the restaurant with all sorts of needs, from physiological ones, including the emotions that accompany hunger, to a sometimes complicated desire for human contact. Her tip depended on how well she responded to these needs, and so she became adept at reading social cues and managing feelings, both the customers' and her own. No wonder, then, that Rosie was intrigued by psychology. The restaurant became the place where she studied human behavior, puzzling over the problems of her regular customers and refining her ability to deal with people in a difficult world. She took pride in *being among the public,* she'd say. *There isn't a day that goes by in the restaurant that you don't learn something.*

Intelligence is closely associated with formal education, and most people seem to move comfortably from that notion to a belief that work requiring less schooling requires less intelligence. These assumptions run through our cultural history, from the post-Revolutionary War period, when mechanics were characterized by political rivals as illiterate and therefore incapable of participating in government, until today. Generalizations about intelligence, work, and social class deeply affect our assumptions about ourselves and each other, guiding the ways we use our minds to learn, build knowledge, solve problems, and make our way through the world.

Although writers and scholars have often looked at the working class, they have generally focused on the values such workers exhibit rather than on the thought their work requires—a subtle but pervasive omission. Our cultural iconography promotes the muscled arm, sleeve rolled tight against biceps, but no brightness behind the eye, no image that links hand and brain.

One of my mother's brothers, Joe Meraglio, left school in the ninth grade to work for the Pennsylvania Railroad. From there he joined the Navy, returned to the railroad, which was already in decline, and eventually joined his older brother at General Motors, where, over a 33-year career, he moved from working on the assembly line to supervising the paint-and-body department. When I was a young man, Joe took me on a tour of the factory. The floor was loud—in some places deafening—and when I turned a corner or opened a door, the smell of chemicals knocked my head back. The work was repetitive and taxing, and the pace was inhumane.

Most people seem to move . . . to a belief that work requiring less schooling requires less intelligence.

Still, for Joe the shop floor was a school. He learned the most efficient way to use his body by acquiring a set of routines that were quick and preserved energy. Otherwise he never would have survived on the line.

As a foreman, Joe constantly faced new problems and became a consummate multi-tasker, evaluating a flurry of demands quickly, parceling out physical and mental resources, keeping a number of ongoing events in his mind, returning to whatever task had been interrupted, and maintaining a cool head under the pressure of grueling production schedules. In the midst of all this, Joe learned more and more about the auto industry, the technological and social dynamics of the shop floor, the machinery and production processes, and the basics of paint chemistry and of plating and baking. With further promotions, he not only solved problems but also began to find problems to solve: Joe initiated the redesign of the nozzle on a paint sprayer, thereby eliminating costly and unhealthy overspray. And he found a way to reduce the energy costs of the baking ovens without affecting the quality of the paint. He lacked formal knowledge of how the machines under his supervision worked, but he had direct experience with them, hands-on knowledge, and was savvy about their quirks and operational capabilities. He could experiment with them.

In addition, Joe learned about budgets and management. Coming off the line as he did, he had a perspective of workers' needs and management's demands, and this led him to think of ways to improve efficiency on the line while relieving some of the stress on the assemblers. He had each worker in a unit learn his or her coworkers' jobs so they could rotate across stations to relieve some of the monotony. He believed that rotation would allow assemblers to get longer and more frequent breaks. It was an easy sell to the people on the line. The union, however, had to approve any modification in job duties, and the managers were wary of the change. Joe had to argue his case on a number of fronts, providing him a kind of rhetorical education.

Eight years ago I began a study of the thought processes involved in work like that of my mother and uncle. I catalogued the cognitive demands of a range of blue-collar and service jobs, from waitressing and hair styling to plumbing and welding. To gain a sense of how knowledge and skill develop, I observed experts as well as novices. From the details of this close examination, I tried to fashion what I called "cognitive biographies" of blue-collar workers. Biographical accounts of the lives of scientists, lawyers, entrepreneurs, and other professionals are rich with detail about the intellectual dimension of their work. But the life stories of working-class people are few and are typically accounts of hardship and courage or the achievements wrought by hard work.

Our culture—in Cartesian fashion—separates the body from the mind, so that, for example, we assume that the use of a tool does not involve abstraction. We reinforce this notion by defining intelligence solely on grades in school and numbers on IQ tests. And we employ social biases pertaining to a person's place on the occupational ladder. The distinctions among blue, pink, and white collars carry with them attributions of character, motivation, and intelligence. Although we rightly acknowledge and amply compensate the play of mind in white-collar and professional work, we diminish or erase it in considerations about other endeavors—physical and service work particularly. We also often ignore the experience of everyday work in administrative deliberations and policymaking.

Here's what we find when we get in close. The plumber seeking leverage in order to work in tight quarters and the hair stylist adroitly handling scissors and comb manage their bodies strategically. Though work-related actions become routine with experience, they were learned at some point through observation, trial and error, and, often, physical or verbal assistance from a coworker or trainer.

The use of tools requires the studied refinement of stance, grip, balance, and fine-motor skills. Workers must also know the characteristics of the material they are engaging—how it reacts to various cutting or compressing devices, to degrees of heat, or to lines of force. Some of these things demand judgment, the weighing of options, the consideration of multiple variables, and, occasionally, the creative use of a tool in an unexpected way.

Carpenters have an eye for length, line, and angle; mechanics troubleshoot by listening; hair stylists are attuned to shape, texture, and motion. Sensory data merge with concept, as when an auto mechanic relies on sound, vibration, and even smell to understand what cannot be observed.

Planning and problem solving have been studied since the earliest days of modern cognitive psychology and are considered core elements in Western definitions of intelligence. To work is to solve problems. The big difference between the psychologist's laboratory and the workplace is that in the former the problems are isolated and in the latter they are embedded in the real-time flow of work with all its messiness and social complexity.

Verbal and mathematical skills drive measures of intelligence in the Western Hemisphere, and many of the kinds of work I studied are thought to require relatively little proficiency in either. Compared to certain kinds of white-collar occupations, that's true. But written symbols flow through physical work.

Numbers are rife in most workplaces: on tools and gauges, as measurements, as indicators of pressure or concentration or temperature, as guides to sequence, on ingredient labels, on lists and spreadsheets, as markers of quantity and price. Certain jobs require workers to make, check, and verify calculations, and to collect and interpret data. Basic math can be involved, and some workers develop a good sense of numbers and patterns. Consider, as well, what might be called material mathematics: mathematical functions embodied in materials and actions, as when a carpenter builds a cabinet or a flight of stairs.

A simple mathematical act can extend quickly beyond itself. Measuring, for example, can involve more than recording the dimensions of an object. As I watched a cabinetmaker measure a long strip of wood, he read a number off the tape out loud, looked back over his shoulder to the kitchen wall, turned back to his task, took another measurement, and paused for a moment in thought. He was solving a problem involving the molding, and the measurement was important to his deliberation about structure and appearance.

In the blue-collar workplace, directions, plans, and reference books rely on illustrations, some representational and others, like blueprints, that require training to interpret. Esoteric symbols—visual jargon—depict switches and receptacles, pipe fittings, or types of welds. Workers themselves often make sketches on the job. I frequently observed them grab a pencil to sketch something on a scrap of paper or on a piece of the material they were installing.

Though many kinds of physical work don't require a high literacy level, more reading occurs in the blue-collar workplace than is generally thought, from manuals and catalogs to work orders and invoices, to lists, labels, and forms. With routine tasks, for example, reading is integral to understanding production quotas, learning how to use an instrument, or applying a product. Written notes can initiate action, as in restaurant orders or reports of machine malfunction, or they can serve as memory aids.

True, many uses of writing are abbreviated, routine, and repetitive, and they infrequently require interpretation or analysis. But analytic moments can be part of routine activities, and seemingly basic reading and writing can be cognitively rich. Because workplace language is used in the flow of other activities, we can overlook the remarkable coordination of words, numbers, and drawings required to initiate and direct action.

If we believe everyday work to be mindless, then that will affect the work we create in the future. When we devalue the full range of everyday cognition, we offer limited educational opportunities and fail to make fresh and meaningful instructional connections among disparate kinds of skill and knowledge. If we think that whole categories of people—identified by class or occupation—are not that bright, then we reinforce social separations and cripple our ability to talk across cultural divides.

If we think that whole categories of people—identified by class or occupation—are not that bright, then we reinforce social separations.

Affirmation of diverse intelligence is not a retreat to a softhearted definition of the mind. To acknowledge a broader range of intellectual capacity is to take seriously the concept of cognitive variability, to appreciate in all the Rosies and Joes the thought that drives their accomplishments and defines who they are. This is a model of the mind that is worthy of a democratic society.

DISCUSSION

1. Take a closer look at this essay's title. How do you interpret the phrase "blue-collar brilliance"? To what extent does this phrase challenge or rewrite the norms we are taught to use when thinking about blue-collar work? What alternative vision of such work does a phrase like this suggest?
2. Using his mother's experiences on the job as a kind of case study, Rose presents readers with a list of the particular skills and knowledge that one blue-collar job requires. His mother, Rose tells us, "took customers' orders, pencil poised over pad, while fielding questions about the food. She walked full tilt through the room with plates stretching up her left arm and two cups of coffee somehow cradled in her right hand. She stood at a table or booth and removed a plate for this person, another for that person, then another, remembering who had the hamburger, who had the fried shrimp, almost always getting it right" (p. 281). Does this list, in your view, successfully make the case that blue-collar jobs can call on and foster brilliance in workers? Do the skills, talents, and knowledge necessary to perform this job fit your definition of *brilliance*? How or how not?
3. Can you think of an example of blue-collar work that fits Rose's definition of *brilliance*? What kind of job is it? What aptitudes and skills does it require? How are these skills and aptitudes typically viewed?

WRITING

4. This essay asks you to think about the relationship between blue- and white-collar work. Write an essay in which you compare the particular rules, scripts, roles, and norms that teach us how to think about each of these two categories. How is each type of work typically defined? What tasks, skills, or abilities are we told each conventionally involves? And, perhaps most important, how are we taught to value these types of work differently? In your view, are these value distinctions fair? Accurate? How or how not?
5. What would a school curriculum look like that values and teaches the skills and abilities Rose showcases in this essay? What types of work would it require? What assignments or tests would it include? How would teachers evaluate these? Assess how this curriculum would differ from the one typically seen operating in schools. How do its rules differ? What role does it script for students? What are the underlying norms it is designed to support? And which do you find preferable? Why?
6. How do you think Rose's dissection of "blue-collar brilliance" relates to John Taylor Gatto's (p. 271) critique of school? Does Rose's attempt to rewrite the conventional norms regarding class, learning, and "smarts" seem similar to Gatto's attempt to rewrite the conventional scripts regarding school? In your view, would Gatto's plan for changing the rules for school better accommodate the types of aptitudes, skills, and knowledge described by Rose? How or how not?

BELL HOOKS

Learning in the Shadow of Race and Class

How does one's race and class affect one's experience of school? To what extent is modern education shaped by the unspoken norms connected to these two questions? Recounting her own experiences at one of America's elite institutions of higher education, bell hooks examines some of the core assumptions, ideals, and double standards that go into scripting the ideal "minority" student. As a cultural critic, feminist theorist, poet, and writer, hooks focuses on the intersections of race, class, and gender. She is the author of over thirty books, including *Talking Back: Thinking Feminist, Thinking Black* (1989), *Teaching to Transgress* (1994), *Rock My Soul: Black People and Self-Esteem* (2002), and *Outlaw Culture: Resisting Representations* (2006). hooks's most recent book is *Writing Beyond Race: Living Theory and Practice* (2013). She was born Gloria Jean Watkins in Hopkinsville, Kentucky. Currently, hooks is a Distinguished Professor of English at City College in New York. The following essay first appeared in the November 17, 2000, issue of the *Chronicle of Higher Education*.

AS A CHILD, I OFTEN WANTED THINGS MONEY COULD BUY THAT MY parents could not afford and would not get. Rather than tell us we did not get some material thing because money was lacking, mama would frequently manipulate us in an effort to make the desire go away. Sometimes she would belittle and shame us about the object of our desire. That's what I remember most. That lovely yellow dress I wanted would become in her storytelling mouth a really ugly mammy-made thing that no girl who cared about her looks would desire. My desires were often made to seem worthless and stupid. I learned to mistrust and silence them. I learned that the more clearly I named my desires, the more unlikely those desires would ever be fulfilled.

I learned that my inner life was more peaceful if I did not think about money, or allow myself to indulge in any fantasy of desire. I learned the art of sublimation and repression. I learned it was better to make do with acceptable material desires than to articulate the unacceptable. Before I knew money mattered, I had often chosen objects to desire that were costly, things a girl of my class would not ordinarily desire. But then I was still a girl who was *unaware of class*, who did not think my desires were

I was still a girl who was unaware of class, who did not think my desires were stupid and wrong.

stupid and wrong. And when I found they were, I let them go. I concentrated on *survival*, on making do.

When I was choosing a college to attend, the issue of money surfaced and had to be talked about. While I would seek loans and scholarships, even if everything related to school was paid for, there would still be transportation to pay for, books, and a host of other hidden costs. Letting me know that there was no extra money to be had, mama urged me to attend any college nearby that would offer financial aid. My first year of college, I went to a school close to home. A plain-looking white woman recruiter had sat in our living room and explained to my parents that everything would be taken care of, that I would be awarded a full academic scholarship, that they would have to pay nothing. They knew better. Still they found this school acceptable.

After my parents dropped me at the predominately white women's college, I saw the terror in my roommate's face that she was going to be housed with someone black, and I requested a change. She had no doubt also voiced her concern. I was given a tiny single room by the stairs—a room usually denied a first-year student—but I was a first-year black student, a scholarship girl who could never in a million years have afforded to pay her way or absorb the cost of a single room. My fellow students kept their distance from me. I ate in the cafeteria and did not have to worry about who would pay for pizza and drinks in the world outside. I kept my desires to myself, my lacks, and my loneliness; I made do.

I rarely shopped. Boxes came from home, with brand-new clothes mama had purchased. Even though it was never spoken, she did not want me to feel ashamed among privileged white girls. I was the only black girl in my dorm. There was no room in me for shame. I felt contempt and disinterest. With their giggles and their obsession to marry, the white girls at the women's college were aliens. We did not reside on the same planet. I lived in the world of books. The one white woman who became my close friend found me there reading. I was hiding under the shadows of a tree with huge branches, the kinds of trees that just seemed to grow effortlessly on well-to-do college campuses. I sat on the "perfect" grass reading poetry, wondering how the grass around me could be so lovely, and yet, when daddy had tried to grow grass in the front yard of Mr. Porter's house, it always turned yellow or brown and then died. Endlessly, the yard defeated him, until finally he gave up. The outside of the house looked good, but the yard always hinted at the possibility of endless neglect. The yard looked poor.

Foliage and trees on the college grounds flourished. Greens were lush and deep. From my place in the shadows, I saw a fellow student sitting alone weeping. Her sadness had to do with all the trivia that haunted our day's classwork, the fear of not being smart enough, of losing financial aid (like me she had loans and scholarships, though her family paid some), and boys. Coming from an Illinois family of Czechoslovakian immigrants, she understood class.

When she talked about the other girls who flaunted their wealth and family background, there was a hard edge of contempt, anger, and envy in her voice. Envy was always something I pushed away from my psyche. Kept too close for comfort, envy could lead to infatuation and on to desire. I desired nothing that they had. She desired everything, speaking her desires openly, without shame. Growing up in the kind of community where there was constant competition to see who could buy the bigger better whatever, in a world of organized labor, of unions and strikes, she understood a world of bosses and workers, of haves and have-nots.

White friends I had known in high school wore their class privilege modestly. Raised, like myself, in church traditions that taught us to identify only with the poor, we knew that there was evil in excess. We knew rich people were rarely allowed into heaven. God had given them a paradise of bounty on earth, and they had not shared. The rare ones, the rich people who shared, were the only ones able to meet the divine in paradise, and even then it was harder for them to find their way. According to the high-school friends we knew, flaunting wealth was frowned upon in our world, frowned upon by God and community.

The few women I befriended my first year in college were not wealthy. They were the ones who shared with me stories of the other girls flaunting the fact that they could buy anything expensive—clothes, food, vacations. There were not many of us from working-class backgrounds; we knew who we were. Most girls from poor backgrounds tried to blend in, or fought back by triumphing over wealth with beauty or style or some combination of the above. Being black made me an automatic outsider. Holding their world in contempt pushed me further to the edge. One of the fun things the "in" girls did was choose someone and trash their room. Like so much else deemed cute by insiders, I dreaded the thought of strangers entering my space and going through my things. Being outside the in crowd made me an unlikely target. Being contemptuous made me first on the list. I did not understand. And when my room was trashed, it unleashed my rage and deep grief over not being able to protect my space from violation and invasion. I hated the girls who had so much, took so much for granted, never considered that those of us who did not have mad money would not be able to replace broken things, perfume poured out, or talcum powder spread everywhere—that we did not know everything could be taken care of at the dry cleaner's, because we never took our clothes there. My rage fueled by contempt was deep, strong, and long lasting. Daily it stood as a challenge to their fun, to their habits of being.

Nothing they did to win me over worked. It came as a great surprise. They had always believed black girls wanted to be white girls, wanted to possess their world. My stony gaze, silence, and absolute refusal to cross the threshold of their world was total mystery; it was for them a violation they needed to avenge. After trashing my room, they tried to win me over with apologies and urges to talk and understand. There was nothing about me I wanted them to understand. Everything about their world was overexposed, on the surface.

One of my English professors had attended Stanford University. She felt that was the place for me to go—a place where intellect was valued over foolish fun and games and dress up, and finding a husband did not overshadow academic work. I had never thought about the state of California. Getting my parents to agree to my leaving Kentucky to attend a college in a nearby state had been hard enough. They had accepted a college they could reach by car, but a college thousands of miles away was beyond their imagination. Even I had difficulty grasping going that far away from home. The lure for me was the promise of journeying and arriving at a destination where I would be accepted and understood.

All the barely articulated understandings of class privilege that I had learned my first year of college had not hipped me to the reality of class shame. It still had not dawned on me that my parents, especially mama, resolutely refused to acknowledge any difficulties with money because her sense of shame around class was deep and intense. And when this shame was coupled with her need to feel that she had risen above the low-class backwoods culture of her family, it was impossible for her to talk in a straightforward manner about the strains it would put on the family for me to attend Stanford.

All I knew then was that, as with all my desires, I was told that this desire was impossible to fulfill. At first, it was not talked about in relation to money, it was talked about in relation to sin. California was an evil place, a modern-day Babylon where souls were easily seduced away from the path of righteousness. It was not a place for an innocent young girl to go on her own. Mama brought the message back that my father had absolutely refused to give permission.

I expressed my disappointment through ongoing unrelenting grief. I explained to mama that other parents wanted their children to go to good schools. It still had not dawned on me that my parents knew nothing about "good" schools. Even though I knew mama had not graduated from high school, I still held her in awe.

When my parents refused to permit me to attend Stanford, I accepted the verdict for awhile. Overwhelmed by grief, I could barely speak for weeks. Mama intervened and tried to change my father's mind, as folks she respected in the outside world told her what a privilege it was for me to have this opportunity, that Stanford University was a good school for a smart girl. Without their permission, I decided I would go. And even though she did not give her approval, mama was willing to help.

My decision made conversations about money necessary. Mama explained that California was too far away, that it would always "cost" to get there, that if something went wrong, they would not be able to come and rescue me, that I would not be able to come home for holidays. I heard all this, but its meaning did not sink in. I was just relieved I would not be returning to the women's college, to the place where I had truly been an outsider.

There were other black students at Stanford. There was even a dormitory where many black students lived. I did not know I could choose to live there. I went where I was assigned. Going to Stanford was the first time I flew somewhere. Only mama stood and waved farewell as I left to take the bus to the airport. I left with a heavy heart, feeling both excitement and dread. I knew nothing about the world I was journeying to. Not knowing made me afraid, but my fear of staying in place was greater.

I had no idea what was ahead of me. In small ways, I was ignorant. I had never been on an escalator, a city bus, an airplane, or a subway. I arrived in San Francisco with no understanding that Palo Alto was a long drive away—that it would take money to find transportation there. I decided to take the city bus. With all my cheap overpacked bags, I must have seemed like just another innocent immigrant when I struggled to board the bus.

This was a city bus with no racks for luggage. It was filled with immigrants. English was not spoken. I felt lost and afraid. Without words the strangers surrounding me understood the universal language of need and distress. They reached for my bags, holding and helping. In return, I told them my story—that I had left my village in the South to come to Stanford University and that, like them, my family were workers.

On arriving, I called home. Before I could speak, I began to weep as I heard the faraway sound of mama's voice. I tried to find the words to slow down, to tell her how it felt to be a stranger, to speak my uncertainty and longing. She told me this is the lot I had chosen. I must live with it. After her words, there was only silence. She had hung up on me—let me go into this world where I am a stranger still.

Stanford University was a place where one could learn about class from the ground up. Built by a man who believed in hard work, it was to have been a place where students of all classes would come, women and men, to work together and learn. It was to be a place of equality and communalism. His vision was seen by many as almost communist. The fact that he was rich made it all less threatening. Perhaps no one really believed the vision could be realized. The university was named after his son, who had died young, a son who had carried his name but who had no future money could buy. No amount of money can keep death away. But it could keep memory alive.

Everything in the landscape of my new world fascinated me, the plants brought from a rich man's travels all over the world back to this place of water and clay. At Stanford University, adobe buildings blend with Japanese plum trees and leaves of kumquat. On my way to study medieval literature, I ate my first kumquat. Surrounded by flowering cactus and a South American shrub bougainvillea of such trailing beauty it took my breath away, I was in a landscape of dreams, full of hope and possibility. If nothing else would hold me, I would not remain a stranger to the earth. The ground I stood on would know me.

Class was talked about behind the scenes. The sons and daughters from rich, famous, or notorious families were identified. The grown-ups in charge of us were always looking out for a family who might give their millions to the college. At Stanford, my classmates wanted to know me, thought it hip, cute, and downright exciting to have a black friend. They invited me on the expensive vacations and ski trips I could not afford. They offered to pay. I never went. Along with other students who were not from privileged families, I searched for places to go during the holiday times when the dormitory was closed. We got together and talked about the assumption that everyone had money to travel and would necessarily be leaving. The staff would be on holiday as well, so all students had to leave. Now and then the staff did not leave, and we were allowed to stick around. Once, I went home with one of the women who cleaned for the college.

Now and then, when she wanted to make extra money, mama would work as a maid. Her decision to work outside the home was seen as an act of treason by our father. At Stanford, I was stunned to find that there were maids who came by regularly to vacuum and tidy our rooms. No one had ever cleaned up behind me, and I did not want them to. At first I roomed with another girl from a working-class background—a beautiful white girl from Orange County who looked like pictures I had seen on the cover of *Seventeen* magazine. Her mother had died of cancer during her high-school years, and she had since been raised by her father. She had been asked by the college officials if she would find it problematic to have a black roommate. A scholarship student like myself, she knew her preferences did not matter and, as she kept telling me, she did not really care.

Like my friend during freshman year, she shared the understanding of what it was like to be a have-not in a world of haves. But unlike me, she was determined to become one of them. If it meant she had to steal nice clothes to look the same as they did, she had no problem taking these risks. If it meant having a privileged boyfriend who left bruises on her body now and then, it was worth the risk. Cheating was worth it. She believed the world the privileged had created was all unfair—all one big cheat; to get ahead, one had to play the game. To her, I was truly an innocent, a lamb being led to the slaughter. It did not surprise her one bit when I began to crack under the pressure of contradictory values and longings.

Like all students who did not have seniority, I had to see the school psychiatrists to be given permission to live off campus. Unaccustomed to being around strangers, especially strangers who did not share or understand my values, I found the experience of living in the dorms difficult. Indeed, almost everyone around me believed working-class folks had no values. At the university where the founder, Leland Stanford, had imagined different classes meeting on common ground, I learned how deeply individuals with class privilege feared and hated the working classes. Hearing classmates express contempt and hatred toward people who did not come from the right backgrounds shocked me.

To survive in this new world of divided classes, this world where I was also encountering for the first time a black bourgeois elite that was as contemptuous of working people as their white counterparts were, I had to take a stand, to get clear my own class affiliations. This was the most difficult truth to face. Having been taught all my life to believe that black people were inextricably bound in solidarity by our struggles to end racism, I did not know how to respond to elitist black people who were full of contempt for anyone who did not share their class, their way of life.

I did not know how to respond to elitist black people who were full of contempt for anyone who did not share their class, their way of life.

At Stanford, I encountered for the first time a black diaspora. Of the few black professors present, the vast majority were from African or Caribbean backgrounds. Elites themselves, they were only interested in teaching other elites. Poor folks like myself, with no background to speak of, were invisible. We were not seen by them or anyone else. Initially, I went to all meetings welcoming black students, but when I found no one to connect with, I retreated. In the shadows, I had time and books to teach me about the nature of class—about the ways black people were divided from themselves.

Despite this rude awakening, my disappointment at finding myself estranged from the group of students I thought would understand, I still looked for connections. I met an older black male graduate student who also came from a working-class background. Even though he had gone to the right high school, a California school for gifted students, and then to Princeton as an undergraduate, he understood intimately the intersections of race and class. Good in sports and in the classroom, he had been slotted early on to go far, to go where other black males had not gone. He understood the system. Academically, he fit. Had he wanted to, he could have been among the elite, but he chose to be on the margins, to hang with an intellectual artistic avant-garde. He wanted to live in a world of the mind where there was no race or class. He wanted to worship at the throne of art and knowledge. He became my mentor, comrade, and companion.

Slowly, I began to understand fully that there was no place in academe for folks from working-class backgrounds who did not wish to leave the past behind. That was the price of the ticket. Poor students would be welcome at the best institutions of higher learning only if they were willing to surrender memory, to forget the past and claim the assimilated present as the only worthwhile and meaningful reality.

Students from nonprivileged backgrounds who did not want to forget often had nervous breakdowns. They could not bear the weight of all the contradictions they had to confront. They were crushed. More often than not, they dropped out with no trace of their inner anguish recorded, no institutional record of the myriad ways their take on the world was assaulted by an elite vision of class and privilege. The records merely indicated that, even after receiving financial aid and other support, these students simply could not make it, simply were not good enough.

At no time in my years as a student did I march in a graduation ceremony. I was not proud to hold degrees from institutions where I had been constantly scorned and shamed. I wanted to forget these experiences, to erase them from my consciousness. Like a prisoner set free, I did not want to remember my years on the inside. When I finished my doctorate, I felt too much uncertainty about who I had become. Uncertain about whether I had managed to make it through without giving up the best of myself, the best of the values I had been raised to believe in—hard work, honesty, and respect for everyone no matter their class—I finished my education with my allegiance to the working class intact. Even so, I had planted my feet on the path leading in the direction of class privilege. There would always be contradictions to face. There would always be confrontations around the issue of class. I would always have to reexamine where I stand.

DISCUSSION

1. Take a few moments to consider the title of this piece. What are the shadows that, according to hooks, most directly affect or shape her experiences of school? To what extent do these shadows operate in her life as powerful, unspoken scripts, drawing the lines around the particular role she felt allowed to play?
2. As hooks relates, she became familiar with the standards and expectations being placed on her in college largely by indirection and inference. The norms and scripts to which she was expected to conform, she makes clear, remained invisible and unspoken. How would you put some of these norms and scripts into words? What script would you write?
3. For hooks, the prospect of succeeding in school revolved around the experience of loss: giving up connections and relationships that had formerly defined how she viewed herself. In your experience, has anything similar defined your relationship to school?

WRITING

4. Race and class, hooks argues, are the unspoken norms that structure everyday college life, the invisible scripts that set the boundaries around what different types of students are encouraged or allowed to expect from school. Write an essay in which you analyze how hooks makes this argument. How does she present her own experience as a student as an example? What unspoken (or spoken) scripts about schooling, education, race, or class does hooks expose in her writing?
5. For hooks, there is a complicated relationship between education and desire. Write an essay in which you analyze how this relationship works, according to hooks. Describe the particular role imposed on hooks as a black working-class student, and assess the particular ways this role seems designed to set boundaries around the educational designs and desires she was allowed to have.
6. On pages 275–76, John Taylor Gatto lists Alexander Inglis's six basic functions of modern schooling. Write an essay in which you analyze whether any of these functions also appear in hooks's assessment of education. How do you think hooks would respond to Gatto's critique of the educational system? Would any of Gatto's suggestions alleviate the issues of race and class that hooks faced?

RACHEL TOOR

Unconscious Plagiarism

Do we really have a handle on what exactly plagiarism is and why exactly it's wrong? And what might happen if we were to rethink these assumptions? According to Rachel Toor, it's possible that such an effort might actually result in a new kind of educational opportunity: a chance to explore not only how we think about cheating, but also how we think about the purpose and goals of learning altogether. Toor is an assistant professor of creative writing at Eastern Washington University. This essay first appeared in the *Chronicle of Higher Education* in 2011.

IT AMUSES ME IN THE CLASSROOM WHEN I HEAR STUDENTS QUOTING me back to myself. As my peculiar sentences and ideas come out of their mouths, I smile and wonder if they are aware they are parroting me. They repeat things I've said as if they were Platonic forms of ideas.

It kind of makes me think I'm doing my job. Thomas Jefferson wrote, "He who receives an idea from me, receives instruction himself without lessening mine; as he who lights his taper at mine, receives light without darkening me."

One of the things I say to my students is that good writers steal. By that, I mean that when you read like a writer, you look to see the moves and tricks that other authors are using, and you seek to emulate them. Of course I don't mean copying specific words or sentences, but adopting ways to build tension on a line-by-line level, tricks to make fluid transitions, and the ability to create beauty by putting unlike things next to each other.

So in my writing courses, we look at Martin Luther King Jr.'s sentences and copy his structure. We examine what happens between John McPhee's paragraphs, and we study Joan Didion's curious juxtapositions.

It amuses me in the classroom when I hear students quoting me back to myself.

Sometimes reading like a student means imitating. That was the idea behind ancient "copy books," where pupils simply retranscribed the writing of others. Rote memorization used to be a popular form of learning. How many of us had to be able to recite, as English majors, the first 10 lines of *The Canterbury Tales* in the original middle-muddle of the language? How many English majors still do?

So when I hear my own words and ideas come flying back at me, I try to take it as the sincerest form of flattery. At least when it comes from my students.

In our teaching, we all stand on the shoulders of those giants who have lectured and seminar-ed us. Does it make any sense to say where we learned what we learned?

Years ago, I dated a scholar who was well and widely published. When I saw my ideas and sentences appear in print in his books and articles, it did not please me. If you're such a big fat deal, I thought (and may have said), come up with your own damn ideas and sentences. As an editor, I never maintained ownership over things I added to manuscripts. It was my job to improve a manuscript. As a girlfriend, however, it was a different story. I felt ripped off.

Recently a friend, a graduate student in another discipline I've informally mentored for years, sent me a draft of an essay he was working on. I read it with interest; my interest piqued when I recognized neologisms, linguistic tics, and ideas on his pages. At first I thought: Gee, this sounds familiar. Then I thought: Are you freaking kidding me?

When we exchanged e-mails, I told him I was surprised to see him making choices in his writing that sounded so much like mine.

Unapologetic, he responded, "I do everything I can to steal (I mean learn) from you, whether it's word choice or big ideas. How the hell else am I supposed to get any better at this?"

I don't want to be chary with either my ideas or my willingness to help friends. But sometimes that kind of thing can feel like a blow, even though I know it does nothing to diminish me.

Attribution is as easy as appropriation, or it should be. I may go too far to make sure that I give credit to those whose words, phrases, or ideas so delight me that I can't help but filch them. If I use someone else's writing exercise in class, for example, I say, "I stole this from my thesis adviser, Judy Blunt." Or I'll write, "As my friend Jeff-the-economist likes to say." In certain cases, I love citing the provenance: I once heard Mary Karr quoting Martin Amis who quoted Ian McEwen as saying something like, "When you publish a book you become an employee of your former self." Putting myself in that company makes me feel good.

But there are so many things—phrases, exercises, classroom tricks—I've pilfered from others that for many of them, I couldn't tell you the original source. Sometimes phrases from Wallace Stevens or Milton show up in my prose, sometimes a line from an Elvis Costello song. Even if my aim is true, I don't know how much I'm stealing at any given time. Unconscious plagiarism is the cost of paying attention to language.

My friend Nancy pointed out, when I was in mid-fume about this issue, that Mark Twain said Adam was the only person who could be certain he wasn't a plagiarist. When I got home, I Googled the quote and found Twain actually wrote, "What a good thing Adam had. When he said a good thing he knew nobody had said it before."

Nancy's version was, I thought, funnier. Only she and I would know if I tried to pass off her version as my own. But the fact is, she and I would know.

I also found a passage from Twain about how a friend complimented the dedication in *The Innocents Abroad*, saying he'd always admired it, even before he'd seen it in Twain's book. "Of course, my first impulse was to prepare this man's remains for burial," Twain wrote, but then the two friends went to a bookstore and found the original in Oliver Wendell Holmes's book. To Twain's surprise, he discovered, "I had really stolen that dedication, almost word for word. I could not imagine how this curious thing had happened; for I knew one thing, for a dead certainty—that a certain amount of pride always goes along with a teaspoonful of brains, and that this pride protects a man from deliberately stealing other people's ideas."

Twain then remembered reading and rereading Holmes's poems until his "mental reservoir was filled with them to the brim." He wrote to Holmes to apologize, and the gracious guy wrote back that he "believed we all unconsciously worked over ideas gathered in reading and hearing, imagining they were original with ourselves."

What I'm talking about here is clearly nothing new. In a 2007 *Harper's* essay called "The Ecstasy of Influence," Jonathan Lethem looked carefully, historically, and smartly at this phenomenon called "cryptomnesia," and at related concepts of plagiarism, collage art, and the limits of copyright. More recently, David Shields published a cranky book, *Reality Hunger,* a large chunk of which is unattributed quotes to make his argument about all art being theft. There is much talk in the wider culture about memes, and about the spreading and replicating of ideas.

How much, though, do we talk about this in academe?

In our teaching, we all stand on the shoulders of those giants who have lectured and seminar-ed us. Does it make any sense to say where we learned what we learned? Do students care? Should we? Even though scholars make a fetish out of footnoting, where do we give credit to ideas or innovations whose provenance we're not exactly sure of? Sometimes it's hard to tell where your original notion ended and where it was driven further by conversation with a friend or colleague. We're in the business of intellectual exchange; it's an economy with little currency in the real world, so we have to value in-group bartering. I wonder if that makes us more possessive of what we think is ours.

I used to be surprised when academics so worried about being scooped they were reluctant to take ideas for test-drives at conferences. But then I heard horror stories about stolen research and plagiarized theses, about grad students and junior colleagues having their names left off published papers to which they had contributed substantially. What scholar would do something like that? Where is the pride that goes along with a teaspoonful of brains? Is unconscious plagiarism less morally icky than outright theft, even if the result is the same?

I think about the trope-stealing boyfriend, sentence-parroting students, and the friend who plays dress-up in my linguistic quirks, and wonder if petty pissiness might give way to rage if what these imitators pilfered was something that mattered.

DISCUSSION

1. The conventional view of plagiarism is that it is a conscious or intentional act. How does the essay's title, "Unconscious Plagiarism," challenge this view? What definition of plagiarism does it suggest? And how does this definition compare to your own?
2. Toor draws a distinction between "stealing" and "imitating." How do you understand this difference? Do you agree with Toor that, when it comes to academic plagiarism, there is a valid line to be drawn between the two? Why or why not?
3. One of Toor's central premises is that the rise in incidents of plagiarism is less the result of a decline in the morality of current students than of a fundamental misunderstanding about what truly constitutes academic cheating. Do you agree? Is plagiarism more a problem of understanding than intention? Can you think of an example from your own experience as a student that supports your view?

WRITING

4. Cast yourself in the role of a teacher or an administrator whose job is to devise a new policy for dealing with academic plagiarism. Then write an essay in which you describe and defend what this policy should be. How does it define cheating? What punishments or consequences does it impose for such infractions? What incentives does it offer for students who do the right thing? And why do you feel this is correct? What educational goals does it advance?
5. Toor addresses her essay to an audience of college instructors like herself. What would be different about the argument here if it were directed toward a readership of students? Write an essay in which you reformulate Toor's argument for a student audience. How might you go about re-presenting or rewording her key points? In place of the anecdotes she includes, what examples or stories would you offer as support instead?
6. Identifying one of the key ironies in the ways we think about plagiarism, Toor notes that the very behavior college professors decry in their students (i.e., borrowing the ideas of others) is exactly what so many of them engage in themselves. How do you think John Taylor Gatto (p. 271) would respond to this observation? Do you think he would regard it as evidence of how and why students find themselves so "bored" in school?

JONATHAN KOZOL

Preparing Minds for Markets

Whether or not we want to admit it, many of our public schools play a formative role in shaping how children come to see themselves as workers. Presenting an eye-opening account of the ways that corporate logos and workplace terminology have permeated the modern classroom, Jonathan Kozol offers a spirited critique of the work-related scripts children today are often compelled to take up. Kozol is a writer and educator best known for his works on inequality in American education. He graduated from Harvard University and was awarded a Rhodes Scholarship to study at Magdalen College, Oxford. Rather than finishing at Oxford, however, he moved to Paris to work on a novel. When he returned to the United States, he began teaching in the Boston public schools, but he was fired for teaching a Langston Hughes poem that was not in the curriculum. His experiences in Boston's segregated classrooms led to his first book, *Death at an Early Age* (1967), which won the National Book Award. His other books include *Savage Inequalities* (1991), *Amazing Grace* (1995), *Letters to a Young Teacher* (2007), and most recently, *Fire in the Ashes: Twenty-Five Years Among the Poorest Children in America* (2012). The following selection is from *The Shame of the Nation*, published in 2005.

THREE YEARS AGO, IN COLUMBUS, OHIO, I WAS VISITING A SCHOOL in which the stimulus-response curriculum that Mr. Endicott was using in New York had been in place for several years.[1] The scripted teaching method started very early in this school. ("Practice Active Listening!" a kindergarten teacher kept repeating to her children.) So too did a program of surprisingly explicit training of young children for the modern marketplace. Starting in kindergarten, children in the school were being asked to think about the jobs that they might choose when they grew up. The posters that surrounded them made clear which kinds of jobs they were expected to select.

"Do you want a manager's job?" the first line of a kindergarten poster asked.

"What job do you want?" a second question asked in an apparent effort to expand the range of choices that these five-year-olds might wish to make.

But the momentary window that this second question seemed to open into other possible careers was closed by the next question on the wall. "How will you do the manager's job?" the final question asked.

The tiny hint of choice afforded by the second question was eradicated by the third, which presupposed that all the kids had said yes to the first. No written question asked the children: "Do you want a lawyer's job? a nurse's job? a doctor's job? a poet's job? a preacher's job? an engineer's job? or an artist's job?" Sadly enough, the teacher had not even thought to ask if anybody in the class might someday like to be a teacher.

In another kindergarten class, there was a poster that displayed the names of several retail stores: JCPenney, Wal-Mart, Kmart, Sears, and a few others. "It's like working in a store," a classroom aide explained. "The children are learning to pretend that they're cashiers."

Work-related themes and managerial ideas were carried over into almost every classroom of the school. In a first grade class, for instance, children had been given classroom tasks for which they were responsible. The names of children and their tasks were posted on the wall, an ordinary thing to see in classrooms everywhere. But in this case there was a novel twist: All the jobs the kids were given were described as management positions!

There was a "Coat Room Manager" and a "Door Manager," a "Pencil Sharpener Manager" and a "Soap Manager," an "Eraser, Board, and Marker Manager," and there was also a "Line Manager." What on earth, I was about to ask, is a "Line Manager"? My question was answered when a group of children filing in the hallway grew a bit unruly and a grown-up's voice barked out, "Who is your line manager?"

In the upper grades, the management positions became more sophisticated and demanding. In a fourth grade, for example, I was introduced to a "Time Manager" who was assigned to hold the timer to be sure the teacher didn't wander from her schedule and that everyone adhered to the prescribed number of minutes that had been assigned to every classroom task.

Turning a corner, I encountered a "HELP WANTED" sign. Several of these signs, I found, were posted on the walls at various locations in the school. These were not advertisements for school employees, but for children who would be selected to fill various positions as class managers. "Children in the higher grades are taught to file applications for a job," the principal explained—then "go for interviews," she said, before they can be hired. According to a summary of schoolwide practices she gave me, interviews "for management positions" were intended to teach values of "responsibility for . . . jobs."

"Children in the higher grades are taught to file applications for a job."

In another fourth grade class, there was an "earnings chart" that had been taped to every child's desk, on which a number of important writing skills had been spelled out and, next to each, the corresponding earnings that a child would receive if written answers he or she provided in the course of classroom exercises such as mini-drills or book reports displayed the necessary skills.

"How Much Is My Written Answer Worth?" the children in the class were asked. There were, in all, four columns on the "earnings charts" and children had been taught the way to fill them in. There was also a Classroom Bank in which the children's earnings were accrued. A wall display beneath the heading of the Classroom Bank presented an enticing sample of real currency—one-dollar bills, five-dollar bills, ten-dollar bills—in order to make clear the nexus between cash rewards and writing proper sentences.

Ninety-eight percent of children in the school were living in poverty, according to the school's annual report card; about four-fifths were African-American. The principal said that only about a quarter of the students had been given preschool education.

At another elementary school in the same district, in which 93 percent of children were black or Hispanic, the same "HELP WANTED" posters and the lists of management positions were displayed. Among the positions open to the children in this school, there was an "Absence Manager," a "Form-Collector Manager," a "Paper-Passing Manager," a "Paper-Collecting Manager," a "Paper-Returning Manager," an "Exit Ticket Manager," even a "Learning Manager," a "Reading Manager," a "Behavior Manager," and a "Score-Keeper Manager." Applications for all management positions, starting with the second graders, had to be "accompanied by references," according to the principal.

On a printed application form she handed me—"Consistency Management Manager Application"[2] was its title—children were instructed to fill in their name, address, phone number, teacher, and grade level, and then indicate the job that they preferred ("First job choice. . . . Why do you want this job? Second job choice. . . . Why do you want this job?"), then sign and date their application. The awkwardly named document, the principal explained, originated in a program aimed at children of minorities that had been developed with financial backing from a businessman in Texas.

The silent signals I'd observed in the South Bronx and Hartford were in use in this school also. As I entered one class, the teacher gave his students the straight-arm salute, with fingers flat. The children responded quickly with the same salute. On one of the walls, there was a sign that read "A Million Dollars Worth of Self-Control." It was "a little incentive thing," the teacher told me when I asked about this later in the afternoon.

As I was chatting with the principal before I left, I asked her if there was a reason why those two words "management" and "manager" kept popping up throughout the school. I also summoned up my nerve to tell her that I was surprised to see "HELP WANTED" signs within an elementary school.

"We want every child to be working as a manager while he or she is in this school," the principal explained. "We want to make them understand that, in this country, companies will give you opportunities to work, to prove yourself, no matter what you've done."

I wasn't sure of what she meant by that—"no matter what you've done"—and asked her if she could explain this. "Even if you have a felony arrest," she said, "we want you to understand that you can be a manager someday."

I told her that I still did not quite understand why management positions were presented to the children as opposed to other jobs—being a postal worker, for example, or construction worker, or, for that matter, working in a field of purely intellectual endeavor—as a possible way to earn a living even if one once had been in trouble with the law. But the principal was interrupted at this point and since she had already been extremely patient with me, I did not believe I had the right to press her any further. So I left the school with far more questions in my mind than answers.

When I had been observing Mr. Endicott at P.S. 65, it had occurred to me that something truly radical about the way that inner-city children are perceived was presupposed by the peculiar way he spoke to students and the way they had been programmed to respond. I thought of this again here in these classes in Ohio. What is the radical perception of these kids that underlies such practices? How is this different from the way most educated friends of mine would look at their own children?

"Primitive utilitarianism"—"Taylorism in the classroom"—were two of the terms that Mr. Endicott had used in speaking of the teaching methods in effect within his school. "Commodification"—"of the separate pieces of the learning process, of the children in themselves"—is the expression that another teacher uses to describe these practices. Children, in this frame of reference, are regarded as investments, assets, or productive units—or else, failing that, as pint-sized human deficits who threaten our competitive capacities. The package of skills they learn, or do not learn, is called "the product" of the school. Sometimes the educated child is referred to as "the product" too.

These ways of viewing children, which were common at the start of the last century, have reemerged over the past two decades in the words of business leaders, influential educators, and political officials. "We must start thinking of students as workers . . . ," said a high official of one of the nation's teachers unions at a forum convened by *Fortune* magazine in 1988.[3] I remember thinking when I read these words: Is this, really, what it all comes down to? Is future productivity, from this point on, to be the primary purpose of the education we provide our children? Is this to be the way in which we will decide if teachers are complying with their obligations to their students and society? What if a child should grow ill and die before she's old enough to make her contribution to the national economy? Will all the money that our government has spent to educate that child have to be regarded as a bad investment?

Admittedly, the economic needs of a society are bound to be reflected to some rational degree within the policies and purposes of public schools. But, even so, most of us are inclined to ask, there must be *something* more to life as it is lived by six-year-olds or ten-year-olds, or by teenagers for that matter, than concerns about "successful global competition." Childhood is not merely basic training for utilitarian adulthood. It should have some claims upon our mercy, not for its future value to the economic interests of competitive societies but for its present value as a perishable piece of life itself.

Listening to the stern demands we hear for inculcating worker ideologies in the mentalities of inner-city youth—and, as we are constantly exhorted now, for "getting tough" with those who don't comply—I am reminded of a passage from the work of Erik Erikson, who urged us to be wary of prescriptive absoluteness in the ways we treat and think about our children. "The most deadly of all possible sins" in the upbringing of a child, Erikson wrote, derive too frequently from what he called "destructive forms of conscientiousness."[4] Erikson's good counsel notwithstanding, the momentum that has led to these utilitarian ideas about the education of low-income children has been building for a long, long time and, at least in public discourse as it is presented in the press and on TV, has not met with widespread opposition. Beginning in the early 1980s and continuing with little deviation right up to the present time, the notion of producing "products" who will then produce more wealth for the society has come to be embraced by many politicians and, increasingly, by principals of inner-city schools that have developed close affiliations with the representatives of private business corporations.

The notion of producing "products" who will then produce more wealth for the society has come to be embraced by many politicians and . . . principals.

"Dismayed by the faulty products being turned out by Chicago's troubled public schools," the *Wall Street Journal* wrote in 1990, "some 60 of the city's giant corporations have taken over the production line themselves," a reference to the efforts that these corporations had invested in creation of a model school in a predominantly black neighborhood that was intended to embody corporate ideas of management and productivity. "I'm in the business of developing minds to meet a market demand," the principal of the school announced during a speech delivered at "a power breakfast" of the top executives of several of these corporations. "If you were manufacturing Buicks, you would have the same objectives," said a corporate official who was serving as the school's executive director.[5]

Business jargon has since come to be commonplace in the vocabularies used within the schools themselves. Children in the primary grades are being taught they must "negotiate" with one another for a book or toy or box of crayons or a pencil-sharpener—certainly not a normal word for five- or six-year-olds to use. In many schools, young children have been learning also to "sign contracts" to complete their lessons rather than just looking up and telling Miss O'Brien they will "try real hard" to do what she has asked.

Learning itself—the learning of a skill, or the enjoying of a book, and even having an idea—is now defined increasingly not as a process or preoccupation that holds satisfaction of its own but in proprietary terms, as if it were the acquisition of an object or stock-option or the purchase of a piece of land. "Taking ownership" is the accepted term, which now is used both by the kids themselves and also by their teachers. Most people like to think they "get" ideas, "understand" a process, or "take pleasure" in the act of digging into a good book. In the market-driven classroom, children are encouraged to believe they "own" the book, the concept, the idea. They don't *engage* with knowledge; they possess it.

In the Columbus schools, as we have seen, children are actively "incentivized" (this is another term one hears in many inner-city schools) by getting reimbursements for the acquisition of a skill in terms of simulated cash. At P.S. 65 in the South Bronx, I was shown another Classroom Bank, out of which a currency called "Scholar Dollars" was disbursed. Some of these things may be dismissed as little more than modern reembodiments of ordinary rituals and phrases known to schoolchildren for decades. We all got gold stars in my elementary school if we brought in completed homework; many teachers give their students sticky decals with a picture of a frog or mouse or cat or dog, for instance, as rewards for finishing a book report or simply treating one another with politeness. Most Americans, I think, would smile at these innocent and pleasant ways of giving children small rewards. But would they smile quite so easily if their own children were provided earnings charts to calculate how much they will be paid for learning to write sentences?

Some of the usages that I have cited here ("ownership," "negotiate," for instance) have filtered into the vocabularies of suburban schools as well, but in most of these schools they are not introduced to children as the elements of acquisitional vocabulary and are more likely to be used, unconsciously perhaps, as borrowings from language that has come to be familiar in the world of pop psychology—"learning to 'take ownership' of one's emotions," for example. It is a different story when they are incorporated into a much broader package of pervasive corporate indoctrination.

Very few people who are not involved with inner-city schools have any idea of the extremes to which the mercantile distortion of the purposes and character of education have been taken or how unabashedly proponents of these practices are willing to defend them. The head of a Chicago school, for instance, who was criticized by some for emphasizing rote instruction which, his critics said, was turning children into "robots," found no reason to dispute the charge. "Did you ever stop to think that these robots will never burglarize your home?" he asked, and "will never snatch your pocket books. . . . These robots are going to be producing taxes. . . ."[6]

These ways of speaking about children and perceiving children are specific to the schools that serve minorities.

Would any educator feel at ease in using terms like these in reference to the children of a town like Scarsdale or Manhasset, Glencoe or Winnetka, or the affluent suburban town of Newton, Massachusetts, in which I attended elementary school and later taught? I think we know this is unlikely. These ways of speaking about children and perceiving children are specific to the schools that serve minorities. Shorn of unattractive language about "robots" who will be producing taxes and not burglarizing homes, the general idea that schools in ghettoized communities must settle for a different set of goals than schools that serve the children of the middle class and upper middle class has been accepted widely. And much of the rhetoric of "rigor" and "high standards" that we hear so frequently, no matter how egalitarian in spirit it may sound to some, is fatally belied by practices that vulgarize the intellects of children and take from their education far too many of the opportunities for cultural and critical reflectiveness without which citizens become receptacles for other people's ideologies and ways of looking at the world but lack the independent spirits to create their own.

Perhaps the clearest evidence of what is taking place is seen in schools in which the linkage between education and employment is explicitly established in the names these schools are given and the work-related goals that they espouse. When badly failing schools are redesigned—or undergo "reconstitution," as the current language holds—a fashionable trend today is to assign them names related to the world of economics and careers. "Academy of Enterprise" or "Corporate Academy" are two such names adopted commonly in the renaming of a segregated school. Starting about ten years ago, a previously unfamiliar term emerged to specify the purposes these various academies espouse. "School-to-work" is the unflinching designation that has since been used to codify these goals, and "industry-embedded education" for the children of minorities has now become a term of art among practitioners.

Advocates for school-to-work do not, in general, describe it as a race-specific project but tend instead to emphasize the worth of linking academic programs to the world of work for children of all backgrounds and insisting that suburban children too should be prepared in school for marketplace demands, that children of all social classes ought to have "some work experience" in high school, for example. But the attempt at even-handedness in speaking of the ways that this idea might be applied has been misleading from the start. In most suburban schools, the school-to-work idea, if educators even speak of it at all, is little more than seemly decoration on the outer edges of a liberal curriculum. In many urban schools, by contrast, it has come to be the energizing instrument of almost every aspect of instruction.

Some business leaders argue that this emphasis is both realistic and humane in cases, for example, where a sixteen-year-old student lacks the skills or motivation to pursue a richly academic course of study or, indeed, can sometimes barely write a simple paragraph or handle elementary math. If the rationale for this were so defined in just so many words by the administrators of our schools, and if it were not introduced until the final years of secondary education at a point when other options for a student may appear to be foreclosed, an argument could certainly be made that school-to-work is a constructive adaptation to the situation many teenage students actually face.

But when this ethos takes control of secondary education almost from the start, or even earlier than that, before a child even enters middle school, as is the case in many districts now, it's something very different from an adaptation to the needs of students or the preferences they may express. It's not at all an "adaptation" in these cases; it's a prior legislation of diminished options for a class of children who are not perceived as having the potential of most other citizens. It's not "acceding" to their preferences. It's manufacturing those preferences and, all too frequently, it's doing this to the direct exclusion of those options other children rightly take as their entitlement.

There are middle schools in urban neighborhoods today where children are required, in effect, to choose careers before they even enter adolescence. Children make their applications to a middle school when they're in the fifth grade. . . . [A] South Bronx middle school [bears] Paul Robeson's name. "Robeson," however, as I subsequently learned, wasn't the complete name of this school. "The Paul Robeson School for Medical Careers and Health Professions" was the full and seemingly enticing designation that it bore; and, sadly enough, this designation and the way the school described itself in a brochure that had been given to the fifth grade students in the local elementary schools had led these girls into believing that enrolling there would lead to the fulfillment of a dream they shared: They wanted to be doctors.

"An understanding and embracement of medical science and health," said the brochure in a description of the school's curriculum, "is developed through powerful learning opportunities. . . . To be successful at the Paul Robeson School . . . , a student is expected to be highly motivated to broaden their horizons." Not many ten-year-olds in the South Bronx would likely know that this description represented an outrageous overstatement of the academic offerings this middle school provided. Unless they had an older sibling who had been a student there, most would have no way of knowing that the Robeson School, perennially ranking at the lowest level of the city's middle schools, sent very few students into high schools that successfully prepared a child for college and that any likelihood of moving from this school into a medical career, as these girls understood the term, was almost nonexistent.

"It's a medical school," another child, named Timeka, told me when I asked her why she had applied there. "I want to be a baby doctor," she explained, a goal that a number of the girls had settled on together, as children often do in elementary school. But the program at the Robeson School did not provide the kind of education that could lead her to that goal. A cynic, indeed, might easily suspect it was designed instead to turn out nursing aides and health assistants and the other relatively low-paid personnel within a hospital or nursing home, for instance, all of which might be regarded as good jobs for children with no other options, if they continued with their education long enough to graduate; but even this was not the usual pattern for a child who had spent three years at Robeson.

Timeka went from Robeson to another of those "industry-embedded" schools,[7] a 97 percent black and Hispanic school called "Health Opportunities," in which only one in five ninth graders ever reached twelfth grade and from which Timeka dropped out in eleventh grade.[8] I had known Timeka since she was a jubilant and energetic eight-year-old. I used to help her with her math and reading when she was in the fourth grade. She was smart and quick and good with words, and very good in math. If she had gone to school in almost any middle-class suburban district in this nation, she'd have had at least a chance of realizing her dream if she still wanted to when she completed high school. And if she changed her mind and settled on a different dream, or many different dreams, as adolescents usually do, she would have been exposed to an array of options that would have permitted her to make a well-informed decision. The choice of a career means virtually nothing if you do not know what choices you may actually have.

The choice of a career means virtually nothing if you do not know what choices you may actually have.

"In recent years, business has taken ownership of school-to-work . . . ," according to an advocate for these career academies.[9] National and regional industry associations, he reports, are "linking students" to "standards-driven, work-based learning opportunities while they are in school" and then, he says, providing students with job offers from participating businesses. One such program has taken place for several years at a high school in Chicago where an emphasis on "Culinary Arts" has been embedded in curriculum.[10] A teacher at the school, where 98 percent of students are black or Hispanic (many of Mexican descent), told me of a student she had grown attached to when she taught her in eleventh grade. The student, she said, showed academic promise—"I definitely thought that she was capable of going on to college"—so she recommended her to be admitted to a senior honors class.

It was a big school (2,200 students) and the teacher said she didn't see this girl again until the following September when she happened to run into her during a class break on an escalator in the building, and she asked her if she'd been admitted to the honors class. The student told her, "No," she said. "I couldn't figure out why." Then, she said, "I realized she'd been placed in Culinary Arts."

Students, she explained, were required "to decide on a 'career path' at the end of freshman year," and "once you do this, your entire program is determined by that choice." Technically, she said, a student could select a college education as "career path," but this option, she reported, wasn't marketed to many of the students at the school as forcefully as were the job-related programs. The career programs in the upper-level grades, moreover, were blocked out "as a double period every day," the teacher said, which made it harder for the students in these programs who so wished to take an honors class or other academic classes that appealed to them.[11]

The program in culinary arts, in which the students were prepared to work in restaurant kitchens, had been set up in coordination with Hyatt Hotels, which offered jobs or internships to students on completion of their education.[12] The program was promoted to the students so effectively that many who initially may have had academic goals "appear to acquiesce in this"—"they will defend it, once they've made the choice," she said—even though some recognize that this will lead them to a relatively lower economic role in later years than if they somehow found the will to keep on and pursue a college education. "If you talk with them of college options at this point," and "if they trust you," said the teacher, "they will say, 'Nobody ever told me I could do it.' If you tell them, 'You *could* do it,' they will say, 'Why didn't someone tell me this before?'"

She told me she felt torn about expressing her concern that college education as a possible career path for such students was, in her words, either "not presented" or else "undersold," because she said there were outstanding teachers in the work-related programs and she did not want to speak of them with disrespect or compromise their jobs. At the same time, she clearly was upset about this since she spoke with deep emotion of the likelihood that "we may be trapping these young ones" in "low-paying jobs."

The teacher's story of her brief encounter with her former student reminded me of the disappointment I had felt about Timeka. The teacher seemed to blame herself to some degree, wishing, I guess, that she could have remained in closer touch with this bright student in the months since she had been a pupil in her class, perhaps believing that she might have intervened somehow on her behalf. The teacher didn't speak of a career in cooking in a restaurant, or work in a hotel, with any hint of condescension or disparagement. She was simply cognizant of other possibilities her student might have entertained; and she was saddened by this memory.

NOTES

[1]I visited these schools in November 2002, following a preliminary visit in October 2001.

Poverty and racial data for both schools described: School Year Report Cards, Columbus City School District, 2003–2004 (race and poverty data from 2002–2003).

[2]This document, part of a self-described "comprehensive classroom management program" known as "Consistency Management and Cooperative Discipline," is published by Project Grad USA, based in Houston, Texas.

[3]Albert Shanker, American Federation of Teachers, cited in *Fortune*, November 7, 1988.

[4]*Young Man Luther*, by Erik Erikson (New York: Norton, 1962).

[5]*Wall Street Journal*, February 9, 1990.

[6]"Learning in America," a MacNeil/Lehrer Production, PBS, April 3, 1989.

[7]Clara Barton High School for Health Professionals (95 percent black and Hispanic) had 633 ninth graders and 301 twelfth graders in 2002–2003. Graphic Arts Communications High School (94 percent black and Hispanic) had 1,096 ninth graders and 199 twelfth graders. Metropolitan Corporate Academy (98 percent black and Hispanic) had 90 ninth graders and 55 twelfth graders, of whom 34 graduated in 2003. Metropolitan Corporate Academy was conceived as a partnership with the financial firm Goldman Sachs, which provided mentors and internships for students. A school's reliance on resources from the private sector carries risks of instability, however. After serious layoffs at Goldman Sachs in 2002, according to Insideschools, an online service of Advocates for Children, "the number of mentors was cut in half." (Annual School Reports for all three schools, New York City Public Schools, 2002–2003 and 2003–2004; Insideschools 2002.)

[8]Of 294 ninth graders in the fall of 1999, only 60 remained as twelfth graders in 2003. White students made up 1.6 percent of the school's enrollment of 665. (Annual School Report for Health Opportunities High School, New York City Public Schools, 2002–2003; Common Core of Data, National Center for Education Statistics, U.S. Department of Education, 1999–2000 and 2002–2003.)

[9]Tim Barnicle, director of the Workforce Development Program at the National Center on Education and the Economy, Washington, D.C., in a letter to *Education Week*,

February 3, 1999. "The most viable school-to-work partnerships," Mr. Barnicle writes, are "tied to high academic standards . . . , supported by business and industry partners that provide students with technical skills needed to succeed in a job. . . ." He concedes that "too often school-to-work" has not been "viewed as being connected to higher academic performance in the classroom," but nonetheless believes that career-embedded schools, if properly conceived, can improve retention and increase "access to postsecondary education."

[10]The program is sited at the Roberto Clemente High School. For racial demographics, see Illinois School Report Card for Roberto Clemente Community High School, 2002, and Roberto Clemente Community High School Profile 2003–2004, Chicago Public Schools, 2004.

[11]Interview with teacher (unnamed for privacy concerns), July 2003, and subsequent correspondence in 2004 and 2005.

[12]"Project Profile, Roberto Clemente Community Academy," Executive Service Corps of Chicago, 2002–2003. An early evaluation of the program is provided in "The Millennium Breach: The American Dilemma, Richer and Poorer," a report by the Milton S. Eisenhower Foundation and the Corporation for What Works, Washington, D.C., 1998.

DISCUSSION

1. For many minority or low-income children in the United States today, school is primarily a dress rehearsal for one's future life on the job — what Kozol refers to as "vocational" or "utilitarian" learning. What do you think of this educational model? Are the market-driven roles Kozol describes the ones best for children to practice and master in school?
2. What do you make of the phrase "school-to-work"? In your view, does it suggest an approach to education that is legitimate or even useful? Does it reflect the way we're usually taught to think about education? Can you think of an alternative term that would suggest an educational approach that is preferable?
3. Kozol describes visiting one kindergarten classroom in which posters of different retail stores (JCPenney, Wal-Mart, Kmart, Sears) were displayed. "'It's like working in a store,' a classroom aide explained. 'The children are learning to pretend that they're cashiers'" (p. 302). What, in your opinion, is either good or bad about this kind of educational setting? This particular lesson? Are these types of roles worth modeling?

WRITING

4. Here is a list of the job titles to which the students in the classroom Kozol observes can aspire: coat room manager; door manager; pencil sharpener manager; soap manager; eraser, board, and marker manager; and line manager. Write an essay in which you assess the particular kind of learning environment this classroom seems to offer. What rules and what roles are present for students and teachers alike? Do you find anything redeeming about this classroom model? Why or why not?
5. "A fashionable trend today," Kozol writes, "is to assign [schools] names related to the world of economics and careers" — names like "Academy of Enterprise" or "Corporate Academy" (p. 307). Write an essay in which you analyze how this practice might or might not represent a shift in the way we think about the purposes of education. How would you go about arguing in favor of this market-oriented approach to education? What advantages or benefits of this model would you play up?
6. From very different perspectives, Kozol and Mike Rose (p. 280) invite readers to take a closer look at the way cultural stereotypes about different jobs can influence how we define legitimate or valid intelligence. Write an essay in which you identify and assess how these writers' respective commentaries compare. How does each understand the connection between work and learning? What sort of conclusions or critique does each offer? And which do you find more convincing or compelling? Why?

Rule **Maker** >>>>>>>>> *Rule* **Breaker**

"Earning a post-secondary degree or credential is no longer just a pathway to opportunity for a talented few; rather, it is a prerequisite for the growing jobs of the new economy. Over this decade, employment in jobs requiring education beyond a high school diploma will grow more rapidly than employment in jobs that do not; of the 30 fastest growing occupations, more than half require postsecondary education. With the average earnings of college graduates at a level that is twice as high as that of workers with only a high school diploma, higher education is now the clearest pathway into the middle class."

WHITE HOUSE WEBSITE ON HIGHER EDUCATION, 2012

HTTP://WWW.WHITEHOUSE.GOV/ISSUES/EDUCATION/HIGHER-EDUCATION

"Is this, really, what it all comes down to? Is future productivity, from this point on, to be the primary purpose of the education we provide our children? Is this to be the way in which we decide if teachers are complying with their obligations to their students and society? . . . [T]here must be something *more to life as it is lived by six-year-olds or ten-year-olds, or by teenagers for that matter, than concerns about 'successful global competition.'"*

JONATHAN KOZOL, EDUCATION WRITER AND ACTIVIST, 2005

Jeff Greenberg/Alamy

Miami, Florida, Little Haiti Edison Park Elementary School Career Day student uniforms

THE WHITE HOUSE VS. JONATHAN KOZOL

Over the last several years, the public debate over the future of education has increasingly pitted two antithetical educational models against each other. The quotation from the White House website captures the first model: The goal of schooling is to prepare students to become productive workers and contributors to America's market-driven economy. Jonathan Kozol sums up the second model: The goal of education is to make students into critical thinkers, to foster a familiarity with a diverse range of viewpoints, and to instill an appreciation for how varied and complex the world around us truly is. Envisioning school as a kind of preprofessional training ground, the first model defines education as an economic resource, a set of discrete skills whose value is measured in terms of usefulness in the marketplace. Casting school as the setting for disinterested inquiry, the liberal arts model defines the nature and value of learning intrinsically, independent of any vocational purpose to which it might be put. Taken together, they present us with fundamental questions about what learning is for, and what a "quality" education should include.

FIND THE RULES: Write a brief essay in which you list all the ways you normally hear education described — in the news, in your classes, in your personal relationships with friends and families. Which of the two models represented by the quotations in this feature do these descriptions seem to align with?

ANALYZE THE RULES: Write an essay in which you evaluate the relative merits of each model. What specific advantages to education does each bring? What particular challenges or downsides does each pose? And which do you find preferable?

MAKE YOUR OWN RULES: Write an essay in which you argue in favor of one of the characterizations of education featured here. Is there any way to reconcile these points of view so that a definition of education can encompass both models? How is that possible?

DAN HURLEY

Can You Make Yourself Smarter?

For many pundits, the rise in video-game use by young people ranks among the primary factors contributing to our nation's cultural decline. But what if this attitude is all wrong? Considering just this possibility, Dan Hurley explores the growing trend of using video games as learning tools within the classroom. Hurley is a science writer and journalist who regularly contributes to the *New York Times*. He has also been senior writer at the *Medical Tribune* and contributing editor to *Psychology Today*. This article first appeared in the *New York Times Magazine* in 2012.

EARLY ON A DRAB AFTERNOON IN JANUARY, A DOZEN THIRD GRADers from the working-class suburb of Chicago Heights, Ill., burst into the Mac Lab on the ground floor of Washington-McKinley School in a blur of blue pants, blue vests and white shirts. Minutes later, they were hunkered down in front of the Apple computers lining the room's perimeter, hoping to do what was, until recently, considered impossible: increase their intelligence through training.

"Can somebody raise their hand," asked Kate Wulfson, the instructor, "and explain to me how you get points?"

On each of the children's monitors, there was a cartoon image of a haunted house, with bats and a crescent moon in a midnight blue sky. Every few seconds, a black cat appeared in one of the house's five windows, then vanished. The exercise was divided into levels. On Level 1, the children earned a point by remembering which window the cat was just in. Easy. But the game is progressive: the cats keep coming, and the kids have to keep watching and remembering.

"And here's where it gets confusing," Wulfson continued. "If you get to Level 2, you have to remember where the cat was two windows ago. The time before last. For Level 3, you have to remember where it was three times ago. Level 4 is four times ago. That's hard. You have to keep track. O.K., ready? Once we start, anyone who talks loses a star."

So began 10 minutes of a remarkably demanding concentration game. At Level 2, even adults find the task somewhat taxing. Almost no one gets past Level 3 without training. But most people who stick with the game do get better with practice. This isn't surprising: practice improves performance on almost every task humans engage in, whether it's learning to read or playing horseshoes.

What is surprising is what else it improved. In a 2008 study, Susanne Jaeggi and Martin Buschkuehl, now of the University of Maryland, found that young adults who practiced a stripped-down, less cartoonish version of the game also showed improvement in a fundamental cognitive ability known as "fluid" intelligence: the capacity to solve novel problems, to learn, to reason, to see connections and to get to the bottom of things. The implication was that playing the game literally makes people smarter.

Psychologists have long regarded intelligence as coming in two flavors: crystallized intelligence, the treasure trove of stored-up information and how-to knowledge (the sort of thing tested on *Jeopardy!* or put to use when you ride a bicycle); and fluid intelligence. Crystallized intelligence grows as you age; fluid intelligence has long been known to peak in early adulthood, around college age, and then to decline gradually. And unlike physical conditioning, which can transform 98-pound weaklings into hunks, fluid intelligence has always been considered impervious to training.

How could watching black cats in a haunted house possibly increase something as profound as fluid intelligence?

That, after all, is the premise of I.Q. tests, or at least the portion that measures fluid intelligence: we can test you now and predict all sorts of things in the future, because fluid intelligence supposedly sets in early and is fairly immutable. While parents, teachers, and others play an essential role in establishing an environment in which a child's intellect can grow, even Tiger Mothers generally expect only higher grades will come from their children's diligence—not better brains.

How, then, could watching black cats in a haunted house possibly increase something as profound as fluid intelligence? Because the deceptively simple game, it turns out, targets the most elemental of cognitive skills: "working" memory. What long-term memory is to crystallized intelligence, working memory is to fluid intelligence. Working memory is more than just the ability to remember a telephone number long enough to dial it; it's the capacity to manipulate the information you're holding in your head—to add or subtract those numbers, place them in reverse order or sort them from high to low. Understanding a metaphor or an analogy is equally dependent on working memory; you can't follow even a simple statement like "See Jane run" if you can't put together how "see" and "Jane" connect with "run." Without it, you can't make sense of anything.

Over the past three decades, theorists and researchers alike have made significant headway in understanding how working memory functions. They have developed a variety of sensitive tests to measure it and determine its relationship to fluid intelligence. Then, in 2008, Jaeggi turned one of these tests of working memory into a training task for building it up, in the same way that push-ups can be used both as a measure of physical fitness and as a strength-building task. "We see attention and working memory as the cardiovascular function of the brain," Jaeggi says. "If you train your attention and working memory, you increase your basic cognitive skills that help you for many different complex tasks."

Jaeggi's study has been widely influential. Since its publication, others have achieved results similar to Jaeggi's not only in elementary-school children but also in preschoolers, college students, and the elderly. The training tasks generally require only 15 to 25 minutes of work per day, five days a week, and have been found to improve scores on tests of fluid intelligence in as little as four weeks. Follow-up studies linking that improvement to real-world gains in schooling and job performance are just getting under way. But already, people with disorders including attention-deficit hyperactivity disorder (A.D.H.D.) and traumatic brain injury have seen benefits from training. Gains can persist for up to eight months after treatment.

In a town like Chicago Heights, where only 16 percent of high schoolers met the Illinois version of the No Child Left Behind standards in 2011, finding a clear way to increase cognitive abilities has obvious appeal. But it has other uses too, at all ages and aptitudes. Even high-level professionals have begun training their working memory in hopes of boosting their fluid intelligence—and, with it, their job performance. If the effect is real—if fluid intelligence can be raised in just a few minutes a day, even by a bit, and not just on a test but in real life—then it would seem to offer, as Jaeggi's 2008 study concluded with Spock-like understatement, "a wide range of applications."

Since the first reliable intelligence test was created just over a hundred years ago, researchers have searched for a way to increase scores meaningfully, with little success.

Since the first reliable intelligence test was created just over a hundred years ago, researchers have searched for a way to increase scores meaningfully, with little success. The track record was so dismal that by 2002, when Jaeggi and her research partner (and now her husband), Martin Buschkuehl, came across a study claiming to have done so, they simply didn't believe it.

The study, by a Swedish neuroscientist named Torkel Klingberg, involved just 14 children, all with A.D.H.D. Half participated in computerized tasks designed to strengthen their working memory, while the other half played less challenging computer games. After just five weeks, Klingberg found that those who played the working-memory games fidgeted less and moved about less. More remarkable, they also scored higher on one of the single best measures of fluid intelligence, the Raven's Progressive Matrices. Improvement in working memory, in other words, transferred to improvement on a task the children weren't training for.

Even if the sample was small, the results were provocative (three years later Klingberg replicated most of the results in a group of 50 children), because matrices are considered the gold standard of fluid-intelligence tests. Anyone who has taken an intelligence test has seen matrices like those used in the Raven's: three rows, with three graphic items in each row, made up of squares, circles, dots, or the like. Do the squares get larger as they move from left to right? Do the circles inside the squares fill in, changing from white to gray to black, as they go downward? One of the nine items is missing from the matrix, and the challenge is to find the underlying patterns—up, down and across—from six possible choices. Initially the solutions are readily apparent to most people, but they get progressively harder to discern. By the end of the test, most test takers are baffled.

If measuring intelligence through matrices seems arbitrary, consider how central pattern recognition is to success in life. If you're going to find buried treasure in baseball statistics to give your team an edge by signing players unappreciated by others, you'd better be good at matrices. If you want to exploit cycles in the stock market, or find a legal precedent in 10 cases, or for that matter, if you need to suss out a woolly mammoth's nature to trap, kill and eat it—you're essentially using the same cognitive skills tested by matrices.

When Klingberg's study came out, both Jaeggi and Buschkuehl were doctoral candidates in cognitive psychology at the University of Bern, Switzerland. Since his high-school days as a Swiss national-champion rower, Buschkuehl had been interested in the degree to which skills—physical and mental—could be trained. Intrigued by Klingberg's suggestion that training working memory could improve fluid intelligence, he showed the paper to Jaeggi, who was studying working memory with a test known as the N-back. "At that time there was pretty much no evidence whatsoever that you can train on one particular task and get transfer to another task that was totally different," Jaeggi says. That is, while most skills improve with practice, the improvement is generally domain-specific: you don't get better at Sudoku by doing crosswords. And fluid intelligence was not just another skill; it was the ultimate cognitive ability underlying all mental skills, and supposedly immune from the usual benefits of practice. To find that training on a working-memory task could result in an increase in fluid intelligence would be cognitive psychology's equivalent of discovering particles traveling faster than light.

Together, Jaeggi and Buschkuehl decided to see if they could replicate the Klingberg transfer effect. To do so, they used the N-back test as the basis of a training regimen. As seen in the game played by the children at Washington-McKinley, N-back challenges users to remember something—the location of a cat or the sound of a particular letter—that is presented immediately before (1-back), the time before last (2-back), the time before that (3-back), and so on. If you do well at 2-back, the computer moves you up to 3-back. Do well at that, and you'll jump to 4-back. On the other hand, if you do poorly at any level, you're nudged down a level. The point is to keep the game just challenging enough that you stay fully engaged.

To make it harder, Jaeggi and Buschkuehl used what's called the dual N-back task. As a random sequence of letters is heard over earphones, a square appears on a computer screen moving, apparently at random, among eight possible spots on a grid. Your mission is to keep track of both the letters and the squares. So, for example, at the 3-back level, you would press one button on the keyboard if you recall that a spoken letter is the same one that was spoken three times ago, while simultaneously pressing another key if the square on the screen is in the same place as it was three times ago.

The point of making the task more difficult is to overwhelm the usual task-specific strategies that people develop with games like chess and Scrabble. "We wanted to train underlying attention and working-memory skills," Jaeggi says.

Jaeggi and Buschkuehl gave progressive matrix tests to students at Bern and then asked them to practice the dual N-back for 20 to 25 minutes a day. When they retested them at the end of a few weeks, they were surprised and delighted to find significant improvement. Jaeggi and Buschkuehl later expanded the study as postdoctoral fellows at the University of Michigan, in the laboratory of John Jonides, professor of psychology and neuroscience.

"Those two things, working memory and cognitive control, I think, are at the heart of intellectual functioning," Jonides told me when I met with him, Jaeggi, and Buschkuehl in their basement office. "They are part of what differentiates us from other species. They allow us to selectively process information from the environment, and to use that information to do all kinds of problem-solving and reasoning."

When they finally published their study, in a May 2008 issue of *Proceedings of the National Academy of Sciences*, the results were striking. Before training, participants were able to correctly answer between 9 and 10 of the matrix questions. Afterward, the 34 young adults who participated in dual N-back training for 12 weeks correctly answered approximately one extra matrix item, while those who trained for 17 weeks were able to answer about three more correctly. After 19 weeks, the improvement was 4.4 additional matrix questions.

"It's not just a little bit higher," Jaeggi says. "It's a large effect."

The study did have its shortcomings. "We used just one reasoning task to measure their performance," she says. "We showed improvements in this one fluid-reasoning task, which is usually highly correlated with other measures as well." Whether the improved scores on the Raven's would translate into school grades, job performance, and real-world gains remained to be seen. Even so, accompanying the paper's publication in *Proceedings* was a commentary titled, "Increasing Fluid Intelligence Is Possible After All," in which the senior psychologist Robert J. Sternberg (now provost at Oklahoma State University) called Jaeggi's and Buschkuehl's research "pioneering." The study, he wrote, "seems, in some measure, to resolve the debate over whether fluid intelligence is, in at least some meaningful measure, trainable."

For some, the debate is far from settled. Randall Engle, a leading intelligence researcher at the Georgia Tech School of Psychology, views the proposition that I.Q. can be increased through training with a skepticism verging on disdain. "May I remind you of 'cold fusion'?" he says, referring to the infamous claim, long since discredited, that nuclear fusion could be achieved at room temperature in a desktop device. "People were like, 'Oh, my God, we've solved our energy crisis.' People were rushing to throw money at that science. Well, not so fast. The military is now preparing to spend millions trying to make soldiers smarter, based on working-memory training. What that one 2008 paper did was to send hundreds of people off on a wild-goose chase, in my opinion."

"Fluid intelligence is not culturally derived," he continues. "It is almost certainly the biologically driven part of intelligence. We have a real good idea of the parts of the brain that are important for it. The prefrontal cortex is especially important for the control of attention. Do I think you can change fluid intelligence? No, I don't think you can. There have been hundreds of other attempts to increase intelligence over the years, with little or no—just no—success."

At a meeting of cognitive scientists last August, and again in November, Engle presented a withering critique of Jaeggi and her colleagues' 2008 paper. He pointed to a variety of methodological weaknesses (many of which have been addressed in subsequent papers by Jaeggi and others) and then presented the results from his own attempt to replicate the study, which found no effect whatsoever. (Those results have yet to be published.)

The most prominent takedown of I.Q. training came in June 2010, when the neuroscientist Adrian Owen published the results of an experiment conducted in coordination with the BBC television show *Bang Goes the Theory*. After inviting British viewers to participate, Owen recruited 11,430 of them to take a battery of I.Q. tests before and after a six-week online program designed to replicate commercially available "brain building" software. (The N-back was not among the tasks offered.) "Although improvements were observed in every one of the cognitive tasks that were trained," he concluded in the journal *Nature*, "no evidence was found for transfer effects to untrained tasks, even when those tasks were cognitively closely related."

But even Owen, reached by telephone, told me that he respects Jaeggi's studies and looks forward to seeing others like it. If before Jaeggi's study, scientists' attempts to raise I.Q. were largely unsuccessful, other lines of evidence have long supported the view that intelligence is far from immutable. While studies of twins suggest that intelligence has a fixed genetic component, at least 20 to 50 percent of the variation in I.Q. is due to other factors, whether social, school, or family-based. Even more telling, average I.Q.'s have been rising steadily for a century as access to schooling and technology expands, a phenomenon known as the Flynn Effect. As Jaeggi and others see it, the genetic component of intelligence is undeniable, but it functions less like the genes that control for eye color and more like the complex of interacting genes that affect weight and height (both of which have also been rising, on average, for decades). "We know that height is heavily genetically determined," Jonides told me during our meeting at the University of Michigan. "But we also know there are powerful environmental influences on height, like nutrition. So the fact that intelligence is partly heritable doesn't mean you can't modify it."

Harold Hawkins, a cognitive psychologist at the Office of Naval Research who oversees most of the U.S. military's studies in the area, expressed a common view. For him, the question now is not whether cognitive training works but how strongly and how best to achieve it. "Until about four or five years ago, we believed that fluid intelligence is immutable in adulthood," Hawkins told me. "No one believed that training could possibly achieve dramatic improvements in this very fundamental cognitive ability. Then Jaeggi's work came along. That's when I started to move my funding from some other areas into this area. I personally believe, and if I didn't believe it I wouldn't be making an investment of the taxpayers' money, that there's something here. It's potentially of extremely profound importance." A similar view was expressed by Jason Chein, assistant professor of psychology at Temple University in Philadelphia, who published a series of studies—using another method, not N-back, for training working memory—that showed an increase in cognitive abilities. "My findings support what they've done," he says, referring to the work of Jaeggi and her colleagues. "I've never replicated exactly what they do. But across a number of labs, using similar but different approaches to training, we have related successes. I think there's a great deal of work to be done, but on the whole we are seeing positive signs."

This past winter, I went to visit Jason Chein's lab in Philadelphia, where he has begun to train subjects with something called a complex working memory span task. "It's a terrible name," he said with a laugh. "And you could call it a gimmicky psychological task. But there are 20 years of research behind it." Chein invited me to try my hand at it. Once he clicked "start" on the computer program, the screen showed a checkerboard of 16 squares, with all of them white except 1; I was supposed to remember the red square's location. Then it showed a series of three checkerboard patterns; for each, I had to decide whether the pattern was symmetrical or not. This sequence—having to remember the one red square, and then having to decide on symmetry—was repeated three more times. At the end, I had to click, in order, on the location of those four red squares.

I got only three right.

"Everyone gets better with practice," he said. "Some people get up to being able to remember a string of 11 or higher."

Of course, the goal is not to get better at remembering the location of red squares on a checkerboard but to expand a subject's underlying working memory. Doing so, Chein has found, translates into the kind of real-world improvements associated with increases in cognitive capabilities. "We've seen, in college kids who do it, improvements in their reading-comprehension scores," Chein said. "And in a sample of adults, 65 and older, it appears to improve their ability to keep track of what they recently said, so they don't repeat themselves."

Despite continuing academic debates, other commercial enterprises are rushing in to offer an array of "brain building" games that make bold promises to improve all kinds of cognitive abilities.

In addition to working memory, researchers are seeking to improve fluid intelligence by training other basic mental skills—perceptual speed (deciding, in a matter of seconds, whether a number is odd or even), visual tracking (on a shoot-'em-up computer game, for instance), or quickly switching between a variety of tasks. Ulman Lindenberger and colleagues at the Max Planck Institute for Human Development in Berlin used 12 different tasks to train 101 younger and 103 older adults. Compared with those who received no training, those who participated in 100 daily one-hour training sessions (both young and old) showed significant improvements on tests that measured reasoning, working memory, perceptual speed (in young adults only), and episodic memory (the ability to remember a short list, for example). A statistical measure of how those improvements correlated to one another suggested, Lindenberger concluded, systematic improvements "at the level of broad abilities."

At the University of California, Berkeley, Silvia Bunge, director of a laboratory on the building blocks of cognition, takes what she calls "an everything-but-the-kitchen-sink approach." Working with 28 children from low socioeconomic backgrounds, she assigned half of them to play games designed to boost the speed of response times, and the other half to play games that target reasoning skills. "Quirkle," for instance, challenges children to align tiles on a grid to match shapes and colors. After eight weeks of training—75 minutes per day, twice a week—Bunge found that the children in the reasoning group scored, on average, 10 points higher on a nonverbal I.Q. test than they had before the training. Four of the 17 children who played the reasoning games gained an average of more than 20 points. In another study, not yet published, Bunge found improvements in college students preparing to take the LSAT.

Torkel Klingberg, meanwhile, has continued studying the effects of training children with his own variety of working-memory tasks. In October 2010, a company he founded to offer those tasks as a package through psychologists and other training professionals, was bought by Pearson Education, the world's largest provider of educational assessment tools.

Despite continuing academic debates, other commercial enterprises are rushing in to offer an array of "brain building" games that make bold promises to improve all kinds of cognitive abilities. Within a block of each other in downtown San Francisco are two of the best known. Posit Science, among the oldest in the field, remains relatively small, giving special attention to those with cognitive disorders. Lumosity began in 2007 and is now by far the biggest of the services, with more than 20 million subscribers. Its games include a sleeker, more entertaining version of the N-back task.

In Chicago Heights, the magic was definitely not happening for one boy staring blankly at the black cats in the Mac Lab. Sipping from a juice box he held in one hand, jabbing at a computer key over and over with the other, he periodically sneaked a peak at his instructor, a look of abject boredom on his freckled face.

"That's the biggest challenge we have as researchers in this field," Jaeggi told me, "to get people engaged and motivated to play our working-memory game and to really stick with it. Some people say it's hard and really frustrating and really challenging and tiring."

In a follow-up to their 2008 study in young adults, Jaeggi, Buschkuehl, and their colleagues published a paper last year that described the effects of N-back training in 76 elementary- and middle-school children from a broad range of social and economic backgrounds. Only those children who improved substantially on the N-back training had gains in fluid intelligence. But their improvement wasn't linked to how high they originally scored on Raven's; children at all levels of cognitive ability improved. And those gains persisted for three months after the training ended, a heartening sign of possible long-term benefits. Although it's unknown how much longer the improvement in fluid intelligence will last, Jaeggi doubts the effects will be permanent without continued practice. "Do we think they're now smarter for the rest of their lives by just four weeks of training?" she asks. "We probably don't think so. We think of it like physical training: if you go running for a month, you increase your fitness. But does it stay like that for the rest of your life? Probably not."

If future studies confirm the benefits of working-memory training on fluid intelligence, the implications could be enormous. Might children with A.D.H.D. receive working-memory training rather than stimulant drugs like Ritalin? Might students in high school and college do N-back training rather than cramming for their finals? Could a journalist like me write better articles?

Of course, in order to improve, you need to do the training. For some, whether brilliant or not so much, training may simply be too hard—or too boring.

To increase motivation, the study in Chicago Heights offers third graders a chance to win a $10 prepaid Visa card each week. In collaboration with researchers from the University of Chicago's Initiative on Chicago Price Theory (directed by Steven D. Levitt, of *Freakonomics* fame), the study pits the kids against one another, sometimes one on one, sometimes in groups, to see if competition will spur them to try harder. Each week, whichever group receives more points on the N-back is rewarded with the Visa cards. To isolate the motivating effects of the cash prizes, a group of fourth graders is undergoing N-back training with the same black-cats-in-haunted-house program, but with no Visa cards, only inexpensive prizes—plastic sunglasses, inflatable globes—as a reward for not talking and staying in their seats.

The boy tapping randomly at his computer without even paying attention to the game? He was in the fourth-grade class. Although the study is not yet complete, perhaps it will show that the opportunity to increase intelligence is not motivation enough. Just like physical exercise, cognitive exercises may prove to be up against something even more resistant to training than fluid intelligence: human nature.

DISCUSSION

1. What are some of the stereotypes you have been taught to associate with video games? What image of the typical video-game user comes to mind when you hear the term? Based on your own experience, are these images and stereotypes accurate? How or how not?
2. From standardized tests to IQ exams, Hurley notes, educators have long searched for the best instrument for measuring student intelligence. What do you think the best instrument is for accomplishing this goal? Why?
3. Hurley cites scientific research that divides intelligence into two distinct categories: "crystallized intelligence" and "fluid intelligence" (p. 317). How are these two categories defined? How do they differ? Can you think of an example or experience that illustrates this difference?

WRITING

4. Write a description of a video game you think could be used as an effective tool for teaching academic skills. What does this game look like? By what rules does it operate? What tasks is it designed to accomplish? When you're done, lay out the rationale for why you think this game would make such an effective educational tool. What specific learning goals would it advance? And why are these goals worthwhile?
5. Underneath the debate over technology and education, Hurley notes, is a deeper debate over whether intelligence is biologically or culturally derived. Write an essay in which you present and defend your own views on this question. Do you think intelligence is largely a matter of intrinsic or inherited ability? Or is it possible that changes in our external circumstances can actually make us smarter? And on the basis of what evidence do you make this claim?
6. Jonathan Kozol (p. 301) warns against the dangers of using commercial tools and commercial concepts to achieve educational goals. Do you think Kozol would regard Hurley's discussion of games and gaming as an example of what he is decrying? In your view, what aspects of Hurley's essay support or reinforce Kozol's critique? What aspects challenge or complicate it?

Tying It All Together

Matthew Crawford ("The Case for Working with Your Hands," p. 368) is another writer who challenges the ways our ideas about and attitudes toward so-called blue-collar work have been scripted. How does Crawford's discussion compare to the viewpoint espoused by Mike Rose in "Blue-Collar Brilliance" (p. 280)? In your view, does Crawford's portrayal of motorcycle-repair work support Rose's argument about the unacknowledged complexity of manual labor? How, specifically?

Like John Taylor Gatto, Virginia Heffernan ("The Attention-Span Myth," p. 113) is interested in whether young people today are demonstrating greater degrees of indifference and inattention. Unlike Gatto, however, Heffernan is far more skeptical that such concerns need to be taken seriously. Write an essay in which you compare the parallels and differences between Heffernan's discussion of the "attention-span myth" and Gatto's critique of boredom in school. What specific problem is each writer describing? What attitude toward this problem does each writer display? And which treatment of this issue do you find more compelling? Why?

Scenes and Un-Scenes: **Looking at Learning**

How do we define what learning looks like? What a good education looks like? Underneath every definition of the ideal school, every vision of the perfect teacher or model student, there lies an even more fundamental vision: of what it means to be truly educated. Think for a moment about all of the different material that gets proffered and promoted in our culture that, in one way or another, claims to answer this question. There are all of the advice books, offering parents and educators "expert" instruction on how to enhance kids' learning. There are all of the "enrichment" games, toys, and programs currently on the market. There are all of the TV shows — from *Dora the Explorer* to *Sesame Street* to *Mr. Rogers' Neighborhood* — that model the proper way of "doing school." Whatever its individual purview, each of these can be understood as an effort to script for us the standards and ideals that define "real" education. Each of the following examples invites you to conduct this kind of analysis: to decode the vision of learning, the model of schooling each presents.

Though school environments like the one pictured here are less and less the norm (with the advent of pods and grouping), nonetheless this stereotype of school remains relevant. How many scripts can you spot here regarding teacher authority, student interaction, learning styles, and so on?

George Marks/Getty Images

Tim Boyle/Getty Images

Much debate on U.S. education focuses not only on what is taught but also on the environment in which it is taught, including concerns about school security. What do images like this make you think about learning environments today? How does this shift the norm from the previous photo?

Bridget Besaw/Aurora Photos

We are much more likely today to think of educational environments as diverse. This photo shows a mother homeschooling her children. What strikes you as inherently different about this environment versus those that we more commonly associate with school?

Kobal Collection/Picture Desk

Films for teenagers, such as* Mean Girls *(2005), have always used school as a central locale for their stories' settings. Why do you think this is? How closely do the portrayals of school in television or film reflect your experiences as a student? How do these movies present education? What factors of education do they ignore?

Lawren/Getty Images

Photos like this one show how our culture values learning by even the youngest children before they enter formal schooling. How does this photo present the learning process? Are there any elements of this photo that critics who oppose pushing children into formal learning too soon would alter?

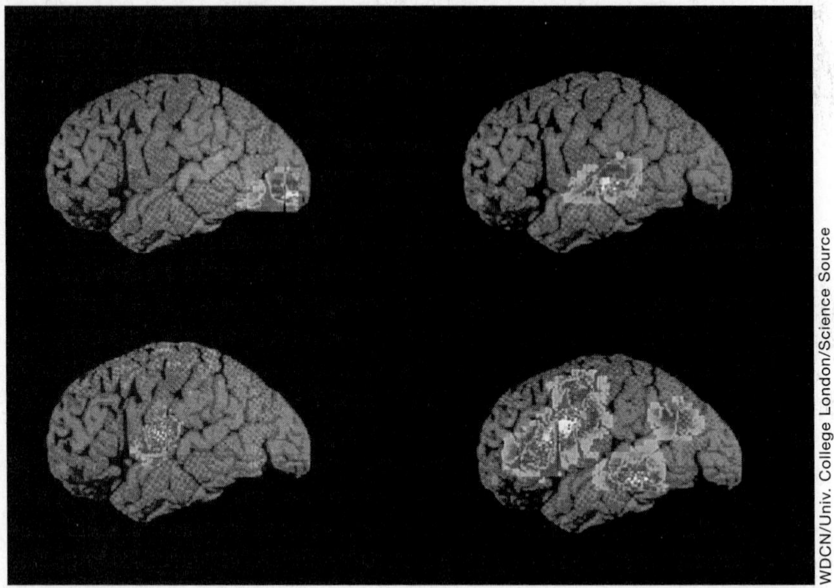

WDCN/Univ. College London/Science Source

This photo shows activity in the brain during the learning process. Without any knowledge of the environment or context for the learning process shown here, how does this photo change your impression of what learning looks like?

DISCUSSION

1. Which of these images best captures your experiences in school? Which of them would you most want to use as a model for rewriting the scripts by which your experiences as a student unfolded?
2. Do you think any of these depictions promote educational messages that are problematic or dangerous?
3. Are there any educational ideals that you think this collection of images leaves out? If so, what are they? And what, in your view, makes them so valuable?

WRITING

4. Choose a television show or movie that sketches a portrait of modern school life. How does it depict school? What specific aspects of schooling (e.g., school rules, teacher or student behavior, and so on) get idealized? Which satirized? Write an essay in which you analyze the practices and standards this portrait presents as the ideal. How do they compare with the images of school or learning shown in this feature?
5. Make a list of all the different aspects of contemporary education that you think this collection could critique. Then write an essay in which you identify a particular question or issue that does not get raised or referenced in this collection. What is it, and why in your view does it merit particular focus? Can you find an image of this issue that you would include to better balance this set?
6. Choose one of the images above, one whose depiction clearly lays out an alternative model of schooling. Then choose the writer in this chapter whose own critique of conventional education most closely mirrors this model. Write an essay in which you compare and contrast the specific features within each of these alternative visions.

Putting It into Practice: **Educational Scripts**

Now that you've read the chapter selections, try applying your conclusions to your own life by completing the following exercises.

QUIZZING TEACHERS Prepare an interview questionnaire about attitudes toward teaching and education and ask an instructor, teacher, or education major you know to complete it. Here are some suggested questions: *What do you like most about teaching? Least? What are the biggest challenges you face as an educator? What do you believe is the purpose of education? What do you believe is most important for your students to know?* Feel free to ask any other questions you might think of. When you get his or her answers, write an essay in which you analyze the responses based on what you think are the most common ways we think of education in our culture. How do the answers reflect this common thinking? Where do they differ? Do any of the responses echo the critiques or anxieties of any of the authors in this chapter?

DOING YOUR HOMEWORK Choose some educational issue or controversy that is currently being publicly debated: the value of standardized testing, the growing cost of higher education, and so on. First, research this issue as thoroughly as you can. What are the key points of disagreement? What questions or issues does it involve? What people, organizations, or interest groups are on each side? If you were asked to pick a side in the debate, which would it be, and why? Then read an article that engages this debate and write a description of your observations and responses.

GRADING THE IMPACT Choose one of the educational issues discussed by the writers included in this chapter and write a personal essay in which you discuss how this issue has impacted your life as a student. What new insight have you gained by reading further about this issue? How do you view your education differently? If you could, what would you change about your education?

AP Photo/John Amis

5 How We WORK

What do our jobs say about us?

Introduction

Rules and Roles/Rewards and Punishments

Think back to your last job. Was it waiting tables? Making cold calls as a telemarketer? Perhaps you gave guided tours at a museum or worked construction. Or maybe you delivered pizzas, sold insurance, or interned at a nonprofit. Whatever type of job it was, chances are it didn't take you very long to discover that it had some basic and nonnegotiable rules in place — rules laying out in fairly specific detail the things you were and were not permitted to do. Whether white-collar, blue-collar, or no-collar, every job is defined by certain regulations and instructions, some of which are spelled out explicitly and others of which remain unspoken. Usually, for example, we are told up front what tasks we have to perform and how much we're going to get paid to complete them. Other expectations are laid out less overtly: the norms, for instance, about how employees interact with bosses or dress appropriately for their jobs. Whether formal or informal, overt or implied, however, all of these rules share one thing: They are set in stone long before we ever step behind the counter, sit down at a desk, pick up a shovel, or type our first word on the computer.

Why do so many of us adhere to rules like these written by somebody else? Is this the normal cost of "doing business"? The short answer, of course, is because we *have* to. Adhering to the rules governing a given job, common sense tells us, is required to keep it. And although undoubtedly true, this explanation is incomplete. The rules of work are more than just marching orders, commands we have no choice but to obey simply because we can't think of any alternative. It is more accurate, in fact, to think of these rules as *propositions* or *bargains* in which we choose to adopt a particular role or conform to a particular script in exchange for a payoff that we've decided makes doing so worth it. From the perks or promotions dangled in front of us to the threats of reprimand or dismissal we face, the truth is that our day-to-day lives on the job are shaped less by a set of abstract rules per se than by a set of very tangible rewards and punishments. When we go along with the office mandate to wear "standard business attire" or accede to our supervisor's reminder to "always wear a smile," we're doing so not because we are mindless robots or powerless pawns, but rather because we have made the calculation that such compliance is in our better interest. When reframed in these kinds of cost/benefit terms, we confront a slightly different set of questions: On what

What is normal?

AP Photo/Frank Franklin II

What does this image ask you to believe? What are the ideas/values/ attitudes it asks you to accept as normal?

basis do we decide to make these choices? Where do we learn which standards are the right ones to employ?

SELLING SUCCESS, SCRIPTING FAILURE

It is tempting to answer this last question by saying simply "ourselves." However, as with so many other aspects of our daily lives, it is far more likely that the standards and priorities we use as we navigate our work lives have their origins at least partly in the popular culture that surrounds us. And if you doubt this contention, just think back to all the different television shows, movies, and commercials you've seen in the last few months that convey one message or another about work. Even if we sample this kind of material only sporadically, it's difficult not to come away with a clear sense of the attitudes toward work that it's our "job" to adopt. We quickly learn, for example, that we should covet certain jobs and spurn others. We become adept at identifying, almost instinctively, the things that make one career choice advantageous and another altruistic. We learn that being, say, a corporate CEO is a more "legitimate" undertaking than being a nurse, a social worker, or a high school teacher. The work it involves, the contribution it makes, and therefore the rewards it garners are supposedly far superior. Whether we embrace these lessons or resist them, whether they accurately reflect our personal views and experiences or drastically misrepresent them, one thing seems indisputable: Our culture's tutorial vis-à-vis work goes on constantly.

What is normal?

"I always say: Moms have the toughest job in the world."

Talk-show host and superstar, Oprah Winfrey

Do you share this belief? Should we automatically accept it as normal?

Our world abounds with messages and markers that tell us how to measure not only a job's desirability but also its fundamental worthiness as well as our worthiness in taking it. Perhaps the most obvious of these has to do with money. If we are looking for the quickest way to see where certain jobs rank within the official hierarchy of American employment, we need look no further than at the disparity in salary between them. And this difference is closely related to other, nonmonetary kinds of distinctions we are encouraged to draw between different jobs — between, for instance, the relative respectability or social status accorded to each. All of this thinking gets reinforced and elaborated by the ways these jobs get depicted in our popular media as well — by the clichés and stereotypes that typically attach themselves to each. If you had to write profiles of fictional Wall Street bankers, you could, because you've seen the same depictions of them over and over again on the nightly news.

And the more familiar this instruction becomes, the easier it is to believe that we really do know the difference between worthy and unworthy work. What makes all this more than a little dangerous, of course, is that the conclusions we are encouraged to draw are often wildly off the mark. Put simply, they are cultural stereotypes rather than objective facts. Pointing this out, however, doesn't necessarily diminish their influence. Indeed, we may be drawn to these generalizations precisely *because* they're stereotypes — because they take a situation that otherwise would feel complicated and messy, and render it disarmingly simple. It's no easy task to figure out what really makes work meaningful, to decide what is valid about certain jobs and not valid about others. While commercials depict corporate boardrooms filled with zany pranksters and free-thinking individuals, construction sites populated by truck-driving he-men, and insurance offices staffed with empathetic, dedicated salespeople, we know on some level that these images don't supply us with scripts that adequately explain the true meaning or value of work.

It is precisely this question of valuation that the selections in this chapter invite you to ponder. How is it, their authors ask, that work has come to stand as our culture's preeminent marker of self-worth? What does it mean that we so often turn to our jobs as definitive expressions of who and what we are? To delve into the assumptions and norms around work is to confront one of the key places in our world where we learn to draw distinctions between success and failure, to differentiate being a "winner" from being a "loser." Our job, of course, is hardly to take such distinctions for granted. Rather, it is to make sense of what these instructions mean and what they do: whether these scripts are helpful or harmful, whether they crowd out other, more valid ways to measure our personal value. In doing so, we will devote our energy not only to examining some of the different jobs available in our world, but also to expanding our understanding of what exactly work is.

One of the most versatile, encompassing terms in our modern vocabulary, *work* really describes any activity or undertaking — from doing algebra homework to taking out the garbage — that involves a degree of effort. Because of its very flexibility, in fact, work offers us an especially resonant metaphor for understanding our relationship to popular culture more generally. The term *work* underscores the degree to which the cultural messages conveyed to us, the standards mapped for us, the scripts written for us are presented not as optional things but as requirements. Like a job, our pop culture calls on us to take up particular tasks and perform particular roles. And as with a job, these expectations or rules get enforced in terms of the rewards and punishments facing us for following along or rebelling against. And finally, there is the double meaning of using this term in a cultural context, referring not only to the work our pop culture assigns to us, but also to the ways we respond to these expec-

What is normal?

"200+ Million Members. Manage Your Professional Identity. Build and Engage with Your Professional Peers."

From the home page of LinkedIn, a professional networking website

What kind of social script does this quotation create? What would it feel like to act out this script in our personal lives?

tations, the ways, that is, we "work out" our individual relationship to these scripts. The term reminds us that pop culture, like the jobs we hold, is not just a taskmaster, but also a testing ground. It is the place where we assess whether these rules and roles really "work" for us.

Despite their differences, each of the essays collected here is informed by this particular understanding. Each selection author invites us to look more closely at the places where work and culture most powerfully intersect. Some pieces accomplish this goal by chronicling the ways different kinds of work get done day to day, detailing the real-world pressures and rules that dictate how different jobs are performed. Anthony DePalma, for example, tells the story of Mexican restaurant workers in New York City, whose struggles to remain gainfully employed in a volatile job market underscore how factors like race and class can drastically skew the sorts of opportunities available. Offering a provocative twist on the term "working mother," Arlie Russell Hochschild takes a closer look at the world of surrogate parenting, pondering the economic, psychological, and ethical implications of a job that turns procreation into a for-profit business. Continuing this focus on gender and work, Ashley Nelson reports on the real (and often underreported) costs imposed on professional women who take time away from their careers to raise a family. At the heart of this chapter is an exploration of the question, "Do we work to live, or live to work?" Because work and identity are linked, Louis Uchitelle analyzes under- and unemployment trends in contemporary America to critique some of our most deeply embedded assumptions and beliefs about success and self-worth. Addressing the issue of underemployment from a different perspective, Barbara Ehrenreich chronicles many of the hidden costs — both social and financial — our society imposes on the working poor. Turning our attention to the white-collar/blue-collar divide, Matthew Crawford champions manual labor and the way our culture values it in relation to sitting behind a desk. Mac McClelland, meanwhile, uncovers the darker side of manual work, taking her readers on a guided tour of life in the "modern-day sweatshop" of online factory work. Rounding out these employment portraits is the essay by Catherine Rampell, which urges readers to rethink the myths and stereotypes that have scripted young Americans as the "slacker generation."

What is normal?

"'Nice to meet you. What do you do?'

For many, this is one of the first conversations we have when meeting someone new. But our jobs are more than simply a topic of conversation — they are an important part of our lives. They can be an extension of us and a matter of pride. What we 'do' is part of who we are."

Hilda Solis, Former Secretary of Labor, May 11, 2010

Can social scripts be rewritten? Are there alternative norms to those described here?

e macmillanhighered.com/actingout
Tutorials > Digital Writing > Job Search/Personal Branding
e-Readings > Lauren Orsini, *WorkHands Wants to Become the Blue-Collar LinkedIn*

LOUIS UCHITELLE

The Consequences—Undoing Sanity

Chronicling what he calls the "psychiatric aspect of layoffs," Louis Uchitelle uses a focus on joblessness to better understand the social messages and cultural values that teach Americans to connect their work to their self-worth. In a world ever more frequently marked by downsizing and layoffs, Uchitelle asks whether it's still possible to treat such cherished notions as job security and the dignity of work as indisputable facts of life. Uchitelle writes about business and economics for the *New York Times*, and he won a George Polk Award for the *Times* series "The Downsizing of America," an investigation of layoffs that ran in 1996. He addressed the subject again in his book *The Disposable American: Layoffs and Their Consequences* (2006), from which the following selection is taken.

HARD AS SHE TRIED, STACY BROWN COULD NOT REKINDLE IN HER husband, Erin, the passion for work that he lost when United Airlines laid him off as a mechanic at its giant aircraft maintenance center in Indianapolis. She loved Erin; that is, she loved the engaged and energetic young man she had married three years earlier. "He was just going a million miles a minute before this all happened," she said. She wanted that Erin back, and soon. Not for the income. If need be, she could support the family quite handsomely herself, as a litigator at a white-shoe Indianapolis law firm. But as we talked in late 2004, she was six months pregnant with their second child, and it was time to embrace the roles they had planned for themselves when they married: she as the mother and care-giver, he as the really skilled engineer, mechanic, and craftsman rising adventurously in the corporate world, or going out on his own as an entrepreneur. The layoff had destroyed all this and her distress was unrestrained.[1]

"I think the layoff destroyed his self-esteem," Stacy said, her words coming rapidly and intensely. "I don't think he will ever admit that but I think it has. That is a hard thing to overcome and I don't know how you overcome it to get back into the working world, which is what I think he is going to have to do. When he fills out résumés and applies for jobs, you can see it is not with the extreme belief that he is going to get one. He waits until the last minute and gets the résumé in, but maybe doesn't get it in completely. I think that is because he is probably depressed."

Two years after Erin Brown lost his job at United Airlines, his wife was attempting, in a drastic, risky way, to jump-start her husband's self-confidence—to puncture his inertia and bring him quickly to the point that he would once again want to step into a career and take on the risks involved in pursuing uncertain goals. She had insisted on the purchase of a rundown three-bedroom house half a block from their own home in their once splendid Victorian-era neighborhood, which was now coming back as a downtown enclave for young professionals and executives. Erin had balked at the purchase, as he had balked at earlier opportunities to acquire and renovate rundown houses in the neighborhood, then flip them at a profit. Too risky, he insisted. This time, ignoring her husband's reluctance, Stacy put in a bid anyway, winning the house for a rock-bottom $95,000 at a mortgage foreclosure sale. She closed the deal by doing all the paperwork herself, moving forward decisively once Erin assured her that the eighty-four-year-old dwelling with its spacious front veranda was structurally sound.

They paid cash, drawing on their savings, and immediately put the house up for sale at $165,000, untouched. They were ready in their own minds, or at least Stacy was, to accept a counteroffer of $140,000 for this handyman special. Gentrification alone would bring them a sufficient profit, she reasoned, and that success would rebuild in Erin some of the self-esteem and energy that the layoff had destroyed. Or, faced with ownership—having been pushed by his wife into a gamble—Erin would renovate the house and they would then resell it for at least $195,000, an even greater success for him. Mainly, however, Stacy hoped for the quick resale. She doubted that Erin possessed the self-confidence to carry out the renovation. "He's going to want to start this and then he's not going to be able to finish it in a very timely manner," she said, "so we will end up hanging on to two houses, which is okay, but what it doesn't do is give him that sense of accomplishment and purpose and financial reward, which is what he needs to function effectively again."

"I think the layoff destroyed his self-esteem."

In the cataloging of damage that results from layoffs, incapacitating emotional illness almost never appears on the lists that economists, politicians, sociologists, union leaders, business school professors, management consultants, and journalists compile. There is much discussion of income loss, downward mobility, a decrease in family cohesion, a rise in the divorce rate, the unwinding of communities, the impact on children, the impact on survivors who dodge a layoff but are left feeling insecure and guilty that they kept their jobs while colleagues did not.[2] Extended periods of unemployment bring a cascade of damages, including depression, and these too are documented. One study, for example, found that for every percentage point change in the unemployment rate, up or down, the national suicide rate rose or fell in tandem, and so did the frequency of strokes, heart attacks, crime, and accidents.[3]

The layoff, however, is seldom singled out as damaging in itself, quite apart from the unemployment that follows. But the trauma of dismissal—the "acuteness of the blow," as Dr. Theodore Jacobs, the New York psychoanalyst, put it—unwinds lives in its own right, damaging self-esteem, undoing normal adaptive mechanisms, and erecting the sort of emotional barriers that have prevented Erin Brown and thousands of others, perhaps millions of others, from returning energetically to the workforce in jobs that draw productively on their education and skills. "There are many people who do not want to face that trauma again and to some degree they lose a sense of reality," Dr. Jacobs said. "They give themselves a lot of conscious reasons why they cannot accept this job or that job, but deeper down they don't want to face the rigors and anxieties of work and the fears they won't be up to it and they will be dropped again."[4]

I did not think in the early stages of the reporting for this book that I would be drawn so persistently into the psychiatric aspect of layoffs. But a surprisingly high number of the laid-off people with whom I talked described from every angle and over and over again what, in their minds, had been done to them, the mistakes they had made, their bad luck in being caught in the particular situation that cost them their jobs, the shortsightedness or outright evil of the bosses who failed to protect them or did not want to do so, how cut adrift they felt, or, hiding their loss and hurt in elaborate rationalizations, how comfortable they insisted they were in some new way of life, safely separated from challenging work.

The emotional damage was too palpable to ignore. Whenever I insisted that layoffs were a phenomenon in America beyond their control, they agreed perfunctorily and then went right back to describing their own devaluing experiences, and why it was somehow their fault or their particular bad luck. When I turned to psychiatrists and psychologists for an explanation of what I was finding, they offered similar observations of their own. "Chipping away at human capital," Dr. Jacobs called it. "Even when a person accurately realizes that he has done a good job, that the company is in a bad way, that it has to lay off a lot of people and it is not about me, there is always some sense of diminishment. Others at the company are not laid off, so why me? And that sense of having been judged and found wanting dovetails with older feelings of inadequacy about one's self that were acquired growing up."

Dr. Kim Cameron, an organizational psychologist at the University of Michigan's business school, focuses in his work on developing ways for corporate managers to carry out layoffs benignly, the goal being to limit the damage to the victims and in doing so soften the blow to morale among the survivors. In the same vein, management consultants and business school professors write endlessly about the various techniques for finessing layoffs. Dr. Cameron has concluded, however, that no matter how sophisticated the technique, there is not much balm: layoffs are destructive psychologically for the individuals who lose their jobs.

Layoffs are destructive psychologically for the individuals who lose their jobs.

I told him Brown's story, including the conflicts with his manager at United Airlines over his inspection reports and the related setback in his application to advance to the engineering department at United's maintenance center, and Dr. Cameron replied that Brown seemed to be an example of a "fundamental in-the-bones blow to ego and self-worth."[5]

"You can have all kinds of people like spouses and friends say you are terrific, you are wonderful, you are great," Dr. Cameron said, "but in the core you say, I am not, and I have big evidence that I am not. Layoffs diminish the ability to restart. They are the opposite of life giving; they literally deplete life." In Brown's case and in many others, Dr. Cameron said, the damage is hard to observe. "It is subversive in that it limits all kinds of other activities—for example, the ability to form emotional bonds with people, the ability to be energized and aggressive in pursuing a new job or position, and the ability to try new things. Trial-and-error learning is diminished. If I am feeling awful about myself, I don't want one more failure. If you try new things, the probability seems higher that you will fail, so you don't try them."[6]

Psychiatrists and psychologists uncover these hidden linkages in therapy. Living with Erin, Stacy also gradually saw them, although her husband tried to hide what he was feeling from her, and from himself. The emotional damage from layoffs varies, of course, from case to case. Brown had to contend with his wife's success as a lawyer and her earning power. His parents' divorce when he was a boy may have also undermined his sense of himself as an effective worker. But who among us does not have contributing factors embedded in our lives waiting for a catalyst, like a layoff, to set them off? At age thirty, Erin was frozen, unable to act, not just in home renovation but in elbowing his way back into a job that would draw on his considerable skills. Denial and anger justified his inaction and hid its deeper causes.

A year after her husband's layoff, Stacy prodded him into applying for a job at a Rolls-Royce engine plant in Indianapolis. The opening was for a technical specialist in the engineering department, a job involving research on jet engines that Erin later said he wanted. But his description of his encounter with the human resources manager who interviewed him was laced with resentment and insult, and the manager must have noticed. "I was well-qualified and I went through a lot of effort to get that one," Erin said, "and it turns out the guy who was doing the hiring had not bothered to understand the nature of the job he was in charge of filling."

In Brown's view, the candidate finally selected was inferior to him in education and know-how. "He had no bachelor's degree in engineering and he lacked the analytical skill that the job required," Erin asserted, berating the interviewer for bureaucratically placing too much importance on a relatively insignificant aspect of the job description: shop-floor experience in machining. The winning candidate had that experience and that made the difference, Erin said, despite his plea to the interviewer that he could come up to speed as a machinist in two weeks. "I said to this guy, 'Hey, look, I have the training, I just don't have the experience in the field, but I'll do whatever you want me to do on my own time to get it.' No interest on his part. They want everything exactly according to the specifications. . . . And then, even if you are among the top applicants, they don't have the decency to get back to you and say, 'Thanks, but no thanks.' I mean you have to call them and hound them to see what happened with the position."

His account of the purchase of the house down the street from their home differed alarmingly from his wife's subsequent explanation. He did not mention her decisive role in making the purchase or that she was trying to prod him out of what she described as a mild but incapacitating depression. Instead, he left the impression that he had taken the initiative in making the purchase. If the house did not resell quickly—and it was already on the market—then he would remodel the kitchen and add a garage to increase the resale value. None of Stacy's anguish came through in the optimistic plans that Erin described. Before doing any of the remodeling, he said, sounding sure of himself, he just might move his family into the new dwelling while he completed the long-drawn-out renovation of his own home. The Rolls-Royce debacle, he said, he had put behind him. He had made no further attempt to apply for challenging jobs in big corporations. Henceforth, he said, he would go the entrepreneurial route, relying on himself. As evidence of his determination and effectiveness, he declared that he had finally completed construction of the two-story carriage house behind his and Stacy's home. It was ready to be sold or rented as office space, he said.

This was the project that Erin had started while Stacy was on maternity leave in the winter and spring of 2003, shortly after he lost his job at United. Birth, layoff, and maternity leave melded. During Stacy's leave, Erin did 60 percent of the construction work and then, when she went back to her job, he stopped, not touching the carriage house again for more than a year; caring for Kyle took up too much of his time, he said. Now, after all those months of inactivity, Erin told me by phone that he had completed the project, the work carried out in what appeared to be a spurt of energy and activity despite the time consumed in child care. He e-mailed me a photo of the exterior, freshly painted green and white.

But he had not finished the interior. Inside that cozy two-story house, wiring and electricity were yet to be installed and studs were still exposed.

Stacy set me straight on the status of the carriage house. Her husband had indeed completed the exterior, she said. "He did beautiful work." But he had acted because he had no choice: either he used the materials he had purchased or they would "sit there and rot." As for the interior, Erin found reasons to put off doing that essential work, and Stacy saw the postponements as a signal from her husband—a signal whose true meaning he suppressed—that he did not want to take the risk of actually finishing the carriage house and then somehow having that achievement, too, taken from him.

She had finally concluded that Erin's emotional damage had become a barrier to the family life they both seemed to want. "Our hope is that . . . there will be a time for me to stay home with our children for a while," Stacy told me. "But at the same time, just this morning, we were talking that it was time to make elections next year for my work and my contributions to the medical savings account and things like that, and he says, 'What happens if you have to go back to work?' And I thought, What do you mean what happens if I have to go back to work? I thought the plan was that *you* were going to go to work. So I think at the same time he's just such an optimistic soul, but I think in the back of his mind, I think he is doubting. I mean, I think he is doubting his ability to get gainful employment and employment that supports our family. I mean, all along, even though he wanted to be laid off in the sense that he thought he was ready to leave United, I firmly believe the layoff impacted him very much. To think back to the person he was when I met him—he enjoyed his job, he really thought he had a career going. And to watch the person that he is today, so averse to employment and so averse to being a worker."

Stacy asked me for help. She had appealed to Erin's father, but father and son did not communicate easily, and Erin resisted taking advice from members of her family. "He talks to you," she said. So I waited a couple of weeks and called Erin. I said that he had misled me at times, without meaning to, and that Stacy and I were concerned about his inaction. I suggested that he see a therapist, that therapy might help him get through this crisis. He did not respond directly to my suggestion, nor did he veer from amiability. "What worries Stacy and you is that I am not really concerned about working to my potential," he replied.

That did worry us, but Erin would not be swayed. He had just completed a two-evening-a-week course in air-conditioner repair, learning very little that he did not already know, to get the necessary certification for a $13- or $14-an-hour dead-end job. Driving about in a panel truck making repairs to air-conditioning units would give him health insurance and some income for the family, once Stacy left her law firm, he explained to me. Most important, he would have a nondemanding, unthreatening platform from which to branch out and ample spare time for truly challenging work: renovating and reselling rundown homes, for example. "I know that I will be overqualified for the next position that I take," he said.

Not everyone has as much difficulty as Erin Brown in shaking off the emotional setback that layoffs produce. Some of those whose stories have been told earlier managed to move on to a next stage in their lives with their mental health more or less intact. But the majority did not. Psychiatrists and psychoanalysts view layoffs as catalysts for emotional damage. There is no mechanism, however, for collecting and disseminating what they know so that the consequences of corporate layoffs can be publicly flagged. The Centers for Disease Control and Prevention in Atlanta track the number of cases of flu, AIDS, measles, polio, Lyme disease, and other physical illnesses, and when the number spikes for one of these ailments, the center alerts us that an epidemic may be brewing, one that requires stepped-up medical treatment and a concerted public effort to shrink the number of cases. While doctors and hospitals funnel data about physical illness to the Centers for Disease Control, psychiatrists and psychologists do not similarly report the incidence among their patients of disabling neuroses connected to layoffs. Nor do the organizations that represent them adopt resolutions that declare layoffs to be a source of mental illness and therefore a menace to public health.

The American Psychiatric Association, whose 35,000 members are likely to treat mental illness related to layoffs, has never formally declared that the modern American layoff is hazardous to health. The president of the association, Dr. Steven S. Sharfstein, readily acknowledges the linkage as do other leaders of the organization.[7] Divorce, however, also damages mental health, Dr. Sharfstein said. So does the death of a spouse or a parent, not to mention the trauma of war. For psychiatry to oppose these events on public health grounds would be futile, he argued, and in the case of layoffs very possibly counterproductive. "If a company refrains from a layoff and then, as a result, is forced out of business, everyone would end up laid off," he said. So the American Psychiatric Association acquiesces in the practice and pushes instead to expand treatment of the victims. It lobbies business, for example, to expand coverage for mental illness. "We do see there are major shortcomings with employer health insurance in terms of access to mental health care," Dr. Sharfstein said, "and that is how we go at this issue."

Only one group of psychiatrists that I could find had singled out the layoff, the act in which a worker is sent away, as damaging in itself to mental health. The alert had come from the three hundred members of the Group for the Advancement of Psychiatry, or more specifically from the dozen or so in the group's Committee on Psychiatry in Industry.

These were psychiatrists whose practices focused on working with companies as consultants. Their client companies engaged in layoffs and they had first-hand knowledge of what people went through. In 1982, when the modern layoff was still a raw American experience, they published a monograph, *Job Loss—a Psychiatric Perspective,* in which they declared: "Our experience in industry and with patients suggests that those who lose their functional role as workers may behave as if their society no longer values them. Because they accept that as true, they suffer a consequent loss in the perception of their value in their families and to themselves."[8]

"Company managers were more interested in talking about the coping skills of those who remained on the job . . ."

They distributed that study, with its straightforward, unpleasant observation, and eight years later, three psychiatrists on the committee expanded their findings into a book, *The Psychosocial Impact of Job Loss.*[9] Neither drew any attention. "Company managers were more interested in talking about the coping skills of those who remained on the job than they were about the damage to those they had laid off," Dr. Stephen Heidel, a consultant to businesses and a clinical professor of psychiatry at the University of California, San Diego, told me. I asked the doctors why, in their opinion, they had had so little success in publicizing the message in their monograph and book.[10] Various possibilities were mentioned, but all seemed to agree with Dr. Heidel's observation that managers don't want to be told about damage to mental health that results from a layoff they initiated. "If a psychiatrist goes out and says, I am an expert in job loss, the manager does not want to hear that and the psychiatrist won't be consulted about other services he can provide to a corporation," Dr. Heidel said. "If you lead with that, the door will be shut. You need to put a positive spin on things."

While the nation's psychiatrists remain all but silent as a group, psychologists and sociologists in academic research seldom spot the sorts of debilitating neuroses that are evident in one-on-one therapy. Academics place much more faith in what they can document through empirical studies. They seek quantifiable evidence and shun the diagnostic judgment that is unavoidable in psychotherapy, whose raw material is narrative and free association. Their work, in consequence, relies heavily on surveys that blend together layoffs and unemployment and correlate the undifferentiated experience with measurable reactions: elevated blood pressure; an increased incidence of stomach problems, headaches, and insomnia; noticeably greater anxiety; a tendency to drink and smoke more; an increase in hospital admissions for ostensibly physical ailments. No survey of observable symptoms would pick up Brown's malady.

Psychoanalysts like Dr. Jacobs are also reluctant to single out layoffs publicly as damaging to mental health. By way of explanation, Dr. Jacobs said that people who seek psychoanalysis do so because of "long-standing character problems and in the course of analysis they mention a layoff, which has magnified what is already there or latently there." As a result, the layoff is not a central issue for the 2,500 members of the American Psychoanalytic Association. None of the numerous sessions at the association's four-day semiannual conferences have focused on layoffs and mental health. When I posted a request at the winter meeting in January 2005 to interview psychoanalysts concerned about the linkage, the only response came from Dr. Alexandra K. Rolde, a psychiatrist and psychoanalyst in private practice in Boston and a clinical instructor in psychiatry at Harvard Medical School.[11] For some of her patients, layoffs were indeed a central theme.

Dr. Rolde, a Czech immigrant in her late sixties, lived through the German occupation of Prague during World War II, in "semihiding" with her mother, as she puts it, to escape deportation and death as Jews. It was an experience that familiarized her with trauma, which is now her specialty in psychiatry. After the war she moved to Canada with her mother and stepfather, and the parents thrived in the jewelry business, first in Montreal and then in Toronto. When they moved the business from one city to the other, acting out of concern that Quebec's separatist movement might isolate the province from the rest of Canada, all fifty of the employees moved, too. No one was laid off, Dr. Rolde said, proud of the loyalties that kept her parents and their workers together. She has treated roughly thirty patients over the past twenty years for layoff-related ailments, she said, and she considers the layoffs to have been life-changing for them. Like Dr. Jacobs, she sees children as well as adults, and they, too, are often damaged.

"It is a trauma to the entire family," she said. "You have a parent working at a prestigious full-time job. All of a sudden the parent sits at home and can't find a job and is depressed. And suddenly the child's role model sort of crumbles. Instead of feeling admiration for the parent, the child eventually begins to feel disrespect. Because the children identify with their parents, they begin to doubt that they can accomplish anything. They feel they won't be successful in life and their self-esteem plummets. This of course is a long-term thing. We call it transgenerational trauma; it is similar to what we used to see with Holocaust survivors and their children. The children feel as damaged as their parents, even though they did not experience the trauma directly themselves."

She told me about a woman she had treated for years after the woman was laid off from an executive job at General Electric. "She got back into the workforce quickly enough, but in a job she did not like, yet she clung to it anyway," Dr. Rolde said. "She was so traumatized by the layoff that she did not have the self-confidence to risk moving on to more suitable work."

NOTES

[1]Interview with Stacy Brown, December 27, 2004.

[2]Concerning children, some studies show that children in two-parent families react differently to a father's job loss than to a mother's. In a study of 4,500 school-age children, for example, Ariel Kalil and Kathleen M. Ziol-Guest of the University of Chicago found that "mothers' employment is never significantly associated with children's academic progress. In contrast, we found significant adverse associations between fathers' job losses [and] children's probability of grade repetition and school suspension/expulsion."

[3]M. Merva and R. Fowles, "Effects of Diminished Economic Opportunities on Social Stress: Heart Attacks, Strokes and Crime," Salt Lake City Economic Policy Institute, University of Utah, 1992. The study covered fifteen metropolises over a twenty-year period. For other studies of the effects of unemployment on health, see "Links in the Chain of Adversity Following Job Loss: How Financial Strain and Loss of Personal Control Lead to Depression, Impaired Functioning and Poor Health," by Richard H. Price, Jin Nam Choi, and Amiram D. Vinokur, *Journal of Occupational Health Psychology* 7 (2002).

[4]Interview with Dr. Theodore Jacobs, August 5, 2004. In addition to his posts as a clinical professor of psychiatry at New York University School of Medicine and at the Albert Einstein College of Medicine, Dr. Jacobs is also the supervising analyst at the Psychoanalytic Institute at New York University and at the New York Psychoanalytic Institute.

[5]Interviews with Kim Cameron, January 17, 2005, and February 2, 2005.

[6]Interview with Kim Cameron, February 2, 2005.

[7]Interview with Dr. Steven Sharfstein, January 17, 2005. Dr. Sharfstein's one-year term as president of the APA began in May 2005. He is president and chief executive of Sheppard Pratt Health Care System, a nonprofit organization in Baltimore that provides mental health care for drug addicts and education for mentally disturbed children, among other services. He has a private psychiatric practice in Baltimore and has been a clinical professor of psychiatry at the University of Maryland.

[8]*Job Loss—a Psychiatric Perspective*, published by Mental Health Materials Center, New York, 1982.

[9]Nick Kates, Barrie S. Grieff, and Duane Hagen, *The Psychosocial Impact of Job Loss* (American Psychiatric Press, 1990).

[10]The conversation took place on April 8, 2005, during and after a session of the Committee on Psychiatry and Industry at the spring meeting of the Group for the Advancement of Psychiatry.

[11]The request was posted at the winter meeting, January 2005, at the Waldorf-Astoria. Dr. Rolde is also on the faculty of the Psychoanalytic Institute of New England East (PINE) and is a member of the Psychoanalytic Society of New England East (PSNE) as well as the Boston Psychoanalytic Society and Institute (BPSI).

DISCUSSION

1. It is far more conventional to speak about layoffs in economic rather than emotional terms. How does Uchitelle challenge this convention? In what ways does his examination of the psychiatric aspects of joblessness rewrite the scripts by which we are taught to think about unemployment?
2. "'You can have all kinds of people like spouses and friends say you are terrific, you are wonderful, you are great,'" Uchitelle quotes one medical expert as saying, "'but in the core you say, I am not, and I have big evidence that I am not. Layoffs diminish the ability to restart'" (p. 345). Why are layoffs so often considered such convincing evidence of our self-worth? What does it tell us about the kind of importance we are taught to place on the work we do?
3. "In the cataloging of damage that results from layoffs," writes Uchitelle, "incapacitating emotional illness almost never appears on the lists that economists, politicians, sociologists, union leaders, business school professors, management consultants, and journalists compile" (p. 343). Why doesn't it? What would you say are the assumptions or norms that keep us from viewing emotional illness as a legitimate consequence of unemployment?

WRITING

4. One of the costs of layoffs, according to Uchitelle, is that they deprive people of a primary way to define their self-worth. Write an essay in which you reflect on the role that work plays in anchoring and validating your views of yourself. Can you think of a job you've held or a career path you've pursued (or one you would like to) that you've used to define your self-worth? What would the effect be of having this particular work outlet taken away?
5. Some of the psychological or emotional effects of being laid off that Uchitelle lists are low self-esteem, nervousness, inability to form close bonds, and fear of trying new things. Do you think it is reasonable for employers to consider the emotional costs of layoffs in determining whether to let workers go? How might an employer address the criticisms that Uchitelle is making? Ultimately, is a company responsible for the emotional well-being of its employees? Why or why not?
6. Their many differences aside, Uchitelle does share with Matthew Crawford (p. 368) an interest in exploring what we might call the emotional life of work. Both writers ask us to consider what effects working (or not working) can have on our happiness, contentment, and self-esteem. Write an essay in which you compare how each writer explores this issue. To what extent does Uchitelle's argument about the psychological damage wrought by unemployment recall or help reinforce Crawford's claims about the emotional satisfactions afforded by working with your hands?

ANTHONY DEPALMA

Fifteen Years on the Bottom Rung

America, it is said, is the "land of opportunity." Depending on where you're born, what pressures you face, or what circumstances you find yourself in, however, this myth can play itself out in radically different ways. Anthony DePalma focuses on one group of workers for whom the supposedly universal promise of opportunity bumps up against the hard realities that often confront those on the lower rungs of the socioeconomic ladder. A writer-in-residence at Seton Hall University, DePalma is the author of numerous books, including *The Man Who Invented Fidel* (2006), a study of the *New York Times* reporter who helped to create the myth surrounding Castro, and most recently, *City of Dust: Illness, Arrogance, and 9/11* (2010). DePalma was a staff writer for the *New York Times*, and as bureau chief for Mexico and Canada, he covered political events such as the Zapatista uprising, economic news such as the crisis of the peso, and natural disasters such as the Quebec ice storm. He has also worked as a business correspondent in both the metropolitan and national divisions. The following essay is from *Class Matters* (2005), a collection of essays written by correspondents of the *New York Times.*

IN THE DARK BEFORE DAWN, WHEN MADISON AVENUE WAS ALL BUT deserted and its pricey boutiques were still locked up tight, several Mexicans slipped quietly into 3 Guys, a restaurant that the Zagat guide once called "the most expensive coffee shop in New York."

For the next ten hours they would fry eggs, grill burgers, pour coffee, and wash dishes for a stream of customers from the Upper East Side of Manhattan. By 7:35 a.m., Eliot Spitzer, attorney general of New York, was holding a power breakfast back near the polished granite counter. In the same burgundy booth a few hours later, Michael A. Wiener, cofounder of the multibillion-dollar Infinity Broadcasting, grabbed a bite with his wife, Zena. Just the day before, Uma Thurman slipped in for a quiet lunch with her children, but the paparazzi found her and she left.

More Mexicans filed in to begin their shifts throughout the morning, and by the time John Zannikos, one of the restaurant's three Greek owners, drove in from the north Jersey suburbs to work the lunch crowd, Madison Avenue was buzzing. So was 3 Guys.

"You got to wait a little bit," Zannikos said to a pride of elegant women who had spent the morning at the Whitney Museum of American Art, across Madison Avenue at 75th Street. For an illiterate immigrant who came to New York years ago with nothing but $100 in his pocket and a willingness to work etched on his heart, could any words have been sweeter to say?

With its wealthy clientele, middle-class owners, and low-income workforce, 3 Guys is a template of the class divisions in America. But it is also the setting for two starkly different tales about breaching those divides.

The familiar story is Zannikos's. For him, the restaurant—don't dare call it a diner—with its twenty-dollar salads and elegant décor represents the American promise of upward mobility, one that has been fulfilled countless times for generations of hardworking immigrants.

But for Juan Manuel Peralta, a thirty-four-year-old illegal immigrant who worked there for five years until he was fired in May 2004, and for many of the other illegal Mexican immigrants in the back, restaurant work today is more like a dead end. They are finding the American dream of moving up far more elusive than it was for Zannikos. Despite his efforts to help them, they risk becoming stuck in a permanent underclass of the poor, the unskilled, and the uneducated.

That is not to suggest that the nearly five million Mexicans who, like Peralta, are living in the United States illegally will never emerge from the shadows. Many have, and undoubtedly many more will. But the sheer size of the influx—over 400,000 a year, with no end in sight—creates a problem all its own. It means there is an ever-growing pool of interchangeable workers, many of them shunting from one low-paying job to another. If one moves on, another one—or maybe two or three—is there to take his place.

There is an ever-growing pool of interchangeable workers, many of them shunting from one low-paying job to another.

Although Peralta arrived in New York almost forty years after Zannikos, the two share a remarkably similar beginning. They came at the same age to the same section of New York City, without legal papers or more than a few words of English. Each dreamed of a better life. But monumental changes in the economy and in attitudes toward immigrants have made it far less likely that Peralta and his children will experience the same upward mobility as Zannikos and his family.

Of course, there is a chance that Peralta may yet take his place among the Mexican-Americans who have succeeded here. He realizes that he will probably not do as well as the few who have risen to high office or who were able to buy the vineyards where their grandfathers once picked grapes. But he still dreams that his children will someday join the millions who have lost their accents, gotten good educations, and firmly achieved the American dream.

Political scientists are divided over whether the twenty-five million people of Mexican ancestry in the United States represent an exception to the classic immigrant success story. Some, like John H. Mollenkopf at the City University of New York, are convinced that Mexicans will eventually do as well as the Greeks, Italians, and other Europeans of the last century who were usually well assimilated after two or three generations. Others, including Mexican-Americans like Rodolfo O. de la Garza, a professor at Columbia, have done studies showing that Mexican-Americans face so many obstacles that even the fourth generation trails other Americans in education, home ownership, and household income.

The situation is even worse for the millions more who have illegally entered the United States since 1990. Spread out in scores of cities far beyond the Southwest, they find jobs plentiful but advancement difficult. President Vicente Fox of Mexico was forced to apologize in the spring of 2005 for declaring publicly what many Mexicans say they feel, that the illegal immigrants "are doing the work that not even blacks want to do in the United States." Resentment and race subtly stand in their way, as does a lingering attachment to Mexico, which is so close that many immigrants do not put down deep roots here. They say they plan to stay only long enough to make some money and then go back home. Few ever do.

But the biggest obstacle is their illegal status. With few routes open to become legal, they remain, like Peralta, without rights, without security, and without a clear path to a better future.

"It's worrisome," said Richard Alba, a sociologist at the State University of New York, Albany, who studies the assimilation and class mobility of contemporary immigrants, "and I don't see much reason to believe this will change."

Little has changed for Peralta, a cook who has worked at menial jobs in the United States for fifteen years. Though he makes more than he ever dreamed of in Mexico, his life is anything but middle class and setbacks are routine. Still, he has not given up hope. "*Querer es poder*," he sometimes says—want something badly enough and you will get it.

But desire may not be enough anymore. That is what concerns Arturo Sarukhan, Mexico's consul general in New York. In early 2005, Sarukhan took an urgent call from New York's police commissioner about an increase in gang activity among young Mexican men, a sign that they were moving into the underside of American life. Of all immigrants in New York City, officials say, Mexicans are the poorest, least educated, and least likely to speak English.

The failure or success of this generation of Mexicans in the United States will determine the place that Mexicans will hold here in years to come, Sarukhan said, and the outlook is not encouraging.

"They will be better off than they could ever have been in Mexico," he said, "but I don't think that's going to be enough to prevent them from becoming an underclass in New York."

DIFFERENT RESULTS

There is a break in the middle of the day at 3 Guys, after the lunchtime limousines leave and before the private schools let out. That was when Zannikos asked the Mexican cook who replaced Peralta to prepare some lunch for him. Then Zannikos carried the chicken breast on pita to the last table in the restaurant.

"My life story is a good story, a lot of success," he said, his accent still heavy. He was just a teenager when he left the Greek island of Chios, a few miles off the coast of Turkey. World War II had just ended, and Greece was in ruins. "There was only rich and poor, that's it," Zannikos said. "There was no middle class like you have here." He is seventy now, with short gray hair and soft eyes that can water at a mention of the past.

Because of the war, he said, he never got past the second grade, never learned to read or write. He signed on as a merchant seaman, and in 1953, when he was nineteen, his ship docked at Norfolk, Virginia. He went ashore one Saturday with no intention of ever returning to Greece. He left behind everything, including his travel documents. All he had in his pockets was $100 and the address of his mother's cousin in the Jackson Heights–Corona section of Queens.

Almost four decades later, Juan Manuel Peralta underwent a similar rite of passage out of Mexico. He had finished the eighth grade in the poor southern state of Guerrero and saw nothing in his future there but fixing flat tires. His father, Inocencio, had once dreamed of going to the United States, but never had the money. In 1990, he borrowed enough to give his firstborn son a chance.

"I'm in the middle and I'm happy."

Peralta was nineteen when he boarded a smoky bus that carried him through the deserted hills of Guerrero and kept going until it reached the edge of Mexico. With eight other Mexicans he did not know, he crawled through a sewer tunnel that started in Tijuana and ended on the other side of the border, in what Mexicans call El Norte.

He had carried no documents, no photographs, and no money except what his father gave him to pay his shifty guide and to buy an airline ticket to New York. Deep in a pocket was the address of an uncle in the same section of Queens where John Zannikos had gotten his start. By 1990, the area had gone from largely Greek to mostly Latino.

Starting over in the same working-class neighborhood, Peralta and Zannikos quickly learned that New York was full of opportunities and obstacles, often in equal measure. On his first day there, Zannikos, scared and feeling lost, found the building he was looking for, but his mother's cousin had moved. He had no idea what to do until a Greek man passed by. Walk five blocks to the Deluxe Diner, the man said. He did.

The diner was full of Greek housepainters, including one who knew Zannikos's father. On the spot, they offered him a job painting closets, where his mistakes would be hidden. He painted until the weather turned cold. Another Greek hired him as a dishwasher at his coffee shop in the Bronx.

It was not easy, but Zannikos worked his way up to short-order cook, learning English as he went along. In 1956, immigration officials raided the coffee shop. He was deported, but after a short while he managed to sneak back into the country. Three years later he married a Puerto Rican from the Bronx. The marriage lasted only a year, but it put him on the road to becoming a citizen. Now he could buy his own restaurant, a greasy spoon in the South Bronx that catered to a late-night clientele of prostitutes and undercover police officers.

Since then, he has bought and sold more than a dozen New York diners, but none have been more successful than the original 3 Guys, which opened in 1978. He and his partners own two other restaurants with the same name farther up Madison Avenue, but they have never replicated the high-end appeal of the original.

"When employees come in, I teach them, 'Hey, this is a different neighborhood,'" Zannikos said. What may be standard in some other diners is not tolerated here. There are no Greek flags or tourism posters. There is no television or twirling tower of cakes with cream pompadours. Waiters are forbidden to chew gum. No customer is ever called "Honey."

"They know their place and I know my place," Zannikos said of his customers. "It's as simple as that."

His place in society now is a far cry from his days in the Bronx. He and his second wife, June, live in Wyckoff, a New Jersey suburb where he pampers fig trees and dutifully looks after a bird feeder shaped like the Parthenon. They own a condominium in Florida. His three children all went far beyond his second-grade education, finishing high school or attending college.

They have all done well, as has Zannikos, who says he makes about $130,000 a year. He says he is not sensitive to class distinctions, but he admits he was bothered when some people mistook him for the caterer at fund-raising dinners for the local Greek church he helped build.

All in all, he thinks immigrants today have a better chance of moving up the class ladder than he did fifty years ago.

"At that time, no bank would give us any money, but today they give you credit cards in the mail," he said. "New York still gives you more opportunity than any other place. If you want to do things, you will."

He says he has done well, and he is content with his station in life. "I'm in the middle and I'm happy."

A DIVISIVE ISSUE

Juan Manuel Peralta cannot guess what class John Zannikos belongs to. But he is certain that it is much tougher for an immigrant to get ahead today than fifty years ago. And he has no doubt about his own class.

"*La pobreza*," he says. "Poverty."

It was not what he expected when he boarded the bus to the border, but it did not take long for him to realize that success in the United States required more than hard work. "A lot of it has to do with luck," he said during a lunch break on a stoop around the corner from the Queens diner where he went to work after 3 Guys.

"People come here, and in no more than a year or two they can buy their own house and have a car," Peralta said. "Me, I've been here fifteen years, and if I die tomorrow, there wouldn't even be enough money to bury me."

In 1990, Peralta was in the vanguard of Mexican immigrants who bypassed the traditional barrios in border states to work in far-flung cities like Denver and New York. The 2000 census counted 186,872 Mexicans in New York, triple the 1990 figure, and there are undoubtedly many more today. The Mexican consulate, which serves the metropolitan region, has issued more than 500,000 ID cards just since 2001.

Fifty years ago, illegal immigration was a minor problem. Now it is a divisive national issue, pitting those who welcome cheap labor against those with concerns about border security and the cost of providing social services. Though newly arrived Mexicans often work in industries that rely on cheap labor, like restaurants and construction, they rarely organize. Most are desperate to stay out of sight.

Peralta hooked up with his uncle the morning he arrived in New York. He did not work for weeks until the bakery where the uncle worked had an opening, a part-time job making muffins. He took it, though he didn't know muffins from crumb cake. When he saw that he would not make enough to repay his father, he took a second job making night deliveries for a Manhattan diner. By the end of his first day he was so lost he had to spend all his tip money on a cab ride home.

He quit the diner, but working there even briefly opened his eyes to how easy it could be to make money in New York. Diners were everywhere, and so were jobs making deliveries, washing dishes, or busing tables. In six months, Peralta had paid back the money his father gave him. He bounced from job to job and in 1995, eager to show off his newfound success, went back to Mexico with his pockets full of money, and married. He was twenty-five then, the same age at which Zannikos married. But the similarities end there.

When Zannikos jumped ship, he left Greece behind for good. Though he himself had no documents, the compatriots he encountered on his first days were here legally, like most other Greek immigrants, and could help him. Greeks had never come to the United States in large numbers—the 2000 census counted only 29,805 New Yorkers born in Greece—but they tended to settle in just a few areas, like the Astoria section of Queens, which became cohesive communities ready to help new arrivals.

Peralta, like many other Mexicans, is trying to make it on his own and has never severed his emotional or financial ties to home. After five years in New York's Latino community, he spoke little English and owned little more than the clothes on his back. He decided to return to Huamuxtitlán, the dusty village beneath a flat-topped mountain where he was born.

"People thought that since I was coming back from El Norte, I would be so rich that I could spread money around," he said. Still, he felt privileged: his New York wages dwarfed the $1,000 a year he might have made in Mexico.

He met a shy, pretty girl named Matilde in Huamuxtitlán, married her, and returned with her to New York, again illegally, all in a matter of weeks. Their first child was born in 1996. Peralta soon found that supporting a family made it harder to save money. Then, in 1999, he got the job at 3 Guys.

"Barba Yanni helped me learn how to prepare things the way customers like them," Peralta said, referring to Zannikos with a Greek title of respect that means Uncle John.

The restaurant became his school. He learned how to sauté a fish so that it looked like a work of art. The three partners lent him money and said they would help him get immigration documents. The pay was good.

But there were tensions with the other workers. Instead of hanging their orders on a rack, the waiters shouted them out, in Greek, Spanish, and a kind of fractured English. Sometimes Peralta did not understand, and they argued. Soon he was known as a hothead.

Still, he worked hard, and every night he returned to his growing family. Matilde, now twenty-seven, cleaned houses until their second child, Heidi, was born in 2002. Now Matilde tries to sell Mary Kay products to other mothers at Public School 12, which their son Antony, who is eight, attends.

Most weeks, Peralta could make as much as $600. Over the course of a year that could come to over $30,000, enough to approach the lower middle class. But the life he leads is far from that and uncertainty hovers over everything about his life, starting with his paycheck.

To earn $600, he has to work at least ten hours a day, six days a week, and that does not happen every week. Sometimes he is paid overtime for the extra hours, sometimes not. And, as he found out, he can be fired at any time and bring in nothing, not even unemployment, until he lands another job. In 2004, he made about $24,000.

Because he is here illegally, Peralta can easily be exploited. He cannot file a complaint against his landlord for charging him $500 a month for a nine- by nine-foot room in a Queens apartment that he shares with nine other Mexicans in three families who pay the remainder of the $2,000-a-month rent. All thirteen share one bathroom, and the established pecking order means the Peraltas rarely get to use the kitchen. Eating out can be expensive.

Because they were born in New York, Peralta's children are United States citizens, and their health care is generally covered by Medicaid. But he has to pay out of his pocket whenever he or his wife sees a doctor. And forget about going to the dentist.

As many other Mexicans do, he wires money home, and it costs him $7 for every $100 he sends. When his uncle, his nephew, and his sister asked him for money, he was expected to lend it. No one has paid him back. He has middle-class ornaments, like a cellphone and a DVD player, but no driver's license or Social Security card.

He is the first to admit that he has vices that have held him back; nothing criminal, but he tends to lose his temper and there are nights when he likes to have a drink or two. His greatest weakness is instant lottery tickets, what he calls "*los scratch*," and he sheepishly confesses that he can squander as much as $75 a week on them. It is a way of preserving hope, he said. Once he won $100. He bought a blender.

Years ago, he and Matilde were so confident they would make it in America that when their son was born they used the American spelling of his name, Anthony, figuring it would help pave his passage into the mainstream. But even that effort failed.

"Look at this," his wife said one afternoon as she sat on the floor of their room near a picture of the Virgin of Guadalupe. Peralta sat on a small plastic stool in the doorway, listening. His mattress was stacked against the wall. A roll of toilet paper was stashed nearby because they dared not leave it in the shared bathroom for someone else to use.

She took her pocketbook and pulled out a clear plastic case holding her son's baptismal certificate, on which his name is spelled with an *H*. But then she unfolded his birth certificate, where the *H* is missing.

"The teachers won't teach him to spell his name the right way until the certificate is legally changed," she said. "But how can we do that if we're not legal?"

PROGRESS, BUT NOT SUCCESS

An elevated subway train thundered overhead, making the afternoon light along Roosevelt Avenue blink like a failing fluorescent bulb. Peralta's daughter and son grabbed his fat hands as they ran some errands. He had just finished a ten-hour shift, eggs over easy and cheeseburgers since 5:00 a.m.

It had been especially hard to stand the monotony that day. He kept thinking about what was going on in Mexico, where it was the feast day of Our Lady of the Rosary. And, oh, what a feast there was—sweets and handmade tamales, a parade, even a bullfight. At night, fireworks, bursting loud and bright against the green folds of the mountains. Paid for, in part, by the money he sends home.

But instead of partying, he was walking his children to the Arab supermarket on Roosevelt Avenue to buy packages of chicken and spare ribs, and hoping to get to use the kitchen. And though he knew better, he grabbed a package of pink and white marshmallows for the children. He needed to buy tortillas, too, but not there. A Korean convenience store a few blocks away sells La Maizteca tortillas, made in New York.

The swirl of immigrants in Peralta's neighborhood is part of the fabric of New York, just as it was in 1953, when John Zannikos arrived. But most immigrants then were Europeans, and though they spoke different languages, their Caucasian features helped them blend into New York's middle class.

In 1953, . . . most immigrants . . . were Europeans, and . . . their Caucasian features helped them blend into New York's middle class.

Experts remain divided over whether Mexicans can follow the same route. Samuel P. Huntington, a Harvard professor of government, takes the extreme view that Mexicans will not assimilate and that the separate culture they are developing threatens the United States.

Most others believe that recent Mexican immigrants will eventually take their place in society, and perhaps someday muster political clout commensurate with their numbers, though significant impediments are slowing their progress. Francisco Rivera-Batiz, a Columbia University economics professor, says that prejudice remains a problem, that factory jobs have all but disappeared, and that there is a growing gap between the educational demands of the economy and the limited schooling that the newest Mexicans have when they arrive.

But the biggest obstacle by far, and the one that separates newly arrived Mexicans from Greeks, Italians, and most other immigrants—including earlier generations of Mexicans—is their illegal status. Rivera-Batiz studied what happened to illegal Mexican immigrants who became legal after the last national amnesty in 1986. Within a few years, their incomes rose 20 percent and their English improved greatly.

"Legalization," he said, "helped them tremendously."

Although the Bush administration talks about legalizing some Mexicans with a guest worker program, there is opposition to another amnesty, and the number of Mexicans illegally living in the United States continues to soar. Desperate to get their papers any way they can, many turn to shady storefront legal offices. Like Peralta, they sign on to illusory schemes that cost hundreds of dollars but almost never produce the promised green cards.

Until the 1980s, Mexican immigration was largely seasonal and mostly limited to agricultural workers. But then economic chaos in Mexico sent a flood of immigrants northward, many of them poorly educated farmers from the impoverished countryside. Tighter security on the border made it harder for Mexicans to move back and forth in the traditional way, so they tended to stay here, searching for low-paying unskilled jobs and concentrating in barrios where Spanish, constantly replenished, never loses its immediacy.

"Cuidado!" Peralta shouted when Antony carelessly stepped into Roosevelt Avenue without looking. Although the boy is taught in English at school, he rarely uses anything but Spanish at home.

Even now, after fifteen years in New York, Peralta speaks little English. He tried English classes once, but could not get his mind to accept the new sounds. So he dropped it, and has stuck with Spanish, which he concedes is "the language of busboys" in New York. But as long as he stays in his neighborhood, it is all he needs.

It was late afternoon by the time Peralta and his children headed home. The run-down house, the overheated room, the stacked mattress, and the hoarded toilet paper—all remind him how far he would have to go to achieve a success like John Zannikos's.

Still, he says, he has done far better than he could ever have done in Mexico. He realizes that the money he sends to his family there is not enough to satisfy his father, who built stairs for a second floor of his house made of concrete blocks in Huamuxtitlán, even though there is no second floor. He believes Juan Manuel has made it big in New York and he is waiting for money from America to complete the upstairs.

His son has never told him the truth about his life up north. He said his father's images of America came from another era. The older man does not know how tough it is to be a Mexican immigrant in the United States now, tougher than any young man who ever left Huamuxtitlán would admit. Everything built up over fifteen years here can come apart as easily as an adobe house in an earthquake. And then it is time to start over, again.

A CONFLICT ERUPTS

It was the end of another busy lunch at 3 Guys in the late spring of 2003. Peralta made himself a turkey sandwich and took a seat at a rear table. The Mexican countermen, dishwashers, and busboys also started their breaks, while the Greek waiters took care of the last few diners.

It is not clear how the argument started. But a cross word passed between a Greek waiter and a Mexican busboy. Voices were raised. The waiter swung at the busboy, catching him behind the ear. Peralta froze. So did the other Mexicans.

Even from the front of the restaurant, where he was watching the cash register, Zannikos realized something was wrong and rushed back to break it up. "I stood between them, held one and pushed the other away," he said. "I told them: 'You don't do that here. Never do that here.'"

For the Mexicans it became a class struggle pitting powerless workers against hard-hearted owners.

Zannikos said he did not care who started it. He ordered both the busboy and the waiter, a partner's nephew, to get out.

But several Mexicans, including Peralta, said that they saw Zannikos grab the busboy by the head and that they believed he would have hit him if another Mexican had not stepped between them. That infuriated them because they felt he had sided with the Greek without knowing who was at fault.

Zannikos said that was not true, but in the end it did not matter. The easygoing atmosphere at the restaurant changed. "Everybody was a little cool," Zannikos recalled.

What he did not know then was that the Mexicans had reached out to the Restaurant Opportunities Center, a workers' rights group. Eventually six of them, including Peralta, cooperated with the group. He did so reluctantly, he said, because he was afraid that if the owners found out, they would no longer help him get his immigration papers. The labor group promised that the owners would never know.

The owners saw it as an effort to shake them down, but for the Mexicans it became a class struggle pitting powerless workers against hard-hearted owners.

Their grievances went beyond the scuffle. They complained that with just one exception, only Greeks became waiters at 3 Guys. They challenged the sole Mexican waiter, Salomon Paniagua, a former Mexican army officer who, everyone agreed, looked Greek, to stand with them.

But on the day the labor group picketed the restaurant, Paniagua refused to put down his order pad. A handful of demonstrators carried signs on Madison Avenue for a short while before Zannikos and his partners reluctantly agreed to settle.

Zannikos said he felt betrayed. "When I see these guys, I see myself when I started, and I always try to help them," he said. "I didn't do anything wrong."

The busboy and the Mexican who intervened were paid several thousand dollars and the owners promised to promote a current Mexican employee to waiter within a month. But that did not end the turmoil.

Fearing that the other Mexicans might try to get back at him, Paniagua decided to strike out on his own. After asking Zannikos for advice, he bought a one-third share of a Greek diner in Jamaica, Queens. He said he put it in his father's name because the older man had become a legal resident after the 1986 amnesty.

After Paniagua left, 3 Guys went without a single Mexican waiter for ten months, despite the terms of the settlement. In March, an eager Mexican busboy with a heavy accent who had worked there for four years got a chance to wear a waiter's tie.

Peralta ended up having to leave 3 Guys around the same time as Paniagua. Zannikos's partners suspected he had sided with the labor group, he said, and started to criticize his work unfairly. Then they cut back his schedule to five days a week. After he hurt his ankle playing soccer, they told him to go home until he was better. When Peralta came back to work about two weeks later, he was fired.

Zannikos confirms part of the account but says the firing had nothing to do with the scuffle or the ensuing dispute. "If he was good, believe me, he wouldn't get fired," he said of Peralta.

Peralta shrugged when told what Zannikos said. "I know my own work and I know what I can do," he said. "There are a lot of restaurants in New York, and a lot of workers."

When 3 Guys fired Peralta, another Mexican replaced him, just as Peralta replaced a Mexican at the Greek diner in Queens where he went to work next.

This time, though, there was no Madison Avenue address, no elaborate menu of New Zealand mussels or designer mushrooms. In the Queens diner a bowl of soup with a buttered roll cost two dollars, all day. If he fried burgers and scraped fat off the big grill for ten hours a day, six days a week, he might earn about as much as he did on Madison Avenue, at least for a week.

His schedule kept changing. Sometimes he worked the lunch and dinner shift, and by the end of the night he was worn out, especially since he often found himself arguing with the Greek owner. But he did not look forward to going home. So after the night manager lowered the security gate, Peralta would wander the streets.

One of those nights he stopped at a phone center off Roosevelt Avenue to call his mother. "Everything's okay," he told her. He asked how she had spent the last $100 he sent, and whether she needed anything else. There is always need in Huamuxtitlán.

Still restless, he went to the Scorpion, a shot-and-beer joint open till 4 a.m. He sat at the long bar nursing vodkas with cranberry juice, glancing at the soccer match on TV and the busty Brazilian bartender who spoke only a little Spanish. When it was nearly eleven, he called it a night.

Back home, he quietly opened the door to his room. The lights were off, the television murmuring. His family was asleep in the bunk bed that the store had now threatened to repossess. Antony was curled up on the top, Matilde and Heidi cuddled in the bottom. Peralta moved the plastic stool out of the way and dropped his mattress to the floor.

The children did not stir. His wife's eyes fluttered, but she said nothing. Peralta looked over his family, his home.

"This," he said, "is my life in New York."

Not the life he imagined, but his life. In early March 2005, just after Heidi's third birthday, he quit his job at the Queens diner after yet another heated argument with the owner. In his mind, preserving his dignity is one of the few liberties he has left.

"I'll get another job," he said while babysitting Heidi at home a few days after he quit. The rent is already paid till the end of the month and he has friends, he said. People know him. To him, jobs are interchangeable—just as he is to the jobs. If he cannot find work as a grillman, he will bus tables. Or wash dishes. If not at one diner, then at another.

"It's all the same," he said.

It took about three weeks, but Peralta did find a new job as a grillman at another Greek diner in a different part of New York. His salary is roughly the same, the menu is roughly the same (one new item, Greek burritos, was a natural), and he sees his chance for a better future as being roughly the same as it has been since he got to America.

A LONG DAY CLOSES

It was now dark again outside 3 Guys. About 9:00 p.m. John Zannikos asked his Mexican cook for a small salmon steak, a little rare. It had been another busy ten-hour day for him, but a good one. Receipts from the morning alone exceeded what he needed to take in every day just to cover the $23,000 a month rent.

He finished the salmon quickly, left final instructions with the lone Greek waiter still on duty, and said good night to everyone else. He put on his light tan corduroy jacket and the baseball cap he picked up in Florida.

"'Night," he said to the lone table of diners.

Outside, as Zannikos walked slowly down Madison Avenue, a self-made man comfortable with his own hard-won success, the bulkhead doors in front of 3 Guys clanked open. Faint voices speaking Spanish came from below. A young Mexican who started his shift ten hours earlier climbed out with a bag of garbage and heaved it onto the sidewalk. New Zealand mussel shells. Uneaten bits of portobello mushrooms. The fine grounds of decaf cappuccino.

One black plastic bag after another came out until Madison Avenue in front of 3 Guys was piled high with trash.

"Hurry up!" the young man shouted to the other Mexicans. "I want to go home, too."

DISCUSSION

1. DePalma begins his essay by presenting a list of the powerful or famous people who frequent the 3 Guys café. Why do you think he does this? What sort of framework does this introduction provide for the experiences of the Mexican workers whom the essay goes on to profile?
2. According to DePalma, the workplace portrait sketched here is a "template of the class divisions in America" (p. 354). How accurate does this claim seem to you? In what ways does the essay's depiction of work also function as a commentary on the ideals of class mobility?
3. How would you define the ideal working environment? What kinds of jobs or roles does it offer? How does this hypothetical world compare to or differ from the one depicted in this essay?

WRITING

4. This essay draws a clear connection between work and immigration, exploring the ways that the contemporary landscape for temporary workers threatens to rewrite what DePalma calls the "classic immigrant success story." Write an essay in which you assess the validity of this view. What is the "classic immigrant success story"? What is its typical plotline, its traditional roles? How does this conventional script compare to the immigrant story DePalma relates about either Juan Manuel Peralta or John Zannikos? How closely does this example resemble the ideal?
5. Make a list of the different jobs Peralta performs during his years in the United States. Write an essay in which you describe the particular role you think these jobs script for the workers who undertake them. What is the profile of the typical person who performs these jobs? How accurate and fair do you think these descriptions are? Why?
6. How much of DePalma's discussion here reminds you of what Louis Uchitelle (p. 342) says about the kinds of psychic harm job-related struggles can inflict? Write a review of DePalma's essay that you think Uchitelle might offer. To what extent would Uchitelle's review find parallels in the social and economic hardships profiled here and his argument regarding the emotional costs of unemployment?

MATTHEW B. CRAWFORD

The Case for Working with Your Hands

In our hyperactive, information-based economy, it's easy to assume that any work involving manual skill has become obsolete. According to Matthew B. Crawford, however, ours may well be the moment where precisely such work is most urgently needed. Taking a critical look at current cultural conceits about "knowledge work," he offers a spirited defense of what he calls "working with your hands." Crawford lives in Richmond, Virginia, and is a fellow at the Institute for Advanced Studies in Culture at the University of Virginia. He is the author of the book *Shop Class as Soulcraft: An Inquiry into the Value of Work* (2009). The following essay appeared in the May 21, 2009, issue of the *New York Times Magazine.*

THE TELEVISION SHOW *DEADLIEST CATCH* DEPICTS COMMERCIAL crab fishermen in the Bering Sea. Another, *Dirty Jobs*, shows all kinds of grueling work; one episode featured a guy who inseminates turkeys for a living. The weird fascination of these shows must lie partly in the fact that such confrontations with material reality have become exotically unfamiliar. Many of us do work that feels more surreal than real. Working in an office, you often find it difficult to see any tangible result from your efforts. What exactly have you accomplished at the end of any given day? Where the chain of cause and effect is opaque and responsibility diffuse, the experience of individual agency can be elusive. *Dilbert*, *The Office*, and similar portrayals of cubicle life attest to the dark absurdism with which many Americans have come to view their white-collar jobs.

Is there a more "real" alternative (short of inseminating turkeys)?

High-school shop-class programs were widely dismantled in the 1990s as educators prepared students to become "knowledge workers." The imperative of the last 20 years to round up every warm body and send it to college, then to the cubicle, was tied to a vision of the future in which we somehow take leave of material reality and glide about in a pure information economy. This has not come to pass. To begin with, such work often feels more enervating than gliding. More fundamentally, now as ever, somebody has to actually do things: fix our cars, unclog our toilets, build our houses.

When we praise people who do work that is straightforwardly useful, the praise often betrays an assumption that they had no other options. We idealize them as the salt of the earth and emphasize the sacrifice for others their work may entail. Such sacrifice does indeed occur—the hazards faced by a lineman restoring power during a storm come to mind. But what if such work answers as well to a basic human need of the one who does it? I take this to be the suggestion of Marge Piercy's poem "To Be of Use," which concludes with the lines "the pitcher longs for water to carry/and a person for work that is real." Beneath our gratitude for the lineman may rest envy.

This seems to be a moment when the useful arts have an especially compelling economic rationale. A car mechanics' trade association reports that repair shops have seen their business jump significantly in the current recession: people aren't buying new cars; they are fixing the ones they have. The current downturn is likely to pass eventually. But there are also systemic changes in the economy, arising from information technology, that have the surprising effect of making the manual trades—plumbing, electrical work, car repair—more attractive as careers. The Princeton economist Alan Blinder argues that the crucial distinction in the emerging labor market is not between those with more or less education, but between those whose services can be delivered over a wire and those who must do their work in person or on site. The latter will find their livelihoods more secure against outsourcing to distant countries. As Blinder puts it, "You can't hammer a nail over the Internet." Nor can the Indians fix your car. Because they are in India.

A gifted young person who chooses to become a mechanic rather than to accumulate academic credentials is viewed as eccentric, if not self-destructive.

If the goal is to earn a living, then, maybe it isn't really true that 18-year-olds need to be imparted with a sense of panic about getting into college (though they certainly need to learn). Some people are hustled off to college, then to the cubicle, against their own inclinations and natural bents, when they would rather be learning to build things or fix things. One shop teacher suggested to me that "in schools, we create artificial learning environments for our children that they know to be contrived and undeserving of their full attention and engagement. Without the opportunity to learn through the hands, the world remains abstract and distant, and the passions for learning will not be engaged."

A gifted young person who chooses to become a mechanic rather than to accumulate academic credentials is viewed as eccentric, if not self-destructive. There is a pervasive anxiety among parents that there is only one track to success for their children. It runs through a series of gates controlled by prestigious institutions. Further, there is wide use of drugs to medicate boys, especially, against their natural tendency toward action, the better to "keep things on track." I taught briefly in a public high school and would have loved to have set up a Ritalin fogger in my classroom. It is a rare person, male or female, who is naturally inclined to sit still for 17 years in school, and then indefinitely at work.

The trades suffer from low prestige, and I believe this is based on a simple mistake. Because the work is dirty, many people assume it is also stupid. This is not my experience. I have a small business as a motorcycle mechanic in Richmond, Virginia, which I started in 2002. I work on Japanese and European motorcycles, mostly older bikes with some "vintage" cachet that makes people willing to spend money on them. I have found the satisfactions of the work to be very much bound up with the intellectual challenges it presents. And yet my decision to go into this line of work is a choice that seems to perplex many people.

After finishing a Ph.D. in political philosophy at the University of Chicago in 2000, I managed to stay on with a one-year postdoctoral fellowship at the university's Committee on Social Thought. The academic job market was utterly bleak. In a state of professional panic, I retreated to a makeshift workshop I set up in the basement of a Hyde Park apartment building, where I spent the winter tearing down an old Honda motorcycle and rebuilding it. The physicality of it, and the clear specificity of what the project required of me, was a balm. Stumped by a starter motor that seemed to check out in every way but wouldn't work, I started asking around at Honda dealerships. Nobody had an answer; finally one service manager told me to call Fred Cousins of Triple O Service. "If anyone can help you, Fred can."

I called Fred, and he invited me to come to his independent motorcycle-repair shop, tucked discreetly into an unmarked warehouse on Goose Island. He told me to put the motor on a certain bench that was free of clutter. He checked the electrical resistance through the windings, as I had done, to confirm there was no short circuit or broken wire. He spun the shaft that ran through the center of the motor, as I had. No problem: it spun freely. Then he hooked it up to a battery. It moved ever so slightly but wouldn't spin. He grasped the shaft, delicately, with three fingers, and tried to wiggle it side to side. "Too much free play," he said. He suggested that the problem was with the bushing (a thick-walled sleeve of metal) that captured the end of the shaft in the end of the cylindrical motor housing. It was worn, so it wasn't locating the shaft precisely enough. The shaft was free to move too much side to side (perhaps a couple of hundredths of an inch), causing the outer circumference of the rotor to bind on the inner circumference of the motor housing when a current was applied. Fred scrounged around for a Honda motor. He found one with the same bushing, then used a "blind hole bearing puller" to extract it, as well as the one in my motor. Then he gently tapped the new, or rather newer, one into place. The motor worked!

Then Fred gave me an impromptu dissertation on the peculiar metallurgy of these Honda starter-motor bushings of the mid-'70s. Here was a scholar.

Over the next six months I spent a lot of time at Fred's shop, learning, and put in only occasional appearances at the university. This was something of a regression: I worked on cars throughout high school and college, and one of my early jobs was at a Porsche repair shop. Now I was rediscovering the intensely absorbing nature of the work, and it got me thinking about possible livelihoods.

As it happened, in the spring I landed a job as executive director of a policy organization in Washington. This felt like a coup. But certain perversities became apparent as I settled into the job. It sometimes required me to reason backward, from desired conclusion to suitable premise. The organization had taken certain positions, and there were some facts it was more fond of than others. As its figurehead, I was making arguments I didn't fully buy myself. Further, my boss seemed intent on retraining me according to a certain cognitive style—that of the corporate world, from which he had recently come. This style demanded that I project an image of rationality but not indulge too much in actual reasoning. As I sat in my K Street office, Fred's life as an independent tradesman gave me an image that I kept coming back to: someone who really knows what he is doing, losing himself in work that is genuinely useful and has a certain integrity to it. He also seemed to be having a lot of fun.

Seeing a motorcycle about to leave my shop under its own power, several days after arriving in the back of a pickup truck, I don't feel tired even though I've been standing on a concrete floor all day. Peering into the portal of his helmet, I think I can make out the edges of a grin on the face of a guy who hasn't ridden his bike in a while. I give him a wave. With one of his hands on the throttle and the other on the clutch, I know he can't wave back. But I can hear his salute in the exuberant "bwaaAAAAP!" of a crisp throttle, gratuitously revved. That sound pleases me, as I know it does him. It's a ventriloquist conversation in one mechanical voice, and the gist of it is "Yeah!"

After five months at the think tank, I'd saved enough money to buy some tools I needed, and I quit and went into business fixing bikes. My shop rate is $40 per hour. Other shops have rates as high as $70 per hour, but I tend to work pretty slowly. Further, only about half the time I spend in the shop ends up being billable (I have no employees; every little chore falls to me), so it usually works out closer to $20 per hour—a modest but decent wage. The business goes up and down; when it is down I have supplemented it with writing. The work is sometimes frustrating, but it is never irrational.

And it frequently requires complex thinking. In fixing motorcycles you come up with several imagined trains of cause and effect for manifest symptoms, and you judge their likelihood before tearing anything down. This imagining relies on a mental library that you develop. An internal combustion engine can work in any number of ways, and different manufacturers have tried different approaches. Each has its own proclivities for failure. You also develop a library of sounds and smells and feels. For example, the backfire of a too-lean fuel mixture is subtly different from an ignition backfire.

As in any learned profession, you just have to know a lot. If the motorcycle is 30 years old, from an obscure maker that went out of business 20 years ago, its tendencies are known mostly through lore. It would probably be impossible to do such work in isolation, without access to a collective historical memory; you have to be embedded in a community of mechanic-antiquarians. These relationships are maintained by telephone, in a network of reciprocal favors that spans the country. My most reliable source, Fred, has such an encyclopedic knowledge of obscure European motorcycles that all I have been able to offer him in exchange is deliveries of obscure European beer.

There is always a risk of introducing new complications when working on old motorcycles, and this enters the diagnostic logic. Measured in likelihood of screw-ups, the cost is not identical for all avenues of inquiry when deciding which hypothesis to pursue. Imagine you're trying to figure out why a bike won't start. The fasteners holding the engine covers on 1970s-era Hondas are Phillips head, and they are almost always rounded out and corroded. Do you really want to check the condition of the starter clutch if each of eight screws will need to be drilled out and extracted, risking damage to the engine case? Such impediments have to be taken into account. The attractiveness of any hypothesis is determined in part by physical circumstances that have no logical connection to the diagnostic problem at hand. The mechanic's proper response to the situation cannot be anticipated by a set of rules or algorithms.

There probably aren't many jobs that can be reduced to rule-following and still be done well. But in many jobs there is an attempt to do just this, and the perversity of it may go unnoticed by those who design the work process. Mechanics face something like this problem in the factory service manuals that we use. These manuals tell you to be systematic in eliminating variables, presenting an idealized image of diagnostic work. But they never take into account the risks of working on old machines. So you put the manual away and consider the facts before you. You do this because ultimately you are responsible to the motorcycle and its owner, not to some procedure.

There probably aren't many jobs that can be reduced to rule-following and still be done well.

Some diagnostic situations contain a lot of variables. Any given symptom may have several possible causes, and further, these causes may interact with one another and therefore be difficult to isolate. In deciding how to proceed, there often comes a point where you have to step back and get a larger gestalt. Have a cigarette and walk around the lift. The gap between theory and practice stretches out in front of you, and this is where it gets interesting. What you need now is the kind of judgment that arises only from experience; hunches rather than rules. For me, at least, there is more real thinking going on in the bike shop than there was in the think tank.

Put differently, mechanical work has required me to cultivate different intellectual habits. Further, habits of mind have an ethical dimension that we don't often think about. Good diagnosis requires attentiveness to the machine, almost a conversation with it, rather than assertiveness, as in the position papers produced on K Street. Cognitive psychologists speak of "metacognition," which is the activity of stepping back and thinking about your own thinking. It is what you do when you stop for a moment in your pursuit of a solution, and wonder whether your understanding of the problem is adequate. The slap of worn-out pistons hitting their cylinders can sound a lot like loose valve tappets, so to be a good mechanic you have to be constantly open to the possibility that you may be mistaken. This is a virtue that is at once cognitive and moral. It seems to develop because the mechanic, if he is the sort who goes on to become good at it, internalizes the healthy functioning of the motorcycle as an object of passionate concern. How else can you explain the elation he gets when he identifies the root cause of some problem?

This active concern for the motorcycle is reinforced by the social aspects of the job. As is the case with many independent mechanics, my business is based entirely on word of mouth. I sometimes barter services with machinists and metal fabricators. This has a very different feel than transactions with money; it situates me in a community. The result is that I really don't want to mess up anybody's motorcycle or charge more than a fair price. You often hear people complain about mechanics and other tradespeople whom they take to be dishonest or incompetent. I am sure this is sometimes justified. But it is also true that the mechanic deals with a large element of chance.

I once accidentally dropped a feeler gauge down into the crankcase of a Kawasaki Ninja that was practically brand new, while performing its first scheduled valve adjustment. I escaped a complete tear-down of the motor only through an operation that involved the use of a stethoscope, another pair of trusted hands, and the sort of concentration we associate with a bomb squad. When finally I laid my fingers on that feeler gauge, I felt as if I had cheated death. I don't remember ever feeling so alive as in the hours that followed.

Often as not, however, such crises do not end in redemption. Moments of elation are counterbalanced with failures, and these, too, are vivid, taking place right before your eyes. With stakes that are often high and immediate, the manual trades elicit heedful absorption in work. They are punctuated by moments of pleasure that take place against a darker backdrop: a keen awareness of catastrophe as an always-present possibility. The core experience is one of individual responsibility, supported by face-to-face interactions between tradesman and customer.

Contrast the experience of being a middle manager. This is a stock figure of ridicule, but the sociologist Robert Jackall spent years inhabiting the world of corporate managers, conducting interviews, and he poignantly describes the "moral maze" they feel trapped in. Like the mechanic, the manager faces the possibility of disaster at any time. But in his case these disasters feel arbitrary; they are typically a result of corporate restructurings, not of physics. A manager has to make many decisions for which he is accountable. Unlike an entrepreneur with his own business, however, his decisions can be reversed at any time by someone higher up the food chain (and there is always someone higher up the food chain). It's important for your career that these reversals not look like defeats, and more generally you have to spend a lot of time managing what others think of you. Survival depends on a crucial insight: you can't back down from an argument that you initially made in straightforward language, with moral conviction, without seeming to lose your integrity. So managers learn the art of provisional thinking and feeling, expressed in corporate doublespeak, and cultivate a lack of commitment to their own actions. Nothing is set in concrete the way it is when you are, for example, pouring concrete.

Those who work on the lower rungs of the information-age office hierarchy face their own kinds of unreality, as I learned some time ago. After earning a master's degree in the early 1990s, I had a hard time finding work but eventually landed a job in the Bay Area writing brief summaries of academic journal articles, which were then sold on CD-ROMs to subscribing libraries. When I got the phone call offering me the job, I was excited. I felt I had grabbed hold of the passing world—miraculously, through the mere filament of a classified ad—and reeled myself into its current. My new bosses immediately took up residence in my imagination, where I often surprised them with my hidden depths. As I was shown to my cubicle, I felt a real sense of being honored. It seemed more than spacious enough. It was my desk, where I would think my thoughts—my unique contribution to a common enterprise, in a real company with hundreds of employees. The regularity of the cubicles made me feel I had found a place in the order of things. I was to be a knowledge worker.

But the feel of the job changed on my first day. The company had gotten its start by providing libraries with a subject index of popular magazines like *Sports Illustrated*. Through a series of mergers and acquisitions, it now found itself offering not just indexes but also abstracts (that is, summaries), and of a very different kind of material: scholarly works in the physical and biological sciences, humanities, social sciences, and law. Some of this stuff was simply incomprehensible to anyone but an expert in the particular field covered by the journal. I was reading articles in *Classical Philology* where practically every other word was in Greek. Some of the scientific journals were no less mysterious. Yet the categorical difference between, say, *Sports Illustrated* and *Nature Genetics* seemed not to have impressed itself on the company's decision makers. In some of the titles I was assigned, articles began with an abstract written by the author. But even in such cases I was to write my own. The reason offered was that unless I did so, there would be no "value added" by our product. It was hard to believe I was going to add anything other than error and confusion to such material. But then, I hadn't yet been trained.

My job was structured on the supposition that in writing an abstract of an article there is a method that merely needs to be applied, and that this can be done without understanding the text. I was actually told this by the trainer, Monica, as she stood before a whiteboard, diagramming an abstract. Monica seemed a perfectly sensible person and gave no outward signs of suffering delusions. She didn't insist too much on what she was telling us, and it became clear she was in a position similar to that of a veteran Soviet bureaucrat who must work on two levels at once: reality and official ideology. The official ideology was a bit like the factory service manuals I mentioned before, the ones that offer procedures that mechanics often have to ignore in order to do their jobs.

My starting quota, after finishing a week of training, was 15 articles per day. By my 11th month at the company, my quota was up to 28 articles per day (this was the normal, scheduled increase). I was always sleepy while at work, and I think this exhaustion was because I felt trapped in a contradiction: the fast pace demanded complete focus on the task, yet that pace also made any real concentration impossible. I had to actively suppress my own ability to think, because the more you think, the more the inadequacies in your understanding of an author's argument come into focus. This can only slow you down. To not do justice to an author who had poured himself into the subject at hand felt like violence against what was best in myself.

The quota demanded, then, not just dumbing down but also a bit of moral re-education, the opposite of the kind that occurs in the heedful absorption of mechanical work. I had to suppress my sense of responsibility to the article itself, and to others—to the author, to begin with, as well as to the hapless users of the database, who might naïvely suppose that my abstract reflected the author's work. Such detachment was made easy by the fact there was no immediate consequence for me; I could write any nonsense whatever.

Now, it is probably true that every job entails some kind of mutilation. I used to work as an electrician and had my own business doing it for a while. As an electrician you breathe a lot of unknown dust in crawl spaces, your knees get bruised, your neck gets strained from looking up at the ceiling while installing lights or ceiling fans, and you get shocked regularly, sometimes while on a ladder. Your hands are sliced up from twisting wires together, handling junction boxes made out of stamped sheet metal, and cutting metal conduit with a hacksaw. But none of this damage touches the best part of yourself.

You might wonder: Wasn't there any quality control? My supervisor would periodically read a few of my abstracts, and I was sometimes corrected and told not to begin an abstract with a dependent clause. But I was never confronted with an abstract I had written and told that it did not adequately reflect the article. The quality standards were the generic ones of grammar, which could be applied without my supervisor having to read the article at hand. Rather, my supervisor and I both were held to a metric that was conjured by someone remote from the work process—an absentee decision maker armed with a (putatively) profit-maximizing calculus, one that took no account of the intrinsic nature of the job. I wonder whether the resulting perversity really made for maximum profits in the long term. Corporate managers are not, after all, the owners of the businesses they run.

At lunch I had a standing arrangement with two other abstracters. One was from my group, a laconic, disheveled man named Mike whom I liked instantly. He did about as well on his quota as I did on mine, but it didn't seem to bother him too much. The other guy was from beyond the partition, a meticulously groomed Liberian named Henry who said he had worked for the C.I.A. He had to flee Liberia very suddenly one day and soon found himself resettled near the office parks of Foster City, California. Henry wasn't going to sweat the quota. Come 12:30, the three of us would hike to the food court in the mall. This movement was always thrilling. It involved traversing several "campuses," with ponds frequented by oddly real seagulls, then the lunch itself, which I always savored. (Marx writes that under conditions of estranged labor, man "no longer feels himself to be freely active in any but his animal functions.") Over his burrito, Mike would recount the outrageous things he had written in his abstracts. I could see my own future in such moments of sabotage—the compensating pleasures of a cubicle drone. Always funny and gentle, Mike confided one day that he was doing quite a bit of heroin. On the job. This actually made some sense.

How was it that I, once a proudly self-employed electrician, had ended up among these walking wounded, a "knowledge worker" at a salary of $23,000? I had a master's degree, and it needed to be used. The escalating demand for academic credentials in the job market gives the impression of an ever-more-knowledgeable society, whose members perform cognitive feats their unschooled parents could scarcely conceive of. On paper, my abstracting job, multiplied a millionfold, is precisely what puts the futurologist in a rapture: we are getting to be so smart! Yet my M.A. obscures a more real stupidification of the work I secured with that credential, and a wage to match. When I first got the degree, I felt as if I had been inducted to a certain order of society. But despite the beautiful ties I wore, it turned out to be a more proletarian existence than I had known as an electrician. In that job I had made quite a bit more money. I also felt free and active, rather than confined and stultified.

A good job requires a field of action where you can put your best capacities to work and see an effect in the world.

A good job requires a field of action where you can put your best capacities to work and see an effect in the world. Academic credentials do not guarantee this.

Nor can big business or big government—those idols of the right and the left—reliably secure such work for us. Everyone is rightly concerned about economic growth on the one hand or unemployment and wages on the other, but the character of work doesn't figure much in political debate. Labor unions address important concerns like workplace safety and family leave, and management looks for greater efficiency, but on the nature of the job itself, the dominant political and economic paradigms are mute. Yet work forms us, and deforms us, with broad public consequences.

The visceral experience of failure seems to have been edited out of the career trajectories of gifted students. It stands to reason, then, that those who end up making big decisions that affect all of us don't seem to have much sense of their own fallibility, and of how badly things can go wrong even with the best of intentions (like when I dropped that feeler gauge down into the Ninja). In the boardrooms of Wall Street and the corridors of Pennsylvania Avenue, I don't think you'll see a yellow sign that says "Think Safety!" as you do on job sites and in many repair shops, no doubt because those who sit on the swivel chairs tend to live remote from the consequences of the decisions they make. Why not encourage gifted students to learn a trade, if only in the summers, so that their fingers will be crushed once or twice before they go on to run the country?

There is good reason to suppose that responsibility has to be installed in the foundation of your mental equipment—at the level of perception and habit. There is an ethic of paying attention that develops in the trades through hard experience. It inflects your perception of the world and your habitual responses to it. This is due to the immediate feedback you get from material objects and to the fact that the work is typically situated in face-to-face interactions between tradesman and customer.

An economy that is more entrepreneurial, less managerial, would be less subject to the kind of distortions that occur when corporate managers' compensation is tied to the short-term profit of distant shareholders. For most entrepreneurs, profit is at once a more capacious and a more concrete thing than this. It is a calculation in which the intrinsic satisfactions of work count—not least, the exercise of your own powers of reason.

Ultimately it is enlightened self-interest, then, not a harangue about humility or public-spiritedness, that will compel us to take a fresh look at the trades. The good life comes in a variety of forms. This variety has become difficult to see; our field of aspiration has narrowed into certain channels. But the current perplexity in the economy seems to be softening our gaze. Our peripheral vision is perhaps recovering, allowing us to consider the full range of lives worth choosing. For anyone who feels ill suited by disposition to spend his days sitting in an office, the question of what a good job looks like is now wide open.

DISCUSSION

1. What are some of the stereotypes we are taught to associate with "working with your hands"? What are the social scripts that teach us to define and evaluate this type of labor? In your view, are these attitudes accurate or fair? Why or why not?
2. For Crawford, cultural norms around work are intimately entwined with cultural norms around school. "Some people," he writes, "are hustled off to college, then to the cubicle, against their own inclinations and natural bents, when they would rather be learning to build things or fix things" (p. 369). In your view, is Crawford correct? Do you agree that there exists a bias within our educational system against manual labor? And do you share Crawford's sense that this educational script needs to be rewritten? Why or why not?
3. "Ultimately," Crawford writes, "it is enlightened self-interest, then, not a harangue about humility or public-spiritedness, that will compel us to take a fresh look at the trades" (p. 378). Do you agree? In your view, is it ultimately in our better interests — whether individually or societally — to change our public attitudes toward manual work? If so, how?

WRITING

4. Part of Crawford's argument in favor of manual work rests on the claims he makes about "knowledge work." In a brief essay, explore what characterizes white-collar or "knowledge work." What rules dictate what this kind of labor is supposed to look like and what it is supposed to be for? What specific forms of work does it involve? What skills does it require? Next, explain what, specifically, Crawford finds wanting or problematic about this type of work. Do you agree?
5. Write an essay in which you apply Crawford's analysis to your own experiences with work. How do you define the ideal job? Does this ideal resemble or differ from Crawford's portrait of his own work? Does your ideal confirm or challenge the claims Crawford makes about hands-on versus knowledge work? How or how not?
6. Like Crawford, Catherine Rampell (p. 388) is interested in challenging entrenched stereotypes around work. Write an assessment of how the messages in these two essays compare with one another. Does Rampell's attempt to explode the myth of the "slacker generation" remind you in any way of Crawford's desire to rewrite the boundary between white-collar and manual labor? Do these writers challenge such stereotypes in order to say similar or different things about the meaning and value of work?

BARBARA EHRENREICH

How the Poor Are Made to Pay for Their Poverty

We've all heard the complaints that government needs to become leaner, more efficient, more cost effective. But what happens when the brunt of such efforts is borne by those least able to withstand it? Offering a portrait of the unique and punitive costs society imposes upon the working poor, Barbara Ehrenreich asks some hard questions about fairness, responsibility, and social class in America today. Ehrenreich is a writer and political activist who has written for a variety of magazines and newspapers including the *Nation*, the *Atlantic*, *Ms.*, and the *Progressive*. She has published over a dozen books of journalism and social commentary. *Nickel and Dimed: On (Not) Getting By in America* (2002) is an undercover investigation of low-wage jobs, and a chapter of it won Ehrenreich a Sydney Hillman Award for Journalism. Among her other books are *Bait and Switch: The (Futile) Pursuit of the American Dream* (2005) and, most recently, *Living with a Wild God* (2014). The selection below was first published in the *Guardian* in 2012.

INDIVIDUALLY, THE POOR ARE NOT TOO TEMPTING TO THIEVES, FOR obvious reasons. Mug a banker and you might score a wallet containing a month's rent. Mug a janitor and you will be lucky to get away with bus fare to flee the crime scene. But as *Businessweek* helpfully pointed out in 2007, the poor *in aggregate* provide a juicy target for anyone depraved enough to make a business of stealing from them.

The trick is to rob them in ways that are systematic, impersonal, and almost impossible to trace to individual perpetrators. Employers, for example, can simply program their computers to shave a few dollars off each paycheck, or they can require workers to show up 30 minutes or more before the time clock starts ticking.

Lenders, including major credit companies as well as payday lenders, have taken over the traditional role of the street-corner loan shark, charging the poor insanely high rates of interest. When supplemented with late fees (themselves subject to interest), the resulting effective interest rate can be as high as 600% a year, which is perfectly legal in many states.

It's not just the private sector that's preying on the poor. Local governments are discovering that they can partially make up for declining tax revenues through fines, fees, and other costs imposed on indigent defendants, often for crimes no more dastardly than driving with a suspended license. And if that seems like an inefficient way to make money, given the high cost of locking people up, a growing number of jurisdictions have taken to charging defendants for their court costs and even the price of occupying a jail cell.

The poster case for government persecution of the down-and-out would have to be Edwina Nowlin, a homeless Michigan woman who was jailed in 2009 for failing to pay $104 a month to cover the room-and-board charges for her 16-year-old son's incarceration. When she received a back paycheck, she thought it would allow her to pay for her son's jail stay. Instead, it was confiscated and applied to the cost of her own incarceration.

Being poor itself is not yet a crime, but in at least a third of the states, being in debt can now land you in jail.

GOVERNMENT JOINS THE LOOTERS OF THE POOR

You might think that policymakers would take a keen interest in the amounts that are stolen, coerced, or extorted from the poor, but there are no official efforts to track such figures. Instead, we have to turn to independent investigators, like Kim Bobo, author of *Wage Theft in America,* who estimates that wage theft nets employers at least $100 billion a year and possibly twice that. As for the profits extracted by the lending industry, Gary Rivlin, who wrote *Broke USA: From Pawnshops to Poverty, Inc—How the Working Poor Became Big Business*, says the poor pay an effective surcharge of about $30 billion a year for the financial products they consume and more than twice that if you include sub-prime credit cards, sub-prime auto loans, and sub-prime mortgages.

These are not, of course, trivial amounts. They are on the same order of magnitude as major public programs for the poor. The government distributes about $55 billion a year, for example, through the largest single cash-transfer program for the poor, the Earned Income Tax Credit; at the same time, employers are siphoning off *twice that amount*, if not more, through wage theft.

And while government generally turns a blind eye to the tens of billions of dollars in exorbitant interest that businesses charge the poor, it is notably chary with public benefits for the poor. Temporary Assistance to Needy Families, for example, our sole remaining nationwide welfare program, gets only $26 billion a year in state and federal funds. The impression is left of a public sector that's totally self-contradictory: on the one hand, offering safety net programs for the poor; on the other, enabling large scale private sector theft from the very people it is supposedly trying to help.

At the local level though, government is increasingly opting to join in the looting. In 2009, a year into the Great Recession, I first started hearing complaints from community organizers about ever more aggressive levels of law enforcement in low-income areas. Flick a cigarette butt and get arrested for littering; empty your pockets for an officer conducting a stop-and-frisk operation and get cuffed for a few flakes of marijuana. Each of these offenses can result, at a minimum, in a three-figure fine.

And the number of possible criminal offenses leading to jail and/or fines has been multiplying recklessly. All across the country—from California and Texas to Pennsylvania—counties and municipalities have been toughening laws against truancy and ratcheting up enforcement, sometimes going so far as to handcuff children found on the streets during school hours. In New York City, it's now a crime to put your feet up on a subway seat, even if the rest of the car is empty, and a South Carolina woman spent six days in jail when she was unable to pay a $480 fine for the crime of having a "messy yard." Some cities—most recently, Houston and Philadelphia—have made it a crime to share food with indigent people in public places.

Before we can "do something" for the poor, there are some things we need to stop doing* to *them.

Being poor itself is not yet a crime, but in at least a third of the states, being in debt can now land you in jail. If a creditor like a landlord or credit card company has a court summons issued for you and you fail to show up on your appointed court date, a warrant will be issued for your arrest. And it is easy enough to miss a court summons, which may have been delivered to the wrong address or, in the case of some bottom-feeding bill collectors, simply tossed in the garbage—a practice so common that the industry even has a term for it: "sewer service." In a sequence that National Public Radio reports is "increasingly common," a person is stopped for some minor traffic offense—having a noisy muffler, say, or broken brake light—at which point, the officer discovers the warrant and the unwitting offender is whisked off to jail.

LOCAL GOVERNMENTS AS PREDATORS

Each of these crimes, neo-crimes, and pseudo-crimes carries financial penalties as well as the threat of jail time, but the amount of money thus extracted from the poor is fiendishly hard to pin down. No central agency tracks law enforcement at the local level, and local records can be almost willfully sketchy.

According to one of the few recent nationwide estimates, from the National Association of Criminal Defense Lawyers, 10.5 million misdemeanors were committed in 2006. No one would risk estimating the average financial penalty for a misdemeanor, although the experts I interviewed all affirmed that the amount is typically in the "hundreds of dollars." If we take an extremely lowball $200 per misdemeanor, and bear in mind that 80–90% of criminal offenses are committed by people who are officially indigent, then local governments are using law enforcement to extract, or attempt to extract, at least $2 billion a year from the poor.

And that is only a small fraction of what governments would like to collect from the poor. Katherine Beckett, a sociologist at the University of Washington, estimates that "deadbeat dads" (and moms) owe $105 billion in back child-support payments, about half of which is owed to state governments as reimbursement for prior welfare payments made to the children. Yes, parents have a moral obligation to their children, but the great majority of child-support debtors are indigent.

Attempts to collect from the already-poor can be vicious and often, one would think, self-defeating. Most states confiscate the drivers' licenses of people owing child support, virtually guaranteeing that they will not be able to work. Michigan just started suspending the drivers' licenses of people who owe money for parking tickets. Las Cruces, New Mexico, just passed a law that punishes people who owe overdue traffic fines by cutting off their water, gas, and sewage.

Once a person falls into the clutches of the criminal justice system, we encounter the kind of slapstick sadism familiar to viewers of *Wipeout*. Many courts impose fees without any determination of whether the offender is able to pay, and the privilege of having a payment plan will itself cost money.

In a study of 15 states, the Brennan Center for Justice at New York University found 14 of them contained jurisdictions that charge a lump-sum "poverty penalty" of up to $300 for those who cannot pay their fees and fines, plus late fees and "collection fees" for those who need to pay over time. If any jail time is imposed, that too may cost money, as the hapless Edwina Nowlin discovered, and the costs of parole and probation are increasingly being passed along to the offender.

The predatory activities of local governments give new meaning to that tired phrase "the cycle of poverty." Poor people are far more likely than the affluent to get into trouble with the law, either by failing to pay parking fines or by incurring the wrath of a private sector creditor like a landlord or a hospital.

Once you have been deemed a criminal, you can pretty much kiss your remaining assets goodbye. Not only will you face the aforementioned court costs, but you'll have a hard time ever finding a job again once you've acquired a criminal record. And then, of course, the poorer you become, the more likely you are to get in fresh trouble with the law, making this less like a "cycle" and more like the waterslide to hell. The further you descend, the faster you fall—until you eventually end up on the streets and get busted for an offense like urinating in public or sleeping on a sidewalk.

I could propose all kinds of policies to curb the ongoing predation on the poor. Limits on usury should be reinstated. Theft should be taken seriously even when it's committed by millionaire employers. No one should be incarcerated for debt or squeezed for money they have no chance of getting their hands on. These are no-brainers, and should take precedence over any long term talk about generating jobs or strengthening the safety net.

Before we can "do something" for the poor, there are some things we need to stop doing *to* them.

DISCUSSION

1. Ehrenreich uses the concept of thievery to describe such everyday practices as employers deducting extra pay from workers who fail to show up for work early or payday lenders who loan out money at interest rates that can top 600 percent. Do you agree with her characterization? In your view, is it accurate or valid to describe such practices as theft? Why or why not?
2. "Before we can 'do something' for the poor," Ehrenreich writes, "there are some things we need to stop doing *to* them" (p. 384). How do you understand this distinction? And what larger point is Ehrenreich trying to make by drawing this distinction here?
3. "I could propose," writes Ehrenreich, "all kinds of policies to curb the ongoing predation on the poor. Limits on usury should be reinstated. Theft should be taken seriously even when it's committed by millionaire employers. No one should be incarcerated for debt or squeezed for money they have no chance of getting their hands on" (p. 384). What do you think of the solutions Ehrenreich proposes here? Are they adequate responses to the problems she describes in this essay? Do you think they would make a substantial or meaningful difference? How or how not?

WRITING

4. "Being poor," writes Ehrenreich, "itself is not yet a crime, but in at least a third of the states, being in debt can now land you in jail. If a creditor like a landlord or credit card company has a court summons issued for you and you fail to show up on your appointed court date, a warrant will be issued for your arrest" (p. 382). In a short essay, respond to the scenario Ehrenreich lays out here. What larger argument about the challenges and injustices of "being poor" is she using this example to make? And do you find yourself convinced by the evidence she presents here? Why or why not?
5. Here is a partial list of the concepts Ehrenreich uses to describe the way employers, local governments, and creditors treat the working poor: *robbery*, *persecution*, *predatory*. In an essay, conduct a close reading of the language Ehrenreich uses. What picture of the plight confronting the working poor do these terms evoke? What critique of employers, government, and creditors does it imply? And how valid do you find this commentary?
6. Anthony DePalma (p. 353) is another writer who chronicles the challenges confronting the working poor. How does his profile of immigrant workers compare to Ehrenreich's discussion of the working poor? Based on the argument she makes here, which specific aspects of DePalma's essay do you think Ehrenreich would find most persuasive? Why?

Rule Maker >>>>>>>>> Rule Breaker

"*Give me a W!*
Give me an A!
Give me an L!
Give me a squiggly!
Give me an M!
Give me an A!
Give me an R!
Give me a T!
What's that spell?
Wal-Mart!
Whose Wal-Mart is it?
It's my Wal-Mart!
Who's number one?
The customer! Always!"

— THE WAL-MART CHEER

"*While Wal-Mart isn't the only big box store criticized for its policies, it has become a symbol for much of what is wrong with employers. Wal-Mart reported a net income of over $11 billion last year—surely plenty of money to remedy some questionable workplace practices—yet stories persist about wage law violations, inadequate health care, exploitation of workers, and the retailer's anti-union stance.*"

WORKPLACE FAIRNESS INSTITUTE, 2013

WAL-MART VS. WORKPLACE FAIRNESS INSTITUTE

How does the promise of work compare to the reality? Whether in television commercials or magazine spreads, Internet job sites or help-wanted ads, it is hardly a secret that virtually every job gets hyped in ways calculated to cast it in the best possible light. As many of us know from personal experience, however, sooner or later most such rosy predictions bump up against the kinds of pressures and limitations that these promotions rarely mention. We know, for example, that in the "real world" discrepancies in economic and educational background or barriers of race and class can drastically restrict the opportunities available to people looking for work. Or that when we actually find ourselves in a given job, the interests of employers and the rights of employees are not always in sync. Take, for instance, the controversy surrounding Wal-Mart's employment practices. While it may be commonplace for corporate boosters to describe their workforce as one big, happy family, it is also true that such feel-good language can serve to direct attention away from more serious and pressing discussions—about things like fair wages, hiring discrimination, or unionization. In this case, the gap between the promise and the reality suggests that we may need to rethink the ways we talk about work. Should we rewrite the scripts that teach us what to expect from our jobs? And if so, what would these new scripts look like?

FIND THE RULES: Make a list of the different expectations big retail companies like Wal-Mart have for their workers. What attitudes and behaviors are such workers expected to follow as the norm? Then write a paragraph in which you discuss the ways these expectations are being reinforced or challenged in the quotations above.

ANALYZE THE RULES: In a one-page essay, evaluate the attitudes toward the workplace this cheer scripts for the typical Wal-Mart employee. Are they reasonable attitudes to expect Wal-Mart workers to adopt? Do these attitudes serve the interests of the Wal-Mart corporation in any particular way? In your view, are these attitudes Wal-Mart workers should be encouraged to adopt? Why or why not?

MAKE YOUR OWN RULES: How do you think the Workplace Fairness Institute or others critical of Wal-Mart's employment practices would respond to the "Wal-Mart Cheer"? Rewrite the cheer to reflect such criticism of Wal-Mart, and write a brief response explaining why you rewrote the cheer the way you did.

JD Pooley/Getty Images

CATHERINE RAMPELL

A Generation of Slackers? Not So Much

According to popular myth, young people today rank among the most entitled, coddled, and laziest in history. But this cultural conceit, says Catherine Rampell, is more the result of generational misunderstanding than it is any accurate assessment of reality. Rebutting stereotypes about America's "slacker generation," Rampell sketches a portrait of work among "millennials" in which commitment, sacrifice, and ambition have not so much disappeared as taken on new forms. Rampell writes about economics for the *New York Times*, where she served as the founding editor of the Economix blog. She previously wrote for the *Washington Post* and the *Chronicle of Higher Education.* This article appeared in the *New York Times* in 2011.

YOU'D THINK THERE WOULD BE A LITTLE SYMPATHY. THIS MONTH, college graduates are jumping into the job market, only to land on their parents' couches: the unemployment rate for 16- to 24-year-olds is a whopping 17.6 percent.

The reaction from many older Americans? This generation had it coming.

Generation Y—or Millennials, the Facebook Generation, or whatever you want to call today's cohort of young people—has been accused of being the laziest generation ever. They feel entitled and are coddled, disrespectful, narcissistic, and impatient, say authors of books like *The Dumbest Generation* and *Generation Me*.

And three in four Americans believe that today's youth are less virtuous and industrious than their elders, a 2009 survey by the Pew Research Center found.

[M]any of the behaviors that older generations interpret as laziness may actually enhance young people's productivity.

In a sign of humility or docility, young people agree. In that 2009 Pew survey, two-thirds of millennials said older adults were superior to the younger generation when it came to moral values and work ethic.

After all, if there's a young person today who's walked 10 miles barefoot through the snow to school, it was probably on an iPhone app.

So is this the Laziest Generation? There are signs that its members benefit from lower standards. Technology has certainly made life easier. But there may also be a generation gap; the way young adults work is simply different.

It's worth remembering that to some extent, these accusations of laziness and narcissism in "kids these days" are nothing new—they've been leveled against Generation X, Baby Boomers, and many generations before them. Even Aristotle and Plato were said to have expressed similar feelings about the slacker youth of their times.

But this generation has had it easy in some ways.

They can access just about any resource, product, or service anywhere from a mere tap on a touch screen. And as many critics have noted, it's also easier to get A's. The typical grade-point average in college rose to about 3.11 by the middle of the last decade, from 2.52 in the 1950s, according to a recent study by Stuart Rojstaczer, professor emeritus at Duke, and Christopher Healy of Furman University.

College students also spend fewer hours studying each week than did their counterparts in 1961, according to a new working paper by Philip S. Babcock of the University of California, Santa Barbara, and Mindy Marks of the University of California, Riverside. That doesn't mean all this leftover time is spent on PlayStation 3's.

There is ample evidence that young people today are hard-working and productive. The share of college students working full time generally grew from 1985 onward—until the Great Recession knocked many millennials out of the labor force, according to the Labor Department.

And while many college students today—like those of yesterday—get financial help from their parents, 44 percent of students today say that work or personal savings helped finance their higher educations, according to a survey of recent graduates by Rutgers University.

"I don't think this is a generation of slackers," said Carl Van Horn, a labor economist at Rutgers. "This image of the kid who goes off and skis in Colorado, I don't think that's the correct image. Today's young people are very focused on trying to work hard and to get ahead."

It's worth remembering that to some extent, these accusations of laziness and narcissism in "kids these days" are nothing new. . . .Even Aristotle and Plato were said to have expressed similar feelings about the slacker youth of their times.

Defying the narcissism stereotype, community service among young people has exploded. Between 1989 and 2006, the share of teenagers who were volunteering doubled, to 26.4 percent from 13.4 percent, according to a report by the Corporation for National and Community Service. And the share of incoming college freshmen who say they plan to volunteer is at a record high of 32.1 percent, too, U.C.L.A.'s annual incoming freshman survey found.

Perhaps most important, many of the behaviors that older generations interpret as laziness may actually enhance young people's productivity, say researchers who study Generation Y.

Members of Gen Y, for example, are significantly more likely than Gen X'ers and boomers to say they are more productive working in teams than on their own, according to Don Tapscott, author of *Grown Up Digital: How the Net Generation is Changing Your World*, a book based on interviews with 11,000 millennials.

To older workers, wanting help looks like laziness; to younger workers, the gains that come from teamwork have been learned from the collaborative nature of their childhood activities, which included social networks, crowd-sourcing, and even video games like World of Warcraft that "emphasize cooperative rather than individual competition," Mr. Tapscott says.

Employers also complain about millennials checking Facebook and Twitter on the job, or working with their ear buds in.

Older workers have a strong sense of separate spheres for work and play: the cubicle is for work, and home is for fun. But to millennials, the boundaries between work and play are fuzzier, said Michael D. Hais, coauthor of *Millennial Makeover: MySpace, YouTube, and the Future of American Politics*.

Think of the corporate cultures at prototypical Gen Y employers like Facebook and Google, he says, where foosball, volleyball courts, and subsidized massages are office fixtures.

The prevailing millennial attitude is that taking breaks for fun at work makes people more, not less, productive. Likewise, they accept that their work will bleed into evenings and weekends.

Some experts also believe that today's young people are better at quickly switching from one task to another, given their exposure to so many stimuli during their childhood and adolescence, said John Della Volpe, the director of polling at Harvard's Institute of Politics. (The jury is still out on that one.)

Of course, these explanations may be unconvincing to older bosses, co-workers, and teachers on the other side of this culture clash. But at least they can take comfort in one fact: someday, millennials will have their own new generation of know-it-all ne'er-do-wells to deal with.

DISCUSSION

1. What do you make of the phrase "slacker generation"? What image does it conjure in your mind? And in your view, does it serve as an accurate descriptor for young people today?
2. As Rampell notes, "Accusations of laziness and narcissism in 'kids these days' are nothing new — they've been leveled against Generation X, Baby Boomers, and many generations before them" (p. 389). How important do you think this observation is? In your view, does it matter that there is historical precedent for today's attitude toward millennials? Does having this historical context give you a different way of thinking about the accusations leveled against young people today?
3. "In a sign of humility or docility," writes Rampell, "two-thirds of millennials said older adults were superior to the younger generation when it came to moral values and work ethic" (p. 388). If you were asked this same question in a poll, how would you respond? Do you share the majority view that there exists a measurable, generational difference where moral values and work ethic are concerned?

WRITING

4. Much of the pessimism directed toward younger workers these days, Rampell argues, stems from the fact that the norms around work have undergone such dramatic change. While older workers continue to define hard work in terms of such ideals as self-sufficiency and competition, younger workers subscribe to more contemporary values like teamwork and collaboration. Write an essay in which you evaluate the merits of this argument. What do you make of the distinction between older and younger workers Rampell draws here? Do you find her claim about the power of cultural norms to change personal attitudes toward work persuasive? How does this compare to your own view?
5. Rampell lists some of the skills and attitudes she believes young people bring to the workplace: a familiarity with working in teams; a willingness to blur the boundaries between work and play; a capacity to switch easily from one task to another. What do you make of this list? Do you think it itemizes a set of skills that are genuinely valuable? And how accurately does this list reflect your own workplace attitudes and skills? Can you cite an example from your own work experience that either confirms or challenges the accuracy of this list?
6. Mac McClelland (p. 394) is another writer who offers a portrait of young workers on the job. Her essay, however, paints a picture of workplace norms and employment pressures that is far different from the one presented by Catherine Rampell here. How do these two depictions of work compare? What are the key differences between them? And do you think McClelland's essay challenges or supports Rampell's thesis about the cultural misconceptions surrounding the so-called slacker generation?

Then and Now: **Dressing for Success**

The rules establishing proper workplace attire have changed markedly over the years. But are these changes merely cosmetic? Or do they tell us something about the ways our attitudes toward work, or perhaps even our social or cultural attitudes, have changed? To be sure, there is a long and storied history in America of treating workplace wardrobe as a kind of societal barometer. In the case of the 1950s office worker, for example, the "gray flannel suit" came to be widely viewed as a metaphor for the corporate standardization, political conformity, and social conservatism that for many defined American life during this period. For countless commentators, this unadorned and anonymous business uniform not only captured the supposedly faceless, robotic nature of 1950s office work, but it also symbolized a pervasive hostility in midcentury America toward individuality, creativity, and dissent.

When compared to the corporate dress codes that prevail today, it's hard not to feel we've come a long way from this buttoned-down, bygone era. Nowadays the drab uniformity of gray flannel has given way to the more flexible and informal wardrobe norms of so-called business casual — a shift, we are told, that proves how much more liberated, freewheeling, and

J. R. Eyerman/Time Life Pictures/Getty Images

creative office work has become. No longer the faceless drone of yore, the corporate employee of the twenty-first century (at least according to what we see in countless commercials) plies his or her trade in an environment where individuality and diversity are prized, a world in which employees are members of teams, professional colleagues are also personal friends, and creativity rather than conformity is the rule of thumb.

But is this actually true? Does this shift in dress code really prove how much more liberated office life — or life in general — has become? In answering this question, we might begin by pointing out a paradox: Despite its emphasis on nonconformity and individual choice, business casual is nonetheless still a *style*, a wardrobe standard established for and marketed to us. Just because we get to wear khakis and sandals to the office these days doesn't automatically mean we're now using clothes to express our individuality — particularly when we may well have gotten the idea for this outfit by paging through a clothing catalog. Even when an office wardrobe is informal, it isn't necessarily any less of an office uniform. What the rise of business casual may well demonstrate, in fact, is not how nonconformist modern American culture has become, but rather how the terms defining such conformity have simply changed. It certainly seems a stretch to claim that white-collar work is no longer hierarchical or rigidly organized, or that the contemporary business landscape has grown any less "corporate." Perhaps this shift toward casualness is best understood not as a movement beyond conformity but as a compensation for conformity: a style change designed to add a gloss of informality and autonomy to a work world still largely dictated by scripts we ourselves do not write.

© Larry Williams/Corbis

WRITING

1. Write an essay in which you analyze the norms about work being conveyed by the style of dress in these two examples. What, if anything, seems to have changed between the work dress in the 1950s versus today? In your opinion, which of these photographs seems more typical of the concepts of work and career? Why?
2. One of the most visible differences between white-collar and blue-collar work is the difference in dress. How do you think Anthony DePalma (p. 353) would respond to the idea of business-casual dress? In your opinion, does the idea of business casual highlight or diminish the differences between white- and blue-collar work? Why?

MAC MCCLELLAND

I Was a Warehouse Wage Slave

In the eyes of many pundits and commentators, the rise of online commerce has been a boon for companies and consumers alike. But what about all the anonymous workers who labor behind the scenes to make all of these dazzling new commercial opportunities possible? This is the question journalist Mac McClelland takes up here. Chronicling her experiences working as a "warehouse wage slave" for an online retailer order-fulfillment center, McClelland presents a portrait that dramatically challenges the feel-good narrative of life and work in the age of the Internet. McClelland is a human rights reporter for *Mother Jones* magazine. She is also the author of *For Us Surrender is Out of the Question: A Story from Burma's Never-Ending War* (2010). This article appeared in *Mother Jones* in 2012.

"DON'T TAKE ANYTHING THAT HAPPENS TO YOU THERE PERSONALLY," the woman at the local chamber of commerce says when I tell her that tomorrow I start working at "Amalgamated Product Giant Shipping Worldwide Inc." She winks at me. I stare at her for a second.

"*What?*" I ask. "Why, is somebody going to be mean to me or something?"

She smiles. "Oh, yeah." This town somewhere west of the Mississippi is not big; everyone knows someone or is someone who's worked for Amalgamated. "But look at it from their perspective. They need you to work as fast as possible to push out as much as they can as fast as they can. So they're gonna give you goals, and then you know what? If you make those goals, they're gonna increase the goals. But they'll be yelling at you all the time. It's like the military. They have to break you down so they can turn you into what they want you to be. So they're going to tell you, 'You're not good enough, you're not good enough, you're not good enough,' to make you work harder. Don't say, 'This is the best I can do.' Say, 'I'll try,' even if you know you can't do it. Because if you say, 'This is the best I can do,' they'll let you go. They hire and fire constantly, every day. You'll see people dropping all around you. But don't take it personally and break down or start crying when they yell at you."

Several months prior, I'd reported on an Ohio warehouse where workers shipped products for online retailers under conditions that were surprisingly demoralizing and dehumanizing, even to someone who's spent a lot of time working in warehouses, which I have. And then my editors sat me down. "We want you to go work for Amalgamated Product

Giant Shipping Worldwide Inc.," they said. I'd have to give my real name and job history when I applied, and I couldn't lie if asked for any specifics. (I wasn't.) But I'd smudge identifying details of people and the company itself. Anyway, to do otherwise might give people the impression that these conditions apply only to one warehouse or one company. Which they don't.

So I fretted about whether I'd have to abort the application process, like if someone asked me why I wanted the job. But no one did. And though I was kind of excited to trot out my warehouse experience, mainly all I needed to get hired was to confirm 20 or 30 times that I had not been to prison.

The application process took place at a staffing office in a run-down city, the kind where there are boarded-up businesses and broken windows downtown and billboards advertising things like "Foreclosure Fridays!" at a local law firm. Six or seven other people apply for jobs along with me. We answer questions at computers grouped in several stations. Have I ever been to prison? the system asks. No? Well, but have I ever been to prison for assault? Burglary? A felony? A misdemeanor? Raping someone? Murdering anybody? Am I sure? There's no point in lying, the computer warns me, because criminal-background checks are run on employees. Additionally, I have to confirm at the next computer station that I can read, by taking a multiple-choice test in which I'm given pictures of several album covers, including Michael Jackson's *Thriller*, and asked what the name of the Michael Jackson album is. At yet another set of computers I'm asked about my work history and character. How do I feel about dangerous activities? Would I say I'm not really into them? Or *really* into them?

I realize that for whatever relative youth and regular exercise and overachievement complexes I have brought to this job, I will never be able to keep up with the goals I've been given.

In the center of the room, a video plays loudly and continuously on a big screen. Even more than you are hurting the company, a voice-over intones as animated people do things like accidentally oversleep, you are hurting yourself when you are late because you will be penalized on a point system, and when you get too many points, you're fired—unless you're late at any point during your first week, in which case you are instantly fired. Also because when you're late or sick you miss the opportunity to maximize your overtime pay. And working more than eight hours is mandatory. Stretching is also mandatory, since you will either be standing still at a conveyor line for most of your minimum 10-hour shift or walking on concrete or metal stairs. And be careful, because you could seriously hurt yourself. And watch out, because some of your coworkers will be the kind of monsters who will file false workers' comp claims. If you know of someone doing this and you tell on him and he gets convicted, you will be rewarded with $500.

The computers screening us for suitability to pack boxes or paste labels belong to a temporary-staffing agency. The stuff we order from big online retailers lives in large warehouses, owned and operated either by the retailers themselves or by third-party logistics contractors, a.k.a. 3PLs. These companies often fulfill orders for more than one retailer out of a single warehouse. America's largest 3PL, Exel, has 86 million square feet of warehouse in North America; it's a subsidiary of Deutsche Post DHL, which is cute because Deutsche Post is the German post office, which was privatized in the 1990s and bought DHL in 2002, becoming one of the world's biggest corporate employers. The $31 billion "value-added warehousing and distribution" sector of 3PLs is just a fraction of what large 3PLs' parent companies pull in. UPS's logistics division, for example, pulls in more than a half a billion, but it feeds billions of dollars of business to UPS Inc.

Anyhow, regardless of whether the retailer itself or a 3PL contractor houses and processes the stuff you buy, the actual stuff is often handled by people working for yet another company—a temporary-staffing agency. The agency to which I apply is hiring 4,000 drones for this single Amalgamated warehouse between October and December. Four thousand. Before leaving the staffing office, I'm one of them.

I'm assigned a schedule of Sunday through Thursday, 7 a.m. to 5:30 p.m. When additional overtime is necessary, which it will be soon (Christmas!), I should expect to leave at 7 or 7:30 p.m. instead. Eight days after applying, i.e., after my drug test has cleared, I walk through a small, desolate town nearly an hour outside the city where I was hired. This is where the warehouse is, way out here, a long commute for many of my coworkers. I wander off the main road and into the chamber of commerce to kill some afternoon time—though not too much since my first day starts at 5 a.m.—but I end up getting useful job advice.

"Well, what if I do start crying?" I ask the woman who warns me to keep it together no matter how awfully I'm treated. "Are they really going to fire me for that?"

"Yes," she says. "There's 16 other people who want your job. Why would they keep a person who gets emotional, especially in this economy?"

Still, she advises, regardless of how much they push me, don't work so hard that I injure myself. I'm young. I have a long life ahead of me. It's not worth it to do permanent physical damage, she says, which, considering that I got hired at elevensomething dollars an hour, is a bit of an understatement.

As the sun gets lower in the curt November sky, I thank the woman for her help. When I start toward the door, she repeats her "No. 1 rule of survival" one more time.

"Leave your pride and your personal life at the door." If there's any way I'm going to last, she says, tomorrow I have to start pretending like I don't have either.

Though it's inconvenient for most employees, the rural location of the Amalgamated Product Giant Shipping Worldwide Inc. warehouse isn't an accident. The town is bisected by a primary interstate, close to a busy airport, serviced by several major highways. There's a lot of rail out here. The town became a station stop on the way to more important places a hundred years ago, and it now feeds part of the massive transit networks used to get consumers anywhere goods from everywhere. Every now and then, a long line of railcars rolls past my hotel and gives my room a good shake. I don't ever get a good look at them, because it's dark outside when I go to work, and dark again when I get back.

"Leave your pride and your personal life at the door." If there's any way I'm going to last, she says, tomorrow I have to start pretending like I don't have either.

Inside Amalgamated, an employee's first day is training day. Though we're not paid to be here until 6, we have been informed that we need to arrive at 5. If we don't show up in time to stand around while they sort out who we are and where they've put our ID badges, we could miss the beginning of training, which would mean termination. "I was up half the night because I was so afraid I was going to be late," a woman in her 60s tells me. I was, too. A minute's tardiness after the first week earns us 0.5 penalty points, an hour's tardiness is worth 1 point, and an absence 1.5; 6 is the number that equals "release." But during the first week even a minute's tardiness gets us fired. When we get lined up so we can be counted a third or fourth time, the woman conducting the roll call recognizes the last name of a young trainee. "Does your dad work here? Or uncle?" she asks. "Grandpa," he says, as another supervisor snaps at the same time, sounding not mean but very stressed out, "We gotta get goin' here."

The culture is intense, an Amalgamated higher-up acknowledges at the beginning of our training. He's speaking to us from a video, one of several videos—about company policies, sexual harassment, etc.—that we watch while we try to keep our eyes open. We don't *want* to be so intense, the higher-up says. But our customers demand it. We are surrounded by signs that state our productivity goals. Other signs proclaim that a good customer experience, to which our goal-meeting is essential, is the key to growth, and growth is the key to lower prices, which leads to a better customer experience. There is no room for inefficiencies. The gal conducting our training reminds us again that we cannot miss any days our first week. There are *NO* exceptions to this policy. She says to take Brian, for example, who's here with us in training today. Brian already went through this training, but then during his first week his lady had a baby, so he missed a day and he had to be fired. Having to start the application process over could cost a brand-new dad like Brian a couple of weeks' worth of work and pay. Okay? Everybody turn around and look at Brian. Welcome back, Brian. Don't end up like Brian.

Soon, we move on to practical training. Like all workplaces with automated and heavy machinery, this one contains plenty of ways to get hurt, and they are enumerated. There are transition points in the warehouse floor where the footing is uneven, and people trip and sprain ankles. Give forklifts that are raised up several stories to access products a wide berth: "If a pallet falls on you, you won't be working with us anymore." Watch your fingers around the conveyor belts that run waist-high throughout the entire facility. People lose fingers. Or parts of fingers. And about once a year, they tell us, someone in an Amalgamated warehouse gets caught by the hair, and when a conveyor belt catches you by the hair, it doesn't just take your hair with it. It rips out a piece of scalp as well.

If the primary message of one-half of our practical training is Be Careful, the takeaway of the other half is Move As Fast As Humanly Possible. Or superhumanly possible. I have been hired as a picker, which means my job is to find, scan, place in a plastic tote, and send away via conveyor whatever item within the multiple stories of this several-hundred-thousand-square-foot warehouse my scanner tells me to. We are broken into groups and taught how to read the scanner to find the object among some practice shelves. Then we immediately move on to practicing doing it faster, racing each other to fill the orders our scanners dictate, then racing each other to put all the items back.

"Hurry up," a trainer encourages me when he sees me pulling ahead of the others, "and you can put the other items back!" I roll my eyes that my reward for doing a good job is that I get to do more work, but he's got my number: I am exactly the kind of freak this sort of motivation appeals to. I win, and set myself on my prize of the bonus errand.

That afternoon, we are turned loose in the warehouse, scanners in hand. And that's when I realize that for whatever relative youth and regular exercise and overachievement complexes I have brought to this job, I will never be able to keep up with the goals I've been given.

The place is immense. Cold, cavernous. Silent, despite thousands of people quietly doing their picking, or standing along the conveyors quietly packing or box-taping, nothing noisy but the occasional whir of a passing forklift. My scanner tells me in what exact section—there are nine merchandise sections, so sprawling that there's a map attached to my ID badge—of vast shelving systems the item I'm supposed to find resides. It also tells me how many seconds it thinks I should take to get there. Dallas sector, section yellow, row H34, bin 22, level D: wearable blanket. Battery-operated flour sifter. Twenty seconds. I count how many steps it takes me to speed-walk to my destination: 20. At 5-foot-9, I've got a decently long stride, and I only cover the 20 steps *and* locate the exact shelving unit in the allotted time if I don't hesitate for one second or get lost or take a drink of water before heading in the right direction as fast as I can walk or even occasionally jog. Olive-oil mister. Male libido enhancement pills. Rifle strap. Who the fuck buys their paper towels off the internet? Fairy calendar. Neoprene lunch bag. Often as not, I miss my time target.

Plenty of things can hurt my goals. The programs for our scanners are designed with the assumption that we disposable employees don't know what we're doing. Find a Rob Zombie Voodoo Doll in the blue section of the Rockies sector in the third bin of the A-level in row Z42, my scanner tells me. But if I punch into my scanner that it's not there, I have to prove it by scanning every single other item in the bin, though I swear on my life there's no Rob Zombie Voodoo Doll in this pile of 30 individually wrapped and bar-coded batteries that take me quite a while to beep one by one. It could be five minutes before I can move on to, and make it to, and find, my next item. That lapse is supposed to be mere seconds.

This week, we newbies need to make 75 percent of our total picking-volume targets. If we don't, we get "counseled." If the people in here who've been around longer than a few weeks don't make their 100 percent, they get counseled. *Why* aren't you making your targets? the supervisors will ask. You *really* need to make your targets.

From the temp agency, Amalgamated has ordered the exact number of humans it should take to fill this week's orders if we work at top capacity. Lots of retailers use temporary help in peak season, and online ones are no exception. But lots of warehousing and distribution centers like this also use temps year-round. The Bureau of Labor Statistics found that more than 15 percent of pickers, packers, movers, and unloaders are temps. They make $3 less an hour on average than permanent workers. And they can be "temporary" for years. There are so many temps in this warehouse that the staffing agency has its own office here. Industry consultants describe the temp-staffing business as "very, very busy." "On fire." Maximizing profits means making sure no employee has

If the primary message of one-half of our practical training is Be Careful, the takeaway of the other half is Move As Fast As Humanly Possible.

a slow day, means having only as many employees as are necessary to get the job done, the number of which can be determined and ordered from a huge pool of on-demand labor literally by the day. Often, temp workers have to call in before shifts to see if they'll get work. Sometimes, they're paid piece rate, according to the number of units they fill or unload or move. Always, they can be let go in an instant, and replaced just as quickly.

Everyone in here is hustling. At the announcement to take one of our two 15-minute breaks, we hustle even harder. We pickers close out the totes we're currently filling and send them away on the conveyor belt, then make our way as fast as we can with the rest of the masses across the long haul of concrete between wherever we are and the break room, but not before passing through metal detectors, for which there is a line—we're required to be screened on our way out, though not on our way in; apparently the concern is that we're sneaking Xbox 360s up under our shirts, not bringing in weapons. If we *don't* set off the metal detector and have to be taken aside and searched, we can run into the break room and try to find a seat among the rows and rows and long-ass rows of tables. We lose more time if we want to pee—and I do want to pee, and when amid the panic about the time constraints it occurs to me that I don't have my period I toss a fist victoriously into the air—between the actual peeing and the waiting in line to pee in the nearest one of the two bathrooms, which has eight stalls in the ladies' and I'm not sure how many in the men's and serves thousands of people a day. Once I pare this process down as much as possible, by stringing a necktie through my belt loops because I can't find a metal-less replacement for my belt at the local Walmart—and if my underwear or butt-crack slips out, I've been warned, I can get penalized—and by leaving my car keys in the break room after a manager helps me find an admittedly "still risky" hiding place for them because we have no lockers and "things get stolen out of here all the time," I get myself up to seven minutes' worth of break time to inhale as many high-fat and -protein snacks as I can. People who work at Amalgamated are always working this fast. Right now, because it's almost Black Friday, there are just more of us doing it.

Then as quickly as we've come, we all run back. At the end of the 15 minutes, we're supposed to be back at whichever far-flung corner of the warehouse we came from, scanners in hand, working. We run to grab the wheeled carts we put the totes on. We run past each other and if we do say something, we say it as we keep moving. "How's the job market?" a supervisor says, laughing, as several of us newbies run by. "Just kidding!" Ha ha! "I know why you guys are here. That's why I'm here, too!" At another near collision between employees, one wants to know how complaining about not being able to get time off went and the other spits that he was told he was lucky to *have* a job. This is no way to have a conversation, but at least conversations are not forbidden, as they were in the Ohio warehouse I reported on—where I saw a guy get fired for talking, specifically for asking another employee, "Where are you from?" So I'm allowed the extravagance of smiling at a guy who is always so unhappy and saying, "How's it goin'?" And he can respond, "Terrible," as I'm running to the big industrial cage-lift that takes our carts up to the second or third floors, which involves walking under a big metal bar gating the front of it, and which I should really take my time around. Within the last month, three different people have needed stitches in the head after being clocked by these big metal bars, so it's dangerous. Especially the lift in the Dallas sector, whose bar has been installed wrong, so it is extra prone to falling, they tell us. Be careful. Seriously, though. We really need to meet our goals here.

At lunch, the most common question is "Why are you here?" like in prison.

Amalgamated has estimated that we pickers speed-walk an average of 12 miles a day on cold concrete, and the twinge in my legs blurs into the heavy soreness in my feet that complements the pinch in my hips when I crouch to the floor—the pickers' shelving runs from the floor to seven feet high or so—to retrieve an iPad protective case. iPad anti-glare protector. iPad one-hand grip-holder device. Thing that looks like a land-line phone handset that plugs into your iPad so you can pretend that rather than talking via iPad you are talking on a phone.

I've started cringing every time my scanner shows a code that means the item I need to pick is on the ground, which, in the course of a 10.5-hour shift—much less the mandatory 12-hour shifts everyone is slated to start working next week—is literally hundreds of times a day. "How has OSHA signed off on this?" I've taken to muttering to myself. "*Has* OSHA signed off on this?" ("The thing about ergonomics," OSHA says when I call them later to ask, "is that OSHA doesn't have a standard. Best practices. But no laws.")

At lunch, the most common question is "Why are you here?" like in prison. A guy in his mid-20s says he's from Chicago, came to this state for a full-time job in the city an hour away from here because "Chicago's going down." His other job doesn't pay especially well, so he's here—pulling 10.5-hour shifts and commuting two hours a day—anytime he's not there. One guy says he's a writer; he applies for grants in his time off from the warehouse. A middle-aged lady near me used to be a bookkeeper. She's a peak-season hire, worked here last year during Christmas, too. "What do you do the rest of the year?" I ask. "Collect unemployment!" she says, and laughs the sad laugh you laugh when you're saying something really unfunny. All around us in the break room, mothers frantically call home. "Hi, baby!" you can hear them say; coos to children echo around the walls the moment lunch begins. It's brave of these women to keep their phones in the break room, where theft is so high—they can't keep them in their cars if they want to use them during the day, because we aren't supposed to leave the premises without permission, and they can't take them onto the warehouse floor, because "nothing but the clothes on your backs" is allowed on the warehouse floor (*anything* on your person that Amalgamated sells can be confiscated—"And what does Amalgamated sell?" they asked us in training. "Everything!"). I suppose that if I were responsible for a child, I would have no choice but to risk leaving my phone in here, too. But the mothers make it quick. "How are you doing?" "Is everything okay?" "Did you eat something?" "I love you!" and then they're off the phone and eating as fast as the rest of us. Lunch is 29 minutes and 59 seconds—we've been reminded of this: "Lunch is *not* 30 minutes and 1 second"—that's a penalty-point-earning offense—and that includes the time to get through the metal detectors and use the disgustingly overcrowded bathroom—the suggestion board hosts several pleas that someone do something about that smell—and time to stand in line to clock out and back in. So we chew quickly, and are often still chewing as we run back to our stations.

The days blend into each other. But it's near the end of my third day that I get written up. I sent two of some product down the conveyor line when my scanner was only asking for one; the product was boxed in twos, so I should've opened the box and separated them, but I didn't notice because I was in a hurry. With an hour left in the day, I've already picked 800 items. Despite moving fast enough to get sloppy, my scanner tells me that means I'm fulfilling only 52 percent of my goal. A supervisor who is a genuinely nice person comes by with a clipboard listing my numbers. Like the rest of the supervisors, she tries to create a friendly work environment and doesn't want to enforce the policies that make this job so unpleasant. But her hands are tied. She needs this job, too, so she has no choice but to tell me something I have never been told in 19 years of school or at any of some dozen workplaces. "You're doing really bad," she says.

I'll admit that I did start crying a little. Not at work, thankfully, since that's evidently frowned upon, but later, when I explained to someone over Skype that it hurts, oh, how my body hurts after failing to make my goals despite speed-walking or flat-out jogging and pausing every 20 or 30 seconds to reach on my tiptoes or bend or drop to the floor for 10.5 hours, and isn't it awful that they fired Brian because he had a baby, and, in fact, when I was hired I signed off on something acknowledging that anyone who leaves without at least a week's notice—whether because they're a journalist who will just walk off or because they miss a day for having a baby and are terminated—has their hours paid out not at their hired rate but at the legal minimum. Which in this state, like in lots of states, is about $7 an hour. Thank God that I (unlike Brian, probably) didn't need to pay for opting into Amalgamated's "limited" health insurance program. Because in my 10.5-hour day I'll make about $60 after taxes.

"This is America?" my Skype pal asks, because often I'm abroad.

Indeed, and I'm working for a gigantic, immensely profitable company. Or for the staffing company that works for that company, anyway. Which is a nice arrangement, because temporary-staffing agencies keep the stink of unacceptable labor conditions off the companies whose names you know. When temps working at a Walmart warehouse sued for not getting paid for all their hours, and for then getting sent home without pay for complaining, Walmart—not technically their employer—wasn't named as a defendant. (Though Amazon has been named in a similar suit.) Temporary staffers aren't legally entitled to decent health care because they are just short-term "contractors" no matter how long they keep the same job. They aren't entitled to raises, either, and they don't get vacation and they'd have a hell of a time unionizing and they don't have the privilege of knowing if they'll have work on a particular day or for how long they'll have a job. And that is how you slash prices and deliver products superfast and offer free shipping and still post profits in the millions or billions.

Temporary staffers aren't legally entitled to decent health care because they are just short-term "contractors" no matter how long they keep the same job.

"This really doesn't have to be this awful," I shake my head over Skype. But it is. And this job is just about the only game in town, like it is in lots of towns, and eventually will be in more towns, with US internet retail sales projected to grow 10 percent every year to $279 billion in 2015 and with Amazon, the largest of the online retailers, seeing revenues rise 30 to 40 percent year after year and already having 69 giant warehouses, 17 of which came online in 2011 alone. So butch up, Sally.

"You look way too happy," an Amalgamated supervisor says to me. He has appeared next to me as I work, and in the silence of the vast warehouse, his presence catches me by surprise. His comment, even more so.

"Really?" I ask.

I don't really *feel* happy. By the fourth morning that I drag myself out of bed long before dawn, my self-pity has turned into actual concern. There's a screaming pain running across the back of my shoulders. "You need to take 800 milligrams of Advil a day," a woman in her late 50s or early 60s advised me when we all congregated in the break room before work. When I arrived, I stashed my lunch on a bottom ledge of the cheap metal shelving lining the break room walls, then hesitated before walking away. I cursed myself. I forgot something in the bag, but there was no way to get at it without crouching or bending over, and any extra times of doing that today were times I couldn't really afford. The unhappy-looking guy I always make a point of smiling at told me, as we were hustling to our stations, that this is actually the second time he's worked here: A few weeks back he missed some time for doctors' appointments when his arthritis flared up, and though he had notes for the absences, he was fired; he had to start the application process over again, which cost him an extra week and a half of work. "Zoom zoom! Pick it up! Pickers' pace, guys!" we were prodded this morning. Since we already felt like we were moving pretty fast, I'm quite dispirited, in fact.

"*Really?*" I ask.

"Well," the supervisor qualifies. "Just everybody else is usually really sad or mad by the time they've been working here this long."

It's my 28th hour as an employee.

I probably look happier than I should because I have the extreme luxury of not giving a shit about keeping this job. Nevertheless, I'm tearing around my assigned sector hard enough to keep myself consistently light-headed and a little out of breath. I'm working in books today. "Oh," I smiled to myself when I reached the paper-packed shelves. I love being around books.

Picking books for Amalgamated has a disadvantage over picking baby food or Barbies, however, in that the shelving numbers don't always line up. When my scanner tells me the book I need is on the lowest level in section 28 of a row, section 28 of the eye-level shelf of that row may or may not line up with section 28 of the lowest level. So when I spot eye-level section 28 and squat or kneel on the floor, the section 28 I'm looking for might be five feet to my right or left. Which means I have to stand up and crouch back down again to get there, greatly increasing the number of times I need to stand and crouch/kneel in a day. Or I can crawl. Usually, I crawl. A coworker is choosing the crouch/kneel option. "This gets so tiring after a while," he says when we pass each other. He's 20. It's 9:07 a.m.

There are other disadvantages to working in books. In the summer, it's the heat. Lots of the volumes are stored on the second and third floors of this immense cement box; the job descriptions we had to sign off on acknowledged that temperatures can be as low as 60 and higher than 95 degrees, and higher floors tend to be hotter. "They had to get fans because in the summer people were dying in here," one of the supervisors tells us. The fans still blow now even though I'm wearing five shirts. "If you think it's cold in *here*," one of my coworkers told me when she saw me rubbing my arms for warmth one morning, "just hope we don't have a fire drill." They evacuated everyone for one recently, and lots of the fast-moving employees had stripped down to T-shirts. They stood outside, masses of them, shivering for an hour as snow fell on their bare arms.

In the books sector, in the cold, in the winter dryness, made worse by the fans and all the paper, I jet across the floor in my rubber-soled Adidas, pant legs whooshing against each other, 30 seconds according to my scanner to take 35 steps to get to the right section and row and bin and level and reach for *Diary of a Wimpy Kid* and a hot spark shoots between my hand and the metal shelving. It's not the light static-electric prick I would terrorize my sister with when we got bored in carpeted department stores, but a solid shock, striking enough to make my body learn to fear it. I start inadvertently hesitating every time I approach my target. One of my coworkers races up to a shelving unit and leans in with the top of his body first; his head touches the metal, and the shock knocks him back. "Be careful of your head," he says to me. In the first two hours of my day, I pick 300 items. The majority of them zap me painfully.

"Please tell me you have suggestions for dealing with the static electricity," I say to a person in charge when the morning break comes. This conversation is going to cost me a couple of my precious few minutes to eat/drink/pee, but I've started to get paranoid that maybe it's not good for my body to exchange an electric charge with metal several hundred times in one day.

"Oh, are you workin' in books?"

"Yeah."

"No. Sorry." She means this. I feel bad for the supervisors who are trying their damnedest to help us succeed and not be miserable. "They've done everything they can"—"they" are not aware, it would appear, that anti-static coating and matting exist—"to ground things up there but there's nothing you can do."

I produce a deep frown. But even if she did have suggestions, I probably wouldn't have time to implement them. One suggestion for minimizing work-related pain and strain is to get a stepladder to retrieve any items on shelves above your head rather than getting up on your toes and overreaching. But grabbing one of the stepladders stashed few and far between among the rows of merchandise takes time. Another is to alternate the hand you use to hold and wield your cumbersome scanner. "You'll feel carpal tunnel start to set in," one of the supervisors told me, "so you'll want to change hands." But that, too, he admitted, costs time, since you have to hit the bar code at just the right angle for it to scan, and your dominant hand is way more likely to nail it the first time. Time is not a thing I have to spare. I'm still only at 57 percent of my goal. It's been 10 years since I was a mover and packer for a moving company, and only slightly less since I worked ridiculously long hours as a waitress and housecleaner. My back and knees were younger then, but I'm only 31 and feel pretty confident that if I were doing those jobs again I'd still wake up with soreness like a person who'd worked out too much, not the soreness of a person whose body was staging a revolt. I can break into goal-meeting suicide pace for short bouts, sure, but I can't keep it up for 10.5 hours.

"Do not say that," one of the workampers tells me at break. Workampers are people who drive RVs around the country, from temporary job to temporary job, docking in trailer camps. "We're retired but we can't . . ." another explains to me about himself and his wife, shrugging, "*make* it. And there's no jobs, so we go where the jobs are."

Amalgamated advertises positions on websites workampers frequent. In this warehouse alone, there are hundreds of them.

"Never say that you can't do it," the first workamper emphasizes. "When they ask you why you aren't reaching your goals—"

"Say, 'It's because they're totally unreasonable'?" I suggest.

"Say you'll do better, even if you know you can't," she continues, ignoring me. "Say you'll try harder, even if the truth is that you're trying your absolute hardest right now, no matter how many times they tell you you're not doing good enough."

There *are* people who make the goals. One of the trainers does. She works here all year, not just during Christmas. "I hated picking for the first month," she told me sympathetically the other day. "Then you just get used to it." She's one of many hardcore workers here, a labor pool studded with dedicated and solid employees. One of the permanent employees has tried to encourage me by explaining that he *always* makes his goals, and sometimes makes 120 percent of them. When I ask him if that isn't totally exhausting, he says, "Oh yeah. You're gonna be crying for your mommy when today's over." When I ask him if there's any sort of incentive for his overperformance, if he's rewarded in any way, he says occasionally Amalgamated enters him in drawings for company gift cards. For $15 or $20. He shrugs when he admits the size of the bonus. "These days you need it." Anyway, he says, he thinks it's important to have a good attitude and try to do a good job. Even some of the employees who are total failures are still trying really hard. "I heard you're doing good," one of the ladies in my training group says to me. Her eyebrows are heavy with stress. I am still hitting less than 60 percent of my target. Still, that's better than she's doing. "Congratulations," she says, and smiles sadly.

We will be fired if we say we just can't or won't get better, the workamper tells me. But so long as I resign myself to hearing how inadequate I am on a regular basis, I can keep this job. "Do you think this job has to be this terrible?" I ask the workamper.

"Oh, no," she says, and makes a face at me like I've asked a stupid question, which I have. As if Amalgamated couldn't bear to lose a fraction of a percent of profits by employing a few more than the absolute minimum of bodies they have to, or by storing the merchandise at halfway ergonomic heights and angles. But that would cost space, and space costs money, and money is not a thing customers could possibly be expected to hand over for this service without huffily taking their business elsewhere. Charging for shipping does cause high abandonment rates of online orders, though it's not clear whether people wouldn't pay a few bucks for shipping, or a bit more for the products, if they were guaranteed that no low-income workers would be tortured or exploited in the handling of their purchases.

"The first step is awareness," an e-commerce specialist will tell me later. There have been trickles of information leaking out of the Internet Order Fulfillment Industrial Complex: an investigation by the Allentown, Pennsylvania, *Morning Call* in which Amazon workers complained of fainting in stifling heat, being disciplined for getting heat exhaustion, and otherwise being "treated like a piece of crap"; a workampers' blog picked up by *Gizmodo*; a *Huffington Post* exposé about the lasting physical damage and wild economic instability temporary warehouse staffers suffer. And workers have filed lawsuits against online retailers, their logistics companies, and their temp agencies over off-the-clock work and other compensation issues, as well as at least one that details working conditions that are all too similar. (That case has been dismissed but is on appeal.) Still, most people really don't know how most internet goods get to them. The e-commerce specialist didn't even know, and she was in charge of choosing the 3PL for her midsize online-retail company. "These decisions are made at a business level and are based on cost," she says. "I never, ever thought about what they're like and how they treat people. Fulfillment centers want to keep clients blissfully ignorant of their conditions." If you called major clothing retailers, she ventured, and asked them "what it was like at the warehouse that ships their sweaters, no one at company headquarters would have any fucking clue."

Further, she said, now that I mentioned it, she has no idea how to go about getting any information on the conditions at the 3PL she herself hired. Nor how to find a responsible one. "A standard has to be created. Like fair trade or organic certification, where social good is built into the cost. There is a segment of the population"—like the consumers of her company's higher-end product, she felt—"that cares and will pay for it."

If they are aware how inhumane the reality is. But awareness has a long way to go, and logistics doesn't just mean online retail; food packagers and processors, medical suppliers, and factories use mega-3PLs as well. And a whole lot of other industries—hotels, call centers—take advantage of the price controls and plausible deniability that temporary staffing offers.

"Maybe awareness will lead to better working conditions," says Vinod Singhal, a professor of operations management at Georgia Tech. "But . . ." Given the state of the economy, he isn't optimistic.

This is the kind of resignation many of my coworkers have been forced to accept. At the end of break, the workamper and I are starting to fast-walk back to our stations. A guy who's been listening to our conversation butts in. "They can take you for everything you've got," he says. "They know it's your last resort."

At today's pickers' meeting, we are reminded that customers are waiting. We *cannot* move at a "comfortable pace," because if we are comfortable, we will never make our numbers, and customers are not willing to wait. And it's Christmastime. We got 2.7 million orders this week. People need—*need*—these items and they need them right now. So even if you've worked here long enough to be granted time off, you are not allowed to use it until the holidays are over. (And also forget about Election Day, which is today. "What if I want to vote?" I ask a supervisor. "I think you should!" he says. "But if I leave I'll get fired," I say. To which he makes a sad face before saying, "Yeah.") No time off includes those of you who are scheduled to work Thanksgiving. There are two Amalgamated-catered Thanksgiving dinners offered to employees next week, but you can only go to one of them. If you attend one, your employee badge will be branded with a nonremovable sticker so that you cannot also attempt to eat at the other. Anyway, good luck, everybody. Everybody back to work. Quickly!

Speed-walking back to the electro-trauma of the books sector, I wince when I unintentionally imagine the types of Christmas lore that will prevail around my future household. I feel genuinely sorry for any child I might have who ever asks me for anything for Christmas, only to be informed that every time a "Place Order" button rings, a poor person takes four Advil and gets told they suck at their job.

I suppose this is what they were talking about in the radio ad I heard on the way to work, the one that was paid for by a coalition of local businesses, gently begging citizens to buy from them instead of off the internet and warning about the importance of supporting local shops. But if my coworker Brian wants to feed his new baby any of these 24-packs of Plum Organics Apple & Carrot baby food I've been picking, he should probably buy them from Amazon, where they cost only $31.16. In my locally owned grocery store, that's $47.76 worth of sustenance. Even if he finds the time to get in the car to go buy it at a brick-and-mortar Target, where it'd be less convenient but cost about the same as on Amazon, that'd be before sales tax, which physical stores, unlike Amazon, are legally required to charge to help pay for the roads on which Brian's truck, and more to the point Amazon's trucks, drive.

Back in books, I take a sharp shock to my right hand when I grab the book the scanner cramping my left hand demands me to and make some self-righteous promises to myself about continuing to buy food at my more-expensive grocery store, because I can. Because I'm not actually a person who makes $7.25 an hour, not anymore, not one of the 1 in 3 Americans who is now poor or "near poor." For the moment, I'm just playing one.

"Lucky girl," I whisper to myself at the tail of a deep breath, as soon as fresh winter air hits my lungs. It's only lunchtime, but I've breached the warehouse doors without permission. I've picked 500 items this morning, and don't want to get shocked anymore, or hear from the guy with the clipboard what a total disappointment I am. "Lucky girl, lucky girl, lucky girl," I repeat on my way to my car. I told the lady from my training group who's so stressed about her poor performance to tell our supervisor not to look for me—and she grabbed my arm as I turned to leave, looking even more worried than usual, asking if I was sure I knew what I was doing. I don't want our supervisor to waste any time; he's got goals to make, too. He won't miss me, and nobody else will, either. The temp agency is certainly as full of applicants as it was when I went to ask for a job.

"Just look around in here if you wanna see how bad it is out there," one of the associates at the temp office said to me, unprompted, when I got hired. It's the first time anyone has ever tried to comfort me *because* I got a job, because he knew, and everyone in this industry that's growing wildfire fast knows, and accepts, that its model by design is mean. He offered me the same kind of solidarity the workers inside the warehouse try to provide each other at every break: *Why are you here? What happened that you have to let people treat you like this?* "We're all in the same boat," he said, after shaking my hand to welcome me aboard. "It's a *really* big boat."

DISCUSSION

1. What do you make of the phrase "wage slave"? What does the conjunction of these two terms suggest about the larger argument McClelland is trying to make here?
2. "I feel genuinely sorry," McClelland writes, "for any child I might have who ever asks me for anything for Christmas, only to be informed that every time a 'Place Order' button rings, a poor person takes four Advil and gets told they suck at their job" (p. 408). What point is she trying to make here? What kind of connection is she suggesting exists between the customer who places an online order and the worker who labors to fill this order?
3. The number-one piece of advice McClelland receives upon being hired is: "Leave your pride and your personal life at the door" (p. 397). To what extent does this advice capture the broader critique McClelland is advancing here? In what ways does this kind of job strip workers of their "personal" or human qualities?

WRITING

4. Much of McClelland's critique of warehouse work involves detailing her attempts to follow her employers' draconian rules about efficient time management. "At the end of the 15 minutes, we're supposed to be back at whichever far-flung corner of the warehouse we came from, scanners in hand, working. We run to grab the wheeled carts we put the totes on. We run past each other and if we do say something, we say it as we keep moving" (p. 400). In an essay, identify and analyze the specific critique this passage is designed to convey. To what aspects of warehouse work does a description like this draw your attention? And what sort of criticism of this work does it ask you to consider?
5. Near the end of the essay, McClelland identifies what she believes is the fundamental question underlying all of her interactions with her coworkers: "*Why are you here? What happened that you have to let people treat you like this?*" (p. 409). Based on the portrait of "wage slave" work she presents here, how do you think McClelland would answer her own question? According to this essay, what are some of the key factors that compel workers to seek and keep this kind of job? Do you find this explanation persuasive? Why or why not?
6. McClelland not only chronicles the physical toll warehouse work can exact; she examines the psychological toll as well. How does her account of the psychological pressures she experienced on the job compare to the portrait of the unemployed Louis Uchitelle (p. 342) presents? Do you find any similarities or parallels in the ways each essay explores this issue?

ASHLEY NELSON

Confessions of a Stay-at-Home Mom

The airwaves have been filled lately with advice enjoining working mothers to "lean in": that is, to share their stories and pool their resources in order to find new and creative ways to remain active and productive in their professional lives. But does this advice reflect a genuine understanding of the challenges and pitfalls working women face when they choose to take a leave from the professional ranks and care for their family? Ashley Nelson suspects that it doesn't, and she asks some pointed questions in this essay about the hard choices working moms really face. Nelson writes on women, politics, and culture for the *New York Times*, the *Guardian*, and the *Washington Post.* This essay appeared in the *Nation* in 2013.

A YEAR AFTER I QUIT MY JOB TO STAY HOME WITH MY FIRST CHILD, I read Linda Hirshman's *Get to Work* (2006), which chided well-educated women for doing just that. Why, she wondered, would a congressman "listen to someone whose life so resembles that of a toddler's?" Although my daughter was napping on me, I still managed to scrawl in the margins, "Because they vote!" I was her target audience, and I felt under attack.

Since then, similar books have followed, notably Leslie Bennetts's *The Feminine Mistake* (2007) and Sheryl Sandberg's *Lean In*, published this year. While Sandberg pays more lip service to the hard work stay-at-home mothers do, her thesis is largely the same as that of her predecessors. She is quick to point out the risks of taking time off. "Women who take time out of the workforce," she warns, "pay a big career penalty. Only 74 percent of professional women will rejoin the workforce in any capacity, and only 40 percent will return to full-time jobs. Those who do rejoin will often see their earnings decrease dramatically."

Although her argument was familiar, the unease Sandberg's book brought me was distinctly different from that caused by either Hirshman's or Bennetts's. Or perhaps I was just different. Older. The truth was, I hadn't followed Sandberg's advice. Career-wise, I leaned out when I should have leaned in. I anticipated children before I had them. When they did arrive, I scaled back my work. And recently I've been feeling some regret about that.

I was not the likeliest candidate for this position. Before I had kids, I wrote a master's thesis on the importance of women's economic independence. I wrote articles on feminism and getting women to the top. In other words, I knew this stuff. But I also knew that shortly after giving birth, I'd be moving to another city. My husband was finishing up his PhD, and there were no local positions in his field. So I left my job, figuring I could freelance while the baby napped.

I leaned out when I should have leaned in.

Rookie mistake.

I hired a sitter, but for a time my work took a back seat to life. We moved and, two years later, moved again so my husband could take a job overseas. A second daughter arrived. Then, shortly after, I found myself in a situation I never predicted: sitting across from a divorce lawyer who didn't even bother writing down my annual freelance income. I had published well and often, but my compensation was less robust. It would barely have covered a month of her costs.

I spent the next year or two beating myself up. I had, after all, made a choice of sorts. Though divorce is common, I never anticipated it, or the vulnerability even an amicable one could inspire. So, now more than ever, I get Sandberg's point, often echoed by some on the left, who remind women that despite feminism's emphasis on choice, not all choices are equal.

And yet lately I've come to believe that there is more to this story, especially given that nearly every mother I know who scaled back or quit work to care for children feels a similar anxiety about what the decision has cost her. Like myself, most never felt they were relinquishing their "work selves" completely, just momentarily turning down the tap. Many do some work, but it feels supplemental and underpaid. The climb back into full-time employment seems monumental. "I'll be 40 next year, with a PhD—I will not be an intern," my friend recently vented, with perhaps a few expletives.

The tone is melancholy, but laced with frustration and anger. After all, we hadn't spent our time home doing nothing. Children don't raise themselves, and for various reasons, usually economic and personal, we decided to devote ourselves primarily to this task, at least for a time.

And yet, while we are hardly alone—more than a third of mothers lean back from the workforce for an average of two years—much of what we hear about "stay-at-home" moms bears little resemblance to our lives. We don't care overmuch about scones. And we take care of toddlers; we don't resemble them. In fact, polls suggest most mothers want to return to full-time employment by the time their children are school-age. If we have failed, it is only in recognizing how, for mothers, discrimination and bias make this much easier said than done.

Even minor career breaks have dire economic consequences. Over a lifetime, women lose 18 percent of their earning power by leaving the workforce for only two years. A 2011 Harvard study revealed that female MBAs who took "a job interruption equivalent to 18 months" earned 41 percent less than male MBAs.

> ***She is also a reminder that mothers who do continue working—the majority of moms out there—routinely face discrimination that, when it doesn't push them out of the workforce, makes their lives miserable.***

And these are the lucky ones: the ones who find work at all. A study published by the *American Journal of Sociology* found that people were significantly less willing to hire mothers over nonmothers. Moreover, "the recommended starting salary for mothers was $11,000 less than that offered to nonmothers."

I spoke to about a dozen women for this piece, and none of these numbers surprised them. "I feel like I'm in a holding pattern," one told me. Like many, she feels tired and underappreciated: "The other day, my husband asked me what I wanted to be when I grow up."

Until recently, she had been the family breadwinner: a lawyer who, shortly after giving birth, left her law firm for a bigger one, hoping for more flexibility. But this didn't go as planned. "On my second day back, they wanted me to stay till 11 p.m.," she said. "I don't want to feel when I'm leaving at 5 p.m. that I'm this bad person and that people are questioning my work ethic."

After repeated failed attempts to negotiate a reasonable schedule, she decided to leave. Her preference is to stay home longer with her young daughter, but her family needs the money. On interviews, she never mentions her desire for flextime, and she confesses that her recruiter is skeptical about her prospects with large, prestigious firms.

Stuck between two reasonable desires—to care for her child and to find fulfilling work—this woman is typical of many stay-at-home mothers I met. She is also a reminder that mothers who do continue working—the majority of moms out there—routinely face discrimination that, when it doesn't push them out of the workforce, makes their lives miserable.

First, there is the paycheck problem. Much attention is paid to the wage gap between men and women, but in reality it's mostly a "mommy gap." Labor statistics show that while full-time working women without children earn 7 percent less than their male counterparts, women with children earn 23 percent less. A mother is also 50 percent less likely to be promoted than a woman without children. It's no wonder there's a saying among work-life experts: "If you want equality, die childless at 30."

Other forms of discrimination are more subtle. A frequent complaint among the working moms I met is that when they return from maternity leave, they have been in effect demoted—clients moved, cases shifted. "Compared to what I was doing before, it was not important work," confessed one woman who left an investment bank for this reason.

The sense is that employers, consciously or not, demote mothers, assuming they cannot live up to the hours and demands of the workplace. Ironically, some new mothers I met privately welcomed the break, needing all the "flexibility" they could get, while also resenting the lost pay and prestige. Others, like the woman at the investment bank, felt bored and frustrated that it was so difficult to find work that was both challenging and family-friendly. When a colleague encouraged her to join a business she was starting, promising she would be able to leave at 5 and work from home, she jumped ship. Unfortunately, that promise fell flat: her flextime requests were denied, and she felt stigmatized for even asking. "My boss always suggested I looked tired because of the kids." Eventually, she left.

Technically, stereotyping of this sort is illegal. The nonprofit A Better Balance (ABB), dedicated to work-life issues, notes that although "there is no federal law that explicitly prohibits employers from discriminating against their employees on the basis of their family status or family caregiving responsibilities," women who are treated as less committed or capable because they are mothers are protected by laws against "family responsibilities discrimination," or FRD.

But there are three main problems with FRD. One, few women know their rights. "Moms get tons of advice about what to eat, which stroller to buy, and how to get their bodies back in shape, but what's missing is clear and comprehensive advice about how to keep and protect their paycheck after their baby arrives," observes Dina Bakst, co-founder of ABB and co-author of the newly published *Babygate: What You Really Need to Know About Pregnancy and Parenting in the American Workplace.*

But the second problem is that many mothers are happy just to have a job. Those women are tired, not often in positions of power, and scared to rock the boat. "We hear from low-wage women who can't even get an extra bathroom break or a water bottle," Bakst says. Suing is another realm altogether.

Finally, discrimination can be hard to prove. One woman I spoke with described telling the chairman of her law firm that she was getting married. His immediate response: "Pregnant yet?" The subtext was clear, the woman notes, but "I knew I couldn't build a case off just that." Her work assignments declined, and she left the firm soon after.

Proving discrimination can also be difficult when 62 percent of private sector workers are discouraged or prohibited from comparing their wages with co-workers. The Paycheck Fairness Act, recently introduced by Senator Barbara Mikulski and Representative Rosa DeLauro, could change that by prohibiting employers from punishing workers who share wage information and further requiring them to prove that any pay discrepancies are unrelated to gender.

A few large legal victories wouldn't hurt either. "What we really need are some big Supreme Court rulings that shake employers the way that sexual harassment did in the '80s and '90s," says Bakst, although she is quick to point out the limits of litigation. The recently reintroduced Pregnant Workers Fairness Act, she notes, would significantly help by protecting pregnant women's right to modest workplace accommodations so they are less likely to have to resort to litigation.

Another idea would be to strengthen benefits for new mothers so that if they take time off, they are not penalized so onerously. I saw this approach in England, where I had my second child. Like much of Europe, England has generous family benefits, with new mothers receiving a year of job protection and thirty-nine weeks paid leave, in some cases up to 90 percent of one's salary. New fathers get some paid leave, too, and can, during the first year, stay at home with pay for up to twenty-six weeks if the mother chooses to work.

England also offers universal preschool after a child's fourth birthday and fifteen hours of free "nursery" after their third (and sometimes second) birthday. Parents also have the right to request flexible work schedules, including the right to scale back to part time either temporarily or permanently. Employers do not have to grant the request, but they must provide an explicit reason for denying it. Finally, part-time workers, the vast majority of whom are women, must be paid on the same scale and receive the same benefits as full-time workers.

These benefits can act as lifelines for women by significantly reducing that scramble time in the United States—the time between birth and kindergarten—when many women just give up, if they don't get pushed out first. Further, when women are granted paid maternity leave, they are more likely to return to work and maintain higher wages than women without leave.

One of the biggest challenges, however, is tackling resistance to government regulation of employee benefits and access to workplace flexibility. Also in Europe, governments generally pay for benefits like family leave, but there is little political support for that here. And getting employers to foot the bill seems unlikely. While some corporations, like Google, appear to be amenable to this approach, others that set the parameters of the debate do not—and politicians seem increasingly beholden to them. The GOP-sponsored Working Families Flexibility Act of 2013, for example, is a pale shadow of the legislation sponsored under the same name by Ted Kennedy in 2007 and Carolyn Maloney in 2012.

Kennedy's and Maloney's versions would have guaranteed employees the right to request flextime without penalty, as they can already do in England and other parts of Europe. Both efforts failed. The latest version, though it proposes to support employees, panders to employers instead, allowing them to give their workers comp time instead of overtime pay. It passed the House in May.

There is some reason to hope the tide is turning. President Obama just proposed a $75 billion plan for universal preschool. And, perhaps more significant, a recent poll released by the National Partnership for Women & Families shows that the majority of voters, both Republican (73 percent) and Democrat (96 percent), feel it's important to consider enacting laws that provide for paid family leave and paid sick days. These figures are up from similar polls conducted just a few years ago.

But until this happens, mothers must fend for themselves. When I ask Allison O'Kelly, founder of Mom Corps, a staffing organization that helps connect mothers with flexible employment, what advice she has for new mothers struggling between childcare and work, she hesitates. "Honestly, I'm a big believer in staying in, because re-entry is so tricky," she says. "But if you do take time off, do something, even if it's small—even if it's ten hours a week. Something paid is preferable to volunteer work, but if you have nothing else, then volunteer. Keep your résumé fresh."

It's difficult to argue with such a practical approach. And yet it seems equally important to reframe this issue by focusing on the hurdles women face, not the individual "choices" they make. The latter may be a salable approach, pitting women against women, but it distracts from the more pressing issue of discrimination. Moreover, while choices seem black-and-white from afar, what you learn from sitting down with mothers is that life is more complicated than that. I'm not going to argue with the woman who tried for six years to have a child and then stayed home with her for three. Nor can I blame the many who leave work because they are tired of spending their entire paycheck on childcare.

The stories I heard from such women are the stories of half the population, stories that politicians and businesses need to hear, and that women need to voice. "Show them how ready and motivated you are." This is Allison O'Kelly's advice on how to win over an employer, but it's good advice all around.

DISCUSSION

1. What is your reaction to the term "stay-at-home mom"? What sort of image or associations does it evoke for you? In your view, are these images and associations fair? Accurate? How or how not?
2. "[D]espite feminism's emphasis on choice," Nelson writes, "not all choices are equal" (p. 412). Do you agree? Can you think of an example of a "choice" that illustrates or reinforces Nelson's point?
3. In Nelson's view, one way to begin resolving the work/family dilemma that so many professional women confront is "to reframe this issue by focusing on the hurdles women face, not the individual 'choices' they make" (p. 416). What is your response to this suggestion? Do you agree that it's important to focus on "hurdles" as well as "choices"? Why or why not?

WRITING

4. According to Nelson, many women find themselves caught between the desire for "fulfilling work" and the desire "to care for [their] child." In an essay, identify and analyze the cultural norms that cast these two "desires" as incompatible or mutually exclusive. According to the conventional wisdom, what is it that supposedly makes it so difficult – if not impossible – to fulfill these two goals simultaneously? And how much validity do you think there is to this view?
5. "Much attention is paid," Nelson writes, "to the wage gap between men and women, but in reality it's mostly a 'mommy gap.' Labor statistics show that while full-time working women without children earn 7 percent less than their male counterparts, women with children earn 23 percent less. A mother is also 50 percent less likely to be promoted than a woman without children" (p. 413). Write an essay in which you offer a hypothesis that would help explain these statistics. What cultural stereotypes might be partly responsible for such stark discrepancies in earning potential and promotion rates?
6. Arlie Russell Hochschild (p. 418) offers a very different take on the issues of work and motherhood. How do you think Ashley Nelson would respond to the portrait of surrogacy Hochschild presents in her essay? In your view, does Hochschild's account of the surrogacy industry lend any support or credibility to Nelson's argument about the economic and cultural obstacles confronting working women? If so, how specifically?

ARLIE RUSSELL HOCHSCHILD

Our Baby, Her Womb

Few experiences are more momentous and deeply personal than the birth of a child. But what happens when this experience gets turned into a job for hire? Offering a quick portrait of the "surrogacy" industry, Arlie Russell Hochschild takes a closer look at what happens when we agree to treat pregnancy and childbirth as a business transaction. Russell Hochschild is a professor of sociology at the University of California, Berkeley. She is the author of numerous books, among them: *The Managed Heart: Commercialization of Human Feeling* (1983), *The Time Bind: When Work Becomes Home and Home Becomes Work* (1997), and most recently, *The Outsourced Self: Intimate Life in Market Times* (2012), from which this selection is excerpted.

AS WE DROVE INTO THE VAST PARKING LOT AT 10:45 IN THE morning, mothers in floral summer dresses and flip-flops, fathers in short-sleeved shirts, and girls in strapless tops and capri pants were slowly streaming from every direction toward the auditorium of the Holy Mission Baptist megachurch in Jackson, Louisiana. At the entrance, a young man in a dark suit passed out sheets listing "Events of the Day" and pointed parents with toddlers toward one door, older children toward another. I was led into a great auditorium filled with nearly five thousand seated parishioners facing three enormous screens. Looming above us was the projected image of two earnest singers in a loud and rousing vocal duet of "Jesus Lives," set to the 1960s tune "Celebration Time."

[The clinic] encourages highly businesslike relationships between surrogate and client so as to facilitate the easy transfer of the baby.

The singers moved on to "Christ Is Alive" and "The Empty Grave Rejoices." Parishioners were tapping their feet, rocking, bouncing gently in their chairs. A few stood. Hands clapping, hips swaying. Soon a dozen smiling ushers roamed the aisles, tossing in the air dozens of red, white, and blue beach balls for the audience to catch and pitch about the festive auditorium. When the music drew to a close, the Director of the Youth Ministry, dressed in jeans and a blue shirt with rolled-up sleeves, led us in prayer. He then called on parishioners to stand and shake hands with their neighbors, left and right. "Ask them, What's your favorite Beach Boys song?" Laughter arose. "I can't remember . . .

'California Girls'? 'Do it Again'?" "Now," the minister said, "ask the person in front and in back." More laughter. " 'Good Vibrations.' 'Fun, Fun, Fun' . . . I like that one, too."

This lighthearted ritual of greeting was part of the church's open-arms philosophy—one that had attracted Tim and Lili Mason, both born-again Christians. Before they married six years ago, they had been American nomads, moving several times each to new cities and, once settled in Jackson, from one neighborhood to another. The parents of both Lili and Tim lived in other states, and the couple knew neighbors only enough to "wave at." So it was through Holy Mission Baptist—which served 17,000 believers, Tim told me proudly—that they had discovered a community. In fact, soon after they joined the church, a facilitator proposed that they join a group of young couples looking forward to parenthood. To improve their marriage, they also signed up for church-sponsored marital counseling. All of it offered them a welcome relief from the lonely, restless lives they had lived before marriage and church, though this sense of community also felt, to Tim, somehow moveable. As he said cheerfully, "If we move again, we can find a satellite campus and still feel part of the same community."

Despite the thousands of people in the audience that Sunday morning, the pastor's message seemed directed specifically at Lili and Tim and their thwarted hopes for a baby. After describing the heartache of waiting for something that just didn't happen, the pastor told the biblical story of Sarah, the wife of Abraham, who found herself too old to conceive the child she yearned to have. She "foolishly took tools into her own hands," the pastor said, and talked Abraham into sleeping with her servant Hagar. When Hagar conceived a son, Sarah flew into a jealous rage and banished her and her baby, Ishmael. Abraham was, the pastor commented wryly, "a wimp for going along with Sarah's wild scheme," and now found himself in a fine mess. A murmur of appreciation for the pastor's frank remarks rose from the rapt congregation.

The message of the sermon was to "leave the tools in God's hands" and not, like Sarah, take them into one's own. Little could the pastor have known that two listeners in the front middle row had actually flown halfway around the globe to hire a "Hagar" to bear their child.

This was to be their biological child—the product of Tim's sperm and Lili's egg—implanted in the womb of a surrogate who lived in India. The science, the technology, the very idea would have been beyond the wildest fantasies of my grandparents, not to mention Sarah and Abraham. Yet Tim and Lili were not even venturing into the farthest reaches of today's reproductive possibilities. For a person can now legally purchase an egg from one continent, sperm from another, and implant it in a "womb for rent" in yet another. An Israeli entrepreneur who calls himself "Doron" in the 2009 documentary *Google Baby* assembles such parts of life for a fee.

A client can even purchase the sperm and egg online, have them delivered in liquid nitrogen to a clinic in India, have them implanted in the Indian surrogate, and pick up the baby nine months later. Where, I wondered, was the human touch in all this—the spirit of the gift? I was visiting Lili and Tim to see how they were feeling their way along this part of the market frontier.

After lunch at a nearby mall, we returned to the Mason home through a quiet, leafy neighborhood of dandelion-free lawns, small ornate water fountains, and two-car garages. All was quiet except for the distant roar of a leaf blower and weed whacker down the street near a truck marked *top turf lawn care*. The elegant homes, the sculpted shrubs, the manicured grass, all spoke of a desire for order and control.

"I'm a talker," Lili began, handing me a tall glass of iced tea on a porch behind their spacious three-story redbrick home. A pretty, bright-eyed, petite woman, the daughter of Indian immigrants, and a computer programmer, Lili was wearing cutoff shorts, a white shift, and plastic sandals, an outfit she had worn to church earlier that day. "I'll tell you anything you want to know," she offered.

In recent years, Lili had suffered from osteoarthritis and scoliosis, and after a double hip replacement, her doctor advised her to give up on trying to bear a child. But physical problems were not, she offered, the entire reason why she had never had a baby. Like many working women, she had delayed the decision to conceive and, even now at forty, approached the idea of a baby with caution: "I was slow to really *want* a baby. I was never one of those women who knew from day one she had to be a mother. But I don't beat myself up about it."

When I asked Lili about her early years, she slowly tucked her lustrous black hair behind her ears and described, with surprising detachment, the painful memory of her father's relentless tirades ("You're filthy. You're a slut. You're no good") and her after-school job cleaning blood and vomit off the floors of mussed rooms in her father's small hotel. "He didn't want me to turn out like the women who stayed in his hotel. I used to cry, hit myself, pull my hair, and slap myself. There was a railroad track behind the hotel. I used to think about lying down on it. So going through all that, I learned to be numb."

Ironically, her father seemed to push Lili into the very nightmare he imagined himself protecting her from. In her teen years, Lili began experimenting with drugs and sex. "I'm a 'try stuff' sort of person," she said, "so I thought I could handle it. But I couldn't." After a series of boyfriends, four abortions, and one failed marriage, Lili found herself living alone in a high-rise apartment building in New Orleans, working a temp job as a file clerk during the day, flipping channels on her television at night, and accepting monthly checks from her worried parents.

"I was so depressed," she continued. But one late weekend afternoon, she switched the channel to a plain-talking spiritual adviser, Joyce Meyer, and that day, alone in her apartment, she "submitted to Jesus." Some while later, she moved to another apartment building and met Tim, also a recent convert, who told her he very much wanted a child. They married. With a brightened outlook, a desire to strengthen her bond with Tim and to be a good Christian wife to him, Lili began to try to want to have a child. "There's still part of me that says, 'Gaaa . . . no!' But another part says, 'I'd like to do it for Tim.' Tim is the real *go go go* guy on getting a baby."

When I spoke to Tim later, he made no secret of his desire for a child. He was seated on the living-room couch, his leg in a full-length plaster cast propped up on a stack of pillows, the result of a recent fall in their backyard. Stocky, blond, with cherubic blue eyes, it was in a soft voice and slow measures that he described his day job managing warehouse shipments and Saturday afternoons coaching soccer and baseball. "I'm thirty-four and have gotten to a certain stage in my career," Tim said. "I want to devote the next chapter of my life to being a father." When he imagined being a parent, Tim pictured quitting his warehouse job, while Lili continued to work, and after Lili got home in the evening, teaching guitar in his basement office.

Refusing to be disheartened by four years of fruitless effort to get pregnant, Tim turned to other possibilities. Before their marriage, he had assumed it would be easy for Lili to get pregnant. But after four years of trying, they turned to in vitro fertilization. For this, the doctor harvested Lili's eggs, combined them in a petri dish with Tim's sperm, in hopes of creating an embryo that could be implanted in Lili's uterus. But try after try, the procedure failed and costs mounted. After Lili's double hip replacement and her doctor's disappointing counsel not to carry a child, Tim started to research surrogacy.

I was Googling around and found some articles online about this infertility clinic in Anand, Gujarat, that offers very inexpensive IVF and surrogacy. I gave it to Lili to read and said, "Tell me what you think." She read it and said, "You want me to go to *India* for a medical procedure? You must be out of your mind."

Lili's parents, naturalized Americans who had been born in India, had never heard of Indian infertility clinics. Nor had word of them come through the *samaj*, the local Indian community in Jackson that kept up on eligible marriage partners and local dowry prices. Instead, word came to Tim via Google. Lili remembered her response: "No way! I wouldn't be caught dead in an Indian hospital!" But Tim persisted: "I brought up online images of their modern equipment; it looked just like the IVF equipment the clinics have in Jackson."

Had they considered adoption? I asked. Yes, but only as a last resort. Had they thought of asking a friend or relative to be their surrogate? Tim replied:

Actually, my brother's wife and the wife of a friend both offered. We weren't really entertaining the idea of my brother's wife as much as Betty, the wife of my childhood buddy. We're pretty close to them. I was overwhelmed that she offered us this huge gift and was excited to do it for us. They had to stop at one child for financial reasons and she'd enjoyed her pregnancy and wanted to go through it again.

They also felt bad for us. My buddy is a fireman and he told us he goes on calls in bad neighborhoods at 3:30 a.m. or 4:00 a.m. and will see a toddler in the middle of the street. There are so many people with babies that just don't take care of them. And yet it's so hard for responsible people to become parents.

"Why not accept Betty's offer?" I asked. "It's the cost," Lili replied. "Insurance doesn't cover the cost of medically preparing me to produce eggs, the cost of preparing the surrogate's body to receive them, or the cost of the surrogacy itself." Tim continued:

Then there's the cost of the psychological evaluations. Plus lawyer fees. Altogether it would come to between $20,000 and $22,000 just to try. Then if Betty got pregnant, there are labor costs. The total could come to $50,000. We'd obviously want to pay Betty, too. If we hired a stranger here in the States, that alone could range from $25,000 to $40,000. So the total bill could be $80,000 here—and that's if you have a normal baby. In India the total could be $10,000.

Lili and Tim earned a combined $172,000 a year. I asked them if they had considered moving to a smaller home to save money so they could pay for a surrogate in America. No, they liked the house and needed the basement for Tim's music lessons. The SUV? It was handy, and at least they didn't have two cars. Could they accept a gift, I asked Lili, from her well-to-do parents?

My parents wouldn't hesitate to give us money. But now, at age forty, I have a fifteen percent chance of having it work with my egg and another woman's womb. I wouldn't want to spend their money for such a slim chance of success. Who goes with these odds? Do you invest in a stock with such terrible odds of return? No. Even if you have the money, it's not a wise decision.

So, despite Lili's hesitation, Tim e-mailed Dr. Nayna Patel at the Akanksha Clinic in Anand. She replied with a series of medical questions. Tim answered these, inquired further, and asked for names and e-mail addresses of references. Thinking over the events that had led them to Anand, still painfully fresh in their minds, Tim recalled: "She gave us the names of three couples, all of whom ended up with babies. We e-mailed all three and spoke by phone with two. They said sometimes you e-mail Dr. Patel and she doesn't answer and you have to e-mail again, or call late at night. She's very curt, but it's not a scam."

A few months later, Tim and Lili flew to India. "When we decided to go I began to feel, 'Hey, I really want this baby,'" Lili said. They checked into a small hotel in Anand. The next morning, they took an auto-rickshaw to the clinic, where Dr. Patel's amiable husband ushered them into her office.

Dr. Patel herself graciously greeted Lili and Tim and, after a short interview, drew back a white curtain separating the front of her office from two examining tables in the back. She asked Lili to undress and lie down. As Lili recalled: "When Dr. Patel examined me with the wand [a medical device used in pelvic exams], it felt like she was driving a stick shift around my abdomen: first gear, reverse. In the United States, a doctor might warn you, 'You'll feel a little pressure here or there. . . .'"

Lying on the same table, Lili prepared to have blood drawn. Tim described the scene: "There's no rain for ten months of the year in Anand. So the ground is very dry with big cracks in the soil, dust over the cars, rickshaws. So this blood-work guy comes into the clinic office with dusty feet." Lili added:

> He looked like a street vendor. He pulled syringes out of what I thought was a dirty camera bag. He entered the exam room with his rubber gloves already on. I thought, "What the heck is this?"

To collect semen, Tim was conducted to a room with a bed (he recalled grimy sheets) and a loose faucet hung over a dirty sink. "They tell you to wash your hands," another client who completed his task in the same room told Tim, "but my hands were already cleaner than that water." Lili was then sedated and the doctor retrieved two eggs, which were mixed with Tim's sperm in a petri dish. Five days later, an embryo formed. They were elated.

THE QUIET, THIN SURROGATE

The Akanksha Clinic houses the world's largest-known group of commercial surrogates. A baby a week is born there. Dr. Patel, the director, is especially proud of her clinic's attention to quality control (most surrogates live on a supervised high-quality diet, often in secluded dormitories) and efficiency (Akanksha encourages highly businesslike relationships between surrogate and client so as to facilitate the easy transfer of the baby).

When Lili and Tim arrived at the clinic to meet the surrogate into whom their precious embryo would be implanted, Dr. Patel handed them her profile. At the top was her name and under it:

Age: 25
Weight: 44 kilos
Height: 5 feet

Complexion: wheatish
HIV: negative
Hepatitis: negative
Occupation: housewife
Marital Status: married
Children: one
Cast [*sic*]: Hindu
Education: uneducated

The surrogate, recruited by Dr. Patel herself, was ushered into the main office, her eyes fixed on the floor, as were those of her husband, who filed in behind her. As Tim recounted:

The surrogate was very, very short and very, very, very skinny and she didn't speak any English at all. She sat down and she smiled. She was bashful and her husband, too. You could tell they were both very nervous. We would ask a question and the translator would give a one- or two-word response. We asked what her husband did for a living, and the age of their child, just to make conversation. I don't remember the answers. I don't remember her name.

Surrogates earn more money if they agree to live in the dormitory for the full nine months, which nearly all of them do. Tim continued:

We asked whether she planned to stay in the dormitory or stay with her husband. She said she would live in the dormitory the whole time. Dr. Patel told us her husband would only be allowed to visit for a couple hours and in a crowded room, so there would be no chance they would have sex or that he would transmit any infection.

Lili remembered being nervous about meeting the surrogate:

It was because of this Indian-to-Indian dynamic. Other client couples—American, Canadian—tend to react more emotionally. They hold hands with their surrogate. But to me, that's weird; we don't do that touchy-feely thing—especially not for services rendered. You know, "I'm so glad you are doing this for me, let me hold your hand." I'm a little bit rough around the edges anyway. But to me it's simple: This girl is poor and she's just doing it for the money.

But when Lili saw the diminutive woman enter the room, she did feel an urge to reach out.

I didn't want her to think of me as this big rich American coming in with my money to buy her womb for a while. So I did touch her at some point, I think, her hair or her shoulder. I tried to smile a lot. Through the interpreter I told her, "I am very glad and grateful you are doing this." I explained that we'd tried to have a baby but couldn't. I told her not to worry for herself; she would be taken care of. I asked her about her own child. She didn't look at ease. It was not the unease of "I can't believe I'm doing this," but more the unease of the subordinate meeting her boss.

The surrogate and her husband asked Tim and Lili no questions about themselves. "I'm sure to them it's a pure business transaction," Tim said. "Payment for surrogacy could equal ten years' of salary in India. Still, if she'd been more cheerful, maybe we would have talked more."

The encounter lasted fifteen minutes. The second and last time the Masons met the surrogate, she was lying on a table preparing to have their embryo implanted in her womb. Lili stood by the table and held the surrogate's hand for about half an hour. A day later, Tim and Lili flew back to Louisiana. Two weeks after that they received an abrupt e-mail from Dr. Patel: "Sorry to inform you that Beta HCG of your surrogate is less than 2, hence pregnancy test negative. Herewith attached is the report of Beta HCG." In other words, the egg had failed to grow in the surrogate's uterus.

The second and last time the Masons met the surrogate, she was lying on a table preparing to have their embryo implanted in her womb.

Had the surrogate been malnourished? Had the procedure been done correctly? It was hard to know. Dr. Patel recommended trying again with Tim's sperm and a donor's egg. Weary of the roller coaster of hope and disappointment, they asked about the chances of success. "Sixty percent," Dr. Patel responded. But she had told a television interviewer it was 44 percent, and still other gynecologists estimated 20 percent. "We couldn't tell what the real rate was," Tim said, adjusting his leg cast on the sofa.

But the Masons decided to take the next step. They agreed to purchase a donor egg that would be artificially fertilized by Tim's sperm and implanted in the womb of another surrogate. For this, Dr. Patel's clinic needed to locate the right donor.

Several months went by.

At last, Dr. Patel wrote to say that she had found an egg donor. She was already on her seventh day of medication, the doctor explained, to help stimulate egg production. But who was paying for the medication she was already on, Tim and Lili wondered. Other clients? Had they dropped out? If so, why? "It seemed strange, but we wired her the $4,500 she requested," Tim said. Egg donors at the clinic, Tim later discovered, received $100 to $500 per donation.

Lili and Tim asked to see a photograph of the donor so they could have some idea of what their child might look like. Weeks passed. No photo arrived. Lili called Dr. Patel. In the notes Tim kept at the time, the exchange between them went like this: "Doctor asked, 'If you don't like the picture, will you pull out of the egg donation?' We said, 'No, it would just be nice to see the picture.'" A day later, a photo arrived.

She was "small, thin, and fairly pretty," Lili recalled. Soon after, Dr. Patel implanted the donor egg fertilized with Tim's sperm into the second surrogate. (To increase the chance of success, the doctor routinely implanted about five embryos at a time, aborting fetuses if they numbered more than two.)

Two weeks later another dispiriting e-mail message appeared on Tim's computer: "Hello. Sorry to inform you that Beta HCG of your surrogate is less than 2, hence pregnancy test negative. Herewith attach the report of Beta HCG."

Tim and Lili never met their egg donor or second surrogate, nor did they see their first surrogate again, nor did they see the dormitory where both surrogates had promised to live for nine months. And when I asked them whether they would have kept in touch with their surrogate had a baby been born, both paused in slight surprise at the question: "I would have left that up to the surrogate," Lili said.

If she had no preference one way or another, and just gave some polite answer, I probably would have sent some photos of the baby or a letter. If there had been no response, I'd probably have given up. She probably can't write. The Surrogate Profile Form said "no education." Even if she could write, I can't read Gujarati. It's probably a big cost for them to write letters. And who knows if they'd still be living at the same address.

Although Tim and Lili had no real interest in forming a friend or family-like bond with their surrogates, it was not a sign of callousness or moral unease. They were caring people who faithfully tithed their income for the poor in India. They objected to any suggestion of exploitation and were disturbed to hear surrogacy mentioned in the same breath as the black market for organs. As Tim reflected:

There are so many activists out there saying that "wombs for rent" are a violation of human rights. I think it's just a decision people make on their own. It's not the same as one person buying and another selling a liver on the black market in Mexico. These Indian surrogates are very poor. They may not be the people you drive by, living beneath a blue tarp by the edge of some Indian road. But they're not much above that. So why would you not want to help somebody out? What's wrong with that? If they have a financial incentive, that's fine.

Simply, Tim and Lili saw their relationship with the surrogate as a mutually beneficial transaction. They imagined themselves as outsourcers paying a stranger to provide a professionally supervised service. They hoped to establish a pleasant, temporary bond with the surrogate, to pay her, thank her, and leave. They sought to create the sort of relationship one might establish with an obstetrician or dentist. In the outsourcer ideal, relations are pleasant and honest, but the point of them is to facilitate the exchange of money for service. In the course of a modern day, the outsourcer manages many such relationships—with a babysitter, psychiatrist, physical trainer, for example—and can't get "entangled" with them all.

Tim and Lili's relationship with the Akanksha Clinic came to a decisive end after they received the last of Dr. Patel's cryptic, disheartening messages, and Tim declared the search for a surrogacy baby at Akanksha over. "We're now looking into adoption in Nepal," he said. To prepare for that, they took an adoption class that Lili said had transformed her thinking.

When we were doing the surrogacy, I wasn't so aware of the mother-child bond. I didn't know a baby could recognize the voice of the mother who carried it. I guess I felt detached.

But after we took the adoption class, I realized how important contact between the surrogate and baby might be, and so how important it was for me to feel connected to the surrogate. If you're carrying a child for nine months, and then suddenly it's delivered and gone, there would inevitably be a void. God didn't create our bodies to work with IVF and surrogacy. So I now think I would have wanted some relationship with the surrogate—for the sake of the child.

EVERYTHING FOR SALE

The international search for a baby immersed Tim and Lili in a globe-spanning stream of "medical tourists" for which India is a particularly popular destination. Since India declared surrogacy legal in 2002, an estimated three thousand Assisted Reproductive Technology (ART) clinics have sprung up nationwide and are predicted to add, from 2012 onward, an annual average $2.3 billion to the nation's gross domestic product. Advertisements describe India as a "global doctor," offering First World skills at Third World prices, short waits, privacy, and—especially important in the case of surrogacy—a minimum of legal red tape. The Indian government encourages First World patients to come to India by granting lower tax rates and import duties on medical supplies to private hospitals that treat foreign patients.

The fertility market is flourishing in the United States as well. Had Tim and Lili decided to purchase an egg in the United States, they could have entered the world of ads placed by fertility clinics and prospective parents in college newspapers, on Facebook, and on Craigslist. In a 2006 study of more than one hundred advertisements seeking egg donors published in sixty-three college papers, Dr. Aaron Levine, a professor of public policy at the Georgia Institute of Technology, found that a quarter of these offered potential compensation exceeding $10,000. Guidelines issued by the American Society for Reproductive Medicine, the nonprofit arm of an industry group, take no issue with the commercial purchase of eggs but urge limits on their price. A client should pay no more than $10,000 for an egg, they suggest. But ads in newspapers at Harvard, Princeton, and Yale on average promise donors $35,000.

The society also recommends that fertility clinics forbid clients from paying additional fees in return for special "traits" such as a gift for math or music. The society has no means to enforce its guidelines, however. With its Corporate Council members from Good Start Genetics, Freedom Fertility Pharmacy, Merck & Co., Pfizer Inc., and other for-profit companies with a financial interest in the matter, the society is unlikely to question the wisdom of placing reproduction on the market frontier. Dr. Levine discovered that for every extra one hundred points in a university student's SAT score, the advertised fee rose by two thousand dollars. And dozens of American clinics now offer would-be parents detailed profiles of the characteristics of sperm and egg donors. Xytex Corporation in Atlanta, Georgia, for example, provides potential clients a list of genetically coded attributes—including the length of eyelashes, the presence of freckles, and results of the Keirsey Temperament Sorter test.

Students themselves found the fertility clinic ads unremarkable. One twenty-two-year-old Brown University undergraduate told the *New York Times* that she was shocked at first that they would target "what they were looking for, like religion, SAT score, and hair color." But like other things she was first exposed to in college, "the shock wore off." I asked one of my students at University of California, Berkeley, how she felt about ads for human eggs in the *Daily Californian*, the college newspaper: "Our tuition is rising," she said, "and we're less and less a public university that regular families can afford. I have friends who are looking seriously at those ads. I don't blame them."

Tim and Lili had themselves come to accept things that had once seemed unthinkable. In the meantime, they had placed their name on a waiting list, number 375, to adopt a Nepalese child and had settled in for a long wait. It might be a year or two. The minister at Holy Mission Baptist Church was right, they felt, sometimes waiting can be painfully hard. Still, Lili now saw meaning in the wait. "I need to work on my anxiety and anger issues. Maybe God is giving us time to truly prepare."

When I contacted the Masons a year later, Lili told me that the Nepal adoption agency had been accused of corruption and that several countries had pulled out, including the United States, through which they had put in their application papers. But Tim had gone online again and discovered a clinic in Hyderabad, which he visited with his father, leaving behind a check for $7,000 and a semen sample. "This clinic keeps trying with surrogates and donors for as long as it takes until one succeeds," he explained. "The next payment isn't due until a pregnancy is confirmed at three months. The total will come to $25,000, including the payment to the surrogate, the egg donor, the delivery, everything." The first donor's eggs yielded sixteen embryos, which were implanted in three tries over several months. The couple had recently learned that, perhaps due to storage problems, Tim's sperm had died and the clinic needed more samples.

Lili was resigning herself, it seemed, to life without a child. But Tim, "the upbeat spirit" in their home, as Lili described him, could not. His injured leg had healed badly, robbing him of much feeling in his left foot. This made it impossible to play soccer and took much of the joy out of coaching—another great love in his life. Perhaps for that reason, the wish for a baby loomed ever larger, and, cautiously hopeful, Tim was planning a second trip to Hyderabad.

DISCUSSION

1. The term Hochschild uses to describe the job of bearing another couple's child is "commercial surrogate." How do you react to this phrase? What image or associations does it conjure in your mind? And do you think it accurately or fairly describes what this work involves?
2. The married couple, Hochschild tells us, "objected to any suggestion of exploitation and were disturbed to hear surrogacy mentioned in the same breath as the black market for organs" (p. 426). Do you share this view? In your estimation, is surrogacy free of any "exploitation"?
3. The book from which this selection is excerpted is titled *The Outsourced Self*. What do you think this title means? How well does the story of surrogacy here capture or reflect this meaning?

WRITING

4. One of the key tensions surrounding surrogacy is that it transforms what is normally considered an entirely private, personal matter into a financial arrangement. As Hochschild puts it: "Tim and Lili [the married couple] saw their relationship with the surrogate as a mutually beneficial transaction. They imagined themselves as outsourcers paying a stranger to provide a professionally supervised service" (p. 426). In an essay, evaluate the business model sketched out here. In your view, is it valid to regard the interactions between couples and surrogates as a "mutually beneficial transaction"? Does it seem right to you to treat surrogacy itself as a "service" like any other? Why or why not?
5. Write an essay in which you present your views on the specific rules that you think should govern the surrogacy process. What rights should surrogates be able to claim? How should these be balanced against those of parents? Should there be rules concerning contact between parents, surrogates, and the child? Next, offer an explanation or defense of why you think these rules would be the best ones to adopt. What larger objectives do they serve? What advantages or benefits do they bring?
6. Hochschild, like Barbara Ehrenreich (p. 380), connects her examination of work to the issue of poverty. Both essays ask readers to consider the difficult choices confronting those whose work-related options are so drastically limited by circumstance. Write an essay in which you compare the ways each writer uses a focus on work to make a larger point about poverty. What does each writer want her readers to understand about the experience of being poor? And how effective do you find each commentary?

Tying It All Together

As both Matthew B. Crawford and Catherine Rampell suggest, there is often a close connection between the norms that underlie cultural attitudes toward work and those that shape our assumptions about education. First, choose a selection from "How We Learn" (Chapter 4) that, in your view, highlights the same connection between work and education-related norms. Possible selections include Alfie Kohn ("From Degrading to De-Grading," p. 238), Jonathan Kozol ("Preparing Minds for Markets," p. 301), and Mike Rose ("Blue-Collar Brilliance," p. 280). Then write a short essay in which you identify and assess the ways this writer's examination of work and education-related norms compares to the examination presented by Crawford or Rampell. What relationship between these two types of norms does each writer showcase? What are key similarities and differences?

Like Arlie Russell Hochschild, Keith O'Brien ("The Empathy Deficit," p. 464) is interested in the ways the norms around intimacy and connection are being transformed. In a three- to five-page essay, describe and analyze how each writer explores this question. To what extent does Hochschild's profile of the "surrogacy industry" parallel or reinforce the data O'Brien cites about our growing "empathy deficit"? What larger argument about the changing nature of intimacy does each writer make? And do you find these arguments persuasive? Why or why not?

Scenes and Un-Scenes: A Woman's Work

For decades, if not centuries, Americans have been encouraged not only to draw firm boundaries between men's work and women's work, but also to *value* these kinds of work in radically different ways. As many of us know firsthand, gender stereotypes continue to play a prominent role in scripting the ways we are taught to think about and evaluate life on the job. Whether measured in terms of annual income, social prestige, or professional clout, we know, for example, that we are supposed to view being a kindergarten teacher and being a corporate CEO very differently. We know how to assess and rank these respective occupations because our culture has supplied us with a set of ready-made and highly gendered assumptions (for example, about the kind of person who is the most natural fit for the job, about the rewards and respect such a jobholder is allowed to expect, and so on). But do these assumptions really offer us an accurate guide? Do they frame choices or script norms that actually "work" for us? And if they don't, to what extent can they be challenged or revised? Each of the following images presents us with an image that rewrites stereotypical scripts by which we have been taught to segregate men's work from women's work. What do these acts of revision involve? What particular norms do their portraits of women and work seem to parody or critique? And what new norms do they posit in their place?

An image initially created as part of a government-led effort during World War II to recruit women into industries that had lost their all-male workforces to overseas fighting, Rosie the Riveter was originally intended to represent the country's short-term employment crisis. One of the most iconic work images of the twentieth century, Rosie the Riveter stands as a pointed rebuke to the ways Americans have traditionally been taught to think about "women's work."

World History Archive/Newscom

"What do you say, gentlemen—ready for some girltalk?"

Jim Sizemore/Cartoonstock.com

Other cultural texts have built on Rosie's legacy in different ways. Unlike its preceding counterparts, this image works much more clearly to redirect traditional gender stereotypes toward nontraditional ends. Rather than a sexist shorthand used to marginalize the contributions of working women, the phrase* girltalk *– uttered here by a female executive – gets transformed into a sly joke, one that inverts conventional gender hierarchies by making men the object of humor.

In the 1980 film* 9 to 5*, three women office workers end up running their company when, through a series of comic misunderstandings, they end up holding their boss hostage. Over the last few decades, our airwaves have been filled with movies and television shows that attempt the very Rosie-like feat of placing women within positions of workplace authority traditionally occupied by men. However, this sort of role reversal has often been undertaken for comic effect: a way of poking fun at conventional gender norms and gender hierarchies by turning them upside down. In the end, though, how much of the film's comedy rests on the assumption that a woman running a company is inherently funny?

Michael Ochs Archives/Getty Images

Mark Wilson/Getty Images

In 2007, Representative Nancy Pelosi (D-CA) became the first woman Speaker of the U.S. House of Representatives. Is there anything about the composition of this news photo that could be said to be reminiscent of the depiction of Rosie the Riveter from the 1940s? In what ways does it differ?

DISCUSSION

1. How does the Rosie the Riveter image seem to define the ideal job? What kinds of work? What particular roles? And to what extent does this definition challenge or rewrite conventional gender stereotypes?
2. How accurately do the work portraits presented in this feature capture or comment on your experiences on the job? Do they convey messages or model norms that would be considered acceptable within the work environments you know personally? How or how not?
3. How valid do you think the distinction between men's work and women's work is in this day and age? Is it a distinction that continues to exert influence in our culture? Does it present a script we are still encouraged to use?

WRITING

4. Choose the image in this feature that you think most directly reinforces the connection between work and self-worth. Write an essay in which you assess the merits and/or flaws of this depiction. In what ways does this image encourage viewers to forge a connection between their work and their self-worth? What, in your view, are the implications of embracing this message? Of using it as the basis for living one's own life?
5. In addition to the distinction between men's and women's work, the examples here also underscore certain differences between white-collar and blue-collar jobs. What are the scripts in our culture by which we are taught to differentiate these two types of employment? Choose one of the images and write an essay in which you analyze how particular gender stereotypes influence the depiction of white- or blue-collar work. What gender roles or gender scripts get associated with this kind of work? How does the photo convey them? Does this portrayal seem accurate? Fair? How or how not?
6. In "Our Baby, Her Womb," Arlie Russell Hochschild (p. 418) writes about the ways motherhood has been transformed into a business. How do you think she would respond to the images you have just seen, all of which depict women in stereotypically male-dominated types of work? What images can you think of from popular culture that might be added to the preceding set that would corroborate the view of motherhood as a for-pay undertaking?

Putting It into Practice: **Working Hard or Hardly Working?**

Now that you've read the chapter selections, try applying your conclusions to your own life by completing the following exercises.

BUILDING THE PERFECT WORK ENVIRONMENT The selections in this chapter cover many different types of jobs, but they also describe, sometimes indirectly, different work *environments*. Write an essay in which you describe the different environments in two or three of these selections. What are the standards of dress or behavior you think these environments condone? What isn't allowed? What type of work environment do you believe is most suited to your personality? Why? What does your ideal "office" (whether or not it's a traditional workspace) look like? What are the standards of conduct you would implement?

EVALUATING SALARIES The U.S. Department of Labor Bureau of Labor Statistics has compiled a list of mean salaries for 800 jobs (www.bls.gov/oes/current/oes_nat.htm). Select several different occupations and see how each one compares in terms of its related salary. Write an essay in which you discuss what salary tells us about the "value" of work. What sorts of skills or training seem to lead to larger salaries? In your opinion, do the higher-earning jobs truly merit their larger salaries? Why or why not? If you could reassign rank to the jobs you've chosen, how would your list compare with the real salaries for those jobs?

PUTTING YOUR BEST FOOT FORWARD Visit your school's Career Services office and ask to see sample resumes. Think about a job or career path that you are interested in pursuing, and use these resources to write a résumé for an entry-level job (or one commensurate with your experience) in this field.

Sean Gallup/Getty Images

6 How We CONNECT

What forces help — and hinder — our relationships with others?

Introduction

"Let's stay in touch"

We hear a lot these days about the virtues of being connected. From commercials touting the latest smart phone app to pundits making pronouncements about our "shrinking planet," we find ourselves at the center of a new world in which the pleasures and pay-offs of "connectedness" are increasingly taken as an indisputable fact of life. But does this newfound cultural ideal truly live up to its billing? Whether through Google searches or Facebook posts, YouTube videos or Twitter feeds, it's undeniable that we now inhabit a wired environment in which our access to each other has come to feel almost limitless. And yet it is far from clear whether we've fully confronted all the questions these dazzling new possibilities raise. In a world where our interactions are increasingly mediated through online technologies, are we becoming less practiced in the art of face-to-face conversation? As we grow ever more accustomed to tracking the daily minutiae of each others' lives, do we find the notion of privacy slipping away? As we spend more and more of the day plugged in, are we losing the capacity to think of ourselves as a community? Living at the center of a world in which we are perpetually in contact, constantly communicating, and boundlessly informed, are we using all our vaunted access to remain *truly* connected?

This book began by asking you to take a closer look at your own underlying beliefs: what they are, where they come from, and what role they play in shaping how you think, talk, and act. In doing so, as you no doubt recall, you also found yourself confronting some fundamental questions: What is our relationship to the larger culture? In what ways does our culture actively teach us what to believe? We now come full circle with these questions by concluding with a chapter that invites you to look closely at what has arguably become our culture's newest and most widely-embraced belief: "connectedness." Consider the flip side of the questions posed above—not just "How does culture teach us what is normal?" but "To what extent can we define what is normal for ourselves?" This chapter asks you to take seriously the proposition that we are more than just the passive recipients of our culture's rules and scripts, that we in fact have a hand in *shaping* these rules and scripts as well.

You have received this same invitation, of course, throughout the book. Our investigation into the societal rules and public roles, cultural norms and social scripts has consistently been underwritten by a healthy belief in our own agency: the power and prerogative to make our own decisions and choose our own path — even in the face of a culture bent on making these choices for us. We have come to see that the views, values, attitudes, and actions promoted in our world as norms — what everybody, everywhere accepts as simply "the way things are" — are not timeless verities set in stone but social constructs: the products of particular forces in particular times and places. And as we have also come to see, if these are things that have been written out for us, then they can be rewritten as well.

Writers can spur changes in our thinking about cultural norms often whether they intend to or not. The act of recording our impressions about the world around us creates a record not only of how we see ourselves in relation to society but also a reverse negative that shows our perfect, ideal world. When Henry David Thoreau offered his own take on the idea of being connected, deciding to forsake the world for a simpler life at Walden Pond, the act in itself did not change the world. Rather, it was his writing about that experience in *Walden* that made sense of his endeavor, that set forth his principles for a perfect life, and that passed down his set of beliefs for future generations to discover and contend with. As Thoreau proved, good writing has the potential to bend the arc of society in ever-new directions. As you practice your own writing, think about how you are rescripting the rules you live by.

What is normal?

"I never found the companion that was so companionable as solitude."

Henry David Thoreau, *Walden*

What does this quotation ask you to believe? What are the ideas, values, or attitudes it asks you to accept as normal?

The Plugged-in World

To look more closely at the cultural ideal of connectedness is to follow in the footsteps of Thoreau: to ask our own questions about how cultural ideas become cultural norms, and how such norms themselves change over time. What are the factors and forces that cause one collection of rules, one set of norms, one body of scripts to be replaced by another? And to what extent do we, as individual actors within our culture, participate in this process? "How We Connect" offers an opportunity to begin answering these questions not only by presenting us with examples of individuals whose own views and values have been shaped by this newly ascendant ideal but also by encouraging us to use their writing as a catalyst for rethinking the role it plays in our own lives.

As you delve more deeply into the notion of connectedness, you might begin by reflecting on the ways our relationship to this cultural ideal has evolved over the years. Think, for example, about what it meant to be connected generations ago. In the era before Twitter, Instagram, and Skype, the task of staying in touch involved very different investments of time and energy. In the nineteenth century, for example, staying in touch involved composing and responding to actual handwritten letters. A couple of decades later, the telephone, an invention that made instantaneous connection an option for millions of people for the first time, made this task far easier. A few years later, mass media such as radio and television put countless Americans into regular daily contact with characters, stories, and viewpoints very different from their own immediate experience. In each case, these technological advances brought concomitant cultural change as well. As innovations like the telephone and television supplied Americans with new ways to connect, they also raised a number of key questions whose answers were far from self-evident. As we find ourselves increasingly able to stay in touch, where do we draw the line between what can be made public and what should remain private? In a world that affords us more opportunities to speak out on topics of importance, whose voices get to be heard? As digital technology has once again remade our communications landscape over the last decade, we find ourselves confronting anew the complex cultural questions that arise from living in such a profoundly interconnected world.

What is normal?

"Your world delivered. Connecting to your world, everywhere you live and work."

AT&T Slogan

Do you share the attitude this quotation reflects? Should we automatically accept it as normal?

DENIS CHARLET/AFP/Getty Images

The selections assembled in this chapter revolve around precisely these kinds of questions. Taking aim at the cultural norms surrounding connection, each of these essays showcases the ways individual people negotiate and remake this norm to suit their own purposes. The goal behind these selections is to lay out the range of possibilities for responding to a norm as widely touted and broadly accepted as the notion of connectedness. In the face of the growing cultural orthodoxy around the value of being "connected," what choices do individual people have? Do they respond with anxiety and trepidation? Do they embrace the prospect of being perpetually connected with confidence and gusto? Curtis Silver and Evgeny Morozov both examine how social technology has fostered important changes in the way we socialize and share information with each other, for better or worse. Nathan Jurgenson continues this line of inquiry by exploring the rise of digital photo-sharing programs, such as Snapchat and Instagram, and what photography has come to mean in our online society. Keith O'Brien poses his own questions about technology-aided connection, asking whether our growing dependence upon social media has diminished our capacity to empathize with each other. Countering such techno-pessimism, Hanna Rosin delves into recent studies that suggest kids may actually have something to gain from "screen time." Joel Kotkin chronicles a different kind of trend, one which finds more and more Americans returning to their hometowns in an attempt to reclaim a sense of community. In a counterpoint to this piece, Peter Lovenheim discovers just how little he knows about his neighbors living right next door. And finally, Claire Suddath rounds out our selections by making a powerful case for *dis*connection, profiling a retreat dedicated to what she calls "digital detox."

What is normal?

"Over the course of your lives, I promise you will have many opportunities to use technology to make your world bigger: to meet more different kinds of people, and to keep in touch with more of the people you meet. . . . I want you to connect because I believe it will inspire you to do something, to make a difference in the world."

Commencement speech at Duke University by Melinda Gates, 2013

What kind of social script do these instructions write? What would it feel like to act out this script in our own lives? And can this kind of social script be rewritten?

macmillanhighered.com/actingout
Tutorials > Digital Writing > Photo Editing Basics with GIMP
> Audio Editing with Audacity
> Presentations
> Word Processing
e-Readings > Casey Neistat, *Texting While Walking*

CURTIS SILVER

The Quagmire of Social Media Friendships

The explosive growth and burgeoning popularity of online social networking sites raise important questions about the ways we are redefining friendship. It is beyond dispute that these new technologies have reconfigured the ways we think about, talk to, and define our friends. Less clear, however, is whether these changes are for the better. Taking up this question, Curtis Silver shares his thoughts about the ways social media have eroded more traditional notions of friendship. Silver writes about technology and culture for Technorati and Medium, and is a frequent contributor to the GeekDad column for Wired.com where this essay appeared in 2012.

UP UNTIL ABOUT FIVE YEARS AGO I ONLY HAD A HANDFUL OF people that I would consider friends. These people knew me well, and I them. These were the kinds of people to help a guy move on short notice or jump your car in the rain. Now, times have changed and considering all the social networks I'm attached to, I have thousands of friends. I'm the most popular person in the world!

Until the reality of that thought crumbles, which tends to happen more often than not. Regardless of what we think or what our social media statistics indicate, as functioning humans we can only maintain a set number of actual relationships, straining what exactly a friend is. The best way to contemplate how many "friends" we can maintain and effectively care about in even the simplest sense is with Dunbar's number theory.

Dunbar's number is a cognitive theory that states that we can only maintain 150 "friendships" in social relationships. That is, the number of people we keep some sort of social contact with but does not include those we know personally with a dead social relationship (such as childhood friends we no longer have any contact with) or people we might know casually but don't maintain a social relationship [with]. These [exceptions] might produce a number much bigger than 150, and depend on our long-term memory.

Evolutionary psychologist and anthropologist Robin Dunbar came up with the theory back in the early 1990's during primate study. This behavioral study was quickly applicable to humans, as our social interactions can be pretty similar (in more ways than one, you crazy monkeys you). More recently, the theory has been applied to social networks, [and the results suggest] that having an exponentially high number of Facebook friends means nothing as you can only maintain 150 social relationships.

I think that is a false assertion of Dunbar's number and doesn't take into account the constantly shifting nature of social networks. Not only that, but Dunbar's number was developed using personal, physical relationships rather than online ones. Online relationships are a different beast. However, I think that the theory itself, perhaps not the exact number, holds plenty of weight when applied to social relationships. First, we need to understand what these relationships really are. That means asking ourselves, what is a friend?

[C]onsidering all the social networks I'm attached to, I have thousands of friends. I'm the most popular person in the world!

Author Anaïs Nin once said, "Each friend represents a world in us, a world possibly not born until they arrive, and it is only by this meeting that a new world is born." While people we maintain social relationships with are casually called "friends" on social sites. Some may be, but those cases would have other extenuating circumstances. According to the cosmically understood, Oxford dictionary definition of a friend, it is "a person with whom one has a bond of mutual affection, typically one exclusive of sexual or family relations."

The argument can be made that we have a mutual affection for everyone we interact with on a social network, but those mutual affections in most cases are quite minute and we're possibly grasping at tiny strings in order to justify the usage of the word "friend." For example, in ancient Greek both "friend" and "lover" were the same word, so it's under no slight amount of amazement that the concept of a friend has been debated across all disciplines of psychology. The advent of social networks has given us more "friends," yet at the same time has diminished true friendships.

According to a 2006 study in the journal *American Sociological Review*, Americans have been suffering a loss in number and quality of friendships since 1985. The study states that 25% of Americans have no close friends, and the average of that overall per person has dropped from four to two. Yet, at the same time we hop on Facebook and broadcast our personal business to the world at large. So what exactly does this mean? Does this mean we've lost the personal touch and no longer have any sense of privacy or confidence in confidants?

I think what it means is that we have friends, because we have too many acquaintances that we share too much with to keep them filed at such a base level. As we put more of our lives online, we bring the people in our networks up to a higher sociological level in our brains because we somehow feel they know us. Personally, I don't even start to classify someone as that until I've shaken their hand in person. While there are plenty of people online that I'd loosely consider a "friend" the harsh truth is that they are ghosts in the machine.

Because to me, friendship is what its philosophical definition suggests. Friendship is "a distinctively personal relationship that is grounded in a concern on the part of each friend for the welfare of the other, for the other's sake, and that involves some degree of intimacy." To put it bluntly, a friend is someone who cares about you: Not just the fact that you exist, but the fact they contribute to your existence and the quality of your existence. In that, "friend" is still reserved for a biological response, rather than a social one. Yet, our online friends elicit similar emotional responses. So in effect, the word "friend" has split into two definitions of itself, one being in the classical sense, the other being in the modern social sense.

My friend (in the classical sense, having worked together for several years) Stephen put it quite eloquently on a Facebook response:

> It's a folksy attempt by Big Social to convince us we all are really friends and that this is something we need to feel wanted (and in turn, something Big Social needs for ad clicks and return visits). But it could just be an outdated term that hasn't been changed when the paradigm of a web only contact was introduced; the resultant being a web only "friend" becoming included under the "Friend" banner by default. When Facebook introduced things like Subscriptions and Acquaintances, we can now delineate between a real friend and just some person we chat with. However, a lot of people just won't know how to keep perspective on which is which (simply because they don't care and just really want that sense of belonging, even if it's a lie).

So now that we've basically defined a friend, let's go back to Dunbar's number and apply it to social relationships. I believe we have to look at each social network differently, but still generally. As an aside, Dunbar himself did consult Facebook back in 2010 in relation to his work on the theory. With the exception of celebrities on social networks, I think that 150 is like an IP address that changes every time you connect to the internet. Think of it like a sliding scale with thousands of data points on it, and the slider contains 150 points. It slides up and down the scale depending on interaction. There are some folks on Twitter I go weeks without talking to, then suddenly we're back and forth all week.

[W]hen it comes down to it, anyone we don't know on a personal level is nothing more than a stranger.

In the modern definition of it, we can't [help but] say that everyone that we interact with are friends. In truth, and I credit LinkedIn with popularizing this term, they are connections. They are our audience and we theirs. Outside of business, social media is a stage and every single one of us is on our stage interacting with the crowd, which we are also in. It's very metaphysical. Social media has created a new sociological definition of existence and really needs to be studied further, because as time goes on it's just going to go deeper and deeper into sociological and psychological territory.

Here is where it is already getting tricky. Because of how casual social media "friendships" are, and our general nature of interaction, actual physical encounters have been affected. Those of us who are inundated in social media tend to carry over that causal attitude when we meet new people, whether they be quick encounters or new co-workers. There is less trepidation and that period of base nervousness when meeting new people in the physical realm. On one hand, this has made talking to people easier and strangely less awkward. On the other hand, it's created a comfortability with strangers that shouldn't exist. Because when it comes down to it, anyone we don't know on a personal level is nothing more than a stranger.

Yet at the same time, that's when the Dunbar number slider slides over to include in that 150 people you are interacting with in your physical life. Think about when you are buried in work or other physical interactions, your social media interactions decrease. That's because that slider has slid off the social media and into your physical life.

Here's what some of my "friends" had to say on the subject. Actually, two of these people are actual real "I can count on" friends in my physical life.

> "A friend is someone you can always trust. They are someone if you haven't seen in awhile you can always pick right up and talk like it was yesterday. A friend is always there for you no matter what. Someone you can be silly with and knows you inside and out . . . and still loves you. Ta da!"—Emily (via FB)

> "People on social networks CAN be friends, but it's not automatic. A friend is someone who actually cares about you, & acts on it."—@jennywilliams

> "Just as we've lost the distinction between 'want' and 'need', we've also lost the distinction between 'acquaintance' and 'friend.'"—@tmoney941

> "Friend & Like are sadly bastardized in today's world. Is Friend better than Follower (or minion) to define the new abstract?"—@endashes

The new abstract is a good definer of what a friend is these days. We call them all friends because we have nothing else to call them that relays the same emotional attachment, even if it's not sincere or totally real. But, as evidenced by the quote from another of my connections below, "friend" in the social media age is still being defined.

> "I call you my friend, but my wife says you don't count cuz we've never met IRL."—@timlav

DISCUSSION

1. As the title suggests, the essay addresses its critique toward social media in general. Can you think of a specific example of such media that illustrates the points Silver is making here? How does this example exemplify the ways social media have more broadly reshaped our definitions of friendship? In your opinion, have these changes been for better or worse? How?
2. To support his argument, Silver cites the theory of evolutionary psychologist Robin Dunbar. What does his reference to this theory contribute to Silver's overall argument? Do you agree that a theory originally applied to primates can be transferred to a discussion of human interaction and social media?
3. One possible counterargument to Silver's critique of social media is to see online technologies as instruments or aids for creating closer and more meaningful connections rather than a "quagmire" in which such connections get confused and lost. Is it valid to think of the virtual connections we forge online as a supplement to the actual connections we forge face to face? And if so, how might this impact the overall effectiveness of Silver's argument?

WRITING

4. For Silver, online relationships will always exist as an inferior or incomplete version of friendship that can be fulfilled only through face-to-face contact: "Personally, I don't even start to classify someone as that until I've shaken their hand in person. While there are plenty of people online that I'd loosely consider a 'friend' the harsh truth is that they are ghosts in the machine" (p. 446). Write an essay in which you assess the key claims Silver makes here. Do you agree that online friendship represents a merely "ghostly" version of actual friendships? How or how not?
5. Silver writes: "To put it bluntly, a friend is someone who cares about you. Not just the fact that you exist, but the fact they contribute to your existence and the quality of your existence" (p. 446). In a brief essay, analyze and assess the definition of friendship presented here. What's the difference between a friend who only "cares about the fact you exist" and one who "contribute[s] to the quality of your existence"? Is this distinction part of your own definition of friendship?
6. Peter Lovenheim (p. 458) is another writer interested in exploring the ways modern American culture might be fostering habits of social and emotional disconnection. Write an essay in which you speculate about how Lovenheim might respond to the argument Silver is advancing about "the quagmire of social media friendship." Do you think Lovenheim would find much commonality between this argument and the portrait of contemporary neighbor relations his essay presents? How or how not?

EVGENY MOROZOV

Open and Closed

In our increasingly wired world, it's become an article of faith that more openness is always better than less, that greater and greater degrees of transparency will automatically improve our dealings with each other. But is it possible that we have embraced this ideal a little too enthusiastically? Are there situations in which — prevailing wisdom notwithstanding — it's actually better to be more closed than open, more opaque than transparent? Outlining just this contrarian view, Evgeny Morozov makes a spirited case for the importance, indeed the necessity, of *un*transparency. Morozov is a contributing editor at the *New Republic* and has written extensively about digital culture. His writings have appeared in such publications as the *New York Times*, the *Economist,* and the *Wall Street Journal.* He is the author of two books, *The Net Delusion: The Dark Side of Internet Freedom* (2011) and *To Save Everything, Click Here: The Folly of Technological Solutionism* (2013). The essay below was published in the *New York Times* in 2013.

"CAN 3D PRINTING BE SUBVERSIVE?" ASKS A VOICE IN THE CREEPIEST Internet video you'll be likely to watch this month. It's a trailer for Defcad.com, a search engine for 3D-printable designs for things "institutions and industries have an interest in keeping from us," including "medical devices, drugs, goods, guns."

The voice belongs to Cody Wilson, a law student in Texas who last year founded Defense Distributed, a controversial initiative to produce a printable "wiki weapon." With Defcad, he is expanding beyond guns, allowing, say, drone enthusiasts to search for printable parts.

Mr. Wilson plays up Defcad's commitment to "openness," the latest opiate of the (iPad-toting) masses. Not only would Defcad's search engine embrace "open source"—the three-minute trailer says so twice—but it would also feature "open data." With so much openness, Defcad can't possibly be evil, right?

Certified as "open," the most heinous and suspicious ideas suddenly become acceptable."

One doesn't need to look at projects like Defcad to see that "openness" has become a dangerously vague term, with lots of sex appeal but barely any analytical content. Certified as "open," the most heinous and suspicious ideas suddenly become acceptable. Even the Church of Scientology boasts of its "commitment to open communication."

Openness is today a powerful cult, a religion with its own dogmas. "Owning pipelines, people, products, or even intellectual property is no longer the key to success. Openness is," proclaims the Internet pundit Jeff Jarvis.

This fascination with "openness" stems mostly from the success of open-source software, publicly accessible computer code that anyone is welcome to improve. But lately it has been applied to everything from politics to philanthropy; recent book titles include *The Open-Source Everything Manifesto* and *Radical Openness*. There's even "OpenCola"—a true soda drink for the masses.

For many institutions, "open" has become the new "green." And in the same way that companies will "greenwash" their initiatives by invoking eco-friendly window dressing to hide less-palatable practices, there has also emerged a term to describe similar efforts to read "openness" into situations and environments where it doesn't exist: "openwashing."

Alas, "openwashing," as catchy as it sounds, only questions the authenticity of "open" initiatives; it doesn't tell us what kinds of "openness," if any, are worth pursuing. We must differentiate the many different types of "open."

Take the "openness" celebrated by the philosopher Karl Popper, who defined the "open society" as the apotheosis of liberal political values. This is not the same openness implied by open-source. While Popper's openness is primarily about politics and a free flow of ideas, open-source is about cooperation, innovation, and efficiency—useful outcomes, but not in all situations.

For many institutions, "open" has become the new "green."

Take how George Osborne, the British chancellor of the Exchequer, defined "open-source politics" recently. "Instead of relying on politicians" and "civil servants to have a monopoly of wisdom," he said, "you'd be engaged through the Internet" with the "whole of the public, or as many of the public are interested, in solving a particular problem."

As an add-on to existing politics, this is wonderful. As a replacement for existing politics, though, this is terrifying.

Of course, it's important to involve citizens in solving problems. But who gets to decide which "particular problem" citizens tackle in the first place? And how does one delineate the contours of this "problem"? In open-source software, such decisions are often made by managers and clients. But in democratic politics, citizens both steer the ship (with some delegation) and do the rowing. In open-source politics, all they do is row.

Likewise, "open government"—a term once reserved for discussing accountability—today is used mostly to describe how easy it is to access, manipulate, and "remix" chunks of government information. "Openness" here doesn't measure whether such data increase accountability, only how many apps can be built on top of it, even if those apps pursue trivial goals. This ambiguity of "openness" allows British Prime Minister David Cameron to champion open government while also complaining that freedom of information laws are "furring up the arteries of government."

This confusion isn't limited to government. Take the obsession with massive open online courses. In what sense are they open? Well, they are available online for free. But to celebrate this as a triumph of openness is premature. A more ambitious openness agenda would not just expand access to courses but also give users the ability to reuse, remix, and repurpose their content. I could take somebody's lecture notes, add a few paragraphs, and distribute them further as part of my own course. This is not what most MOOCs currently offer: their terms of use often ban such repurposing.

Will "openness" win, as the digital Pollyannas assure us? It well might. But a victory for "openness" might also signify defeat for democratic politics, ambitious policy reform, and much else. Perhaps we should impose a moratorium on the very word "open." Just imagine the possibilities this could open up!

DISCUSSION

1. "Openness," writes Morozov, "is today a powerful cult, a religion with its own dogmas" (p. 450). What do you make of this analogy? Do you agree that we are encouraged these days to adopt a "cult-like" or "dogmatic" faith in the power of openness? Can you think of an example that either confirms or challenges the validity of this comparison?
2. Morozov draws a distinction between "openness" and "open-sourcing." Popper's openness, he states, "is primarily about politics and a free flow of ideas, [while] open-source is about cooperation, innovation, and efficiency" (p. 450). Do you share Morozov's view that there is a key difference between these two definitions? And do you think the distinction he draws here offers a helpful or revealing way to think about the dangers of openness online?
3. In a tongue-in-cheek conclusion, Morozov suggests that "[p]erhaps we should impose a moratorium on the very word 'open'" (p. 451). If we were to take this suggestion seriously, what term do you think would serve as a useful substitute? What alternative norm might this substitute term promote? And do you think this norm would be more beneficial?

WRITING

4. "For many institutions," Morozov declares, "'open' has become the new 'green.' And in the same way that companies will 'greenwash' their initiatives by invoking eco-friendly window dressing to hide less-palatable practices, there has also emerged a term to describe similar efforts to read 'openness' into situations and environments where it doesn't exist: 'openwashing'" (p. 450). Choose an example of a corporate practice that fits the analogy Morozov offers here. Then write an essay in which you describe and evaluate the ways this example either confirms or contradicts the argument Morozov uses this analogy to advance. What are the particular ways "openness" gets presented or discussed in your example? And to what extent does the use of this term serve to "hide" or "whitewash" practices that are potentially problematic or wrong?
5. For Morozov, the problem with our current cultural obsession with "openness" is that it encourages us to apply this ideal to areas of life (e.g., government, education) where it isn't entirely applicable. First, choose an area of life that you think exemplifies Morozov's point. Then make an argument about the specific ways the ideal of "openness" would not prove useful. What limits would it face? What problems would it raise?
6. For all their differences, Morozov's argument about the dangers of online "openness" shares a fundamental skepticism about the promise and potential of the Web with Claire Suddath's portrait of the digital detox (p. 500). How do you think Morozov would respond to the "digital detox" retreat Suddath depicts? Given his own argument about the dangers of access and "openness," do you think Morozov would regard the retreat's efforts to disconnect from the digital world to be a viable solution? How or how not?

JOEL KOTKIN

There's No Place Like Home

It has become a cliché in recent years to observe that Americans are more and more disconnected from each other. But how much truth does this old saw actually contain? Taking a closer look at some of the data that belies this assumption, Joel Kotkin sketches a portrait of what he calls the "new localism": a trend, increasingly prevalent, that finds more and more people settling down, establishing roots, finding themselves more and more invested in the people and places around them. Kotkin frequently writes on the economy, politics, and society. He is the author of the books *The City: A Global History* (2005) and *The Next Hundred Million: America in 2050* (2010). He is the Roger Hobbs Distinguished Fellow in Urban Studies at Chapman University in Orange, California, and executive editor of www.newgeography.com. In addition, he writes a weekly column for Forbes.com and is a regular contributor to the Daily Beast. The following article originally appeared in the October 9, 2009, edition of *Newsweek.*

ON ALMOST ANY NIGHT OF THE WEEK, CHURCHILL'S RESTAURANT is hopping. The 10-year-old hot spot in Rockville Centre, Long Island, is packed with locals drinking beer and eating burgers, with some customers spilling over onto the street. "We have lots of regulars—people who are recognized when they come in," says co-owner Kevin Culhane. In fact, regulars make up more than 80 percent of the restaurant's customers. "People feel comfortable and safe here," Culhane says. "This is their place."

Thriving neighborhood restaurants are one small data point in a larger trend I call the new localism. The basic premise: the longer people stay in their homes and communities, the more they identify with those places, and the greater their commitment to helping local businesses and institutions thrive, even in a downturn. Several factors are driving this process, including an aging population, suburbanization, the Internet, and an increased focus on family life. And even as the recession has begun to yield to recovery, our commitment to our local roots is only going to grow more profound. Evident before the recession, the new localism will shape how we live and work in the coming decades, and may even influence the course of our future politics.

Perhaps nothing will be as surprising about 21st-century America as its settledness. For more than a generation Americans have believed that "spatial mobility" would increase, and, as it did, feed an inexorable trend toward rootlessness and anomie. This vision of social disintegration was perhaps best epitomized in Vance Packard's 1972 bestseller *A Nation of Strangers*, with its vision of America becoming "a society coming apart at the seams." In 2000, Harvard's Robert Putnam made a similar point, albeit less hyperbolically, in *Bowling Alone*, in which he wrote about the "civic malaise" he saw gripping the country. In Putnam's view, society was being undermined, largely due to suburbanization and what he called "the growth of mobility."

Yet in reality Americans actually are becoming less nomadic. As recently as the 1970s as many as one in five people moved annually; by 2006, long before the current recession took hold, that number was 14 percent, the lowest rate since the census starting following movement in 1940. Since then tougher times have accelerated these trends, in large part because opportunities to sell houses and find new employment have dried up. In 2008, the total number of people changing residences was less than those who did so in 1962, when the country had 120 million fewer people. The stay-at-home trend appears particularly strong among aging boomers, who are largely eschewing Sunbelt retirement condos to stay tethered to their suburban homes—close to family, friends, clubs, churches, and familiar surroundings.

The trend will not bring back the corner grocery stores and the declining organizations—bowling leagues, Boy Scouts, and such—cited by Putnam and others as the traditional glue of American communities. Nor will our car-oriented suburbs replicate the close neighborhood feel so celebrated by romantic urbanists like the late Jane Jacobs. Instead, we're evolving in ways congruent with a postindustrial society. It will not spell the demise of Wal-Mart or Costco, but will express itself in scores of alternative institutions, such as thriving local weekly newspapers, a niche that has withstood the shift to the Internet far better than big-city dailies.

The longer people stay in their homes and communities, the more they identify with those places.

Our less mobile nature is already reshaping the corporate world. The kind of corporate nomadism described in Peter Kilborn's recent book, *Next Stop, Reloville: Life Inside America's Rootless Professional Class*, in which families relocate every couple of years so the breadwinner can reach the next rung on the managerial ladder, will become less common in years ahead. A smaller cadre of corporate executives may still move from place to place, but surveys reveal many executives are now unwilling to move even for a good promotion. Why? Family and technology are two key factors working against nomadism, in the workplace and elsewhere.

Family, as one Pew researcher notes, "trumps money when people make decisions about where to live." Interdependence is replacing independence. More parents are helping their children financially well into their 30s and 40s; the numbers of "boomerang kids" moving back home with their parents has also been growing as job options and the ability to buy houses has decreased for the young. Recent surveys of the emerging millennial generation suggest this family-centric focus will last well into the coming decades.

Nothing allows for geographic choice more than the ability to work at home. By 2015, suggests demographer Wendell Cox, there will be more people working electronically at home full time than taking mass transit, making it the largest potential source of energy savings on transportation. In the San Francisco Bay Area and Los Angeles, almost one in 10 workers is a part-time telecommuter. Some studies indicate that more than one quarter of the U.S. workforce could eventually participate in this new work pattern. Even IBM, whose initials were once jokingly said to stand for "I've Been Moved," has changed its approach. Roughly 40 percent of the company's workers now labor at home or remotely from a client's location.

We are seeing a return to placeness, along with more choices for individuals, families, and communities.

These home-based workers become critical to the localist economy. They will eat in local restaurants, attend fairs and festivals, take their kids to soccer practices, ballet lessons, or religious youth-group meetings. This is not merely a suburban phenomenon; localism also means a stronger sense of identity for urban neighborhoods as well as smaller towns.

Could the new localism also affect our future politics? Ever greater concentration of power in Washington may now be all the rage as the federal government intervenes, albeit often ineffectively, to revive the economy. But throughout our history, we have always preferred our politics more on the home-cooked side. On his visit to America in the early 1830s, Alexis de Tocqueville was struck by the de-centralized nature of the country. "The intelligence and the power are dispersed abroad," he wrote, "and instead of radiating from a point, they cross each other in every direction."

This is much the same today. The majority of Americans still live in a patchwork of smaller towns and cities, including many suburban towns within large metropolitan regions. There are well over 65,000 general-purpose governments, and with so many "small towns," the average local jurisdiction population in the United States is 6,200, small enough to allow nonprofessional politicians to have a serious impact.

After decades of frantic mobility and homogenization, we are seeing a return to placeness, along with more choices for individuals, families, and communities. For entrepreneurs like Kevin Culhane and his workers at Churchill's, it's a phenomenon that may also offer a lease on years of new profits. "We're holding our own in these times because we appeal to the people around here," Culhane says. And as places like Long Island become less bedroom community and more round-the-clock locale for work and play, he's likely to have plenty of hungry customers.

DISCUSSION

1. How do you understand the term *placeness*? How do you define this concept? Does it, in your view, suggest a value or ideal that you consider important? How or how not?
2. Much of Kotkin's argument rests on recent statistical findings regarding what he calls the "stay-at-home trend" in American life. How convincing do you find this argument to be? In your view, do these statistics effectively prove his thesis that Americans are becoming more connected to each other? Can you think of a countertrend in American life that might lead to the opposite conclusion?
3. Counter to popular thinking, according to Kotkin, advances in technology are actually leading more Americans to become rooted within and committed to a single place. To what extent does this view challenge the norms we typically use to think about technology?

WRITING

4. "For more than a generation," Kotkin writes, "Americans have believed that 'spatial mobility' would increase, and, as it did, feed an inexorable trend toward rootlessness" (p. 453). Is Kotkin right in suggesting that this trend has been overstated? In an essay, make clear your own views on this question of rootlessness in modern American life. Can you think of a context or setting in which the rules, norms, and scripts produce a sense of disconnection? Can you, conversely, think of an example in which the rules, norms, and scripts produce the opposite? Which, in your view, is representative of American life more generally?
5. Choose a specific technology such as e-mail, text messages, or Skype. Write a one-page essay in which you argue for the ways this technology either fosters or inhibits greater connection among people. Does this technology, in your view, render us closer to each other? Or does it serve, rather, to make us more alone? In either case, how?
6. Write an essay in which you evaluate how Kotkin's examination of home and roots compares to Silver's discussion of online friendship (p. 444). Does Silver's essay, in your view, confirm or complicate the conclusions Kotkin draws about Americans' increasing commitment to place and each other?

PETER LOVENHEIM

Won't You Be My Neighbor?

In a "wired" age often celebrated for its interactivity and interconnectedness, it may come as a surprise to hear how disconnected from each other so many of us have become. For Peter Lovenheim, this disconnection has become the signature condition of our times. Reflecting on how this has come to be and what it means, he offers some suggestions — at once both unorthodox and commonsensical — about how to ameliorate the loneliness at the heart of modern life. Lovenheim is the author of *In the Neighborhood: The Search for Community on an American Street, One Sleepover at a Time* (2010), the culmination of a project he discusses in the following essay, originally published in the *New York Times* on June 23, 2008. He teaches writing at Rochester Institute of Technology and is also the author of *Portrait of a Burger as a Young Calf: The Story of One Man, Two Cows, and the Feeding of a Nation* (2002).

THE ALARM ON MY CELLPHONE RANG AT 5:50 A.M., AND I AWOKE TO find myself in a twin bed in a spare room at my neighbor Lou's house.

Lou was 81. His six children were grown and scattered around the country, and he lived alone, two doors down from me. His wife, Edie, had died five years earlier. "When people learn you've lost your wife," he told me, "they all ask the same question. 'How long were you married?' And when you tell them 52 years, they say, 'Isn't that wonderful!' But I tell them no, it isn't. I was just getting to know her."

Lou had said he gets up at six, but after 10 more minutes, I heard nothing from his room down the hall. Had he died? He had a heart ailment, but generally was in good health. With a full head of silver-gray hair, bright hazel-blue eyes, and a broad chest, he walked with the confident bearing of a man who had enjoyed a long and satisfying career as a surgeon.

The previous evening, as I'd left home, the last words I heard before I shut the door had been, "Dad, you're crazy!" from my teenage daughter. Sure, the sight of your 50-year-old father leaving with an overnight bag to sleep at a neighbor's house would embarrass any teenager, but "crazy"? I didn't think so.

There's talk today about how as a society we've become fragmented by ethnicity, income, city versus suburb, red state versus blue. But we also divide ourselves with invisible dotted lines. I'm talking about the property lines that isolate us from the people we are physically closest to: our neighbors.

It was a calamity on my street, in a middle-class suburb of Rochester, several years ago that got me thinking about this. One night, a neighbor shot and killed his wife and then himself; their two middle-school-age children ran screaming into the night. Though the couple had lived on our street for seven years, my wife and I hardly knew them. We'd see them jogging together. Sometimes our children would carpool.

Some of the neighbors attended the funerals and called on relatives. Someone laid a single bunch of yellow flowers at the family's front door, but nothing else was done to mark the loss. Within weeks, the children had moved with their grandparents to another part of town. The only indication that anything had changed was the "For Sale" sign on the lawn.

A family had vanished, yet the impact on our neighborhood was slight. How could that be? Did I live in a community or just in a house on a street surrounded by people whose lives were entirely separate? Few of my neighbors, I later learned, knew others on the street more than casually; many didn't know even the names of those a few doors down.

According to social scientists, from 1974 to 1998, the frequency with which Americans spent a social evening with neighbors fell by about one-third. Robert Putnam, the author of *Bowling Alone*, a groundbreaking study of the disintegration of the American social fabric, suggests that the decline actually began 20 years earlier, so that neighborhood ties today are less than half as strong as they were in the 1950s.

Why is it that in an age of cheap long-distance rates, discount airlines, and the Internet . . . we often don't know the people who live next door?

Why is it that in an age of cheap long-distance rates, discount airlines, and the Internet, when we can create community anywhere, we often don't know the people who live next door?

Maybe my neighbors didn't mind living this way, but I did. I wanted to get to know the people whose houses I passed each day—not just what they do for a living and how many children they have, but the depth of their experience and what kind of people they are.

What would it take, I wondered, to penetrate the barriers between us? I thought about childhood sleepovers and the insight I used to get from waking up inside a friend's home. Would my neighbors let me sleep over and write about their lives from inside their own houses?

A little more than a year after the murder-suicide, I began to telephone my neighbors and send e-mail messages; in some cases, I just walked up to the door and rang the bell. The first one turned me down, but then I called Lou. "You can write about me, but it will be boring," he warned. "I have nothing going on in my life—nothing. My life is zero. I don't do anything."

That turned out not to be true. When Lou finally awoke that morning at 6:18, he and I shared breakfast. Then he lay on a couch in his study and, skipping his morning nap, told me about his grandparents' immigration, his Catholic upbringing, his admission to medical school despite anti-Italian quotas, and how he met and courted his wife, built a career, and raised a family.

Later, we went to the Y.M.C.A. for his regular workout; he mostly just kibitzed with friends. We ate lunch. He took a nap. We watched the business news. That evening, he made us dinner and talked of friends he'd lost, his concerns for his children's futures, and his own mortality.

Before I left, Lou told me how to get into his house in case of an emergency, and I told him where I hide my spare key. That evening, as I carried my bag home, I felt that in my neighbor's house lived a person I actually knew.

I was privileged to be his friend until he died, just this past spring.

Remarkably, of the 18 or so neighbors I eventually approached about sleeping over, more than half said yes. There was the recently married young couple, both working in business; the real estate agent and her two small children; the pathologist married to a pediatrician who specializes in autism.

Eventually, I met a woman living three doors away, the opposite direction from Lou, who was seriously ill with breast cancer and in need of help. My goal shifted: could we build a supportive community around her—in effect, patch together a real neighborhood? Lou and I and some of the other neighbors ended up taking turns driving her to doctors' appointments and watching her children.

Our political leaders speak of crossing party lines to achieve greater unity. Maybe we should all cross the invisible lines between our homes and achieve greater unity in the places we live. Probably we don't need to sleep over; all it might take is to make a phone call, send a note, or ring a bell. Why not try it today?

DISCUSSION

1. For Lovenheim, the relations among the neighbors on his street become a barometer of how "community" has come to be defined in our culture. "Did I live in a community," he asks, "or just in a house on a street surrounded by people whose lives were entirely separate?" (p. 459) Do you share Lovenheim's concerns? In your view, does a belief in the importance of community constitute one of our culture's vanishing norms?
2. How would you define the ideal neighborhood? What kinds of relationships among neighbors would you most like to see? Why did you choose these types of connections?
3. Many of his neighbors, Lovenheim observes, didn't seem to mind living next door to people they barely knew. How do you think you would feel? Would you find this kind of anonymity acceptable? Troubling? Why?

WRITING

4. "There's talk today," writes Lovenheim, "about how as a society we've become fragmented by ethnicity, income, city versus suburb, red state versus blue. But we also divide ourselves with invisible dotted lines. I'm talking about the property lines that isolate us from the people we are physically closest to: our neighbors" (p. 458). Write an essay in which you respond to this claim. Is Lovenheim correct, in your opinion? Do the physical barriers in our lives divide us from each other as deeply as do social differences in income, age, ethnicity, or gender? How or how not?
5. How well do you know your neighbors? And how well do they, in turn, know you? In a two-page essay, reflect on how much of Lovenheim's argument about neighborliness and community applies to your experiences. Based on your interactions with the people who live in your neighborhood, would you say Lovenheim's insights are valid? In what ways do your experiences either confirm or challenge his insights?
6. In many ways, Lovenheim's response to the crisis of neighborliness could be read as a commentary on what Keith O'Brien calls the "empathy deficit" (p. 464) and the way modern communications technology renders us more distanced from each other. Write an essay in which you identify and assess the parallels connecting Lovenheim's examination of neighborhoods and O'Brien's discussion of empathy.

Then and Now: Personal Shopping

In America, few relationships have undergone as many changes over the years as the one between retailers and consumers. For those living outside of major cities a hundred years ago, for example, the primary lifeline connecting them to the world of purchasable goods was the mail-order catalog. Filled with images and descriptions of every product imaginable — from children's toys and formal clothing, household gadgets to beauty aids — the catalog evoked for millions of nineteenth-century readers a vision of the commercial marketplace as an exotic, mysterious, and faraway world. Today this vision has long since been superseded by a model of shopping in which the distance between seller and buyers has almost entirely collapsed. In place of the mail-order catalog, we now have sites like eBay and Craigslist, online venues that allow people to play the role of consumer and retailer simultaneously — hunting for bargains on the one hand while hawking their own wares to the highest bidder on the other.

Sears, Roebuck and Co.

NICHOLAS KAMM/AFP/Getty Images

And yet while today's digital marketplace puts buyers and sellers into far more immediate and intimate contact, it's still an open question whether all this new proximity has entirely dispelled all of the mystery from the shopping experience. True, goods no longer arrive at our doorstep like exotic talismans from a far-off land. And, yes, shoppers in the do-it-yourself world of online retail no longer have to base their purchasing decisions on a catalog's stylized images or idealized portraits. But this doesn't automatically mean that the allure of these products is any less powerful. Even though we've forsaken the mail-order catalog for the personal shopping website, the marketplace may well remain just as inscrutable and mysterious as it ever was.

WRITING

1. What are some of the social scripts that govern the way people typically shop online? And do you think these scripts are useful or effective? Pick an example of a product that gets marketed online. How is this product marketed to potential customers? What particular strategies does its seller use to persuade customers to "buy into" what is on display? How would you respond if you were among this target audience?
2. What example in our current popular culture comes closest to the Sears & Roebuck catalog? What are the key similarities and differences between them? And which do you find a more effective or persuasive vehicle for selling products? Why?

KEITH O'BRIEN

The Empathy Deficit

Few would disagree that it's far easier nowadays to keep in touch than it was a generation ago. As face-to-face meetings have given way to Skype, as letters and postcards have been replaced by e-mail, and as the telephone has found itself superseded by texts and Tweets, our ability to reach each other (often at a moment's notice) has grown exponentially. But has all this increased access led us to become more tolerant, more sympathetic, more understanding? Journalist and author Keith O'Brien answers "no." Culling the most recent findings about the "millennial generation," he tries to make sense of one of our era's great paradoxes: The more connected to each other young people grow, the less interested and concerned about each other they seem to become. O'Brien is a former reporter for the *Boston Globe* and is now a New Orleans-based writer. His work has appeared in the *New York Times Magazine*, the *Boston Globe Magazine*, *Boston Magazine*, *Runner's World*, and the *Dallas Morning News*. This piece appeared in the *Boston Globe* in 2010.

YOUNG AMERICANS TODAY LIVE IN A WORLD OF ENDLESS CONNECTIONS and up-to-the-minute information on one another, constantly updating friends, loved ones, and total strangers—"Quiz tomorrow . . . gotta study!"—about the minutiae of their young, wired lives. And there are signs that Generation Wi-Fi is also interested in connecting with people, like, face-to-face, in person. The percentage of high school seniors who volunteer has been rising for two decades.

But new research suggests that behind all this communication and connectedness, something is missing. The study, conducted by researchers at the University of Michigan Institute for Social Research, found that college students today are 40 percent less empathetic than they were in 1979, with the steepest decline coming in the last 10 years.

According to the findings, today's students are generally less likely to describe themselves as "soft-hearted" or to have "tender, concerned feelings" for others. They are more likely, meanwhile, to admit that "other people's misfortunes" usually don't disturb them. In other words, they might be constantly aware of their friends' whereabouts, but all that connectedness doesn't seem to be translating to genuine concern for the world and one another.

"To me, that's the basic glue," said Sara Konrath, a research assistant professor and the lead author of the study on empathy. "It's so rewarding to connect with human beings. It's so good for our bodies to do this. Everything we know as psychologists tells us it's the most wonderful thing. So if we're losing that, I think that is distressing."

Empathy might seem like a hard-to-define, touchy-feely idea, and it's fair to say that most of us don't spend our days wondering if we're empathetic. Yet psychologists have been trying to measure empathy for decades, recognizing its inherent value to humanity. A world without empathy, they say, is a world we wouldn't want to live in.

Today's students . . . might be constantly aware of their friends' whereabouts, but all that connectedness doesn't seem to be translating to genuine concern for the world and one another.

"Do a thought experiment," said Mark Davis, a professor of psychology at Eckerd College in Florida who's spent the last 30 years studying empathy. "Imagine if humans didn't have the capacity for empathy. What would it mean if, in fact, we never gave a damn about what happened to other people? That's an almost an inconceivable world."

It's so inconceivable that Davis counts himself among the skeptics of the new research that documents the decline. "Put me down," he said, "as intrigued by it." He points out that Konrath, along with coauthors Edward O'Brien and Courtney Hsing, are drawing their conclusions from a relatively small sample size—just 72 studies over three decades. He and others would like to see more work on the matter before making any final conclusions about how much young people care, or don't care, about others. But even some skeptics agree that it's disturbing to consider the trend laid out in the new research and then play out the string.

"As awful a species as we can be—and we certainly have the capacity for terrible things—we're also capable of some pretty wonderful things, noble things, self-sacrifice," said Davis. "And the fear would be, if there really is a genuine decline in our ability to act on this capacity we have, the world becomes meaner."

Empathy is such a basic ingredient of the human experience that even babies exhibit it, crying when other children cry or reacting to the facial expressions of adults and parents. Yet the word itself is relatively new: It didn't enter the English lexicon until the early 1900s, derived from the German word *einfühlung*, according to Daniel Batson, a researcher of empathy and professor emeritus at Kansas University. And psychologists studying empathy still disagree on some basic questions about how it should be defined: Is it feeling for others? Feeling as others feel? Understanding how others feel? Or some combination of the above?

"It's all over the place," Batson said. "There's no agreed-upon definition."

But at the most basic level, most concur that empathy is some sort of emotional response to another person's plight, pain, state, or suffering. "It's not just putting oneself in another's shoes," said Aaron L. Pincus, a professor of psychology at Penn State University. "It's truly grasping what they're experiencing. . . . Your emotional state will move in a direction more similar to the person you're empathizing with."

In small ways, psychologists say, empathy is constantly driving our daily lives, as we take into consideration how other people might feel before we act. Some suggest that empathy is the foundation for social norms, even basic etiquette. We typically don't insult people to their faces, Davis explained, in part because we know they're not going to like how that feels.

In small ways, psychologists say, empathy is constantly driving our daily lives, as we take into consideration how other people might feel before we act.

Given its obvious importance to relationships and the human experience, psychologists began studying the issue in the early to mid-20th century. Some researchers have conducted live experiments, staging scenes where someone is suffering and then gauging how observers respond to watching the pain. Others, meanwhile, have developed surveys where people are asked to self-report how they feel, or don't feel, about others or themselves in certain situations. The survey respondents usually then receive a score, essentially assigning a number to describe just how empathetic they are or aren't.

Such studies have obvious flaws. Some people, when surveyed, want to give answers that reflect positively on them. However, researchers have found that these scales are actually effective at predicting how people will behave. Spouses who score higher on empathic concern are more likely to offer emotional support to their partners. People capable of seeing another person's perspective are more likely to help and less likely to exhibit aggression. And those who are narcissistic are probably going to be less empathetic. "Generally speaking," said Pincus, "there's a lack of empathy as narcissism increases."

That link between empathy and narcissism drove the Michigan study. In recent years, some psychologists, including Konrath, have offered evidence that narcissism may be on the rise, leading to a debate about whether that's actually happening and, if so, whether it's a problem. A certain amount of narcissism is healthy, psychologists point out, helping give people the confidence to compete, succeed, or lead others. But it can also tip the other way, creating a world of increased self-absorption. Konrath and her coauthors, hoping to get to the bottom of this debate, set out to measure how empathy had changed over time. If narcissism was truly on the rise, they postulated, then empathy had to be in decline. They began to analyze the results of 72 different surveys, given to almost 14,000 college students, beginning in 1979, charting how the students answered the same questions over time.

Initially, they found little shift. "It's looking sort of flat, or no real pattern, up until 2000," Konrath said. "And then there's this sudden, sharp drop."

Starting around a decade ago, scores in two key areas of empathy begin to tumble downward. According to the analysis, perspective-taking, often known as cognitive empathy—that is, the ability to think about how someone else might feel—is declining. But even more troubling, Konrath noted, is the drop-off the researchers have charted in empathic concern, often known as emotional empathy. This is the ability to exhibit an emotional response to someone else's distress.

Perhaps more than any other characteristic, one's capacity for empathic concern dictates how much one cares about others. Those who score high in empathic concern, according to past research, are more likely to return incorrect change to a cashier, let someone else ahead of them in line, carry a stranger's belongings, give money to a homeless person, volunteer, donate to a charity, look after a friend's pet or plant, or even live on a vegetarian diet. And what's alarming, Konrath said, is that empathic concern has fallen more than any other aspect of empathy. Between 1979 and 2009, according to the new research, empathic concern dropped 48 percent.

The results have led to the obvious follow-up questions: What cultural changes may have shaped children in the 1980s and '90s, giving rise to a less empathetic generation? Why do we care less? And is there any way we can reverse the trend?

The answers, to date, are all speculative. What's clear, Konrath said, is that something critical began happening about a decade ago when a new crop of college students began taking these standard surveys.

These students, Konrath points out, would have been born in the 1980s, raised in the '90s on video games, 24-hour cable television, and widespread divorce, and sent off to college with laptops and cellphones—the young pioneers of the digital age. Perhaps, some suggest, technology has connected them in one sense, but pushed them away from each other in another. "It's very shallow, a lot of these connections," said Jean Twenge, coauthor of *The Narcissism Epidemic: Living in the Age of Entitlement*. "You don't really have an emotional connection with someone on Facebook."

Perhaps, others argue, the problem is the advent of 24-hour cable and Internet news; young people today have been inundated with news to the point that they cannot care anymore. The oil spill in Louisiana this week, the flood in Pakistan next week—the tragedies all run together, making it harder to care in any sort of sustained way. Parenting could also be at fault, Konrath speculated. Perhaps today's less empathetic children were raised by more narcissistic parents. Or the problem could be a hypercompetitive world in which everyone is trying to get into the best schools, get ahead, get more.

It's possible, some psychologists argue, that people haven't changed so much as the world around us has. Innately, they suggest, young people today still care as much as they once did. But at a time when jobs are scarce, the economy is sputtering, our politics are filled with anger, and people often feel powerless to address the problems in their own lives—much less affect big issues like climate change—perhaps young Americans are just evolving to focus on what matters most: their own tiny worlds.

"I'd be extremely surprised if it turns out that students were now less capable of caring for other people—their friends, romantic partners, family, or pets," Batson said. "The idea that they're less capable of caring than they were 20 years ago—that just seems unlikely. I don't think we change like that. But our situation may have changed. One may feel pressure to pull back on the scope of one's concern. Pull it back and say, 'I've got to deal with the needs that are pressing right here.' "

Konrath also warns that it's hard to know if the problem is as acute as the study shows. College students aren't a representative slice of America. In order to know if empathy is truly declining, Konrath said, she would need to run a study that captures the full picture of the populace—research that her group has already started. And though the findings aren't published yet, Konrath said, the early indications are that the national findings support what they have already found. "People who were born in the '80s or later," she said, "are lowest in empathy, regardless of whether they have a college degree or not."

Still, she is trying to stay upbeat about the present and the future. If empathy can go down, she said, it can also go up. It's malleable. But still there's reason for concern, just knowing how a lack of empathy can affect society.

In recent years, W. Keith Campbell, Twenge's coauthor and a professor of psychology at the University of Georgia, has run a series of experiments where he places four people in charge of forestry companies harvesting an imaginary 200-hectare forest. He gives them permission to cut down 10 hectares a year, stipulating that 10 percent will grow back. The question before the participants is: Will they limit their short-term gains for the long-term good of the group? Or will they cut down as many trees as possible, thereby exhausting the resource for everyone much faster?

The narcissists—those focused primarily on themselves—always do well, Campbell said, harvesting more trees than the others in the group. But soon enough, the system is destroyed and everyone is worse off.

"So if you have a society where a lot of people are narcissistic, the whole thing blows up," he said. "It implodes."

DISCUSSION

1. O'Brien refers to the millennials under examination here as "Generation Wi-Fi." How do you respond to this term? What does O'Brien mean to suggest about this generation (i.e., its habits, its views, its values) by describing them in this way? In your view, is this an accurate or fair characterization? Why or why not?
2. The main goal behind this essay is to make sense of what, in O'Brien's view, is the central paradox about young people today: While they are "constantly aware of their friends' whereabouts . . .all that connectedness doesn't seem to be translating to genuine concern for the world and one another" (p. 464). Do you share O'Brien's dismay here? Do you find it surprising or troubling to come across findings that show a gap between "connectedness" and a "concern for the world and one another"? Do these findings accord with your own experiences?
3. According to the experts O'Brien interviews, the opposite of empathy is narcissism: a predominant or exclusive concern for one's own needs and interests. Would you say we live in a culture in which empathy or narcissism is more widely promoted as a social or cultural norm? Can you think of an example from contemporary life that supports your hypothesis?

WRITING

4. In reviewing the data about empathy, O'Brien cites one researcher who offers what he calls a "thought experiment": "Imagine if humans didn't have the capacity for empathy. What would it mean if, in fact, we never gave a damn about what happened to other people? That's an almost an inconceivable world" (p. 465). Write an essay in which you take up the invitation to conduct this "thought experiment." What do you think it would mean to live in such a world? What would be the specific consequences in a society where the value, indeed the necessity, of empathizing no longer held sway as a cultural norm?
5. At the "most basic level," writes O'Brien, " . . .empathy is some sort of emotional response to another person's plight, pain, state, or suffering" (p. 466). Choose a cultural text (i.e., film, website, advertisement, image) that you think promotes this definition of empathy as a social or cultural norm. First describe this text. What are its key features or characteristics? What material does it include? Where is it found? Then analyze the specific ways it attempts to promote its message about empathy. What, according to this text, makes empathizing with others so important? What benefits does it claim embracing this ideal will bring? And finally, evaluate how persuasive you find this message to be. Are you convinced by the argument this text advances? Why or why not?
6. In many ways, O'Brien's investigation into empathy provides us with a useful context for thinking about the experiment in "unplugging" that Claire Suddath profiles ("Digital Detox," p. 500). What specific aspects of O'Brien's thesis about the "empathy deficit" do you think are most directly in line with the goals of the "tech addicts" Suddath describes? Does this "deficit," in your view, help explain why some people might be tempted to try an experience like this? How?

Rule **Maker** >>>>>>>>> *Rule* **Breaker**

"What's blocking us right now is sort of hyper-partisanship in Washington that, frankly, I was hoping to overcome in 2008. And in the midst of crisis, I think the other party reacted, rather than saying now is the time for us all to join together, decided to take a different path. My thinking was after we beat them in 2012, well, that might break the fever, and it's not quite broken yet. But I am persistent. And I am staying at it. And I genuinely believe that there are actually Republicans out there who would like to work with us but they're fearful of their base and they're concerned about what Rush Limbaugh might say about them. And, as a consequence, we get the kind of gridlock that makes people cynical about government and inhibits our progress."

— PRESIDENT BARACK OBAMA,
MAY 13, 2013

"Obama said . . . he'd get a lot more done without Fox News and Rush Limbaugh. The rest of the media's in the tank. Everybody else has fallen in line. There is no opposition other than Fox News and Limbaugh. The way it works, and what this all boils down to: the Republicans, everybody knows they want to get along with Democrats. Everybody knows they want to socialize. They want their lives to have meaning, but Limbaugh is the one standing in the way 'cause what happens? The Republicans are simply afraid that I'm gonna criticize them if they do something that is cooperative with the Democrats. And so that's a problem."

— RUSH LIMBAUGH,
REMARKS ON HIS RADIO SHOW, JANUARY 28, 2013

BARACK OBAMA VS. RUSH LIMBAUGH

No single term more aptly encapsulates the problems of our current political culture than *gridlock*. As countless commentators and pundits have lamented, our model of governance seems to have devolved from one that values the art of compromise into one that practices the scorched-earth tactics of destroying the opponent at all costs. Surveying this dysfunctional scene, many have begun to wonder whether it's possible any longer for policymakers to set aside their differences and forge genuine political connections.

The exchange between President Obama and Rush Limbaugh showcased above offers a case in point. According to the President, all of our current political troubles can be laid at the feet of the Republicans, whose knee-jerk opposition is responsible for paralyzing the operation of government. For critics like Rush Limbaugh, meanwhile, such intransigence is not an impediment or a problem but rather a legitimate and necessary act of political critique. So how do you know whom to believe? When one person's partisan sabotage is another person's civic duty, how do you tell the difference between gridlock and governance?

AP Photo/Julie Smith

FIND THE RULES: Choose a current political issue that is the subject of polarizing, even paralyzing, political debate (examples include healthcare or financial reform, environmental legislation, or immigration reform). Write about how this issue gets debated within our current political culture. What makes this issue controversial? What different groups does it pit against each other? How do their views and values differ?

ANALYZE THE RULES: Next, analyze why you think this particular issue is so polarizing. What specific social or cultural norms does this debate pit against each other? And what factors account for why there exists so little common ground between the opposing sides?

MAKE YOUR OWN RULES: Imagine that you are a political strategist tasked with creating a new model for conducting this particular debate. First, write a description of the specific strategies this effort would entail. What specific aspects of or elements within the current debate would you change in order to bridge the ideological differences this debate currently involves? What specific groups or constituencies would you target? What groups or constituencies would you not target? When you're done, write an assessment of why you made these particular choices. How do you think these strategies would help lead to greater political collaboration and connection?

NATHAN JURGENSON

Pics and It Didn't Happen

We've all heard the worried commentary about the ways social media are "dumbing down" the language we use to communicate. But what about our ability to communicate through pictures? Given how visually oriented today's digital culture is, it is possible that the communication norms of the future may include no words at all. This is the startling possibility Nathan Jurgenson explores in his examination of Snapchat, a mobile app that allows users to communicate by sharing videos and photos that automatically delete. What effect, Jurgenson asks, does such a technology have on the ways we think both about — and through — pictures? Jurgenson is a contributing editor at the online journal the *New Inquiry*, where this piece appeared in 2013.

A PHOTOGRAPH IS MADE OF TIME AS MUCH AS IT IS OF LIGHT—A frozen shutter-speed-size gap of the present captured within a photo border. Despite this, photographs have always been a way to cheat death, or at least to declare the illusion of immortality through lasting visual evidence. There's always the possibility that the next photo you take will one day be lovingly removed from a box by some unborn great-grandchild; the Polaroid developing in your hands might come to be pinned to someone's bedpost in posterity. To update that to more contemporary terms, your selfie on Instagram might be a signpost for the future you of what it was like to be this young.

On Snapchat, images have no such future. Fittingly, its logo is a ghost.

By refuting the assumption of the permanence of the image, Snapchat is a radical departure. It inaugurates *temporary photography,* in which photos are seen once by their chosen audience and then are gone in 10 seconds or less. Snapchat recipients can take a screenshot, though the app discourages this by notifying the sender. Millions of people have done this a billion times with the Snapchat app (to say nothing of Facebook's copycat, Poke).

The temporary photograph's abbreviated lifespan changes how it is made and seen, and what it comes to mean. Snaps could be likened to other temporary art such as ice sculptures or decay art (e.g., Yoko Ono's famous rotting apple) that takes seriously the process of disappearance, or the One Hour Photo project from 2010 that has as its premise to "project a photograph for one hour, then ensure that it will never be seen again." There was once a Temporary Art Museum in Washington, D.C. However, whatever changes in the aesthetics of photographic vision

Snapchat is effecting are difficult to assess, given that no one really knows what its self-deleting photos collectively look like. In many ways, this is exactly the point.

To understand the emergence of temporary photography, one must understand it in relation to the inflating archive of persistent images and their significance on how we perceive and remember the world.

The logic of the camera is that reality is real only to the extent that it is photographable. It pulls individuals out of the moment and makes them see it (and themselves) as an object for the future as well as always already of the past. This seizing of experience's ephemerality—to possess the present, docile and durable—is what Andreas Kitzmann called a "museal gesture," what Jean Baudrillard called "museumification," and what André Bazin called the "mummy complex," the "need to have the last word in the argument with death by means of the form that endures." It's ownership of the present by proxy.

The temporary photograph's abbreviated lifespan changes how it is made and seen, and what it comes to mean.

As Susan Sontag wrote in *On Photography,*

> there is something predatory in the act of taking a picture. To photograph people is to violate them, by seeing them as they never see themselves, by having knowledge of them they can never have; it turns people into objects that can be symbolically possessed.

Sontag notes that this makes for a nostalgic gaze, an understanding of the world as primarily documentable. For those who live with status updates, check-ins, likes, retweets, and ubiquitous photography, such an understanding is near inescapable. Social media have invited users to adopt a sort of documentary vision, through which the present is always apprehended as a potential past. This is most triumphantly exemplified by Instagram's faux-vintage filters.

There's always tension between experience-for-itself and experience-for-documentation, but social media have brought that strain to its breaking point. Temporary photography is in part a response to social-media users' feeling saddled with the distraction of documentary vision. It rejects the burden of creating durable proof that you are here and you did that. And because temporary photographs are not made to be collected or archived, they are elusive, resisting other museal gestures of systemization and taxonomization, the modern impulse to classify life according to rubrics. By leaving the present where you found it, temporary photographs feel more like life and less like its collection.

The photograph, for all its promised immortality, always hinted at death. This was central to Roland Barthes's analysis in *Camera Lucida,* that the enduring image "produces Death while trying to preserve life." Documenting the present as a future past, as conventional photographs do, asserts the facts of change, impermanence, and mortality. The temporary photograph does the opposite: It interrupts the traditional photographic fixation of the present as impending history by positing a present moment that's not concerned with the past or the future. As such, the temporary photograph is necessarily less sentimental and nostalgic. By being quick, the temporary photograph is a tiny protest against time.

Let's face it, much of photography was already becoming Snapchat even before Snapchat existed. While much is justifiably, if hyperbolically, made of "the death of privacy" in the age of information immortality, the likely fate of the vast majority of images today is to be briefly consumed and quickly forgotten. As well as offering relief from deepening documentary vision, the temporary photograph also responds to this photographic abundance, which has deflated the value of images. As making more and more photos becomes easier, each individual shot means less and less. Snapchat is an attempt at re-inflation.

Snapchat inspires memory because it welcomes the possibility of forgetting.

In their scarcity, photographs can age like wine, with grace and importance. In their abundance, photos can sometimes curdle, spoil, and rot. But from the beginning, technological innovation in photography has driven toward creating visual abundance. Daguerre is widely credited as inventing photography, in 1839, in part because earlier mechanical image-capturing techniques—most famously Niepce's so-called heliography—did not create as many images as quickly and reliably. In subsequent decades, major advances shortened exposure times and made images even more easily reproducible, chiefly through replacing photographic plates with paper. Photography democratized dramatically with the introduction of Kodak's small, cheap, and easy-to-use personal cameras at the turn of the 20th century. The ads proclaimed, "You press the button, we do the rest." And then there is the rise of digital photography and smartphone cameras that make taking, duplicating, and viewing photos something many people do almost anytime and anywhere.

As photographic technology expanded photography's user base, the photograph went from a rare prized possession to common keepsake to a nuisance that clutters our visual memories. Writing of this visual oversaturation, Michael Sacasas worries that

> digital photography and sites like Facebook have brought us to an age of memory abundance. The paradoxical consequence of this development will

> be the progressive devaluing of such memories and severing of the past's hold on the present. Gigabytes and terabytes of digital memories will not make us care more about those memories, they will make us care less.

By simulating the aesthetic of photographic scarcity, Instagram works as a response to (or overcompensation for) this fear—the enchanting landscape, disarming portrait, the bold statements and delicate textures look like moments captured from the past for posterity. These are the visual cues of photography pre-digital-devaluation, right down to the warm colors, faded glow, and false paper scratches and borders. Instagram's faux-vintage filters . . . reassure that present lives are just as authentic and worthy of nostalgia as the life captured in the seemingly scarce images from the analog past. *Photographs are becoming too easy, so, dammit, here's my life framed like it's 1942.*

But having an Instagram account is like having an abundance of money in a dead currency. So much nostalgia and meaning have been shoveled at us that the aesthetic has lost much of its ability to affect. Merely making your photos evocative of photo scarcity doesn't make them actually scarce or make others covet them. There's a deep mismatch between the aesthetic language of Instagram and the affordances of the network. Despite all the manufactured nostalgia, your photo disappears down the stream, largely unnoticed.

So whereas Instagram merely evokes the look of scarcity, temporary photography by definition enforces a certain rarity that imbues the image with a heightened aura of meaningfulness. Snapchat inspires memory because it welcomes the possibility of forgetting. Instead of being shared with a large number of people on a popular website, temporary photographs are taken specifically for and shared with one other person or a small group of people. The meaning of the photo doesn't rest just in its content but in the choice to restrict its consumption—the choice to send that particular image to that particular person at that particular time, to the exclusion of other images, other recipients, and other times.

The ephemerality sharpens viewers' focus: Once received, a Snapchat count-down is a kind of time-bomb that demands an urgency of vision, a challenge to exhaust the meaning from the image before the clock runs out. Unlike a paper photo that fades slowly over the years, the temporary photo disappears suddenly. Given only a peek, you look hard.

The temporary photo will wrongly be called frivolous or trivial—after all, only unimportant images could be so easily parted with. But as we have seen, there is meaning in witnessing ephemerality itself, an appreciation of impermanence for its own sake. By carving a space away from the growing necessity to record and collect life into database museums, temporary photography encourages an appreciation of the importance of experiencing the present for its own sake.

We might be witnessing an extraordinarily rare, even if minor, countertrend to photography's increasing abundance—a sort of photographic population control. In this way, the rise of self-deleting photographs might be as much about reinstating the importance of nontemporary photos as it is the enactment of photographic disposability.

If everyday photography becomes temporary photography—if more people switch to apps like Snapchat and Poke—photos saved to more permanent locations like Facebook will become correspondingly more scarce and perhaps seem more important. Photographs taken and shared as temporary will impart more meaning to those chosen to be permanent. In the age of digital abundance, photography desperately needs this introduction of intentional and assured mortality, so that some photos can become immortal again.

DISCUSSION

1. Take a moment to reflect upon the name "Snapchat." What images or associations does this term evoke? What vision of communication does it suggest?
2. "Snapchat," writes Jurgenson, "inspires memory because it welcomes the possibility of forgetting" (p. 475). What do you think he means here? In what way do you think Snapchat photos might feel especially memorable? And how might this differ from the memories inspired by conventional photographs?
3. Think back to a moment when you used a photo-sharing app. What types of images did you record? To whom did you send them? And what larger goal(s) were you hoping to accomplish by doing so?

WRITING

4. Central to the purpose Snapchat serves, notes Jurgenson, is its temporariness: "The temporary photograph's abbreviated lifespan changes how it is made and seen, and what it comes to mean" (p. 472). In a short essay, make an argument about the ways the "abbreviated lifespan" of Snapchat photos changes the ways these photos are seen. In your view, how does the temporary quality of such images change how a viewer might respond? And how does your view compare to Jurgenson's?
5. Choose an experience that you think lends itself best to being recorded via Snapchat. What kind of experience is this? What aspects in particular do you think Snapchat would best help you capture? Then put yourself in the position of a viewer to whom these photos might be sent. How do you think the Snapchat format would affect the way you respond to these images? How would this technology shape your attitudes and/or reaction?
6. Evgeny Morozov ("Open and Closed," p. 449) is deeply skeptical about the kinds of openness frequently championed by boosters of social media. Compare his thesis to Jurgenson's argument about the social and aesthetic significance of Snapchat. Is Snapchat an example of the type of online openness Morozov decries? Or does this "temporary" photography represent the kind of "opaque" technology Morozov endorses?

Scenes and Un-Scenes: "Hello, Neighbor"

It has become cliché to bemoan the demise of community in contemporary life. But what exactly do we mean by the term *community*? Ritually invoked by politicians and pundits, commentators and educators, community stands as one of the most frequently lauded, and yet chronically unspecified, ideals in public life — defined as much by what it's not and where it's missing as by anything else. To speak of community is, on some level, to pose the questions "What do we have in common? What interests or sympathies, experiences or background, bind us to one another?" To watch the news and listen to pundits, one is always hearing declarations that the nature of community is changing and, by many accounts, eroding. But do you agree?

How we answer such questions depends in large measure on where we stand. Different vantages generate different notions of community. This, in the broadest sense, is what the images assembled here make clear. Sampling some of the more representative perspectives on community within our culture, these visuals show us the extent to which our definitions of community are determined by our given perspective.

An iconic figure in American pop culture, Mr. Rogers embodied for generations of American children what it means to be part of a community. The gentle invitation with which he opened every show — "Won't you be my neighbor?" — grew over the years into one of the most universally recognized and endlessly imitated phrases in all of television. In its own way, this phrase encapsulated the concept of community that guided the entire show. To be a "neighbor" meant joining a community that placed no restrictions on belonging, a world in which differences of race and class, gender and age were dissolved in the vision of an all-inclusive neighborhood in which all were recognized as equals. What do you make of this ethic? Does such acceptance and inclusiveness still constitute a norm in our society?

Fotos International/Getty Images

When we think of community, many of us think of the physical space we inhabit. Looking at a community from a distance, how does our idea of it change? How is this space dependent on who lives inside it? Does an image like this say "community" to you? When looking at an aerial image, does community still evoke the same communal ideals?

Creative Images/Getty Images

Loic Venance/Getty Images

What happens when community goes online? In the wake of technologies that now allow us to invent, control, or even fabricate our chosen community, we have seen the emergence of an entirely new set of rules and norms around how this ideal can be defined. Virtual relationships, those that exist nowhere except online, now routinely fall within the category of community. But should they? What are the differences between an online and a so-called real-world community? Are communities we create online any less authentic than those we join in our everyday lives?

"NOW THAT WE'VE LEARNED TO TALK, WE'D BETTER ESTABLISH SOME LOCAL COMMUNITY STANDARDS."

Rex May Baloo/Cartoonstock.com

This cartoon takes a tongue-in-cheek look at the idea of communal living, namely that we collaborate on rules by which we live. But it also skewers this notion. How does it do that? What does this cartoon seem to say about the existence of community standards? Are they good or bad?

United Way

▲ *For many, the term* **community** *is a rallying cry, a call to tackle and redress a pressing social problem. In this context,* **community** *denotes less a specific group or place than a program or plan for implementing some type of policy. This United Way campaign is designed to advocate for community involvement in urban areas. What ideas about community are present in this image? Which are missing?*

DISCUSSION

1. Which of these images most resembles your notion of community? Why is that?
2. Which of these images seems most foreign to you? How does its depiction of community or community ideals fail to relate to your experience?
3. Do you think any images are missing from this portfolio? What would they be? How would they represent your opinion on the way community is changing?

WRITING

4. Pick one of the images in this portfolio and write a brief essay in which you evaluate how well it reflects your notion of what community ideals are. Be sure to focus on specific aspects of the image in your critique. What might you change, if anything, about this image to bring it in line with your own experience of community?
5. Do the images in this portfolio represent fundamental changes in the nature of community? Write an essay in which you argue how they do or do not.
6. Peter Lovenheim (p. 458) writes about bygone ideals of community. Write an essay in which you use his definition of community to evaluate the images shown in this portfolio. Do any images in particular fit his ideal? Would he find any of them undesirable? Why or why not?

HANNA ROSIN

The Touch-Screen Generation

Few worries rank higher in the minds of parents these days than those concerning kids and video games. Among educators, advocates, and other experts, it has become an article of faith that excessive "screen time" poses one of the most dire risks children face. But is there proof to support this belief? Or is this ironclad orthodoxy more a reflection of cultural stereotype than the result of hard data? Hanna Rosin answers this question by wading into the research about childhood development and screen time. What she uncovers is a portrait of kids and their video games that is far more complex than the prevailing norms would have us believe. Rosin is a writer and journalist who began her career as a staff writer for the *New Republic.* She is currently a writer for the *Atlantic* as well as the cofounder of DoubleX, *Slate* magazine's women's section. In addition to these publications, Rosin has also written for the *Washington Post*, the *New Yorker*, *GQ*, and *New York*. Her book, *The End of Men and the Rise of Women*, was published in 2012. This article appeared in the *Atlantic* in 2013.

ON A CHILLY DAY LAST SPRING, A FEW DOZEN DEVELOPERS OF children's apps for phones and tablets gathered at an old beach resort in Monterey, California, to show off their games. One developer, a self-described "visionary for puzzles" who looked like a skateboarder-recently-turned-dad, displayed a jacked-up, interactive game called Puzzingo, intended for toddlers and inspired by his own son's desire to build and smash. Two 30-something women were eagerly seeking feedback for an app called Knock Knock Family, aimed at 1-to-4-year-olds. "We want to make sure it's easy enough for babies to understand," one explained.

The gathering was organized by Warren Buckleitner, a longtime reviewer of interactive children's media who likes to bring together developers, researchers, and interest groups—and often plenty of kids, some still in diapers. It went by the Harry Potter-ish name Dust or Magic, and was held in a drafty old stone-and-wood hall barely a mile from the sea, the kind of place where Bathilda Bagshot might retire after packing up her wand. Buckleitner spent the breaks testing whether his own remote-control helicopter could reach the hall's second story, while various children who had come with their parents looked up in awe and delight. But mostly they looked down, at the iPads and other tablets displayed around the hall like so many open boxes of candy. I walked around and talked with developers, and several paraphrased a famous saying of Maria Montessori's, a quote imported to ennoble a touch-screen age when very young kids, who once could be counted on only to chew on a square of aluminum, are now engaging with it in increasingly sophisticated ways: "The hands are the instruments of man's intelligence."

What, really, would Maria Montessori have made of this scene? The 30 or so children here were not down at the shore poking their fingers in the sand or running them along mossy stones or digging for hermit crabs. Instead they were all inside, alone or in groups of two or three, their faces a few inches from a screen, their hands doing things Montessori surely did not imagine. A couple of 3-year-old girls were leaning against a pair of French doors, reading an interactive story called *Ten Giggly Gorillas* and fighting over which ape to tickle next. A boy in a nearby corner had turned his fingertip into a red marker to draw an ugly picture of his older brother. On an old oak table at the front of the room, a giant stuffed Angry Bird beckoned the children to come and test out tablets loaded with dozens of new apps. Some of the chairs had pillows strapped to them, since an 18-month-old might not otherwise be able to reach the table, though she'd know how to swipe once she did.

Not that long ago, there was only the television, which theoretically could be kept in the parents' bedroom or locked behind a cabinet. Now there are smartphones and iPads, which wash up in the domestic clutter alongside keys and gum and stray hair ties.

Not that long ago, there was only the television, which theoretically could be kept in the parents' bedroom or locked behind a cabinet. Now there are smartphones and iPads, which wash up in the domestic clutter alongside keys and gum and stray hair ties. "Mom, everyone has technology but me!" my 4-year-old son sometimes wails. And why shouldn't he feel entitled? In the same span of time it took him to learn how to say that sentence, thousands of kids' apps have been developed—the majority aimed at preschoolers like him. To us (his parents, I mean), American childhood has undergone a somewhat alarming transformation in a very short time. But to him, it has always been possible to do so many things with the swipe of a finger, to have hundreds of games packed into a gadget the same size as *Goodnight Moon*.

In 2011, the American Academy of Pediatrics updated its policy on very young children and media. In 1999, the group had discouraged television viewing for children younger than 2, citing research on brain development that showed this age group's critical need for "direct interactions with parents and other significant care givers." The updated report began by acknowledging that things had changed significantly since then. In 2006, 90 percent of parents said that their children younger than 2 consumed some form of electronic media. Nonetheless, the group took largely the same approach it did in 1999, uniformly discouraging passive media use, on any type of screen, for these kids. (For older children, the academy noted, "high-quality programs" could have "educational benefits.") The 2011 report mentioned "smart cell phone" and "new screen" technologies, but did not address interactive apps. Nor did it broach the possibility that has likely occurred to those 90 percent of American parents, queasy though they might be: that some good might come from those little swiping fingers.

I had come to the developers' conference partly because I hoped that this particular set of parents, enthusiastic as they were about interactive media, might help me out of this conundrum, that they might offer some guiding principle for American parents who are clearly never going to meet the academy's ideals, and at some level do not want to. Perhaps this group would be able to articulate some benefits of the new technology that the more cautious pediatricians weren't ready to address. I nurtured this hope until about lunchtime, when the developers gathering in the dining hall ceased being visionaries and reverted to being ordinary parents, trying to settle their toddlers in high chairs and get them to eat something besides bread.

I fell into conversation with a woman who had helped develop Montessori Letter Sounds, an app that teaches preschoolers the Montessori methods of spelling.

She was a former Montessori teacher and a mother of four. I myself have three children who are all fans of the touch screen. What games did her kids like to play?, I asked, hoping for suggestions I could take home.

"They don't play all that much."

Really? Why not?

"Because I don't allow it. We have a rule of no screen time during the week," unless it's clearly educational.

No screen time? None at all? That seems at the outer edge of restrictive, even by the standards of my overcontrolling parenting set.

"On the weekends, they can play. I give them a limit of half an hour and then stop. Enough. It can be too addictive, too stimulating for the brain."

Her answer so surprised me that I decided to ask some of the other developers who were also parents what their domestic ground rules for screen time were. One said only on airplanes and long car rides. Another said Wednesdays and weekends, for half an hour. The most permissive said half an hour a day, which was about my rule at home. At one point I sat with one of the biggest developers of e-book apps for kids, and his family. The toddler was starting to fuss in her high chair, so the mom did what many of us have done at that moment—stuck an iPad in front of her and played a short movie so everyone else could enjoy their lunch. When she saw me watching, she gave me the universal tense look of mothers who feel they are being judged. "At home," she assured me, "I only let her watch movies in Spanish."

By their pinched reactions, these parents illuminated for me the neurosis of our age: as technology becomes ubiquitous in our lives, American parents are becoming more, not less, wary of what it might be doing to their children. Technological competence and sophistication have not, for parents, translated into comfort and ease. They have merely created yet another sphere that parents feel they have to navigate in exactly the right way. On the one hand, parents want their children to swim expertly in the digital stream that they will have to navigate all their lives; on the other hand, they fear that too much digital media, too early, will sink them. Parents end up treating tablets like precision surgical instruments, gadgets that might perform miracles for their child's IQ and help him win some nifty robotics competition—but only if they are used just so. Otherwise, their child could end up one of those sad, pale creatures who can't make eye contact and has an avatar for a girlfriend.

[A]s technology becomes ubiquitous in our lives, American parents are becoming more, not less, wary of what it might be doing to their children.

Norman Rockwell never painted *Boy Swiping Finger on Screen*, and our own vision of a perfect childhood has never adjusted to accommodate that now-common tableau. Add to that our modern fear that every parenting decision may have lasting consequences—that every minute of enrichment lost or mindless entertainment indulged will add up to some permanent handicap in the future—and you have deep guilt and confusion. To date, no body of research has definitively proved that the iPad will make your preschooler smarter or teach her to speak Chinese, or alternatively that it will rust her neural circuitry—the device has been out for only three years, not much more than the time it takes some academics to find funding and gather research subjects. So what's a parent to do?

In 2001, the education and technology writer Marc Prensky popularized the term *digital natives* to describe the first generations of children growing up fluent in the language of computers, video games, and other technologies. (The rest of us are *digital immigrants*, struggling to understand.) This term took on a whole new significance in April 2010, when the iPad was released. iPhones had already been tempting young children, but the screens were a little small for pudgy toddler hands to navigate with ease and accuracy. Plus, parents tended to be more possessive of their phones, hiding them in pockets or purses. The iPad was big and bright, and a case could be made that it belonged to the family. Researchers who study children's media immediately recognized it as a game changer.

Previously, young children had to be shown by their parents how to use a mouse or a remote, and the connection between what they were doing with their hand and what was happening on the screen took some time to grasp. But with the iPad, the connection is obvious, even to toddlers. Touch technology follows the same logic as shaking a rattle or knocking down a pile of blocks: the child swipes, and something immediately happens. A "rattle on steroids," is what Buckleitner calls it. "All of a sudden a finger could move a bus or smush an insect or turn into a big wet gloopy paintbrush." To a toddler, this is less magic than intuition. At a very young age, children become capable of what the psychologist Jerome Bruner called "enactive representation"; they classify objects in the world not by using words or symbols but by making gestures—say, holding an imaginary cup to their lips to signify that they want a drink. Their hands are a natural extension of their thoughts.

I have two older children who fit the early idea of a digital native—they learned how to use a mouse or a keyboard with some help from their parents and were well into school before they felt comfortable with a device in their lap. (Now, of course, at ages 9 and 12, they can create a Web site in the time it takes me to slice an onion.) My youngest child is a whole different story. He was not yet 2 when the iPad was released. As soon as he got his hands on it, he located the Talking Baby Hippo app that one of my older children had downloaded. The little purple hippo repeats whatever you say in his own squeaky voice, and responds to other cues. My son said his name ("Giddy!"); Baby Hippo repeated it back. Gideon poked Baby Hippo; Baby Hippo laughed. Over and over, it was funny every time. Pretty soon he discovered other apps. Old MacDonald, by Duck Duck Moose, was a favorite. At first he would get frustrated trying to zoom between screens, or not knowing what to do when a message popped up. But after about two weeks, he figured all that out. I must admit, it was eerie to see a child still in diapers so competent and intent, as if he were forecasting his own adulthood. Technically I was the owner of the iPad, but in some ontological way it felt much more his than mine.

Without seeming to think much about it or resolve how they felt, parents began giving their devices over to their children to mollify, pacify, or otherwise entertain them. By 2010, two-thirds of children ages 4 to 7 had used an iPhone, according to the Joan Ganz Cooney Center, which studies children's media. The vast majority of those phones had been lent by a family member; the center's researchers labeled this the "pass-back effect," a name that captures well the reluctant zone between denying and giving.

The market immediately picked up on the pass-back effect, and the opportunities it presented. In 2008, when Apple opened up its App Store, the games started arriving at the rate of dozens a day, thousands a year. For the first 23 years of his career, Buckleitner had tried to be comprehensive and cover every children's game in his publication, *Children's Technology Review*. Now, by Buckleitner's loose count, more than 40,000 kids' games are available on iTunes, plus thousands more on Google Play. In the iTunes "Education" category, the majority of the top-selling apps target preschool or elementary-age children. By age 3, Gideon would go to preschool and tune in to what was cool in toddler world, then come home, locate the iPad, drop it in my lap, and ask for certain games by their approximate description: "Tea? Spill?" (That's Toca Tea Party.)

As these delights and diversions for young children have proliferated, the pass-back has become more uncomfortable, even unsustainable, for many parents:

> He'd gone to this state where you'd call his name and he wouldn't respond to it, or you could snap your fingers in front of his face . . .
>
> But, you know, we ended up actually taking the iPad away for—from him largely because, you know, this example, this thing we were talking about, about zoning out. Now, he would do that, and my wife and I would stare at him and think, *Oh my God, his brain is going to turn to mush and come oozing out of his ears*. And it concerned us a bit.

This is Ben Worthen, a *Wall Street Journal* reporter, explaining recently to NPR's Diane Rehm why he took the iPad away from his son, even though it was the only thing that could hold the boy's attention for long periods, and it seemed to be sparking an interest in numbers and letters. Most parents can sympathize with the disturbing sight of a toddler, who five minutes earlier had been jumping off the couch, now subdued and staring at a screen, seemingly hypnotized. In the somewhat alarmist *Endangered Minds: Why Children Don't Think—and What We Can Do About It*, author Jane Healy even gives the phenomenon a name, the "'zombie' effect," and raises the possibility that television might "suppress mental activity by putting viewers in a trance."

Ever since viewing screens entered the home, many observers have worried that they put our brains into a stupor. An early strain of research claimed that when we watch television, our brains mostly exhibit slow alpha waves—indicating a low level of arousal, similar to when we are daydreaming. These findings have been largely discarded by the scientific community, but the myth persists that watching television is the mental equivalent of, as one Web site put it, "staring at a blank wall."

These common metaphors are misleading, argues Heather Kirkorian, who studies media and attention at the University of Wisconsin at Madison. A more accurate point of comparison for a TV viewer's physiological state would be that of someone deep in a book, says Kirkorian, because during both activities we are still, undistracted, and mentally active.

Because interactive media are so new, most of the existing research looks at children and television. By now, "there is universal agreement that by at least age 2 and a half, children are very cognitively active when they are watching TV," says Dan Anderson, a children's-media expert at the University of Massachusetts at Amherst. In the 1980s, Anderson put the zombie theory to the test, by subjecting roughly 100 children to a form of TV hell. He showed a group of children ages 2 to 5 a scrambled version of *Sesame Street*: he pieced together scenes in random order, and had the characters speak backwards or in Greek. Then he spliced the doctored segments with unedited ones and noted how well the kids paid attention. The children looked away much more frequently during the scrambled parts of the show, and some complained that the TV was broken. Anderson later repeated the experiment with babies ages 6 months to 24 months, using *Teletubbies*. Once again he had the characters speak backwards and chopped the action sequences into a nonsensical order—showing, say, one of the Teletubbies catching a ball and then, after that, another one throwing it. The 6- and 12-month-olds seemed unable to tell the difference, but by 18 months the babies started looking away, and by 24 months they were turned off by programming that did not make sense.

Anderson's series of experiments provided the first clue that even very young children can be discriminating viewers—that they are not in fact brain-dead, but rather work hard to make sense of what they see and turn it into a coherent narrative that reflects what they already know of the world.

Anderson's series of experiments provided the first clue that even very young children can be discriminating viewers—that they are not in fact brain-dead, but rather work hard to make sense of what they see and turn it into a coherent narrative that reflects what they already know of the world. Now, 30 years later, we understand that children "can make a lot of inferences and process the information," says Anderson. "And they can learn a lot, both positive and negative." Researchers never abandoned the idea that parental interaction is critical for the development of very young children. But they started to see TV watching in shades of gray. If a child never interacts with adults and always watches TV, well, that is a problem. But if a child is watching TV instead of, say, playing with toys, then that is a tougher comparison, because TV, in the right circumstances, has something to offer.

How do small children actually experience electronic media, and what does that experience do to their development? Since the '80s, researchers have spent more and more time consulting with television programmers to study and shape TV content. By tracking children's reactions, they have identified certain rules that promote engagement: stories have to be linear and easy to follow, cuts and time lapses have to be used very sparingly, and language has to be pared down and repeated. A perfect example of a well-engineered show is Nick Jr.'s *Blue's Clues*, which aired from 1996 to 2006. Each episode features Steve (or Joe, in later seasons) and Blue, a cartoon puppy, solving a mystery. Steve talks slowly and simply; he repeats words and then writes them down in his handy-dandy notebook. There are almost no cuts or unexplained gaps in time. The great innovation of *Blue's Clues* is something called the "pause." Steve asks a question and then pauses for about five seconds to let the viewer shout out an answer. Small children feel much more engaged and invested when they think they have a role to play, when they believe they are actually helping Steve and Blue piece together the clues. A longitudinal study of children older than 2 and a half showed that the ones who watched *Blue's Clues* made measurably larger gains in flexible thinking and problem solving over two years of watching the show.

For toddlers, however, the situation seems slightly different. Children younger than 2 and a half exhibit what researchers call a "video deficit." This means that they have a much easier time processing information delivered by a real person than by a person on videotape. In one series of studies, conducted by Georgene Troseth, a developmental psychologist at Vanderbilt University, children watched on a live video monitor as a person in the next room hid a stuffed dog. Others watched the exact same scene unfold directly, through a window between the rooms. The children were then unleashed into the room to find the toy. Almost all the kids who viewed the hiding through the window found the toy, but the ones who watched on the monitor had a much harder time.

A natural assumption is that toddlers are not yet cognitively equipped to handle symbolic representation. (I remember my older son, when he was 3, asking me if he could go into the TV and pet Blue.) But there is another way to interpret this particular phase of development. Toddlers are skilled at seeking out what researchers call "socially relevant information." They tune in to people and situations that help them make a coherent narrative of the world around them. In the real world, fresh grass smells and popcorn tumbles and grown-ups smile at you or say something back when you ask them a question. On TV, nothing like that happens. A TV is static and lacks one of the most important things to toddlers, which is a "two-way exchange of information," argues Troseth.

A few years after the original puppy-hiding experiment, in 2004, Troseth reran it, only she changed a few things. She turned the puppy into a stuffed Piglet (from the Winnie the Pooh stories). More important, she made the video demonstration explicitly interactive. Toddlers and their parents came into a room where they could see a person—the researcher—on a monitor. The researcher was in the room where Piglet would be hidden, and could in turn see the children on a monitor. Before hiding Piglet, the researcher effectively engaged the children in a form of media training. She asked them questions about their siblings, pets, and toys. She played Simon Says with them and invited them to sing popular songs with her. She told them to look for a sticker under a chair in their room. She gave them the distinct impression that she—this person on the screen—could interact with them, and that what she had to say was relevant to the world they lived in. Then the researcher told the children she was going to hide the toy and, after she did so, came back on the screen to instruct them where to find it. That exchange was enough to nearly erase the video deficit. The majority of the toddlers who participated in the live video demonstration found the toy.

Blue's Clues was on the right track. The pause could trick children into thinking that Steve was responsive to them. But the holy grail would be creating a scenario in which the guy on the screen did actually respond—in which the toddler did something and the character reliably jumped or laughed or started to dance or talk back.

Like, for example, when Gideon said "Giddy" and Talking Baby Hippo said "Giddy" back, without fail, every time. That kind of contingent interaction (I do something, you respond) is what captivates a toddler and can be a significant source of learning for even very young children—learning that researchers hope the children can carry into the real world. It's not exactly the ideal social partner the American Academy of Pediatrics craves. It's certainly not a parent or caregiver. But it's as good an approximation as we've ever come up with on a screen, and it's why children's-media researchers are so excited about the iPad's potential.

A couple researchers from the Children's Media Center at Georgetown University show up at my house, carrying an iPad wrapped in a bright-orange case, the better to tempt Gideon with. They are here at the behest of Sandra Calvert, the center's director, to conduct one of several ongoing studies on toddlers and iPads. Gideon is one of their research subjects. This study is designed to test whether a child is more likely to learn when the information he hears comes from a beloved and trusted source. The researchers put the iPad on a kitchen chair; Gideon immediately notices it, turns it on, and looks for his favorite app. They point him to the one they have invented for the experiment, and he dutifully opens it with his finger.

Onto the screen comes a floppy kangaroo-like puppet, introduced as "DoDo." He is a nobody in the child universe, the puppet equivalent of some random guy on late-night public-access TV. Gideon barely acknowledges him. Then the narrator introduces Elmo. "Hi," says Elmo, waving. Gideon says hi and waves back.

An image pops up on the screen, and the narrator asks, "What is this?" (It's a banana.)

"This is a banana," says DoDo.

"This is a grape," says Elmo.

I smile with the inner glow of a mother who knows her child is about to impress a couple strangers. My little darling knows what a banana is. Of course he does! Gideon presses on Elmo. (The narrator says, "No, not Elmo. Try again.") As far as I know, he's never watched *Sesame Street*, never loved an Elmo doll or even coveted one at the toy store. Nonetheless, he is tuned in to the signals of toddler world and, apparently, has somehow figured out that Elmo is a supreme moral authority. His relationship with Elmo is more important to him than what he knows to be the truth. On and on the game goes, and sometimes Gideon picks Elmo even when Elmo says an orange is a pear. Later, when the characters both give made-up names for exotic fruits that few children would know by their real name, Gideon keeps doubling down on Elmo, even though DoDo has been more reliable.

As it happens, Gideon was not in the majority. This summer, Calvert and her team will release the results of their study, which show that most of the time, children around age 32 months go with the character who is telling the truth, whether it's Elmo or DoDo—and quickly come to trust the one who's been more accurate when the children don't already know the answer. But Calvert says this merely suggests that toddlers have become even more savvy users of technology than we had imagined. She had been working off attachment theory, and thought toddlers might value an emotional bond over the correct answer. But her guess is that something about tapping the screen, about getting feedback and being corrected in real time, is itself instructive, and enables the toddlers to absorb information accurately, regardless of its source.

Calvert takes a balanced view of technology: she works in an office surrounded by hardcover books, and she sometimes edits her drafts with pen and paper. But she is very interested in how the iPad can reach children even before they're old enough to access these traditional media.

"People say we are experimenting with our children," she told me. "But from my perspective, it's already happened, and there's no way to turn it back. Children's lives are filled with media at younger and younger ages, and we need to take advantage of what these technologies have to offer. I'm not a Pollyanna. I'm pretty much a realist. I look at what kids are doing and try to figure out how to make the best of it."

Despite the participation of Elmo, Calvert's research is designed to answer a series of very responsible, high-minded questions: Can toddlers learn from iPads? Can they transfer what they learn to the real world? What effect does interactivity have on learning? What role do familiar characters play in children's learning from iPads? All worthy questions, and important, but also all considered entirely from an adult's point of view. The reason many kids' apps are grouped under "Education" in the iTunes store, I suspect, is to assuage parents' guilt (though I also suspect that in the long run, all those "educational" apps merely perpetuate our neurotic relationship with technology, by reinforcing the idea that they must be sorted vigilantly into "good" or "bad"). If small children had more input, many "Education" apps would logically fall under a category called "Kids" or "Kids' Games." And many more of the games would probably look something like the apps designed by a Swedish game studio named Toca Boca.

The founders, Emil Ovemar and Björn Jeffery, work for Bonnier, a Swedish media company. Ovemar, an interactive-design expert, describes himself as someone who never grew up. He is still interested in superheroes, Legos, and animated movies, and says he would rather play stuck-on-an-island with his two kids and their cousins than talk to almost any adult. Jeffery is the company's strategist and front man; I first met him at the conference in California, where he was handing out little temporary tattoos of the Toca Boca logo, a mouth open and grinning, showing off rainbow-colored teeth.

In late 2010, Ovemar and Jeffery began working on a new digital project for Bonnier, and they came up with the idea of entering the app market for kids. Ovemar began by looking into the apps available at the time. Most of them were disappointingly "instructive," he found—"drag the butterfly into the net, that sort of thing. They were missing creativity and imagination." Hunting for inspiration, he came upon Frank and Theresa Caplan's 1973 book *The Power of Play*, a quote from which he later e-mailed to me:

> What is it that often puts the B student ahead of the A student in adult life, especially in business and creative professions? Certainly it is more than verbal skill. To create, one must have a sense of adventure and playfulness. One needs toughness to experiment and hazard the risk of failure. One has to be strong enough to start all over again if need be and alert enough to learn from whatever happens. One needs a strong ego to be propelled forward in one's drive toward an untried goal. Above all, one has to possess the ability to play!

Ovemar and Jeffery hunted down toy catalogs from as early as the 1950s, before the age of exploding brand tie-ins. They made a list of the blockbusters over the decades—the first Tonka trucks, the Frisbee, the Hula-Hoop, the Rubik's Cube. Then they made a list of what these toys had in common: None really involved winning or losing against an opponent. None were part of an effort to create a separate child world that adults were excluded from, and probably hostile toward; they were designed more for family fun. Also, they were not really meant to teach you something specific—they existed mostly in the service of having fun.

In 2011 the two developers launched Toca Tea Party. The game is not all that different from a real tea party. The iPad functions almost like a tea table without legs, and the kids have to invent the rest by, for example, seating their own plushies or dolls, one on each side, and then setting the theater in motion. First, choose one of three tablecloths. Then choose plates, cups, and treats. The treats are not what your mom would feed you. They are chocolate cakes, frosted doughnuts, cookies. It's very easy to spill the tea when you pour or take a sip, a feature added based on kids' suggestions during a test play (kids love spills, but spilling is something you can't do all that often at a real tea party, or you'll get yelled at). At the end, a sink filled with soapy suds appears, and you wash the dishes, which is also part of the fun, and then start again. That's it. The game is either very boring or terrifically exciting, depending on what you make of it. Ovemar and Jeffery knew that some parents wouldn't get it, but for kids, the game would be fun every time, because it's dependent entirely on imagination. Maybe today the stuffed bear will be naughty and do the spilling, while naked Barbie will pile her plate high with sweets. The child can take on the voice of a character or a scolding parent, or both. There's no winning, and there's no reward. Like a game of stuck-on-an-island, it can go on for five minutes or forever.

Soon after the release of Toca Tea Party, the pair introduced Toca Hair Salon, which is still to my mind the most fun game out there. The salon is no Fifth Avenue spa. It's a rundown-looking place with cracks in the wall. The aim is not beauty but subversion. Cutting off hair, like spilling, is on the list of things kids are not supposed to do. You choose one of the odd-looking people or creatures and have your way with its hair, trimming it or dyeing it or growing it out. The blow-dryer is genius; it achieves the same effect as Tadao Cern's Blow Job portraits, which depict people's faces getting wildly distorted by high winds. In August 2011, Toca Boca gave away Hair Salon for free for nearly two weeks. It was downloaded more than 1 million times in the first week, and the company took off. Today, many Toca Boca games show up on lists of the most popular education apps.

Are they educational? "That's the perspective of the parents," Jeffery told me at the back of the grand hall in Monterey. "Is running around on the lawn educational? Every part of a child's life can't be held up to that standard." As we talked, two girls were playing Toca Tea Party on the floor nearby. One had her stuffed dragon at a plate, and he was being especially naughty, grabbing all the chocolate cake and spilling everything. Her friend had taken a little Lego construction man and made him the good guy who ate neatly and helped do the dishes. Should they have been outside at the beach? Maybe, but the day would be long, and they could go outside later.

The more I talked with the developers, the more elusive and unhelpful the "Education" category seemed. (Is *Where the Wild Things Are* educational? Would you make your child read a textbook at bedtime? Do you watch only educational television? And why don't children deserve high-quality fun?) Buckleitner calls his conference Dust or Magic to teach app developers a more subtle concept than pedagogy. By *magic*, Buckleitner has in mind an app that makes children's fingers move and their eyes light up. By *dust*, he means something that was obviously (and ploddingly) designed by an adult. Some educational apps, I wouldn't wish on the naughtiest toddler. Take, for example, Counting With the Very Hungry Caterpillar, which turns a perfectly cute book into a tedious app that asks you to "please eat 1 piece of chocolate cake" so you can count to one.

Before the conference, Buckleitner had turned me on to Noodle Words, an app created by the California designer and children's-book writer Mark Schlichting. The app is explicitly educational. It teaches you about active verbs—*spin*, *sparkle*, *stretch*. It also happens to be fabulous. You tap a box, and a verb pops up and gets acted out by two insect friends who have the slapstick sensibility of the Three Stooges. If the word is *shake*, they shake until their eyeballs rattle. I tracked down Schlichting at the conference, and he turned out to be a little like Maurice Sendak—like many good children's writers, that is: ruled by id and not quite tamed into adulthood. The app, he told me, was inspired by a dream he'd had in which he saw the word *and* floating in the air and sticking to other words like a magnet. He woke up and thought, *What if words were toys?*

Every new medium has, within a short time of its introduction, been condemned as a threat to young people.

During the course of reporting this story, I downloaded dozens of apps and let my children test them out. They didn't much care whether the apps were marketed as educational or not, as long as they were fun. Without my prompting, Gideon fixated on a game called LetterSchool, which teaches you how to write letters more effectively and with more imagination than any penmanship textbooks I've ever encountered. He loves the Toca Boca games, the Duck Duck Moose games, and random games like Bugs and Buttons. My older kids love The Numberlys, a dark fantasy creation of illustrators who have worked with Pixar that happens to teach the alphabet. And all my kids, including Gideon, play Cut the Rope a lot, which is not exclusively marketed as a kids' game. I could convince myself that the game is teaching them certain principles of physics—it's not easy to know the exact right place to slice the rope. But do I really need that extra convincing? I like playing the game; why shouldn't they?

Every new medium has, within a short time of its introduction, been condemned as a threat to young people. Pulp novels would destroy their morals, TV would wreck their eyesight, video games would make them violent. Each one has been accused of seducing kids into wasting time that would otherwise be spent learning about the presidents, playing with friends, or digging their toes into the sand. In our generation, the worries focus on kids' brainpower, about unused synapses withering as children stare at the screen. People fret about television and ADHD, although that concern is largely based on a single study that has been roundly criticized and doesn't jibe with anything we know about the disorder.

There are legitimate broader questions about how American children spend their time, but all you can do is keep them in mind as you decide what rules to set down for your own child. The statement from the American Academy of Pediatrics assumes a zero-sum game: an hour spent watching TV is an hour not spent with a parent. But parents know this is not how life works. There are enough hours in a day to go to school, play a game, and spend time with a parent, and generally these are different hours. Some people can get so drawn into screens that they want to do nothing else but play games. Experts say excessive video gaming is a real problem, but they debate whether it can be called an addiction and, if so, whether the term can be used for anything but a small portion of the population. If your child shows signs of having an addictive personality, you will probably know it. One of my kids is like that; I set stricter limits for him than for the others, and he seems to understand why.

In her excellent book *Screen Time*, the journalist Lisa Guernsey lays out a useful framework—what she calls the three C's—for thinking about media consumption: content, context, and your child. She poses a series of questions—Do you think the content is appropriate? Is screen time a "relatively small part of your child's interaction with you and the real world?"—and suggests tailoring your rules to the answers, child by child. One of the most interesting points Guernsey makes is about the importance of parents' attitudes toward media. If they treat screen time like junk food, or "like a magazine at the hair salon"—good for passing the time in a frivolous way but nothing more—then the child will fully absorb that attitude, and the neurosis will be passed to the next generation.

"The war is over. The natives won." So says Marc Prensky, the education and technology writer, who has the most extreme parenting philosophy of anyone I encountered in my reporting. Prensky's 7-year-old son has access to books, TV, Legos, Wii—and Prensky treats them all the same. He does not limit access to any of them. Sometimes his son plays with a new app for hours, but then, Prensky told me, he gets tired of it. He lets his son watch TV even when he personally thinks it's a "stupid waste." *SpongeBob SquarePants*, for example, seems like an annoying, pointless show, but Prensky says he used the relationship between SpongeBob and Patrick, his starfish sidekick, to teach his son a lesson about friendship. "We live in a screen age, and to say to a kid, 'I'd love for you to look at a book but I hate it when you look at the screen' is just bizarre. It reflects our own prejudices and comfort zone. It's nothing but fear of change, of being left out."

Prensky's worldview really stuck with me. Are books always, in every situation, inherently better than screens? My daughter, after all, often uses books as a way to avoid social interaction, while my son uses the Wii to bond with friends. I have to admit, I had the exact same experience with *SpongeBob*. For a long time I couldn't stand the show, until one day I got past the fact that the show was so loud and frenetic and paid more attention to the story line, and realized I too could use it to talk with my son about friendship. After I first interviewed Prensky, I decided to conduct an experiment. For six months, I would let my toddler live by the Prensky rules. I would put the iPad in the toy basket, along with the remote-control car and the Legos. Whenever he wanted to play with it, I would let him.

Gideon tested me the very first day. He saw the iPad in his space and asked if he could play. It was 8 a.m. and we had to get ready for school. I said yes. For 45 minutes he sat on a chair and played as I got him dressed, got his backpack ready, and failed to feed him breakfast. This was extremely annoying and obviously untenable. The week went on like this—Gideon grabbing the iPad for two-hour stretches, in the morning, after school, at bedtime. Then, after about 10 days, the iPad fell out of his rotation, just like every other toy does. He dropped it under the bed and never looked for it. It was completely forgotten for about six weeks.

Now he picks it up every once in a while, but not all that often. He has just started learning letters in school, so he's back to playing LetterSchool. A few weeks ago his older brother played with him, helping him get all the way through the uppercase and then lowercase letters. It did not seem beyond the range of possibility that if Norman Rockwell were alive, he would paint the two curly-haired boys bent over the screen, one small finger guiding a smaller one across, down, and across again to make, in their triumphant finale, the small z.

DISCUSSION

1. What are some of the most prevalent anxieties parents have about the dangers of "screen time"? In your view, are these worries valid? Why or why not?
2. Rosin describes children's engagement with screen-based technology as "swim[ming] in the digital stream." What does she mean by this phrase? What kind of relationship to these devices is she using this phrase to evoke?
3. Rosin writes: "The reason many kids' apps are grouped under 'Education' in the iTunes store, I suspect, is to assuage parents' guilt" (p. 494). Why do you think so many smartphone apps are marketed as educational? In your view, is this an accurate or valid way to describe them? Can you think of an app that serves a legitimately educational purpose?

WRITING

4. "Norman Rockwell," writes Rosin, "never painted *Boy Swiping Finger on Screen*, and our own vision of a perfect childhood has never adjusted to accommodate that now-common tableau" (p. 487). In an essay, respond to this statement. Why doesn't the image of a child interacting with a computer fit our conception of the "perfect childhood"? What vision of "perfection" have we been taught to accept instead? And do you agree with Rosin's suggestion that our notions of childhood are going to have to change to "accommodate" the dramatic changes in the way kids now entertain themselves? If so, how?
5. "There are legitimate broader questions about how American children spend their time," Rosin declares, "but all you can do is keep them in mind as you decide what rules to set down for your own child" (p. 497). Write an essay in which you take up the implied invitation contained within this statement. What sort of rules regarding technology and screen time would you "set down" for kids? What specific restrictions and guidelines would these rules include? And, finally, what kind of argument can you make in favor of following these particular rules over others?
6. In a certain sense, this essay could be viewed as a response to the attitudes showcased in the essay by Claire Suddath (p. 500), which emphasize the need to renounce our reliance on digital technology. In what ways can Hanna Rosin's discussion here be read as a critique of the views that Suddath explores? To what extent does the research cited by Rosin challenge or complicate this kind of effort to "unplug"? And how sympathetic are you to such efforts?

CLAIRE SUDDATH

Digital Detox, a Tech-Free Retreat for Internet Addicts

So pervasive have digital technologies become, so deeply ingrained in our everyday lives, that it's virtually impossible to imagine a day — let alone a week or a month — without them. But it is precisely such an effort to forgo these tools that Claire Suddath examines here. Suddath is a tech reporter for *Bloomberg Businessweek,* in which this article appeared in 2013.

JULIA TEST, A 28-YEAR-OLD FREELANCE PHOTOGRAPHER, CAN'T stop checking Facebook. Her last relationship failed partly because she and her ex kept fighting over texts instead of talking things out in person. "It wasn't a long-distance relationship or anything," she says. "It's just easier to say something mean in a text than watching someone's face when you say it." Jen McDowell, a director of entertainment at the travel company Olivia, says her bosses have told her she's too tethered to her job. "I never took vacation," she says. "Finally, they came to me and said, 'We'll have legal problems if you don't take at least three days off. Please leave.'" A woman named Monika, who says only that she works for "a very large company in Redmond, Wash.," also never takes vacation. Unfortunately for her, her bosses are fine with that.

This isn't a group therapy session. It's Digital Detox, a three-day retreat at Shambhalah Ranch in Northern California for people who feel addicted to their gadgets. For 72 hours, the 11 participants, who've paid from $595 for a twin bed to $1,400 for a suite, eat vegan food, practice yoga, swim in a nearby creek, take long walks in the woods, and keep a journal about being offline. (Typewriters are available for anyone not used to longhand.) The ranch is two-and-a-half hours north of San Francisco, so most guests come from the Bay Area, although a few have flown in from Seattle and New York. They're here for a variety of reasons—bad breakups, career troubles—but there's one thing everyone has in common: They're driven to distraction by the Internet.

Isn't everyone? Checking e-mail in the bathroom and sleeping with your cell phone by your bed are now considered normal. According to the Pew Research Center, in 2007 only 58 percent of people used their phones to text; last year it was 80 percent. More than half of all cell phone users have smartphones, giving them Internet access all the time. As a result, the number of hours Americans spend collectively online has almost doubled since 2010, according to ComScore, a digital analytics company. Teens and twentysomethings are the most wired. In 2011, Diana Rehling and Wendy Bjorklund, communications professors at St. Cloud State University in Minnesota, surveyed their undergraduates and found that the average college student checks Facebook 20 times an hour.

Some are starting to rebel against this constant compulsion to connect. Webby Awards founder Tiffany Shlain, an advocate of unplugging, self-corrects by instituting one technology-free day each week. "It's the slowest day in the world," she says. Shlain lectures frequently about the benefits of her "technology shabbats." Sherry Turkle, director of the MIT Initiative on Technology and Self and the author of *Alone Together*, which explores the way the Internet constrains offline relationships, has also observed this shift. "I don't want to say it's a movement just yet, but it does seem like a lot of people have gotten to the point with technology where common sense is starting to kick in," she says. "We've finally realized that we have to start making healthier choices."

Checking e-mail in the bathroom and sleeping with your cell phone by your bed are now considered normal.

That's what happened to Digital Detox's co-founder, Levi Felix. In 2009, Felix, now 29, was a vice president at a Los Angeles Internet startup, Causecast, working 80 hours a week and sleeping with his cell phone under his pillow. He was diagnosed with an esophageal tear that doctors told him was "related to too much stress, too much coffee, too much work, and too much Thai takeout." So he and his girlfriend, Brooke Dean, quit their jobs and traveled the world for nine months, eventually landing at a communal farm in Cambodia. When they returned, they noticed their friends had grown even more attached to social media. "I couldn't figure out why people were staring down at their phones all the time," Felix says. He read Turkle's *Alone Together* and came up with the idea of Digital Detox.

Felix and Dean hosted the first retreat in June 2012. Since then their venture has grown to a series of vacation-esque unplugging seminars in places such as Costa Rica and Cambodia. Earlier this year they hosted an adult summer camp where 300 professionals made lanyards and performed talent show routines. The program's core remains small, 10- to 15-person retreats in the redwoods. Digital Detox feels kind of like a camping trip with some particularly touchy-feely California friends.

Minus the pot. There's not even alcohol or coffee, just some weak black tea to stave off caffeine headaches. When guests arrive, Felix takes their digital devices and stores them in paper bags, along with any watches and clocks. Shambhalah Ranch is surrounded by redwoods—at one point, participants actually hug a tree—but since cameras are gadgets, detoxers aren't allowed to take pictures. When they want to remember an experience, they make a square with their thumbs and index fingers, bring it up to their eyes, and say, "Click!" They're ordinarily forbidden from discussing ages or jobs (exceptions are made for nosy reporters). That way everyone from the recent college grad to the company executive will feel as if he's among peers.

On the second day of Digital Detox, Anna Trautman, a quality-control lab assistant at Gordon Biersch Brewing, spends several hours sitting quietly by a lake contemplating whether she has the guts to quit her job and travel alone. "I'd never make the time to sit and think about this if I had my phone," she says later that night. "I would've just spent hours looking at strangers' photos on Instagram instead."

"It feels like the 1990s again!" says Laura Monfredini, 39, an in-house lawyer for the Federal Reserve Bank of San Francisco. "Things were so much slower back then. I used to be able to read a whole book at a time. Now I can only do one or two chapters before I think, Oh, what's on Facebook?" While Monfredini appreciates getting her attention span back, she's not sure that reverting to a pre-Web lifestyle is better. The Internet makes our lives more convenient, she argues.

One attendee keeps feeling phantom cell phone vibrations. Another misses texting her best friend.

She's not the only one struggling to live without technology, even for just a few days. One attendee keeps feeling phantom cell phone vibrations. Another misses texting her best friend. Monika from Washington has the hardest time: She spends the weekend making a mental list of things she wants to Google when she gets back online. Still, she and everyone else say they end the weekend refreshed. "You know when a computer is on too long, and it starts overheating and making those whirring noises?" says Evan Kleiman, who works in business development and lives in Los Angeles. "I feel like my brain had been doing that. This weekend I finally managed to turn it off."

On the last morning everyone discusses how long they think they'll last before turning their phones back on. They wonder if being bombarded with three days of e-mail is really the best way to reenter the world. Kleiman says he feels as if he doesn't even need his phone anymore, though he admits he won't get rid of it. McDowell says she still won't take any of her vacation days, but from now on she vows to go device-free every morning before work. (A month later, she confesses she hasn't kept this promise.) "I know it's not PC to say this here, but I miss my phone," Monfredini says. When she leaves the ranch, the first thing she does is turn it back on.

DISCUSSION

1. The goal behind projects like Digital Detox is to help people work against the increasingly pervasive impulse to connect. What do you make of this goal? Do you think that disconnecting ourselves from the trappings of modern technology carries particular benefits? If so, what?
2. Take a moment to reflect upon the term "Digital Detox." What vision of the digital world does this phrase evoke for you? Does this vision accurately reflect your own experiences with digital technology? How or how not?
3. Speaking about those who attend the "Digital Detox" retreat, Suddath writes: "They're here for a variety of reasons — bad breakups, career troubles — but there's one thing everyone has in common: They're driven to distraction by the Internet" (p. 500). In your view, what types of "distraction" is this retreat designed to remedy? And do you agree that such "distraction" constitutes a legitimate problem? Why or why not?

WRITING

4. Write an essay in which you identify, analyze, and evaluate the mission of the "Digital Detox" program. How would you describe its key goals? What specific changes or improvements is it designed to achieve? And do you think this program is worth attempting? Why or why not?
5. Choose an example of a digital tool that you think would be targeted by "Digital Detox" as harmful or problematic. Then write an essay in which you lay out your own program for redressing the negative effect this tool has on its users. What uses of this tool would you allow and disallow? Why?
6. Suddath writes: "The program's core remains small, 10- to 15-person retreats in the redwoods. Digital Detox feels kind of like a camping trip with some particularly touchy-feely California friends" (p. 501). How do you think Joel Kotkin (p. 453) would respond to this description? Does this synopsis of the Digital Detox community resemble or echo in any way the definition of home Kotkin presents in his piece? Which vision of community do you find more appealing? Why?

Tying It All Together

As we noted at the beginning of the chapter, connectedness stands as one of the preeminent beliefs in contemporary culture. Choose one of the cultural beliefs under examination in the chapter "How We Believe" (i.e., patriotism, consumerism, fame, religious faith, etc.) and discuss the particular ways it compares to the ideal of connection. What are the key similarities and differences between the two? What social scripts does each belief create? What cultural norms does each promote? And which, finally, do you find more valid or compelling? Why?

For Peter Lovenheim ("Won't You Be My Neighbor?" p. 458) and Joel Kotkin ("There's No Place Like Home," p. 453), the idea of connectedness is deeply tied to the question of community. Do we live in a world, they ask, where it is possible to truly know each other? Or do too many factors and forces conspire to keep us separated, detached, and disconnected? In fact, a number of essays throughout the book pose these kinds of questions. Among them: John Paul Titlow ("#Me: Instagram Narcisissm and the Scourge of the Selfie," p. 122), bell hooks ("Learning in the Shadow of Race and Class," p. 287), and David Brooks ("People Like Us," p. 62). In a two- to three-page essay, consider how one of these pieces compares with Lovenheim's or Kotkin's essay. What sort of argument is each writer making about the meaning and value of community? In each case, what are the factors that prevent people from forging connections? And what response or solution to this problem does each writer propose?

Putting It into Practice: **The More Things Change . . .**

Now that you've read the chapter selections, try applying your conclusions to your own life by completing the following exercises.

DESIGNING YOUR IDEAL COMMUNITY Write a one-page description of the community in which you live, whether it represents your school, home, church, or other institution. Be as specific as possible about the types of connection (i.e., social, cultural, professional, etc.) this community make possible. Then write another page in which you evaluate aspects of these types of connections that do not measure up to your own ideal. What aspects about this community would you change to make it fit your ideal of the truly connected community?

BRIDGING THE PARTISAN DIVIDE Think of a divisive or polarizing social issue that interests you and research groups in your community that advocate for different positions on this issue. What are their goals, and how do they go about achieving them? What are the key differences that define their respective positions? If possible, interview a member of one organization and find out what about this group appeals to him or her. Using all the information you have collected, write an essay in which you propose a plan for how these differences might be overcome.

PERSONAL CONNECTIONS Write a personal reflection in which you identify and address a particular moment in your life when you felt (physically, socially, culturally) disconnected from the larger world around you. What did this experience of disconnection feel like? What factors caused or contributed to it? How did you respond to this situation? And as you think about it now, do you regard this experience as positive or negative? Why?

Index of Authors and Titles

Missing something? Instructors may assign the online materials that accompany this text. For access to them, visit **macmillanhighered.com/actingout.**

Inside LaunchPad Solo for *Acting Out Culture*

LearningCurve

Commas

Fragments

Run-ons and comma splices

Active and passive voice

Appropriate language

Subject-verb agreement

Working with sources (MLA)

Working with sources (APA)

Topic sentences and supporting details

Topics and main ideas

Critical reading

e-Readings

Edudemic.com, *Anti-Bullying Public Service Announcement* [video]

Duke University, Fuqua School of Business, *The Context of Our Character* [video]

Linda Stone, *On Continuous Partial Attention* [video]

Casey Neistat, *Calorie Detective* [video]

The American Academy of Arts & Sciences, *The Heart of the Matter* [video]

Lauren Orsini, *WorkHands Wants to Become the Blue-Collar LinkedIn* [multi-modal reading]

Casey Neistat, *Texting While Walking* [video]

Tutorials

Working with Sources
- Do I need to cite that?
- How to cite a book in MLA style
- How to cite an article in MLA style
- How to cite a database in MLA style
- How to cite a Web site in MLA style
- How to cite a database in APA style
- How to cite a Web site in APA style

Critical Reading
- Active reading strategies
- Reading visuals: Purpose
- Reading visuals: Audience

Digital Writing
- Online Research Tools
- Job Search/Personal Branding
- Photo Editing Basics with GIMP
- Audio Editing with Audacity
- Presentations
- Word Processing